W9-BFE-373

American Diversity
Contested Visions of the U.S. Experience

HIS 111
Custom Edition for Illinois State University

Selections taken from:
Strangers to These Shores, Eleventh Edition
by Vincent N. Parrillo

Occupied America: A History of Chicanos, Eighth Edition
by Rodolfo F. Acuña

First Americans: A History of Native Peoples, Combined Volume
by Kenneth W. Townsend and Mark A. Nicholas

Prentice Hall Reference Guide, Eighth Edition
by Muriel Harris and Jennifer L. Kunka

ISBN 10: 1-323-44034-8
ISBN 13: 978-1-323-44034-6

CONTRIBUTORS

Senior Editor
Mitch Lerner

Managing Editor
David Staley

Copy Editor
Ann Heiss

Assistant Managing Editor
Hunter Price

Contributing Editors

Tyler Anbinder
Kenneth J. Andrien
Jean Harvey Baker
Michael Les Benedict
Mansel Blackford
Paul C. Bowers
Rowland Brucken
John D. Buenker
John C. Burnham
Joan E. Cashin
William R. Childs
Albert J. Churella
Steven Conn
Saul Cornell
Nick Cullather
Jeanette Davis
Merton L. Dillon
Daniel Feller
Charles Coleman Finlay
Emily Greenwald
Mark Grimsley
Bernard N. Grindel
Peter L. Hahn
James Hansen
Susan M. Hartmann
Mary Ann Heiss
Earl J. Hess
Michael J. Hogan
R. Douglas Hurt

Bruce Karhoff
Michael Kazin
Terence Kehoe
K. Austin Kerr
Frank Lambert
Valerie Mendoza
James McCaffrey
Allan R. Millett
Pamela J. Mills
Daniel Nelson
Margaret E. Newell
Josef Ostyn
Carla Gardina Pestana
Patrick D. Reagan
Randolph A. Roth
Hal K. Rothman
John A. M. Rothney
Leila J. Rupp
Richard D. Shiels
David Sicilia
C. Edward Skeen
Amy L. S. Staples
David L. Stebenne
David Steigerwald
Marshall F. Stevenson, Jr.
Warren R. Van Tine
Christopher Waldrep
J. Samuel Walker

Table of Contents

Diversity in America - Third Edition

The Chicago Manual of Style

"Brief and True Report of the New Found Land of Virginia"

In 1588, as dark rumors about the New World swirled in England, Thomas Harriot (1560–1621) produced the most important promotional work of the day. Harriot's A Brief and True Report of the New Found Land of Virginia *is the first original English book describing the first English colony in America. Sent by Sir Walter Raleigh to gather information about the New World, Harriot settled on Roanoke Island, off the coast of present day North Carolina, in 1585. He would return to England a few years later, eventually becoming a leading mathematician and one of England's foremost scientists.*

Evidence of Harriot's meticulous mind is apparent in his report. His careful record of the resources of the area made Virginia more tempting than any of the vague accounts then circulating. He describes in detail the flora and fauna of the region, as well as including astronomical observations that later led to the drawing of the most accurate map of English exploration at the time. Many of the Native Americans, the southeastern Algonquians, that Harriot wrote about would succumb to epidemic diseases in the coming decades, and his account offers the best descriptions of these lives lost. He was able to be so accurate because he both traveled widely and became one of the few colonists to learn Carolina Algonquian. The following passage is his report on the Algonquians whom he encountered.

It resteth [remains to be done] I speake a word or two of the naturall inhabitants, their natures and maners, leaving large discourse thereof until time more convenient hereafter: nowe onely so farre foorth, as that you may know, how that they in respect of troubling our inhabiting and planting, are not to be feared, but

From Thomas Harriot, *A Brief and True Report of the New Found Land of Virginia*, The History Book Club, (New York, 1951).

that they shall have cause both to feare and love us, that shall inhabite with them.

They are a people clothed with loose mantles made of deere skinnes, and aprons of the same round about their middles, all eels naked, of such a difference of statures onely as wee in England, having no edge tools or weapons of yron or steele to offend us withal, neither knowe they how to make any: those weapons that they have, are onely bowes made of Witch-hazle, and arrows of reedes, flat edged truncheons also of wood about a yard long, neither have they any thing to defend themselves but targets [round shields] made of barkes, and some armours made of sticks wickered together with thread.

Their townes are but small and neere the Sea coast but fewe, some containing but tenne or twelve houses; some 20. the greatest that we have seene hath bene but of 30. houses: if they bee walled, it is onely done with barkes of trees made fast to stakes, or eels with poles onely fixed upright, and close one by another. . . .

Their maner of warres amongst themselves is either by sudden surprising one an other most commonly about the dawning of the day, or moone-light, or eels by ambushes, or some subtile devises. Set battles are very rare, except it fall out where there are many trees, where either part may have some hope of defence, after the delivery of every arrow, in leaping behind some or other. . . .

Some religion they have already, which although it be farre from the trueth, yet being as it is, there is hope it may be the easier and sooner reformed.

They believe there are many gods. . . . First (they say) were made waters, out of which by the gods was made all diversitie of creatures that are visible or invisible.

For mankinde they say a woman was made first, which by the working of one of the gods, conceived and brought foorth children: And in such sort they say they had their beginning. But how many yeeres or ages have passed since, they say they can make no relation, having no letters nor other such meanes as we to keepe Records of the particularities of times past, but only tradition from father to sonne.

First Encounters with Native Americans

In this selection taken from his history of the "Lost Colony" of Roanoke, Captain John Smith—promoter, soldier of fortune, and key figure in the colonization of Virginia—recounts the Algonquin Indians' response to the outbreak of disease following the English landing in North Carolina in 1585.

One other strange Accident . . . will I mention before I end, which mooved the whole Country that either knew or heard of us, to have us in wonderfull admiration.

There was no Towne where they had practised any villany against us . . . but within a few dayes after our departure, they began to dye; in some Townes twenty, in some forty, in some sixty, and in one an hundred and twenty, which was very many in respect of their numbers. And this hapned in no place (we could learn) but where we had bin. . . . And this disease was so strange, they neither knew what it was, nor how to cure it; nor had they knowne the like time out of minde. . . . [T]hey were perswaded it was the worke of God through our meanes: and that we by him might kill and slay whom we would, without weapons, and not come neare them. . . .

This marveilous Accident in all the Country wrought so strange opinions of us, that they could not tell whether to thinke us gods or men. And the rather that all the space of their

From John Smith, "The Generall Historie of Virginia, the Somer Iles, and New England . . ." in *The Complete Works of Captain John Smith (1580–1631)*, Vol. 2, ed. Philip L. Barbour, copyright © by University of North Carolina Press, (Chapel Hill, 1986), 2:80–81.

sicknesse, there was no man of ours knowne to die, or much sicke. They noted also we had no women, nor cared for any of theirs: some therefore thought we were not borne of women, and therefore not mortall. . . . Some would Prophesie there were more of our generation yet to come, to kill theirs and take their places.

The Virginia Charter

During the 1500s and 1600s, it was customary for European monarchs to grant charters for overseas colonies as rewards to loyal, wealthy subjects and/or military leaders. This practice was beneficial to both the monarchs and to the recipients of the charter since it would, potentially, bring great wealth to each through prosperous trade, and the discovery, hopefully, of precious metals and stones. In 1606, King James I of England granted a group of nobles and businessmen the right to establish a colony between the thirty-fourth and thirty-eighth parallels along the eastern coast of the so-called "New World." This land totaled approximately six million acres, a vast amount of land particularly for England, an island. The colony was named Virginia, after Elizabeth I, the "Virgin Queen." The English were motivated by the enormous riches that Spain had found during their conquests of the Aztec Empire in present-day Mexico and the Incan Empire in present-day Peru. They believed that this new colony would also yield fabulous wealth in the form of gold, silver, and copper mines, and easily transportable goods in high demand in Europe. They did not expect to have to farm and perform manual labor simply in order to survive. However, this was the reality of life in their new settlement of Jamestown on the James River for the first two decades. In the larger, international context, this land had actually been claimed by Spain through the Treaty of Tordesillas in 1494 signed with Portugal. By also laying claim to this land, the King of England was directly challenging the right of Spain to claim all of North America and a substantial portion of South America.

Notice in the following document how King James describes himself and the justification he offers for laying claim to this land along the coast of the "New World." What reasons does the Charter offer for the colonization of this land and its inhabitants, and what does this tell you about the

From *National Documents: State Papers Arranged to Illustrate the Growth of the North American Colonies and the United States from 1606 to the Present Day*, Sun Dial Classics, (New York, 1908), 5–7, 9, 10–11, 13, 17.

assumptions made by the English about the native peoples? What specifically does the Charter lay claim to and why? What type of government does the charter establish for the colony? Keep in mind that the charter was given to the leaders of the Virginia Company, a joint-stock venture, which raised money for settlement and trade through the selling of shares.

I, James, by the Grace of God, King of England, Scotland, France and Ireland, Defender of the Faith, &c. WHEREAS our loving and well-disposed Subjects, Sir Thomas Gates, and Sir George Somers, Knights, Richard Hackluit, Prebendary of Westminster, and Edward-Maria Wingfield, Thomas Hanham and Ralegh Gilbert, Esqrs. William Parker, and George Popham, Gentlemen, and divers others of our loving Subjects, have been humble Suitors unto us, that We would vouchsafe unto them our License, to make Habitation, Plantation, and to deduce a colony of sundry of our People into that Part of America commonly called VIRGINIA, and other Parts and Territories in America, either appertaining unto us, or which are not now actually possessed by any Christian Prince or People, situate, lying, and being all along the Sea Coasts, between four and thirty Degrees of Northerly Latitude from the Equinoctial Line, and five and forty Degrees of the same Latitude, and in the main Land between the same four and thirty and five and forty Degrees, and the Islands thereunto adjacent, or within one hundred Miles of the Coast thereof;

And to that End, and for the more speedy Accomplishment of their said intended Plantation and Habitation there, are desirous to divide themselves into two several Colonies and Companies; the one consisting of certain Knights, Gentlemen, Merchants, and other Adventurers, of our City of London and elsewhere, which are, and from time to time shall be, joined unto them, which do desire to begin their Plantation and Habitation in some fit and convenient Place, between four and thirty and one and forty Degrees of the said Latitude, along the Coasts of Virginia, and the Coasts of America aforesaid . . .

We, greatly commending, and graciously accepting of, their Desires for the Furtherance of so noble a Work, which may, by the Providence of Almighty God, hereafter tend to the Glory of his Divine Majesty, in propagating of Christian Religion to such People, as yet live in Darkness and miserable Ignorance of the true Knowledge and Worship of God, and may in time bring the Infidels and Savages, living in those parts, to human Civility, and to a settled and quiet Government: DO, by these our Letters Patents, graciously accept of, and agree to, their humble and well-intended Desires.

And do therefore, for Us, our Heirs, and Successors, GRANT and agree, that the said Sir Thomas Gates, Sir George Somers, Richard Hackluit, and Edward-Maria Wingfield, Adventurers of and for our City of London, and all such others, as are, or shall be, joined unto them of that Colony, shall be called the first Colony; And they shall and may begin their said first Plantation and Habitation, at any Place upon the said-Coast of Virginia or America, where they shall think fit and convenient, between the said four and thirty and one and forty Degrees of the said Latitude; And that they shall have all the Lands, Woods, Soil, Grounds, Havens, Ports, Rivers, Mines, Minerals, Marshes, Waters, Fishings, Commodities, and Hereditaments, whatsoever, from the said first Seat of their Plantation and Habitation by the Space of fifty Miles of English Statute Measure, all along the said Coast of Virginia and America, towards the West and Southwest, as the Coast lyeth, with all the Islands within one hundred Miles directly over against the same Sea Coast; And also all the Lands, Soil, Grounds, Havens, Ports, Rivers, Mines, Minerals, Woods, Waters, Marshes, Fishings, Commoditites, and Hereditaments, whatsoever, from the said Place of their first Plantation and Habitation for the space of fifty like English Miles, all along the said Coasts of Virginia and America, towards the East and Northeast, or towards the North, as the Coast lie, together with all the Islands within one hundred Miles, directly over against the said Sea Coast, And also all the Lands, Woods, Soil, Grounds, Havens, Ports, Rivers, Mines, Minerals, Marshes, Waters, Fishings, Commodities, and Hereditaments, whatsoever, from the same fifty Miles every way on the Sea Coast, directly into the main Land by the Space of one hundred like English Miles; And shall and may inhabit and remain there; and shall and may also build and fortify within any the same, for their better Safeguard and Defense, according to their best Discretion, and the Discretion of the Council of that Colony; And that no other of our Subjects shall be permitted, or suffered, to plant or inhabit behind, or on the Backside of them, towards the main Land, without the Express License or Consent of the Council of that Colony, thereunto in Writing; first had and obtained.

. . .

And we do also ordain, establish, and agree, for Us, our Heirs, and Successors, that each of the said Colonies shall have a Council, which shall govern and order all Matters and Causes, which shall arise, grow, or happen, to or within the same several Colonies, according to such Laws, Ordinances, and Instructions, as shall be, in that behalf, given and signed with Our Hand or Sign Manual, and pass under the Privy Seal of our Realm of England; Each of which Councils shall consist of thirteen Persons, to be ordained, made, and removed, from time to time, according as shall be directed and comprised in the same instructions; And shall have a several Seal, for all Matters that shall pass or concern the same several Councils; . . .

And moreover, we do GRANT and agree, for Us, our Heirs and Successors; that that the said several Councils of and for the said several Colonies, shall and lawfully may, by Virtue hereof, from time to time, without any Interruption of Us, our Heirs or Successors, give and take Order, to dig, mine, and search for all Manner of Mines of Gold, Silver, and Copper, as well within any Part of their said several Colonies, as of the said main Lands on the Backside of the same Colonies; And to HAVE and enjoy the Gold, Silver, and Copper, to be gotten thereof, to the Use of the same Colonies, and the Plantations thereof; YIELDING therefore to Us, our Heirs and Successors, the fifth Part only of all the same Gold and Silver, and the fifteenth Part of all the same Copper, so to be gotten or had, as is aforesaid, without any other Manner of Profit or Account, to be given or yielded to Us, our Heirs, or Successors, for or in Respect of the same:

And that they shall, or lawfully may, establish and cause to be made a Coin, to pass current there between the people of those several Colonies, for the more Ease of Traffic and Bargaining between and amongst them and the Natives there, of such Metal, and in such Manner and Form, as the said several Councils there shall limit and appoint.

. . .

Moreover, we do, by these Presents, for Us, our Heirs, and Successors, GIVE AND GRANT License unto the said Sir Thomas Gates, Sir George Somers, Richard Hackluit, Edward-Maria Wingfield, Thornas Hanham, Ralegh Gilbert, William Parker, and

George Popham, and to every of the said Colonies, that they, and every of them, shall and may, from time to time, and at all times forever hereafter, for their several Defenses, encounter, expulse, repel, and resist, as well by Sea as by Land, by all Ways and Means whatsoever, all and every such Person or Persons, as without the especial License of the said several Colonies and Plantations, shall attempt to inhabit within the said several Precincts and Limits of the said several Colonies and Plantations, or any of them, or that shall enterprise or attempt, at any time hereafter, the Hurt, Detriment, or Annoyance, of the said several Colonies or Plantations:

. . .

Also we do, for Us, our Heirs, and Successors, DECLARE, by these Presents, that all and every the Persons being our Subjects, which shall dwell and inhabit within every or any of the said several Colonies and Plantations, and every of their children, which shall happen to be born within any of the Limits and Precincts of the said several Colonies and Plantations, shall HAVE and enjoy all Liberties, Franchises, and Immunities, within any of our other Dominions, to all Intents and Purposes, as if they had been abiding and born, within this our Realm of England, or any other of our said Dominions.

. . .

IN Witness whereof, we have caused these our Letters to be made Patent; Witness Ourself at Westminster, the tenth Day of April, in the fourth Year of our Reign of England, France, and Ireland, and of Scotland the nine and thirtieth.

Chief Powhatan's Speech to Captain John Smith

Prior to the arrival of the English colonists, Wahunsonacock (1550–1631) had organized thirty Algonquian communities, numbering more than 14,000 Native Americans and almost 140 villages into a confederacy to better defend themselves against other, hostile tribes in the area. Historically, he is known as Powhatan; the English settlers referred to him by the name of his confederacy rather than by his given name. The people of the Powhatan Confederacy were primarily agricultural and lived along the rivers in this area of what became known as Virginia. They fished and hunted deer to supplement the food that they grew. John Smith (1580–1631) became the leader of the early Virginia settlement at Jamestown. He arrived in Chesapeake Bay in the spring of 1607 with 105 English colonists following the failed attempt to settle at Roanoke in the 1590s. Many of the first colonists at Jamestown were not well trained or eager to engage in hard, manual labor. Smith rose to the leadership position through his installations of basic, practical laws designed to ensure the colony's survival, essentially requiring the colonists to work if they wished to eat.

The night the colonists first landed at Chesapeake Bay, Powhatan's warriors attacked, wounding two of the colonists. Relationships between the two groups continued to remain tense, although the Powhatan Confederacy did provide the colonists with food in exchange for English goods such as axes, swords and pots. Smith first met Powhatan in December 1607, after he was captured by Powhatan's warriors. He narrowly escaped a death sentence when Powhatan's daughter, Pocahontas, begged her father to spare Smith's life. He was initiated into the tribe and taken into their confidence. Due to a serious food shortage and mass starvation among the English colonists in 1609, they desperately began to

---

From Captain John Smith, *A Map of Virginia* (Oxford, 1612), 60–65.

attack Powhatan's people in search of food. The fighting between the two groups, which lasted about four years, resulted in major territorial gains for the English along the James River. The wariness with which Powhatan and other Algonquins had initially greeted the English was replaced with outright hostility.

Captain Smith, you may understand that I, having seen the death of all my people thrice, and not any one living of those three generations but myself, I know the difference of peace and war, better than any in my Country. But now I am old and before long must die. My brothers, namely Opichapam, Opechankanough, and Kekataugh, my two sisters, and their two daughters, are distinctly each others' successors. I wish their experiences no less then mine, and your love to them no less then mine to you.

But this brute from Nansamud, that you are come to destroy my Country, so much frighten all my people, as they dare not visit you. What good will it do you to take that by force you may quietly have by love, or to destroy those who provide you food. What can you get by war, when we can hide our provisions and fly to the woods? Whereby you must famish by wronging us your friends. And why are you jealous of our loves, seeing us unarmed, and willing still to feed you, with that you cannot get but by our hard labors? Think you I am so simple, not to know it is better to eat good meat, lay well, and sleep quietly with my women and children, laugh and be merry with you, have copper, hatchets, or what I want being your friend? Then be forced to flee from all, to lie cold in the woods, feed upon acorns, roots, and such trash, and be so hunted by you, that I can neither rest, eat, nor sleep; but my tired men must watch, and if a twig does break, every one cries out "here comes Captain Smith."

Then I must fly. I know not whether, and thus with miserable fear end my miserable life, leaving my pleasures to such youths as you, which through your reckless ways may quickly as miserably end, for want of that, you never know how to find? Let this therefore assure you of our families, and every year our friendly continues we shall furnish you with corn. And also if you would come in friendly manner to see us, and thus not with your guns and swords, as to invade your foes.

Chief Powhatan's Speech to Captain John Smith

Captain Smith replied: Seeing you will not rightly understand our words, we try to make you know our thoughts by our deeds. The vow I made you of my love, both myself and my men have kept, as for your promise, I find it violated, by some of your subjects, yet we finding your love and kindness (our custom is so far from being ungrateful) that for your sake only, we have curbed our thirsting desire for revenge. Had they known as well the cruelty we give to our enemies as our true love to our friends. And I think that your judgement sufficient to convince as well by the adventures we have undertaken, as by the advantage we have by our arms of yours, that has we intended any of you to be hurt, long before this, we could have affected this. Your people coming to meet me at Jamestown are entertained with their bows and arrows without exception; we seeming as it is with you to wear our arms as part of our apparel. As for the dangers of our enemies, in such wars consists our chiefest pleasure, for your riches we have no use, as for the hiding of your provision, or by fleeing into the woods, we shall so unadvisedly do as you conclude, your friendly care in that behalf in needless, for we have a rule to find beyond your knowledge.

The Mayflower Compact

In 1606, King James of England laid claim to all the land along the eastern portion of North America from the thirty-fourth parallel to the forty-fifth parallel. The area in between the thirty-fourth and the thirty-eighth parallel was granted to the Virginia Company, a joint-stock venture. The so-called Plymouth group was granted control over the land between the forty-first and forty-fifth parallels, and the land in between was open to settlement by people from both groups. Unlike the settlers of the Chesapeake Bay region, the colonists of the Plymouth group came in search of peace and religious freedom rather than quick riches. Those aboard the Mayflower had been blown off course by a storm. Rather than landing near Chesapeake Bay, they disembarked on Cape Cod and established the colony of Plymouth.

Since the group lacked a royal charter giving them claim to the land, the leaders of the group of 101 settlers wrote the following Mayflower Compact establishing a government for their tiny community and claiming legitimate ownership of the land. It emphasized their relationship with God and their determination to found a godly community. Known also as "pilgrims," these settlers all followed a strict Protestant sect of Puritanism called Separatism. Even though their agreement acknowledges the political sovereignty of King James, their religious group had decisively split from the Church of England, Anglicanism, of which King James was the spiritual head. Anglicanism had been established by King Henry VIII in 1534 following a dispute with the Pope over the annulment of his marriage to Catherine of Aragon. The Puritan community had developed over the latter half of the sixteenth century with the aim of "purifying" the Church of England; essentially, Puritans believed that the Church of England was too Catholic and that it did not follow the path established by other strains of Protestantism, such as Lutheranism

---

From *Great Charters of Americanism* (Iowa City, 1920), 5.

and Calvinism, as closely as it should. Separatists, such as the pilgrims, had renounced the goal of reforming the Church of England, and sought instead to establish a separate, religiously-pure community.

In the name of God, Amen. We, whose names are underwritten, the loyal subjects of our dread sovereign Lord, King James, by the grace of God, of Great Britain, France and Ireland king, defender of the faith, etc., having undertaken for the glory of God, and advancement of the Christian faith, and honor of our king and country, a voyage to plant the first colony in the northern parts of Virginia, do, by these presents solemnly and mutually in the presence of God, and one of another, covenant and combine ourselves together into a civil body politic, for our better ordering and preservation and furtherance of the ends aforesaid; and by virtue hereof to enact, constitute, and frame such just and equal laws, ordinances, acts, constitutions, and offices, from time to time, as shall be thought most meet and convenient for the general good of the colony, unto which we promise all due submission and obedience. In witness whereof we have hereunder subscribed our names at Cape Cod the 11th of November, in the year of the reign of our sovereign Lord, King James, of England, France and Ireland, the eighteenth, and of Scotland, the fifty-fourth. Anno. Dom. 1620.

The Role of the Puritan Congregation

The Congregationalist Church was the center of Puritan society, both literally (the meeting house was usually placed in the center of each new community) and figuratively. Membership in the Puritan Church was an enormous spiritual and social commitment; it entailed joining a spiritual community full of reciprocal responsibilities to other church members, to God, and to the community as a whole. All church members entered into a "covenant," a sort of spiritual contract with both God and the other members of the congregation/community. Joining the church and entering into its covenant was a public act. The covenant below, from the First Church of Salem, Massachusetts (founded 1629), gives some idea of the simultaneous private and public commitments that joining a Puritan Church entailed.

As Calvinists, Puritans believed in the doctrine of predestination, the belief that an individual's spiritual fate was predetermined by an all-knowing God. Only those individuals believed by the congregation to be destined for salvation were permitted to join the church and enter into the covenant. The contractual nature of the covenant below, and its promises that members will actively and willfully "oppose all contrarie ways" and "resolve to prove our selves to the Lord" suggest the paradoxes of free will and fate inherent in Puritan society. The Puritans inhabited a spiritual world controlled utterly by an omniscient and all-powerful God yet nevertheless full of false paths, personal temptations, and potential failures of the will.

Wee whose names are here under written, members of the present Church of Christ in Salem, haveing found by sad experience how dangerous it is to sitt loose to the Covenant wee make

From *The Records of the First Church in Salem Massachusetts, 1629–1736*, ed. Richard D. Pierce, Essex Institute, (Salem, Mass., 1974), copyright © 1974 by Essex Institute, Salem, Massachusetts, 3–5.

with our God: and how apt wee are to wander into by pathes, even to the looseing of our first aimes in entring into Church fellowship: Doe therefore, solemnly in the presence of the Eternall God both for our owne comforts and those which shall or maye be joyned unto us renewe that Church covenant we find this Church bound unto at theire first begining. vizt: That we Covenant with the Lord and one with an other, and doe bynd our selves in the presence of God, to walke together in all his waies, according as he is pleased to reveale him selfe unto us in his Blessed word of truth. And doe more explicitly in the name and feare of God, profess and protest to walke as followeth through the power and grace of our Lord Jesus.

1. first wee avowe the Lord to be our God, and our selves his people in the truth and simplicitie of our Spirits

2. Wee give our selves to the Lord Jesus Christ, and the word of his grace, fore the teaching, ruleing and sanctifyeing of us in matters of worship, and conversation resolveing to cleave to him alone for life and glorie; and oppose all contrarie wayes, cannons and constitutions of men in his worship.

3. Wee promise to walk with our brethren and sisters in the Congregation with all watchfullness, and tendernis avoyding all jelousies, suspitions, backbyteings, conjurings, provoakings, secrete riseings of spirit against them, but in all offences to follow the rule of the Lord Jesus, and to beare and forbeare, give and forgive as he hath taught us.

4. In publick or private, we will willingly doe nothing to the ofence of the Church but will be willing to take advise for ourselves and ours as ocasion shall be presented.

5. Wee will not in the Congregation be forward eyther to show our owne gifts or parts in speaking or scrupuling [2] or there discover the fayling of our brethren or sisters butt attend an orderly cale there unto; knowing how much the Lord may be dishonoured, and his Gospell in the profession of it, sleighted by our distempers, and weaknesses in publyck.

6. Wee bynd ourselves to studdy the advancment of the Gospell in all truth and peace, both in regard of those that are within, or without, noe waye sleighting our sister Churches, but useing theire Counsell as need shalbe; nor laying a stumbling block, before any, noe not the Indians, whose good we desire to promote, and soe to converse, as wee may avoyd the verrye appearance of evill,

7. Wee hereby promise to carrye ourselves in all lawfull obedience, to those that are over us in Church or Common weale, knowing how well pleasing it wilbe to the Lord, that they should have incouragement in theire places, by our not greiveing theyre spirites through our iregulareties.

8. Wee resolve to prove our selves to the Lord in our particular calings, shunning ydlenes as the bane of any state, nor will wee deale hardly, or opressingly with Any, wherein wee are the Lords stewards: alsoe

9. promyseing to our best abilitie to teach our children and servants, the knowledge of God and his will, that they may serve him alsoe and all this, not by any strength of our owne, but by the Lord Christ, whose bloud we desire may sprinckle this our Covenant made in his name.

The Trial of Puritan Dissenter
Anne Hutchinson

Arriving in Boston in 1634, Anne Hutchinson (1591–1643) soon challenged both religious and gender traditions of the fledgling Massachusetts Bay Colony. During the voyage to Boston, Hutchinson was unhappy with the sermons of the minister onboard and had held religious discussions with fellow passengers. On shore, this criticism continued, and this mother of fourteen children and wife of a merchant found herself leading religious discussion groups of as many as sixty participants. Her fundamental problem was the Puritan community's emphasis on good works, as if a person could "buy" his or her way into heaven or influence God. To her, the covenant of good works preached in Boston was too close to Catholicism. Hutchinson believed that Puritans should look inward to find grace. Her ideas spread throughout the community, and her meetings came to the attention of John Winthrop, Governor of the Colony. He brought her before the General Court, which was composed of the governor and representatives who were selected by towns. This court, which had both political and religious authority, dealt very harshly with anyone whose words or actions went against the Puritan way.

In the following excerpts from the transcript, the religious and gender transgressions of Anne Hutchinson come through quite clearly. Initially, she, who had been well educated by her father, traded interpretations of the Bible with Winthrop, often winning the war of words. Then, she claimed God had spoken with her, which was considered heresy by Puritans. Whereas she believed that direct communication with God, revelation, was central to one's faith, the Puritan community at Boston thought that the only way that God communicated with human beings was through the Bible. Her idea threatened the role of ministers within the community by diminishing their importance. The General Court found Anne Hutchinson guilty of heresy. They also condemned her for overstepping her proper

From Thomas Hutchinson, *The History of the Colony and Province of Massachusetts-Bay,* Harvard University Press, (Cambridge, Mass., 1936), copyright © 1936 by the President and Fellows of Harvard College, 366–391.

role within society. Although Puritans believed that women and men were equal in terms of their ability to be saved, they rejected the idea that women should be involved in matters of political or religious governance. As part of her sentence, Anne Hutchinson and her family were banished from Massachusetts Bay. They briefly joined Roger Williams in his exile community in Providence. After leaving Providence, they moved to present-day Westchester County in N.Y., where she and almost all her family were killed by Native Americans. Puritan leaders saw her death as proof that their religious beliefs were correct.

November, 1637: The Examination of Mrs. Ann Hutchinson at the court at Newtown.

"Governor Winthrop: Mrs. Hutchinson, you are called here as one of those who have troubled the peace of the commonwealth and the churches here; you are known to be a woman that hath a great share in the promoting and divulging of those opinions that are causes of this trouble, and to be nearly joined not only in affinity and affection with some of those the court had taken notice of and passed censure upon, but you have spoken divers things as we have been informed very prejudicial to the honor of the churches and the ministers thereof, and you have maintained a meeting and an assembly in your house that hath been condemned by the general assembly as a thing not tolerable nor comely in the sight of God nor fitting for your sex, and notwithstanding that was cried down you have continued the same, therefore, we have thought good to send for you to understand how things are, that if you be in an erroneous way we may reduce you that so you may become a profitable member here among us, otherwise if you be obstinate in your course that then the court may take such course that you may trouble us no further, therefore I would entreat you to express whether you do not assent and hold in practice to those opinions and factions that have been handled in court already, that is to say, whether you do not justify Mr. Wheelwright's sermon and the petition. [Mr. Wheelwright's sermon was one of those criticized by Anne Hutchinson for emphasizing good works rather than faith.]

Mrs. Hutchinson: I am called here to answer before you but I hear no things laid to my charge.

Governor: I have told you some already and more I can tell you.

Mrs. Hutchinson: Name one Sir.

Governor: Have I not named some already?

Mrs. Hutchinson: What have I said or done?

Governor: Why for your doings, this you did harbor and countenance those that are parties in this faction that you have heard of.

Mrs. Hutchinson: That's a matter of conscience, Sir."

[They continued on to debate whether agreeing with those who emphasized faith over good works broke the law of the community.] . . .

"Governor: We do not mean to discourse with those of your sex but only this; you do adhere unto them and do endeavor to set forward this faction and so you do dishonor us.

Mrs. Hutchinson: I do acknowledge no such thing neither do I think that I ever put any dishonor upon you.

Governor: Why do you keep such a meeting at your house as you do every week upon a set day?

Mrs. Hutchinson: It is lawful for me to do so, as it is all your practices and can you find a warrant for yourself and condemn me for the same thing? The ground of my taking it up was, when I first came to this land because I did not go to such meetings as those were, it was presently reported that I did not allow of such meetings but held them unlawful and therefore in that regard they said I was proud and did despise all ordinances, upon that a friend came to me and told me of it, and I to prevent such aspersions took it up, but it was in practice before I came therefore I was not the first.

Governor: For his, that you appeal to our practice you need no confutation. If your meeting had answered to the former it had not been offensive, but I will say that there was no meeting of women alone, but your meeting is of another sort for there are sometimes men among you.

Mrs. Hutchinson: There was never any man with us.

Governor: Well, admit that there was no man at your meeting and that you was sorry for it, there is no warrant for your doings, and by what warrant do you continue such a course?

Mrs. Hutchinson: I conceive there lies a clear rule in Titus, that the elder women should instruct the younger and then I must have a time wherein I must do it.

Governor: All this I grant you, I grant you a time for it, but what is this to the purpose that you Mrs. Hutchinson must call a company together from their callings to come to be taught of you?

Mrs. Hutchinson: Will it please you to answer me this and to give me a rule for them I will willingly submit to any truth. If any come to my house to be instructed in the ways of God what rule do I have to put them away?

Governor: But suppose that a hundred men come unto you to be instructed will you forbear to instruct them?

Mrs. Hutchinson: As far as I conceive I cross a rule in it.

Governor: Very well and do you not so here?

Mrs. Hutchinson: No Sir for my ground [reason] is they are men.

Governor: Men and women all is one for that, but suppose that a man should come and say Mrs. Hutchinson, I hear that you are a woman that God hath given his grace unto and you have knowledge in the word of God I pray instruct me a little, ought you not to instruct this man?

Mrs. Hutchinson: I think I may.—Do you think it not lawful for me to teach women and why do you call me to teach the court?

Governor: We do not call you to teach the court but to lay open yourself [confess].

Mrs. Hutchinson: I desire you that you would then set me down a rule by which I may put them away that come unto me and so have peace in so doing.

Governor: You must show your rule to receive them.

Mrs. Hutchinson: I have done it.

Governor: I deny it because I have brought more arguments than you have.

Mrs. Hutchinson: I say, to me it is a rule."

[Debate over whether Mrs. Hutchinson should be able to hold religious discussions in her house continued.] . . .

"Governor: Your course is not to be suffered for, besides that we find such a course as this to be greatly prejudicial to the state, besides the occasion that it is to seduce many honest persons that are called to those meetings and your opinions being known to be different from the word of God may seduce many simple souls that resort unto you, besides that the occasion with hath come of late hath come from none but such as have frequented your meetings, so that they are now flown off from magistrates and ministers and this since they have come to you, and besides that it will not well stand with the commonwealth that families should be neglected for so many neighbors and dames and so much time spent, we see no rule of God for this, we see not that any should have authority to set up any other exercises besides what authority hath already set up and so what hurt comes of this you will be guilty of and we for suffering you.

Mrs. Hutchinson: Sir I do not believe that to be so.

Governor: Well, we see how it is, we must therefore put it away from you or restrain you from maintaining this course.

Mrs. Hutchinson: If you have a rule for it from God's word you may.

Governor: We are your judges, not you ours and we must compel you to it."

. . . [The Governor than called seven ministers to testify how the ideas and teaching of Mrs. Hutchinson went against their own beliefs and therefore represented a risk to the well-being of the community. The court then adjourned for the day.]

"The next morning

Governor: We proceeded last night as far as we could in hearing of this cause of Mrs. Hutchinson. There were divers things laid to her charge, but ordinary meetings about religious exercises, her speeches in derogation of the ministers among us, and the weakening of hands and hearts of the people towards them. Here was sufficient proof made of that which she was accused of in that point concerning the ministers and their ministry, as that they did preach a covenant of works when others did preach a covenant of grace, and that they were not able ministers of the new testament, and that they had not the seal of the spirit, and this was spoken not as was pretended out of private conference, but out of conscience and warrant from scripture alleged the fear of man is a snare and seeing God had given her a calling to it she would freely speak. Some other speeches she used, as that the letter of the scripture held forth a covenant of works, and this is offered to be proved by provable grounds. If there be anything else that the court hath to say they may speak.

Mrs. Hutchinson: The ministers come in their own cause. Now the Lord hath said that an oath is the end of all controversy; though there be a sufficient number of witnesses yet they are not according to the word, therefore I desire that they may speak on oath."

[This statement by Mrs. Hutchinson then sent off a lengthy discussion as to whether the ministers who had testified should be compelled to take an oath as to the veracity of their testimony in the court. This was followed by the testimony of Reverend Cotton who agreed with Mrs. Hutchinson's views on the overemphasis placed by Puritan ministers on good works.]

Mrs. Hutchinson: "... The Lord knows that I could not open scripture; he must by his prophetical office open it unto me. So after that being unsatisfied in the thing, the Lord was pleased to bring this scripture out of the Hebrews. He that denies the testament denies the testator, and in this did open unto me and give me to see that those which did not teach the new covenant has the spirit of antichrist, and upon this he did discover the ministry unto me . . . ."

The Bloody Tenant of Persecution

Roger Williams

Roger Williams (1603-1683) was born in England, studied at Cambridge University, and was an ordained minister of the Church of England. As a young man, Williams was attracted to Puritanism, a Calvinist reform movement within the Church of England. In 1630, as toleration for the Puritans declined, Williams severed his ties with the Church and joined the Puritans in their exodus to Massachusetts Bay in North America.

Once in Boston, Williams began espousing separatist ideals and refused to serve the Puritan congregation as long as it recognized the Church of England. Furthermore, he denounced the Puritans for imposing religious conformity on the colonists. Perhaps most radical was his refusal to acknowledge the validity of the Massachusetts Bay Charter, arguing that the King of England had no right to land that belonged to the Natives. In 1635, Governor John Winthrop banished Williams from the colony. The exiled minister moved south to found Providence, Rhode Island, as a haven of religious freedom. In 1643, facing encroachments from neighboring colonies, Williams returned to England to obtain a royal charter for the "Providence Plantations in Narragansett Bay." While in England he penned "The Bloody Tenant of Persecution," an eloquent explanation of his views on the freedom of religion.

Modern readers interested in freedom of religion and the separation of church and state will find Williams's words apt and applicable. Relentlessly chastising both Protestants and Catholics for their intolerance, Williams called for peace among the religions of the world. To persecute anyone of any faith directly contradicted "the doctrine of Christ Jesus the Prince of Peace."

First, that the blood of so many hundred thousand souls of Protestants and Papists, spilt in the wars of present and former ages, for their respective consciences, is not required nor accepted by Jesus Christ the Prince of Peace.

Secondly, pregnant scriptures and arguments are throughout the work proposed against the doctrine of persecution for cause of conscience.

Thirdly, satisfactory answers are given to scriptures, and objections produced by Mr. Calvin, Beza, Mr. Cotton, and the ministers of the New English churches and others former and later, tending to prove the doctrine of persecution for cause of conscience.

Fourthly, the doctrine of persecution for cause of conscience is proved guilty of all the blood of the souls crying for vengeance under the altar.

Fifthly, all civil states with their officers of justice in their respective constitutions and administrations are proved essentially civil, and therefore not judges, governors, or defenders of the spiritual or Christian state and worship.

Sixthly, it is the will and command of God that (since the coming of his Son the Lord Jesus) a permission of the most paganish, Jewish, Turkish, or antichristian consciences and worships, be granted to all men in all nations and countries; and they are only to be fought against with that sword which is only (in soul matters) able to conquer, to wit, the sword of God's Spirit, the Word of God.

Seventhly, the state of the Land of Israel, the kings and people thereof in peace and war, is proved figurative and ceremonial, and no pattern nor president for any kingdom or civil state in the world to follow.

Eighthly, God requireth not a uniformity of religion to be enacted and enforced in any civil state; which enforced uniformity (sooner or later) is the greatest occasion of civil war, ravishing of conscience, persecution of Christ Jesus in his servants, and of the hypocrisy and destruction of millions of souls.

Ninthly, in holding an enforced uniformity of religion in a civil state, we must necessarily disclaim our desires and hopes of the Jew's conversion to Christ.

Tenthly, an enforced uniformity of religion throughout a nation or civil state, confounds the civil and religious, denies the principles of Christianity and civility, and that Jesus Christ is come in the flesh.

Eleventhly, the permission of other consciences and worships than a state professeth only can (according to God) procure a firm and lasting peace (good assurance being taken according to the wisdom of the civil state for uniformity of civil obedience from all forts).

Twelfthly, lastly, true civility and Christianity may both flourish in a state or kingdom, notwithstanding the permission of divers and contrary consciences, either of Jew or Gentile. . . .

TRUTH. I acknowledge that to molest any person, Jew or Gentile, for either professing doctrine, or practicing worship merely religious or spiritual, it is to persecute him, and such a person (whatever his doctrine or practice be, true or false) suffereth persecution for conscience.

But withal I desire it may be well observed that this distinction is not full and complete: for beside this that a man may be persecuted because he holds or practices what he believes in conscience to be a truth (as Daniel did, for which he was cast into the lions' den, Dan. 6), and many thousands of Christians, because they durst not cease to preach and practice what they believed was by God commanded, as the Apostles answered (Acts 4 & 5), I say besides this a man may also be persecuted, because he dares not be constrained to yield obedience to such doctrines and worships as are by men invented and appointed. . . .

Dear TRUTH, I have two sad complaints:

First, the most sober of the witnesses, that dare to plead thy cause, how are they charged to be mine enemies, contentious, turbulent, seditious?

Secondly, thine enemies, though they speak and rail against thee, though they outrageously pursue, imprison, banish, kill thy faithful witnesses, yet how is all vermilion'd o'er for justice against the heretics? Yea, if they kindle coals, and blow the flames of devouring wars, that leave neither spiritual nor civil state, but burn up branch and root, yet how do all pretend an holy war? He that kills, and he that's killed, they both cry out: "It is for God, and for their conscience."

'Tis true, nor one nor other seldom dare to plead the mighty Prince Christ Jesus for their author, yet (both Protestant and Papist) pretend they have spoke with Moses and the Prophets who all, say they (before Christ came), allowed such holy persecutions, holy wars against the enemies of holy church.

TRUTH. Dear PEACE (to ease thy first complaint), 'tis true, thy dearest sons, most like their mother, peacekeeping, peace-making sons of God, have borne and still must bear the slurs of troublers of Israel, and turners of the world upside down. And 'tis true again, what Solomon once spake: "The beginning of strife is as when one letteth out water, therefore (saith he) leave off contention before it be meddled with. This caveat should keep the banks and sluices firm and strong, that strife, like a breach of waters, break not in upon the sons of men."

Yet strife must be distinguished: It is necessary or unnecessary, godly or Ungodly, Christian or unchristian, etc.

It is unnecessary, unlawful, dishonorable, ungodly, unchristian, in most cases in the world, for there is a possibility of keeping sweet peace in most cases, and, if it be possible, it is the express command of God that peace be kept (Rom. 13).

Again, it is necessary, honorable, godly, etc., with civil and earthly weapons to defend the innocent and to rescue the oppressed from the violent paws and jaws of oppressing persecuting Nimrods (Psal. 73; Job 29).

It is as necessary, yea more honorable, godly, and Christian, to fight the fight of faith, with religious and spiritual artillery, and to contend earnestly for the faith of Jesus, once delivered to the saints against all opposers, and the gates of earth and hell, men or devils, yea against Paul himself, or an angel from heaven, if he bring any other faith or doctrine. . . .

PEACE. I add that a civil sword (as woeful experience in all ages has proved) is so far from bringing or helping forward an opposite in religion to repentance that magistrates sin grievously against the work of God and blood of souls by such proceedings. Because as (commonly) the sufferings of false and antichristian teachers harden their followers, who being blind, by this means are occasioned to tumble into the ditch of hell after their blind leaders, with more inflamed zeal of lying confidence. So, secondly, violence and a sword of steel begets such an impression in the sufferers that certainly they conclude (as indeed that religion cannot be true which needs such instruments of violence to uphold it so) that persecutors are far from soft and gentle commiseration of the blindness of others. . . .

For (to keep to the similitude which the Spirit useth, for instance) to batter down a stronghold, high wall, fort, tower, or castle, men bring not a first and second admonition, and after obstinacy, excommunication, which are spiritual weapons concerning them that be in the church: nor exhortation to repent and be baptized, to believe in the Lord Jesus, etc., which are proper weapons to them that be without, etc. But to take a stronghold, men bring cannons, culverins, saker, bullets, powder, muskets, swords, pikes, etc., and these to this end are weapons effectual and proportionable.

On the other side, to batter down idolatry, false worship, heresy, schism, blindness, hardness, out of the soul and spirit, it is vain, improper, and unsuitable to bring those weapons which are used by persecutors, stocks, whips, prisons, swords, gibbets, stakes, etc. (where these seem to prevail with some cities or kingdoms, a stronger force sets up again, what a weaker pull'd down), but against these spiritual strongholds in the souls of men, spiritual artillery and weapons are proper, which are mighty through God to subdue and bring under the very thought to obedience, or else to bind fast the soul with chains of darkness, and lock it up in the prison of unbelief and hardness to eternity. . . .

PEACE. I pray descend now to the second evil which you observe in the answerer's position, viz., that it would be evil to tolerate notorious evildoers, seducing teachers, etc.

TRUTH. I say the evil is that he most improperly and confusedly joins and couples seducing teachers with scandalous livers.

PEACE. But is it not true that the world is full of seducing teachers, and is it not true that seducing teachers are notorious evildoers?

TRUTH. I answer, far be it from me to deny either, and yet in two things I shall discover the great evil of this joining and coupling seducing teachers, and scandalous livers as one adequate or proper object of the magistrate's care and work to suppress and punish.

First, it is not an homogeneal (as we speak) but an hetergeneal commixture or joining together of things most different in kinds and natures, as if they were both of one consideration. . . .

TRUTH. I answer, in granting with Brentius that man hath not power to make laws to bind conscience, he overthrows such his tenent and practice as restrain men from their worship, according to their conscience and belief, and constrain them to such worships (though it be out of a pretense that they are convinced) which their own souls tell them they have no satisfaction nor faith in.

Secondly, whereas he affirms that men may make laws to see the laws of God observed.

I answer, God needeth not the help of a material sword of steel to assist the sword of the Spirit in the affairs of conscience, to those men, those magistrates, yea that commonwealth which makes such magistrates, must needs have power and authority from Christ Jesus to fit judge and to determine in all the great controversies concerning doctrine, discipline, government, etc.

And then I ask whether upon this ground it must not evidently follow that:

Either there is no lawful commonweal nor civil state of men in the world, which is not qualified with this spiritual discerning (and then also that the very commonweal hath more light concerning the church of Christ than the church itself).

Or, that the commonweal and magistrates thereof must judge and punish as they are persuaded in their own belief and conscience (be their conscience paganish, Turkish, or antichristian) what is this but to confound heaven and earth together, and not only to take away the being of Christianity out of the world, but to take away all civility, and the world out of the world, and to lay all upon heaps of confusion? . . .

PEACE. The fourth head is the proper means of both these powers to attain their ends.

First, the proper means whereby the civil power may and should attain its end are only political, and principally these five. First, the erecting and establishing what form of civil government may seem in wisdom most meet, according to general rules of the world, and state of the people.

Secondly, the making, publishing, and establishing of wholesome civil laws, not only such as concern civil justice, but also the free passage of true religion; for outward civil peace ariseth and is maintained from them both, from the latter as well as from the former.

Civil peace cannot stand entire, where religion is corrupted (2 Chron. 15. 3. 5. 6; and Judges 8). And yet such laws, though conversant about religion, may still be counted civil laws, as, on the contrary, an oath doth still remain religious though conversant about civil matters.

Thirdly, election and appointment of civil officers to see execution to those laws.

Fourthly, civil punishments and rewards of transgressors and observers of these laws.

Fifthly, taking up arms against the enemies of civil peace.

Secondly, the means whereby the church may and should attain her ends are only ecclesiastical, which are chiefly five.

First, setting up that form of church government only of which Christ hath given them a pattern in his Word.

Secondly, acknowledging and admitting of no lawgiver in the church but Christ and the publishing of His laws.

Thirdly, electing and ordaining of such officers only, as Christ hath appointed in his Word.

Fourthly, to receive into their fellowship them that are approved and inflicting spiritual censures against them that o end.
Fifthly, prayer and patience in suffering any evil from them that be without, who disturb their peace.
So that magistrates, as magistrates, have no power of setting up the form of church government, electing church officers, punishing with church censures, but to see that the church does her duty herein. And on the other side, the churches as churches, have no power (though as members of the commonweal they may have power) of erecting or altering forms of civil government, electing of civil officers, inflicting civil punishments (no not on persons excommunicate) as by deposing magistrates from their civil

authority, or withdrawing the hearts of the people against them, to their laws, no more than to discharge wives, or children, or servants, from due obedience to their husbands, parents, or masters; or by taking up arms against their magistrates, though he persecute them for conscience: for though members of churches who are public officers also of the civil state may suppress by force the violence of usurpers, as Iehoiada did Athaliah, yet this they do not as members of the church but as officers of the civil state.

TRUTH. Here are divers considerable passages which I shall briefly examine, so far as concerns our controversy.

First, whereas they say that the civil power may erect and establish what form of civil government may seem in wisdom most meet, I acknowledge the proposition to be most true, both in itself and also considered with the end of it, that a civil government is an ordinance of God, to conserve the civil peace of people, so far as concerns their bodies and goods, as formerly hath been said.

But from this grant I infer (as before hath been touched) that the sovereign, original, and foundation of civil power lies in the people (whom they must needs mean by the civil power distinct from the government set up). And, if so, that a people may erect and establish what form of government seems to them most meet for their civil condition; it is evident that such governments as are by them erected and established have no more power, nor for no longer time, than the civil power or people consenting and agreeing shall betrust them with. This is clear not only in reason but in the experience of all commonweals, where the people are not deprived of their natural freedom by the power of tyrants.

And, if so, that the magistrates receive their power of governing the church from the people, undeniably it follows that a people, as a people, naturally consider (of what nature or nation soever in Europe, Asia, Africa, or America), have fundamentally and originally, as men, a power to govern the church, to see her do her duty, to correct her, to redress, reform, establish, etc. And if this be not to pull God and Christ and Spirit out of heaven, and subject them unto natural, sinful, inconstant men, and so consequently to Satan himself, by whom all peoples naturally are guided, let heaven and earth judge. . . .

PEACE. Some will here ask: What may the magistrate then lawfully do with his civil horn or power in matters of religion?

TRUTH. His horn not being the horn of that unicorn or rhinoceros, the power of the Lord Jesus in spiritual cases, his sword not the two-edged sword of the spirit, the word of God (hanging not about the loins or side, but at the lips. and proceeding out of the mouth of his ministers) but of an humane and civil nature and constitution, it must consequently be of a humane and civil operation, for who knows not that operation follows constitution; And therefore I shall end this passage with this consideration:

The civil magistrate either respecteth that religion and worship which his conscience is persuaded is true, and upon which he ventures his soul; or else that and those which he is persuaded are false.

Concerning the first, if that which the magistrate believeth to be true, be true, I say he owes a threefold duty unto it:

First, approbation and countenance, a reverent esteem and honorable testimony, according to Isa. 49, and Revel. 21, with a tender respect of truth, and the professors of it.

Secondly, personal submission of his own soul to the power of the Lord Jesus in that spiritual government and kingdom, according to Matt. 18 and 1 Cor. 5.

Thirdly, protection of such true professors of Christ, whether apart, or met together, as also of their estates from violence and injury, according to Rom. 13.

Now, secondly, if it be a false religion (unto which the civil magistrate dare not adjoin, yet) he owes:

First, permission (for approbation he owes not what is evil) and this according to Matthew 13. 30 for public peace and quiet's sake.

Secondly, he owes protection to the persons of his subjects (though of a false worship), that no injury be offered either to the persons or goods of any. . . .

. . . The God of Peace, the God of Truth will shortly seal this truth, and confirm this witness, and make it evident to the whole world, that the doctrine of persecution for cause of conscience, is most evidently and lamentably contrary to the doctrine of Christ Jesus the Prince of Peace. Amen.

A Puritan Justifies Intolerance

The New England Puritans were criticized for more than leaving England at a time of intense struggle; they were also attacked as religious bigots. In the following selection, Puritan legal scholar Nathaniel Ward (1570–1653) attempts to justify intolerance. Although he and his co-religionists were criticized for these attitudes in their own day, we must bear in mind that principled opposition to religious diversity was fairly common among their contemporaries. This passage is taken from The Simple Cobler of Aggawam in America, *5th ed. Aggawam was an early name for the town of Ipswich, Massachusetts.*

My heart hath natura'ly detested four things: The standing of the Apocrypha in the Bible; Forainers dwelling in my Country, to crowd out Native Subjects into the corners of the Earth; Alchymized Coines; Tolerations of divers Religions, or of one Religion in segregant shapes: He that willingly assents to the last, if he examines his heart by day-light, his Conscience will tell him, he is either an Atheist, or an Heretick, or an Hypocrite, or at best a captive to some Lust: Poly-piety is the greatest impiety in the World. True Religion is *Ignis probation is* which doth *congregare homogenea & segregare heterogenea* [*True Religion is a Testing Fire which doth Bring Together the alike and drive away the different or heterodox*].

Not to tolerate things meerly indifferent to weak Consciences, argues a Conscience too strong: pressed uniformity in these, causes much disunity: To tolerate more than indifferents, is not to deal indifferently with God: He that doth it, takes his Scepter out of his hand, and bids him stand by. Who hath to do to institute

From *The Simple Cobler of Aggawam in America*, 5th ed., by Nathaniel Ward a.k.a. Theodore de la Guard, printed by J.D. & R.I., reprinted for Daniel Henchman at his shop in King Street, Boston, Massachusetts, 1713, 5–6.

Religion but God. The power of all Religion and Ordinances, lies in their Purity: their Purity in their Simplicity: then are mixtures pernicious. I lived in a City, where a Papist Preached in one Church, a Lutheran in another, a Calvinist in a third; a Lutheran one part of the day, a Calvinist the other, in the same Pulpit: the Religion of that Place was but motly and meagre, their affections Leopard-like.

If the whole Creature should conspire to do the Creator a mischief, or offer him an insolency, it would be in nothing more, than in erecting untruths against his Truth, or by sophisticating his Truths with humane medleyes: the removing of some one iota in Scripture, may draw out all the life, and traverse all the Truth of the whole Bible: but to authorize an untruth, by a Toleration of State, is to build a Sconce against the walls of Heaven, to batter God out of his Chair: To tell a practical lye, is a great Sin, but yet transient; but to set up a Theorical untruth, is to warrant every lye that lyes from its root to the top of every branch it hath, which are not a few.

Bringing the Salem Witch Trials to an End

Witchcraft scares had taken place in other communities throughout Puritan New England during the middle and late 1600s. Unlike the events in Salem, however, previous outbreaks of witchcraft generally involved one or a handful of accused and subsided after one round of accusations and trials. The accused were usually obvious scapegoats. In Salem, however, afflictions, accusations, and arrests continued well beyond the first outbreak, and as the trials continued, charges of witchcraft began to spread up the social ladder. By June of 1692, nineteen had been executed and hundreds more, including prominent and respected members of the community, had been arrested or accused. The notion that a community of the Godly could be so overrun by the forces of Satan did serious violence to the Puritan worldview.

The Salem witch trials represented to Puritan society a problem of jurisprudence as well as a problem of spiritual and social decay. Those who began to challenge the course and conduct of the trials often did so not out of disbelief in the underlying spiritual accusations (the existence of witches was never questioned by Puritan society) but out of a sense that the legal system had spiraled out of control. The most famous statement of this perspective, by prominent Boston minister and politician Increase Mather, challenged the trials' sloppy procedures and questionable use of evidence. Note that Mather went out of his way, in a postscript to his criticisms of the trials, to affirm his belief in the reality of witchcraft and the dangers it posed to Puritan society. The statement below, signed by Mather and a group of other prominent New England ministers, brought the trials to an end.

The Return of several Ministers consulted by his Excellency, and the Honourable Council, upon the present Witchcrafts in *Salem* Village.

From *Cases of Conscience*, by Increase Mather, (Boston, 1693), unpaginated appendix.

Boston, June 15. 1692

I. The afflicted State of our poor Neighbours, that are now suffering by Molestations from the Invisible World, we apprehend so deplorable, that we think their Condition calls for the utmost help of all Persons in their several Capacities.

II. We cannot but with all Thankfulness acknowledge, the Success which the merciful God has given unto the sedulous and assiduous Endeavors of our honourable Rulers, to detect the abominable Witchcrafts which have been committed in the Country; humbly *praying that the discovery of these mysterious and mischievous Wickednesses, may be perfected.*

III. We judge that in the prosecution of these, and all such Witchcrafts, there is need of a very critical and exquisite Caution, left by too much Credulity for things received only upon the Devil's Authority, there be a Door opened for a long Train of miserable Consequences, and Satan get an Advantage over us, for we should not be ignorant of his Devices.

IV. . . . 'tis necessary that all Proceedings thereabout be managed with an exceeding tenderness toward those that may be complained of; especially if they have been Persons formerly of an unblemished Reputation.

V. When the first Enquiry is made into the Circumstances of such as may lie under any just Suspicion of Witchcrafts, we could wish that there may be admitted as little as is possible, of such Noise, Company, and Openness, as may too hastily expose them that are examined; and that there may nothing be used as a Test, for the Trial of the suspected, the Lawfulness whereof may be doubted among the People of God; but that the Directions given by such Judicious Writers as Perkins and Bernard, be consulted in such a Case.

At the close of his pamphlet opposing the witch trials, Increase Mather added a postscript protesting that he did not want to be misunderstood. In particular, Mather feared that readers might think he did not believe in witches or that he intended to criticize the trial judges. These excerpts from his postscript reveal how uncomfortable New England elites felt about publishing their differences; in addition they suggest that Mather did not want to be seen as contributing to irreligion by denying again the existence of the supernatural.

The Design of the preceding *Dissertation,* is not to plead for Witchcrafts, or to appear as an Advocate for Witches: I have therefore written another Discourse proving that there are such horrid Creatures as Witches in the World; and that they are to be extripated and cut off from amongst the People of God, which I have Thoughts and Inclinations in due time to publish; and I am abundantly satisfied that there have been, and are still most cursed Witches in the Land. More then one or two of those now in Prison, have freely and credibly acknowledged their Communion and Familiarity with the Spirits of Darkness; and have also declared unto me the Time and Occasion, with the particular Circumstances of their Hellish Obligations and Abominations.

Nor is there designed any Reflection on those worthy Persons who have been concerned in the late Proceedings at *Salam:* They are wise and good Men, and have acted with all Fidelity according to their Light, and have out of tenderness declined the doing of some things, which in our own Judgments they were satisfied about: Having therefore so arduous a Case before them, Pitty and Prayers rather than Censures are their due; on which account I am glad that there is published to the World (by my Son) a *Breviate of the Tryals* of some who were lately executed, whereby I hope the thinking part of Mankind will be satisfied, that there was more than that which is called *Spectre Evidence* for the Conviction of the Persons condemned.

Seventeenth-Century Eastern Woodlands, 1607–1689

From Chapter 4 of *First Americans: A History of Native Peoples*, Combined Volume, First Edition. Kenneth W. Townsend, Mark A. Nicholas.

Worlds Apart

The Wampanoag Indians of Cape Cod had welcomed the Pilgrims, and they allowed the first Englishmen on the Cape to share their lands. But the first settlers turned Wampanoag homelands into the colony of New Plymouth, and in that colony Englishmen and the Wampanoags maintained peaceful but fragile relationships. To make room for farms and houses in their new colony, the Englishmen, over the course of forty years, stripped the Wampanoags of the most fertile soil and best harbors and beachheads. After hearing complaints, New Plymouth's leaders conceded that they would not take any more of

King Philip (Metacomet), Sachem of the Wampanoags.

the Indians' lands. This was nothing short of a lie. Indian-white relations in New Plymouth started to tailspin in 1663, when the colonists established the town of Swansea. Swansea's residents quickly noticed warriors associated with the sachem, or chief, Metacom (known to the English as King Philip) around the town's borders. The settlers had taken Wampanoag hunting grounds to turn them into Swansea's farmsteads. In 1671, the colonists increased the pressure on Metacom, demanding that he cede additional Wampanoag land to Plymouth and pay tribute to the colony. Meeting these conditions would have made Plymouth sovereign over the Wampanoags. Desperate, Metacom turned to another group of English colonists, the residents of the Massachusetts Bay colony, for support. Not surprisingly, the English colonists sided with each other.

In acting as they did, the English destroyed a longstanding treaty brokered in 1621 by Massasoit, Metacom's father, to benefit the Wampanoags. The agreement had allowed the English to share the Wampanoag homelands. In 1621, Massasoit was on friendly terms with the colonists, but now his son Metacom faced a direct challenge to the Wampanoags' existence as an independent people. Metacom felt he had no choice but to go to war and, in 1675, King Philip's War began. The war, as it turned out, was one of the bloodiest conflicts in American history.

Around the same time, far to the west in the *pays d'en haut*, as the French called the vast territory reaching from the Great Lakes through parts of the Ohio Country into present-day Illinois, there were very different sorts of cross-cultural interactions. Horrific lighting raids out of New York by the Five Nations Iroquois Confederacy displaced many tribal peoples. Extreme violence on the part of the Iroquois turned the *pays d'en haut* into a vast multitribal zone of exiled Indians who were both physically and emotionally shattered. In this portion of the Eastern Woodlands, people were not warring against each other but searching for ways to keep the peace. In the 1660s, a group of Indians welcomed the French explorer Nicholas Perrot to a village of Miami and Mascouten Indians near Green Bay. An elderly man and a woman first greeted Perrot. The Mascouten man, probably a chief, carried a pipe with a long stem, known as a calumet, a sign of his friendly intentions. The man presented the pipe to the Frenchman for him to smoke, but first he performed a ritual, pointing the calumet in all the cardinal directions surrounding the visitors. The Indians inhaled from the calumet then blew smoke near Perrot's face as an Algonquian greeting of peace.

Entering the village, Perrot witnessed the ritual practice of binding friends together. Holding their own calumets, several Miami chiefs stood at the village entrance, ready to celebrate into the evening. The following day, Perrot reciprocated the Indians' generosity. He gave the Mascoutens and Miamis a kettle and a gun. Then right before he left, Perrot proclaimed to the villagers that he was ". . . the dawn of that light, which

CHRONOLOGY	
1607–1608	Jamestown settlement and interaction with Powhatan Confederacy
1608	Champlain settles Quebec along the St. Lawrence River
1609–1610	Champlain and Indian alliance defeat Mohawks
1610–1614	First Anglo-Powhatan War
1621	Pilgrim treaty with Massasoit
1622–1632	Second Anglo-Powhatan War
1644	Opechancanough's last rebellion in Virginia
1640s	"Praying Town" model established in Massachusetts
1630s–1650s	Great Puritan migration to Massachusetts and development of Rhode Island and Connecticut First Five Nations "Beaver Wars"
1660s–1690s	Rise of the "Middle Ground" in western Great Lakes region
1675–1676	King Philip's War (Metacom's War)
1676	Bacon's Rebellion
1689	Start of King William's War in the colonies and the end of the last Iroquois "Beaver Wars"
1701	Final negotiation of grand settlement between Five Nations and New France

is beginning to appear in your lands." After years of dark times stained by bloodshed, Perrot's words in the Algonquian tongue would have brought some healing to the Indians' broken hearts. The two sides may not have fully understood each other yet, but one thing was for certain: both the French and the multitribal villagers of the *pays d'en haut* had a sincere desire to bring peace and friendship to the region.

As these events demonstrate, relations between Indians and Europeans in the Eastern Woodlands varied widely. Along the Atlantic seaboard, Indians and English colonists headed into war. In the *pays d'en haut,* French and Algonquian peoples worked hard to find ways to live in peace. Misunderstanding, miscommunication, and bad faith could, and did, lead to conflict, violence, and outright war. It was also true, however, that a spirit of accommodation and adaptation was sometimes enough to hold together fragile, complex relations between Indians and Europeans. And some Indian peoples took a third choice, turning inward to their communities for strength rather than relying on European goods, religions, and relationships. All of this was part of the makeup of the seventeenth-century Eastern Woodlands. This chapter begins with the Powhatan Confederacy and the English in the Algonquian homelands of *Tsenacommacah*, called Virginia by the English. It then traces Indian and English interactions in early New England. Moving into a world in the northeast near the Great Lakes region, the chapter then looks at how brewing antagonisms among the Iroquois, Huron, and surrounding Algonquian peoples became worse as the French introduced trade, disease, Catholicism, and unfamiliar diplomatic tactics. The chapter ends by looking at two major wars involving native peoples that closed out the century: King Philip's War in New England and Bacon's Rebellion in Virginia.

KEY QUESTIONS

1. How was the Powhatan Confederacy structured, and what sort of relationships did the English create with the confederacy?

2. How did intercultural encounters unfold between New England Indians and the Puritans?

3. With the creation of New France, how did the combination of trade, diplomacy, war, and Catholicism reshape Indian lives in the Northeast?

4. What made the "middle ground" different from other parts of the Eastern Woodlands?

5. What were the causes of Metacom's War?

6. What were the causes of Bacon's Rebellion?

TSENACOMMACAH

Before the English arrived, Algonquian-speaking Native Americans in the region surrounding the Chesapeake Bay had already experienced significant changes to their ways of life. Historians and archaeologists remain uncertain about exactly when Chesapeake tribal groups first coalesced into larger chiefdoms, although scholars generally agree that warfare with the Iroquois to the north and the Susquehannocks to the south was the key factor in the transformation. Over time, hereditary chiefs known as **weroances** came to hold key positions in Chesapeake society. From fellow villagers they received tribute in trade. Weroances also mustered men for war, primarily to attack northern and southern rivals in the Iroquois and the Susquehannocks. Smaller villages became tributaries to a paramount chief. The threat of raids by both northern and southern tribes compelled the chiefdoms to pursue intertribal friendships to protect settlements and trade networks. *Weroances* who traced descent through their mothers' lines entered into intertribal marriages that led to new relations of kinship. Matrilineal lines also had an important role to play in village politics. Clan mothers appointed particular village *weroances* to leadership positions, had say over the land as women tilled the soil, and often had to give their consent before men could go to war. Creating a confederacy involved a high frequency of war and trade to bring other tribes into a system of owing tribute to a leading *weroance* and his elite matrilineages. The paramount chief, Wahunsunacock, known to the English as Powhatan, and his elite village *weroances* had consolidated a massive confederacy by the time the English came to settle Jamestown in 1607. He had conquered many neighbors, created an effective system of tribute to rule over local groups, and established a shared set of beliefs. They claimed a homeland in *Tsenacommacah* ("our land") in present-day Virginia. Making comparisons with their experiences with monarchial rule, the English viewed Powhatan as a king, a man capable of ruling over lesser lords. Powhatan was no king, although in truth *Tsenacommacah* was immense. Powhatan's confederacy included close to thirty tribes in a territory extending from the southern shores of the James River up to the Potomac River (see Map 1). *Tsenacommacah* under Powhatan's rule generally remained unchecked by other Indians in the area.

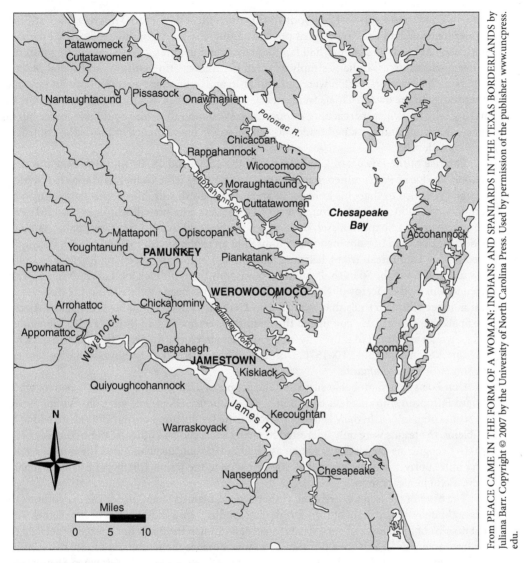

From PEACE CAME IN THE FORM OF A WOMAN: INDIANS AND SPANIARDS IN THE TEXAS BORDERLANDS by Juliana Barr. Copyright © 2007 by the University of North Carolina Press. Used by permission of the publisher. www.uncpress.edu.

Map 1   Indian landscape and tribal locations

The Rise of the Powhatan Confederacy

The Powhatan Indians' confederacy came to hold a powerful place in the Chesapeake world. In an environment of growing European trade, elite intermarriage with multiple wives, and intertribal conflict, Wahunsunacock—most likely in the 1560s or 1570s—built an Atlantic-coast Indian confederacy around *Tsenacommacah*. The size of Powhatan's confederacy was rivaled only by those of the Great Lakes Huron and New York Iroquois (see later in this chapter). Powhatan consolidated his power through war and marriage, and also in patterns of trade goods exchange specific to the internal workings of a stratified chiefdom. The conspicuous display of prestige items from foreign sources and the distribution of goods and food increased a *weroance's* sacred and political authority. A *weroance* of an elite lineage who accumulated more trade items and gave more to other villages could hope to rise to become a paramount chief. Thus, *weroances* were always interested in acquiring rare trade goods from distant lands, including mica, copper, shells, and various precious stones. The first European travelers to the Chesapeake coastline brought a new and exotic set of goods to this dynamic. Glass beads, mirrors, and utilitarian copper items all had their own spirit powers among coastal Algonquians like the Powhatans. Some such as beads and copper had familiar colors and textures, closely resembling traditional indigenous resources. Indians simply adapted them to existing cultural and social practices. Others such as mirrors, which were unfamiliar in appearance and texture, brought new status and prestige to the owner. Chiefs were expected to display their wealth and to share it. Decision making relied on villagers reaching a consensus. *Weroances* therefore could not coerce but only persuade. Strong and sustained trade was crucial to the maintenance of Powhatan control over their confederacy.

The rise of the Powhatan Confederacy in the 1560s and 1570s was also linked to the incredible voyage of Paquiquineo. Paquiquineo was a young, elite Indian who traveled to Mexico City and returned to share his knowledge about the Spanish with his people. Paquiquineo most certainly traced his descent through one of Powhatan's elite matrilineal lines. In 1561, Paquiquineo boarded a Spanish vessel, the *Santa Catalina*, and headed for New Spain. As he traveled to Mexico City, Paquiquineo found himself in an exotic world. In Mexico City, Paquiquineo lived among Dominican friars, learning Spanish and eventually receiving baptism as well as a new name. Among the Spanish, Paquiquineo was now the Catholic Don Luís de Velasco, a name given to him by the Viceroy of New Spain. Soon Don Luís began to talk about the riches and the vast number of Indian souls that were ripe for Catholic conversion in his homeland—Ajacán to the Spanish explorers. He convinced the Spanish governor of La Florida, Pedro Menéndez de Avilés, a man appointed to protect Spanish provinces in North America, to send him back to the Chesapeake; on September 10, 1570, Don Luís, along with some Jesuit missionaries, landed on the shores of *Tsenacommacah*.

Don Luís's return probably surprised the people of *Tsenacommacah*, as few natives who left aboard European ships made it back home. *Tsenacommacah*'s people were also disappointed in his Jesuit companions. In their heavy black robes, the Jesuits stood out as oddities. To add to their problems, the Jesuits were only interested in saving souls and had little to offer in the way of trade goods. Recognizing the Jesuits as not an asset, Don Luís quickly abandoned them to move about forty miles upriver. During a horrible, starving winter, the Jesuits finally gave in and exchanged some useful items for food.

The head of the Jesuit expedition, Father Segura, blamed Don Luís for the expedition's troubles and publicly lashed out at him for his "backsliding" into Indian ways of life. Father Segura had no idea of the danger of such tirades against an Indian from an elite lineage, especially coming from someone in as weak a position as he was. Because the Jesuits were more of a hindrance than a help, Don Luís decided to kill them. An opportunity presented itself when Segura further insulted Don Luís by sending two Jesuits to the Indian village without proper offerings of trade. Seizing the moment, Don Luís killed the two priests. Then with a small party of warriors he went to the mission and killed Father Segura and the other Jesuits. By deciding to kill the Jesuits with Spanish-made axes, Don Luís and his warriors made an important statement. The bloody event let the Spanish know that to land on *Tsenacommacah* soil meant trading prestige items with elite leaders on their own terms.

The only member of the mission party to survive the attack was Alonso, a Spanish boy who had traveled with the Jesuits. Rescuing Alonso from the coast then using his limited knowledge of the Indians, Menéndez the governor decided to lead an expedition to kill Don Luís. After a fray in which the Spanish killed twenty Indians and took thirteen as captives, the Spanish entered into negotiations with the Indians. They could not find Don Luís. The governor then traded his way back to his ship with the captives, where he ordered the hanging of eight or nine of the captives if Don Luís continued to elude the Spanish. The Spanish hoped that the hangings would persuade Don Luís to surrender himself. However, in minds of the Powhatan Indians the death of eight or nine lesser tribesmen at the hands of unwilling traders was perhaps a lesser sacrifice compared with the life of an elite chief.

Don Luís vanished from the historical record, but his odyssey and subsequent return had incredible consequences for Powhatan's growing confederacy. Don Luís's special knowledge made Powhatan and his *weroances* more aware of European intentions and more appreciative of the power of European weapons. The Powhatan also now knew that the European newcomers did not understand the importance of offering goods to the paramount chief and other elites. Unless Europeans learned to follow the proper rules of diplomatic and economic engagement in *Tsenacommacah*, the end result would always be violent confrontation.

Powhatan and the English: Trade and Conflict

Christopher Newport led the initial Jamestown expedition up the James River in 1607. The entire area from Jamestown up the James River to the falls fell within Powhatan's confederacy. The tiny settlement of Jamestown was sixty miles from the Chesapeake Bay. Newport and his men had selected an inappropriate place to build an outpost, particularly a settlement not of farmers but of soldiers and gentlemen. Jamestown began more as a military outpost than a self-sustaining colony. Water was brackish. Food was scarce because the soldiers and their leaders had little interest in planting and growing crops.

Some local natives were, at first, eager to trade with the English, exchanging corn for glass beads and other small items. Newport and his men, however, were not interested in establishing a minor trading post. Their goal was to bring the Indians' land under English control by any means necessary, to find profit from the lands of Virginia. To mark his intentions, Newport placed a crucifix at the head of the falls on his first expedition upriver in 1607. Because Newport had violated the rules of sharing the land only after negotiating with Powhatan, Algonquian warriors from upriver villages joined warriors from the Jamestown area in a joint attack on the English settlement. Only their guns and cannon allowed Jamestown's men to survive the offensive.

Powhatan most likely ordered the Indian strike against Jamestown as a way of gauging the colonists' intentions and their military strength. Not knowing when the next attack might come, Newport ordered the construction of increased fortifications around Jamestown. This move only intensified Indian mistrust of the colonists, as it signaled English permanency on the land without Powhatan's approval. From the beginning, Newport and the other Jamestown settlers did not grasp that building a colony in *Tsenacommacah* meant getting Powhatan's approval. Newport had to first conduct business with the paramount chief. This meant trading prestige goods in an appropriate diplomatic setting and not spending time among tributary villages trading trinkets.

Relations with Powhatan's confederacy shifted for the worse once Captain John Smith took power over Jamestown. Smith claimed his own role as Jamestown's leader in 1607–1608, right after Newport departed for England to recruit new settlers and bring back new stocks of food and goods. Jamestown faced disease and starvation in its first winter. The Indians were uninterested in trading corn; their own winter stocks were low, and without Indian corn the colony could not survive. Smith was an experienced military man—aggressive and often brutal. He refused to let the colony starve. Trading where he could and using force where he could not, Smith gathered corn for his colony. Tributary villages traded reluctantly with what corn they could spare, but they soon grew disgruntled with Smith's aggressive tactics and lack of reciprocity.

Pamunkeys, one of the tribes within the Powhatan confederacy, captured Smith during his travels. Smith's life was spared because Powhatan's brother, Opechancanough, recognized Smith as a valuable captive, one worthy of meeting with his brother. To prevent another attack on Jamestown, Smith promised Opechancanough prestige goods from Jamestown. The captain sent a letter to his men, warning them of potential approaching Indian war parties, but also telling them to send along guns, beads, and other items.

Opechancanough took Smith to his home village in 1607, where the Pamunkeys held a ceremony to prepare Smith for his introduction to Powhatan. Smith found the Pamunkey rituals strange and could make nothing of them. According to Smith, priests covered in red and white paint danced around him. Among Algonquians, rituals and ceremonies reminded villagers of the power of the spiritual world, the beginning of the human world, and what were appropriate behaviors. With offers of cornmeal as a gift, and descriptions of the earth, the Pamunkeys tried to make Smith understand that *Tsenacommacah* was a spiritual land populated by people who were hospitable in the proper settings with foreigners.

Algonquian everyday life had many ceremonies and rituals to appease spiritual beings. Virginia Indians called spirits **manitous**. *Manitous* inhabited the forests, trees, and the waters; they were among the living and the dead; they were on the earth and in the cosmos. *Manitous* were everywhere. As a consequence, *manitous* provided Algonquian peoples with **manit** (power) that was essential to maintaining community balance and harmony. If Smith came to *Tsenacommacah* with good intentions, then Powhatan's confederacy and the *manitous* would offer friendship in return.

Powhatans, and probably other tribes within the confederacy, worshipped a god named Ahone, as the creator of all things, the heavens and earth, and the yearly bounty of corn. When it came to day-to-day activities, though, the god Okeus prevailed. With a watchful eye, Okeus made sure that men and women behaved properly and punished them when they did not. Disease, thunderstorms, and flooding were the result of Okeus punishing the Powhatans for their wrongdoings. In a stratified chiefdom like the Powhatan confederacy, having a pantheon of gods all villagers could looked to for help further consolidated the spiritual power and authority of both *weroances* and spiritual specialists.

After his stay with Opechancanough, Smith left for Powhatan's village of Werowocomoco, along the York River. Powhatan wanted to reinforce the bond of goodwill between Anglo-Virginians and the Powhatan people. He proposed a new relationship between the Indians and the English. To control the Jamestown settlers as a tribute village, Powhatan asked Smith to move the outpost to the York River, south of Werowocomoco. Smith also had to declare complete loyalty to Powhatan by a continuous exchange of goods. In return, Powhatan would feed the English. Smith did not agree to Powhatan's terms, and Jamestown remained as it was.

Smith remembered the event much differently. To Smith, it was another moment where he almost lost his life at the hands of Indians. During a ceremony in which Powhatan wanted to cement the new relationship, Smith believed that Powhatan's followers tried to club him to death. According to Smith, Pocahontas, the ten-year old daughter of Powhatan, saved him from certain doom. Indeed, the story of Pocahontas saving Smith has become part of American lore. Pocahontas, who had served as a negotiator between the Powhatans and the English and would later marry the Englishman John Rolfe, had an important role as a cultural broker, which may account for why Smith gave her credit for saving his life. But most likely the ceremony was an Algonquian rite of acceptance into their culture. The clubs with Smith on the altar were symbols of the captain's death as an Englishmen. Because women had their own *manit* as the givers of life, the presence of elite females such as Pocahontas brought Smith back from the dead as an adopted, elite "Anglo-Powhatan." The Powhatan Indians did not want Smith to pose a threat to the balance of relations within the confederacy.

That same year, however, a carefully orchestrated coronation ceremony for Powhatan revealed the settlers' unchanged desire to pacify and control the chief. Newport returned to Jamestown in October of 1608. Following the London Company's orders, he staged a dramatic coronation of Powhatan, one in which he was to acknowledge his submission to the English crown. Smith returned to Werowocomoco to entice Powhatan to come to Jamestown for the coronation. Powhatan refused, insisting that the English come to him. Acquiescing to Powhatan's demand, Newport led fifty men to Werowocomoco for the coronation of Powhatan, bringing a boatload of copper, a basin, a bed, a pitcher, bedclothes, and a scarlet cloak and a crown. At the climax of the coronation, Powhatan was supposed to kneel, showing his submission to the English crown. Again, Powhatan refused. He did, however, take the crown and cloak as a gesture of kindness and to increase his own status and prestige among his people. The two sides saw the ceremony very differently. Newport believed Powhatan had submitted to the crown. To his followers, Powhatan had turned the ceremony around in his favor, demonstrating that he was a powerful man capable of bending the English to his will. Leaving the English, Powhatan—with the scarlet cloak and crown in his hands—had even more prestige items to conspicuously display.

Indian War and the Emergence of Virginia

The coronation ceremony was one of the last times Powhatan's confederacy and the Anglo-Virginians met on anything like friendly terms. Relations deteriorated quickly in

Detail of John Smith being saved by Pocahontas. These sets of drawings appeared in John Smith's own account of his harrowing experiences in Virginia. In the top middle is Powhatan, to the right of that image is Opechancanough facing off against Smith, and in the bottom right is the image of Pocahontas saving Smith.

University Library; Univ of North Carolina Chapel Hill

the years that followed. Once Newport departed for the second time for London to convince his sponsors to keep up their support of Jamestown, Smith again took over and began to aggressively enter *Tsenacommacah* villages. Starvation had taken a toll on Jamestown during the winter of 1608–1609, with Powhatan's people contributing to the situation by refusing to trade corn. Searching for food, and looking to reassert his authority by subduing Powhatan's people by force, Smith entered Pamunkey villages hunting for corn. In January of 1609, Smith held Opechancanough hostage, demanding corn from the *weroance*'s warriors in exchange for the safe release of their leader. That same year, Englishmen continued to enter numerous other villages, stealing corn and killing Indians. In 1609–1610, solider-settlers, food, and a newly appointed governor in the person of Sir Thomas West all came to Jamestown from London. Smith departed for England, and West began to strengthen and consolidate the colony of Virginia.

All of this was a recipe for war. The first Anglo-Powhatan war (1610–1614) raged mostly along the James River, but it spilled into the Chesapeake Bay region. The war did not go well for Powhatan and his confederated villages. Powhatan was in his sixties and stayed in hiding during the war, allowing Opechancanough and the Pamunkeys to deal with the Anglo-Virginians. Englishmen pillaged inland villages and killed numerous Indians. They also settled on *Tsenacommacah* lands along the James River and in the interior without offering tribute to Powhatan. Opechancanough and the Pamunkeys were battered in their attempts to save their villages.

The English capture of Pocahontas in 1613 marked a turning point in the war. Pocahontas abandoned her status as a Powhatan elite, converted to Anglicanism, and married an Anglo-Virginian of status, John Rolfe. With his most prized daughter and useful cultural negotiator now married to an Englishmen, and with the war shifting in favor of the English, Powhatan was a defeated man. The once mighty paramount chief of a massive confederacy agreed to English terms in the spring of 1614, receiving in return a shaving knife, combs of bone, fishhooks, and a dog and cat. By the summer of 1617, Powhatan retired to a village along the Potomac. He then officially turned his leadership duties over to Opechancanough. Grieving over his daughter's transformation, Powhatan died in 1618.

Virginia was now more secure for its English colonists, but it lacked a viable export commodity. Without such a commodity, its backers could not get a return on their investment. In 1616, Orinoco tobacco came to Virginia from the West Indies. The tidewater soil was perfect for the crop. Planters and indentured servants flocked to Virginia's tidewater region to strike it rich by planting as much tobacco as possible. Powhatan Indians, in a position of subordination, supplied greedy Virginians with corn, water to drink, and meat of various kinds, while the English offered goods in exchange.

After the first Anglo-Powhatan war, Opechancanough sought to preserve the Powhatan confederacy's autonomy amid the onslaught of English settlement. Tobacco was an immensely profitable crop, sometimes turning small planters into rich men. Virginians rushing onto Indian lands throughout the tidewater established small hamlets and plantations. Opechancanough tried to accommodate the new settlers, while also protecting any Native American sovereignty in *Tsenacommacah*. He allowed some Powhatans to convert to Christianity under the tutelage of the Anglican missionary George Thorpe in a show that the Powhatan Indians could live side by side with the English. Opechancanough, using his political savvy, convinced the English to allow Powhatans to train with muskets, although the English strictly monitored the trade in guns with local Indians.

Not all Powhatans were interested in accommodation. A medicine man named Nemattanew, called "Jack the Feathers" by the English, resented the planters and indentured servants on his people's homelands. A self-proclaimed prophet, Nemattanew preached a message of Powhatan regeneration, of a return of *Tsenacommacah* to the Indians. Nemattanew, who held immense control over sacred powers, claimed English bullets could not even kill him.

The politician and war leader Opechancanough listened to the prophet's message. When the English killed Nemattanew in 1622 by shooting him for spreading his message, Opechancanough and his followers began a campaign of violence against the English who now occupied most of *Tsenacommacah*. On March 22, 1622, Opechancanough and an alliance of the Indians once within the confederacy struck all the English settlements along the James River. Many Indians entered the lands of the English, showing signs of peace only to take English knives and axes and brutally kill the settlers. The initial rebellion resulted in the death of 347 English colonists, approximately one-quarter of the colony's total population.

Virginia's governor, Sir Francis Wyatt, mounted a counterattack to help ignite the second Anglo-Powhatan war (1622–1632). Both sides sought to wipe out the other, but by 1632 the English realized that the complete extermination of the Virginia Indians was impossible and the war ceased. During the war, the united Indians showed their determination to keep some of the tidewater for themselves.

That same year, a major tobacco boom had Englishmen searching for more land. In 1634, there were only 5,200 colonists in Virginia, but by 1640 there were 8,100. To accommodate this influx of settlers, the English pushed farther north along the York and Potomac rivers, still demanding that local Indians provide food and water. As the colony grew, Englishmen fenced in Indian hunting grounds and allowed livestock to roam and trample the small tended Indian fields. In 1644, Opechancanough, nearly one hundred years old, led the last attempt to push the English out of the tidewater. The tidewater Indians killed an estimated four or five hundred English colonists and took many captive as they retreated to their interior villages. The new governor, William Berkeley, organized his militia units to spread out over the tidewater and piedmont regions. English militia entered the remaining villages of the Powhatans, Appamattucks, Chickahominies, Nansemonds, and Pamunkeys. Indian defenses were so weak that the English took Opechancanough hostage and brought him to the governor at Jamestown. Opechancanough died at the old fort, shot by an insubordinate English soldier.

PROFILE

POCAHONTAS IN THE ATLANTIC WORLD

Pocahontas, the daughter of Powhatan, remains one of the most famous women in American history. As the courageous girl moving through the violent climate between her people and the settlers of Jamestown, Pocahontas became Lady Rebecca Rolfe after marrying John Rolfe in Virginia. Lady Rolfe and a few traveling friends sailed to London and were the first female migrants from the British colonies to make the trek across the Atlantic. She arrived in June of 1616 with her husband, baby boy, and ten other Powhatan men. At the time of her arrival, her father's followers were waging a devastating war against the English colonists.

According to most reports, London's upper class saw Lady Rolfe as a princess, a young lady who carried herself as the daughter of a king, another English misinterpretation of leadership structures among the Virginia Indians. Lady Rolfe was also the only woman to achieve celebrity status out of numerous colonial-era voyagers to London, and the only Virginia Indian ever baptized in the Anglican Church before traveling to London. Lady Rolfe received much attention from both the crown and the church; her female friends stayed in London for five years. Pocahontas, a young girl who at one point sacrificed so much for her people, did not end her life in Virginia as the head of a Powhatan matrilineal household. As the final symbol of her transformation from Powhatan Indian to trans-Atlantic, Anglican voyager, Lady Rebecca Rolfe died in London in 1617.

Library of Congress

POWHATANS AND THE ENGLISH, 1560–1644

1560–1570s	Consolidation of the Powhatan Confederacy
Circa 1595	Birth of Pocahontas
1561	Paquiquineo begins his trans-Atlantic voyage to New Spain
1570	Paquiquineo arrives in *Tsenacommacah* with Jesuits
1607	Establishment of the Jamestown Colony
1607–1608	Faltering relations between Powhatan Confederacy and Captain John Smith
1608	Coronation ceremony
1609–1610	New Governor Sir Thomas West arrives in Virginia
1610–1614	First Anglo-Powhatan war
1616	Pocahontas arrives in London
1616	First Tobacco boom in Virginia
1617	Powhatan turns over the leadership of the Confederacy to Opechancanough
1622–1632	Second Anglo-Powhatan war
1644	Opechancanough attacks Virginia settlements for the last time

Indians in Virginia did not vanish after the bloody events of 1644, but the English started to use English law to guard their plantations and homes from native peoples. A treaty in 1646 designated a Pamunkey *weroance* named Necotawance as the sole ruler over his people. With Necotawance as a subject to the English king, Virginia's native peoples owed the English an annual tribute of twenty beaver skins. Under the new laws, Indians were not allowed to roam into colonists' lands, nor could Indians sell their land unless the governor approved the sale. Native Americans also had to give up all their guns and captives. Any lands remaining in Indian hands were islands in a sea of English settlers. Livestock destroyed native harvests, and disputes over animal rights provoked greater tension between tidewater planters and Native Americans. The English destroyed native hunting grounds, transforming forests full of game into cleared tobacco fields and plantation homes. Virginia moved quickly to a plantation economy. To speed the growth of their new economy, Virginians relied on on another group of people that they also eventually came to see as "savage"—imported African slaves.

SOUTHERN NEW ENGLAND INDIANS ENCOUNTER THE ENGLISH

There was no massive confederacy of Indians like that of the Powhatans in New England, an area encompassing present-day Massachusetts, Connecticut, and Rhode Island. In Southern New England in and around present-day Cape Cod, the lower portions of Massachusetts, and Rhode Island, elite Indian leaders were called sachems. Sachems were not coercive leaders. Sachems led by charisma and persuasion and inherited their positions through elite lines of descent. They were generous with the return of gifts once villagers paid tribute in meats, hides, crops, and even labor. Advised by an elite council of relations, sachems managed justice, welcomed important visitors, and upheld relations with other Indian groups. Sachem duties passed down from father to the oldest son, and, in rare moments, to the youngest son, an uncle, or even a daughter.

Before the English arrived, **sachemships**, linking villages under a sachem's control, were extended territories that also served as social units. Sachemships included numerous villages where land was held collectively, but also villages that had **usufruct property rights**. Under the latter system, sachems allowed families to grow crops on particular tracts of land, and to reap the benefits of that land for themselves. Families usually had fields for long periods of time, and then abandoned them when the land became unfertile. This practice allowed for the sharing of resources on particular tracts, exclusive of the crops or other resources claimed by individual houses, or wigwams. Sachems also determined which families settled wigwams on unused sachemship lands. At the same time, sachems allowed villagers to hunt on sachemship lands because wigwams moved with the seasons in search of game. Because of their position, sachems claimed some power over the homeland, but they did not own the sachemship or assume absolute control over the people who used the lands. Disaffected villagers could pick up and leave and choose to owe tribute to another sachem. In other words, the homelands were sovereign as a sachemship, but sachems never used threats or violence to keep people bound to their sachemship. The Indians of southern New England moved within the bounds of their homelands as the seasons and circumstances dictated. Thus, they were not wholly nomadic, but they still traveled from time to time according to the seasonal demands of fishing and hunting, to find better farming grounds, and to find new sources of a variety of other resources.

Algonquian-speaking Indians of southern New England shared cultural traits with the Virginia Indians. For example, *manitous* moved throughout all sachemships, among the villages, wigwams, hunting grounds, trails, and cultivated fields. Harvesting, fishing, hunting, warring, and trailblazing—all daily activities—occurred with rituals and ceremonies that upheld a spiritual balance between humans and the natural world. Like the Algonquian-speakers of Virginia, New England Indians also believed in a universe suffused by *manit* (power). Mediating Algonquian relations between humans and spirits were medicine men—called ***powwaws*** in New England. New England Indians prized *Powwaws* for their sacred abilities in dreaming, healing, and prophesying and these spiritual healers only maintained their respect and influence by continually demonstrating their powers.

The Algonquians along the New England coast were not wholly unfamiliar to the English. Before the settlement of larger colonies in New England, an ambitious group of explorers first encountered groups of New England Indians. A stockholding firm known as the Plymouth Company established the Sagadahoc settlement in Maine in 1607 along the present-day Kennebec River. There they hoped to build a productive outpost. Local Abenaki, who had some connections with the French, attacked and killed eleven of the English settlers, which led to the small outpost's demise. The local Abenaki particularly hated when the English took captives. In 1605, five had been taken captive by Captain George Weymouth and went back to London and eventually learned English. In 1611, Captain Edward Harlow took several Algonquians from the Cape Cod region captive. One captive was Epenow from Martha's Vineyard. Speaking enough English to deceive his London captors into returning to the Vineyard under the pretense that the colonists would harvest gold-like corn, Epenow soon escaped to be with his people. Such early lessons about potential violence over trade and the occupation of native lands certainly exerted some influence on the future settlements in New England, giving both Indians and the English some knowledge of the potential problems of intercultural encounters.

Native Americans and Plymouth Bay

Religious separatists known as Pilgrims were the first English people to build a permanent colony within the Algonquian world of sachemships and *manitous*. Dissatisfied with England's official church, the Church of England (the Anglican Church), the Pilgrims left England and went to the Netherlands to practice their faith. From there, they boarded the Mayflower and set off for New England. The Pilgrims came to North America not as traders or fishermen, but as people who sought to create a new and, in their minds, purer form of Christian community. The Pilgrims secured financial backing from a group of London-based explorers. Arriving in 1620, the Pilgrims already had knowledge of New England's plentiful wildlife, clear running streams, and open land.

Following their stockholders' orders, the Pilgrims established their New World community with a group of nonseparatist soldiers led by Captain Miles Standish. Captain Standish had two missions: to claim new land in the name of King James I and to become engaged in the fish and fur trade. Standish's search for profits and the Pilgrims' search for religious freedom and community security meant there were different English purposes for the colony and understandings of the nature of its leadership. Such confusion resulted in miscommunication and tension between the colonists and the New England Indians.

To the Pilgrims the landscape appeared empty just waiting for them to plow, plant, and fence. Diseases European traders spread had torn through New England's Indian communities during the previous three years. Estimates suggest that in some areas up to 90 percent of village populations died. With elders hit particularly hard by the disease, Wampanoag leadership vanished quickly and many sachemships shrunk to smaller collections of villages. On the other hand, the epidemics largely did not affect the Narragansetts of Rhode Island. Their newfound strength gave the Narragansetts profound influence over the diplomatic proceedings between the Pilgrims and the tattered remnants of both Plymouth Bay and Cape Cod sachemships. Thus, a shift in the balance of power between Wampanoags and Narragansetts had already started when the Pilgrims began their colony.

Struggling Pilgrims first settled at Patuxet (Plymouth). The local Patuxet Indians watched the colonists very closely. In the past, these Indians had traded with sporadic visitors, but had also witnessed captive raiders kidnapping coastal Algonquians. To compound matters, when the Mayflower originally anchored in Cape Cod Bay before reaching Patuxet, Captain Standish and his men had pilfered corn and other items to help sustain the ship's passengers.

In spite of the potential abundance of the land around Plymouth Bay, without adequate knowledge of local conditions and agricultural practices, the settlers barely lived through their first winter. Half of them died of starvation. The members of the small Plymouth Bay colony realized that without the aid of local Native Americans, their project was doomed.

After the starving time, the Wampanoags, with the aid of Samoset and Squanto (Squanto a former captive of the sea captain George Weymouth) who both spoke broken English, sought negotiations with the Plymouth Bay settlers. From the perspective of the lead Wampanoag sachem, Massasoit, an alliance with the English meant help for the diminished Wampanoags in their efforts to exert new influence over nearby Indians. In March of 1621, Squanto and Samoset arranged for a meeting between the Plymouth Bay colonists and Massasoit. Wampanoags agreed to ally with the English in times of attacks from outsiders, bear no arms during meetings, and return stolen property. Massasoit would use his authority as sachem over other local natives to exact justice against any Indians who attacked the English settlers. As in Virginia, the English granted royal powers to the leaders of southern New England tribes, calling them "kings," or "governors."

But the English interpreted Massasoit's willingness to negotiate as submission. Massasoit, the Wampanoag sachem, or royal governor, was now in their minds a subject of King James and under English sovereignty. The Wampanoags understood the treaty differently. Exchanges of prestige goods and words, not written documents, indicated that the settlers had bound themselves by ties of tribute to the Wampanoag sachem. The Plymouth Bay colonists, moreover, did not own the land, nor did the English crown; they now shared the land with the Wampanoags who were still free to use the land within the Plymouth colony's territory. But to the colonists, Massasoit had admitted his subjection to the crown, had divested his people of a large tract of land, and was now bound to serve the English settlers' interests.

Different interpretations of the treaty of 1621 strained Wampanoags relationships with the Plymouth Bay colonists. Roaming Indians were a problem for Plymouth farmers because Wampanoag hunters jumped fences, ran across fields, and scared away the Pilgrims' livestock. From the Indians' point of view, fences and fields changed the ecology of their hunting grounds, threatening an important source of Wampanoag men's spiritual power. Standish believed they had subjugated the Wampanoags, and English authority now extended from Patuxet west toward the Narragansetts. Violent exchanges and the spread of rumors of a joint Narragansett and Wampanoag war party resulted in Standish advising William Bradford, the appointed leader of New Plymouth, and the Pilgrims, to fortify their tiny colony. In the winter of 1623, as word spread of the Indian war in Virginia, Standish asserted his authority in Indian villages, in many cases by attempting to usurp the power of local sachems. He ordered the release of corn, skins and furs, and stolen goods, and demanded that sachems punish native criminals. Standish's aggression violated the 1621 treaty of friendship and hospitality. Standish continued his attempts at military submission, particularly among the Indians to the north known as the Massachusett. Standish and his men killed several Massachusett leaders to assure Standish's standing among the Wampanoags. Standish's behavior only increased miscommunication with the Indians of southern New England, who thought they had negotiated a peace with the English.

Other colonists such as Edward Winslow sought peace with the Indians through the spread of Christianity. Winslow reached out to offer the Indians teachings in the precepts and practices of his faith. In an effort to highlight similarities between Indian and Puritan sources of sacred power, Winslow recanted a previous claim that Algonquian speakers had no religion. He began to preach that the Algonquian spirit, Kiehtan, bore many similarities to the Christian God. Yet Winslow also sought to undermine the work of the *powwaws*, the spiritual leaders among Southern New England Indians, by arguing that their belief in *powwaws* as the one who cured wounds and diseases was the devil's work. Asserting his own healing powers, Winslow visited and cured many sick Indians. Local sachems questioned who actually led the new colony. Wampanoag sachems refused to defer to Standish as the king's subjects, but at the colony of Plymouth Bay, the separatists greeted the Indians with notions of Christian friendship.

New England Indians Face English Expansion

The Great Puritan Migration under the auspices of the Massachusetts Bay Company and religious leaders led by John Winthrop was much larger than the Plymouth colony in terms of both population and territory occupied. Between 1630 and 1633, approximately three thousand Puritan families came to Massachusetts. They saw New England as a new "Canaan." Canaan was the land the Hebrews traveled to when Moses led them out of bondage in Egypt. Like the Hebrews, the Puritans saw themselves as fleeing oppression. And, like the Hebrews, they saw themselves as traveling to a land of plenty promised to them by God. These families followed the **"New England town model."** Puritans spread out across Massachusetts in small communities with fenced-in farms, fields, and common grounds. Farming and fencing quickly transformed Massachusetts's landscape, destroying the hunting grounds that were so important to the Indians' way of life. Town patriarchs ruled communities, and at the center of each town was the community church. Coming on the heels of the epidemic of 1617–1619, English settlement was another heavy blow for the local Indians. English traders offered the few remaining Indians cloth and metal tools in exchange for corn. The Indians were also subject to English laws, although they did not live within English-styled towns.

There were other transformations to the native ecology in New England. The Quahog clam along the Long Island shore and Rhode Island was an indispensable source of native food. Moreover, the clamshells were used to make wampum beads, sacred items painted in various colors and used among Algonquian and Iroquoian-speaking people for rituals and ceremonies. Strung into wampum belts for circulation between villages and tribes, the beads became mnemonic devices from which Indians could translate messages. The Dutch, who had established the colony of New Netherland in 1624 as an economic enterprise, had experience with Africans who strung cowry shells to trade for slaves and goods. Building on this experience, Dutch traders provided the Narragansetts and other coastal Algonquians with metal lathes to manufacture wampum in massive amounts. In a short time, once sacred items became a form of common currency for interior Algonquian and Iroquois hunters involved in the expanding fur trade. Farther inland, with their hunting grounds bounded by English towns and their forests cleared for grazing animals, Indians turned to a more sedentary existence. The result in coastal and inland areas was more fishing and hunting to the point of almost depleting coastal and inland animal resources. The search for pelts and furs to sell to the Dutch and the English put pressure on beavers, deer, and other animal populations closer to the Atlantic seaboard. At the same time, Indian agriculture declined as Indians were pushed onto marginal lands with less and less productive soil.

As their numbers increased, the Puritans moved west and south. The Puritans did not find a wilderness as they expected, but instead territories of the Narragansetts, Mohegans, Pequots, and other groups tied to the interior fur trade. One of the first Puritans to push west was not a land-hungry settler but a religious dissenter named Roger Williams. Williams had taken a public stance against theocratic rule and was banished from Massachusetts in 1636 as a result. Williams purchased a tract of land, the Providence Plantation, from the Narragansett Indians. His purchase opened what would later become Rhode Island for English settlement. In 1643, Williams published his *A Key to the Language of America*, a seminal study of the Narragansett language that was designed to help English settlers deal with the Indians on a fair basis.

Unfortunately, in the 1630s and 1640s there were not many Puritans like Williams who befriended Native Americans. Seeking to increase the interior trade in wampum from which they profited, in 1633 the Pequots invited the Dutch to establish a trading post in southern Connecticut. The Puritans, on the other hand, saw the Dutch as their enemies and as competitors for Pequot lands in Connecticut. For example, in 1636 William Pynchon led a party of family and friends from Roxbury to the Connecticut River, purchased lands from the local sachem, and began the community of Agawam. He profited in the beaver trade, eventually competing with the Dutch traders who had preceded him into the region. By English standards, Pynchon became

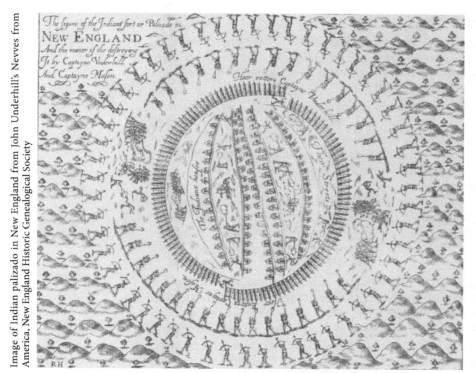

Image of Indian palizado in New England from John Underhill's Nevves from America, New England Historic Genealogical Society

English and Narragansett Indian attack on the Pequot fort at Mystic, CT.

an expert at dealing with native peoples. As English settlers streamed into Massachusetts as the Great Migration reached twenty thousand by 1642, land-grabbing profit-minded men like Pynchon became more common.

With an English presence in Rhode Island under Williams's charge after 1636, and with Pynchon settled near Connecticut that same year, the Puritans went to war with the Pequots, who had lost many to a recent epidemic, and attacked the English at Fort Saybrook in 1636. Using their Mohegan and Narragansett allies to their advantage, the Anglo-Indian alliance attacked the Pequots in 1637. Uncas, the Mohegan sachem, and one of the last leaders of that group to hold power in the Connecticut region, had refused Pequot overtures to change sides, as did the Narragansetts who competed heavily with the Pequots in the trade of wampum. Surrounding a Pequot stronghold at a village at Mystic, the Anglo-Indian alliance ravaged a hamlet largely comprised of elders, women, and children. Englishmen rushed into the village, razing homes and killing Pequots. Outside of the fortified village, Narragansett and Mohegan warriors killed any Pequots who sought to escape. Under the leadership of their sachem, Sassacus, Pequot warriors who were not in the village when it was attacked hurried west to live among the Mohawks. However, the Mohawks were allies of the Narragansetts, and killed all of the Pequots on their lands. The 1638 Treaty of Hartford brought the war to an end. The treaty was designed to rewrite the history of the Connecticut River territory. According to the treaty, the Pequots no longer existed as a tribe and could be sold into slavery to the West Indies.

The supposed extinguishment of the Pequots opened a power vacuum in Connecticut. Both the Narragansetts and Uncas's Mohegans sought to fill that vacuum and take over Pequot lands, going to war over which group would hold the dominant position. The Mohegans were savvy diplomats signing a peace accord with the English to control the Connecticut River valley but remain allied to the English in trade and war. Wealthy western merchants like Pynchon, however, were able to maintain the peace by keeping both groups happy with a highly lucrative fur and wampum trade. By the 1640s, an imperial rivalry for furs and wampum that extended into New York and the Great Lakes and involved Dutch, French, Algonquian, and Iroquois peoples further changed the geopolitics of Connecticut.

Christianity and the Praying Town Model

Puritans in Massachusetts wanted to reform the Church of England by creating perfect, model Christian communities that would shine back overseas like small beacons of light. Having the perfect Christian society meant Native Americans who lived next to Puritans had to fall in line with the Puritan social order. Thus, it was only a matter of time before Puritans began targeting native peoples as potential converts to Christianity. Believing that well-ordered Godly, Indian communities could coexist with the Puritans, John Eliot began his missionary efforts in Massachusetts in the 1640s. Educated at Cambridge, England, Eliot became head of the Roxbury church in Massachusetts in 1631 and began his visits to local native groups in the 1640s.

The seal of the Massachusetts Bay Colony held out the promise of conversion, with an Indian on the front speaking the words "come over and help us." The Puritan mission project organized by Eliot centered on the principle of wholesale cultural change in the context of Christian conversion. Learning the Algonquian tongue, Eliot followed the strict rules of Puritan conversion among his first series of native converts. For the Indians, as with the Puritans, strict scriptural knowledge was a requisite for full membership into any congregation, as were believable signs of a conversion experience before other "visible saints" who were people already in the church. At the village of Nonatum, an aspiring spiritual leader, Waban, encouraged Eliot to make frequent visits. Eliot spoke of the fragility of mankind and the supremacy of God, who sent divine vengeance against sinners. He spoke of God's commandments, the benefits of life in heaven, and the fiery depths of hell. Eliot recognized that to convert the Indians of Nonatum meant to work through native social structures. Converting sachems was key here because if Eliot could transform village leaders others might follow. Such notions of converting leaders were similar to the Spanish-Franciscan understandings of spreading mission zeal. Eliot also believed that if he could somehow display the healing power of his Christian medicine, he would undermine the work of Algonquian *powwaws*.

In 1649, with funding from the benevolent New England Company, Eliot initiated his **"praying town"** model. Natick became the first of his praying towns. Waban and his followers requested a tract of land to create their own English-styled town, and they received a grant along the Charles River. Natick was carved out of the Puritan town of Dedham, which had a population of Indians that Eliot had worked among near Roxbury. Many of the Indians who joined Natick found Algonquian cosmology inadequate in explaining the destruction English colonization wrought, and so they turned to Christianity as a new source of spiritual guidance. Other Indians found Natick a safe haven from the war amid English settlers.

Natick became a model community. Indians built houses, fenced in farms, built a bridge, and changed traditional Algonquian gender roles. Some men no longer hunted but instead farmed, and some women imitated traditionally English wifely roles. Natick laws forbade former Algonquian customs such as premarital sex and the growing of long hair. An Indian-led civil body governed the town of Natick, while Massachusetts took its own measures to guard the praying Indians by appointing Daniel Gookin in 1656 superintendent of Indian affairs. In 1660, under the watch of Gookin, Eliot, and other local church leaders, eight Indian confessors were finally brought into full communion with the church. By the close of the 1660s, Eliot and Gookin had a connected network of six additional praying towns.

In the Plymouth colony, Christianity spread among the Wampanoags from a new source along the Cape. Richard Bourne, one of the founders of the town of Sandwich, near Barnstable, began in 1660 to preach to nearby Wampanoags. In 1665 and 1666, a group of Christian Indians known as the Mashpees secured a tract of land for a new praying town with Bourne's help. By the 1670s, there were both itinerant Indian and white preachers moving throughout the Cape and other parts of the New Plymouth Colony who sought to create new Indian Christian communities.

Christianity followed a different course on the island of Martha's Vineyard, where Indians were in the majority. The unique nature of Martha's Vineyard enabled Indian-Christian communities to grow and dampened any potential violence between Indians and colonists. A Wampanoag Hiacoomes invited Thomas Mayhew Jr. to begin Christian work among his people. Mayhew offered a brand of Puritan conversion that was not like the praying town model. With the help of Hiacoomes, Vineyard Indian ministers gained considerable control over religious practices and church authority on the island to tailor Christianity closely to Indian spirituality in a bid to gain more converts. Between the 1640s and 1670s, Martha's Vineyard became a stronghold of Wampanoag Christianity. John Eliot's 1663 translation of the Bible to Massachusett, a dialect closely related to Wampanoag, helped the mission effort on the island. Puritan ministers learned the importance of "translating" Christianity into terms that made sense to the Indians. Ministers learned to substitute *Manitoo* for "God." Praying in church to *Manitoo* channeled the same sense of spiritual power that customarily brought community balance. On the other hand, *Cheepi* represented the god of the deceased, and in translated Puritan texts, missionaries often drew parallels between *Cheepi*, Satan, and hell.

PROFILE

UNCAS, THE LAST SACHEM OF THE MOHEGANS

Uncas was born in 1588 near the Thames River in present-day Connecticut. He was the son of the Mohegan sachem Owaneoc. Uncas spoke broken English and Dutch. His ability to create Mohegan alliances with the English made the Mohegans a leading regional tribe of southern New England.

In 1626, Uncas married the daughter of the Pequot sachem Tatobem, a marriage designed by Owaneoc to create a Mohegan-Pequot alliance. When his father died, Uncas had to follow the guidance of Tatobem, as he had married the sachem's daughter and because of the brokered agreement of the Pequot-Mohegan alliance that put Uncas into a subordinate leadership role under the much more experienced Tatobem. When Tatobem died, Uncas began to challenge Pequot claims to dominance in an alliance where originally the Mohegans and the Pequots had a shared balance of power. In 1634, Uncas challenged Pequot power and authority to the point that the Pequots banished him to live among the Narragansett in present-day Rhode Island. Uncas went back home, only to find few Mohegans willing to follow his leadership and Mohegan lands diminished to small parcels.

Around 1635, Uncas forged alliances with leading Connecticut traders and settlers. Uncas warned the Connecticut settlers of an impending Pequot attack, as the English observed that Uncas was "faithful to the English." Uncas threw his support behind the English during the Pequot war in 1637. Uncas and his Mohegan followers led several strikes against the Pequots. Once the English-Mohegan forces defeated the Pequots, Uncas absorbed many remaining Pequots, making them Mohegans through a process of adoption. Uncas then signed the Treaty of Hartford in 1638 that made the Mohegans a "tributary" of the Connecticut colony. With the treaty, Uncas could lead the Mohegans into the former lands of the Pequots, but only under the supervision of the colony. The treaty, in short, made the Mohegans the strongest tribe in Connecticut. In 1643, Uncas lead the Mohegans into war against the Narragansetts, as both groups wanted the former Pequot lands. Uncas received help from the English. When he captured the Narragansett sachem Miantonomo, Uncas gave him to the English, and the English brought Miantonomo to court. Found guilty of war crimes, Miantonomo was sentenced to death, and the English ordered Uncas to carry out the act in Mohegan territory. Uncas's brother, Wawequa, killed Miantonomo with a blow from a tomahawk, but only after Uncas had given his approval. With their leading sachem dead, the Narragansetts had to sign a treaty of peace.

When King Philip's War broke out in 1675, Uncas again supported the English. The Mohegans assaulted both the Wampanoags and the Narragansetts. Uncas's involvement in the war was short lived, however. By July of 1676, the Mohegans, weak in numbers, stopped any involvement in the war. Uncas, the last Mohegan sachem to play a decisive role in New England society, died in 1683 or 1684.

ALGONQUIANS IN AN EVER-EXPANDING NEW ENGLAND, 1606–1660S

Date	Event
1606	Establishment of the failed Sagadahoc colony among the Abenakis in Maine
1617–1619	Epidemic destroys the native populations of southern New England
1620	Pilgrims arrive and establish the colony of Plymouth Bay
1621	Wampanoag sachem Massasoit brokers peace agreement with the Pilgrims
1630–1633	Beginning of Great Puritan Migration to Massachusetts Bay colony
1633	Pequots allow Dutch to establish a post in Connecticut to extend wampum and fur trade
1634–1638	Pequot War
1649	John Eliot establishes "praying town" model at Natick
1660s	"Praying towns" spread throughout southern New England

Natives who ran prayer sessions, schools, and churches cemented kinship and community networks by educating and converting family members and Wampanoags who resided within the boundaries of particular sachemships. At the same time, they also provided individuals and households with a source of strength to deal with emerging colonial forces on the island such as alcoholism, disease, land loss, and debt servitude. Keeping intercultural relationships on Martha's Vineyard from spiraling downward into violent conflict involved the cultivation of deeply felt religious conviction that brought together converted island Indians, their ministers, and the English missionaries.

CONFEDERACIES, EMPIRES, AND VILLAGES

Two important institutions played key roles in Iroquois collective life: the Iroquois League and the Five Nations Confederacy. The Iroquois League represented the source of spiritual strength and political stability of the Five Nations, with a council of sachems and spiritual leaders providing a backbone of myth, tradition, peace, and unity for the Five Nations. The league was one symbolically united longhouse of the Haudenosaunee, as the New York Iroquois called themselves. The Senecas, in the setting of the longhouse, were the "Keepers of the Western Door." Moving east were the Cayugas, Onondagas, Oneidas, and the Mohawks. The Mohawks were the "Keepers of the Eastern Door" of the league's longhouse. The Five Nations Confederacy acted as the face of the league, serving in foreign diplomacy, trade, and warfare. Confederacy leaders convened at Onondaga, but league sachems did not always attend. Five Nations' chiefs and warriors from specific village clans met in council at Onondaga, the "central castle" of Iroquoia, to discuss matters concerning the overall survival of the Five Nations. If Five Nations' leaders could not reach consensus on decisions of diplomacy and war, confederacy members parted ways on good terms. Within each Iroquois nation, matrilineal longhouses were at the center of village life. A husband married into his wife's clan and lived in her longhouse. Iroquois women appointed clan leaders, divided between civil chiefs and war chiefs. Civil chiefs controlled diplomacy, whereas war chiefs oversaw military activities. Women could remove both civil chiefs and war chiefs, and they had much power in determining the nature of diplomatic relations and whether or not specific nations went to war.

Hurons were also Iroquoian speakers. Huronia was an expansive portion of the upper Great Lakes, just northwest of Lake Ontario. Hurons shared many cultural traditions with the tribes of the Iroquois Confederacy. The Huron origin myth, for example, was much like the one of the Five Nations. The Huron lived in extended longhouses consisting of matrilineal households, and village social structures and practices were Iroquoian in nature. Women controlled clan households and also appointed and removed leaders. The Huron differed from the Iroquois primarily in their geographical location around the Great Lakes. Such proximity to the French when they arrived gave the Huron immediate access to New France's economic lifeline (see Map 2).

The Huron Ascendancy

Four nations were in the Huron Confederacy. Farthest to the west were the Arendarhonon who were probably the largest of the Huron Confederacy members. To the east were the lands of the Attignawantan. Nestled in between these two groups were the Attigneenongnahac and

From THE ORDEAL OF THE LONGHOUSE: PEOPLES OF THE IROQUOIS LEAGUE IN THE ERA OF EUROPEAN COLONIZATION by Daniel K. Richter. Published for the Omochundro Institute of Early American History and Culture. Copyright © 1992 by the University of North Carolina Press. Used by permission of the publisher

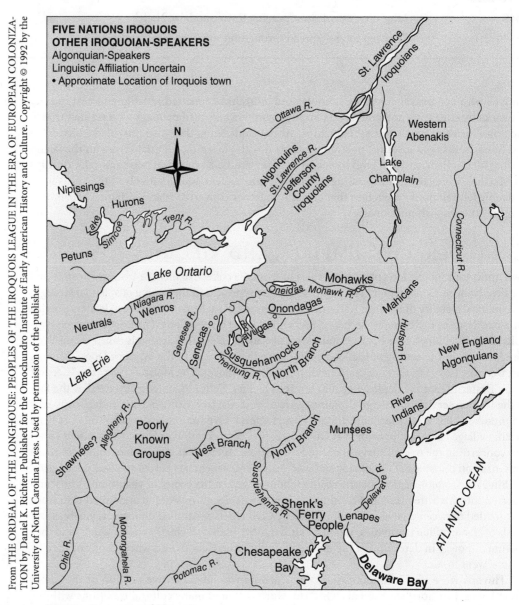

Map 2   Iroquoia and Huronia

Tahontaenrat tribes. The Ataronchronon were a fifth tribe, but other Hurons probably considered them a branch of the Attignawantan. Sparse French records indicate that only four tribes met in council as part of the Huron Confederacy.

In 1608, Samuel de Champlain established New France's center of operations at Quebec. Champlain's goal was to strengthen New France's trade in furs and pelts and fend off Dutch and English efforts to penetrate the region. Quebec's location, between the lands of the rival Iroquois and Huron confederacies, all but guaranteed that the French would be caught up in the competition between the two groups. The situation was further complicated by the presence of a number of peoples who did not belong to either confederacy. They included the Montagnais and Algonkins who settled along the St. Lawrence River, and the Mahicans who lived in the Hudson River valley close to the Iroquois Mohawks.

Seeking to balance French interests with Indian ones, Champlain courted strong relations with the Indians nearest to Quebec: the Hurons, Montagnais, and Algonkins. A threat to Huron-French relations came from the Mohawks to the south, who also sought to benefit from trading with the French at Quebec at the expense of their Huron rivals. Mohawk warriors clad in their traditional wooden armor moved into French territory in 1609 and 1610. To protect his trade alliances with the Hurons and Algonquian speakers closer to Quebec, Champlain agreed to support his trading friends in two decisive blows against the Mohawks. The matchlock muskets of the French overwhelmed the Mohawks.

Huron war chief in wooden armor.

Trade increased the power of the Huron Confederacy at the same time as it enriched the French. From 1619 to 1629, economic interests on both sides made a trading alliance desirable. Each year, Huron traders went up the St. Lawrence to trade at Quebec, bringing with them the furs and pelts of many animals, the most important being beaver pelts. Demand for beaver pelts in Europe pushed prices ever higher which, in turn, resulted in intensified trapping. A Montagnais hunter, tied so much to the French lifeline of goods, said "The Beaver does everything perfectly well; it makes kettles, hatchets, swords, knives, bread—in short, it makes everything." The Huron-French trade had become an economic force to be reckoned with in the Great Lakes region. After 1630, when the trade reached its peak and the beaver population appeared depleted in Huronia, the Huron Confederacy's savvy hunters used their intertribal alliances to extend Huron trade outside of their homelands. Huron traders bartered extra corn from the fields of their women for pelts from Ottawas, Algonkins, Neutrals, Eries, Petuns and other village-based Algonquians. The Hurons received guns and other important items in exchange for the pelts. The trade in pelts started to substantially alter Huron culture by bringing French traders, goods, and diseases into their villages.

In 1634 Jesuits began to enter Huron villages. Jesuits helped French traders and merchants by conducting marriages that brought Frenchmen into matrilineal households. But the Jesuits also created factionalism between Hurons who supported Catholicism and those who refused the faith. Whereas some Huron turned to Catholicism to explain their changing circumstances and to benefit from Catholic marriages for practical reasons, other Huron held the Jesuits accountable for the arrival of new diseases in their communities and turned to traditional spiritual practices to help them survive. Conflict and diseases such as smallpox and typhoid combined into a spiritual and social crisis in Huronia. Many Huron turned to their spiritual leaders and their own cosmology for help against the epidemics that wiped out half of their kin and communities and some saw the Jesuits as a potential source of the evil spirits causing the unending spread of disease. However, most Hurons, seeing the link among the Jesuits, Catholicism, and relations with French traders, became Catholics. Still, by the 1640s, disease and factionalism had taken their toll and the Huron Confederacy was clearly weakening.

Mohawks, on the other hand, grew stronger. After 1623, they turned their economic interests toward Fort Orange and the Dutch. The Dutch had established Fort Orange (present-day Albany, New York), but the Mahicans controlled Mohawk access to Dutch trade. For the Indians, the Dutch trade in furs for muskets and other metal items at Fort Orange was so lucrative that Mohawks called Dutch merchants *Kristoni*, meaning, "I am a metal maker." The Mahicans and their Algonquian allies had a monopoly on trade with the Dutch. To wage unencumbered war against the Mahicans to take control over the Fort Orange trade, Mohawk leaders made peace with New France and the Algonquian peoples to the north. Four years of continuous warfare known as the Mohawk-Mahican war followed. By 1628, the Mohawks pushed the Mahicans out of important western lands and opened a Mohawk trade route to Fort Orange, and the Mahicans settled to the north and east of the Dutch trading post. Under the terms of their pact with northern-Algonquian speakers, the Mohawks prevented Indian traders from the north from carrying furs to Fort Orange. The Mohawk conducted their battles on their own; they did not consult the other Five Nations or Iroquois League sachems. As the Mohawk-Mahican war demonstrates, the wealth that came with European trade also changed the political and military climate of Iroquoia.

War and Mourning: Five Nations' Ferocity

Iroquois warfare continued to change as epidemics hit villages and as Dutch and English traders exchanged guns with Five Nations' warriors for furs. Now armed with a new weapon, the Five Nations waged ferocious and relentless warfare from the 1640s to the 1660s to the north against New France, the Hurons, and the Algonquian speakers.

The Beaver Wars (1648–1657) were particularly intense. As the name indicates, the war centered on competition for increasingly scarce beaver pelts, a trade in which the Iroquois were equal players with the Europeans, but searching for different gains other than just the beavers. Disease also played a role in the bloodshed. Daniel K. Richter has described the Iroquois' need to wage battle at this time in history as part of the Iroquois "mourning war complex." Epidemic disease took its toll on the Five Nations, who had no developed immunity. Persistent outbreaks of disease ripped clans, families, and villages apart, killing the young and the old first, but brutalizing people of all ages. Longhouse life in close quarters most certainly contributed to the rapid-fire spread of pathogens, as did the use of sweat lodges and other communal curing ceremonies. Seeking to replace lost kin, clan mothers grieved and commanded that young Iroquois warriors take captives from the Five Nations' enemies. Such captives could be adopted within clans after a period of indoctrination.

Iroquois consistently raided Huron villages throughout the 1640s. In 1642, for instance, Senecas descended on villagers among the western most of the Huron, the Arendarhonon. The attack was a vicious example of the mourning wars. Senecas took captives, but then left the rest of the Arendarhonon for dead in the burning remnants of their village. The Senecas also took what furs were in the village along with other items. Between 1643 and 1647, the western Senecas and the Hurons continued raids against each other. To the east, Mohawks and Oneidas gave up the occasional raiding of previous decades and instead waged a sustained war against their northern St. Lawrence neighbors.

The Five Nations abandoned its separate western and eastern military tactics in 1648 and through coordinated operations destroyed the Huron Confederacy. During the destructive campaigns against the Senecas, the Arendarhonon fled all of their villages to live among their neighbors. In 1648, Senecas and Mohawks routed Attigneenongnahac villages. The evidence suggests that out of four hundred families, seven hundred people either died or were taken captive. In 1649, about a thousand Iroquois conducted massive raids against the Attigneenongnahac in three major towns. Saint Ignace, a Jesuit mission town, fell to the Iroquois first, followed by the communities known as Saint-Louis and the Jesuit-run mission settlement of Sainte-Marie. Estimates suggest that the Iroquois lost one-third of their warriors, but they had spread such fear among their enemies that the enemies left Huronia. During the 1650s, Five Nations warriors spent most of their time chasing down remaining Huron in Iroquoian-speaking villages near Huronia. After the Five Nations broke the back of the Huron Confederacy, they spent the next seven years going after other Iroquoian-speakers such as the Petuns, Eries, and Neutrals out of the Great Lakes region. By the 1660s, the Five Nations had fought every tribe and village in the Great Lakes territory.

Captives that endured the brutal trek back to Iroquois villages were then put through the gauntlet, an incredible ordeal that was part of the process of becoming a member of an Iroquois clan. Awaiting the captives at the village gates were two lines of men, women, and children, bearing clubs and other weapons. The Iroquois pulled captives slowly through the gauntlet, as Five Nations' villagers hurled words of vengeance and beat the captives with their fists and weapons. Captives lucky enough to survive the gauntlet then had to spend a period as "slaves" among particular clans. During this period, the captives had to display, at some point, that they had become Iroquois in appearance and behavior. Once indoctrinated, captives received all of the benefits of clan membership, even to the point of adopting the name of the deceased clan member they replaced. There are no precise numbers of how many captives were subsumed by the Five Nations, but one thing is for certain: the period of the Beaver Wars changed the entire Native American landscape of the Great Lakes region.

Middle Grounding: The Pays d'en haut

While the Five Nations raged ferocious mourning warfare in the east, a different kind of world took shape to the west. The French called the region the *pays d'en haut* (up country). Refugee communities formed in this vast region as the Iroquois pushed thousands of Indians out of the eastern Great Lakes. Flowing west to avoid the Five Nations' wrath were Miamis, Ottawas, Kickapoos, Illinois, Foxes, Mascoutens, Ojibwas, Potawatomis, and a host of other Algonquian-speaking people. They joined with the Iroquoian-speaking Huron and Siouan dialect groups such as the Winnebagos. Theirs was a multiethnic world where Indians from different groups interacted frequently, often living in the same village, and had to learn to live with one another by sharing cultural and social practices. A blending of cultures took place. Major *pays d'en haut* Indian settlements included Ft. St. Louis and Kaskaskia, both south of Lake Michigan, and Michilmackinac, located at the northern tip of Lake Michigan. A host of other villages stood within a triangular swath of land between Lake Michigan and Lake Superior. It was a place of fertile land with easily accessible rivers, portages, and hunting grounds. Adding to the rich texture of life in the *pays d'en haut* were French Jesuits, military personnel, and the ***coureurs de bois***—French traders who avoided imperial restrictions on trade and lived among the Indians. Indians sought to benefit from the inclusion of Jesuits, soldiers, and traders into their world of villages.

Richard White has described the *pays d'en haut* as "the middle ground." In the *pays d'en haut,* no one power held sway. Cultural negotiation, misunderstandings, and miscommunication were all part of day-to-day life. To gain a foothold among Indian villagers, for instance, Jesuits did not present themselves as *manitous,* but only the bearers of the message of Christ. But Algonquian peoples did not understand the Christian version of Jesus, so the Jesuits adapted and referred to the "Master of Life," a native view of a Great Spirit, or being, who brought balance and harmony to their lives. Because Indians, and not the French, were in control in the *pays d'en haut,* the Jesuits did not try to dominate the Indians or attempt to eliminate the Algonquian belief system in its entirety. Instead, both the Jesuits and Indians adapted and accommodated in whatever ways were necessary to create friendly relations. Each governor of New France was known as "Onontio," which meant father. From the French perspective, this familial language implied that the Indians had subjugated themselves to the crown as its "children." From the Indians' viewpoint, the term suggested that the French were locked into a set of symbolic kinship relations that the French could not violate. Although the two sides interpreted the word differently, they both understood that they had agreed to a set of relations that carried with them specific obligations. The French offered gifts of kindness and entered villages in peace. The ***coureurs de bois*** were the most effective in operating in the tricky world of Indian villages. They learned the languages, often married Indian women, and formed strong friendships. Some of the French in Quebec viewed the *coureurs de bois* as white Indians, but such traders played a key role in keeping the *pays d'en haut* peaceful. In return for French gifts and friendship, the Indians remain allied to the French. If any village group broke that alliance, civil chiefs convened with the French to broker peace with the calumet ceremony. Adopted from the western Pawnees, the calumet was a long-stemmed pipe, and when smoked by all parties during ritual and ceremonies, it restored peace and order and washed away bad feelings.

In the Great Lakes region, where no one Indian group dominated the fur trade, Algonquian villagers controlled the access to the highly prized furs and pelts. In 1680, there were about eight hundred *coureurs de bois* who moved through the world of native villages looking for opportunities to trade. For such men, Indian women were the gateway to a profitable trade, because French traders had to forge networks of kinship and friendship with Indian villagers if they were to succeed.

At village winter posts, French traders tried to make their way into the kin networks of local Indian villages, which included the Iliniwek (Illinois), Miamis, Ojibwa, and other groups. As Susan Sleeper-Smith has noted "Marriage, either in the 'manner of the country,' or performed by missionary priests (Jesuits), assured traders inclusion as Native allies, secured personal safety, and facilitated access to furs." French traders with the good luck to marry elite women entered extensive kin networks, opening the door to greater profits from furs.

Catholicism provided another link between women and the French fur trade. An Illinois woman named Marie Rouensa used Catholic conversion to control her own personal autonomy. When her father tried to arrange a marriage between Marie and a French fur trader whose Catholic devotion was in question, Marie disobeyed her father. Marie's conversion was important in many ways. From her family's standpoint, Marie's conversion to Catholicism opened new avenues to goods from the French. Marie herself became an important promoter of the faith, eventually helping convert her entire family and village. Marie eventually enjoyed the benefits of a church-sanctioned marriage. Catholic marriages offered Indian women protection from the potential abuses of French traders. Marriage also brought the approval of the Jesuits, approval that brought important goods directly to Marie's family. French traders who married Catholic Indian women moved into their wife's household. Thus, kin, women, and Catholicism combined in a unique social system that linked Indian villagers to French traders and a frontier economy.

Transformation of the Five Nations

By the 1660s and 1670s, Five Nations' villagers faced a new series of challenges. When the Dutch trader Ardent van Curler was relieved of his post, the Iroquois had to look elsewhere to trade. The peace treaties of 1665–1667 with New France allowed the Five Nations to trade along the St. Lawrence at Quebec. However, one of the provisions to the treaty was that Jesuits were given permission to enter the villages of the Five Nations. Many captives within Iroquois villages were Hurons who had converted to Catholicism before their capture, and their presence, along with the conversion of other Iroquois, factionalized village life. Catholic captives used the black-robed Jesuits and their faith as a way to stave off full integration into Iroquois society. Other Catholic Iroquois chose to leave their homes rather than face the hostility of non-Catholic villagers. Beginning in the 1660s and with a huge wave after 1673, many Catholic members of the Five Nations moved north into New France. The largest and most prominent of these migrant Catholic villages was Kahnawake (Caughnawaga). By 1679, hundreds of Catholic Iroquois had taken up residence at Kahnawake and other mission villages surrounding Quebec and along the St. Lawrence. For their home villages back in New York, the migration of Catholic members of the Five Nations only added to the ongoing demographic crisis.

The Five Nations were under new pressure from a variety of sources to the east. In 1674, the English took New York from the Dutch. Without Dutch support, New England Indians were now in a position to target the Mohawks as enemies in reprisal for Mohawk raids a decade earlier. Southern New England Indians such as the Narragansetts, Pequots, and Nipmucs became permanent enemies of the Mohawks, who, like the other Five Nations, no longer so heavily depended on the wampum trade from Rhode Island and Connecticut. From New York, Governor Edmund Andros sided with a group of anti-French Iroquois in constructing the **"Covenant Chain alliance,"** an alliance between the Iroquois and the British colonies. In the 1670s, Andros intervened with the Mohawks to strike several key negotiations with New England and with the southern colonies of Virginia and Maryland (see next section). Andros and the English colonists in New York believed the Covenant Chain marked New York's ascendancy in Indian-English diplomacy. For the Five Nations, the Covenant Chain, particularly in the northeast, served as a diplomatic tool that allowed the Iroquois to assert dominance over other tribes who lacked similar powerful alliances.

Throughout Iroquoia disease ran rampant, Catholic kin left, and economic insecurity prevailed. Five Nations villagers, under duress, started a new series of Beaver Wars. In the early 1680s, the Iroquois found themselves in the middle of English Hudson Valley traders, the western Indian nations, and New France to the north. Warriors from the Five Nations took on the Miamis, Illinois, Ojibwas, Fox, and small settlements of Shawnees, Wyandots, and Ottawas. The Five Nations' western attacks were also part of the mourning war complex of previous years. The Iroquois brought captives home, and trade with the English prospered. With the Covenant Chain extending southward, Five Nations warriors attacked Conoys, Piscataways, and raided even as far south as among the Catawbas of South Carolina.

Under a new governor, Jacques-René de Brisay de Denonville, New France in 1687 invaded and destroyed Seneca villages that resided closest to the *pays d'en haut* where the French had worked so hard to establish valuable trading partners among the multitribal villages. Denonville

PROFILE

KATERI TEKAKWITHA

The most famous Catholic Iroquois was Kateri Tekakwitha, a captive whose Algonquin mother and Mohawk father both succumbed to smallpox. Their deaths left Kateri with no kinship ties in her Mohawk village. As the tension created by the Jesuits' activities among the Iroquois mounted, clan and kin pressure would sometimes pull members from the Catholic faith. In Kateri's case this was not so. She became one of the many migrants to Kahnawake. Visited daily by Father Claude Chauchetiére, Kateri was venerated throughout the Catholic community for her extreme physical and emotional devotion to the faith.

Although she lived in relative isolation, she joined a group of Catholic Five Nations women who devoted themselves to chastity, fasting, self-flagellation, and constant exposure to the pains of hot and cold. In 1680, she died at the age of twenty-four. In death she became a powerful symbol to both Jesuits and Mohawks.

Public Archives of Canada

She was a woman, Native American but a devout Catholic, whose devotion to the faith was as strong as any Jesuit in New France. Kateri, in life and death, blurred cultural boundaries. The painting by Claude Chauchetiére included here is the only known image of Kateri. In the painting, Kateri appears in both French and Mohawk dress, and she floats above the ground with an almost saintly quality about her.

led two thousand soldiers, including some members of western tribes, to invade Seneca territory. Although only four villages were burned to the ground, and only twenty Seneca warriors died, Denonville and his party destroyed an estimated 1.2 million bushels of food. At the same time, the warriors and French dug up the Senecas' ancestors looking for buried prestige items. In short, they laid waste to the Seneca landscape and many of the sources of the lands' spiritual power. The destruction of sacred ground infuriated the Senecas and other Five Nations warriors, who mounted a counterattack against New France from multiple directions. To the north, the Iroquois raided Montreal, where the Onondagas took Fort Frontenac and took a Jesuit priest hostage. To the west, they attacked the numerous French-allied Algonquian-speakers among the Wyandots, Miamis, and Ottawas. Along the way, the Five Nations forced the abandonment of every French fort in the western portion of the Great Lakes. Indian and European motivations to control trade and diplomacy in the *pays d'en haut* resulted in continued warfare between the French and the Five Nations.

Iroquois fortunes continued to shift dramatically. England and France waged an imperial war in Europe, known in the colonies as King William's War (1689–1697). Louis de Buade de Frontenac wanted to seize the opportunity and lay waste to the Iroquois to the south. New York, embroiled in an internal rebellion (Leisler's Rebellion) against a group of remaining Dutch settlers, offered little support, violating the rules of Andros's Covenant Chain. During King William's War, New France mustered support from the Ottawas and other western groups, the Abenaki bordering New England and New France, and their Catholic Iroquois friends from Kahnawake to stave off the Five Nations. Iroquois losses were enormous. The attacks left an estimated two thousand Iroquois dead out of a total population of about eight thousand. With few remaining options, the Iroquois began a peace process with New France in the late 1690s that resulted in the Grand Settlement of 1701. In the settlement, the Iroquois agreed to remain neutral in any conflict involving France and England and received the right to hunting grounds in the west. Yet the Iroquois still upheld the Covenant Chain with the English, allowing the Five Nations to continue to exert considerable influence over Indian affairs well into the eighteenth century.

MATURING COLONIES ENDING A CENTURY IN CONFLICT: METACOM'S WAR AND BACON'S REBELLION

Relative to population, King Philip's War was the deadliest conflict ever fought on American soil. Almost half of all towns in New England burned to the ground. In contrast, Bacon's Rebellion was not so much an Indian war as a series of raids and counterraids between Indians and colonists that sparked a larger rebellion of small farmers against Virginia's elite planter class. In both cases, however, the fighting reflected the changing relations between and among native peoples and Anglo-Americans, as well as social and economic developments in the northern and southern colonies. Both conflicts weakened smaller Indian groups, who fell under the control of the Anglo-Iroquois Covenant Chain alliance extending into New England and as far south as Virginia. Both New England and Virginia had maturing economies and governments led by wealthy elites who asserted newer forms of racial and class authority over imported African slaves and small farmers. And although still interested in the highly lucrative trades with interior Indians for furs and pelts, after King Philip's War and Bacon's Rebellion colonists in both regions pushed to the margins any Native Americans remaining within their borders.

Metacom's War

The pressure the growing population of the British colonies created was a key factor in the outbreak of Metacom's War (1675–1676), also known as King Philip's War (see Map 3). As the British population grew naturally and from continued immigration, so did its need for more

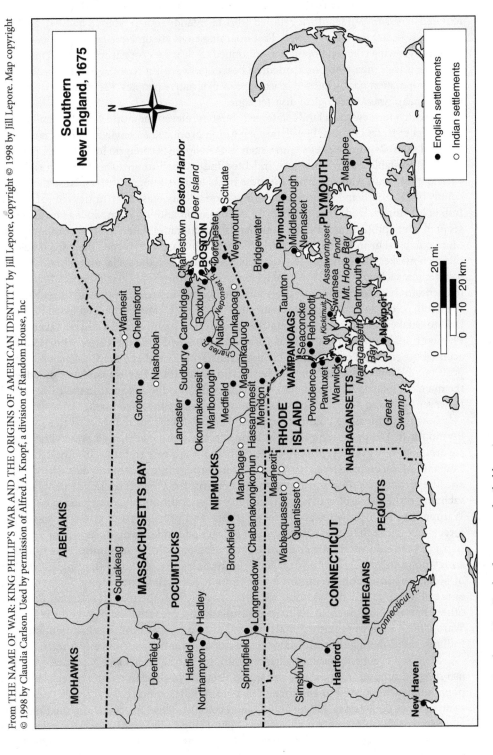

From THE NAME OF WAR: KING PHILIP'S WAR AND THE ORIGINS OF AMERICAN IDENTITY by Jill Lepore, copyright © 1998 by Jill Lepore. Map copyright © 1998 by Claudia Carlson. Used by permission of Alfred A. Knopf, a division of Random House, Inc

Map 3   Southern New England: towns and tribal locations

land and the construction of more towns. Settlers cut down trees, cleared forests, and dammed rivers. Following English tradition, each town had a commons, an unfenced piece of land where all townspeople could let their pigs and cows graze. These animals and the new towns being founded across Indian territories ruined what farmlands Indian women had left, and wild hogs destroyed coastal resources as well. Free-roaming cows ate up New England's open grasslands, while the growing colonial population continued to clear new forests for more farms and grazing grounds. Native men who once procured beaver pelts within New England's borders found the beaver population nearly hunted to extinction. For native peoples, the paradise of the colonist's new "Canaan" was an ecological disaster zone.

A search for new town lands squeezed the some eleven thousand New England natives onto ever-smaller tracts of lands. Population explosion produced an environment of land consolidation and sales. Because western tribes such as the Nipmucs could no longer trade pelts, they fell into debt to stable trading outposts. Indebted Indians had to turn their sachem rights to lands over to merchants, who, in turn, sold these tracts to land-hungry settlers. Near the coast, in the colony of Plymouth and Rhode Island, migration and increased birthrates led to a demand for Indian territories. Under the treaty of 1621, Massasoit and his Wampanoags believed they had secured some protection for their homelands. A generation later, his two sons, Wamsutta and Metacom, lived in an entirely new world. Christian Indians who owned their tracts sold them on the open market, undermining the power of the sachem and the social unit of the sachemship. In some areas, sachems themselves looked to profit, and they sold their homelands right out from underneath their people. Wamsutta also dabbled in the land trade. Although he had appeased the Plymouth colonists by changing his name to Alexander (Metacom changed his to Philip), he sold land to Quakers and other nonseparatists from Rhode Island and elsewhere. Taken prisoner by Plymouth soldiers to curtail his land sales, Wamsutta died soon thereafter. Infuriated, Metacom accused the colonists of poisoning his brother. After his brother's death, Metacom assumed the position of Wampanoag sachem, but he also turned to some English land-use practices. One of the main complaints Indians had about the colonists was the destruction their livestock caused. However, Metacom owned his own pigs and sold them on the open market.

Bowing to pressure colonists applied on him, Metacom recognized the sovereignty of Plymouth in 1674 as a temporary solution to his tribe's weakened state. The question of sovereignty, however, eventually fueled a pan-Indian war to force the English out of New England. Metacom mustered his warriors for battle, while seeking to ally with the Nipmucs and the more numerous and powerful Narragansetts. One of the major problems facing a sachem on the brink of war was an inability to restrain unruly young men. Because young Wampanoag men gained sacred power, status, and prestige from going to war, Metacom's forces were more than ready to raze local villages and kill colonists. In July of 1675, a Christian Harvard-educated former counselor to Metacom, John Sassamon, was found dead in an icy pond named Assawompset. Apparently, Sassamon had told the English of Plymouth of Metacom's intentions to mount a pan-Indian war against the colony. Three of Metacom's enraged warriors killed Sassamon for betraying the Wampanoags. Going on little evidence other than the testimony of a Christian Indian who reported having seen the murder, two Wampanoag men were immediately hanged after a jury of both Englishmen and Christian Indians found them guilty. Metacom could not contain his warriors any longer.

Metacom eventually secured alliances with the Narragansetts and Nipmucs, while the English received support from the few remaining Pequots, Massachusett, and other marginal Indian populations who looked to enhance their own standing among the English. Metacom's men swarmed first on Swansea, killing animals and colonists alike. In retaliation, the English tried to take Metacom by surprise at his village near Mount Hope, but Metacom and the villagers escaped. In response, Metacom's warriors carried out lightning raids against small hamlets throughout the Plymouth colony. In some areas, the war assumed a greater racial tone as frustrated English settlers refused to differentiate between friendly Christian Indians and their enemies, killing many praying town natives. Protecting Indians who remained out of the conflict, Massachusetts's government agreed to keep the Christian Indians on islands off of Boston's coastline such as Deer Island. Then the English preemptively struck Rhode Island's Great Swamp, where the English suspected the Narragansetts had built a fort. The strike on the fort killed the women, children, and the elderly, which forced the Narragansetts into an anti-English posture. The now-united anti-English Wampanoag, Narragansett, and Nipmuc forces moved closer and closer to Boston, burning settlements as they went. From an English perspective, all of New England seemed in peril.

Mohawk intervention changed the course of the war and the state of Indian-English relations in the northeast. In January of 1676, Mohawk allies heard that Metacom was in their territory, near the Hudson River, looking for support from Mahicans and other Native Americans. Sir Edmund Andros, who received word of a potential meeting between Metacom and the Mahicans, armed the Mohawks for an attack on the would-be allies. An epidemic became a friend of the Mohawks as it struck the meeting before any serious proceedings took place. Once the Mohawks cemented an accord with New England, Mohawk warriors killed Mahicans, Wampanoags, and other Algonquian-speakers. To cement their position as the most important Indian group in the region, the Mohawks followed the retreating Algonquians into New England to kill them. That spring, Anglo-Indian forces faced off with Narragansetts and Wampanoags in the southwest part of New England and dealt them a devastating blow.

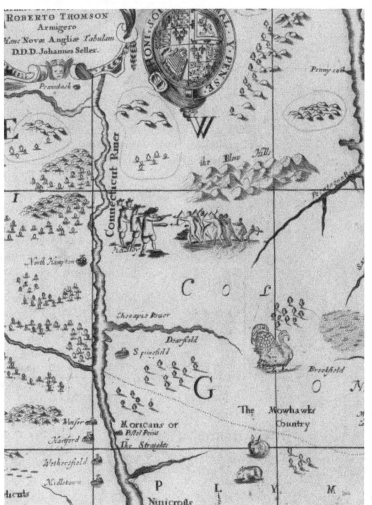

Detail from John Seller, "A Mapp of New England 1675."
Original in the John Carter Brown Library at Brown University.

As the war turned in favor of the English, many Indians switched sides. Numerous Wampanoags abandoned Metacom's cause. An important female sachem, Awashunkes, was a key traitor, as she became pro-English in return for her sachemship lands. Under the leadership of Benjamin Church, and with the help of Wampanoag warriors who had turned against their former leader, a former praying town Indian shot and killed Metacom near the Wampanaog leader's home.

Warfare had tremendous consequences at the local and regional level; forty percent of the native population was killed. According to one English account, brutality of the war waged by "the most barbarous and cruel" enemies of the English resulted in "1,200 houses burned 8,000 head of cattle killed," while the Indians sustained losses of upwards of three thousand people. Indians never again had a strong presence in southern New England.

Englishmen sold many captured Indians into slavery, with many of the enslaved natives transported to Virginia and the West Indies. Both Indians and English settlers were left homeless and starving at the end of the war. New England lay in smoldering rubble with half its homes burned to the ground. The bloodfest now compelled many Puritans to question their faith, as the wrath of

God's hand had come to New England. Why had God punished them? What sins had they committed? Was the Puritan experiment in New England a failure? Such questions loomed—as did memories of the war—in their minds as they tried to rebuild their communities. The war shook the foundations of Puritan society.

Puritan memories of the war lived on in intensified animosity toward Indians. The English confined surviving New England Indians to small government-supervised tracts, the earliest forms of reservations in North America. Limited to low-paying jobs and businesses, Native Americans in New England no longer exerted an influence on the regional economy. In their place were imported slaves who now buttressed the growing urban and rural economies of New England.

Because the Mohawk joined the war on the English side, the Iroquois Confederacy extended its reach into New England in the postwar period. In April 1677, an Albany conference attended by delegates from New York, Massachusetts, Connecticut, and from the Mohawk communities set out to determine a new set of regional relationships. The Mohawks were to release any Indians who had taken refuge in Iroquoia, and those Indians agreed to no longer attack New England. New York was to mediate between the Mohawks and New England. New York and the Mohawks, under Sir Edmund Andros's guidance, established some of the first links in the Covenant Chain alliance between English colonists and the Iroquois.

Reading History

Mary Rowlandson's Captivity Narrative, 1682

Mary Rowlandson, wife to the Reverend Joseph Rowlandson, lived with her family in Lancaster, Massachusetts, on the frontier at the outbreak of King Philip's War. She and her three children, Joseph, Mary, and Sarah, all became wartime captives, enduring hardship for eleven weeks with their Native American captors. Once she returned home, Mary wrote the account of her experience, The Sovereignty and Goodness of God: Being a Narrative of the Captivity and Restoration of Mrs. Mary Rowlandson, which is now considered a classic in the fields of early American literature and the captivity genre.

At length they came and beset our own house, and quickly it was the dolefulest day that ever mine eyes saw. The house stood upon the edge of a hill; some of the Indians got behind the hill, others into the barn, and others behind anything that could shelter them; from all which places they shot against the house, so that the bullets seemed to fly like hail; and quickly they wounded one man among us, then another, and then a third. About two hours (according to my observation, in that amazing time) they had been about the house before they prevailed to fire it (which they did with flax and hemp, which they brought out of the barn, and there being no defense about the house, only two flankers at two opposite corners and one of them not finished); they fired it once and one ventured out and quenched it, but they quickly fired it again, and that took. Now is the dreadful hour come, that I have often heard of (in time of war, as it was the case of others), but now mine eyes see it. Some in our house were fighting for their lives, others wallowing in their blood, the house on fire over our heads, and the bloody heathen ready to knock us on the head, if we stirred out. Now might we hear mothers and children crying out for themselves, and one another, "Lord, what shall we do?" Then I took my children (and one of my sisters', hers) to go forth and leave the house: but as soon as we came to the door and appeared, the Indians shot so thick that the bullets rattled against the house, as if one had taken an handful of stones and threw them, so that we were fain to give back. We had six stout dogs belonging to our garrison, but none of them would stir, though another time, if any Indian had come to the door, they were ready to fly upon him and tear him down. The Lord hereby would make us the more acknowledge His hand, and to see that our help is always in Him. But out we must go, the fire increasing, and coming along behind us, roaring, and the Indians gaping before us with their guns, spears, and hatchets to devour us. No sooner were we out of the house, but my brother-in-law (being before wounded, in defending the house, in or near the throat) fell down dead, whereat the Indians scornfully shouted, and hallowed, and were presently upon him, stripping off his clothes, the bullets flying thick, one went through my side, and the same (as would seem) through the bowels and hand of my dear child in my arms. One of my elder sisters' children, named William, had then his leg broken, which the Indians perceiving, they knocked him on [his] head. Thus were we butchered by those merciless heathen, standing amazed, with the blood running down to our heels. My eldest sister being yet in the house, and seeing those woeful sights, the infidels hauling mothers one way, and children another, and some wallowing in their blood: and her elder son telling her that her son

William was dead, and myself was wounded, she said, "And Lord, let me die with them," which was no sooner said, but she was struck with a bullet, and fell down dead over the threshold. I hope she is reaping the fruit of her good labors, being faithful to the service of God in her place. In her younger years she lay under much trouble upon spiritual accounts, till it pleased God to make that precious scripture take hold of her heart, "And he said unto me, my Grace is sufficient for thee" (2 Corinthians 12.9). More than twenty years after, I have heard her tell how sweet and comfortable that place was to her. But to return: the Indians laid hold of us, pulling me one way, and the children another, and said, "Come go along with us"; I told them they would kill me: they answered, if I were willing to go along with them, they would not hurt me.

Source: *From the introduction of Mary Rowlandson,* The Sovereignty and Goodness of God: Being a Narrative of the Captivity and Restoration of Mrs. Mary Rowlandson *(1682).*

Questions

1. What does Rowlandson's narrative tell us about how Indians conducted warfare in New England?

2. Did Rowlandson and her Indian captors share anything in common?

From the Introduction of Mary Rowlandson, Sovereignty and Goodness of God: Being a Narrative of the Captivity and Restoration of Mrs. Mary Rowlandson (Cambridge, MA: Samuel Green, 1862)

Bacon's Rebellion

In 1676, the same year Metacom's War ended in New England, Bacon's Rebellion erupted in Virginia. A rebellion that began with relatively minor skirmishes against Indians on the Virginia frontier turned into a civil war pitting small farmers against Virginia's planter aristocracy. As was the case in New England after Metacom's War, Bacon's Rebellion ended a tenuous period of peaceful coexistence in Virginia between settlers and Indians. In its wake, a new, racially defined social order emerged with sharp distinctions between the rights and opportunities of whites, blacks, and Indians. Entangled in the war from the start were Indians on the margins of the tidewater, including the Susqehannocks, Doegs, Piscataways, as well as the tributary Indians of the tidewater including the Pamunkeys, Occoneechee, and Mattaponi. All these Indians lived on land Virginia's small farmers believed should belong to them.

In July of 1675, a dispute between settlers and Indians over some hogs resulted in the killing of several Doegs. Seeking revenge, the Doegs murdered the servant of a local planter. This, in turn, prompted a counterattack. A Captain Brent marched with the Westmoreland County militia under the pretense of peacefully negotiating with the Doegs. His group proceeded to kill a Doeg *weroance* and then fourteen Susqehannocks, simply killing the Doegs because of their association with frontier violence. The Susqehannocks pushed by the Iroquois into Maryland and living among the Piscataways now conducted multiple raids into Virginia in revenge. Under orders of Governor William Berkeley (royal governor of Virginia, 1641–1652 and 1660–1677), in September of 1675 Colonel John Washington and Major Isaac Allerton, with militia units from Virginia and Maryland, descended on the Piscataway's fort. Five more *weroances* died who had met the Anglo-American party to negotiate. After the attack on the fort, the Susqehannocks pushed into the forests of Virginia. Although small in number in comparison to a white male population of Virginia of thirteen thousand, Susqehannock warriors terrorized the Virginia countryside, particularly large planters' homes. To put down the Susqehannocks, Governor Berkeley mustered men from the lower rungs of Virginia society and the tributary Indians in the Pamunkeys, Occoneechee, and Mattaponi.

Under the terms of a law the House of Burgesses enacted on March 7, 1676, at the head of each river was a fort, manned by five hundred men drawn from the ranks of small farmers. Seeing the law as an effort to keep small farmers off of prime land and to protect the interests of elite planters, a group of men, led by Nathaniel Bacon, decided to take up arms to resist the governor's policies. In the process, Bacon and his followers took Indian policy into their own hands, roaming the countryside and killing as many Indians as possible. Bacon and his men wanted to drive all Indians out of Virginia, even the tributary Pamunkeys, Occoneechee, and Mattaponi who had been trade partners up to that point and were under the protection of the governor. The rebels murdered and enslaved men, women, and children and pillaged villages. The uprising against the governor and Indians became known as Bacon's Rebellion. What began as a dispute over Indians and land turned into a class war between Bacon and his militia on one side and the governor and planter elites on the other. Bacon and his men made their way to Virginia's capital, Jamestown, offering freedom to any servants or slaves who joined their ranks. With them were many Indian captives, symbolic of the war's beginning. Governor Berkeley took flight from Jamestown aboard ship. On September 9, 1676, Bacon burned Jamestown to the ground. The rebellion ended when Bacon died in October of a fever.

After the rebellion, English officials forced the Virginia government to reestablish the peace with the tributary Indians. The Treaty of Middle Plantation in 1677 recognized a female *weroance* as the sole leader of the Indians remaining within Virginia's borders. As with the treaty of 1646, the Treaty of Middle Plantation included provisions to control the settlement and movement of the Indians. The governor had the duty to handle any disputes or dealings between English planters and native peoples. Planters or farmers were to remain three miles from any Indian village to limit disputes over the trampling of Indian farmlands by livestock. Indians needed a local official's approval to travel to fish, hunt, or gather berries and plants. Indians and Anglo settlers lived together but separate. Virginians, in short, strictly regulated the Indians on reserves, as they did the lives of the numerous African slaves brought to Virginia to support the growing tobacco economy.

Susqehannocks fled north. Governor Edmund Andros reached out to them, negotiating a peace that made the Susqehannocks subjects of the Iroquois Confederacy. Andros concluded the treaty to extend the Iroquois Confederacy as guardians of the Susqehannocks and to challenge the elite leadership in Maryland and Virginia. In June 1677, Maryland and Virginia accepted Andros's terms. As a tributary group of the Iroquois, the Susqehannocks could never raid the plantation colonies again, and the Five Nations also agreed never to raid the two colonies. Now the Covenant Chain alliance had another link as it had extended its reach into the South.

WAR, TRADE, AND THE EASTERN WOODLANDS IN TURMOIL, 1608–1701

Date	Event
1608	Samuel Champlain established Quebec as New France's headquarters
1609–1630	Huron-French alliance for the beaver trade wages war against the Mohawks
1639	Dutch establish Fort Orange in Hudson Valley to compete in fur trade with the Iroquois
1640s–1660s	Escalation of the mourning wars by the Iroquois, displacing thousands of Indians into the *pays d'en haut*
1665–1667	Iroquois peace with New France and Jesuits begins to enter Iroquois villages
1670s	Massive migration of Catholic Iroquois to New France
1674	English take New York from the Dutch Sir Edmund Andros begins the "Covenant Chain" alliance with the Iroquois
1675–1676	Metacom's War in New England
1676	Bacon's Rebellion
1689–1697	King William's War and decline of Iroquois warfare
1701	Peace settlement between New France and the Iroquois

CONCLUSION

The seventeenth century was a time of radical change and disruption for both Native Americans and Europeans in the Eastern Woodlands. French and British imperialism brought disease, war, trade, diplomacy, and new religions. Native Americans from Virginia to the Great Lakes often dictated the terms of intercultural encounters. In the *pays d'en haut,* developing peaceful relationships was a necessity for both the French and Indians who had been dispossessed by years of devastating wars with the Iroquois. At the same time, Europeans tried to impose systems of land ownership, international markets, and politics on native peoples.

As both Native Americans and Europeans competed for control of the Eastern Woodlands, efforts at coexistence were often short lived. In Virginia and New England, the English sought to grab land as much land as possible and viewed the Indians as impediments to progress. By the 1660s and 1670s, Indians and English colonists, in both New England and Virginia, were at war. When these wars were over, it was clear that English colonists in New England and Virginia no longer saw coexistence with the Indians within their borders as a viable option. From an English viewpoint, Indians would have to submit to their authority or go. Native Americans chose their own paths.

Review Questions

1. Compare and contrast Native American relations in Virginia and New England.

2. How and in what ways did native peoples clash with European colonists in New France and New England?

3. Analyze the similarities and differences between King Philip's War and Bacon's Rebellion.

RECOMMENDED READINGS

Horn, James. *A Land As God Made It: Jamestown and the Birth of America* (New York: Basic Books, 2005). A new, very useful, and readable study of the Jamestown settlement and the Powhatan Indians.

Lepore, Jill. *The Name of War: King Philip's War and the Origins of American Identity* (New York: Knopf, 1998). A lively account of King Philip's War.

Morgan, Edmund S. *American Slavery, American Freedom: The Ordeal of Colonial Virginia* (New York: Norton, 1975). Remains a seminal study of the early settlement and development of Virginia that also focuses on English-Powhatan relations.

Richter, Daniel K. *The Ordeal of the Longhouse: The Peoples of the Iroquois League in the Era of European Colonization* (Chapel Hill: University of North Carolina Press, 1992). The best work on the Iroquois in the seventeenth century that covers their relationships with the French, Dutch, and English, and a study that offers the best analysis of the mourning wars.

Salisbury, Neil. *Manitou and Providence: Indians, Europeans, and the Making of New England, 1500–1643* (New York: Oxford University Press, 1982). The classic account of early relations between southern New England Indians and the English.

Silverman, David J. *Faith & Boundaries: Colonists, Christianity, and Community among the Wampanoag Indians of Martha's Vineyard, 1600–1871* (New York: Cambridge University Press, 2005). The most important study of Southern New England to appear in some time, and the best examination of religious change on Martha's Vineyard.

White, Richard. *The Middle Ground: Indians, Empires, and Republics in the Great Lakes Region, 1650–1815* (New York: Cambridge University Press, 1991). The most important study of the Great Lakes territory and intercultural relationships between the multitribal villages and the French.

NATIVE AMERICAN HISTORY ONLINE

General Sites

John Eliot, *Indian Grammar Begun: Or, An Essay to Bring the Indian Language into Rules, For the Help of Such As Desire to Learn the Same, for the Furtherance of the Gospel Among Them* **(Cambridge, 1666).** http://books.google. com/books?id=vz3IoF-bRi8C&printsec=frontcover&dq= John+Eliot,+Indian+Grammar+Begun:+Or,+An+Essay+ to+Bring+the+Indian+Language+into+Rules,+For+the+ Help+of+Such+As+Desire+to+Learn+the+Same,+for+the+ Furtherance+of+the+Gospel+Among+Them&hl=en&ei= iq5OTpelIqL00gHDx8HkBg&sa=X&oi=book_result&ct= result&resnum=2&ved=0CC4Q6AEwAQ#v=onepage&q&f= false One of many tracts published by John Eliot, it shows how New England missionaries tried to make sense of the Algonquian tongue to spread Christianity.

Roger Williams, *A Key Into the Language of America.* http:// books.google.com/books?id=wOfpAPRxlVYC&pg=PA1&dq =%22a+key+to+the+language+of+Americ%22&lr=&source =gbs_toc_r&cad=4#v=onepage&q&f=false=mgUMAAAAY AAJ&pg=PA211&dq=%22New+Netherland%22%2B%22doc uments%22&lr=. Roger Williams's full text of the Narragansett language is an invaluable source for understanding Indian life in southern New England in the seventeenth century.

S. G. Drake, *The Old Indian Chronicle: Being A Collection of Rare Tracts, Published in the Time of King Philip's War, By People Residing in the Country* **(1836).** http://books. google.com/books?id=hA0TAAAAYAAJ&printsec=front cover&dq=%22King+Philp%27s+war+tracts%22&lr=. A compilation of tracts published at the time of King Philip's War allows students to see how colonists viewed the war and the Indians who fought it.

Historical Sites

Mashantucket Pequot Museum and Research Center, Mashantucket, Connecticut. http://www.pequotmuseum. org/. The Pequot Museum provides a visual history of the Pequots and other southern New England Indians.

America in 1607: Jamestown and the Powhatan. http:// ngm.nationalgeographic.com/2007/05/jamestown/ jamestown-standalone.

The New Netherland Institute and New Netherland Project, Albany, New York. http://www.nnp.org/index. shtml. This site provides both a virtual tour of New Netherland and access to documents and other historical resources.

MySearchLab Connections: Sources Online
www.mysearchlab.com

Read and Review

Review this chapter by using the study aids and these related documents available on MySearchLab.

Study Plan
Chapter Test
Essay Test

Documents

Samuel de Champlain, The Journal of Samuel de Champlain (1609)
Champlain recounts his journey down the "River of the Iroquois" (Richelieu River).

Remarks by Chief Powhatan to John Smith (c. 1609)
Powhatan explains his concerns for the relationship between the Jamestown settlers and the Algonquian people.

Captain John Smith to Queen Anne (1617)
Smith's imprisonment by the Algonquian people and his relationship with Pocahontas and her father, Powhatan.

Jean De Brébeuf, What the Hurons Think about Their Origins (1639)
Huron accounts of their origins as recorded by Jesuit Jean de Brebeuf.

Micmac Chief's Observations of the French (1691)
The response of a Micmac chief to European arguments of cultural superiority.

Onandogas and Cayugas, Two Iroquois Chiefs
Arguments spoken by Iroquois chiefs sought to resolve difficulties caused by an ever-expanding colonial population.

Research and Explore

Use the databases available within MySearchLab to find additional primary and secondary sources on the topics within this chapter.

Image
King Philip's War91

BIBLIOGRAPHY

Cronon, William. *Changes in the Land: Indians, Colonists, and the Ecology of New England.* New York: Hill & Wang, 1983.

Mandell, Daniel. *Behind the Frontier: Indians in Eighteenth-Century Eastern Massachusetts.* Lincoln: University of Nebraska Press, 1996.

Pulsipher, Jenny Hale. *Subjects unto the Same King: Indians, English, and the Contest for Authority in Colonial New England.* Philadelphia: University of Pennsylvania Press, 2005.

Sleeper-Smith, Susan. *Indian Women and French Men: Rethinking Cultural Encounter in the Western Great Lakes.* Amherst: University of Massachusetts Press, 2001.

Trigger, Bruce G. *The Children of Aataentsic: A History of the Huron People to 1660.* Montreal: McGill-Queen's University Press, 1976.

_____. *Natives and Newcomers: Canada's "Heroic Age" Reconsidered.* Montreal: McGill-Queen's University Press, 1985.

Native Americans Challenge
Massachusetts Bay's Authority

In the 1640s, the English colony of Massachusetts Bay moved aggressively to incorporate new lands and to extend its jurisdiction over nearby Indians. The Narragansetts of Rhode Island, who earlier had fought alongside English colonists in a common war against the Pequot tribe, began to fear their former allies. When their leader, Miantonomo, was captured and executed by Mohegin Indians at Massachusetts's instigation, the Narragansetts fought back in a way that demonstrated a sophisticated grasp of English imperial politics. They submitted directly to English royal authority in 1644, which gave them equal status with the Bay Colony, and announced their intention to seek mediation in London, not Boston, in the future.

KNOW ALL MEN, Colonies, Peoples, and Nations, unto whom the fame hereof shall come; that wee, the chiefe Sachems, Princes or Governours of the Nanhigansets (in that part of America, now called New-England), together with the joynt and unanimous consent of all our people and subjects, inhabitants thereof, do upon serious consideration, . . . submit, subject, and give over ourselves, peoples, lands, rights, inheritances, and possessions whatsoever, in ourselves and our heires successively for ever, unto the protection, care and government of that worthy and royal Prince, Charles, King of Great Britaine and Ireland, his heires and successors forever, to be ruled and governed according to the ancient and honorable lawes and customes, established in that so renowned realme and kingdome of Old England; . . . *upon*

From "The Act and Deed of the Voluntary and Free Submission of the Chiefe Sachem . . . of the Nanhigansets . . . ," in *Records of the Colony of Rhode Island* . . . , ed. John Russell Bartlett, (Providence, Rhode Island, 1856), 1:134–37.

condition of His Majesties' royal protection, and wrighting us of what wrong is, or may be done unto us, according to his honorable lawes and customes, exercised amongst his subjects, in their preservation and safety, and in the defeating and overthrow of his, and their enemies; not that we find ourselves necessitated hereunto, . . . with any of the natives in these parts, knowing ourselves sufficient defence and able to judge in any matter or cause in that respect; but have just cause of jealousy and suspicion of some of His Majesty's pretended subjects. Therefore our desire is, to have our matters and causes heard and tried according to his just and equall lawes, in that way an order His Highness shall please to appoint: *Nor can we yield over ourselves unto any, that are subjects themselves in any case;* having ourselves been the chief Sachems, or Princes successively, of the country, time out of mind. . . .

Here followeth a copy of a letter sent to the Massachusetts, by the Sachems of the Narrangansetts, (shortly after their subjection to the State and Government of Old England) they being sent unto by the Massachusetts, to make their appearance at their General Court, then approacing [approaching].

We understand your desire is, that we should come downe into the Massachusetts, at the time of your Courte, now approaching. Our occasions at this same time are very great; and the more because of the loss . . . of our late deceased brother [Miantonomo]. . . . Our brother was willing to stir much abroad to converse with men, and we see a sad event at the last thereupon. Take it not ill, therefore, though we resolve to keep at home, . . . and so, at this time, do not repair unto you, according to your request. . . . [We] have subjected ourselves, our lands and possessions, with all the rights and inheritances of us and our people, either by conquest, voluntary subjection or otherwise, unto that famous and honorable government of that Royal King, Charles, and that State of Old England, . . . hereby being subjects now (and that with joint and voluntary consent), unto the same King and State yourselves are. So that if any small things of difference should fall out betwixt us, only the sending of a messenger may bring it to right again; but if any great matter should fall (which we hope and desire will not . . .), then neither yourselves, nor we are to be judges; and both of us are to have recourse, and repair unto that honorable and just Government.

Nathaniel Bacon Justifies Rebellion on Behalf of "The People"

Bacon's Rebellion began in 1676 when Governor William Berkeley of Virginia refused to allow English settlers to confiscate Native American land. The planters had already been angered by the passage of Navigation Acts that restricted the sale of tobacco to English merchants only. As a result of this restricted market, the price of tobacco dropped, and an economic depression began in Virginia. While the planters chafed at English rule, conflict with Native Americans constituted a more pressing problem. The English had been encroaching upon Native American lands and the Indians had retaliated by raiding farms. To solve the land issue, the settlers proposed to acquire property by killing all the Indians in the area, both friends and foes. Berkeley suggested building a series of forts to protect the frontier.

While the English debated policy, a few Indians stole a hog, and whites under the leadership of planter Nathaniel Bacon retaliated by massacring members of the Susquehanna, Algonquin, and Pamunkey tribes. Within months, the colony divided into factions that supported either Berkeley or Bacon, and both sides took up arms. On July 30, 1676, Bacon issued "The Declaration of the People," in which he defended his actions and attacked the policies of Berkeley's government. Bacon's Rebellion ended when Bacon succumbed to a fever, but by that time most of the coastal tribes had been decimated. Berkeley remained in power and executed a number of the rebels.

1st. For haveing . . . raised great unjust taxes vpon the Comonality for the aduancement of private favorites & other sinister ends, but [without having] . . . in any measure aduanced this hopefull Colony either by fortifications Townes or Trade.

From the *Collections of the Massachusetts Historical Society,* 4th Series, (Boston, 1871), 9:184–85.

2d. For haveing abused & rendred contemptable the Magistrates of Justice, by aduanceing to places of Judicature, scandalous and Ignorant favorites.

3. For haveing wronged his Majestys prerogative & interest, by assumeing Monopolony of the Beaver trade, & for haveing in that unjust gaine betrayed & sold his Majestys Country & the lives of his loyall subiects to the barbarous heathen.

4. For haveing, protected, favoured, & Imboldned the Indians against his Majestys loyall subiects, never contriveing, requireing, or appointing any due or proper meanes of satisfaction for theire many Inuasions, robbories, & murthers comitted vpon vs.

5. For haveing when the Army of English was just vpon the track of those Indians, who now in all places burne, spoyle, murther & when we might with ease have distroyed them who then were in open hostillity, for then haveing expressly countermanded, & sent back our Army, by passing his word for the peaceable demeanour of the said Indians, who imediately p'secuted theire evill intentions, comitting horred murthers & robberies in all places, being p'tected by the said ingagement & word past of him the said Sir Wm Berkeley, haveing ruined & laid desolate a greate part of his Majestys Country, & have now drawne themselves into such obscure & remote places, & are by theire success soe imboldned & confirmed, by theire confederacy soe strengthned that the cryes of blood are in all places, & the terror, & constirnation of the people soe greate, are now become, not onely a difficult, but a very formidable enimy, who might att first with ease haue beene distroyed.

6th. And lately when vpon the loud outcryes of blood the Assembly had with all care raised & framed an Army for the preventing of further mischiefe & safeguard of this his Majestys Colony.

7th. For haveing with onely the privacy of some few favorites, without acquainting the people, onely by the alteration of a figure, forged a Comission, by we know not what hand, not onely without, but even against the consent of the people, for the raiseing & effecting civill warr & destruction, which being happily & without blood shed prevented, for haveing the second time attempted the same, thereby calling downe our forces from the defence of the fronteeres & most weekely exposead places.

8. For the prevention of civill mischeife & ruin amongst ourselues, whilst the barbarous enimy in all places did invade, murther & spoyle vs, his majestys most faithfull subiects.

Interdependence and
Exchange in Colonial Louisiana

When the French began to settle the Lower Mississippi region in the late seventeenth century, they quickly sought to ally themselves with the twenty thousand member Choctaw Nation. France's settlements at New Orleans and Biloxi, which never contained more than five thousand white and four thousand black inhabitants, relied on the Choctaws for food, deerskins, and military aid against the English. This anonymous French account from the early 1700s details how the Indians sought trade contacts with the Europeans, but set the terms of exchange, demanded "presents" in the form of yearly tribute, and forced the French to use Indian ceremonies.

The Chaquetas [Choctaws] are a hundred leagues north of Mobile. There are about four thousand bearing arms.... This nation is warlike against similar people.... The French always having needed to depend upon them in war, it has made them so insolent that they despise the French and would receive the English among them. They are much accustomed to receiving presents from the French.... They think that it is a right, that the French pay them for the lands which they occupy. It is this which they try to make them understand in the speeches which they make to the commandants of the posts where they go, saying:

> Formerly our ancestors occupied the place where you now live and came there to hunt; they have ceded it to you as to people who wished to be their friends, in consideration for

From John R. Swanton, "An Early Account of the Choctaw Indians," in *Memoirs of the American Anthropological Association* (Lancaster, Pennsylvania, 1918), 5:54–55.

which you have promised them a certain quantity of goods, and length of time has not cancelled the continuance of the gift, and of the friendship, which, having reigned between our ancestors and the French, reigns still between you and us. You know that every time you have asked us to take vengeance on your enemies who have insulted you, we have had pity, since, being few in numbers, you were unable to go to war, and that we, regarding you as our brothers, have left our wives, children, houses, villages, harvests, and periods of hunting to attack your enemies and stain our arms with their blood; that we have often lost our people there. You know that many times on returning from war we have taken credit for the goods that you have promised us, gained at the price of our blood, because they had not yet arrived by vessel from France. You know that the English are always at our doors importuning us to make an alliance with them, and sell them our deerskins at fairer prices than you offer. We have hopes then that in consideration of all these things you will look with pity on us and will share with us as your brothers in order that we may return to our village loaded with the presents you shall have given us.

Chief Pontiac and Dreams of Rebellion

After the French and Indian War (1756–1763), Native Americans lost their bargaining power, placing them at the mercy of the English. During the war, English and French forces augmented their troops through Indian alliances. Native American leaders used their position to regain their autonomy, collecting rents on lands and negotiating better pay for alliances. The French defeat and departure was devastating to the Native Americans, forcing them to redefine their relationship with the English settlers.

British colonists treated the Native Americans poorly, encroaching on their lands and disregarding treaties. An Ottowa chief, Pontiac, retaliated by creating a confederacy among Indian tribes and began attacking English forts and settlements in the Northeast. His goal was to drive the settlers out and reclaim Native American sovereignty. Although Pontiac's Uprising was put down quickly, the push for Indian independence would continue to gain strength. The motivation for many Indian movements came from the prophet Neolin, who had envisioned a united Indian front against the whites. In the following document Neolin recounts his dream vision where he was instructed to reject European culture and heed the call of the "Master of Life."

I am the Master of Life, whom thou wishest to see, and to whom thou wishest to speak. Listen to that which I will tell thee for thyself and for all the Indians. I am the Maker of Heaven and earth, the trees, lakes, rivers, men, and all that thou seest or hast seen on the earth or in the heavens; and because I love you, you must do my will; you must also avoid that which I hate; I hate you to drink as you do, until you lose your reason; I wish you not to

From *The Death and Rebirth of the Seneca*, by Anthony F. C. Wallace with the assistance of Sheila C. Steen, Alfred A. Knopf, (New York, 1970), copyright © 1970 by Anthony Wallace, 117–118.

fight one another; you take two wives, or run after other people's wives; you do wrong; I hate such conduct; you should have but one wife, and keep her until death. When you go to war, . . . you sing the medicine song, thinking you speak to me; you deceive yourselves; it is to the Manito that you speak; he is a wicked spirit who induces you to evil, and, for want of knowing me, you listen to him.

The land on which you are, I have made for you, not for others: wherefore do you suffer the whites to dwell upon your lands? Can you not do without them? I know that those whom you call the children of your great Father supply your wants. But, were you not wicked as you are, you would not need them. Before those whom you call your brothers had arrived, did not your bow and arrow maintain you? You needed neither gun, powder, nor any other object. The flesh of animals was your food, their skins your raiment. But when I saw you inclined to evil, I removed the animals into the depths of the forests, that you might depend on your brothers for your necessaries, for your clothing. Again become good and do my will, and I will send animals for your sustenance. I do now, however, forbid suffering among you your Father's children; I love them, they know me, they pray to me; I supply their own wants, and give them that which they bring to you. Not so with those who are come to trouble your possessions. Drive them away; wage war against them. I love them not. They know me not. They are my enemies, they are your brothers' enemies. Send them back to the lands I have made for them. Let them remain there.

Here is a written prayer which I give thee; learn it by heart, and teach it to all the Indians and children. It must be repeated morning and evening. Do all that I have told thee, and announce it to all the Indians as coming from the Master of Life. Let them drink but one draught [of liquor], or two at most, in one day. Let them have but one wife, and discontinue running after other people's wives and daughters. Let them not fight one another. Let them not sing the medicine song, for in singing the medicine song they speak to the evil spirit. Drive from your lands those dogs in red clothing; they are only an injury to you. When you want anything, apply to me, as your brothers [i.e., the Christian whites] do, and I will give to both. Do not sell to your brothers that which I have placed on the earth as food. In short, become good, and you shall want nothing.

Petition of the Chickasaw Headmen

During the late 1600s and 1700s a series of colonial wars were fought between England and France for the North American continent. Throughout this period, Native Americans secured their position by creating alliances with the two European powers. Indian leaders devised tactics to take advantage of the animosity between the French and English. However, such strategies were not always advantageous to the Native Americans. Shrewd government officials and traders throughout the English colonies undermined indigenous attempts to manipulate European settlers, using treaties and trading debts to deplete Indian resources and power. The Chickasaws of the Carolinas were not immune to such misfortune. The following document is a letter they wrote to South Carolina Governor James Glen in which they explained their situation and petitioned him for firearms.

To His Excellency James Glen, Esq., Governor of South Carolina, and the Honourable Council from the Head Men and Warriours of the Chickesaw Nation.

We have heard your friendly Talk . . . which together with your kind Presents confirms in us the Oppinion we have long had of your Desire that we should live and injoy our Lands against all the Attempts of our Enemies. Though your Lands and ours is far distant from each other, and that of our Enemies, the French, but a little Way from us, yet we look on you not only as our best Friends, but as our Fathers haveing always found a Readyness in you to assist us whenever we made Application to you, and although we are Red People, we can and ever will make a true

From *Colonial Records of South Carolina, Documents Relating to Indian Affairs, May 21, 1750–August 7, 1754*, ed. William L. McDowell, Jr., (Columbia, South Carolina, 1958), 512–513. Reprinted by permission of South Carolina Department of Archives and History.

Distinction between the English and ever other Nation, and shall love and esteem them all our Days.

It's true some Years ago we did not mind how many our Enemies were, but that is not our case at Present, our Number being reduced to a Handful of Men, and thereby we are rendered uncapable of keeping our Ground without a Continuance of your friendly Assistance, we not being able to hunt nor are we free from the Hands of our Enemies even in our Towns, so that it is impossible for us to kill Dear to buy Cloathing for ourselves, our Wives, and Children, or even to purchase Amunition. This the English Traders that comes amongst us is too sencable off from the small Quantity of Skins they have carried out of this Nation these two last Years to what they used to do formerly. It's needless to trouble you with an Account of what People we have lost in a few Months. . . . Nothing but our present Necessity could oblige us at this Time to ask you for a further Suply of Guns and Ammunition, without which we must either stand and be shott, or defend the Enemies' Bullets with our Hatchets as we have nothing else at Present. Our Traders is tired out with trusting us with Ammunition and Guns, nor can we be angry with them as it has not been in our Power to pay them for it, and many other Things we had from them, so that we may now say our Lives is in your Power to save or to let the Enemy have their Desire off us. It has always been your Desire as well as our own that we should keep this Ground from the French which we have hitherto done, but now this is our very case; we must either run from it and save our Lives or die upon it, and either Ways give it up to them unless assisted by you. In former Times when we either went or sent to you we had Presents of all kinds of Cloths, Duffels, Red Coats, and a great many good Things, but now we do not desire any other then Guns and Amunition to preserve our Lives with. We still love our Lands and Liberties nor shall we chuse ever to give it up but with the Loss of our Lives.

A great many of our People has left us; a Thing we are sorry at, but young People will rather go from us to live in Peace than stay here where they are in Danger every Day. . . . If you think good to take Pity on us and send us some Ammunition and at the same Time four of your Guns that make a great Noise and will kill our Enemys at a great Distance we will either keep our Land or die along side of them Guns, and if we should be all killed the

Guns would still remain on our Ground to shew the French how much the English loved us. All your old good Talks is still fresh with us, and so shall this your last Talk nor shall we ever throw them away.

Worcester v. the State of Georgia

In the years after the War of 1812, if not sooner, large numbers of Americans began to view Native American societies as destined to either assimilate with or—as most thought more likely—die out under the pressure of an expanding, encroaching American civilization. This view was based partly in ethnocentric assumptions about the superiority of white "civilization," partly in American attitudes about race, and partly in political and economic rivalry. By 1830, few Native Americans remained east of the Mississippi River; those who did held land highly coveted by white farmers, especially land in Georgia, Alabama, and the Mississippi delta region held by the so-called Civilized Tribes: the Choctaw, Chickasaw, Creek, and Cherokee. In 1832, the Andrew Jackson Administration forcibly removed the remaining Cherokee tribes to reservations west of the Mississippi River.

*Despite the growing consensus among white Americans that Native American societies were not destined to survive in proximity with white "civilization," the tribes did have supporters in their battle to remain on land reserved to them by previous federal treaty. The Supreme Court was one. The court handed down two decisions in the 1830s—*Cherokee Nation v. Georgia *in 1831 and* Worcester v. Georgia *in 1832—which upheld, at least in theory, the existing land rights of the Cherokee. In* Worcester v. Georgia *the Supreme Court ruled that efforts by Georgia to meddle with the land rights and internal affairs of the Cherokee were unconstitutional. Georgia ignored the court's decision; Andrew Jackson ignored it as well. That such a blatant disregard of both federal supremacy and the established authority of the Supreme Court did not result in a major Constitutional crisis is an indication of the growing sense among white Americans in the nineteenth century that Native American societies were doomed either to move west or disappear.*

From *Reports of Decisions in the Supreme Court of the United States*, vol. 10, ed. B. R. Curtis, Little, Brown & Company, (Boston, 1855), 10:214, 240, 242–44.

A return to a writ of error from this court to a state court, certified by the clerk of the court which pronounced the judgment, and to which the writ is addressed, and authenticated by the seal of the court, is in conformity to law, and brings the record regularly before this court.

The law of Georgia, which subjected to punishment all white persons residing within the limits of the Cherokee nation, and authorized their arrest within those limits, and their forcible removal therefrom, and their trial in a court of the State, was repugnant to the constitution, treaties, and laws of the United States, and so void; and a judgment against the plaintiff in error, under color of that law, was reversed by this court, under the 25th section of the Judiciary Act, (1 Stats. at Large, 85.)

The relations between the Indian tribes and the United States examined. . . .

From the commencement of our government, congress has passed acts to regulate trade and intercourse with the Indians; which treat them as nations, respect their rights, and manifest a firm purpose to afford that protection which treaties stipulate. All these acts, and especially that of 1802, which is still in force, manifestly consider the several Indian nations as distinct political communities, having territorial boundaries, within which their authority is exclusive, and having a right to all the lands within those boundaries, which is not only acknowledged, but guaranteed by the United States.

In 1819, congress passed an act for promoting those humane designs of civilizing the neighboring Indians, which had long been cherished by the executive. It enacts, "that, for the purpose of providing against the further decline and final extinction of the Indian tribes adjoining to the frontier settlements of the United States, and for introducing among them the habits and arts of civilization, the President of the United States shall be, and he is hereby authorized, in every case where he shall judge improvement in the habits and condition of such Indians practicable, and that the means of instruction can be introduced with their own consent, to employ capable persons, of good moral character, to instruct them in the mode of agriculture suited to their situation; and for teaching their children in reading, writing, and arithmetic; and for performing such other duties as may be enjoined, according to such instructions and rules as the President may give and prescribe for the regulation of their conduct in the discharge of their duties."

This act avowedly contemplates the preservation of the Indian nations as an object sought by the United States, and proposes to effect this object by civilizing and converting them from hunters into agriculturists. Though the Cherokees had already made considerable progress in this improvement, it cannot be doubted that the general words of the act comprehend them. Their advance in the "habits and arts of civilization," rather encouraged perseverance in the laudable exertions still further to meliorate their condition. This act furnishes strong additional evidence of a settled purpose to fix the Indians in their country by giving them security at home. . . .

The Indian nations had always been considered as distinct, independent political communities, retaining their original natural rights, as the undisputed possessors of the soil, from time immemorial, with the single exception of that imposed by irresistible power, which excluded them from intercourse with any other European potentate than the first discoverer of the coast of the particular region claimed; and this was a restriction which those European potentates imposed on themselves, as well as on the Indians. The very term "nation," so generally applied to them, means "a people distinct from others." The constitution, by declaring treaties already made, as well as those to be made, to be the supreme law of the land, has adopted and sanctioned the previous treaties with the Indian nations, and consequently admits their rank among those powers who are capable of making treaties. The words "treaty" and "nation" are words of our own language, selected in our diplomatic and legislative proceedings, by ourselves, having each a definite and well understood meaning. We have applied them to Indians, as we have applied them to the other nations of the earth. They are applied to all in the same sense. . . .

The Cherokee nation, then, is a distinct community, occupying its own territory, with boundaries accurately described, in which the laws of Georgia can have no force, and which the citizens of Georgia have no right to enter, but with the assent of the Cherokees themselves, or in conformity with treaties and with the acts of congress. The whole intercourse between the United States and this nation is, by our constitution and laws, vested in the government of the United States. . . .

. . . If the review which has been taken be correct, and we think it is, the acts of Georgia are repugnant to the constitution, laws, and treaties of the United States.

They interfere forcibly with the relations established between the United States and the Cherokee nation, the regulation of which, according to the settled principles of our constitution, are committed exclusively to the government of the Union.

They are in direct hostility with treaties, repeated in a succession of years, which mark out the boundary that separates the Cherokee country from Georgia, guarantee to them all the land within their boundary, solemnly pledge the faith of the United States to restrain their citizens from trespassing on it, and recognize the preëxisting power of the nation to govern itself.

They are in equal hostility with the acts of congress for regulating this intercourse, and giving effect to the treaties.

Cherokee Removal as Benevolent Policy

In the years after the War of 1812, if not sooner, large numbers of Americans began to view Native American societies as destined to either assimilate with or—as most thought more likely—die out under the pressure of an expanding, encroaching American civilization. This view was based partly in ethnocentric assumptions about the superiority of white "civilization," partly in American attitudes about race, and partly in political and economic rivalry. By 1830, few Native Americans remained east of the Mississippi River; those who did held land highly coveted by white farmers, especially land in Georgia, Alabama, and the Mississippi delta region held by the so-called Civilized Tribes: the Choctaw, Chickasaw, Creek, and Cherokee. In 1832, the Andrew Jackson Administration forcibly removed the remaining Cherokee tribes to reservations west of the Mississippi River.

In his second annual message to Congress in 1830, President Andrew Jackson—whose earlier career as a general in the U.S. Army involved extensive action both with and against these tribes—argued for their permanent removal west of the Mississippi and the opening of their land to white settlement. Jackson's message weaves together most of the major contemporary arguments in favor of Indian removal, including the notion, often argued by self-styled "friends of the Indian," that such a course of action was in the best interests of the Native Americans themselves as their only alternative to extinction.

It gives me pleasure to announce to Congress that the benevolent policy of the Government, steadily pursued for nearly thirty years, in relation to the removal of the Indians beyond the white settlements is approaching to a happy consummation. Two

From *A Compilation of the Messages and Papers of the Presidents, 1789–1897,* ed. James D. Richardson, (Washington, 1896), 2:519–523.

important tribes have accepted the provision made for their removal at the last session of Congress, and it is believed that their example will induce the remaining tribes also to seek the same obvious advantages.

The consequences of a speedy removal will be important to the United States, to individual States, and to the Indians themselves. The pecuniary advantages which it promises to the Government are the least of its recommendations. It puts an end to all possible danger of collision between the authorities of the General and State Governments on account of the Indians. It will place a dense and civilized population in large tracts of country now occupied by a few savage hunters. By opening the whole territory between Tennessee on the north and Louisiana on the south to the settlement of the whites it will incalculably strengthen the southwestern frontier and render the adjacent States strong enough to repel future invasions without remote aid. It will relieve the whole State of Mississippi and the western part of Alabama of Indian occupancy, and enable those States to advance rapidly in population, wealth, and power. It will separate the Indians from immediate contact with settlements of whites; free them from the power of the States; enable them to pursue happiness in their own way and under their own rude institutions; will retard the progress of decay, which is lessening their numbers, and perhaps cause them gradually, under the protection of the Government and through the influence of good counsels, to cast off their savage habits and become an interesting, civilized, and Christian community. These consequences, some of them so certain and the rest so probable, make the complete execution of the plan sanctioned by Congress at their last session an object of much solicitude.

Toward the aborigines of the country no one can indulge a more friendly feeling than myself, or would go further in attempting to reclaim them from their wandering habits and make them a happy, prosperous people. I have endeavored to impress upon them my own solemn convictions of the duties and powers of the General Government in relation to the State authorities. For the justice of the laws passed by the States within the scope of their reserved powers they are not responsible to this Government. As individuals we may entertain and express our opinions of their acts, but as a Government we have as little right to control them as we have to prescribe laws for other nations.

With a full understanding of the subject, the Choctaw and the Chickasaw tribes have with great unanimity determined to avail themselves of the liberal offers presented by the act of Congress, and have agreed to remove beyond the Mississippi River. Treaties have been made with them, which in due season will be submitted for consideration. In negotiating these treaties they were made to understand their true condition, and they have preferred maintaining their independence in the Western forests to submitting to the laws of the States in which they now reside. These treaties, being probably the last which will ever be made with them, are characterized by great liberality on the part of the Government. They give the Indians a liberal sum in consideration of their removal, and comfortable subsistence on their arrival at their new homes. If it be their real interest to maintain a separate existence, they will there be at liberty to do so without the inconveniences and vexations to which they would unavoidably have been subject in Alabama and Mississippi.

Humanity has often wept over the fate of the aborigines of this country, and Philanthropy has been long busily employed in devising means to avert it, but its progress has never for a moment been arrested, and one by one have many powerful tribes disappeared from the earth. To follow to the tomb the last of his race and to tread on the graves of extinct nations excite melancholy reflections. But true philanthropy reconciles the mind to these vicissitudes as it does to the extinction of one generation to make room for another. In the monuments and fortresses of an unknown people, spread over the extensive regions of the West, we behold the memorials of a once powerful race, which was exterminated or has disappeared to make room for the existing savage tribes. Nor is there anything in this which, upon a comprehensive view of the general interests of the human race, is to be regretted. Philanthropy could not wish to see this continent restored to the condition in which it was found by our forefathers. What good man would prefer a country covered with forests and ranged by a few thousand savages to our extensive Republic, studded with cities, towns, and prosperous farms, embellished with all the improvements which art can devise or industry execute, occupied by more than 12,000,000 happy people, and filled with all the blessings of liberty, civilization, and religion?

The present policy of the Government is but a continuation of the same progressive change by a milder process. The tribes which occupied the countries now constituting the Eastern States were annihilated or have melted away to make room for the whites. The waves of population and civilization are rolling to the westward, and we now propose to acquire the countries occupied by the red men of the South and West by a fair exchange, and, at the expense of the United States, to send them to a land where their existence may be prolonged and perhaps made perpetual. Doubtless it will be painful to leave the graves of their fathers; but what do they more than our ancestors did or than our children are now doing? To better their condition in an unknown land our forefathers left all that was dear in earthly objects. Our children by thousands yearly leave the land of their birth to seek new homes in distant regions. Does Humanity weep at these painful separations from everything, animate and inanimate, with which the young heart has become entwined? Far from it. It is rather a source of joy that our country affords scope where our young population may range unconstrained in body or in mind, developing the power and faculties of man in their highest perfection. These remove hundreds and almost thousands of miles at their own expense, purchase the lands they occupy, and support themselves at their new homes from the moment of their arrival. Can it be cruel in this Government when, by events which it can not control, the Indian is made discontented in his ancient home to purchase his lands, to give him a new and extensive territory, to pay the expense of his removal, and support him a year in his new abode? How many thousands of our own people would gladly embrace the opportunity of removing to the West on such conditions! If the offers made to the Indians were extended to them, they would be hailed with gratitude and joy.

And is it supposed that the wandering savage has a stronger attachment to his home than the settled, civilized Christian? Is it more afflicting to him to leave the graves of his fathers than it is to our brothers and children? Rightly considered, the policy of the General Government toward the red man is not only liberal, but generous. He is unwilling to submit to the laws of the States and mingle with their population. To save him from this alternative, or perhaps utter annihilation, the General Government kindly offers him a new home, and proposes to pay the whole expense of his removal and settlement. . . .

It is, therefore, a duty which this Government owes to the new States to extinguish as soon as possible the Indian title to all lands which Congress themselves have included within their limits. When this is done the duties of the General Government in relation to the States and the Indians within their limits are at an end. The Indians may leave the State or not, as they choose. The purchase of their lands does not alter in the least their personal relations with the State government. No act of the General Government has ever been deemed necessary to give the States jurisdiction over the persons of the Indians. That they possess by virtue of their sovereign power within their own limits in as full a manner before as after the purchase of the Indian lands; nor can this Government add to or diminish it.

May we not hope, therefore, that all good citizens, and none more zealously than those who think the Indians oppressed by subjection to the laws of the States, will unite in attempting to open the eyes of those children of the forest to their true condition, and by a speedy removal to relieve them from all the evils, real or imaginary, present or prospective, with which they may be supposed to be threatened.

Memorial and Protest of the Cherokee Nation

After the War of 1812, large numbers of Americans began to view Native American societies as destined to either assimilate with or—as most thought more likely—die out under the pressure of an expanding, encroaching American civilization. This view was based partly in ethnocentric assumptions about the superiority of white "civilization," partly in American attitudes about race, and partly in political and economic rivalry. By 1830, few Native Americans remained east of the Mississippi River; those who did held land highly coveted by white farmers, especially land in Georgia, Alabama, and the Mississippi delta region held by the so-called Civilized Tribes: the Choctaw, Chickasaw, Creek, and Cherokee. In 1832, the Andrew Jackson Administration forcibly removed the remaining Cherokee tribes to reservations west of the Mississippi River.

*Despite the growing consensus among white Americans that Native American societies were not destined to survive in proximity with white "civilization," the tribes did have supporters in their battle to remain on land reserved to them by previous federal treaty. The Supreme Court was one. The Court handed down two decisions in the 1830s—*Cherokee Nation v. Georgia *in 1831 and* Worcester v. Georgia *in 1832—which, although ignored by Georgia and the Jackson Administration, upheld, at least in theory, the existing land rights of the Cherokee. Among white Americans, the pro-Cherokee position had support primarily among Northeastern philanthropists, evangelical Protestants, advocates of federal over states' rights, and inveterate haters of Andrew Jackson—categories that frequently overlapped. In this 1836 petition to Congress, leaders of the portion of the Cherokee who wished to remain in the southeast protested formally against their forcible removal west of the Mississippi.*

From the "Memorial and Protest of the Cherokee Nation" of 22 June 1836, in *House Documents, 24th Congress, 1st session*, vol. 7, Doc. No. 286, CIS US Serial no. 292, microprint, 2–5.

If it be said that the Cherokees have lost their national character and political existence, as a nation or tribe, by State legislation, then the President and Senate can make no treaty with them; but if they have not, then no treaty can be made for them, binding, without and against their will. Such is the fact, in reference to the instrument intered into at New Echota, in December last. If treaties are to be thus made and enforced, deceptive to the Indians and to the world, purporting to be a contract, when, in truth, wanting the assent of one of the pretended parties, what security would there be for any nation or tribe to retain confidence in the United States? If interest or policy require that the Cherokees be removed, without their consent, from their lands, surely the President and Senate have no constitutional power to accomplish that object. They cannot do it under the power to make treaties, which are contracts, not rules prescribed by a superior, and therefore binding only by the assent of the parties. In the present instance, the assent of the Cherokee nation has not been given, but expressly denied. The President and Senate cannot do it under the power to regulate commerce with the Indian tribes, or intercourse with them, because that belongs to Congress, and so declared by the President, in his message to the Senate of February 22, 1831, relative to the execution of the act to regulate trade and intercourse with the Indian tribes, &c. passed 30th of March, 1802. They cannot do it under any subsisting treaty stipulation with the Cherokee nation. Nor does the peculiar situation of the Cherokees, in reference to the States their necessities and distresses, confer any power upon the President and Senate to alienate their legal rights, or to prescribe the manner and time of their removal.

Without a decision of what ought to be done, under existing circumstances, the question recurs, is the instrument under consideration a contract between the United States and the Cherokee nation? It so purports upon its face, and that falsely. Is that statement so sacred and conclusive that the Cherokee people cannot be heard to deny the fact? They have denied it under their own signatures, as the documents herein before referred to will show, and protested against the acts of the unauthorized few, who have arrogated to themselves the right to speak for the nation. The Cherokees have said they will not be bound thereby. The documents submitted to the Senate show, that when the vote was taken upon considering the propositions of the commissioner, there were but seventy-nine for so doing. Then it comes to this: could this small number of persons attending the New Echota meeting, acting in their individual capacity, dispose of the rights and interests of the Cherokee nation, or by any instrument they might sign, confer such power upon the President and Senate?

If the United States are to act as the guardian of the Cherokees, and to treat them as incapable of managing their own affairs, and blind to their true interests, yet this would not furnish power or authority to the President and Senate, as the treaty making power to prescribe the rule for managing their affairs. It may afford a pretence for the legislation of Congress, but none for the ratification of an instrument as a treaty made by a small faction against the protest of the Cherokee people.

That the Cherokees are a distinct people, sovereign to some extent, have a separate political existence as a society, or body politic, and a capability of being contracted with in a national capacity, stands admitted by the uniform practice of the United States from 1785, down to the present day. With them have treaties been made through their chiefs, and distinguished men in primary assemblies, as also with their constituted agents or representatives. That they have not the right to manage their own internal affairs, and to regulate, by treaty, their intercourse with other nations, is a doctrine of modern date. In 1793, Mr. Jefferson said, "I consider our right of pre-emption of the Indian lands, not as amounting to any dominion, or jurisdiction, or paramountship whatever, but merely in the nature of a remainder, after the extinguishment of a present right, which gives us no present right whatever, but of preventing other nations from taking possession, and so defeating our expectancy. That the Indians *have the full, undivided, and independent sovereignty as long as they choose to keep it, and that this may be forever.*" This opinion was recognised and practised upon, by the Government of the United States, through several successive administrations, also recognised by the Supreme Court of the United States, and the several States, when the question has arisen. It has not been the opinion only of jurists, but of politicians, as may be seen from various reports of Secretaries of War—beginning with Gen. Knox, also the correspondence between the British and American ministers at Ghent in the year 1814. If the Cherokees have power to judge of their own interests, and to make treaties, which, it is presumed, will be denied by none, then to make a contract valid, the assent of a majority must be had, expressed by themselves or through their representatives, and the

President and Senate have no power to say what their will shall be, for from the laws of nations we learn that "though a nation be obliged to promote, as far as lies in its power, the perfection of others, it is not entitled forcibly to obtrude these good offices on them." Such an attempt would be to violate their natural liberty. Those ambitious Europeans who attacked the American nations, and subjected them to their insatiable avidity of dominion, an order, as they pretended, for civilizing them, and causing them to be instructed in the true religion, (as in the present instance to preserve the Cherokees as a distinct people,) these usurpers grounded themselves on a pretence equally unjust and ridiculous." It is the expressed wish of the Government of the United States to remove the Cherokees to a place west of the Mississippi. That wish is said to be founded in humanity to the Indians. To make their situation more comfortable, and to preserve them as a distinct people. Let facts show how this *benevolent* design has been prosecuted, and how faithful to the spirit and letter has the promise of the President of the United States to the Cherokees been fulfilled—that *"those who remain may be assured of our patronage, our aid, and good neighborhood."* The delegation are not deceived by empty professions, and fear their race is to be destroyed by the mercenary policy of the present day, and their lands wrested from them by physical force; as proof, they will refer to the preamble of an act of the General Assembly of Georgia, in reference to the Cherokees, passed the 2d of December, 1835, where it is said, "from a knowledge of the Indian character, and from the present feelings of these Indians, it is confidently believed, that the right of occupancy of the lands in their possession should be withdrawn, *that it would be a strong inducement to them to treat with the General Government, and consent to a removal to the west;* and whereas, the present Legislature openly avow that their primary object in the measures intended to be pursued *are founded on real humanity to these Indians,* and with a view, in a distant region, to perpetuate them with their old identity of character, *under the paternal care of the Government of the United States;* at the same time frankly disavowing *any selfish or sinister motives towards them in their present legislation."* This is the profession. Let us turn to the practice of *humanity,* to the Cherokees, by the State of Georgia. In violation of the treaties between the United States and the Cherokee nation, that State passed a law requiring all white men, residing in that part of the Cherokee country, in her limits, to take an oath of allegiance to the State of Georgia. For a violation of this law, some of the ministers of Christ, missionaries among the Cherokees, were tried, convicted, and sentenced to hard labor in the penitentiary. Their case may be seen by reference to the records of the Supreme Court of the United States.

Valuable gold mines were discovered upon Cherokee lands, within the chartered limits of Georgia, and the Cherokees commenced working them, and the Legislature of that State interfered by passing an act, making it penal for an Indian to dig for gold within Georgia, no doubt *"frankly disavowing any selfish or sinister motives towards them."* Under this law many Cherokees were arrested, tried, imprisoned, and otherwise abused. Some were even shot in attempting to avoid an arrest; yet the Cherokee people used no violence, but humbly petitioned the Government of the United States for a fulfilment of treaty engagements, to protect them, which was not done, and the answer given that the United States could not interfere. Georgia discovered she was not to be obstructed in carrying out her measures, *"founded on real humanity to these Indians,"* she passed an act directing the Indian country to be surveyed into districts. This excited some alarm, but the Cherokees were quieted with the assurance it would do no harm to survey the country. Another act was shortly after passed, to lay off the country into lots. As yet there was no authority to take possession, but it was not long before a law was made, authorizing a lottery for the lands laid off into lots. In this act the Indians were secured in possession of all the lots touched by their improvements, and the balance of the country allowed to be occupied by white men. This was a direct violation of the 5th article of the treaty of the 27th of February, 1819. The Cherokees made no resistance, still petitioned the United States for protection, and received the same answer that the President could not interpose.

The Narrative of a Slave

Slavery in Africa did not begin with the Europeans. Among the African people, men or women became slaves through warfare or as punishment for a crime. As European demand for slaves grew, though, traders began to kidnap Africans and force them into slavery, often quickly moving the captive far away from his or her home. Of the more than eleven million African slaves brought to America between 1518 and 1850, more than six million were transported after 1750. Many of the slaves did not survive the "middle passage" from Africa to the Americas, described below by Olaudah Equiano.

Equiano was born into the Ibo tribe in the Nigerian village of Isseke in 1745. At the age of eleven, slave traders kidnapped him and he became one of the fifty thousand Africans carried to the New World in 1756. He would spend ten years as a slave in the West Indies, in the American colonies, and in the British navy before becoming a free man. In 1789 as people in England and the United States campaigned against the slave trade, Equiano published his life story. One of the first anti-slavery books written by a former slave, Equiano's narrative is the story of an ordinary man forced into extraordinary circumstances.

The first object which saluted my eyes when I arrived on the coast, was the sea, and a slave ship, which was then riding at anchor, and waiting for its cargo. These filled me with astonishment, which was soon converted into terror, when I was carried on board. I was immediately handled, and tossed up to see if I were sound, by some of the crew; and I was now persuaded that I had gotten into a world of bad spirits, and that they were going to kill me. . . . When I looked round the ship too, and saw a large

From Robert J. Allison, ed., *The Interesting Narrative of the Life of Olaudah Equiano: Written by Himself,* (Boston, 1995), copyright © 1995 by Bedford Books, 53–57.

furnace of copper boiling, and a multitude of black people of every description chained together, every one of their countenances expressing dejection and sorrow, I no longer doubted of my fate; and, quite overpowered with horror and anguish, I fell motionless on the deck and fainted. When I recovered a little, I found some black people about me, who I believed were some of those who had brought me on board, and had been receiving their pay; they talked to me in order to cheer me, but all in vain. . . .

I now saw myself deprived of all chance of returning to my native country, or even the least glimpse of hope of gaining the shore. . . . I was not long suffered to indulge my grief; I was soon put down under the decks, and there I received such a salutation in my nostrils as I had never experienced in my life; so that, with the loathsomeness of the stench, and crying together, I became so sick and low that I was not able to eat, nor had I the least desire to taste anything. I now wished for the last friend, death, to relieve me; but soon, to my grief, two of the white men offered me eatables; and, on my refusing to eat, one of them held me fast by the hands, and laid me across, I think, the windlass, and tied my feet, while the other flogged me severely. . . . I would have jumped over the side, but I could not; and besides, the crew used to watch us very closely who were not chained down to the decks, lest we should leap into the water; and I have seen some of these poor African prisoners most severely cut, for attempting to do so, and hourly whipped for not eating. . . .

The stench of the hold while we were on the coast was so intolerably loathsome, that it was dangerous to remain there for any time, and some of us had been permitted to stay on the deck for the fresh air; but now that the whole ship's cargo were confined together, it became absolutely pestilential. The closeness of the place, and the heat of the climate, added to the number in the ship, which was so crowded that each had scarcely room to turn himself, almost suffocated us. This produced copious perspirations, so that the air soon became unfit for respiration, from a variety of loathsome smells, and brought on a sickness among the slaves, of which many died. . . . This wretched situation was again aggravated by the galling of the chains, now became insupportable, and the filth of the necessary tubs [latrines], into which the children often fell, and were almost suffocated. . . .

One day, when we had a smooth and moderate sea, two of my wearied countrymen who were chained together (I was near them at the time), preferring death to such a life of misery, somehow made through the nettings and jumped into the sea; immediately, another quite dejected fellow, who, on account of his illness, was suffered to be out of irons, also followed their example; and I believe many more would very soon have done the same, if they had not been prevented by the ship's crew. . . .

From Fifty Years in Chains

Born in the early 1780s, Charles Ball served more than forty years in bondage before escaping and, eventually, writing of his harrowing experiences in an 1837 autobiography. After his flight from a Georgia cotton plantation, Ball managed to make his way to Philadelphia where he wrote his memoir with the help of Isaac Fisher, a white lawyer. Though this work was intended as an abolitionist tract, Ball provides detailed descriptions of slave religion and African cultural retentions. The following selection depicts and analyzes the various dimensions of slave religion in the Antebellum South. Notice Ball's discussion of the disdain many enslaved African Americans held for white Christian slaveowners. Excerpted from Charles Ball, Fifty Years in Chains *(Mineola, NY: [1837]), 99–100, 134–137.*

Here it is necessary to make my readers acquainted with the rules of polity, which governed us on Sunday, (for I now speak of myself, as one of the slaves on this plantation,) and with the causes which gave rise to these rules.

All over the south, the slaves are discouraged, as much as possible, and by all possible means, from going to any place of religious worship on Sunday. This is to prevent them from associating together, from different estates, and distant parts of the country; and plotting conspiracies and insurrections. On some estates, the overseers are required to prohibit the people from going to meeting off the plantation, at any time, under the severest penalties. White preachers cannot come upon the plantations, to preach to the people, without first obtaining permission of the master; and afterwards procuring the sanction of the overseer. No slave dare leave the plantation to which he belongs, a single mile, without a written pass from the overseer, or master; but by exposing himself to the danger of being taken up and flogged. Any white man who meets a slave off the plantation without a pass, has a right to take him up, and flog him at his discretion.

All these causes combined, operate powerfully to keep the slave at home. But, in addition to these principles of restraint, it is a rule on every plantation that no overseer ever departs from, to flog every slave, male or female, that leaves the estate for a single hour, by night or by day—Sunday not excepted—without a written pass.

The overseer who should permit the people under his charge to go about the neighbourhood without a pass, would soon lose his character, and no one would employ him; nor would his reputation less certainly suffer in the estimation of the planters, were he to fall into the practice of granting passes, except on the most urgent occasions; and for purposes generally to be specified in the pass.

A cotton planter has no more idea of permitting his slaves to go at will, about the neighbourhood on Sunday, than a farmer in Pennsylvania has of letting his horses out of his field on that day. Nor would the neighbours be less inclined to complain of the annoyance, in the former, than in the latter case.

There has always been a strong repugnance, amongst the planters, against their slaves becoming members of any religious society, Not, as I believe, because they are so maliciously disposed towards their people as to wish to deprive them of the comforts of religion—provided the principles of religion did not militate against the principles of slavery—but they fear that the slaves, by attending meetings, and listening to the preachers, may imbibe with the morality they teach, the notions of equality and liberty, contained in the gospel. This, I have no doubt, is the ground of all the dissatisfaction, that the planters express, with the itinerant preachers, who have from time to time, sought opportunities of instructing the slaves in their religious duties.

The cotton planters have always, since I knew any thing of them, been most careful to prevent the slaves from learning to read; and such is the gross ignorance that prevails, that many of them could not name the four cardinal points.

At the time I first went to Carolina, there were a great many African slaves in the country, and they continued to come in for several years afterwards. I became intimately acquainted with some of these men. Many of them believed there were several gods; some of whom were good, and others evil, and they prayed as much to the latter as to the former, I knew several who must have been, from what I have since learned, Mohamedans; though at that time, I had never heard of the religion of Mohamed.

There was one man on this plantation, who prayed five times every day, always turning his face to the east, when in the performance of his devotion.

There is, in general, very little sense of religious obligation, or duty, amongst the slaves on the cotton plantations; and Christianity cannot be, with propriety, called the religion of these people. They are universally subject to the grossest and most abject superstition; and uniformly believe in witchcraft; conjuration, and the agency of evil spirits in the affairs of human life. Far the greater part of them are either natives of Africa, or the descendants of those who have always, from generation to generation, lived in the south, since their ancestors were landed on this continent; and their superstition, for it does not deserve the name of religion, is no better, nor is it less ferocious, than that which oppresses the inhabitants of the wildest regions of Negro-land.

They have not the slightest religious regard for the Sabbath-day, and their masters make no efforts to impress them with the least respect for this sacred institution. My first Sunday on this plantation was but a prelude to all that followed....

In a community of near three hundred persons, governed by laws as severe and unbending as those which regulated our actions, it is not be expected that universal content can prevail, or that crimes will not to be imagined, and even sometimes perpetrated. Ignorant men estimate those things which fortune has placed beyond their reach, not by their real value, but by the strength of their own desires and passions. Objects in themselves indifferent, which they are forbidden to touch, or even approach, excite in the minds of the unreflecting, ungovernable impulses. The slave, who is taught from infancy, to regard his condition as unchangeable, and his fate as fixed, by the laws of nature, fancies that he sees his master in possession of that happiness which he knows has been denied to himself. The lower men are sunk in the scale of civilization, the more violent become their animal passions. The native Africans are revengeful, and unforgiving in their tempers, easily provoked, and cruel in their designs. They generally place little, or even no value upon the fine houses, and superb furniture of their masters; and discover no beauty in the fair complexions, and delicate forms of their mistresses. They feel indignant at the servitude that is imposed upon them, and only want power to inflict the most cruel retribution upon their oppressors; but they desire only the means of subsistence, and temporary gratification in this country, during their abode here.

They are universally of opinion, and this opinion is founded in their religion, that after death they shall return to their own country, and rejoin their former companions and friends, in some happy region in which they will be provided with plenty of food, and beautiful women, from the lovely daughters of their own native land.

The case is different with the American Negro, who knows nothing of Africa, her religion, or customs, and who has borrowed all his ideas of present and future happiness, from the opinions and intercourse of white people, and of Christians. He is, perhaps, not so impatient of slavery, and excessive labour, as the native of Congo; but his mind is bent upon other pursuits, and his discontent works out for itself other schemes; than those which agitate the brain of the imported negro. His heart pants for no heaven beyond the waves of the ocean; and he dreams of no delights in the arms of sable beauties, in groves of immortality, on the banks of the Niger, or the Gambia; nor does he often solace himself with the reflection, that the day will arrive when all men will receive the awards of immutable justice, and live together in eternal bliss, without any other distinctions than those of superior virtue, and exalted mercy. Circumstances oppose great obstacles in the way of these opinions.

The slaves who are natives of the country, (I now speak of the mass of those on the cotton plantations, as I knew them,) like all other people, who suffer wrong in this world, are exceedingly prone to console themselves with the delights of a future state, when the evil that has been endured in this life, will not only be abolished, and all injuries be compensated by proper rewards, bestowed upon the sufferers, but, as they have learned that wickedness is to be punished, as well as goodness compensated, they do not stop at the point of their own enjoyments and pleasures, but believe that those who have tormented them here, will most surely be tormented in their turn hereafter. The gross and carnal minds of these slaves, are not capable of arriving at the sublime doctrines taught by the white preachers; in which they are encouraged to look forward to the day when all distinctions of colour, and of condition, will be abolished, and they shall sit down in the same paradise, with their masters, mistresses, and even with the overseer. They are ready enough to receive the faith, which conducts them to heaven, and eternal rest, on account of their present sufferings; but they by no means so willingly admit the master and mistress to an equal participation in their enjoyments—this would only be partial justice, and half way retribution. According to their notions, the master and mistress are to be, in future, the companions of wicked slaves, whilst an agreeable recreation of the celestial inhabitants of the negro's heaven, will be a return to the overseer of the countless lashes that he has lent out so liberally here.

It is impossible to reconcile the mind of the native slave to the idea of living in a state of perfect equality, and boundless affection, with the white people. Heaven will be no heaven to him, if he is not to be avenged of his enemies. I know, from experience, that these are the fundamental rules of his religious creed; because I learned them in the religious meetings of the slaves themselves. A favourite and kind master or mistress, may now and then be admitted into heaven, but this rather as a matter of favour, to the intercession of some slave, than as matter of strict justice to the whites, who will, by no means, be of an equal rank with those who shall be raised from the depths of misery, in this world.

The idea of a revolution in the conditions of the whites and the blacks, is the corner-stone of the religion of the latter; and indeed, it seems to me, at least, to be quite natural, if not in strict accordance with the precepts of the Bible; for in that book, I find it every where laid down, that those who have possessed an inordinate portion of the good things of this world, and have lived in ease and luxury, at the expense of their fellow men will surely have to render an account of their stewardship, and be punished, for having withheld from others the participation of those blessings, which they themselves enjoyed.

Narrative of the Life of Frederick Douglass

Northern blacks had long struggled for the abolition of slavery but the voices of the slaves proved far more compelling. Slave narratives, some written by ex-slaves but many penned by white abolitionists, became a popular genre in the 1840s. In writing about their own experiences, slave authors wrote not so much to delineate their own lives but to advance abolition for the behalf of the millions of people still in bondage throughout the South.

One of the most remarkable narrators, Frederick Douglass (1818?–1895), burst onto the stage in the 1840s. A slave who had been raised in Maryland, Douglass had been taught to read a few words by his mistress. Upon being chastised by her husband for breaking the law by educating a slave, the woman stopped teaching Douglass but she had already given him a hunger for knowledge. He learned to read on his own and plotted his freedom. In 1838 at the age of twenty, Douglass borrowed the papers of a free black sailor and rode the train to liberty and New York City. Settling in Massachusetts, Douglass found work lecturing about his life as a slave for the Massachusetts Anti-Slavery Society. He proved so eloquent that suspicions were soon raised about whether he had actually been a slave. His 1845 autobiography, excerpted below, was Douglass's response to the charges. To emphasis the truth of his account, Douglass named specific people and places.

There were no beds given the slaves, unless one coarse blanket be considered such, and none but the men and women had these. This, however, is not considered a very great privation. They find less difficulty from the want of beds, than from the

From Frederick Douglass, *Narrative of the Life of Frederick Douglass: An American Slave*, ed. Deborah E. McDowell, Oxford University Press, (Oxford, England, 1999), copyright © 1999 by Deborah E. McDowell, 21–22, 28, 31.

want of time to sleep; for when their day's work in the field is done, the most of them having their washing, mending, and cooking to do, and having few or none of the ordinary facilities for doing either of these, very many of their sleeping hours are consumed in preparation for the field the coming day; and when this is done, old and young, male and female, married and single, drop down side by side, on one common bed,—the cold, damp floor,—each covering himself or herself with their miserable blankets; and here they sleep till they are summoned to the field by the driver's horn. . . . Mr. Severe, the overseer, used to stand by the door of the quarter, armed with a large hickory stick and heavy cowskin, ready to whip any one who was so unfortunate as not to hear. . . .

Mr. Severe was rightly named: he was a cruel man. I have seen him whip a woman, causing the blood to run half an hour at the time; and this, too, in the midst of her crying children, pleading for their mother's release. He seemed to take pleasure in manifesting his fiendish barbarity. . . .

Colonel Lloyd owned so many [slaves] that he did not know them when he saw them; nor did all the slaves of the out-farms know him. It is reported of him, that, while riding along the road one day, he met a colored man, and addressed him in the usual manner of speaking to colored people on the public highways of the south: "Well, boy, whom do you belong to?" "To Colonel Lloyd," replied the slave. "Well, does the colonel treat you well?" "No, sir," was the ready reply. "What, does he work you too hard?" "Yes, sir." "Well, don't he give you enough to eat?" "Yes, sir, he gives me enough, such as it is."

The colonel . . . rode on; the man also went about his business, not dreaming that he had been conversing with his master. He thought, said, and heard nothing more of the matter, until two or three weeks afterwards. The poor man was then informed by his overseer that, for having found fault with his master, he was now to be sold to a Georgia trader. He was immediately chained and handcuffed; and thus, without a moment's warning, he was snatched away, and forever sundered, from his family and friends, by a hand more unrelenting than death. This is the penalty of telling the truth, of telling the simple truth, in answer to a series of plain questions.

It is partly in consequence of such facts, that slaves when inquired of as to their condition and the character of their masters, almost universally say they are contented, and that their masters are kind. The slaveholders have been known to send in spies among their slaves, to ascertain their views and feelings in regard to their condition. The frequency of this has had the effect to establish among the slaves the maxim, that a still tongue makes a wise head. . . .

Mr. Gore once undertook to whip one of Colonel Lloyd's slaves, by the name of Demby. He had given Demby but few stripes, when, to get rid of the scourging, he ran and plunged himself into a creek, and stood there at the depth of his shoulders, refusing to come out. Mr. Gore told him that he would give him three calls, and that, if he did not come out at the third call, he would shoot him. . . . Demby was no more. His mangled body sank out of sight, and blood and brains marked the water where he had stood.

The Trials of Girlhood

Harriet Jacobs, a bondwoman from North Carolina, spoke vividly about the onset of puberty and the increased sexual exploitation she experienced at the hands of her owner, Dr. Flint. It is clear that enslaved women felt the pressure of sexual exploitation as evident in the following excerpt from L. Maria Child, ed., Incidents in the Life of a Slave Girl. Written By Herself *(Massachusetts, 1861), 44–46.*

But I now entered on my fifteenth year—a sad epoch in the life of a slave girl. My master began to whisper foul words in my ear. Young as I was, I could not remain ignorant of their import. I tried to treat them with indifference or contempt. The master's age, my extreme youth, and the fear that his conduct would be reported to my grandmother, made him bear this treatment for many months. He was a crafty man, and resorted to many means to accomplish his purposes. Sometimes he had stormy, terrific ways, that made his victims tremble; sometimes he assumed a gentleness that he thought must surely subdue. Of the two, I preferred his stormy moods, although they left me trembling. He tried his utmost to corrupt the pure principles my grandmother had instilled. He peopled my young mind with unclean images, such as only a vile monster could think of. I turned from him with disgust and hatred. But he was my master. I was compelled to live under the same roof with him— where I saw a man forty years my senior daily violating the most sacred commandments of nature. He told me I was his property; that I must be subject to his will in all things. My soul revolted against the mean tyranny. But where could I turn for protection? No matter whether the slave girl be as black as ebony or as fair as her mistress. In either case, there is no shadow of law to protect her from insult, from violence, or even from death; all these are inflicted by fiends who bear the shape of men. The mistress, who ought to protect the helpless victim, has no other feelings towards her but those of jealousy and rage. The degradation, the wrongs, the vices, that grow out of slavery, are more than I can describe. They are greater than you would willingly believe. Surely, if you credited one half the truths that are told you concerning the helpless millions suffering in this cruel bondage, you at the north would not help to tighten the yoke. You surely would refuse to do for the master, on your own soil, the mean and cruel work which trained bloodhounds and the lowest class of whites do for him at the south.

Every where the years bring to all enough of sin and sorrow; but in slavery the very dawn of life is darkened by these shadows. Even the little child, who is accustomed to wait on her mistress and her children, will learn, before she is twelve years old, why it is that her mistress hates such and such a one among the slaves. Perhaps the child's own mother is among those hated ones. She listens to violent outbreaks of jealous passion, and cannot help understanding what is the cause. She will become prematurely knowing in evil things. Soon she will learn to tremble when she hears her master's footfall. She will be compelled to realize that she is no longer a child. If God has bestowed beauty upon her, it will prove her greatest curse. That which commands admiration in the white woman only hastens the degradation of the female slave. I know that some are too much brutalized by slavery to feel the humiliation of their position; but many slaves feel it most acutely, and shrink from the memory of it. I cannot tell how much I suffered in the presence of these wrongs, nor how I am still pained by the retrospect. My master met me at every turn, reminding me that I belonged to him, and swearing by heaven and earth that he would compel me to submit to him. If I went out for a breath of fresh air, after a day of unwearied toil, his footsteps dogged me. If I knelt by my mother's grave, his dark shadow fell on me even there. The light heart which nature had given me became heavy with sad forebodings. The other slaves in my master's house noticed the change. Many of them pitied me; but none dared to ask the cause. They had no need to inquire. They knew too well the guilty practices under that roof; and they were aware that to speak of them was an offence that never went unpunished.

Incidents in the Life of a Slave Girl

In an attempt to preserve the union in the face of sectional clashes, the United States adopted the Compromise of 1850. Instead of providing time for passions to cool, as moderates within Congress had hoped, the provisions in the compromise regarding fugitive slaves made the conflict between North and South more bitter. The Fugitive Slave Act, one of the points of the compromise, forced Northerners to support slavery and insulted them with blatantly unjust provisions. The commissioners who decided the fate of black Americans charged with being runaways, for example, received ten dollars for every African American returned to his or her master but only five dollars for every person freed. Sheriffs could force bystanders to aid in the capture of an accused fugitive and, if they refused, they faced fines and jail terms. Armed opposition to the slave catchers immediately arose in cities across the North, but most whites offered no opposition, and about two hundred blacks presumed to be runaways were sent south.

No provision of the act terrified African Americans as greatly as the lack of time limitations. No matter how many years had passed since their escape and no matter how established they had become, all former slaves could be captured and returned to their masters. All free blacks stood continually at risk of being kidnapped, as Harriet Jacobs (1818–1896) relates in an excerpt below from her memoirs. Jacobs escaped from slavery at the age of twenty-seven and penned her autobiography during the fugitive slave turmoil. To protect those who aided her from harsh treatment, Jacobs gave fictitious names to all places and people including herself.

I had but one hesitation, and that was my feeling of insecurity in New York, now greatly increased by the passage of the Fugitive

From Linda Brent [Harriet Brent Jacobs], *Incidents in the Life of a Slave Girl*, ed. Lydia Maria Child, (Boston, 1861), 285–287, 290.

Slave Law. However, I resolved to try the experiment. I was again fortunate in my employer. The new Mrs. Bruce was an American, brought up under aristocratic influences, and still living in the midst of them; but if she had any prejudices against color, I was never made aware of it. . . .

About the time that I reentered the Bruce family, an event occurred of disastrous import to the colored people. The slave Hamlin, the first fugitive that came under the new law, was given up by the bloodhounds of the north to the bloodhounds of the south. It was the beginning of a reign of terror to the colored population. The great [New York City] rushed on in its whirl of excitement, taking no note of the "short and simple annals of the poor. . . ." Many families, who had lived in the city for twenty years, fled from it now. Many a poor washerwoman, who, by hard labor, had made herself a comfortable home, was obliged to sacrifice her furniture, bid a hurried farewell to friends, and seek her fortune among strangers in Canada. Many a wife discovered a secret she had never known before—that her husband was a fugitive, and must leave her to insure his own safety. Worse still, many a husband discovered that his wife had fled from slavery years ago, and as "the child follows the condition of its mother," the children of his love were liable to be seized and carried into slavery. Everywhere, in those humble homes, there was consternation and anguish. But what cared the legislators of the "dominant race" for the blood they were crushing out of trampled hearts?

When my brother William spent his last evening with me, before he went to California, we talked nearly all the time of the distress brought on our oppressed people by the passage of this iniquitous law; and never had I seen him manifest such bitterness of spirit, such stern hostility to our oppressors. He was himself free from operation of the law; for he did not run from any Slaveholding State, being brought into the Free States by his master. But I was subject to it; and so were hundreds of intelligent and industrious people all around us. I seldom ventured into the streets; and when it was necessary to do an errand for Mrs. Bruce, or any of the family, I went as much as possible through back streets and by-ways. What a disgrace to a city calling itself free, that inhabitants, guiltless of offence, and seeking to perform their duties conscientiously, should be condemned to live in such incessant fear, and have nowhere to turn for protection! This state of things, of course, gave rise to many impromptu vigilance committees.

Every colored person, and every friend of their persecuted race, kept their eyes wide open. Every evening I examined the newspapers carefully, to see what Southerners had put up at the hotels. I did this for my own sake, thinking my young mistress and her husband might be among the list; I wished also to give information to others, if necessary. . . .

One day . . . I was hurrying through back streets . . . when I saw a young man approaching. . . . As he came nearer, I recognized Luke. I always rejoiced to see or hear of any one who had escaped from the black pit; but, remembering this poor fellow's extreme hardships, I was peculiarly glad to see him on Northern soil, though I no longer call it *free* soil. . . . I told him of the Fugitive Slave Law, and asked him if he did not know that New York was a city of kidnappers. . . . He went to Canada. . . .

All that winter I lived in a state of anxiety. When I took the children out to breathe the air, I closely observed the countenances of all I met. I dreaded the approach of summer, when snakes and slaveholders make their appearance. I was, in fact, a slave in New York, as subject to slave laws as I had been in a Slave State. Strange incongruity in a State called free!

"The Insurrection"

Nat Turner's slave revolt took place in Southampton County, Virginia in 1831 and resulted in the deaths of approximately sixty whites at the hands of slaves as well as about one hundred and twenty slaves who were killed by whites in retaliation. The brutality of the revolt and the response to it forced the American public to discuss the issue of slavery and to debate whether or not it should be abolished. Taking the lead in this debate were northern abolitionists, such as William Lloyd Garrison, founder and editor of **The Liberator,** *a weekly abolitionist newspaper. Unlike some white abolitionists who still regarded blacks as inferior to whites, Garrison believed that not only slavery but also racism should be abolished. From his headquarters in Boston, Garrison helped to organize a large abolitionist organization, the American Anti-Slavery Society (AASS) that advocated for immediate emancipation of all slaves in the United States. He and other members of the AASS also steadfastly refused to agree that slave owners should be compensated by the government for the loss of their "property." They also called upon other Americans to recognize that slavery was an immoral institution, tainting the entire country by association. Garrison placed such intense scrutiny on southern slaveholders that the state legislature of Georgia offered $5,000 to anyone who would kidnap Garrison and bring him to Georgia to stand trial on charges of inciting rebellion.*

In the following article that appeared in **The Liberator** *on September 3, 1831, approximately two weeks after Nat Turner's Revolt, Garrison clearly lays out his reasons for the immediate abolition of slavery. He uses the deeply held religious convictions of Turner, who believed that God had called on him to start a race war in order to free slaves from oppression, to illustrate the potential dangers of the continuation of slavery. He also refutes the claims of southern slave owners that northern*

From "The Insurrection," by William Lloyd Garrison, in *The Liberator,* (Boston, September 3, 1831), 143.

abolitionists, such as himself, were responsible for convincing slaves to rebel. Garrison also reminds the South that slaves did not need to be urged to rebel by outsiders; rather, the abuses suffered on a daily basis were sufficient.

What we have so long predicted,—at the peril of being stigmatized as an alarmist and declaimer,—has commenced its fulfilment. The first step of the earthquake, which is ultimately to shake down the fabric of oppression, leaving not one stone upon another, has been made. The first drops of blood, which are but the prelude to a deluge from the gathering clouds, have fallen. The first flash of the lightning, which is to smite and consume, has been felt. The first wailings of a bereavement, which is to clothe the earth in sackcloth, have broken upon our ears. . . .

True, the rebellion is quelled. Those of the slaves who were not killed in combat, have been secured, and the prison is crowded with victims destined for the gallows!

> 'Yet laugh not in your carnival of crime
> Too proudly, ye oppressors!'

You have seen, it is to be feared, but the beginning of sorrows. All the blood which has been shed will be required at your hands. At your hands alone? No—but at the hands of the people of New-England and of all the free states. The crime of oppression is national. The south is only the agent in this guilty traffic. But, remember! the same causes are at work which must inevitably produce the same effects; and when the contest shall have again begun, it must be again a war of extermination. In the present instance, no quarters have been asked or given.

[Garrison now attempts to voice the slaveholders' justification for revenge against Nat Turner's band:]

But we have killed and routed them [the slaves] now. . . We have the power to kill *all*—let us, therefore, continue to apply the whip and forge new fetters! . . . They were black—brutes, pretending to be men—legions of curses upon their memories! They were black—God made them to serve us! . . .

[Garrison, as an abolitionist, now addresses the slaveholders:]

Ye accuse the pacific friends of emancipation of instigating the slaves to revolt. Take back the charge as a foul slander. The slaves need no incentives at our hands. They will find them in their stripes—in their emaciated bodies—in their ceaseless toil—in their ignorant minds—in every field, in every valley, on every hill-top and mountain, wherever you and your fathers have fought for liberty—in your speeches, your conversations, your celebrations, your pamphlets, your newspapers—voices in the air, sounds from across the ocean, invitations to resistance above, below, around them! What more do they need? Surrounded by such influences, and smarting under their newly made wounds, is it wonderful that they should rise to contend—as other 'heroes' have contended—for their lost rights? It is *not* wonderful.

In all that we have written, is there aught to justify the excesses of the slaves? No. Nevertheless, they deserve no more censure than the Greeks in destroying the Turks, or the Poles in exterminating the Russians, or our fathers in slaughtering the British. Dreadful, indeed, is the standard erected by worldly patriotism!

For ourselves, we are horror-struck at the late tidings. We have exerted our utmost efforts to avert the calamity. We have warned our countrymen of the danger of persisting in their unrighteous conduct. We have preached to the slaves the pacific precepts of Jesus Christ. We have appealed to christians, philanthropists and patriots, for their assistance to accomplish the great work of national redemption through the agency of moral power—of public opinion—of individual duty. How have we been received? We have been threatened, proscribed, vilified and imprisoned—a laughing-stock and a reproach. Do we falter, in view of these things? Let time answer. If we have been hitherto urgent, and bold, and denunciatory in our efforts,—hereafter we shall grow vehement and active with the increase of danger. We shall cry, in trumpet tones, night and day,—Wo to this guilty land, unless she speedily repent of her evil doings! The blood of millions of her sons cries aloud for redress! IMMEDIATE EMANCIPATION can alone save her from the vengeance of Heaven, and cancel the debt of ages!

The American Anti-Slavery Society Declares Its Sentiments

In the 1830s, reformers turned radical. Once content to change attitudes toward social problems by gradual steps, reform-minded men and women now became impatient for change. Like many of his fellow New Englanders, William Lloyd Garrison (1805–1879) recognized the evils of slavery but, in light of the deep roots of this social and economic institution, he had believed that the best way to end slavery lay in returning blacks to Africa. By 1831, persuaded by strong black opposition to colonization, Garrison launched a new and more radical anti-slavery movement. He began publishing a journal, The Liberator, *and demanded the immediate release of slaves.*

In 1833, Garrison and other abolitionists founded the American Anti-Slavery Society and proclaimed this Declaration of Sentiments. In his characteristically impassioned rhetoric, Garrison condemned slavery and set forth the new organization's principles and proposed activities.

More than fifty-seven years have elapsed, since a band of patriots convened in this place, to devise measures for the deliverance of this country from a foreign yoke. The corner-stone upon which they founded the Temple of Freedom was broadly this—'that all men are created equal; that they are endowed by their Creator with certain inalienable rights; that among these are life, LIBERTY, and the pursuit of happiness.' At the sound of their trumpet-call, three millions of people rose up as from the sleep of death, and rushed to the strife of blood; deeming it more glorious to die instantly as freemen, than desirable to live one hour as slaves. They were few in number—poor in resources; but the honest conviction that Truth, Justice and Right were on their side, made them invincible.

From William Lloyd Garrison, *Selections from the Writings and Speeches of William Lloyd Garrison* (Boston, 1852), 66–71.

We have met together for the achievement of an enterprise, without which that of our fathers is incomplete; and which, for its magnitude, solemnity, and probable results upon the destiny of the world, as far transcends theirs as moral truth does physical force. . . .

Their principles led them to wage war against their oppressors, and to spill human blood like water, in order to be free. Ours forbid the doing of evil that good may come, and lead us to reject, and to entreat the oppressed to reject, the use of all carnal weapons for deliverance from bondage; relying solely upon those which are spiritual, and mighty through God to the pulling down of strong holds.

Their measures were physical resistance—the marshalling in arms—the hostile array—the mortal encounter. Ours shall be such only as the opposition of moral purity to moral corruption—the destruction of error by the potency of truth—the overthrow of prejudice by the power of love—and the abolition of slavery by the spirit of repentance.

Their grievances, great as they were, were trifling in comparison with the wrongs and sufferings of those for whom we plead. Our fathers were never slaves—never bought and sold like cattle—never shut out from the light of knowledge and religion—never subjected to the lash of brutal taskmasters.

But those, for whose emancipation we are striving—constituting at the present time at least one-sixth part of our countrymen—are recognized by law, and treated by their fellow-beings, as marketable commodities, as goods and chattels, as brute beasts; are plundered daily of the fruits of their toil without redress; really enjoy no constitutional nor legal protection from licentious and murderous outrages upon their persons; and are ruthlessly torn asunder—the tender babe from the arms of its frantic mother—the heart-broken wife from her weeping husband—at the caprice or pleasure of irresponsible tyrants. For the crime of having a dark complexion, they suffer the pangs of hunger, the infliction of stripes, the ignominy of brutal servitude. They are kept in heathenish darkness by laws expressly enacted to make their instruction a criminal offence.

These are the prominent circumstances in the condition of more than two millions of our people, the proof of which may be found in thousands of indisputable facts, and in the laws of the slaveholding States.

Hence we maintain—that, in view of the civil and religious privileges of this nation, the guilt of its oppression is unequalled by any other on the face of the earth; and, therefore, that it is bound to repent instantly, to undo the heavy burdens, and to let the oppressed go free.

We further maintain—that no man has a right to enslave or imbrute his brother—to hold or acknowledge him, for one moment, as a piece of merchandize—to keep back his hire by fraud—or to brutalize his mind, by denying him the means of intellectual, social and moral improvement.

The right to enjoy liberty is inalienable. To invade it is to usurp the prerogative of Jehovah. Every man has a right to his own body—to the products of his own labor—to the protection of law—and to the common advantages of society. It is piracy to buy or steal a native African, and subject him to servitude. Surely, the sin is as great to enslave an American as an African.

Therefore we believe and affirm—that there is no difference, in principle, between the African slave trade and American slavery:

That every American citizen, who detains a human being in involuntary bondage as his property, is, according to Scripture, (Ex. xxi. 16,) a man-stealer:

That the slaves ought instantly to be set free, and brought under the protection of law:

That if they had lived from the time of Pharaoh down to the present period, and had been entailed through successive generations, their right to be free could never have been alienated, but their claims would have constantly risen in solemnity:

That all those laws which are now in force, admitting the right of slavery, are therefore, before God, utterly null and void . . .

We further believe and affirm—that all persons of color, who possess the qualifications which are demanded of others, ought to be admitted forthwith to the enjoyment of the same privileges, and the exercise of the same prerogatives, as others; and that the paths of preferment, of wealth, and of intelligence, should be opened as widely to them as to persons of a white complexion.

We maintain that no compensation should be given to the planters emancipating their slaves:

Because it would be a surrender of the great fundamental principle, that man cannot hold property in man:

Because slavery is a crime, and therefore is not an article to be sold:

Because the holders of slaves are not the just proprietors of what they claim; freeing the slave is not depriving them of property, but restoring it to its rightful owner; it is not wronging the master, but righting the slave—restoring him to himself:

Because immediate and general emancipation would only destroy nominal, not real property; it would not amputate a limb or break a bone of the slaves, but by infusing motives into their breasts, would make them doubly valuable to the masters as free laborers; and

Because, if compensation is to be given at all, it should be given to the outraged and guiltless slaves, and not to those who have plundered and abused them.

We regard as delusive, cruel and dangerous, any scheme of expatriation which pretends to aid, either directly or indirectly, in the emancipation of the slaves or to be a substitute for the immediate and total abolition of slavery.

We fully and unanimously recognise the sovereignty of each State, to legislate exclusively on the subject of the slavery which is tolerated within its limits; we concede that Congress, under the present national compact, has no right to interfere with any of the slave States, in relation to this momentous subject:

But we maintain that Congress has a right, and is solemnly bound, to suppress the domestic slave trade between the several States, and to abolish slavery in those portions of our territory which the Constitution has placed under its exclusive jurisdiction. . . .

These are our views and principles—these our designs and measures. With entire confidence in the overruling justice of God, we plant ourselves upon the Declaration of our Independence and the truths of Divine Revelation, as upon the Everlasting Rock.

We shall organize Anti-Slavery Societies, if possible, in every city, town and village in our land.

We shall send forth agents to lift up the voice of remonstrance, of warning, of entreaty, and of rebuke.

We shall circulate, unsparingly and extensively, anti-slavery tracts and periodicals.

We shall enlist the pulpit and the press in the cause of the suffering and the dumb.

We shall aim at a purification of the churches from all participation in the guilt of slavery.

We shall encourage the labor of freemen [free African Americans] rather than that of slaves, by giving a preference to their productions: and

We shall spare no exertions nor means to bring the whole nation to speedy repentance.

Our trust for victory is solely in God. We may be personally defeated, but our principles never! Truth, Justice, Reason, Humanity, must and will gloriously triumph. Already a host is coming up to the help of the Lord against the mighty, and the prospect before us is full of encouragement.

A Northern Woman Condemns Prejudice

In an acrimonious split, the anti-slavery movement divided into conservative and radical wings in the early 1830s. Some women supported a gradual end to slavery and, like many male advocates of the repatriation of slaves to Africa, they did not regard blacks as brothers. The radicals, reformers such as William Lloyd Garrison and Lydia Maria Child (1802-1880), were heavily influenced by the religious revival known as the Second Great Awakening. Garrison and his supporters demanded the immediate abolition of slavery and denounced colonization as surrender to un-Christian principles.

The Boston Female Anti-Slavery Society, to which Child belonged, became one of the women's groups that self-destructed in a bitter clash between Garrisonians and their opponents. Child had given up a comfortable career as a children's magazine editor when she joined the radical wing of the anti-slavery movement in 1833 by writing the following essay. In it, Child is nearly as critical of the racial prejudice exhibited by Northerners as she is of slavery itself. For her unfeminine involvement in political matters, Child lost her magazine but became the editor of the National Anti-Slavery Standard *and she devoted the remainder of her career to the abolitionist cause.*

While we bestow our earnest disapprobation on the system of slavery, let us not flatter ourselves that we are in reality any better than our brethren of the South. Thanks to our soil and climate, and the early exertions of the Quakers, the *form* of slavery does not exist among us; but the very *spirit* of the hateful and mischievous thing is here in all its strength. The manner in which we use what power we have, gives us ample reason to be grateful that the nature of our institutions does not intrust us with more. Our prej-

From Lydia Maria Child, *An Appeal in Favor of that Class of Americans Called Africans* (Boston, 1833), 208–209, 211, 232.

udices against colored people is [are] even more inveterate than it is at the South. The planter is often attached to his negroes, and lavishes caresses and kind words upon them, as he would on a favorite hound; but our cold-hearted, ignoble prejudice admits of no exception—no intermission.

The Southerners have long continued habit, apparent interest and dreaded danger, to palliate the wrong they do; but we stand without excuse. They tell us that Northern ships and Northern capital have been engaged in this wicked business; and the reproach is true. Several fortunes in this city [Boston] have been made by the sale of negro blood. If these criminal transactions are still carried on, they are done in silence and secrecy, because public opinion has made them disgraceful. But if the free States wished to cherish the system of slavery forever, they could not take a more direct course than they now do. Those who are kind and liberal on all other subjects, unite with the selfish and the proud in their unrelenting efforts to keep the colored population in the lowest state of degradation; and the influence they unconsciously exert over children early infuses into their innocent minds the same strong feelings of contempt.

The intelligent and well informed have the least share of this prejudice; and when their minds can be brought to reflect upon it, I have generally observed that they soon cease to have any at all. But such a general apathy prevails and the subject is so seldom brought into view, that few are really aware how oppressively the influence of society is made to bear upon this injured class of the community. . . .

. . . [A]n unjust law exists in this Commonwealth [Massachusetts], by which marriages between persons of different color is [are] pronounced illegal. I am perfectly aware of the gross ridicule to which I may subject myself by alluding to this particular; but I have lived too long, and observed too much, to be disturbed by the world's mockery. In the first place, the government ought not to be invested with power to control the affections, any more than the consciences of citizens. A man has at least as good a right to choose his wife, as he has to choose his religion. His taste may not suit his neighbors; but so long as his deportment is correct, they have no right to interfere with his concerns. . . .

There is among the colored people an increasing desire for information, and a laudable ambition to be respectable in manners and appearance. Are we not foolish as well as sinful, in trying to repress a tendency so salutary to themselves, and so beneficial to the community? Several individuals of this class are very desirous to have persons of their own color qualified to teach something more than mere reading and writing. But in the public schools, colored children are subject to many discouragements and difficulties; and into the private schools they cannot gain admission. A very sensible and well-informed colored woman in a neighboring town, whose family have been brought up in a manner that excited universal remark and approbation, has been extremely desirous to obtain for her eldest daughter the advantages of a private school; but she has been resolutely repulsed, on account of her complexion. . . .

By publishing this book I have put my mite into the treasury [expressed my thoughts]. The expectation of displeasing all classes has not been unaccompanied with pain. But it has been strongly impressed upon my mind that it was a duty to fulfil this task; and earthly considerations should never stifle the voice of conscience.

Black Women's Activism

The goals of free black women involved in abolitionism often differed from those of white women. The speeches and writings of Maria Stewart are an example of this. Maria Stewart was born in Hartford, Conn., in 1803. Widowed at an early age, she became involved in the abolition movement in Boston, Mass., which was a focal point of the movement. Stewart gave a total of four speeches between 1831 and 1833 to mixed audiences of black men and women. Stewart challenged her audiences in two important ways. First, by speaking in public to a mixed audience about a political topic, she broke a deeply rooted social taboo. Women were not supposed to be involved in the public sphere, and particularly not with politics. Secondly, she pushed her audiences, composed mainly of free blacks, to reassess their place within society. Stewart strongly encouraged free blacks to actively work to change their status in society and to eliminate racism. After her fourth speech, Stewart was asked by powerful black men in Boston to cease speaking in public. However, her message continued to be spread by The Liberator, *the abolitionist news-paper edited by William Lloyd Garrison, as it printed all four of her speeches.*

In this excerpt from her pamphlet, "Religion and the Pure Prin-ciples of Morality. . . ," Stewart focuses on the steps black women could take to improve their lives and their community. She recommends that the best way to achieve their educational, economic, and political goals is by working together. Working collectively they would be a stronger force for change.

From "Religion and the Pure Principles of Morality. . . ," a pamphlet by Maria Stewart, issued in 1831 and reprinted in *Black Women in Nineteenth-Century American Life: Their Words, Their Thoughts, Their Feelings,* ed. Bert James Loewenberg and Ruth Bogin, (University Park, Pennsylvania, 1976), 189, 190.

Shall it any longer be said of the daughters of Africa, they have no ambition, they have no force? By no means. Let every female heart become united, and let us raise a fund ourselves; and at the end of one year and a half, we might be able to lay the corner-stone for the building of a High School, that the higher branches of knowledge might be enjoyed by us; and God would raise us up, and enough to aid us in our laudable designs. Let each one strive to excel in good house-wifery, knowing that prudence and economy are the road to wealth. Let us not say, we know this, or, we know that, and practise nothing; but let us practise what we do know.

How long shall the fair daughters of Africa be compelled to bury their minds and talents beneath a load of iron pots and kettles? Until union, knowledge and love begin to flow among us. How long shall a mean set of men flatter us with their smiles, and enrich themselves with our hard earnings; their wives' fingers sparkling with rings, and they themselves laughing at our folly? Until we begin to promote and patronize each other. . . . Do you ask, what can we do? Unite and build a store of your own, if you cannot procure a license. Fill one side with dry goods, and the other with groceries. . . . We have never had an opportunity of displaying our talents; therefore the world thinks we know nothing. . . . Do you ask the disposition I would have you possess? Possess the spirit of independence. The Americans do, and why should not you? Possess the spirit of men, bold and enterprising, fearless and undaunted. Sue for your rights and privileges. Know the reason that you cannot attain them. Weary them with your importunities. You can but die, if you make the attempt; and we shall certainly die if you do not. The Americans have practised nothing but head-work these 200 years, and we have done their drudgery. And is it not high time for us to imitate their examples, and practise head-work too, and keep what we have got, and get what we can? We need never to think that any body is going to feel interested for us, if we do not feel interested for ourselves.

Freedom and Slavery in the 1830s Midwest

German traveler Eduard Zimmerman recorded his impressions of Missouri after taking a walking trip through the state in 1838. His primary reason for visiting was to observe some of the communities founded by German settlers. However, he was struck by the inroads that slavery had made in the region and he could not help but wonder if the slave states could continue to coexist with the free states. He also felt moved to comment on some of the characteristics that distinguished Americans from his own countrymen.

On the morning of the fifteenth of October we started on our excursion into the valley of the Missouri. We took a westerly direction, slightly toward the north. We had made up our minds to follow the highway toward Jefferson City, the seat of government of the state of Missouri, and to deflect from this road only for the purpose of seeking out the settlements of the educated Germans. . . . Inns are found only in the cities and towns, or possibly along the mail-routes. The traveler is therefore obliged to make use of the hospitality of the settlers. This sort of hospitality is perhaps no where developed to a higher degree than in this new country where it would indeed be unnatural and inhuman if a stranger were not hospitably and cordially received. For our purpose of becoming acquainted with the land and its people we had chosen the right mode of traveling [walking], for it compelled us to stop several times each day in the huts of the inhabitants. Necessarily we had to enter into conversation, and no theme was nearer at hand for discussion than the nature of the country, the advantages and disadvantages of the settlement, the kind of produce raised, and the means of disposing of it.

From "Travels into Missouri in October, 1838," by Eduard Zimmerman, in *Missouri Historical Review* 9 (October 1914): 38–43.

. . . There are large and beautifully equipped settlements here which have much in common with the plantations of the southern states. Many of the houses of the homesteads are used exclusively as the dwellings of the black slaves. Here the farmers raise tobacco and cotton. Tobacco is said to do exceptionally well in Missouri and to be preferred to all other tobaccos on the market in New Orleans. The practice of cultivating this crop, however, might easily bring the condition of the slaves near to that condition which their unfortunate fellows suffer in the southern states. Up to this time the treatment of the slaves, who are in the country districts, is very good. Their material condition is very endurable. As a rule they live in families, have their own dwelling houses, their own livestock and till a certain amount of land for themselves, in which way they have their own earnings. This tolerable condition of the Missouri slaves by no means excuses the shameful practice of slavery, however, and against this sin committed against humanity one must strive with all energy. The Germans who live in Missouri have no slaves as yet, and are still opposed to the institution of slavery. However, it is possible that in time this feeling may become dulled, and their posterity may grow up with the idea that it is a necessary institution. No German ought to live in a slave state. Illinois, a free state, has a great advantage over its neighboring state. The breech between the free states and the slave states is inevitable, and who shall then like to be found on the wrong side? . . .

. . . The Americans reproach the Germans for selecting the very poorest land at times, and this is on the whole true. The Germans prefer high lying regions because they are more healthful, open and attractive. This the Americans do not comprehend. They call only that land pretty which is rich in fertility. They never become attached to a given region. If they can sell their property to any sort of advantage, they are certain to do so, regardless of the fact that it may be the scene of their happy childhood with its dearest memories. This characteristic of the Americans is not beautiful, but for the rapid settling of a new state is very advantageous. It is also beneficial to the political condition of the Republic that the American is less susceptible to moral and ethical impressions. The more self-satisfied a people is the more easily it is governed, provided the right cords are touched. The so-called man of feeling is the tool of every ambitious person.

A Call for Women to Become Abolitionists

During the first half of the nineteenth century, the United States shifted to a market economy. With this emphasis upon cash, work came to mean employment outside of the home and the skilled labor of women within the household was discounted as a labor of love. The new celebration of domesticity and the separation of spheres turned the house into a haven and sought to keep women within the home in order to protect them from the chaos and impurity of public life.

Some women defied conventional ideas of their proper position by becoming active participants in the anti-slavery movement. To the shock of many, women spoke in public, circulated petitions, and otherwise promoted the abolitionist cause. This essay is one of the earliest appeals to women. It also shows that women's political activism was sometimes opposed even by women themselves. This excerpt is a response to a woman who objected to other women publicly advocating emancipation.

We have been so long accustomed to consider the duty of the female sex, with regard to slavery, as entirely plain, that we had almost imagined it must be equally so to any unprejudiced thinker upon the subject. Not that we expected to find no difference of feeling, or contrariety of sentiment; apathy and prejudices we were prepared for; but we certainly had not thought that the interference of woman in behalf of suffering humanity, could be seriously objected to, as improper, and at variance with right principles. Yet this we are sorry to find is the light in which it is regarded by one of our own sex—a lady, whose talents and character we respect very highly, and whose approbation of the course we are pursuing, we should be proud to have obtained. But as this is withheld, and it is probable she may not be singular in her opin-

From Elizabeth Margaret Chandler, *The Poetical Works of Elizabeth Margaret Chandler,* (Philadelphia, 1836), 21–23.

ions, we have taken the liberty of quoting some of her sentiments, and appending to them a statement of our own ideas on the same subject.

"Should you inquire why I do not devote myself more sedulously to promote the cause of emancipation?—I would tell you, that I think it is a work which requires the energies of *men*."

And so it does; but it requires also the *influence of woman*. She was given to man 'to be a helpmeet [helpmate] for him;' and it is therefore her duty, whenever she can do so, to lend him her aid in every great work of philanthropy. In *this* her cooperation may be of essential service, without leading her one step beyond her own proper sphere. . . .

"It is a subject so connected with those of government, of law and politics, that I should fear the direct or even apparent interference of my own sex, would be a departure from that propriety of character which nature, as well as society, imposes on woman."

It is true that it is a question of government and politics, but it also rests upon the broader basis of humanity and justice; and it is on *this* ground only, that we advocate the interference of women. We have not the least desire to see our own sex transformed into a race of politicians; but we do not think that in this case such consequences are in the least to be apprehended. To plead for the miserable, to endeavour to alleviate the bitterness of their destiny, and to soften the stern bosoms of their oppressors into gentleness and mercy, can never be unfeminine or unbefitting the delicacy of woman! She does not advocate Emancipation because slavery is at variance with the political interests of the state, but because it is an outrage against *humanity* and *morality* and *religion*; because it is *criminal*, and because her own supineness makes her a *sharer in the crime*; and because a great number of *her own sex* are among its victims. It is therefore, that she should steadily and conscientiously rank among the number of its opponents, and refuse to be benefited by its advantages. She does not by this become a partizan of any system of policy—she seeks only to shield from outrage all that is most holy in her religion! She does not seek to direct, or share with men, the government of the state; but she entreats them to lift the iron foot of despotism from the neck of her sisterhood; and this we consider not only quite within the sphere of her privileges, but also of her positive duties.

Sarah Grimké Challenges the Clergy

Sarah Moore Grimké (1792–1873) and her sister Angelina Grimké (1805–1879) were born into the plantation aristocracy of South Carolina. They both converted to Quakerism, rejected the slave-holding lifestyle of their family, and moved to Pennsylvania. The Grimké sisters were involved in both the abolition movement and the early struggle for women's rights. Since they had firsthand knowledge of slavery, their ideas and stories were in demand in the North. They began to speak at "parlor meetings," small gatherings of initially just white women. However, as word of their speaking abilities spread, organizers had to enlarge meetings, and soon they were speaking to mixed audiences of white women and men. Building on these larger talks, the Grimké sisters began to give public speeches in 1836. The response to women speaking in public was largely negative as many viewed the actions of the Grimké sisters as immodest and unfeminine. Some male abolitionists feared that the negative publicity would be detrimental to their cause.

Some of the sharpest criticism of Sarah Grimké came from the leadership of the Congregational Church of Massachusetts in 1837. The clergymen criticized her for speaking to the Massachusetts state legislature, arguing that she had violated the clear-cut boundaries between men and women, between public and private spheres. In addition, they interpreted her actions and words as a serious threat to the traditional role of women as silent and subordinate members of society. They voiced their opinions in a "Pastoral Letter," which they sent to all Congregational ministers in Massachusetts and urged them not to let Sarah Grimké speak from their pulpits. The following year, Sarah Grimké addressed the concerns raised by the church leadership with "Letters on the Equality of the Sexes and the Condition of Women," an excerpt of which follows. In her response, she urges men and women to accept new roles for women in society, including involvement in political matters and equality between the

---

From *The Liberator*, 6 October 1837.

sexes. She uses historical and biblical references to argue that the sub-servient place of women in society is artificial and unnatural and that with the increased discussion of the rights of blacks to be free, so should society rethink the restrictions placed on women.

Dear Friend,— . . . [T]he Pastoral Letter of the General Association . . . is . . . so extraordinary a document, that when the minds of men and women become emancipated from the thraldom of superstition, and 'traditions of men,' it will be recurred to with as much astonishment as the opinions of Cotton Mather and other distinguished men of his day, on the subject of witchcraft; nor will it be deemed less wonderful, that a body of divines should gravely assemble and endeavor to prove that woman has no right to 'open her mouth for the dumb,' than it now is that judges should have sat on the trials of witches, and solemnly condemned nineteen persons and one dog to death for witchcraft.

But to the letter: it says, 'we invite your attention to the dangers which at present seem to threaten the Female Character with wide-spread and permanent injury.' I rejoice that they have called the attention of my sex to this subject, because I believe if woman investigates it, she will soon discover that danger is impending, though from a totally different source from that which the Association apprehends,—danger from those who, having long held the reins of *usurped* authority, are unwilling to permit us to fill that sphere which God created us to move in, and who have entered into league to crush the immortal mind of woman. I rejoice, because I am persuaded that the rights of woman, like the rights of slaves, need only be examined, to be understood and asserted, even by some of those who are now endeavoring to smother the irrepressible desire for mental and spiritual freedom which glows in the breast of many who hardly dare to speak their sentiments. . . .

No one can desire more earnestly than I do, that woman may move exactly in the sphere which her Creator has assigned her; and I believe her having been displaced from that sphere, has introduced confusion into the world. It is therefore of vast importance to herself, and to all the rational creation, that she should ascertain what are her duties and her privileges as a responsible and immortal being. The New Testament has been referred to, and I am willing to abide by its decisions, and must enter my protest against the false translations of some passages by the men who did that work, and against the perverted interpretation by the MEN who undertook to write commentaries thereon. I am inclined to think, when we are admitted to the honor of studying Greek and Hebrew, we shall produce some various readings of the Bible, a little different from those we now have.

I find the Lord Jesus defining the duties of his followers in his sermon on the Mount. . . . giving the same directions to women as to men, never even referring to the distinction now so strenuously insisted upon between masculine and feminine virtues: this is one of the anti-christian 'traditions of men' which are taught instead of the 'commandments of God.' Men and women were CREATED EQUAL: they are both moral and accountable beings, and whatever is right for man to do, is right for woman to do.

But the influence of woman, says the Association, is to be private and unobtrusive; her light is not to shine before man like that of her brethren; but she is passively to let the lords of the creation, as they call themselves, put the bushel over it . . . 'Her influence is the source of mighty power.' This has ever been the language of man since he laid aside the whip as a means to keep woman in subjection. He spares her body, but the war he has waged against her mind, her heart, and her soul, has been no less destructive to her as a moral being. How monstrous is the doctrine that woman is to be dependent on man! Where in all the sacred scriptures is this taught? But, alas, she has too well learned the lesson which he has labored to teach her. She has surrendered her dearest RIGHTS, and been satisfied with the privileges which man has assumed to grant her; whilst he has amused her with the show of power, and absorbed all the reality into himself. He has adorned the creature, whom God gave him as a companion, with baubles and gewgaws, turned her attention to personal attractions, offered incense to her vanity, and made her the instrument of his selfish gratification, a plaything to please his eye, and amuse his hours of leisure. . . . This doctrine of dependence upon man is utterly at variance with the doctrine of the Bible. In that book I find nothing like the softness of woman, nor the sternness of man; both are equally commanded to bring forth the fruits of the Spirit—Love, meekness, gentleness.

. . . [O]ur powers of mind have been crushed, as far as man could do it, our sense of morality has been impaired by his interpretation of our duties, but no where does God say that he made any distinction between us as moral and intelligent beings. . . .

The General Association say that 'when woman assumes the place and tone of man as a public reformer, our care and protection of her seem unnecessary; we put ourselves in self-defence against her, and her character becomes unnatural.' . . . The motto of woman, when she is engaged in the great work of public reformation, should be.—'The Lord is my light and my salvation; whom shall I fear? The Lord is the strength of my life; of whom shall I be afraid?' She must feel, if she feels rightly, that she is fulfilling one of the important duties laid upon her as an accountable being, and that her character, instead of being 'unnatural,' is in exact accordance with the will of Him to whom and to no other, she is responsible for the talents and the gifts confided to her. . . .

And my sex now feel in the dominion so unrighteously exercised over them, under the gentle appellation of protection, that what they have leaned upon has proved a broken reed at best, and oft a spear.

Religion as a Bulwark of Slavery

When slavery began in the English colonies, most slaveowners could easily justify its existence since Africans seldom were Christians, and scruples did not extend to "heathens." As time passed, Christianity continued to be used to support slavery, now helping to convince slaves to be obedient and to work hard for their masters. To rationalize bondage, slavery's supporters traced the descent of Africans to the Biblical story of Ham, the wicked and disobedient son of Noah. By their reasoning, people with black skin possessed an inherently evil nature and deserved punishment. Lunsford Lane, a North Carolina slave, wrote the following excerpt in 1842. He alludes to the story of Ham and illustrates the use of religion for conservative ends.

I had never been permitted to learn to read; but I used to attend church, and there I received instruction which I trust was of some benefit to me. . . .

I often heard select portions of the scriptures read. And on the Sabbath there was one sermon preached expressly for the colored people which it was generally my privilege to hear. I became quite familiar with the texts, "Servants be obedient to your masters."—"Not with eye service as men pleasers."—"He that knoweth his master's will and doeth it not, shall be beaten with many stripes," and others of this class: for they formed the basis of most of these public instructions to us. The first commandment impressed upon our minds was to obey our masters, and the second was like unto it, namely, to do as much work when they or the overseers were not watching us as when they were. But connected with these instructions there was more or less that was truly excellent; though mixed up with much that would sound strangely in the

From *Five Slave Narratives: A Compendium*, (New York, 1968), 20–21, with some minor grammatical corrections.

ears of freedom. There was one very kind hearted Episcopal minister whom I often used to hear; he was very popular with the colored people. But after he had preached a sermon to us in which he argued from the Bible that it was the will of heaven from all eternity we should be slaves, and our masters be our owners, most of us left him; for like some of the faint hearted disciples in early times we said,—"This is a hard saying, who can bear it?"

American Slavery as It Is

The anti-slavery societies that formed in the first decades of the nine-teenth century aimed to end the "peculiar institution" of slavery by per-suading whites that it was sinful to hold a fellow human being in bondage. Northern abolitionists did not advocate political action, nor did they offer an exposé of the South's slave system. In an age that believed in the perfectability of man, reform movements flourished except for the anti-slavery movement. After their plan of moral suasion had failed mis-erably, the movement divided as its members began to bicker over strat-egy and tactics. Many abolitionists, Theodore Weld among them, believed that they needed to adopt a more direct approach in their efforts to arouse greater interest and concern among Northerners over the plight of slaves.

Weld, a frequent abolitionist lecturer, believed that northern audi-ences opposed the anti-slavery movement out of ignorance. Lacking spe-cific evidence of slavery's cruelties, abolitionists could not persuade the citizenry that slaves were underfed, badly housed, and subjected to bru-tal treatment. To remedy the situation, Weld produced American Slav-ery As It Is: A Testimony of a Thousand Witnesses *(1839), a portion of which is excerpted below. The book proved to be invaluable to aboli-tionists because it provided an arsenal of facts about slavery drawn from legal codes and the mouths of slaveholders.*

The case of Human Rights against Slavery has been adjudi-cated in the court of conscience times innumerable. The same ver-dict has always been rendered—"Guilty". . . .

There is a not a man on earth who does not believe slavery is a curse. . . . Two million seven hundred thousand persons in these

From Richard O. Curry and Joanna Dunlap Cowden, *Slavery in America: Theodore Weld's American Slavery As It Is,* F. E. Peacock, (Itasca, Ill., 1839, 1972), 3–6.

States are in this condition. They were made slaves and are held such by force, and by being put in fear, and this for no crime! Reader, what have you to say of such treatment? Is it right, just, benevolent? Suppose I should seize you, rob you of your liberty, drive you into the field, and make you work without pay as long as you live, would that be justice and kindness or monstrous injustice and cruelty? Now, everybody knows that the slaveholders do these things to the slaves every day, and yet it is stoutly affirmed that they treat them well and kindly, and that their tender regard for their slaves restrains the masters from inflicting cruelties upon them. We shall go into no metaphysics to show the absurdity of this pretence. The man who *robs* you every day, is, forsooth, quite too tenderhearted ever to cuff or kick you! True, he can snatch your money, but he does it gently lest he should hurt you. He can empty your pockets, without qualms, but if your *stomach* is empty, it cuts him to the quick. He can make you work a life time without pay, but loves you too well to let you go hungry. He fleeces you of your *rights* with a relish, but is shocked if you work bareheaded in summer, or in winter without warm stockings. He can make you go without your *liberty,* but never without a shirt. He can crush, in you, all hope of bettering your condition, by vowing that you shall die his slave, but though he can coolly torture your feelings, he is too compassionate to lacerate your back—he can break your heart, but he is very tender of your skin. He can strip you of all protection and thus expose you to all outrages, but if you are exposed to the *weather,* half clad and half sheltered, how yearn his tender bowels! What! Slaveholders talk of treating men well, and yet not only rob them of all they get, but rob them of *themselves,* also; their very hands and feet, all their muscles, and limbs, and senses, their bodies and minds, their time and liberty and earnings, their free speech and rights of conscience, their right to acquire knowledge, and property, and reputation;—and yet they, who plunder them of all these, would fain make us believe that their soft hearts ooze out so lovingly toward their slaves that they always keep them well housed and well clad, never push them too hard in the field, never make their dear backs smart, nor let their dear stomachs get empty. . . .

Are slaveholders dunces, or do they take all the rest of the world to be, that they think to bandage our eyes with such thin gauzes?. . . It is no marvel that slaveholders are always talking of their *kind treatment* of their slaves. The only marvel is, that men of sense can be gulled by such professions. . . . When a man's tongue grows thick, and he begins to hiccough and walk cross-legged, we expect him, as a matter of course, to protest that he is not drunk; so when a man is always singing the praises of his own honesty, we instinctively watch his movements and look out for our pocketbooks. Whoever is simple enough to be hoaxed by such professions, should never be trusted in the streets without somebody to take care of him. Human nature works out in slaveholders just as it does in other men.

The Influence of Slavery

During and after the American Revolution a significant number of white Americans recognized the contradiction between the revolutionary rhetoric of liberty and the reality of slavery, prompting them to question the legitimacy and morality of the "peculiar institution." Many of these critics thought that slavery would decline and disappear of its own accord, or that abolition could be accomplished by sending African Americans to a colony in Africa. With the rise of the Cotton Kingdom in the South, however, slave labor became increasingly important to the region's economy. Subsequently, in the 1830s a new abolitionist movement composed of whites and blacks developed in the North. This movement was opposed to colonization and dedicated to achieving the immediate emancipation of slaves without compensation to masters. More than a few of the new abolitionists also believed that blacks should have civil equality with whites.

One of the single most important advocates of immediate emancipation was William Lloyd Garrison, editor of The Liberator *newspaper. Garrison was a "Christian anarchist," critical of the state, institutional religion, and other manifestations of what he considered to be coercion. He also held quite radical views on various important social issues of the day, including women's rights. The following excerpt reflects his distrust of government and churches as well as his disdain for moderation in opposing slavery.*

For more than two centuries, slavery has polluted the American soil. It has grown with the growth, and strengthened with the strength of the republic. Its victims have multiplied, from a single cargo of stolen Africans, to three millions of native-born inhabitants. In our colonial state, it was deemed compatible with loyalty

From William Lloyd Garrison, *Selections from the Writings and Speeches of William Lloyd Garrison,* (Boston, 1852), 137–139.

to the mother country. In our revolutionary struggle for independence, it exchanged the sceptre of monarchy for the star-spangled banner of republicanism, under the folds of which it has found ample encouragement and protection. From the days of the Puritans down to the present time, it has been sanctified by the religion, and upheld by the patriotism of the nation. From the adoption of the American Constitution, it has declared war and made peace, instituted and destroyed national banks and tariffs, controlled the army and navy, prescribed the policy of the government, ruled in both houses of Congress, occupied the Presidential chair, governed the political parties, distributed offices of trust and emolument among its worshippers, fettered Northern industry and enterprise, and trampled liberty of speech and of conscience in the dust.

It has exercised absolute mastery over the American Church. In her skirts is found 'the blood of the souls of the poor innocents.' With the Bible in their hands, her priesthood have attempted to prove that slavery came down from God out of heaven. . . .

If slavery be thus entwined around the civil, social, and pecuniary interests of the republic—if the religious sects and political parties are banded together for its safety from internal revolt and external opposition—if the people, awed by its power and corrupted by its influence, are basely bending their knees at its footstool—is it wonderful that Church and State are shaken to their foundations by the rallying cry of Liberty? . . .

Slavery must be overthrown. No matter how numerous the difficulties, how formidable the obstacles, how strong the foes to be vanquished—slavery must cease to pollute the land. . . . No matter, though, to effect it, every party should be torn by dissensions, every sect dashed into fragments, the national compact dissolved, the land filled with the horrors of a civil and a servile war—still, slavery must be buried in the grave of infamy, beyond the possibility of a resurrection.

If the State cannot survive the anti-slavery agitation, then let the State perish. If the Church must be cast down . . . to be free, then let the Church fall. . . . If the American Union cannot be maintained . . . then let the American Union be consumed by a living thunderbolt, and no tear be shed over its ashes.

Manifest Destiny

Along with slavery, the issue of territorial expansion dominated American politics in the 1840s. By 1845, Americans had filled the new states created by the Louisiana Purchase and coveted British, Mexican, and Native American lands on the far side of the continent. To a burgeoning population, no physical barrier and no foreign force could stop expansion because it was both inevitable and God's will. Many believed that Oregon, Texas, much of North America, and the nearby islands must be part of the United States because it was divine will that democratic government should spread.

Some of the strongest advocates of expansion and conquest were writers of editorials in the popular press, and of these perhaps the most famous was John L. O'Sullivan, editor of The United States Magazine and Democratic Review. *According to O'Sullivan, it had become America's "manifest destiny" to cover the continent. The selection printed below, comprising parts of two O'Sullivan editorials published in 1839 and 1845, conveys the themes and tone of O'Sullivan's advocacy.*

[1839]

The American people having derived their origin from many other nations, and the Declaration of National Independence being entirely based on the great principle of human equality, these facts demonstrate at once our disconnected position as regards any other nation; that we have, in reality, but little connection with the past history of any of them, and still less with all antiquity, its glories, or its crimes. On the contrary, our national birth was the beginning of a new history, the formation and progress of an untried political system, which separates us from the past and connects us with the future only; and so far as

From *The United States Magazine and Democratic Review,* 6: (November 1839): 426–427, 429–430; and 17: (July 1845): 5, 7–8.

regards the entire development of the natural rights of man, in moral, political, and national life, we may confidently assume that our country is destined to be *the great nation* of futurity. . . .

We have no interest in the scenes of antiquity, only as lessons of avoidance of nearly all their examples. The expansive future is our arena, and for our history. We are entering on its untrodden space, with the truths of God in our minds, beneficent objects in our hearts, and with a clear conscience unsullied by the past. We are the nation of human progress, and who will, what can, set limits to our onward march? Providence is with us, and no earthly power can. We point to the everlasting truth on the first page of our national declaration, and we proclaim to the millions of other lands, that "the gates of hell"—the powers of aristocracy and monarchy—"shall not prevail against it."

The far-reaching, the boundless future will be the era of American greatness. In its magnificent domain of space and time, the nation of many nations is destined to manifest to mankind the excellence of divine principles; to establish on earth the noblest temple ever dedicated to the worship of the Most High—the Sacred and the True. Its floor shall be a hemisphere—its roof the firmament of the star-studded heavens, and its congregation an Union of many Republics, comprising hundreds of happy millions, calling, owning no man master, but governed by God's natural and moral law of equality, the law of brotherhood—of "peace and good will amongst men.". . . .

Yes, we are the nation of progress, of individual freedom, of universal enfranchisement. Equality of rights is the cynosure of our union of States, the grand exemplar of the correlative equality of individuals; and while truth sheds its effulgence, we cannot retrograde, without dissolving the one and subverting the other. We must onward to the fulfilment of our mission—to the entire development of the principle of our organization—freedom of conscience, freedom of person, freedom of trade and business pursuits, universality of freedom and equality. This is our high destiny, and in nature's eternal, inevitable decree of cause and effect we must accomplish it. All this will be our future history, to establish on earth the moral dignity and salvation of man—the immutable truth and beneficence of God. For this blessed mission to the nations of the world, which are shut out from the life-giving light of truth, has America been chosen; and her high example shall smite unto death the tyranny of kings, hierarchs, and oligarchs, and carry the glad tidings of peace and good will where myriads now endure an existence scarcely more enviable than that of beasts of the field. Who, then, can doubt that our country is destined to be *the great nation* of futurity?

[1845]

It is time now for opposition to the Annexation of Texas to cease, all further agitation of the waters of bitterness and strife, at least in connexion with this question,—even though it may perhaps be required of us as a necessary condition of the freedom of our institutions, that we must live on for ever in a state of unpausing struggle and excitement upon some subject of party division or other. But, in regard to Texas, enough has now been given to Party. It is time for the common duty of Patriotism to the Country to succeed;—or if this claim will not be recognized, it is at least time for common sense to acquiesce with decent grace in the inevitable and the irrevocable.

Texas is now ours. Already, before these words are written, her Convention has undoubtedly ratified the acceptance, by her Congress, of our proffered invitation into the Union; and made the requisite changes in her already republican form of constitution to adopt it to its future federal relations. Her star and her stripe may already be said to have taken their place in the glorious blazon of our common nationality; and the sweep of our eagle's wing already includes within its circuit the wide extent of her fair and fertile land. She is no longer to us a mere geographical space—a certain combination of coast, plain, mountain, valley, forest and stream. She is no longer to us a mere country on the map. She comes within the dear and sacred designation of Our Country; no longer a *"pays,"* [country] she is part of *"la patrie;"* [the nation] and that which is at once a sentiment and a virtue, Patriotism, already begins to thrill for her too within the national heart. . . .

Why, were other reasoning wanting, in favor of now elevating this question of the reception of Texas into the Union, out of the lower region of our past party dissensions, up to its proper level of a high and broad nationality, it surely is to be found, found abundantly, in the manner in which other nations have undertaken to intrude themselves into it, between us and the proper parties to the case, in a spirit of hostile interference against us, for the avowed object of thwarting our policy and hampering our power, limiting our greatness and checking the fulfilment of our manifest destiny to overspread the continent allotted by Providence for the free development of our yearly multiplying millions. This we have seen done by England, our old rival and enemy; and by France. . . .

. . . Texas has been absorbed into the Union in the inevitable fulfilment of the general law which is rolling our population westward; the connexion of which with that ratio of growth in population which is destined within a hundred years to swell our numbers to the enormous population of *two hundred and fifty millions* (if not more), is too evident to leave us in doubt of the manifest design of Providence in regard to the occupation of this continent. It was disintegrated from Mexico in the natural course of events, by a process perfectly legitimate on its own part, blameless on ours; and in which all the censures due to wrong, perfidy and folly, rest on Mexico alone. And possessed as it was by a population which was in truth but a colonial detachment from our own, and which was still bound by myriad ties of the very heartstrings to its old relations, domestic and political, their incorporation into the Union was not only inevitable, but the most natural, right and proper thing in the world—and it is only astonishing that there should be any among ourselves to say it nay.

Civil Disobedience

In 1846, with the support of Southerners hoping to expand slavery into southwest territory, the U.S. government declared war on Mexico. As a committed abolitionist, Henry David Thoreau (1817–1862) opposed the war, refused to pay his taxes to support it, and as a result, was jailed in Concord, Mass. Supposedly, when fellow abolitionist and transcendentalist Ralph Waldo Emerson came to visit Thoreau in jail he asked, "What are you doing in there?" Thoreau replied, "What are you doing out there?"

Henry David Thoreau followed his brief stay in jail with an essay, originally published as "Resistance to Civil Government," later republished as "On the Duty of Civil Disobedience." Like other transcendentalists, Thoreau was interested in rethinking the human place in nature as well as the role of intuition in the search for truth. But he was also firmly rooted in other American intellectual traditions, including a Lockean tradition of natural rights, and this is very evident in "Civil Disobedience."

John Locke articulated his arguments about natural rights in "Two Treatises on Civil Government" (1690). American colonists later appropriated these arguments when they made a revolution. Thomas Jefferson gave natural rights doctrine a prominent place in the Declaration of Independence (1776). He insisted that rights were granted by God rather than a monarch or parliament, and that people had the right (and duty) to rebel if government became a tyranny by failing to protect those rights. In the excerpt below, Thoreau draws on Lockean philosophy as it came to him through Jefferson.

I heartily accept the motto, "That government is best which governs least," and I should like to see it acted up to more rapidly

From Henry David Thoreau, *Civil Disobedience*, (Westwood, N.J., 1964), 11–18, 21–22, 27–31, 46–47, 49–50, 55–56.

and systematically. Carried out, it finally amounts to this, which also I believe—"That government is best which governs not at all;" and when men are prepared for it, that will be the kind of government which they will have. . . . The government itself, which is only the mode which the people have chosen to execute their will, is equally liable to be abused and perverted before the people can act through it. Witness the present Mexican war, the work of comparatively a few individuals using the standing government as their tool; for, in the outset, the people would not have consented to this measure. . . .

After all, the practical reason why, when the power is once in the hands of the people, a majority are permitted, and for a long period continue, to rule is not because they are most likely to be in the right, nor because this seems fairest to the minority, but because they are physically the strongest. But a government in which the majority rule in all cases cannot be based on justice, even as far as men understand it. Can there not be a government in which majorities do not virtually decide right and wrong, but conscience?—In which majorities decide only those questions to which the rule of expediency is applicable? Must the citizen ever for a moment, or in the slightest degree, resign his conscience to the legislator? Why has every man a conscience, then? I think that we should be men first, and subjects afterward. It is not desirable to cultivate a respect for the law, so much as for the right. The only obligation which I have a right to assume is to do at any time what I think right. It is truly enough said that a corporation has no conscience; but a corporation of conscientious men is a corporation *with* a conscience. Law never made men a whit more just; and by means of their respect for it even the well-disposed are daily made the agents of injustice. A common and natural result of an undue respect for law is that you may see a file of soldiers— colonel, captain, corporal, privates, powder-monkeys, and all— marching in admirable order over hill and dale to the wars against their wills . . . against their common sense and consciences, which makes it very steep marching indeed, and produces a palpitation of the heart. They have no doubt that it is a damnable business in which they are concerned; they are all peaceably inclined. Now, what are they? Men at all? or small movable forts and magazines, at the service of some unscrupulous man in power? . . .

The mass of men serve the state thus, not as men mainly but as machines, with their bodies. They are the standing army, and the militia, jailers, constables, posse comitatus, etc. In most cases there is no free exercise whatever of the judgement or of the moral sense; but they put themselves on a level with wood and earth and stones, and wooden men can perhaps be manufactured that will serve the purpose as well. Such command no more respect than men of straw or a lump of dirt. They have the same sort of worth only as horses and dogs. Yet such as these even are commonly esteemed good citizens. Others—as most legislators, politicians, lawyers, ministers, and office-holders—serve the state chiefly with their heads; and as they rarely make any moral distinctions, they are as likely to serve as Devil, without *intending* it, as God. . . .

How does it become a man to behave toward this American government today? I answer, that he cannot without disgrace be associated with it. I cannot for an instant recognize that political organization as *my* government which is the *slave's* government also.

All men recognize the right of revolution; that is, the right to refuse allegiance to and to resist, the government, when its tyranny or its inefficiency are great and unendurable. But almost all say that such is not the case now. But such was the case, they think, in the Revolution of '75 [American Revolution]. . . . All machines have their friction, and possibly this does enough good to counterbalance the evil. . . . But when the friction comes to have its machine, and oppression and robbery are organized, I say, let us not have such a machine any longer. In other words, when a sixth of the population of a nation which has undertaken to be the refuge of liberty are slaves, and a whole country [Mexico] is unjustly overrun and conquered by a foreign army and subjected to military law, I think that it is not too soon for honest men to rebel and revolutionize. . . .

. . . There are thousands who are *in opinion* opposed to slavery and to the war [Mexican-American War], who yet in effect do nothing to put an end to them; who, esteeming themselves children of Washington and Franklin, sit down with their hands in their pockets, and say that they know not what to do, and do nothing; who even postpone the question of freedom to the question of free-trade, and quietly read the price-current along with the latest advices from Mexico after dinner, and, it may be, fall asleep over them both. What is the price-current of an honest man and patriot today? They hesitate, and they regret, and sometimes they petition; but they do nothing in earnest and with effect. They will wait, well disposed, for others to remedy the evil, that they may no longer have it to regret. At most, they give only a cheap vote. . . .

All voting is a sort of gaming, like checkers or backgammon, with a slight moral tinge to it, a playing with right and wrong, with moral questions; and betting naturally accompanies it. The character of the voters is not staked. I cast my vote, perchance, as I think right; but I am not vitally concerned that the right should prevail. I am willing to leave it to the majority. Its obligation, therefore, never exceeds that of expediency. Even voting *for the right* is *doing* nothing for it. It is only expressing to men feebly your desire that it should prevail. A wise man will not leave the right to the mercy of chance, nor wish it to prevail through the power of the majority. There is but little virtue in the action of masses of men. When the majority shall at length vote for the abolition of slavery, it will be because they are indifferent to slavery, or because there is but little slavery left to be abolished by their vote. *They* will then be the only slaves. Only *his* vote can hasten the abolition of slavery who asserts his own freedom by his vote. . . .

Unjust laws exist: shall we be content to obey them or shall we endeavor to amend them, and obey them until we have succeeded, or shall we transgress them at once? Men generally, under such a government as this, think that they ought to wait until they have persuaded the majority to alter them. They think that, if they should resist, the remedy would be worse than the evil. But it is the fault of the government itself that the remedy is worse than the evil. *It* makes it worse. Why is it not more apt to anticipate and provide for reform? Why does it not cherish its wise minority? Why does it cry and resist before it is hurt? Why does it not encourage its citizens to be on the alert to point out its faults, and *do* better than it would have them? Why does it always crucify Christ, and excommunicate Copernicus and Luther, and pronounce Washington and Franklin rebels? . . .

. . . If the injustice . . . is of such a nature that it requires you to be the agent of . . . injustice to another, then, I say, break the law. Let your life be the counter-friction to stop the machine. What I have to do is to see, at any rate, that I do not lend myself to the wrong which I condemn. . . .

I do not hesitate to say that those who call themselves Abolitionists should at once effectually withdraw their support, both in person and property, from the government of Massachusetts, and not wait till they constitute a majority of one, before they suffer the right to prevail through them. I think that it is enough if they have God on their side, without waiting for that other one. Moreover, any man more right than his neighbors constitutes a majority of one already.

. . . I know this well, that if one thousand, if one hundred, if ten men whom I could name—if ten *honest* men only—aye, if *one* HONEST man in this State of Massachusetts, *ceasing to hold slaves,* were actually to withdraw from this copartnership, and be locked up in the county jail therefore, it would be the abolition of slavery in America. For it matters not how small the beginning may seem to be; what is once well done is done forever. . . .

. . . A minority is powerless while it conforms to the majority; it is not even a minority then; but it is irresistible when it clogs by its whole weight. If the alternative is to keep all just men in prison, or give up war and slavery, the State will not hesitate which to choose. If a thousand men were not to pay their tax-bills this year, that would not be a violent and bloody measure as it would be to pay them and enable the State to commit violence and shed innocent blood. This is, in fact, the definition of a peaceable revolution, if any such is possible. . . .

I have never declined paying the highway tax, because I am as desirous of being a good neighbor as I am of being a bad subject; and as for supporting schools, I am doing my part to educate my fellow countrymen now. It is for no particular item in the tax-bill that I refuse to pay it. I simply wish to refuse allegiance to the State, to withdraw and stand aloof from it effectually. I do not care to trace the course of my dollar, if I could, till it buys a man or a musket to shoot one with—the dollar is innocent—but I am concerned to trace the effects of my allegiance. In fact, I quietly declare war with the State, after my fashion, though I will still make what use and get what advantage of her I can, as is usual in such cases. . . .

This, then, is my position at present. . . .

I do not wish to quarrel with any man or nation. I do not wish to split hairs, to make fine distinctions, or set myself up as better than my neighbors. I seek rather, I may say, even an excuse for conforming to the laws of the land. I am but too ready to conform to them. Indeed, I have reason to suspect myself on this head; and each year, as the tax-gatherer comes round, I find myself disposed to review the acts and position of the general and State governments, and the spirit of the people, to discover a pretext for conformity. . . .

I believe that the State will soon be able to take all my work of this sort out of my hands, and then I shall be no better a patriot than my fellow countrymen. Seen from a lower point of view, the Constitution, with all its faults, is very good; even this State and this American government are in many respects very admirable and rare things to be thankful for, such as a great many have described them; but seen from a point of view a little higher, they are what I have described them; seen from a higher still, and the highest, who shall say what they are, or that they are worth looking at or thinking of at all? . . .

The authority of government, even such as I am willing to submit to—for I will cheerfully obey those who know and can do better than I, and in many things even those who neither know nor can do so well—is still an impure one: to be strictly just, it must have the sanction and consent of the governed. It can have no pure right over my person and property but what I concede to it. The progress from an absolute to a limited monarchy, from a limited monarchy to a democracy, is a progress toward a true respect for the individual. . . . Is a democracy, such as we know it, the last improvement possible in government? Is it not possible to take a step further toward recognizing and organizing the rights of man? There will never be a really free and enlightened State until the State comes to recognize the individual as a higher and independent power, from which all its own power and authority are derived, and treats him accordingly. I please myself with imagining a State at last which can afford to be just to all men, and to treat the individual with respect as a neighbor; which even would not think it inconsistent with its own repose if a few were to live aloof from it, not meddling with it nor embraced by it, who fulfilled all the duties of neighbors and fellow men. A State which bore this kind of fruit, and suffered it to drop off as fast as it ripened, would prepare the way for a still more perfect and glorious State, which also I have imagined, but not yet anywhere seen.

The Expansion of Slavery Condemned

In March of 1845, the United States admitted Texas as a slave state, shifting the political balance to fifteen slave states and thirteen free states. The annexation of Texas by the United States increased tensions with Mexico, leading to the beginning of the Mexican-American War in May of 1846. In response to the likelihood of an American victory and the acquisition of territory from Mexico, David Wilmot, a Representative from Pennsylvania (Democrat) proposed that no land gained during the war should allow slavery because slavery had been abolished in Mexico and should not be reintroduced. This idea, which became known as the Wilmot Proviso, was hotly debated in political and public circles. The House of Representatives, where Northerners held the majority based on the North's larger population, passed the Proviso more than forty times, but each time, the Senate, where Southerners held the majority based on the higher number of slave states, voted against it. It was a harbinger of difficult times ahead for the Democratic and Whig Parties since each vote split their parties in half, with northern Democrats and Whigs voting for the Proviso, and southern Democrats and Whigs voting against it. The pressure on northern Democrats was particularly intense since the upstart Liberty Party, which ran on an anti-slavery platform, had captured tens of thousands of votes in the North during the 1844 elections. The discussion over the Proviso expanded the national debate from moral grounds to economic reasons, and shifted the emphasis from where slavery did exist to where it might exist.

Charles Sumner (1811–1874) was a noted abolitionist from Boston. Trained at Harvard Law School, he entered the political fray on July 4, 1845, when he made a speech denouncing the Mexican-American War. In 1847, Sumner prepared the following explanation of the reasons why the Mexican-American War should be denounced and delivered it to the

From "Report on the War with Mexico," in *Old South Leaflets*, no. 132 (Boston, n.d.), 150–153, 155–156 [separately paginated as 14–17, 19–20].

Massachusetts legislature. He described the war as one of conquest, meaning that the United States agreed to annex Texas and engage in war with the Mexican government solely for the acquisition of additional land—land where slavery was accepted by Americans who settled there. He harshly criticized the reimposition of slavery in territory where it had already been abolished by the Mexican government. Sumner also rebuked the U.S. government, one founded on principles of equality and justice, for allowing slavery to continue to exist. But according to Sumner, the most ominous part of the willingness of the U.S. government to engage in this war was the increasing division between North and South and the desire on the part of southern states to dominate the northern states. Lastly, he protested the enormous sums of money being spent to wage war, arguing that funds would be better spent on education, industrial expansion, and agricultural development.

It can no longer be doubted that this is a war of conquest. . . .

A war of conquest is bad; but the present war has darker shadows. It is a war for the extension of slavery over a territory which has already been purged, by Mexican authority, from this stain and curse. Fresh markets of human beings are to be established; further opportunities for this hateful traffic are to be opened; the lash of the overseer is to be quickened in new regions; and the wretched slave is to be hurried to unaccustomed fields of toil. It can hardly be believed that now, more than eighteen hundred years since the dawn of the Christian era, a government, professing the law of charity and justice, should be employed in war to extend an institution which exists in defiance of these sacred principles.

It has already been shown that the annexation of Texas was consummated for this purpose. The Mexican war is a continuance, a prolongation, of the same efforts; and the success which crowned the first emboldens the partisans of the latter, who now, as before, profess to extend the area of freedom, while they are establishing a new sphere for slavery. . . . But it is not merely proposed to open new markets for slavery: it is also designed to confirm and fortify the "Slave Power.". . . Regarding it as a war to strengthen the "Slave Power," we are conducted to a natural conclusion, that it is virtually, and in its consequences, a war against the free States of the Union. . . . Nor should we be indifferent to the enormous expenditures which have already been lavished upon the war, and the accumulating debt which will hold in mortgage the future resources of the country. It is impossible to estimate the exact amount of these. At this moment the cost of the war cannot be less than seventy millions. It may be a hundred millions.

This sum is so vast as to be beyond easy comprehension. It may be estimated, partly, by reference to the cost of other objects of interest. It is far more than all the funds for common schools throughout the United States. It is ample for the endowment of three or more institutions like Harvard College in every State. It would plant churches in all the neglected valleys of the land. It would bind and interlace every part of the country by new railroads. It would make our broad and rude soil blossom like a garden. . . .

. . . The war is a crime, and all who have partaken in the blood of its well-fought fields have aided in its perpetration. It is a principle of military law that the soldier shall not question the orders of his superior. If this shall exonerate the army from blame, it will be only to press with accumulated weight upon the government, which has set in motion this terrible and irresponsible machine.

The Expansion of Slavery Justified

In March of 1845, the United States admitted Texas as a slave state, shifting the political balance to fifteen slave states and thirteen free states. The annexation of Texas by the United States increased tensions with Mexico, leading to the beginning of the Mexican-American War in May of 1846. In response to the likelihood of an American victory and the acquisition of territory from Mexico, David Wilmot, a representative from Pennsylvania (Democrat) proposed that no land gained during the war should allow slavery because slavery had been abolished in Mexico and should not be reintroduced. This idea, which became known as the Wilmot Proviso, was hotly debated in political and public circles. The House of Representatives, where Northerners held the majority based on the North's larger population, passed the Proviso more than forty times, but each time, the Senate, where Southerners held the majority based on the higher number of slave states, voted against it. It was a harbinger of difficult times ahead for the Democratic and Whig Parties since each vote split their parties in half, with Northern Democrats and Whigs voting for the Proviso, and Southern Democrats and Whigs voting against it. The pressure on Northern Democrats was particularly intense since the upstart Liberty Party, which ran on an anti-slavery platform, had captured tens of thousands of votes in the North during the 1844 elections. The discussion over the Proviso expanded the national debate from moral grounds to economic reasons, and shifted the emphasis from where slavery did exist to where it might exist.

The sentiments expressed in the following anti-Wilmot editorial were common. It demonstrates traditional arguments against the imposition of federal legislation banning slavery. For instance, John C. Calhoun and other champions of states' rights invoked the Fifth Amendment of the Constitution, contending that abolishing slavery in certain areas of the

From *The United States Magazine and Democratic Review* (October 1847), 21:292.

country conflicted with the constitutional guarantee of no deprivation of property without due process of law. Keep in mind that many people at that time in the United States considered slaves to be property. The editorial also insists that whether all citizens of the United States believe slavery to be justified was not the issue; rather, the most important question raised by the Wilmot Proviso was the constitutional rights of citizens.

All the territory of the Union is the common property of all the states—every member, new or old, of the Union, admitted to partnership under the constitution, has a perfect right to enjoy the territory, which is the common property of all. Some of the territory was acquired by treaty from England—much of it by cession from the older states; yet more by treaties with Indians, and still greater quantities by purchase from Spain and France;—large tracts again by the annexation of Texas—and the present war will add still more to the quantity yet to be entered by citizens of the United States, or of those of any of the countries of Europe that choose to migrate thither. All this land, no matter whence it was derived, belongs to all the states jointly. . . . [N]o citizen of the United States can be debarred from moving thither with his property, and enjoying the liberties guaranteed by the constitution. . . . Any law or regulation which interrupts, limits, delays or postpones the rights of the owner to the immediate command of his service or labor, operates a discharge of the slave from service, and is a violation of the constitution. . . . To set up therefore a pretence that if they adhere to the property they possess, they shall be deprived of their rights in the states to be formed in any acquired territory, is an unprincipled violation of a solemn treaty, an attack upon the constitution, and a gross injustice to the rights of neighboring states. If the constitution is respected, then the rights of no member in the common property can be impaired, because it is possessed of other property distasteful to other members.

The Crime Against Sumner

In 1854, an uneasy truce created by the Compromise of 1850 collapsed when Senator Stephen Douglas introduced the Kansas-Nebraska Act. Douglas aimed to aid the rapid settlement of the West by allowing the people of the Kansas and Nebraska territories to determine the slavery question by popular vote. As the time for the vote in Kansas approached, opponents and proponents of slavery moved into the territory and armed themselves to persuade others to vote "correctly." A guerilla war then began in 1855 in which over two hundred people lost their lives.

Violence over Kansas spread to Congress. In May 1856, Massachusetts Senator Charles Sumner delivered a speech before the Senate popularly known as "The Crime against Kansas." In the speech Sumner harshly criticized South Carolina Senator Andrew P. Butler provoking a violent physical assault upon Sumner a few days later by Butler's nephew, U.S. Representative Preston Brooks. These excerpts of the speech focus on Sumner's comments about Butler but also reflect the passion driving the most radically anti-slavery wing of the Republican party. Brooks's attack left Sumner unconscious in a pool of blood. He did not return to the Senate for three years, becoming a "living martyr" to the anti-slavery cause. The assault seemed to prove the Republican charge that the South would stop at nothing to spread slavery and would not even allow civilized debate on the issue. The violence directed at Sumner convinced many Northerners to abandon the Know Nothing party for the Republican cause, as it seemed to indicate that the "Slave Power" posed a more immediate menace than immigrants and Catholics. This helped the Republicans replace the Know Nothings as the most powerful party in the North, initiating the second phase of the slavery crisis.

From the *New York Tribune*, May 21 and 22, 1856.

May 21, 1856

My task will be divided under three different heads; *first,* THE CRIME AGAINST KANSAS, is its origin and extent; *secondly,* THE APOLOGIES FOR THE CRIME; and *thirdly,* the TRUE REMEDY.

But, before entering upon the argument, I must say something of a general character, particularly in response to what has fallen from Senators who have raised themselves to eminence on this floor in championship of human wrongs; I mean the Senator from South Carolina, [Mr. Butler,] and the Senator from Illinois, [Mr. Douglas,] who, though unlike as Don Quixote and Sacho Panza, yet, like this couple, sally forth together in the same adventure. I regret much to miss the elder Senator from his seat; but the cause, against which he has run a tilt, with such activity of animosity, demands that the opportunity for exposing him should not be lost; and it is for the cause that I speak. The Senator from South Carolina has read many books of chivalry, and believes himself a chivalrous knight, with sentiments of honor and courage. Of course he has chosen a mistress to whom he has made his vows, and who, though ugly to others, is always lovely to him; though polluted in the sight of the world, is chaste in his sight—I mean the harlot, Slavery. For her, his tongue is always profuse in words. Let her be impeached in character, or any proposition made to shut her out from the extension of her wantonness, and no extravagance of manner or hardihood of assertion is then too great for this Senator. The frenzy of *Don Quixote,* in behalf of his wench Dulcinea del Toboso, is all surpassed. The asserted rights of Slavery, which shock equality of all kinds, are cloaked by a fantastic claim of equality. If the slave States cannot enjoy what, in mockery of the great fathers of the Republic, he misnames equality under the Constitution—in other words, the full power in the National Territories to compel fellow-men to unpaid toil, to separate husband and wife, and to sell little children at the auction block—then, sir, the chivalric Senator will conduct the State of South Carolina out of the Union! Heroic knight! Exalted Senator! A second Moses come for a second exodus!

May 22, 1856

With regret, I come again upon the Senator from South Carolina (Mr. Butler), who, omnipresent in this debate, overflowed with rage at the simple suggestion that Kansas had applied for admission as a State; and, with incoherent phrases, discharged the loose expectoration of his speech, row upon her Representative and then upon her people. There was no extravagance of the ancient Parliamentary debate which he did not repeat; nor was there any possible deviation from truth which he did not make, with so much of passion, I am glad to add, as to save him from the suspicion of intentional aberration. But the Senator touches nothing which he does not disfigure—with error, sometimes of principle, sometimes of fact. He shows an incapacity of accuracy, whether in stating the Constitution or in stating the law, whether in the details of statistics or the diversions of scholarship. He cannot open his mouth but out there flies a blunder. Surely he ought to be familiar with the life of Franklin; and yet he referred to this household character, while acting as agent of our fathers in England, as above suspicion; and this was done that he might give point to a false contrast with the agent of Kansas—not knowing that, however, they may differ in genius and fame, in this experience they are alike; that Franklin, when intrusted with the petition of Massachusetts Bay, was assaulted by a foul-mouthed speaker, where he could not be heard in defense, and denounced as a "thief," even as the agent of Kansas has been assaulted on this floor, and denounced as a "forger." And let not the vanity of the Senator be inspired by the parallel with the British statesmen of that day; for it is only in hostility to Freedom that any parallel can be recognized. But it is against the people of Kansas that the sensibilities of the Senator are particularly aroused. Coming, as he announces, "from a State"—aye, Sir, from South Carolina—he turns with lordly disgust from this newly-formed community, which he will not recognize even as "a body politic." Pray, Sir, by what title does he indulge in this egotism? Has he read the history of "the State" which he represents? He cannot surely have forgotten its shameful imbecility from Slavery, confessed throughout the Revolution, followed by its more shameful assumptions for Slavery since. He cannot have forgotten its wretched persistence in the slave trade as the very apple of the eye, and the condition of its participation in the Union. He cannot have forgotten its Constitution, which is republican only in name, confirming power in the hands of the few, and founding the qualifications of voters on "a settled freehold estate and ten negroes."

In all this sympathy there is strength. But in the cause itself there is angelic power. Unseen of men, the great spirits of History combat by the side of the people of Kansas, breathing a divine courage. Above all towers the majestic form of Washington once more, as on the bloody field, bidding them to remember those rights of Human Nature for which the War of Independence was waged. Such a cause, thus sustained, is invincible. It may be crushed to earth for day, but it will surely rise to grasp the victory. The contest which, beginning in Kansas, has reached us, will soon be transferred from Congress to a broader stage, where every citizen will be not only spectator, but actor; and to their judgment I confidently appeal. To the People, now on the eve of exercising the electoral franchise in choosing a Chief Magistrate of the Republic, I appeal, to vindicate the electoral franchise in Kansas. Let the ballot-box of the Union, with multitudinous might, protect the ballot-box in that Territory. Let the voters everywhere, while rejoicing in their own rights, help to guard the equal rights of distant fellow citizens; that the shrines of popular institutions, now desecrated, may be sanctified anew; that the ballot-box, now plundered, may be restored; and that the cry, "I am an American citizen," may not be sent forth in vain against outrage of every kind. In just regard for Free labor in rage of every kind. In just regard for Free labor in that Territory, which it is sought to blast by unwelcome association with slave labor; in Christian sympathy with the slave, whom it is proposed to task and sell there; in stern condemnation of the Crime which has been consummated on that beautiful soil; in rescue of fellow-citizens, now subjected to tyrannical Usurpation; in dutiful respect for the early Fathers, who aspirations are now ignobly thwarted; in the name of the Constitution, which has been outraged—of the Laws trampled down—of Justice banished—of Humanity degraded—of Peace destroyed—of Freedom crushed to earth; and in the name of the Heavenly Father, whose service is perfect Freedom, I make this last appeal.

The Dred Scott Decision

The Supreme Court decision in the case of **Dred Scott v. Sanford** *(1857) was one of the most far-reaching and controversial legal rulings in the years leading up to the Civil War. Dred Scott was a slave whose master in 1834 had taken him from Missouri (a slave state) to Illinois (a free state), then into the Wisconsin Territory (a free territory under the provisions of the Missouri Compromise), and finally back to Missouri. Scott sued for his freedom in the Missouri state courts on the grounds that his residence in a free state and a free territory had made him a free man. The case came to the Supreme Court on appeal by Scott after the Missouri Supreme Court reversed a lower court ruling that declared Scott free. Chief Justice Taney, ruling for the majority, dismissed the appeal on the grounds that Scott was not entitled to sue in federal courts because African Americans were not citizens of the United States. Although the decision could have ended with this dismissal, the court went on to examine the constitutionality of federal laws governing the institution of slavery. Taney concluded that slaves were property of their owners, and that these masters were guaranteed their property rights under the Fifth Amendment. As a result neither Congress nor any territorial legislature could deprive a citizen of his property without due process of law. The court then ruled that the Missouri Compromise of 1820, which restricted slavery to the part of the Louisiana Purchase south of the latitude 36°30', was unconstitutional because Congress had no power to prohibit slavery in the territories. The decision was only the second time the Supreme Court declared a law unconstitutional and a significant victory for the slaveholding South. Although the court hoped their decision would reduce anti-slavery agitation, it instead increased tensions with the North, and fed the sectional antagonism that burst into war in 1861.*

From *Dred Scott v. John F.A. Sandford*, 60 U.S. 393 (1856) as reproduced in http://web.lexis-nexis.com.

The question is simply this: Can a negro, whose ancestors were imported into this country, and sold as slaves, become a member of the political community formed and brought into existence by the Constitution of the United States, and as such become entitled to all the rights, and privileges, and immunities, guarantied by that instrument to the citizen? . . .

We think they are not, and that they are not included, and were not intended to be included, under the word 'citizens' in the Constitution, and can therefore claim none of the rights and privileges which that instrument provides for and secures to citizens of the United States. On the contrary, they were at that time considered as a subordinate and inferior class of beings, who had been subjugated by the dominant race, and, whether emancipated or not, yet remained subject to their authority, and had no rights or privileges but such as those who held the power and the Government might choose to grant them. . . .

It is very clear, therefore, that no State can, by any act or law of its own, passed since the adoption of the Constitution, introduce a new member into the political community created by the Constitution of the United States. It cannot make him a member of this community by making him a member of its own. And for the same reason it cannot introduce any person, or description of persons, who were not intended to be embraced in this new political family, which the Constitution brought into existence, but were intended to be excluded from it.

The question then arises, whether the provisions of the Constitution, in relation to the personal rights and privileges to which the citizen of a State should be entitled, embraced the negro African race, at that time in this country, or who might afterwards be imported, who had then or should afterwards be made free in any State; and to put it in the power of a single State to make him a citizen of the United States, and endue him with the full rights of citizenship in every other State without their consent? Does the Constitution of the United States act upon him whenever he shall be made free under the laws of a State, and raised there to the rank of a citizen, and immediately clothe him with all the privileges of a citizen in every other State, and in its own courts?

The court think the affirmative of these propositions cannot be maintained. And if it cannot, the plaintiff in error could not be a citizen of the State of Missouri, within the meaning of the

Constitution of the United States, and, consequently, was not entitled to sue in its courts. . . .

They [negroes] had for more than a century before been regarded as beings of an inferior order, and altogether unfit to associate with the white race, either in social or political relations; and so far inferior, that they had no rights which the white man was bound to respect; and that the negro might justly and lawfully be reduced to slavery for his benefit. He was bought and sold, and treated as an ordinary article of merchandise and traffic, whenever a profit could be made by it. This opinion was at that time fixed and universal in the civilized portion of the white race. It was regarded as an axiom in morals as well as in politics, which no one thought of disputing, or supposed to be open to dispute; and men in every grade and position in society daily and habitually acted upon it in their private pursuits, as well as in matters of public concern, without doubting for a moment the correctness of this opinion. . . .

No one of that race had ever migrated to the United States voluntarily; all of them had been brought here as articles of merchandise. The number that had been emancipated at that time were but few in comparison with those held in slavery; and they were identified in the public mind with the race to which they belonged, and regarded as a part of the slave population rather than the free. It is obvious that they were not even in the minds of the framers of the Constitution when they were conferring special rights and privileges upon the citizens of a State in every other part of the Union. . . .

The case before us still more strongly imposes upon this court the duty of examining whether the court below has not committed an error . . . We proceed, therefore, to inquire whether the facts relied on by the plaintiff entitled him to his freedom. . . . In considering this part of the controversy, two questions arise: 1. Was he, together with his family, free in Missouri by reason of the stay in the territory of the United States hereinbefore mentioned? And 2. If they were not, is Scott himself free by reason of his removal to Rock Island, in the State of Illinois, as stated in the above admissions? . . .

The act of Congress, upon which the plaintiff relies, declares that slavery and involuntary servitude, except as a punishment for crime, shall be forever prohibited in all that part of the territory ceded by France, under the name of Louisiana, which lies north of thirty-six degrees thirty minutes north latitude, and not included within the limits of Missouri. And the difficulty which meets us at the threshold of this part of the inquiry is, whether Congress was authorized to pass this law under any of the powers granted to it by the Constitution; for if the authority is not given by that instrument, it is the duty of this court to declare it void and inoperative, and incapable of conferring freedom upon any one who is held as a slave under the have of any one of the States. . . .

The powers over person and property of which we speak are not only not granted to Congress, but are in express terms denied, and they are forbidden to exercise them. . . .

It seems, however, to be supposed, that there is a difference between property in a slave and other property, and that different rules may be applied to it in expounding the Constitution of the United States. And the laws and usages of nations, and the writings of eminent jurists upon the relation of master and slave and their mutual rights and duties, and the powers which Governments may exercise over it, have been dwelt upon in the argument. . . .

Now, as we have already said in an earlier part of this opinion, upon a different point, the right of property in a slave is distinctly and expressly affirmed in the Constitution. The right to traffic in it, like an ordinary article of merchandise and property, was guarantied to the citizens of the United States, in every State that might desire it, for twenty years. And the Government in express terms is pledged to protect it in all future time, if the slave escapes from his owner. This is done in plain words—too plain to be misunderstood. And no word can be found in the Constitution which gives Congress a greater power over slave property, or which entitles property of that kind to less protection than property of any other description. The only power conferred is the power coupled with the duty of guarding and protecting the owner in his rights. . . .

Upon these considerations, it is the opinion of the court that the act of Congress which prohibited a citizen from holding and owning property of this kind in the territory of the United States north of the line therein mentioned, is not warranted by the Constitution, and is therefore void; and that neither Dred Scott himself, nor any of his family, were made free by being carried into this territory; even if they had been carried there by the owner, with the intention of becoming a permanent resident. . . .

Upon the whole, therefore, it is the judgment of this court, that it appears by the record before us that the plaintiff in error is not a citizen of Missouri, in the sense in which that word is used in the Constitution; and that the Circuit Court of the United States, for that reason, had no jurisdiction in the case, and could give no judgment in it. Its judgment for the defendant must, consequently, be reversed, and a mandate issued, directing the suit to be dismissed for want of jurisdiction.

Northern Opinion on the Eve of Conflict

The following editorials, from the two most widely read and influential newspapers in the nation, remind us that the North was far from united in support of Lincoln and the Republican party in 1860. In the first, the New York Herald *warns that the "black republican" party (the* Herald *so disdained the Republicans that it refused even to capitalize their name) is foolishly dragging the nation into war by threatening the perpetuation of slavery, which the paper holds "is neither an evil nor a crime." The* New York Tribune, *in contrast, argues that Southern threats to secede are empty ones, another attempt by the "Slave Power" to bully the North into submission. The* Tribune *was especially popular in the Midwest, where its weekly national edition brought farmers news about Washington politics and plenty of Republican campaign propaganda. Such comments also emboldened the South, intensifying the polarization that marked the final stage of the political crisis. The* Herald's *stance convinced Southern politicians that many Northerners espoused their pro-slavery views and that the Republicans were fanatics who should be resisted. Editorials such as those in the* Tribune *pushed Southerners to make good on their long-standing promises to secede, rather than compromise and give the appearance that their threats had been empty ones.*

The Northern Idea and Southern Safety— The Coming Collision Between the North and South

It is already becoming evident that the progress of the black republican party in the Northern and Central States is carrying this confederation to the very verge of a fearful abyss, from which only the most sagacious wisdom and the purest patriotism can save it.

From the *New York Herald*, October 19, 1860, and the *New York Tribune*, November 2, 1860.

Everywhere in the South the fires of resistance are already beginning to burn. Among the people a general feeling of apprehension is spreading, and the authorities and corporations of the several Southern States are already taking the initiative steps of action. It must not be supposed that the public men in the South, in announcing their adhesion to the idea of resistance to Northern aggression and dictation, are stirring the Southern people up to a point to which they advance unwillingly. Public men do not often lead public sentiment; they follow it, and reflect the tone and opinions of those around them, and in whose name they assume to speak. We must accept from the facts we already have in view the logical deduction that follows from them; in so doing we shall admit the conclusion that the general sentiment of the Southern people is strongly in support of the significant acts of their representative men. Hence the isolation and unconnected events which are occurring in different Southern localities must be read in a broad and comprehensive spirit, in order to grasp their true meaning and portent.

We published yesterday the proclamation of Gov. Gist of South Carolina, calling together the Legislature of that State for the purpose of electing Presidential electors, and providing, if advisable, for the safety of the State. The Legislature of Alabama provided, some time since, for the contingency of the election of a sectional President, by authorizing the Governor to call a State Convention immediately on the election of a black republican President becoming known. . . . [I]n many places in the South the young men are organizing themselves as minute men, to hold themselves at the orders of the Governors of their respective States.

These are alarming symptoms of the temper of the times, which no wise or prudent man will set aside with contempt, or even with inattention. It is a feeling which springs from the one great fact that no one can ignore. The black republican political organization is founded on one idea, from which its whole development proceeds; and this is, that "slavery is an evil and a crime." Politicians may disclaim any intent to do anything more but to exclude slavery from the Territories; public leaders may deny any wish to make war upon the institution in the States; and law abiding men may proclaim that they will act only within the terms and powers of the constitution; but these are professions which can be of no avail, for they are at war with the one all-pervading idea that underlies them. The natural and logical development of that idea makes the fulfillment of these impressions impossible. If slavery must be excluded from the Territories because it is an evil and a crime, the same results will apply to its exclusion from the States. If the moral sentiment of men must make war upon it in one place, it must do so in all places. Time and place make no excuse for palliating war against a moral evil or a social crime. If it is right at one time and in one place, it is right in all. This is the only logical result of the black republican creed, and to this it must come at last. . . .

The South hold, and hold rightly, that the institution of domestic servitude for the African race among them is neither an evil nor a crime. The greatest problem is, how shall four millions of an inferior race of men remain in society, best for their happiness, for the good of the community of which they form a part, and for the interests of civilization at large?

The Union is not about to be dissolved—the country is not going to the dogs—on the contrary, it is only a corrupt and played-out cabal of office-holders and Treasury leeches that are about to be turned off to get their living like honest folks or steal it a little less safely than they have done. That they should howl and perform all manner of unseemly antics, is but natural; but let them rest assured that the People laugh alike at their mock-fears for their country and their real concern for their precious selves. And so, "Good night to Marmion!"

How the Union Is to be Dissolved

Mr. George N. Sanders, one of Mr. Douglas's lieutenants, has sent us a manifesto showing how the Union is to be dissolved in case of Mr. Lincoln's election. Mr. Sanders professes to be opposed to Disunion, but is evidently not opposed to using the Fire-eaters' threats of it as a means of terrifying and bullying the Free States. We therefore print his bugaboo, and shall proceed to dissect it.

Mr. Sanders says:

> "All that the Union men of the South ask of you [Republicans] is to let the South alone."

Then, George, we are happy to assure you that there can be no chance for Disunion, for we are going to do that very thing. The

South *will* be let alone by Mr. Lincoln's Administration—thoroughly, decisively, undeniably. Then what is there to secede on?

Mr. Sanders informs us that the Fire-eaters will not wait to see whether Mr. Lincoln purposes to do them any wrong or not. They will make their bolt under the rule of the Old Public Functionary, lest they should have no chance, or no excuse, after Mr. Lincoln's inauguration. And he adds that the Cotton States have already given us due and formal notice that they will secede in case of Mr. Lincoln's election.

We beg leave to assure Mr. S. that he is entirely mistaken as to the facts. The Cotton States have given no such notice, and they are not going to cut up any such didoes as he presages. A few noisy politicians have exhaled a large amount of unwholesome gas, but the Southern People regard their bravado with silent contempt. Jeff Davis & Co. tried to make Mississippi get ready for Secession nearly ten years ago; and the result was that Jeff was beaten for Governor of that State by so poor a tool as Henry S. Foote. Iverson & Co. tried the same game in Georgia, and were utterly routed under the lead of Howell Cobb. So Sam Houston badly thrashed the Fire-eating crew in Texas only last year. And if they put themselves in the way of another such exercise, they will get served worse in 1861 than they have ever yet been. There will be no call for Mr. Lincoln to put down rebellion and nullification in the South-West; the People of the Cotton States will do that whenever the opportunity is offered them. They are not going to have their mails stopped and their coast blockaded to gratify the mad ambition of a few self-seeking counterfeiters of Pro-Slavery fanaticism. We dare the Fire-eaters to submit the question of Secession or No Secession because of Lincoln's election to the popular vote of their own people. They will be badly beaten in every State but South Carolina, and probably beaten in the popular vote also. . . .

"But what will you do for Cotton?" ask the appalled Sanderses. Why, Sirs, we will buy it and pay for it, just as other nations do—just as we do now. They who grow or hold Cotton want to sell it just as much as those who spin and wear it want to buy it. Not to insist on the fact that the South already owes the North more than would keep the latter overstocked with Cotton for the next two years, we may observe that the South wants what we have to spare just as much as we want her Cotton. If she thinks she can enrich herself by levying an export duty of twenty-five per cent on her great staple, let her try it, by all means: the Cotton-growers of India, Africa, the West Indies and South America will be very much obliged to her. It will be a good thing also for those engaged in pushing the manufacture of flax and other vegetable fibers. Cotton would cease to be the staple of our Seceding States within five years, were they to levy an export duty of twenty-five per cent on it; and that might be better for the South and for mankind. We do not say it would, but it might be.

Plan for Reconstruction

President Andrew Johnson launched his plan for reconstructing the nation after the Civil War when he issued a pair of proclamations on May 29, 1865. Like Lincoln before him, Johnson desired a speedy restoration of the Union, but he was less concerned about the plight of the freed people in the South. The two proclamations reflected his priorities. The first, the Amnesty Proclamation, permitted most ex-rebels to regain their full rights as American citizens upon swearing a loyalty oath. High-ranking military and political leaders and wealthy planters were excluded from the general grant of amnesty, but they could still seek forgiveness by appealing directly to the president for their pardons.

The second proclamation established the terms under which the former Confederate states would be allowed to rejoin the Union. Although the proclamation affected North Carolina only, similar presidential decrees were issued for most of the other states in the weeks that followed. The May 29 edict placed North Carolina under the rule of a provisional governor and required the state to convene a special convention for the purposes of amending its prewar constitution. Once this condition had been complied with, the state would then have all of its former political privileges restored. Noticeably absent from this proclamation was any reference to extending voting rights to blacks.

Whereas the President of the United States, on the 8th day of December, 1863, and on the 26th day of March, 1864, did, with the object to suppress the existing rebellion, to induce all persons to return to their loyalty, and to restore the authority of the United States, issue proclamations offering amnesty and pardon to certain persons who had directly or by implication participated in the said rebellion; and whereas, many persons who had so

From *The Papers of Andrew Johnson*, ed. Paul H. Bergeron, et al. The University of Tennessee Press, (Knoxville, Tenn., 1989), 128–130, 136–138.

engaged in said rebellion have, since the issuance of said proclamations, failed or neglected to take the benefits offered thereby; and whereas many persons who have been justly deprived of all claim to amnesty and pardon thereunder, by reason of their participation, directly or by implication, in said rebellion, and continued hostility to the government of the United States since the date of said proclamation, now desire to apply for and obtain amnesty and pardon:

To the end, therefore, that the authority of the government of the United States may be restored, and that peace, order, and freedom may be established, I, Andrew Johnson, President of the United States, do proclaim and declare that I hereby grant to all persons who have, directly or indirectly, participated in the existing rebellion, except as hereinafter excepted, amnesty and pardon, with restoration of all rights of property, except as to slaves and except in cases where legal proceedings, under the laws of the United States providing for the confiscation of property of persons engaged in rebellion have been instituted; but upon the condition, nevertheless, that every such person shall take and subscribe the following oath, (or affirmation) and thenceforward keep and maintain said oath inviolate; and which oath shall be registered for permanent preservation and shall be of the tenor and effect following, to wit:

I, _____, do solemnly swear (or affirm); in presence of Almighty God, that I will henceforth faithfully support, protect, and defend the Constitution of the United States, and the union of the States thereunder, and that I will in like manner abide by and faithfully support all laws and proclamations which have been made during the existing rebellion with reference to the emancipation of slaves. So help me God.

The following classes of persons are excepted from the benefits of this proclamation: 1st, all who are or shall have been pretended civil or diplomatic officers or otherwise domestic or foreign agents of the pretended Confederate Government; 2nd, all who left judicial stations under the United States to aid the rebellion; 3rd, all who shall have been military or naval officers of said pretended Confederate government above the rank of colonel in the army or lieutenant in the navy; 4th, all who left seats in the Congress of the United States to aid the rebellion; 5th, all who resigned or tendered resignations of their commissions in the Army or Navy of the United States to evade duty in resisting the rebellion; 6th, all who have engaged in any way in treating otherwise than lawfully as prisoners of war persons found in the United States service as officers, soldiers, seamen, or in other capacities; 7th, all persons who have been or are absentees from the United States for the purpose of aiding the rebellion; 8th, all military and naval officers in the Rebel service who were educated by the government in the Military Academy at West Point or the United States Naval Academy; 9th, all persons who held the pretended offices of governors of states in insurrection against the United States; 10th, all persons who left their homes within the jurisdiction and protection of the United States and passed beyond the Federal military lines into the pretended Confederate States for the purpose of aiding the rebellion; 11th, all persons who have been engaged in the destruction of the commerce of the United States upon the high seas and all persons who have made raids into the United States from Canada or been engaged in destroying the commerce of the United States upon the lakes and rivers that separate the British Provinces from the United States; 12th, all persons who, at the time when they seek to obtain the benefits hereof by taking the oath herein prescribed, are in military naval, or civil confinement or custody, or under bonds of the civil, military, or naval authorities, or agents of the United States as prisoners of war, or persons detained for offenses of any kind, either before or after conviction; 13th, all persons who have voluntarily participated in said rebellion and the estimated value of whose taxable property is over twenty thousand dollars; 14th, all persons who have taken the oath of amnesty as prescribed in the President's Proclamation of December 8, A.D. 1863, or an oath of allegiance to the government of the United States since the date of said proclamation and who have not thenceforward kept and maintained the same inviolate.

Provided, that special application may be made to the President for pardon by any person belonging, to the excepted classes, and such clemency will be liberally extended as may be consistent with the facts of the case and the peace and dignity of the United States.

Proclamation Establishing Government for North Carolina, May 29, 1865

WHEREAS the 4th section of the 4th Article of the Constitution of the United States declares that the United States shall guarantee to every State in the Union a republican form of government, and shall protect each of them against invasion and domestic violence; and whereas the President of the United States is, by the Constitution, made commander-in-chief of the army and navy, as well as chief civil executive officer of the United States, and is bound by solemn oath faithfully to execute the office of President of the United States, and to take care that the laws be faithfully executed; and whereas the rebellion which has been waged by a portion of the people of the United States against the properly constituted authority of the Government thereof in the most violent and revolting form, but whose organized and armed forces have now been almost entirely overcome, has, in its revolutionary progress, deprived the people of the State of North Carolina of all civil government: and whereas it becomes necessary and proper to carry out and enforce the obligations of the United States to the people of North Carolina, in securing them in the enjoyment of a republican form of government:

Now, THEREFORE, in obedience to the high and solemn duties imposed upon me by the Constitution of the United States, and for the purpose of enabling the loyal people of said State to organize a State government; whereby justice may be established, domestic tranquility insured, and loyal citizens protected in all of their rights of life, liberty, and property, I, ANDREW JOHNSON, President of the United States and commander-in-chief of the army and navy of the United States, do hereby appoint William W. Holden provisional governor of the State of North Carolina, whose duty it shall be, at the earliest practicable period, to prescribe such rules and regulations as may be necessary and proper for convening a convention, composed of delegates to be chosen by that portion of the people of the said State who are loyal to the United States, and no others, for the purpose of altering or amending the constitution thereof; and with authority to exercise, within the limits of said State, all the powers necessary and proper to enable such loyal people of the State of North Carolina to restore said State to its constitutional relations to the Federal government, and to present such a republican form of State government as will entitle the said State to the guarantee of the United States therefor, and its people to protection by the United States against invasion, insurrection and domestic violence; *provided* that in any election that may be hereafter held for choosing delegates to any State convention as aforesaid, no person shall be qualified as an elector, or shall be eligible as a member of such convention, unless he shall have previously taken and subscribed to the oath of amnesty, as set forth in the President's proclamation of May 29, A.D. 1865, and is a voter qualified as prescribed by the constitution and laws of the State of North Carolina in force immediately before the 20th of May, A.D. 1861, the date of the so-called ordinance of secession; and the said convention, when convened, or the legislature that may be thereafter assembled, will prescribe the qualifications of electors, and the eligibility of persons to hold office under the constitution and laws of the State, a power the people of the several States comprising the Federal Union have rightfully exercised from the origin of the government to the present time.

And I do hereby direct:

First. That the military commander of the department, and all officers in the military and naval service, aid and assist the said Provisional Governor in carrying into effect this proclamation, and they are enjoined to abstain from, in any way, hindering, impeding, or discouraging the loyal people from the organization of a State government as herein authorized.

Second. That the Secretary of State proceed to put in force all laws of the United States, the administration whereof belongs to the State Department, applicable to the geographical limits aforesaid.

Third. That the Secretary of the Treasury proceed to nominate for appointment assessors of taxes, and collectors of customs and revenue, and such other officers of the Treasury Department as are authorized by law, and put in execution the revenue laws of the United States within the provisional limits aforesaid. In making appointments, the preference shall be given to qualified loyal persons residing in the districts where their respective duties are to be performed. But if suitable residents of the district shall not be found, then persons residing in other States or districts shall be appointed.

Fourth. That the Postmaster General proceed to establish post offices and post routes, and put into execution the postal laws of the United States within the said State, giving to loyal residents the preference of appointments: but if suitable residents are not found, then to appoint agents, etc., from other States.

Fifth. That the district judge for the judicial district in which North Carolina is included, proceed to hold courts within said State, in accordance with the provisions of the Act of Congress. The Attorney General will instruct the proper officers to libel, and bring to judgment, confiscation and sale, property subject to confiscation, and enforce the administration of justice within said State in all matters within the cognizance and jurisdiction of the Federal Courts.

Sixth. That the Secretary of the Navy take possession of all public property belonging to the Navy Department within said geographical limits, and put in operation all acts of Congress in relation to naval affairs having application to said State.

Seventh. That the Secretary of the Interior put in force all laws relating to the Interior Department applicable to the geographical limits aforesaid.

The Black Codes and Reconstruction

Under President Andrew Johnson's plan of reconstruction, Southerners were given a wide degree of latitude in restoring their governments. Left to their own devices, the former confederate states drafted constitutions that denied blacks the right to vote. Predictably, the all-white legislatures elected under these constitutions then proceeded to pass very repressive black codes that abridged the rights of the freedpeople in other fundamental ways. Among the worst of these statutes was the Mississippi Code. As can be seen from the following excerpt, the code granted blacks a few token legal rights, but on the whole the law amounted to little more than slavery by another name.

An Act to confer Civil Rights on Freedmen . . .

Section 1. . . . [A]ll freedmen, free negroes and mulattoes may sue and be sued . . . in all the courts of law and equity of this State, and may acquire personal property . . . by descent or purchase, and may dispose of the same, in the same manner, and to the same extent that white persons may: Provided that the provisions of this section shall not be construed as to allow any freedman, free negro or mulatto to rent or lease any lands or tenements, except in incorporated towns or cities in which places the corporate authorities shall control the same. . . .

Section 5. . . . [E]very freedman, free negro and mulatto, shall . . . . have a lawful home or employment, and shall have written evidence thereof. . . .

Section 7. . . . [E]very civil officer shall, and every person may arrest and carry back to his or her legal employer any freeman, free negro or mulatto, who shall have quit the service of his or her employer before the expiration of his or her term of service without good cause. . . .

From *Laws of the State of Mississippi* . . . (1866), 82–84, 91, 92.

Frederick Douglass Argues in Favor of Black Suffrage

Following the passage of the Fourteenth Amendment, which guaranteed civil rights for all citizens of the United States, including equal protection under the law, the Republican-controlled Congress next set its sights on Radical Reconstruction. In the Congressional elections of 1866, Republican candidates had won a vast majority of seats, almost a three-to-one margin in both the House and the Senate. They believed their landslide victory gave them a mandate for Radical Reconstruction, the complete overhauling of the political, social, economic and cultural system of the South. After they successfully passed the Reconstruction Act of 1867 (with a two-thirds majority over President Johnson's veto) and the eventual impeachment of Johnson, the Congress turned their attention to the issue of the right to vote for blacks. Former abolitionists such as Frederick Douglass spoke out very strongly in favor of a constitutional amendment guaranteeing that blacks had the right to vote. Without this fundamental, democratic right, blacks could not be fully free. He stated that the right to vote was necessary if the blacks were to be treated as equals, if blacks were to be educated, and if blacks were to rid themselves of the stigma of inferiority. Note whose lack of suffrage Douglass also referred to in his impassioned speech that follows. The Fifteenth Amendment, guaranteeing the right to vote for adult males, regardless of race, color, or previous servitude, was passed by Congress in February of 1869, after Ulysses S. Grant had already been elected President.

From *The Frederick Douglass Papers—Series One: Speeches, Debates, and Interviews, Vol. 4: 1864–80,* ed. John W. Blassingame and John R. McKivigan, (New Haven, 1991), 62–63, 66–68.

Frederick Douglass Argues in Favor of Black Suffrage

I have had but one idea for the last three years to present to the American people. . . . I am for the "immediate, unconditional and universal" enfranchisement of the black man, in every State of the Union. (Loud applause.) Without this, his liberty is a mockery; without this, you might as well almost retain the old name of slavery for his condition; for, in fact, if he is not the slave of the individual master, he is the slave of society, and holds his liberty as a privilege, not as a right. . . .

It may be asked, "Why do you want it? Some men have got along very well without it. Women have not this right." Shall we justify one wrong by another? That is a sufficient answer. Shall we at this moment justify the deprivation of the negro of the right to vote because some one else is deprived of that privilege? I hold that women as well as men have the right to vote (applause), and my heart and my voice go with the movement to extend suffrage to woman. But that question rests upon another basis than that on which our right rests. We may be asked, I say, why we want it. I will tell you why we want it. We want it because it is our right, first of all. (Applause.) No class of men can, without insulting their own nature, be content with any deprivation of their rights. We want it, again, as a means for educating our race. Men are so constituted that they derive their conviction of their own possibilities largely from the estimate formed of them by others. If nothing is expected of a people, that people will find it difficult to contradict that expectation. By depriving us of suffrage, you affirm our incapacity to form an intelligent judgment respecting public men and public measures; you declare before the world that we are unfit to exercise the elective franchise, and by this means lead us to undervalue ourselves, to put a low estimate upon ourselves, and to feel that we have no possibilities like other men. . . . [H]ere, where universal suffrage is the rule, where that is the fundamental idea of the government, to rule us out is to make us an exception, to brand us with the stigma of inferiority, and to invite to our heads the missiles of those about us. Therefore I want the franchise for the black man.

. . . It is said that we are ignorant; I admit it. But if we know enough to be hung, we know enough to vote. If the negro knows enough to pay taxes to support the Government, he knows enough to vote—taxation and representation should go together. If he knows enough to shoulder a musket and fight for the flag, fight for the Government, he knows enough to vote. If he knows as much when he is sober as an Irishman knows when drunk, he knows enough to vote, on good American principles. (Laughter and applause.)

... What have you asked the black men of the South, the black men of the whole country to do? Why, you have asked them to incur the deadly enmity of their masters, in order to befriend you and to befriend this government. You have asked us to call down, not only upon ourselves, but upon our children's children, the deadly hate of the entire Southern people. You have called upon us to turn our backs upon our masters, to abandon their cause and espouse yours; to turn against the South and in favor of the North; to shoot down the Confederacy and uphold the flag— the American flag. . . . And now, what do you propose to do when you come to make peace? To reward your enemies, and trample in the dust your friends? . . . Do you mean to give your enemies the right to vote, and take it away from your friends? . . . In time of trouble we are citizens. Shall we be citizens in war, and aliens in peace? Would that be just?

... What I ask for the negro is not benevolence, not pity, not sympathy, but simply justice.

Debate over the Civil Rights Act of 1866

In the immediate aftermath of the Civil War, the issue of political rights for blacks took center stage in the U.S. Congress and became a major point of contention between one group of Congressmen, Radical Republicans, and the president, Andrew Johnson. After the assassination of Lincoln, plans for how the government should deal with the defeated South took a more punishing turn, from Lincoln's proposed reconciliation to radical reconstruction. Radical members of the Republican Party wanted the entire social and political structure of the South to be altered, to ensure that whites and blacks were truly seen and treated as equals. Their goals clashed directly with the path proposed by President Johnson, himself a former slaveholder from Tennessee, which emphasized rapid rebuilding of state governments and included hundreds of pardons for former Confederate soldiers and government members. While both Radical Republicans and President Johnson agreed on the necessity of the Thirteenth Amendment, which abolished slavery, they did not agree that blacks should be granted full civil and economic rights.

The Civil Rights Act of 1866 described the rights that blacks were entitled to, including property ownership and standing in court. It also stated that the federal government had the authority to take to court those who violated these rights. Essentially, this legislation warned southern states that their attempts to avoid compliance with this law would be prosecuted to the fullest extent of the law, and that this prosecution would be taken out of the hands of state courts, which could not be fully trusted. Congress passed this bill in March of 1866, before southern Congressmen had been allowed to return to the legislature. President Johnson vetoed the bill, a huge victory for Democrats over Radical Republicans. But the following year, a tougher, more comprehensive version of the Civil Rights Act was introduced in Congress, which became the Fourteenth Amend-

From *The Congressional Globe*, 39th Congress, 1st Session, 1679–81 (27 March 1866).

ment to the Constitution. In the following selection, Johnson explained the reasons why it was necessary, in his opinion, to veto the Act.

Debate over African American Rights: The Civil Rights Act

Republicans insisted that all Americans, regardless of color, were entitled to the basic rights of citizenship. In response to the black codes and other deprivations of rights in many states, North and South, they proposed a civil rights act.

Congress passed the Civil Rights bill on 15 March 1866, with southern congressmen still not permitted to take their seats. The bill made it a crime for anyone acting "under the color of law" or "custom" to deny the rights specified in Section 1. It also allowed those denied their rights in the states to transfer civil and criminal cases to the federal courts.

President Johnson vetoed the Civil Rights bill, giving his reasons in the message excerpted below from *The Congressional Globe,* 39th Congress, 1st Session, 1679–81 (27 March 1866).

To the Senate of the United States:

I regret that the bill which has passed both Houses of Congress . . . contains provisions which I cannot approve, consistently with my sense of duty to the whole people and my obligations to the Constitution of the United States. . . .

By the first section of the bill, all persons born in the United States, and not subject to any foreign Power, excluding Indians not taxed, are declared to be citizens of the United States. This provision comprends the Chinese of the Pacific States, Indians subject to taxation, the people called Gypsies, as well as the entire race designated as blacks, people of color, negroes, mulattoes, and persons of African blood. . . .

The right of Federal citizenship thus to be conferred on the several excepted races before mentioned, is now, for the first time, proposed to be given by law. If, as is claimed by many, all persons who are native-born already are, by virtue of the Constitution, citizens of the United States, the passage of the pending bill cannot be necessary to make them such. If, on the other hand, such persons are not citizens, as may be assumed from the proposed legislation to make them such, the grave question presents itself, whether when eleven of the thirty-six States are unrepresented in Congress, at this time it is sound policy to make our entire colored population and all other excepted classes citizens of the United States? Four millions of them have just emerged from slavery into freedom. Can it be reasonably supposed that they possess the requisite qualifications to entitle them to all the privileges and immunities of citizens of the United States? . . .

Thus a perfect equality of the white and black races is attempted to be fixed by Federal law in every State of the Union, over the vast field of State jurisdiction covered by these enumerated rights. . . . In the exercise of State policy over matters exclusively affecting the people of each State, it has frequently been thought expedient to discriminate between the two races. By the statutes of some of the States, northern as well as southern, it is enacted, for instance, that no white person shall intermarry with a negro or mulatto. . . .

Hitherto every subject embraced in the enumeration of rights contained in this bill has been considered as exclusively belonging to the States. They all relate to the internal policy and economy of the respective States. . . .

In all our history, in all our experience as a people living under Federal and State law, no such system as that contemplated by the details of this bill has ever before been proposed or adopted. They establish, for the security of the colored race, safeguards which go infinitely beyond any that the General Government has ever provided for the white race. In fact, the distinction of race and color is, by the bill, made to operate in favor of the colored and against the white race. They interfere with the municipal legislation of the States, with the relations existing exclusively between a State and its citizens, or between inhabitants of the same State_an absorption and assumption of power by the General Government which, if acquiesced in, must sap and destroy our federative system of limited powers, and break down the barriers which preserve the rights of the States. It is another step, or rather stride, towards centralization and the concentration of all legislative powers in the national Government. The tendency of the bill must be to resuscitate the spirit of rebellion, and to arrest the progress of those influences which are more closely drawing around the States the bonds of union and peace.

Opposition to Black Suffrage During Reconstruction

In March of 1867, the U.S. Congress passed the Radical Reconstruction Act. This Act, which was much harsher than earlier versions that had been proposed by both President Lincoln and President Johnson, set up the military occupation of the South by federal troops. It divided the ten former Confederate states who had refused to ratify the Fourteenth Amendment (Tennessee was the exception) into five military districts, each supervised by a Union general. The generals were given the responsibility of supervising the drafting of the new state constitutions to ensure that blacks were not excluded from this process. The new state constitutions had to include guarantees of the right to vote for adult black males. The new constitutions had to be ratified by a majority of voters and approved by the U.S. Congress. The ten former Confederate states who had not yet been re-admitted to the Union also had to ratify the Fourteenth Amendment before Congress would consider their reinstatement. Initially, the Radical Reconstruction Act was vetoed by President Johnson, but Congress overrode his veto with a two-thirds majority. The stage was set for political battle in the South. As the following petition to the U.S. House of Representatives from a group of whites in Alabama illustrates, many white Southerners were vehemently opposed to extending suffrage to blacks. On what grounds do the petitioners seek to deny blacks the right to vote? How do they justify their point of view?

The White people of Alabama send this their humble petition. We beseech your Honorable Bodies to withdraw yourselves from the influence of the passions and contests of the hour, and contemplate for a brief period, our miserable condition . . . .

From the Petition and Memorial File, Records of the House of Representatives, 40th Cong., Record Group 233, National Archives, Washington D.C.

... [I]t is well known by all who have knowledge on the subject,—that while the negroes of the South may be more intelligent and of better morals than those of the same race in any other part of the world ... —yet they are in the main, ignorant generally, wholly unacquainted with the principles of free Governments, improvident, disinclined to work, credulous yet suspicious, dishonest, untruthful, incapable of self-restraint, and easily impelled by want or incited by false and specious counsels, into folly and crime. ...

Are these the people in whom should be vested the high governmental functions of establishing institutions and enacting and enforcing laws, to prevent crime, protect property, preserve peace and order in society, and promote industry, enterprise and civilization in Alabama, and the power and honor of the United States? Without property, without industry, without any regard for reputation, without controul over their own caprices and strong passions, and without fear of punishment under laws, by courts and through juries which are ... created by and composed of ... themselves, or of those whom they elect,—how can it be otherwise than that they will bring, to the great injury of themselves as well as of us and our children,—blight, crime, ruin and barbarism on this fair land? ...

Will you, nearly three years after the war has ended, ... suffer a whole State full of your kindred civilized white inhabitants, not only those who had opposed the Government, but women, children, and loyal men who had adhered to it,—to be thus consigned over to the horrid rule of barbarian negroes! ...

... [D]o not, we implore you, abdicate your own rule over us, by transferring us to the blighting, brutalizing and unnatural dominion of an alien and inferior race: A race which has never shown sufficient administrative capacity for the good government of even the tribes, into which it has always been broken up in its native seats; and which in all ages, has itself furnished slaves for all the other races of the earth.

Violent Resistance to Equal Rights
During Reconstruction

Confronted by Congress' determination to use the powers of the federal government to secure equal civil and political rights for blacks after the Civil War, conservative white Southerners turned to violence. Paramilitary groups such as the Ku Klux Klan sprang up throughout the South. The Klan and other white-supremacist bands targeted black leaders, schools, and churches, as well as some white politicians, using terror as a political weapon to cow their opponents. The following documents describe Klan activities from a variety of perspectives. In the first, a black share-cropper bears vivid witness to the Klan's brutal tactics of intimidation. In the second and third, an ex-Senator from South Carolina and a lawyer, respectively, present their views on the underlying racial animosity that fueled the white-on-black violence in the South.

[Amzi Rainey's Testimony]

I looked out of the window, and I see some four or five disguised men coming up, and I ran up in the loft, and they came on; come to the door; and when they come to the door, they commenced beating and knocking. "God damn you, open the door! open the door! open the door!" . . . and my wife run to one of the doors and they knocked the top hinges off of the first, and she run across the house to the other, and agin that time they got the two hinges knocked off the other door, and the bolt held the door from

---

From *Proceedings in the Ku Klux Klan Trials, at Columbia, S.C. in the United States Circuit Court, November Term, 1871,* (Columbia, S.C., 1872), 279–280; and *Testimony Taken by the Joint Select Committee to Inquire into the Condition of Affairs in the Late Insurrectionary States,* vol. 1 and 2, South Carolina, (Washington, D.C., 1872) 1:446, 449, 2:796–797.

falling, and she got it open . . . and when they come in, they struck her four or five licks before they said a word . . . .

They asked her who lived here. She said, "Rainey—Amzi Rainey." "What Amzi Rainey? What Amzi Rainey?" And she said, "Amzi Rainey," and he struck her another lick, and says: "Where is he? God damn him, where is he?" And she says: "I don't know." And one said: "O, I smell him, God damn him; he has gone up in the loft." He says: "We'll kill him, too," and they come up then. . . .

I was in a box, and they said: "Oh, he is in this box, God damn him, I smell him; we'll kill him!" and the other says: "Don't kill him yet;" and they took me down. This man that struck my wife first, ran back to her and says: "God damn her, I will kill her now; I will kill her out;" and the one that went after me, he says: "Don't kill her;" and he commenced beating her then; struck her some four or five more licks, and then run back and struck me; he run back to her then, and drawed his pistol, and says: "Now, I am going to blow your damn brains out;" and the one by me threw the pistol up, and says: "Don't kill her." He aimed to strike me over the head, and struck me over the back and sunk me right down. Then, after he had done that, my little daughter—she was back in the room with the other little children—he says: "I am going to kill him;" and she runs out of the room, and says: "Don't kill my pappy; please don't kill my pappy!" He shoved her back, and says; "You go back in the room, you God damned little bitch; I will blow your brains out!" and fired and shot her . . . .

. . . [A]nd then they took me . . . [o]ff up the road, about a hundred and fifty yards; and they wanted to kill me up there, and one said, "No, don't kill him, let's talk a little to him first." Then, he asked me which way did I vote. I told him I voted the Radical [Republican] ticket. "Well," he says, "now you raise your hand and swear that you will never vote another Radical ticket, and I will not let them kill you." And he made me stand and raise my hand before him and my God, that I never would vote another Radical ticket . . . .

[Ex-Senator Chesnut's Testimony]

There is a deep dissatisfaction . . . in the hearts of the people of this State. . . . Three hundred thousand white people here around us, who had been accustomed to self-government, who had had an orderly government and had participated in that government, whose property had been taxed only by those who paid the taxes, beheld the whole thing suddenly subverted and themselves placed at the mercy of ignorance and of corruption .... These people are under an absolute despotism, and you will find that the countries where governments are most despotic are precisely those in which secret associations appear; small associations of parties ardent and seeking redress for real or fancied wrongs which they think cannot be avenged through the government. That is the true secret of this thing.

[Simpson Bobo's Testimony]

We have gone through one of the most remarkable changes in our relations to each other that has been known, perhaps, in the history of the world. The negro that was our slave has become our master suddenly . . . ; the bottom rail has got on top . . .—any one living here and knowing all about it, will be surprised that there has been as little disturbance as there has been. If the Government had give us a good government; if it had let us remain under a military government, none of these troubles would have been in this country. . . . There have been a great many . . . cases of the whipping of negroes in this county and some of the adjoining counties, some for one purpose and some for another. I think some of them have been political, and some of them have been with a view of answering special ends. . . . [T]he lower class of white people have a great prejudice against the negro, because he is a competitor for common labor, and wherever they come into collision, these fellows form themselves into a Klan, and take up negroes that come in their way, and punish them. . . . [F]or instance, a white man rents a tract of land to a negro. Some white man wants to get the land. The owner prefers giving it to the negro. For the purpose of punishing the negro, he will then get up a parcel of neighbors, and in disguise they will go and whip the negro half to death.

"The Vanishing Indian"

In the years between the end of the Civil War and 1900, the federal government greatly reduced the amount of land held by the western Native American tribes. This process involved the systematic "re-negotiation" of dozens of treaties, usually under duress after those treaties had been breached by aggressive white settlers and/or after bursts of warfare between federal troops and the tribes. This had been the basic pattern of interaction between American governments and Native American tribes for hundreds of years. By the late 1800s, however, this longstanding pattern was exacerbated by the growing sense among white Americans, even those who considered themselves friendly toward Native Americans, that Native American cultures—and perhaps Native Americans themselves—were doomed to succumb to the westward expansion of modern America. This view of the "Indian problem" was shaped by Social Darwinism, by racism, and by the desire of white settlers to exploit the land and mineral resources encompassed within Indian reservations.

The "solution" eventually chosen by the federal government was assimilation. Federal policy toward Native Americans in these years sought consciously to discourage or destroy Native American cultural practices, including tribal social organization, and encourage adoption of "civilized" (i.e., white American) patterns of living by individual Native Americans. It also sought consciously to reduce the acreage encompassed by the reservations and open up the land to white settlement and development. The Dawes General Allotment Act of 1887 encompassed these twin purposes. The Dawes Act called for division of reservation lands into allotments held as private property by individual Native Americans, to be intensively farmed or otherwise "improved" in Jeffersonian fashion; remaining lands could then be opened to white settlement. Here, Massachusetts Senator Henry L. Dawes, the act's spon-

From *Proceedings of the Lake Mohonk Conference Fifth Avenue Meeting (1887)*, 68.

sor, explains his rationale to an 1887 meeting of the Lake Mohonk Conference (a self-styled "Friends of the Indian" organization).

I feel that the Indian is to-day wrestling with his own fate. That he will pass away as an Indian, I don't doubt, and that very rapidly. It will be into citizenship, and into a place among the citizens of this land, or it will be into a vagabond and a tramp. He is to disappear as an Indian of the past; there is no longer any room for such an Indian in this country; he cannot find a place. The Indian of the past has no place to live in in this country. . . . The greed [of white people] for the land has made it utterly impossible to preserve it for the Indian. He must take his place where you have undertaken to put him, or he must go a vagabond throughout this country, and it is for you and me to say which it shall be. He cannot choose for himself, and he does not know where the ways are. However willing he may be, it is for you and me to guide him to this.

Illustration of the Temperance Movement

One of the major reform movements of the Progressive era, the temperance movement underscored the willingness of reformers to resort to government interventionism to solve social problems. (Courtesy of the Library of Congress.)

Professionalism and Social Activism

Strongly influenced by evangelical Protestantism and by his graduate studies in Germany, Richard T. Ely (1854–1943) was the primary founder of the American Economic Association and the chief exponent of its philosophy of "New Economics": the critical role of government as a vehicle for human progress, greater use of historical and empirical studies in place of the theories of classical economics, and amelioration of the conflict between capital and labor through the collaborative intervention of government, church, and other agencies. He was also an important pioneer of the Social Gospel, author of The Social Aspects of Christianity, *and teacher to hundreds of economists and social scientists who became community activists and government officials. In his autobiography,* Ground Under Our Feet, *Ely describes the formation and principles of the American Economic Association.*

When it became evident that the "Society for the Study of National Economy" could not be established, I undertook to draw up a project for the formation of a society to be called "The American Economic Association," which should be broad enough to appeal to all the younger economists who, irrespective of their personal views, felt the stirring of the new life in economics and who wished to unite in order to secure complete liberty of thought and discussion, even if their thought led them to "unorthodox" conclusions. In the statement of our "objects" and "declaration of principles" I retained the central idea of the authors of the constitution of the "Society for the Study of National Economy," namely, that the dogma of "laissez faire" should be abandoned by our leaders. My "program," was a much

From "Sowing the Seeds," by Richard T. Ely, in *Ground Under Our Feet*, Macmillan, (New York, 1938), copyright © 1938 by the Estate of Richard T. Ely, 135–160.

simpler one and differed from theirs in two important particulars. In the first place, it emphasized historical and statistical study rather than deductive speculation, and, in the second place, it laid less stress on government intervention and, on the whole, was "toned down" in the direction of conservatism. It was designed to attract as many members as possible. The prospectus sent out read as follows:

American Economic Association

Objects of This Association

I. The encouragement of economic research.
II. The publication of economic monographs.
III. The encouragement of perfect freedom in all economic discussion.
IV. The establishment of a bureau of information designed to aid all members with friendly counsels in their economic studies.

Platform

1. We regard the state as an educational and ethical agency whose positive aid is an indispensable condition of human progress. While we recognize the necessity of individual initiative in industrial life, we hold that the doctrine of laissez faire is unsafe in politics and unsound in morals; and that it suggests an inadequate explanation of the relations between the state and the citizens.
2. We do not accept the final statements which characterized the political economy of a past generation; for we believe that political economy is still in the first stages of its scientific development, and we look not so much to speculation as to an impartial study of actual conditions of economic life for the satisfactory accomplishment of that development. We seek the aid of statistics in the present, and of history in the past.
3. We hold that the conflict of labor and capital has brought to the front a vast number of social problems whose solution is impossible without the united efforts of church, state, and science.

4. In the study of the policy of government, especially with respect to restrictions on trade and to protection of domestic manufactures, we take no partisan attitude. We are convinced that one of the chief reasons why greater harmony has not been attained is because economists have been too ready to assert themselves as advocates. We believe in a progressive development of economic conditions which must be met by corresponding changes of policy.

The Character of American Citizens

As the twentieth century dawned, President Theodore Roosevelt spoke often about the nature of American national character. In an era of enormous fortunes and monopoly capitalism, he feared for the future of a nation that focused exclusively on material well-being. To Roosevelt, prosperity was simply a component of all that was distinctive about the United States. If the country turned away from the hardship and dangers of life, it would lose its national soul as well as its right to command respect on the international stage.

Roosevelt's worldview centered upon a concept that he called the "strenuous life," an existence filled with toil and effort. Roosevelt employed his concept to define the obligations that citizens have to one another and to themselves, tying it to the moral foundations of democratic society. Healthy states can only exist, he asserts in this speech from 1907, if the character of citizens is formed by wholesome and vigorous lives. The government should create a level playing field and obey a duty to the nation by encouraging hard work.

From his seventh annual message to Congress, December 4, 1907

When our tax laws are revised the question of an income tax and an inheritance tax should receive the careful attention of our legislators. In my judgment both of these taxes should be part of our system of federal taxation. . . . The inheritance tax, however, is both a far better method of taxation and far more important for

From Willis Fletcher Johnson, ed. *Theodore Roosevelt: Addresses and Papers*, Sun Dial Classics, (New York, 1908), 408–413.

the purpose of having the fortunes of the country bear in proportion to their increase in size a corresponding increase and burden of taxation. The government has the absolute right to decide as to the terms upon which a man shall receive a bequest. . . . A heavy progressive tax upon a very large fortune is in no way such a tax upon thrift or industry as a light tax would be upon a small fortune. No advantage comes either to the country as a whole or to the individuals inheriting the money by permitting the transmission in their entirety of the enormous fortunes which would be affected by such a tax, and as an incident to its function of revenue raising such a tax would help to preserve a measurable quality of opportunity for the people of the generations growing to manhood. We have not the slightest sympathy with that socialistic idea which would try to put laziness, thriftlessness and inefficiency on a par with industry, thrift, and efficiency. . . . Such a theory, if ever adopted, would mean the ruin of the entire country—a ruin which would bear heaviest upon the weakest, upon those least able to shift for themselves. . . . Our aim is to recognize what Lincoln pointed out—the fact that there are some respects in which men are obviously not equal—but also to insist that there should be an equality of self-respect and of mutual respect, an equality of rights before the law, and at least, an approximate equality in the conditions under which each man obtains the chance to show the stuff that is in him. . . .

[I]n any community with the solid, healthy qualities which make up a really great nation the bulk of the people should do work which calls for the exercise of both body and mind. Progress cannot permanently exist in the abandonment of physical labor, but in the development of physical labor, so that it shall represent more and more the work of the trained mind in the trained body. Our school system is gravely defective in so far as it puts a premium upon mere literary training, and tends, therefore, to train the boy away from the farm and the workshop. . . . It should be one of our prime objects to put both the farmer and the mechanic on a higher plane of efficiency and reward, so as to increase their effectiveness in the economic world, and therefore the dignity, the remuneration and the power of their positions in the social world.

No growth of cities, no growth of wealth, can make up for any loss in either the number or the character of the farming population. . . . We cannot afford to lose the pre-eminently typical American, the farmer who owns his own medium sized farm. To have his place taken by either a class of small peasant proprietors or by a class of great landlords with tenant farmed estates would be a veritable calamity. The growth of our cities is a good thing, but only in so far as it does not mean a growth at the expense of the country farmer.

"The Race Question"

It is the feeling of intelligent and self-supporting negroes that the victory of JOHNSON over JEFFRIES will prove a misfortune to their race because it will spread the ambition of young colored men to attain like achievements. As one of these remarked on the news of the fight: "We don't need fighters, we need workers." On the other hand it is obvious that the immediate effect of the fight was to stir the animosity of the lower class of whites all over the country, and though this will doubtless be a passing impulse, it is, so far as it goes, regrettable for both races.

But there is another view of the matter which will appeal to the independent judgment of all fair-minded white men in all sections of the country. It is that the negro, in the low arena in which he was challenged by the white man, has held his part with entire credit. JOHNSON showed not only that he had greater available strength and endurance than JEFFRIES, but that he brought to his task greater intelligence and skill, a sounder judgment, equal courage, and a perfectly fair, manly, and honorable standard of behavior. Surrounded by a crowd among whom he had but few friends and in which there were many enemies, he was from the first as courteous as he was brave. He performed an essentially brutal task in as decent a manner as was practicable, respected all the conventions, and, though goaded by insults, betrayed no savagery. By the tests the white man had elected to apply the black was the "better man" in every sense. However disappointing and irritating that may be to those who had longed to see "the nigger licked," it cannot but have some influence on their view of the inherent relations of the two races...

It may strengthen the feeling that has slowly been growing in all parts of the country, and most in those parts where the "negro

Reprinted from *The New York Times*, July 6, 1910.

problem" is most acute, that it is by far the best for both races that the blacks should have the greatest practicable chance to work and live well and to build up for themselves the kind of character that comes with honest prosperity. This feeling does not tend toward what is generally spoken of as "social equality." It is entertained by multitudes of both whites and blacks who profoundly believe in the wisdom and need of the preservation of race integrity. Perhaps the most significant feature in connection with the spread of the feeling is the steady growth among the blacks of a definite race pride, analogous to that among the whites, which is slowly but constantly tending toward a social organization within the race similar to that existing in the other races.

The basis of this possible-solution of the race problem is the progress of the blacks in industrial efficiency, and the conditions of this progress are justice and education, the justice that demands, outside of social relations, the same treatment for one color as for the other, and the education that best fits is recipients for work. It is quite within the range of reasonable expectation that the indirect influence of the black man's victory in the prize ring, where the conditions of strife were rudely but practically framed on the basis of equality and fairness, may be to stimulate respect for equality and fairness in more respectable competitions. In that case an occurrence in itself ignoble enough may prove to have a redeeming effect.

The Second KKK

After World War I, immigrants surged into the United States, most of them from southern and eastern Europe. Unlike the old wave of immigrants from northern Europe, this vast number of new arrivals, with their strange languages and unfamiliar customs, frightened many Americans. Nativism rose to new heights as Congress passed emergency restrictions on immigration. Meanwhile, moral standards changed as sexuality became something to be flaunted, women celebrated their new freedom, and both sexes ignored the Prohibition upon alcohol. Outside of the cities, a backlash developed against the new culture.

The Ku Klux Klan revived in 1915 and flourished among insecure Protestants who longed to protect their way of life from African-Americans, Roman Catholics, Jews, and immigrants. The Klan flogged bootleggers and men who beat their wives. It never achieved much politically and when its leader, D. C. Stevenson went to jail in 1925 for viciously raping a young woman, the Klan faded away. The following extract, written in 1931 by journalist Frederick Lewis Allen, presents on one level, the facts behind the rise and decline of the Klan. On another level, however, the selections reveal where Allen stood in the clash of cultures that the Klan embodied.

The Klan had been founded as far back as 1915 by a Georgian named Colonel William Joseph Simmons, but its first five years had been lean. When 1920 arrived, Colonel Simmons had only a few hundred members in his amiable patriotic and fraternal order, which drew its inspiration from the Ku-Klux Klan of

Reconstruction days and stood for white supremacy and senti-mental Southern idealism in general. But in 1920 Simmons put the task of organizing the Order into the hands of one Edward Y. Clarke of the Southern Publicity Association. Clarke's gifts of salesmanship . . . were prodigious. The time was ripe for the Klan, and he knew it. Not only could it be represented to potential members as the defender of the white against the black, of Gentile against Jew, and of Protestant against Catholic, and thus trade on all the newly inflamed fears of the credulous small-towner, but its white robe and hood, its flaming cross, its secrecy, and the prepos-terous vocabulary of its ritual could be made the vehicle for all that infantile love of hocus-pocus and mummery, that lust for secret adventure, which survives in the adult whose lot is cast in drab places. Here was a chance to dress up the village bigot and let him be a Knight of the Invisible Empire. The formula was per-fect. And there was another inviting fact to be borne in mind. Well organized, such an Order could be made a paying proposition.

The salesmen of memberships were given the entrancing title of Kleagles; the country was divided into Realms headed by King Kleagles, and the Realms into Domains headed by Grand Goblins; Clarke himself, as chief organizer, became Imperial Kleagle, and the art of nomenclature reached its fantastic pinnacle in the title bestowed upon Colonel Simmons: he became the Imperial Wiz-ard. A membership cost ten dollars; and as four of this went into the pocket of the Kleagle who made the sale, it was soon apparent that a diligent Kleagle need not fear the wolf at the door. Kleagling became one of the profitable industries of the decade. The King Kleagle of the Realm and Grand Goblin of the Domain took a small rake-off from the remaining six dollars of the mem-bership fee, and the balance poured into the Imperial Treasury at Atlanta.

. . . [In 1921] Simmons was succeeded as Imperial Wizard by a Texas dentist named Hiram Wesley Evans, who referred to him-self, perhaps with some justice, as "the most average man in America"; but a humming sales organization had been built up and the Klan continued to grow. It grew, in fact, with such inordi-nate rapidity that early in 1924 its membership had reached . . . the staggering figure of nearly four and a half million. It came to wield great political power, dominating for a time the seven states of Oregon, Oklahoma, Texas, Arkansas, Indiana, Ohio, and Cali-fornia. Its chief strongholds were the New South, the Middle

West, and the Pacific coast, but it had invaded almost every part of the country and had even reached the gates of that stronghold of Jewry, Catholicism, and sophistication, New York City. So far had Clarke's genius and the hospitable temper of the times carried it.

The objects of the Order as stated in its Constitution were "to unite white male persons, native-born Gentile citizens of the United States of America, who owe no allegiance of any nature to any foreign government, nation, institution, sect, ruler, person, or people; whose morals are good, whose reputations and vocations are exemplary . . . to cultivate and promote patriotism toward our Civil Government; to practice an honorable Klanishess toward each other; to exemplify a practical benevolence; to shield the sanctity of the home and the chastity of womanhood; to maintain forever white supremacy, to reach and faithfully inculcate a high spiritual philosophy through an exalted ritualism, and by a practical devotion to conserve, protect, and maintain the distinctive institutions, rights, privileges, principles, traditions and ideals of a pure Americanism."

Thus the theory. In practice the "pure Americanism" varied with the locality. At first, in the South, white supremacy was the Klan's chief objective, but as time went on and the organization grew and spread, opposition to the Jew and above all to the Catholic proved the best talking point for Kleagles in most localities. Nor did the methods of the local Klan organizations usually suggest the possession of a "high spiritual philosophy." These local organizations were largely autonomous and beyond control from Atlanta. They were drawn, as a rule, mostly from the less educated and less disciplined elements of the white Protestant community. ("You think the influential men belong here?" commented an outspoken observer in an Indiana city. "Then look at their shoes when they march in parade. The sheet doesn't cover the shoes.") Though Imperial Wizard Evans inveighed against lawlessness, the members of the local Klans were not always content with voting against allowing children to attend parochial schools, or voting against Catholic candidates for office, or burning fiery crosses on the hilltop back of the town to show the niggers that the whites meant business. The secrecy of the Klan was an invitation to more direct action.

If a white girl reported that a colored man had made improper advances to her—even if the charge were unsupported and based on nothing more than a neurotic imagination—a white-sheeted band might spirit the Negro off to the woods and "teach him a lesson" with tar and feathers or with the whip. If a white man stood up for a Negro in a race quarrel, he might be kidnapped and beaten up. If a colored woman refused to sell her land at an arbitrary price which she considered too low, and a Klansman wanted the land, she might receive the K. K. K. ultimatum—sell or be thrown out. Klan members would boycott Jewish merchants, refuse to hire Catholic boys, refuse to rent their houses to Catholics. A hideous tragedy in Louisiana, where five men were kidnapped and later found bound with wire and drowned in a lake, was laid to Klansmen. R. A. Patton, writing in *Current History*, reported a grim series of brutalities from Alabama: "A lad whipped with branches until his back was ribboned flesh; a Negress beaten and left helpless to contract pneumonia from exposure and die; a white girl, divorcée, beaten into unconsciousness in her own home; a naturalized foreigner flogged until his back was a pulp because he married an American woman; a Negro lashed until he sold his land to a white man for a fraction of its value."

Even where there were no such outrages, there was at least the threat of them. The white-robed army paraded, the burning cross glowed across the valley, people whispered to one another in the darkness and wondered "who they were after this time," and fear and suspicion ran from house to house. Furthermore, criminals and gangs of hoodlums quickly learned to take advantage of the Klan's existence: if they wanted to burn someone's barn or raid the slums beyond the railroad tracks, they could do it with impunity now: would not the Klan be held responsible? Anyone could chalk the letters K. K. K. on a fence and be sure that the sheriff would move warily. Thus, as in the case of the Red hysteria, a movement conceived in fear perpetuated fear and brought with it all manner of cruelties and crimes.

Slowly, as the years passed and the war-time emotions ebbed, the power of the Klan waned, until in many districts it was dead and in others it had become merely a political faction dominated by spoilsmen: but not until it had become a thing of terror to millions of men and women.

The City for African Americans

The First World War effectively marked the end of immigration from Europe. Wartime exigencies in Europe, and then xenophobic legislation passed by the United States Congress in the early 1920s, stanched the flood of immigrants to a trickle. Industrial cities, however, continued to be the destination for those seeking larger economic, social, and cultural opportunities, this time not from overseas but from the American South.

The phenomenon that historians refer to as "The Great Migration" began roughly during World War I and continued through the 1960s as hundreds of thousands—perhaps millions—of African Americans left the rural South for northern cities. The Great Migration probably constitutes one of the most significant internal population shifts in any nation during the twentieth century.

African Americans made the journey north for several reasons, chief among them the promise of higher-paying industrial jobs and the opportunity to escape southern segregation and racial oppression. For these African Americans, cities like New York, Chicago, and Philadelphia seemed to be the "promised land."

What these new arrivals found when they got to the city varied. Racial segregation as it was practiced and enforced in the South seemed to be absent. Black areas of cities, like the South Side of Chicago, North Philadelphia, and most especially Harlem in New York, vibrated with all the possibilities and promise of urban life. On the other hand, many would discover new kinds of racial segregation and discrimination, and some would find the experience of the industrial city to be fundamentally alienating and dehumanizing. The following excerpt is from American Hunger *by Richard Wright.*

Chicago in the 1920s

My first glimpse of the flat black stretches of Chicago depressed and dismayed me, mocked all my fantasies. Chicago seemed an unreal city whose mythical houses were built of slabs of black coal wreathed in palls of gray smoke, houses whose foundations were sinking slowly into the dank prairie. Flashes of steam showed intermittently on the wise horizon, gleaming translucently in the winter sun. The din of the city entered my consciousness, entered to remain for years to come. The year was 1927.

What would happen to me here? Would I survive? My expectations were modest. I wanted only a job. Hunger had long been my daily companion. Diversion and recreation, with the exception of reading, were unknown. In all my life—though surrounded by many people—I had not had a single satisfying, sustained relationship with another human being and, not having had any, I did not miss it. I made no demands whatever upon others.

The train rolled into the depot. Aunt Maggie and I got off and walked slowly through the crowds into the station. I looked about to see if there were signs saying: FOR WHITE—FOR COLORED. I saw none. Black people and white people moved about, each seemingly intent upon his private mission. There was no racial fear. Indeed, each person acted as though no one existed but himself. It was strange to pause before a crowded newsstand and buy a newspaper without having to wait until a white man was served. And yet, because everything was so new, I began to grow tense again, although it was a different sort of tension than I had known before. I knew that this machine-city was governed by strange laws and I wondered if I would ever learn them.

As we waited for a streetcar to take us to Aunt Cleo's home for temporary lodging, I looked northward at towering buildings of steel and stone. There were no curves here, no trees; only angles, lines, squares, bricks and copper wires. Occasionally the ground beneath my feet shook from some faraway pounding and I felt that this world, despite its massiveness, was somehow dangerously fragile. Streetcars screeched past over steel tracks. Cars honked their horns. Clipped speech sounded about me. As I stood in the icy wind, I wanted to talk to Aunt Maggie, to ask her questions, but her tight face made me hold my tongue. I was learning already from the frantic light in her eyes the strain that the city imposed upon its people. I was seized by doubt. Should I have come here? But going back was impossible. I had fled a known terror, and perhaps I could cope with this unknown terror that lay ahead.

The streetcar came. Aunt Maggie motioned for me to get on and pushed me toward a seat in which a white man sat looking blankly out the window. I sat down beside the man and looked straight ahead of me. After a moment I stole a glance at the white man out of the corners of my eyes; he was still staring out the window, his mind fastened upon some inward thought. I did not exist for him; I was as far from his mind as the stone buildings that swept past in the street. It would have been illegal for me to sit beside him in the part of the South that I had come from.

The car swept past soot-blackened buildings, stopping at each block, jerking again into motion. The conductor called street names in a tone that I could not understand. People got on and off the car, but they never glanced at one another. Each person seemed to regard the other as a part of the city landscape. The white man who sat beside me rose and I turned my knees aside to let him pass, and another white man sat beside me and buried his face in a newspaper. How could that possibly be? Was he conscious of my blackness?

We went to Aunt Cleo's address and found that she was living in a rented room. I had imagined that she lived in an apartment and I was disappointed. I rented a room from Aunt Cleo's landlady and decided to keep it until I got a job. I was baffled. Everything seemed makeshift, temporary. I caught an abiding sense of insecurity in the personalities of the people around me. I found Aunt Cleo aged beyond her years. Her husband, a product of a southern plantation, had, like my father, gone off and left her. Why had he left? My aunt could not answer. She was beaten by the life of the city, just as my mother had been beaten. Wherever my eyes turned they saw stricken, frightened black faces trying vainly to cope with a civilization that they did not understand. I felt lonely. I had fled one insecurity and had embraced another.

Slumbering Fires in Harlem

Oswald Garrison Villard

Lloyd Hobbs, sixteen, and his brother Russell, both colored, were New York high-school students of excellent standing and character. On the evening of March 19, 1935, these boys came out of a moving picture house and noticed a small crowd standing before a shop near the corner of 128th Street and Seventh Avenue. Eager to see what was happening they joined the crowd, only to behold an amazing spectacle. The windows of the shop had been broken, and colored people inside were passing out to others the contents of the store. Soon afterward a police car drove up to the curb, and one of its two occupants alighted, brandishing a pistol. At once everybody ran. Patrolman John F. McInerny picked out Lloyd Hobbs as his quarry. He swears that he called on Lloyd to halt; other witnesses swear that he did not. Without stopping to fire a shot in the air, this guardian of the peace brought down Lloyd as he was running across 128th Street by a bullet which passed through his body and into his wrist. Lloyd died in the Harlem Hospital a few days later. McInerny has neither been indicted nor tried by the Police Department.

This was in many ways the most tragic and certainly the most unnecessary event of the riots which kept the center of Harlem in turmoil for the entire evening and night of March 19–20. The deaths were few, the injuries and arrests numerous; the damage to plate glass alone ran up to $150,000. It was a passionate but an undirected outbreak. It was not engineered by Communists or anti-Semites, nor was it a racial riot in the sense of white and colored being aligned against each other. The stores that were raided were owned by Jews, white Gentiles, and Negroes. The affair had

---

"Slumbering Fires in Harlem," by Oswald Villard, reprinted by permission from *The Nation*, 1936.

its origin in a wholly unfounded rumor that a boy caught stealing a pen-knife in Kresge's store on 125th Street had been beaten and murdered by employees in the store basement.

The rumor spread like wildfire. The boy was in fact caught in his theft at 2:30 P.M. and released unharmed. But within an hour crowds began to form and refused to believe statements by store employees and some of the police. By 5:30 it was necessary to close the store. At 6:30 a window of the store was smashed, and the disturbance then grew rapidly. At 7:30 the Young Liberators, a radical colored group bent on protecting the rights of the Negroes, issued a false leaflet that a boy had been maltreated in the Kresge store and was near death, and the Young Communist League also spread the statement in a broadside. Neither organization took the trouble to ascertain the facts. There are still Negroes in Harlem who believe to this day that the boy was killed despite the fact that he was photographed with a colored police lieutenant on the night of the riot and that he has twice appeared at public hearings and sworn that he was the guilty lad.

Never did a serious public disorder arise with less immediate provocation. Why, then, did this outburst take place? The answer has been fully established by Mayor LaGuardia's Commission on Conditions in Harlem, headed by Dr. C. H. Roberts, a leading colored dentist, appointed to look into the entire situation. The rumor was simply the match to touch rank a magazine which had been years preparing. The nerves of a considerable portion of a community of 200,000 people snapped because of five and a half years of depression, with an unemployment average of no less than 70 per cent in certain areas, because of economic and social discrimination and prejudice, because of rank misgovernment greatly accentuated by certain specific grievances. Thus the riot was preceded by a determined movement among the colored residents of Harlem to obtain employment for some of their number in the many stores which owe their very existence to Negro patronage. The Kresge store was one of these; it had only two or three Negroes in its employ when the storm broke.

But this was only one grievance. Other wrongs were persistent: grievous mishandlings by the police in violation of the Bill of Rights, seriously inadequate school accommodations, discrimination in the administration of relief to destitute unemployed, inadequate hospitalization and institutional care, bad housing and worse overcrowding in the tenements, indefensibly high rentals, inadequate playgrounds and recreation centers, the closing of one avenue after another to economic advancement—these were some of the conditions which caused the sudden outburst. The wonder is that the emotions of the Negroes did not get out of hand before, and the danger is that there will be other outbreaks if the depression continues and the situation in other respects remains unchanged.

Hispanic Americans

 Listen to Chapter 11 on MySocLab

With the Honduran flag in the background, this girl in a traditional dress typifies the many second-generation Hispanic Americans who celebrate their heritage at the annual festive events throughout the United States, and thus reaffirm their specific ethnic group identity within a larger Hispanic-American cultural framework.

LEARNING OBJECTIVES | After reading this chapter you will be able to:

1 Describe the sociohistorical context for studying Hispanic Americans.

2 Examine what social indicators tell us about Hispanic progress.

3 Describe the immigrant experiences of Mexicans, Puerto Ricans, and Cubans.

4 Describe the immigrant experiences of Caribbean, Central and South Americans.

5 Compare and contrast assimilation paths followed by Hispanic Americans.

6 Discuss insights gained through sociological analysis.

From Chapter 11 of *Strangers to These Shores, Race and Ethnic Relations in the United States*, Eleventh Edition. Vincent N. Parrillo. Copyright © 2014 by Pearson Education, Inc. All rights reserved.

P erhaps no ethnic group attracts more public attention these days than do the Hispanic people. Their large numbers, their residential clustering, and the bilingual programs and signs associated with them make them a recognizable ethnic group. Although those who live in poverty or the small number involved in gangs, drugs, or other criminal activity get attention and generate negative stereotypes, most Hispanic Americans live in the societal mainstream as members of the working or middle class. Their cultural backgrounds, social class, and length of residence in the United States may differ, but Hispanic Americans share a common language and heritage. Because of this commonality, outsiders often lump them all together despite their many differences.

Sociohistorical Perspective

1 Describe the sociohistorical context for studying Hispanic Americans.

Spanish influence in what is now the United States is centuries old. Long before the English settled in their colonies in the New World, Spanish explorers, missionaries, and adventurers roamed through much of the Western Hemisphere, including Florida and the Southwest. In 1518, the Spanish established St. Augustine, Florida, and in the same year that the first permanent English settlement (Jamestown) was established (1609), the Spanish founded Santa Fe in what is now New Mexico. Spanish cultural influence was extensive throughout the New World in language, religion, customs, values, and town planning (for example, locating church and institutional buildings next to a central plaza).

The nation's largest Hispanic groups—Mexicans and Puerto Ricans—became involved with the United States through two nineteenth-century wars 50 years apart. Through the fortunes of war, the places where they lived became part of the United States, requiring them to live under a different set of laws in a country where they now were a minority.

For the Mexicans, the Treaty of Guadalupe Hidalgo ended the Mexican–American War in 1848, brought Texas, New Mexico, Arizona, and California into the United States, and gave U.S. citizenship to approximately 75,000 Mexican nationals still living there one year after the treaty. Viewed as a conquered and inferior people, they soon lost title to the land where they and their ancestors had lived because they could not prove ownership in the Anglo court system. By 1892, official policy toward Mexican Americans was so biased against them that the federal government allowed anyone except them to get grazing privileges on public lands in the Southwest. Nor did the violence end. In fact, the interethnic violence between Anglos and Mexican Americans thereafter was so extensive that some experts believe there were more killings of Mexican Americans than black Americans lynched between 1850 and 1930.[1] Experienced in farming, ranching, and mining—concentrated along the fertile river valleys—the Mexican Americans proved a valuable labor pool and were incorporated within the white economy as lower-strata laborers.

Ruled by Spain for more than 400 years, Puerto Ricans became U.S. nationals when the Treaty of Paris in 1898 ended the Spanish–American War and made their land U.S. territory. Until 1948, when Puerto Rico became a commonwealth with full autonomy and its people could elect their own governor, the island was a colony with appointed governors and its legislative actions subject to annulment by the U.S. Congress, which reserved the right to legislate for the island if it wished. As only one example of the island's colonial status, U.S. officials decreed that all education was to be in English. That edict remained in effect until 1991, when Puerto Ricans voted to restore Spanish as the island's official language.

STRUCTURAL CONDITIONS

The Hispanic American experience varies greatly, depending on the particular ethnic group, area of the country, and period involved (Figure 1). In the Southwest, agricultural needs and the presence of Central and Mexican Americans are crucial factors in

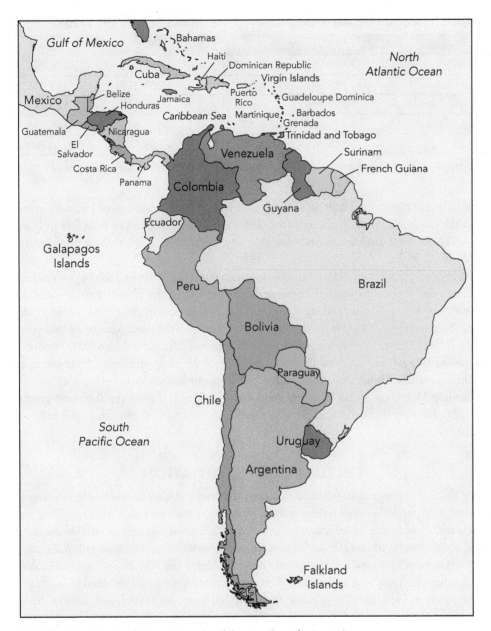

FIGURE 1 Central America, Caribbean, South America

dominant–minority relations. In the East, industrial employment, urban problems, and the presence of Cubans or Puerto Ricans provide the focal points of attitudes and actions.

In the past, low-skilled immigrant groups—including Puerto Ricans and Mexicans—typically obtained jobs such as unskilled factory work that had low status, low pay, and little mobility but at least provided sufficient income to achieve some degree of economic security. Unlike past groups from less industrialized nations, however, today's Hispanic immigrants enter a post-industrial society where fewer unskilled factory jobs are available. Instead, they find work in other physical labor fields such as agriculture, construction and home improvement (demolition, flooring, framing, masonry, painting, and roofing), food service, and landscaping.

Overpopulation throughout Latin America is a significant factor in the continued migration of large numbers of Hispanics to the United States (Table 1). High birth rates, improved sanitation, reduction of child mortality, and negative cultural and religious attitudes toward birth control have led to population booms in countries whose resources

TABLE 1 Legal Hispanic Immigration to the United States, 1971–2012

	1980–1989	1990–1999	2000–2009	2010–2012
Mexico	1,009,586	2,757,418	1,704,166	426,866
Caribbean	789,343	1,004,114	1,053,357	399,016
Central America	339,376	610,189	591,130	126,683
South America	399,803	570,596	856,508	248,218
Total	2,538,108	4,942,317	4,205,161	1,200,783

Source: U.S. Office of Immigration Statistics, *Yearbook of Immigration Statistics: 2012*, Table 2.

and habitable land cannot support so many people. The total population of Latin America and the Caribbean grew from more than 285 million in 1970 to more than 599 million in 2012. Current projections indicate that the population will reach approximately 672 million by 2025.[2]

Suffering from poor living conditions, inadequate schools, limited job opportunities, and economic hardship, many Latinos seek a better life in the United States—indeed, significantly more people than legal channels can accommodate. As a result, some enter illegally along the 2,000-mile border between the United States and Mexico or into port cities by boat. U.S. government agents have been apprehending more than 640,000 **undocumented (illegal) aliens** annually. Most come from Mexico, with other large clusters from Guatemala, Honduras, and El Salvador.[3] Undocumented aliens, by some estimates exceeding 11 million, strain local and state social services and generate dominant-group hostility, but they also make substantial economic contributions as consumers and as low-skilled workers.

CULTURAL DIFFERENTIATION

The cultures of the peoples from the various Caribbean and Central and South American countries differ. Value orientations within a particular country also vary, depending on such factors as degree of urbanization and industrialization, amount of outside contact, and social class. With these qualifications in mind, we will examine some cultural traditions that most Latinos share to a greater or lesser degree and that differ from traditional U.S. values. Before doing so, we should recognize that in areas of considerable acculturation, such as New Mexico, some of these cultural traits are muted, and Latinos have adopted many Anglo (the Latino term for "mainstream white U.S.") behavior patterns.

THE COSMIC RACE. One cultural concept associated with older Hispanics—especially Mexicans—is that of *La Raza Cosmica*, the cosmic race. The Mexican intellectual José Vasconcelos coined the term in 1925 to refer to the amalgamation of the white, black, and Indian races that he believed was occurring in Latin America.[4] In his old age, he dismissed the idea as a juvenile fantasy, but the concept evolved into a group categorization similar to what Kurt Lewin calls the recognition of an "interdependence of fate." In essence, *La Raza Cosmica* suggests that all the Spanish-speaking peoples in the Western Hemisphere share a cultural bond and that God has planned for them a great destiny that yet has to be realized.

From this mythic construct, activists sought to unify compatriots around a common political goal based on the nationalism of an imagined community. Although those cultural resources remained dormant for much of the late twentieth century, *La Raza* lived on as the name of an influential newspaper and of a strong political organization representing Chicano interests. On a broader scale, the realization of that common political goal occurred in the major role played by Hispanic voters in re-electing President Obama. The Latino impact reverberated after the election, causing elected officials of both parties to focus more fully on immigration reform and other issues of concern to this growing segment of the electorate.[5]

HISPANIC AMERICANS

MACHISMO. Overstated in the Anglo stereotype, *machismo* is a basic value governing various qualities of masculinity. To Hispanic males, such attributes as inner strength in the face of adversity, personal daring, bravado, leadership, and sexual prowess are measures of one's manhood.[6] The role of the man is to be a good provider for his family, to protect its honor at all times, and to be strong, reliable, and independent. He should avoid indebtedness, accepting charity, and any kind of relationship, formal or informal, that would weaken his autonomy. Traditional culture and the family system are male dominated. The woman's role is within the family, and women are to be guarded against any onslaught on their honor. Machismo also may find expression in such forms as perceived sexual allure, fathering children, and aggressive behavior. *Marianismo* is the companion value, describing various qualities of femininity, particularly acceptance of male dominance, emphasis on family responsibilities, and the nurturing role of women.

The concept of machismo is not strictly Latin American. Such traditional gender role orientations are common throughout most developing countries, whether African, Eastern, Middle Eastern, Western, or Pacific Island. For Latinos, machismo diminishes with increasing levels of education, assimilation, and multigenerational residence in the United States.

The result of these values not only can be a double standard of sexual morality but also a difficulty adjusting to U.S. culture, as women have more independence in the United States than in most Hispanic countries. Instead of men being the sole providers, women also can find employment, sometimes earning more money than the men of the family. The participation of Hispanic women in the labor force seems to be related to educational level. More highly educated Cuban, Central American, and South American women participate in the labor force at rates similar to those of white women in the United States, whereas Mexican and Puerto Rican women have lower rates. Overall, the participation of Hispanic women in the labor force is about the same as the national average for all women, although more are in less-skilled positions.[7]

DIGNIDAD. The cultural value of *dignidad* is the basis of social interaction; it assumes that the dignity of all humans entitles them to a measure of respect. It is a quality typically attributed to all, regardless of status, race, color, or creed.[8] Regardless of status, each person acknowledges others' *dignidad* in a taken-for-granted reciprocal behavior pattern. Therefore, Hispanics expect to be treated in terms of *dignidad*. Because it is an implicit measure of respect, one cannot demand it from others. Instead, one concludes that others are rude and cold if they do not acknowledge one's *dignidad*. More broadly, the concept includes a strong positive self-image.

STUDENTS SPEAK "Just like any other minority group, Hispanics are not all the same. Each Hispanic country has uniqueness in land, language, people, food, music, government, economic status, education, history, beliefs, and values. What you find in Puerto Rico or Guatemala, you will not find in the Dominican Republic or Mexico. A small example is the *cocui*, a small frog found only in Puerto Rico. Many times Hispanics are categorized as Hispanic just for speaking Spanish but, in truth, it's way beyond that. Spanish culture is an enormously broad range of beauty with many variations. Latinos have much pride of where they come from and even though Hispanic Americans become Americans and assimilate, they never forget where they come from."

—Emna Solares

RACIAL ATTITUDES

In most Latin American countries, skin color is less important than social class as an indicator of social status. An apparent correlation exists between darker skin color and lower social standing, but the racial line between whites and blacks that is drawn sharply in the United States is less distinct in Latin America. A great deal of color integration occurs in social interaction, intermarriage, and shared orientations to cultural values. There also is a much wider range of recognized color gradations, which helps to blunt any color prejudice. Still, in some places, such as Puerto Rico, color prejudice has increased, perhaps as a result of social and economic changes from industrialization.[9]

Color often serves as an unexpected basis of discrimination for Latinos coming to the United States. Being stereotyped, judged, and treated on the basis of one's skin color is

the MINORITY experience

What's in a Name?

What makes someone a Latino? Is it genetics (your blood lines) or geography (where you were born)? For example, a child born in the United States to Dominican immigrant parents would be called "Dominican American." Pope Francis is a native Spanish speaker born and raised in Argentina. However, his parents were born in Italy.

Because of his European heritage, some argue that, even though Pope Francis may be from Latin America and a special inspiration to Spanish-speaking Catholics around the world, he is not a "Latino." Others argue that if you are born in Latin America, and share its language, history and culture, then you indeed are a Latino. The issue rests on whether or not to make a distinction between Latin American (geography) and Latino (genetics).

A related issue is the use of *Hispanic* or *Latino/Latina*. Although *Hispanic* is a long-used governmental term, many people falling under this label reject it because of its association with European conquest of the Americas and/or recent immigrants who speak only Spanish. Instead, they prefer Latino/Latina to identify more accurately their mix of indigenous, African, and European ancestry.

essentially unknown to these brown-skinned peoples in their homeland, so encountering racial prejudice and discrimination can be a traumatic experience. Before long, they realize the extent of this ugly aspect of U.S. society. Some adapt to it, others forsake it and return home, but all resent it.

RELIGION

Throughout Latin America, Catholicism typically means personal relationships with the saints and a community manifestation of faith, and less the individual actions and commitments expected in the United States. Another aspect of religious life in Puerto Rico, Brazil, and other parts of Latin America is the widespread belief in spiritualism and superstition. These practices, which constitute remnants of earlier folk rites, continue to be observed by various cults as well as by many Catholics.[10]

For many people, especially in the lowest socioeconomic class regardless of their racial or ethnic background, religion serves as an emotional escape from the harsh realities of everyday life. **Pentecostalism**, a form of evangelical Christianity, inspires a strong sense of belonging through openly expressive worship participation, thus offering to some a greater attraction than Catholicism. Pentecostal churches represent the largest Hispanic Protestant religious movement in Puerto Rico and the U.S. mainland, as well as throughout Latin America. In the United States, hundreds of such churches, with small and intimate congregations of approximately 60 to 100, offer their largely immigrant members a renewalist Christianity that emphasizes God's ongoing day-to-day intervention in human affairs. Hispanic Catholics practice a distinctive form of Catholicism—a blend of many beliefs and behaviors that constitute Pentecostal or Renewalist Christianity with the main features of traditional Catholic teaching.[11]

Approximately 15 percent of all Latinos identify themselves as evangelical Protestants, while 68 percent are Roman Catholics. Hispanic churches, as other ethnic churches before them, provide both a spiritual haven and a sense of community. As the proportion of Hispanic Catholics increases, the Latino influence on U.S. religious institutions is becoming more pronounced.[12] The 2013 election of Pope Francis, hailed as "the first Latino pope," generated enthusiasm and pride among Hispanic Americans, but also raised questions about determining ethnic identity (see the accompanying box).

HISPANIC AMERICANS

OTHER CULTURAL ATTRIBUTES

Hispanics generally have a more casual attitude toward time than do others in the United States, and they hold a negative attitude toward rushing, believing it robs one of dignity. Another cultural difference—one that easily could lead to misunderstanding—is their attitude about making eye contact with others. To them, not looking directly into the eyes of an authority figure, such as a teacher or police officer, is an act of respect, but native U.S. residents may interpret it as shyness, avoidance, or guilt. Like southern Europeans, Hispanics regard physical proximity in conversation as a sign of friendliness, but Anglos are accustomed to a greater distance between conversationalists. One can envision an Anglo made uncomfortable by the seemingly unusual nearness of a Hispanic person and backing away, the latter reestablishing the physical closeness, the Anglo again backing away, and the Hispanic concluding that the Anglo is a cold or aloof individual. Each has viewed the situation from a different cultural perspective, leading to very different interpretations of the incident.[13]

CURRENT PATTERNS

Hispanics are the largest ethnic group in the United States and steadily are increasing in number all the time. At 51 million residents in 2010 (a 43 percent increase over the 35.3 million in 2000, compared to an overall 10 percent increase), they now constitute approximately 17 percent of the total U.S. population. As the nation's largest minority group, their proportion of the total population will increase, given their higher birth rate than other groups, a high immigration rate from Spanish-speaking countries, and a low average age of these immigrants (36 percent are under age 18).[14]

More than half of all Hispanics live in only three states: California, Texas, and Florida. More than three-fourths live in eight states with Hispanic populations of 1 million or more (California, Texas, New York, Florida, Illinois, Arizona, New Jersey, and Colorado). The Hispanic percentages of some of the nation's nine largest cities are Miami (70 percent), San Antonio (63 percent), Los Angeles (49 percent), Houston (44 percent), Dallas (42 percent), San Jose (33 percent), Chicago, New York, and San Diego (29 percent each).[15]

What do these growing numbers and extensive population clusters suggest for future dominant–minority relations? No simple answer exists because of the variance in Hispanic education, socioeconomic background, and occupational skills. Despite nativist

A common sight in Hispanic neighborhoods is bodegas or stores catering to the needs of the local community, with familiar products and signs in the residents' native language, such as this grocery store on Broadway's Sugar Hill section of New York City.

HISPANIC AMERICANS

the INTERNATIONAL scene

Cultural Diffusion in Argentina

Because nearly all Argentinians are descendants of relatively recent immigrants from Europe, their culture has a stronger European orientation than is found in neighboring Latin American countries. The people of Buenos Aires, the *porteños*, often call their city the Paris of South America, and with its culture and glamour, it probably earns that name. Buenos Aires often is described as Latin America's most European city. The population consists largely of the descendants of immigrants from Spain and Italy who came to Argentina in the late nineteenth or early twentieth century. There also are significant minorities of Germans, British, Jews from central and eastern Europe, and Middle Eastern peoples, who are known collectively as *turcos*.

Since the 1930s, most migrants to the city have come from the northern portion of Argentina, where the population predominantly is *mestizo* (mixed Indian and European). Today, the *mestizos* make up between one-fourth and one-third of the population in the metropolitan area; they tend to live in the poorest sections of the city, in the *villas miserias* and the distant suburbs. The area's black and mulatto population is of negligible size.

There are no ethnic neighborhoods, strictly speaking, but many of the smaller minorities typically settle close to one another in tightly knit communities. Villa Crespo, for example, is known as a Jewish neighborhood; the Avenida de Mayo is a center for Spaniards; and Flores is the home of many *turcos*. The assimilation of these groups has been less than complete, but the Argentinian identity has been flexible enough to allow ethnocentric mutual aid societies and social clubs to emerge. Even the dominant Spanish language has been affected by other European cultures and has undergone changes. In the slums and waterfront districts, an Italianized dialect has emerged, and Italian cuisine is popular in the city.

Another hybrid of the Old and New Worlds is the tango, which emerged from the poor immigrant quarters of Buenos Aires toward the end of the nineteenth century and quickly became famous around the world as Argentina's national dance. Influenced by the Spanish tango and, possibly, by the Argentinian *milonga*, it originally was a high-spirited local dance but soon became an elegant ballroom form danced to melancholy tunes.

The combination of Old and New World cultures also is seen in the Argentinian diet. Southern European influences appear especially in the city where breakfast often is a light serving of rolls and coffee, and supper is taken, in the Spanish tradition, after nine o'clock at night. The Italian influence is seen in the popularity of pasta dishes. But the New World asserts itself in the Argentinian passion for beef, which is overwhelmingly preferred to other meats and fish. *Maté*, a native tea-like beverage brewed from *yerba maté* leaves, is popular in the countryside.

CRITICAL THINKING QUESTION

What examples of Hispanic cultural diffusion in the United States can you name?

---

fears, however, English language mastery is a common goal of Hispanic parents for their children; few in the second generation and hardly any in the third generation are Spanish dominant in their daily conversations.[16] Concerns about ethnic tribalism or about the need to enshrine English as the "official" language of the United States seem unfounded.

Cultural vitality, long an attribute among Mexican Americans in the Southwest living so near their homeland, likely will remain within other Latino communities also. The dynamics of cultural pluralism are fueled by the large Hispanic presence, current migration patterns, psychological ties to the homeland, rapid transportation and communications, government policy, and societal tolerance. Acculturation and mainstreaming no doubt will occur for most Hispanics, as they have for members of other groups, but the dynamics of cultural pluralism suggest that the Hispanic influence will be long-lasting in U.S. society. Although Hispanics may blend in with the rest of society, like the French who influenced the Louisiana region, they well may fundamentally affect U.S. culture itself (see the International Scene box).

Social Indicators of Hispanic Progress

As Figure 2 shows, a much larger percentage of Hispanics than non-Hispanics are young, with proportionately more children and fewer elderly. Higher fertility, particularly among the foreign born, and the high percentage of young adult immigrants in their reproductive years create this differential. However, Hispanic groups vary in their migration and fertility patterns. For example, 21 percent of Cuban Americans are under 18, compared to 36 percent among Mexican Americans. In contrast, children under 15 constitute 22 percent of whites.[17]

Diversity among various Hispanic cultural groups also manifests itself in such social indicators as education, income, and occupation (see Figure 3). These indicators support mixed findings on the status of Hispanic Americans and provide some cause for concern.

2 Examine what social indicators tell us about Hispanic progress.

Read on MySocLab
Document: **The Hispanic Dropout Mystery: A Staggering 30 Percent Leave School, Far More Than Blacks or Whites. Why?**

EDUCATION

Perhaps the most important indicator of societal mainstreaming is education, for it provides the means for greater job opportunities. Unfortunately, far more Latinos ages 25 or older never finished high school compared to the total population (37 to 14 percent). The comparison for holding at least a bachelor's degree is 13 to 28 percent.[18] All Hispanic groups significantly lag behind the non-Hispanic population in producing high school graduates, especially Central Americans and Mexicans.

Reasons cited for the education gap between Hispanics and non-Hispanics include the limited formal education of parents, less preschool experience for Hispanic children compared to whites and blacks, and cultural/linguistic differences encountered in school. Also important is the increased proportion of immigrants in the U.S. Hispanic population. Few educational differences exist between males and females. South Americans and Cuban Americans have the highest percentage of college graduates, and Mexican Americans have the lowest.

We can find two promising notes within other educational data. U.S.-born Hispanics in all ethnic groups are more likely than the foreign born to have higher percentages of high school and college graduates. Approximately 44 percent of foreign-born Hispanic adults are high school graduates compared with 73 percent of U.S.-born Hispanic adults. Further, second-generation Latinos get better grades and their dropout rate is approximately 15 percent compared

STUDENTS SPEAK "Many foreign-born Hispanic parents don't speak English, making it impossible to be involved in their children's schools and their school work. New Hispanic immigrants are coming every day and if this trend of dropouts and parental non-involvement persists, they are going to fall into the poverty cycle as well. As a foreign-born Hispanic myself, I know it is difficult, but we have to look for changes. The Spanish-speaking channels reach people easily and they encourage education, but it is not enough. We have to find other ways to break this cycle."

—Sylvia Barrera

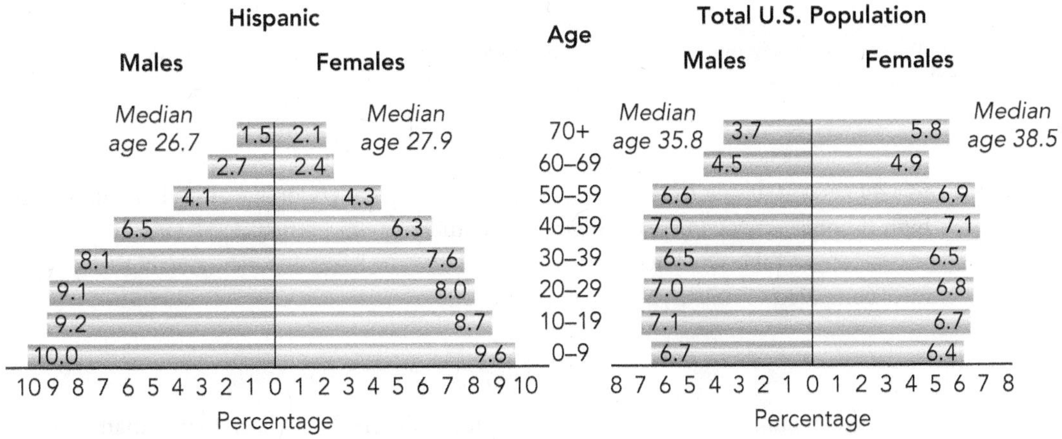

FIGURE 2 **Hispanic-American Population, 2010, in percentages**
Source: U.S. Census Bureau.

FIGURE 3 Social Indicators about Hispanic Subgroups in 2011 (in percentages)

Source: U.S. Census Bureau.

Age

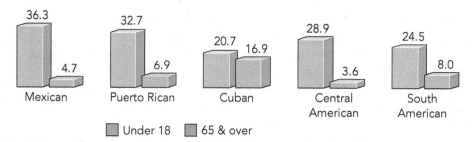

Under 18   65 & over

Education (of persons age 25 and over)

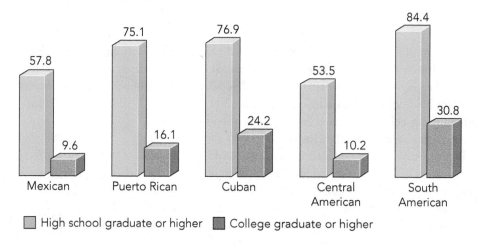

High school graduate or higher   College graduate or higher

Economic Status

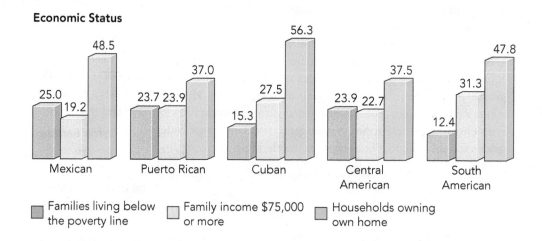

Families living below the poverty line   Family income $75,000 or more   Households owning own home

to a 44 percent dropout rate among Hispanic immigrant children.[19] This is an alarmingly high dropout rate of Hispanic high school students—in particular, Mexican and Puerto Rican teens (Table 2). These statistics translate into lower incomes and higher poverty rates compared to Asians, blacks, and whites.

INCOME

The median family income for Latino families traditionally has been higher than for black families (Table 3). Moreover, the real income gap is growing. Despite a strong Hispanic middle class—22 percent of Hispanic families have incomes of $75,000 or more—another

TABLE 2 High School Dropouts, Ages 16-24, by Race/Ethnicity and Gender (in percentages)

	1980	1990	2000	2010
Blacks	19.1	13.2	13.1	8.0
Females	17.7	14.4	11.1	6.7
Males	20.8	11.9	15.3	9.5
Whites	11.4	9.0	6.9	5.1
Females	10.5	8.7	6.9	4.2
Males	12.3	9.3	7.0	5.9
Hispanics	35.2	32.4	27.8	15.1
Females	33.2	30.3	23.5	12.8
Males	37.2	34.3	31.8	17.3

Source: National Center for Education Statistics, *Digest of Education Statistics: 2011*, Table 116.

TABLE 3 Median Income of Hispanic, Black, and White Families for Selected Years, 1970–2011

YEAR	HISPANIC	BLACK	WHITE	HISPANIC INCOME AS PERCENT OF WHITE
1970	NA	$ 6,279	$10,236	NA
1980	$14,716	$12,674	$21,904	67
1990	$23,431	$21,423	$36,915	64
2000	$33,447	$30,439	$45,904	73
2011	$40,982	$40,140	$66,025	62

Note: NA = not available.
Source: U.S. Census Bureau, *2011 American Community Survey*, Table S0201.

22 percent live in poverty. Generally, Hispanics consistently have had a lower percentage of impoverished families than blacks. A higher percentage of Mexican and Puerto Rican Americans live in poverty than other Hispanic groups, whereas Cuban and South Americans are the least likely of all Hispanic subgroups to live in poverty (Table 4). Also, Puerto Ricans have lessened their poverty numbers slightly in recent years.

TABLE 4 Persons below Poverty Level, 2011 (in percentages)

White	10.4
African American	25.6
All Hispanic	22.4
Mexican American	23.8
Puerto Rican	25.3
Cuban American	15.8
Dominican American	27.5
Central American	18.9
Salvadoran American	17.1
South American	14.0

Source: U.S. Census Bureau, *2011 American Community Survey*, Table S0201.

HISPANIC AMERICANS

Education is the means by which minorities can achieve upward mobility by qualifying for better-paying jobs. Although some Hispanic young adults are graduating from college, the sad reality is that a higher percentage drop out of high school and/or do not attend college in comparison to other U.S. minority groups.

As with the education data, we again must note the impact of immigration on these income and poverty statistics. New entrants into the U.S. labor force typically earn less than those with longer residence because they often lack the education, training, experience, and seniority of other workers. Therefore, they tend to take lower-skill jobs at entry-level salaries. Like past European peasant immigrants, economic survival is their immediate goal. The United States for them is, as William Bradford described North America for the English Puritans in the early seventeenth century, a place "where they must learn a new language and get their livings they knew not how."

OCCUPATION

Occupation provides an important basis for personal esteem, and the occupational distribution of an entire ethnic group thus serves as a comparative measure of its status within the larger society. Table 5 addresses this aspect of Hispanic structural assimilation. As might be expected from the educational data, most Hispanic males (except Cuban, Puerto Rican, and South Americans) are heavily underrepresented in managerial and professional occupations, and an unusually high number of Mexican and Central Americans work in unskilled blue-collar occupations. Reflecting the typical gender occupational distribution in U.S. society, Hispanic females tend to be just as likely to work in sales and administrative support positions as non-Hispanic females. Hispanic women are less likely than non-Hispanics, however, to occupy managerial and professional positions, although Cuban, Puerto Rican, and South American women are more strongly represented in these jobs than are other Hispanic women. All Hispanic women are more likely than non-Hispanics to work in service occupations as well as in unskilled blue-collar positions as operators, in transportation, and as laborers.

TABLE 5 Occupational Distribution, 2011

	NON-HISPANIC	MEXICAN	PUERTO RICAN	CUBAN	CENTRAL AMERICAN	SOUTH AMERICAN
Males						
Managerial, professional	36.0	12.5	22.7	30.3	11.2	24.7
Sales and office occupations	18.5	13.6	20.8	18.5	10.9	19.7
Service occupations	11.3	22.7	23.0	19.4	19.1	15.5
Production, transportation	16.7	22.9	20.0	18.0	22.0	19.3
Construction, extraction, maintenance	16.7	28.3	13.5	13.5	35.6	20.7
Females						
Managerial, professional	41.5	22.1	31.9	37.6	16.2	31.5
Sales and office occupations	35.3	32.0	37.0	30.1	28.2	33.2
Service occupations	17.5	32.3	23.7	21.3	41.1	28.3
Production, transportation	4.9	10.9	6.7	9.4	13.0	6.7
Construction, extraction, maintenance	0.7	2.7	0.8	1.7	1.0	0.3

Source: U.S. Census Bureau, *2011 American Community Survey.*

Mexican Americans

Most of the 33.6 million Mexican Americans live in the southwestern states, with more than three-fourths in California, Texas, Arizona, Illinois, and Colorado. The largest population concentrations live in Los Angeles, Chicago, Houston, San Antonio, and Phoenix.[20]

Much diversity exists within this ethnic group in degree of assimilation and socioeconomic status, ranging along a continuum from the most newly nonacculturated arrivals to the *Hispanos* of northern New Mexico and southern Colorado who trace their ancestry in that region to the days of the Spanish conquest of what is now the southwestern United States.

Throughout New Mexico—which, unlike Texas and California, has limited contact with Mexico through border crossings—the employment pattern is bright. In fact, most Hispanic Americans there hold economically secure jobs and are heavily represented in civil service occupations at the local, state, and federal levels. Like many recent non-Western immigrants, they retain a cultural heritage that includes their diet, child-rearing philosophy, emphasis on the family, and extended family contacts.

Second-generation Mexican Americans living in large cities typically display greater structural assimilation as evidenced by separate residences for nuclear families, English-language competence, fewer children, and comparable family values, jobs, and income than those living in border towns or agricultural regions.[21] However, most present-day Mexican Americans, whether they live in an urban setting or a rural area, lag far behind the rest of the U.S. population on every measure of socioeconomic well-being: education, income, and employment status.

RECRUITING MEXICANS

In the second half of the nineteenth century, Mexicans from south of the border helped fill U.S. labor needs for the construction of railroad lines and the expansion of cotton, fruit, and vegetable farms. Thereafter, the Chinese Exclusion Act of 1882 curtailed one source of laborers, and later the Immigration Acts of 1921 and 1924 curtailed another. However, the demand for labor—especially for agricultural workers—increased, and Mexicans left their poverty-stricken country for the opened economic opportunities in the United States.

3 Describe the immigrant experiences of Mexicans, Puerto Ricans, and Cubans.

Explore on MySocLab
Activity: Navigating Borders: The Lives and Labors of Mexican Americans

Watch on MySocLab
Video: The Basics: Economy and Work

Once the bracero program (1942–1964) provided U.S. farmers with the seasonal help they needed to harvest their crops by allowing Mexicans to enter the United States on temporary visas. Today, mostly Hispanic migrant workers, both legal and illegal immigrants, fill this need, as in this cauliflower field near Santa Cruz, California.

HISPANIC AMERICANS

Despite U.S. government restrictions on immigration, it was easy for Mexicans to cross the largely unpatrolled border and enter the United States illegally, and many did so. The ones who crossed into Texas were known as "wetbacks" because they had crossed the Rio Grande. Some Mexican aliens also entered the United States legally as contract laborers. Under this *bracero* program, Mexican aliens entered the United States on temporary visas and then returned to Mexico after the harvest. This system provided needed workers without incurring the expenses of educating their children and of extending welfare and other social services to them during the off-season. The program lasted from 1942 until 1964, when farm mechanization, labor shortages in Mexico, and the protests of native Hispanics in the United States ended it.

EXPULSION

Although cheap Mexican labor was a boon to the southwestern economy, Mexicans usually found themselves unwelcome during downturns in the U.S. economy. One such time was the 1930s, when many U.S. citizens were jobless. Some Mexicans returned home voluntarily, and others did so under pressure by local residents. Hundreds of thousands who did not leave willingly were rounded up and deported from southern California, from cities throughout the Southwest, and as far north as from Chicago and Detroit:

> In Los Angeles, official trucks would grind into the barrios—the Mexican American neighborhoods—and the occupants would be herded into them. There was little or no determination of national origin. Citizenship or noncitizenship was not considered. Families were divided; the bringing of possessions was not permitted....
>
> "They pushed most of my family into one van," one of the victims, Jorge Acevedo, remembers bitterly. "We drove all day. The driver wouldn't stop for bathroom, nor food nor water. Everyone knew by now we had been deported. Nobody knew why, but there was a lot of hatred and anger....We had always known that we were hated. Now we had proof."[22]

During the recession of the mid-1950s, the U.S. Immigration and Naturalization Service launched "Operation Wetback" to find and return all undocumented Mexican aliens. Between 1954 and 1959, concentrating on California and Texas but ranging as far north and east as Spokane, Chicago, Kansas City, and St. Louis, government officials found and expelled 3.8 million Mexicans, less than 64,000 of whom ever received a formal hearing. Not all were undocumented aliens. INS agents stopped and questioned many U.S. citizens if they "looked Mexican." Those unable to prove their legal status on the spot found themselves arrested and sent "home" without any further opportunity to defend themselves.[23]

VIOLENCE

One infamous incident in which prejudices against Mexicans erupted into violence was the Zoot Suit Riot of 1943. The name came from the popularity among Mexican American youths at that time of wearing long, loose-fitting jackets with wide shoulders; high-waisted, baggy trousers with tight cuffs; and flat-topped hats with broad brims. The gamblers in the original show and the film version of *Guys and Dolls* dressed in this fashion.

On June 3, 1943, two events triggered the riot. Some Mexican boys, returning from a police-sponsored club meeting, were assaulted by a group of non-Mexican hoodlums from the neighborhood in Los Angeles. That same evening, 11 sailors on leave were attacked, and 1 sailor was badly hurt. The sailors said that their assailants were Mexican youths who outnumbered them 3 to 1. When the police, responding late, found no one to arrest in the area, approximately 200 sailors decided to settle the matter themselves the following evening. Cruising through the Mexican section in a caravan of 20 taxicabs, they savagely beat every Mexican they found. The police did nothing to stop them and, as Carey McWilliams reported, the press gave this event and its aftermath wide publicity:

> The stage was now set for the really serious rioting of June seventh and eighth. Having featured the preliminary rioting as an offensive launched by sailors, soldiers, and marines, the press now whipped public opinion into a frenzy by dire warnings that Mexican zoot-suiters planned a mass retaliation. To ensure a riot, the precise street corners were marked at which retaliatory action was expected and the time of the anticipated action was carefully specified. In effect, these stories announced a riot and invited public participation....
>
> On Monday evening, June seventh, thousands of *Angelenos,* in response to twelve hours' advance notice in the press, turned out for a mass lynching. Marching through the streets of downtown Los Angeles, a mob of several thousand soldiers, sailors, and civilians proceeded to beat up every zoot-suiter they could find. Pushing its way into the important motion picture theaters, the mob ordered the management to turn on the house lights and then ranged up and down the aisles dragging Mexicans out of their seats. Street cars were halted while Mexicans, and some Filipinos and Negroes, were jerked out of their seats, pushed into the streets, and beaten with sadistic frenzy....

Here is one of the numerous eyewitness accounts written by Al Waxman, editor of *The Eastside Journal:*

> Four boys came out of a pool hall. They were wearing the zoot-suits that have become the symbols of a fighting flag. Police ordered them into arrest cars. One refused. He asked: "Why am I being arrested?" The police officer answered with three swift blows of the night-stick across the boy's head and he went down. As he sprawled, he was kicked in the face. Police had difficulty loading his body into the vehicle because he was one-legged and wore a wooden limb....
>
> At the next corner, a Mexican mother cried out, "Don't take my boy, he did nothing. He's only fifteen years old. Don't take him." She was struck across the jaw with a night-stick and almost dropped the two-and-a-half-year-old baby that was clinging in her arms....
>
> A Negro defense worker, wearing a defense-plant identification badge on his work clothes, was taken from a street car and one of his eyes was gouged out with a knife. Huge half-page photographs, showing Mexican boys, stripped of their clothes, cowering on the pavements, often bleeding profusely, surrounded by jeering mobs of men and women, appeared in all of the Los Angeles newspapers....
>
> When it finally stopped, the Eagle Rock *Advertiser* mournfully editorialized: "It is too bad the servicemen were called off before they were able to complete the job....Most of the citizens of the city have been delighted with what has been going on."[24]

This bloody incident, like earlier Know-Nothing riots, anti-Chinese race riots, black lynchings, and many other acts of violence, was the result of increasing societal tensions and prejudices against a minority that erupted into aggression far in excess of the triggering incident. Whatever Mexicans thought about Anglo society before this wartime incident, they long would remember this race riot waged against them with approval from the police, the newspapers, and city hall.

URBAN LIFE

In some places, such as Los Angeles and New Mexico, Mexican Americans often are better integrated into the mainstream of society than their compatriots elsewhere. There, they have higher intermarriage rates, nuclear instead of extended family residence patterns, and less patriarchal male roles. They enter more diverse occupations, and many attain middle-class status and move from the barrio to the suburbs and outskirts of the city. Yet in East Los Angeles and in other areas of the Southwest, particularly in smaller cities and towns, Mexican Americans reside in large ethnic enclaves, virtually isolated from participation in Anglo society. Even some *Hispano* middle-class individuals whose families have lived in the United States for generations choose to live among their own people and interact mostly with them.

Many Mexican Americans live in substandard housing under crowded conditions. In the southwestern states where most Mexican Americans live, their housing is more crowded than that of non-whites; in Texas, twice as many Mexicans as blacks live in over-crowded housing. Segregated in the less desirable sections of town, with their children attending schools that warrant the same criticisms as inner-city schools in major cities, they experience many forms of discrimination.

The large influx of Mexican Americans and their residential clustering in urban areas have resulted in a high level of increasingly segregated schools. This trend toward isolation of schoolchildren holds for most urban Hispanics but is pronounced particularly in the Southwest. For example, the percentage of white students in Los Angeles County high schools attended by Mexican American students has dropped from 45 percent in 1970 to less than 15 percent today.[25]

STEREOTYPING

Currently, the two most common stereotypes that Mexican Americans have had to combat involve their identification as undocumented aliens or youth gang members. "Looking" Mexican often raises suspicions about legal residence or makes prospective employers wary of hiring a possible undocumented alien, even if the individual is a legal U.S. resident. In the poor urban barrios of Los Angeles, San Antonio, and El Paso, youth gangs are an integral subculture within the community. Gang fights and killings—particularly in

Olvera Street is located in the oldest section of Los Angeles. Once the residential locale of Mexican Americans, it fell into a seriously deteriorated state until it was revitalized in the late 1920s. Today, it flourishes as a successful commercial area that attracts millions of tourists each year and is LA's center for Cinco de Mayo festivities.

HISPANIC AMERICANS

East Los Angeles—and the associated drug scene create a lasting, negative picture of all Mexican Americans in the minds of many Anglos.

Like blacks and Puerto Ricans, Mexican Americans suffer from culture-of-poverty beliefs held by the dominant society. All too often, outsiders blame their low socioeconomic standing on their supposed cultural values. In reality, Mexican Americans have a participation rate in the labor force comparable to, or higher than, other groups—white, black, Asian, or other Hispanic.[26] Furthermore, the percentage of Mexican Americans receiving welfare assistance is only approximately one-sixth that of blacks and of other Hispanic groups and approximately one-half that of whites. Because Mexican Americans have a large proportion of immigrant workers, the usual pattern of lower wages for the foreign-born wage earners impacts significantly on the median income reported for all Mexican Americans. Studies show that, as their length of time in the United States increases, Mexican immigrants close the earnings gap with U.S.-born Mexican Americans but not with non-Hispanic whites. The gains in earnings associated with age, time in the United States, and English proficiency differ by gender, as women do not close the gap that much.[27]

CHICANO POWER

Until the 1960s, the term *Chicano* was a derogatory name applied in Mexico to the "lower"-class Mexican Indians rather than to the Mexican Spanish. Then, as an outgrowth of the Civil Rights movement and in direct contradiction to the stereotype of the passive, apathetic Mexican community, the Chicano movement emerged. Seeking to instill pride in the group's *mestizo* heritage (mixed Spanish and Indian ancestry), activists adopted the term in their efforts to promote political activism and demands for economic and educational quality. Prominent leaders emerged—César Chávez and his United Farm Workers Union, Rodolfo Gonzales and his *La Raza Unida* political third-party movement, Reies Lópes Tijerina and his Alianza group seeking to recover land lost or stolen throughout the years, and David Sanchez and his militant Brown Berets, who modeled themselves after the Black Panthers. These past militant leaders have been replaced by a new generation of Chicano advocates, such as Janet Murguía, executive director of the National Council of La Raza. Another significant entity is the Mexican-American Legal Defense and Education Fund (MALDEF). This civil rights organization effectively uses its influence in the public arena to address such issues as bilingualism, school financing, segregation, employment practices, and immigration reform.[28]

Before this national movement dawned, rapid expansion in Sunbelt cities in the 1950s and 1960s had generated problems and tensions that led to the formation of community groups opposed to urban renewal plans threatening Mexican American neighborhoods. These organized neighborhood protests were the vanguard of what became known as the Chicano movement. In San Jose, for example, activists of diverse origins and agendas united in opposition to the effects of urban development on the barrios, and this city later became a center for the Chicano movement during its time of phenomenal growth.[29]

Older organizations, such as the League of United Latin American Citizens and the American G. I. Forum, once focused on assimilation and the Anglo world, with a primary emphasis on social functions. Newer groups—such as *La Raza Unida* and *Movimiento Estudiantil Chicano de Aztlán*—served as synthesizers, bringing the two cultures together. The newer groups have focused on political issues, such as the farm workers' plight, while promoting a sense of peoplehood.

Turning away from the third-party politics of the past, Chicanos are integrating into the two main political parties. In states where they are heavily concentrated, Chicanos are developing a powerful political base, now including nearly 6,000 elected and appointed local and state Hispanic public officials, most of whom are in Texas, California, New Mexico, Arizona, and Colorado.[30]

Illinois is now the third highest state of intended residence among new Mexican arrivals, after California and Texas. The Census Bureau reported that in 2011, nearly 1.7 million Mexican Americans lived in Illinois (thanks in large measure to the lure of its meat-packing industry), making it the fourth highest in Mexican American population behind California, Texas, and Arizona. Nearly three times as many Mexican Americans live in Illinois as in New Mexico.[31]

Mexican immigration continues into both rural and urban areas, but most immigrants are settling in urban neighborhoods, although not necessarily in inner cities. In 2011, 76 percent of the Mexican American population was third generation or higher, and thus hardly the newcomers so many Americans assume most of this group to be.[32] Many of the central-city residents are of a low socioeconomic status and live in areas where the school dropout rate of Mexican American youths runs as high as 45 percent, with student alienation serving as a major cause.[33]

Puerto Rican Americans

Originally inhabited by the Arawak and Caribe indigenous tribes, Puerto Rico came under Spanish domination in 1493 and remained so for 400 years. With the decimation of its native population, Spaniards replaced them with African slaves. **Miscegenation** (interracial marriage) was common, resulting in a society that de-emphasized race. Reflecting the high degree of color integration are such words as *moreno, mulatto, pardo,* and *trigueño,* indicating a broad range of color gradations. Today, structural assimilation in the island's multiracial society extends to housing, social institutions, government policy, and cultural identity.[34] A high degree of intermarriage often means that people classified in one racial category have close-kin relationships with people in other racial categories, either by bloodline or by adoption.

Many Latinos—including Puerto Ricans—primarily regard themselves in cultural terms. However, because so many are influenced by the racial categorization of mainstream U.S. society, some usually will answer—when asked about their race—in standard U.S. terms and identify themselves as black, white, or Indian. Others, though, see themselves as a mixture of race and ethnicity and may identify themselves as Afro-Latinos or white Hispanics. In fact, the Latino view of race differs within Latin American countries, social classes, and even families. Not surprisingly, in the 2010 Census more than 18 million Latinos identified themselves as "other," apparently unwilling to accept the government's rigid racial classifications.[35]

Several cultural and historical factors led to the more tolerant racial attitudes found in Puerto Rico (and in other Latin American countries). Spain long ago had experience with dark-skinned people (Moors), who often married white women. Second, in the wars of Christians against Moors and Saracens, captured whites also became slaves, resulting in laws to protect certain fundamental rights of all slaves, a tradition that carried over to the Spanish colonies in the New World. Upper-class men in these colonies recognized their illegitimate children by women of color, frequently freeing the babies at their baptism. Furthermore, through the practice of *compadrazgo* (ritual kinship), leading white members of a community often became godparents of a child of color at baptism. Even in cases where the child's real father was unknown, the *padrino,* or *compadre,* was well respected and became a significant person in the child's life.[36]

EARLY RELATIONS

After the United States annexed Puerto Rico in 1898 after the Spanish–American War, it attempted forced Americanization. Authorities discouraged anything associated with the Spanish tradition and mandated the use of the English language. Presidents appointed governors, usually from the mainland, to rule the territory. The inhabitants received U.S. citizenship in 1917, but otherwise, the island virtually remained an ignored, undeveloped, poverty-stricken land. Citizenship brought open migration because it eliminated the need for passports, visas, and quotas, but it did not give the people the right to vote for president or to have a voting representative in Congress. By 1930, approximately 53,000 Puerto Ricans were living on the mainland. During the Depression and the war years, migration effectively stopped, but then a mass migration occurred during the post–World War II era.

In the 1940s, several improvements occurred. Puerto Rico became a commonwealth, with the people writing their own constitution and electing their own representatives. In addition, the island gained complete freedom in its internal affairs, including the right to maintain its Spanish heritage and elimination of all requirements to use English.

To help the island develop economically, the U.S. government launched Operation Bootstrap in 1945. U.S. industries received substantial tax advantages if they made capital investments in Puerto Rico. These tax breaks and the abundant supply of low-cost labor encouraged businesses to build 300 new factories by 1953 (increasing to 660 by 1960), creating more than 48,000 new jobs. As a result, Puerto Rico became the most advanced industrialized land, with the highest per capita income, in the Caribbean and in most of Central and South America.

By the 1980s, however, expiring tax exemptions prompted numerous industries to leave the island in search of cheaper labor and tax exemptions elsewhere, thereby reducing available job opportunities. Since then, Puerto Rico's unemployment rate consistently has been approximately twice that of the mainland, rising and falling in response to mainland economic conditions. The island's unemployment rate, which peaked at 23 percent in 1983, stood at 13.7 percent in April 2013.[37]

THE PUSH–PULL FACTORS

Despite the creation of thousands of factory jobs through Operation Bootstrap, the collapse of the Puerto Rican sugar industry in the 1950s triggered the beginning of *La Migracion*, one of the most dramatic voluntary exoduses in world history. One of every six Puerto Ricans migrated to the mainland, driven by the island's stagnant agrarian economy and encouraged by inexpensive plane fares and freedom of entry as U.S. citizens. Many were rural people who settled in metropolitan urban centers, drawn by the promise of jobs. The greatest period of Puerto Rican migration was 1946–1964, when approximately 615,000 moved to the mainland. Only the Irish migration of the mid-nineteenth century offers a close comparison, but that was forced in part by the Potato Famine (see the Ethnic Experience box).

After 1964, a significant drop in Puerto Rican migration occurred, aided in part by a revived Puerto Rican sugar industry after a U.S. boycott of all Cuban trade. Other factors contributed to this drop. The pull factor lost its potency, as cities such as New York City lost hundreds of thousands of manufacturing jobs and thus its promise as a job market. An island population of less than 2.4 million at that time and a declining fertility rate made sustaining the previous high exodus rate impossible. Furthermore, the earlier exodus relieved pressure on the home job market as well as increases in U.S. government welfare support, combined with remittances from family members on the mainland, encouraged many to stay on the island. In the 1970s, migration dropped to 65,900, before rising dramatically to 333,000 in the 1980s, prompted in large measure by the high unemployment rates mentioned earlier.

High migration rates and birth rates resulted in an 82 percent increase in the Puerto Rican population living on the mainland—from 2.7 million in 1990 to approximately 4.9 million today.[38] That number exceeds the 4 million currently living on the island.

Like members of most ethnic groups, some Puerto Ricans return to their home-land to visit, and others to stay. Close proximity to the island is an obvious inducement,

the ETHNIC experience

Harassment Against Early Migrants

"My husband and I bought our own house in Brooklyn after the Second World War, and a few years later, we bought other property on Long Island, where we moved to raise our family. In 1956, we were employed by the U.S. Military Academy, West Point, and purchased a lovely home in a so-called exclusive area not too far away. This was a quaint neighborhood where custom-built homes ranged from $40,000 up to $100,000."

"Shortly after we moved in, we went down to Florida on vacation.

When we came back, the house was empty. We slept on the floor and the following day, our attorney by telephone searched every place high and low until he found our possessions in a warehouse in Nyack. Some of our neighbors had learned we were originally from Puerto Rico, were unhappy to have us as neighbors, and had plotted this against us. The harassment continued for a long time. They threw their garbage every night on our lawn. They even sent the police to intimidate us and even tried

to buy us out. We told them they couldn't afford the luxury of buying us out. We felt we had all the rights in the world to enjoy all the privileges others had. We were honest, hard-working, respectable citizens, too. So we took legal action and demanded for damages. The judge was fair and ruled for us."

Source: Puerto Rican woman who came to the mainland in 1946 in her 20s. Taped interview from the collection of Vincent N. Parrillo.

although the reasons for moving back vary. For some, the return migration stems from retirement or the desire for the more family-oriented society without discrimination and urban crime found more often on the mainland. Researchers investigating the motives for this circular migration also found that economic marginality is an important factor. That is, some migrants fail to succeed economically on the mainland and return to the island. The children of these less successful returning migrants are more likely to be impoverished than the children of migrants who remain on the mainland and the children of natives who never left the island. This outcome also could be caused by migration-related disruptions in employment.[39]

THE FAMILY

In Puerto Rico, as in all Latin American countries, an individual's identity, importance, and security depend on family membership. A deep sense of family obligation extends to dating and courtship. Family approval is necessary because of the emphasis on marriage as a joining of two families, not only a commitment between two individuals. An indication of family importance is the use of both the father's and mother's surnames, but in reverse order to the U.S. practice. José Garcia Rivera, whose father's last name is Garcia and whose mother's is Rivera, should be called Mr. Garcia, not Mr. Rivera. Erroneous interpretation of these names in the United States by non-Hispanics can be a source of intercultural awkwardness for Spanish-speaking people.

One common form of Puerto Rican household is the extended family residing either in the same household or in separate households with frequent visits and strong bonds. Another is the nuclear family, increasingly common among the middle class. A third type is the female-headed household, with children of one or more men but with no permanent male in the home.[40] The last type frequently is found among welfare families and thus is the target of much criticism.

HISPANIC AMERICANS

RELIGION

The Catholic Church traditionally played an important role with immigrant groups, assisting in succession the French, Irish, Germans, Italians, Slavics, Poles, Syrians, Lebanese, and others.[41] This pattern at first did not repeat itself with the Puerto Ricans, at least in terms of representation in the church hierarchy, church leadership in the ethnic community, or immigrant involvement in the church. In 1970, Nathan Glazer and Daniel P. Moynihan observed,

> The Puerto Ricans have not created, as others did, national parishes of their own. Thus, the capacities of the Church are weak in just those areas in which the needs of the migrants are great—in creating a surrounding, supporting community to replace the extended families, broken by city life, and to supply a social setting for those who feel lost and lonely in the great city....
>
> Most of the Puerto Ricans in the city are Catholic, but their participation in Catholic life is small.[42]

Several factors contributed to this departure from the usual pattern. Because the island was a colony for so long, first Spanish and then U.S. priests predominated within the church hierarchy on the island. Few Puerto Ricans became priests, and the few who did rarely came to the mainland with the immigrants. The distant and alien nature of the church in Puerto Rico caused Puerto Ricans to internalize the sense of their Catholic identity without formally attending mass and receiving the sacraments. Baptisms, weddings, and funerals all became important as social occasions, and the ceremony itself was of secondary importance. On the mainland, a few other factors weakened any possibility that the Puerto Ricans would develop a strong ethnic church. The movement of white Catholic ethnics out of the cities left behind clusters of old national churches with few parishioners. Church leaders decided to use these existing churches, schools, and other buildings to accommodate the newcomers. Thus, instead of having their own churches, the Puerto Ricans had the services of one or more Spanish-speaking priests, with special masses and services performed in a basement chapel, school hall, or other area of the parish. Although this practice was cost-effective for the Catholic Church, it prevented the parish from becoming the focal point for a strong, stable community because the group could not identify with it.

As the integrated parishes became more Hispanic throughout the years, the New York archdiocese added more Spanish-speaking priests. In time, the annual *Fiesta de San Juan* each June became a widely observed religious festival in New York City. Religious/civic organizations such as the *Centro Católico Puertorriqueño* in Jersey City and the *Caballeros de San Juan* in Chicago became effective support organizations, further uniting the Puerto Rican community.[43]

PUERTO RICAN COMMUNITIES

More than half (53 percent) of all Puerto Ricans live in the Northeast, with another 30 percent residing in the South. Two states—New York (with 1.1 million) and Florida (with 848,000)—account for the lion's share of that total, comprising 41 percent of the Puerto Rican population on the mainland. Puerto Ricans, of course, live in all 50 states, with other large concentrations (more than 266,000) found in New Jersey, Pennsylvania, and Massachusetts.[44]

For many years, the continuous **shuttle migration** prevented an organized community life from fully developing. Hometown clubs—voluntary organizations based on one's place of birth—provided a place to celebrate weddings, birthdays, first communions, and confirmations. However, because they drew members from scattered New York neighborhoods, they did not serve as community centers, nor did any other social institution. Only

Hispanics fuel the growth of Pentecostalism, an energetic form of evangelical Christianity less structured than traditional Christian worship. Already changing their lives by migrating, perhaps, like these worshipers in Tucson, they also seek a worship style more intimate and participatory than ritualistic Catholic masses.

the annual Puerto Rican Day Parade, begun in 1958, served to galvanize group identity. By the late 1970s, however, increased ethnic neighborhood organization was evolving with the establishment of various social institutions. Some were informal, like the *bodega,* or local grocery store, which still serves as more than a source of Hispanic foods. It is a social gathering place where social interaction, gossip, and neighborliness create a rich community center. Here, one can obtain advice on finding a home, getting a job, or buying a car. The *bodega* thus functions as an important part of the community's infrastructure.[45]

Other community institutions are civic and social organizations. Most notable is *Aspira,* founded in 1961. Through guidance, encouragement, and financial assistance, *Aspira* seeks to develop cultural pride and self-confidence in youths and to encourage them to further their education and enter the professions, technical fields, and the arts. Begun in New York City, its grassroots program achieved national fame and expanded to other cities. Another organization begun in New York City is the Puerto Rican Family Institute, which provides professional social services to Puerto Rican families. Parent action groups, athletic leagues, cultural organizations, and social clubs also exist, providing services and fulfilling community needs. Because of their limited political involvement, Puerto Ricans have had less electoral influence than other ethnic groups. Although they have been U.S. citizens since 1917, island Puerto Ricans cannot vote in federal elections.

SOCIOECONOMIC CHARACTERISTICS

Along with Mexican Americans, Puerto Ricans have a higher poverty rate than other Hispanic groups. However, theirs has been declining steadily in recent years, while that of the Mexicans has been increasing steadily. Helping to improve their economic standing is the increased educational attainment of Puerto Ricans. They have more college graduates than Mexican Americans (16 to 10 percent) and a greater percentage of high school graduates (75 to 58 percent).[46]

Approximately the same percentage of Puerto Rican families lives in poverty as do African American families. Even though blacks have a higher educational level (83 to 75 percent high school graduates or more; 18 to 16 percent bachelor's degree or more), Puerto Ricans have a similar proportion below the poverty line.[47] One explanation for this may lie in family structure. A total of 17 percent of all African American families

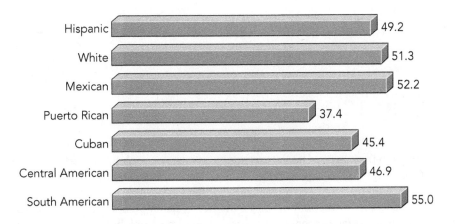

FIGURE 4 Hispanic Married-Couple Families, by origin, in 2011 (in percentages)
Source: U.S. Census Bureau.

have a female head of household with children under age 18, as do 18 percent of Puerto Rican families (see Figure 4).[48] Female-headed households are more vulnerable to living in poverty, and this especially is true for minority women who often lack sufficient education and job skills.

Although these statistics offer cause for concern, at the same time, it would be a mistake to generalize that most Puerto Ricans live in poverty. In fact, many are doing quite well. In 2009, the annual income of 18 percent of Puerto Rican families exceeded $50,000, while the annual income of an additional 24 percent exceeded $75,000.[49]

Cuban Americans

Although the United States granted Cuba independence after the 1898 war with Spain, it continued to exercise *de facto* control over the island. The United States pressured Cuba to relinquish the large naval base it still operates at Guantánamo Bay, and through the Platt Amendment of 1902, it reserved the right to intervene in Cuba if necessary to protect U.S. interests. The Cubans resented these infringements on their newly achieved sovereignty until, in the 1930s, Franklin Roosevelt's Good Neighbor Policy helped ease relations between the two countries.

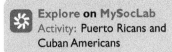

Explore **on MySocLab**
Activity: **Puerto Ricans and Cuban Americans**

MIGRATION

Because the U.S. government did not differentiate Cuban immigrants from others listed as originating in the West Indies until 1950, we do not know the exact numbers of Cuban immigrants prior to that time. Although 500,000 people came to the United States from the West Indies between 1820 and 1950, the Cubans appear to have had little impact on the U.S. scene during that period. Still, a few legacies persisted, such as the Cuban community in northern New Jersey that dates back to 1850 and attracted many immigrants in the 1960s.

Since 1960, more than 1.1 million Cubans have entered the United States. Touched off by Castro's rise to power, Cuban immigration surged in the first years of the Cuban revolution, then ebbed and flowed with shifts in both U.S. and Cuban government policies (see the Ethnic Experience box). In the 1960s and 1970s, the first waves of post-revolutionary refugees (approximately 459,000) were "displaced bourgeoisie"—well-educated middle- and upper-class professionals and businesspeople alienated by the new regime. Sympathetically received as resisters against, and refugees from, the first communist regime in the Western Hemisphere, these Cubans concentrated in several major cities, notably Miami and New York. Initial concern in those cities that the new immigrants might overburden the educational, welfare, and social services systems quickly dissipated as the Cubans made rapid economic progress and became a part of the community.

the ETHNIC experience

Brotherhood in Talk and in Deed

"I have to tell you that the Spanish-speaking people are always talking about brotherhood and the brotherhood of the Latin American countries. They say our brother country Mexico and our brother country Venezuela, and every time they mention a Latin American country, they say the brother country. Well, in reality, it is wrong. When we needed an escape from Cuba, we only had America. America was the only country that opened the door. America is the only place where you can go for freedom and where you can live as a human being."

"I love Cuba very much, but I can tell you that we never had the

freedom that we have here. I can sincerely say that the opportunities in this country—America—are so great and so many, that no matter how bad they say we are as far as economics right now—they're talking about recession and everything—no matter how bad they say, it will never be as bad as it was and it is, actually, in Cuba."

"America took us in and we are grateful to America and to the Americans. And remember, when we came over, we were looking for freedom and liberty. Now we have freedom, we have liberty, and we have the chance to make money. Many Cubans are doing very well, better than me.

I make enough to support my family and to live decently. I am very happy and grateful."

"Believe me, I am not only speaking for myself, but for a large group of Cubans who feel the same way I feel. We are happy here. We miss Cuba. Sometimes we get tearful when we think about the old friends and the old neighborhoods, but we are lucky. We are lucky because we still can say what we want to say, and we can move around wherever we want, and be what we want to be."

Source: Cuban refugee who came to the United States in 1960 at age 18. Taped interview from the collection of Vincent N. Parrillo.

The next influx of Cubans (132,000) occurred in 1980 and was more controversial. Arriving in a so-called "freedom flotilla" of small boats, many chartered by Cuban Americans to bring in other family members, most were urban working-class and lower-class people. However, Castro also forced the departure of several thousand mental patients and prisoners among them—which triggered an unfavorable U.S. response. Called *Marielitos* because they had left Cuba from the port of Mariel, the term became a stigma attached to all these refugees either because of the dubious background of some or the limited education and job skills of many. At first, this group had difficulty adjusting, due partly to their lack of familiarity with a less rigid society in which they must make their own way and find work. Gradually, with help from the longer-established Cuban community, they also were able to acculturate.[50]

ETHNIC COMMUNITIES

Cubans often settled in blighted urban areas, but their motivation, education, and entrepreneurial skills enabled them to bring color, vitality, stability, and improvement to previously declining neighborhoods. Long-time residents of areas heavily populated by Cubans often credited them with restoring or increasing the beauty and vigor of the community.

Miami offers an excellent example. Its climate and nearness to Cuba made it the ideal choice of many exiles, but increased the fears of residents about having so large an ethnic group in their midst. Yet, in the 1960s, the Anglos realized that the Cubans had sparked a real-estate boom, even while other major cities experienced a depressed housing market. Cuban entrepreneurs brought a new commercial vigor to the downtown area, as they created shoe, cigar, and cigarette manufacturing establishments, import houses,

HISPANIC AMERICANS

264

shopping centers, restaurants, and nightclubs. Northwest of Miami, others set up sugar plantations and mills. All this activity marked the beginning of a still-continuing boom period for Miami.[51]

In the early 1980s, however, a series of ethnic-related traumas—labor union restrictions, negative newspaper and public responses to the *Marielitos*, voter approval of a harsh Dade County anti-bilingual ordinance, and four days of anti-Cuban rioting by African Americans—prompted a Cuban reaction that quietly reshaped Miami's political, social, professional, and architectural landscape. Cubans responded to discrimination against them by forming their own economic enclave and entering local politics. Unlike the classical assimilation model of integration and absorption within the dominant society, this movement toward economic and political empowerment enabled Cubans to assert themselves and *then* enter the societal mainstream. Significantly, studies show that Cuban entry into the labor force did *not* negatively affect the city's black population.[52]

THE CONTEMPORARY SCENE

By 2011, the Cuban American population numbered 1.9 million, making them the third largest Hispanic nationality group, after Mexicans and Puerto Ricans. As shown in Figure 4 and Tables 3, 4, and 5, Cuban Americans are doing well according to all social indicators.

It would be a mistake, however, to assume that there is a single Cuban American entity, for within that general patterning are multiple lifestyles. The ethnocultural identity of the first generation, whether early or recent arrivals, remains embedded in Cuban culture, interested in events in Cuba, and fiercely anti-Castro. The Americanized second generation is bilingual but far less active in sociopolitical activity and more interested in the same pop culture, sports, and other matters that appeal to nonethnic young people.[53] Moreover, black Cuban Americans live between two worlds, belonging to both a successful immigrant group yet experiencing the hardships and discrimination of their race.[54]

Because two of every three Cuban Americans live in Florida, the Cuban impact on Miami, now dubbed "Little Havana," has been significant. The city is now 70 percent Hispanic, and Cubans comprise half of that population. More than half of all Cuban Americans live in Miami–Dade County, where Cuban influence has transformed Miami from a resort town to a year-round commercial center with linkages throughout Latin America and has turned it into a leading bilingual cultural center. Approximately 62 percent of Miami–Dade County now is Hispanic, including 894,000 Cubans, 94,000 Puerto Ricans, 56,000 Mexicans, and 236,000 from Central America, and 264,000 from South America.[55]

California has the second-largest Cuban American concentration (84,000), followed by New Jersey (79,000) and New York (75,000). Other Cuban Americans are scattered among the remaining states.[56]

CULTURAL VALUES

In addition to sharing a commonality of values with other Latinos, Cubans share certain subcultural values that differ from those of the dominant U.S. culture.[57] Among these are attitudes toward work, personal qualities, and the role of individuals in society.

Dominant-group values in the United States stress hard work as a means of achieving material well-being, whereas the Cuban orientation is that material success should be pursued for personal freedom, not physical comfort. Cubans do not consider work an end in itself, as they believe Anglos do. Instead, they think one should work to enjoy life. Intellectual pursuits are highly valued; idleness is frowned upon.

Cubans are fervent believers in collective generosity, in contrast to the old Anglo Puritan values of thrift and frugality. Common group traits include sharing good fortune,

In Miami's "Little Havana," some retired Cuban American men, many of them from the first wave of Cuban migration, spend the afternoon playing dominoes in Maximo Gomez Park. This activity is an institutionalized form of ethnic solidarity and social interaction, as card games once were in Italian social clubs a few generations ago.

maintaining a warm open-house policy, and reaching out socially to others. Cubans believe that one of the worst sins is to be a *tacaño,* a cheapskate who does not readily show affection and friendship through kindnesses and hospitality.

Individualism is a value best shown through national and personal pride, which Anglos often misperceive as haughtiness. Yet Cubans believe in expressing individualism not so much through self-assertiveness as through attitudes and actions oriented toward a group, sometimes a large number of people. Hostility needs to be directed through *choteo* and *relajo,* the continuous practice of humor, jokes, and wit, and accepted by others in good part. This is because one should avoid being a *pesado*—someone unlikeable, disagreeable, and without wit—which is the worst of all cultural sins. Cuban Americans thus value *personalismo* (personalized social interactions) more than their Anglo-American counterparts and so tend to spend more leisure time in social activities.

Although they remain the most metropolitan of all Hispanic American groups, Cubans today are as likely to live in such well-groomed suburbs as Coral Gables or Hialeah in Miami–Dade County, Florida—or others in California, New Jersey, or New York—as they are to live in the nearby cities. Except for South Americans, Cubans have a lower fertility rate, lower unemployment rate, higher median family income, greater education rate, and greater middle-class population composition than other Hispanic groups. As Table 5 shows, 22.7 percent of males and 31.9 percent of females are in managerial or professional occupations, a higher proportion than for most other Hispanic groups.

Caribbean, Central and South Americans

4 Describe the immigrant experiences of Caribbean, Central and South Americans.

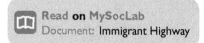

Read on MySocLab
Document: Immigrant Highway

Several push factors—overpopulation, acute shortage of farmland, economic hardship, and political turmoil—triggered a significant increase in **emigration** from several Latin American countries in recent decades. Central and South Americans constitute 13.5 percent of all Hispanic Americans (Figure 5). After Mexico, the largest contingents come from Cuba, the Dominican Republic, El Salvador, Colombia, Guatemala, Ecuador, Peru, and Nicaragua (Figure 6). More than 1.3 million Caribbean immigrants arrived since

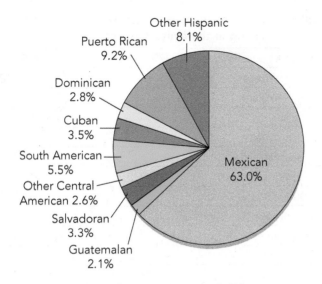

FIGURE 5 Hispanic Americans by Origin, 2010

Source: U.S. Census Bureau.

2000, along with 678,000 from Central America and more than one million from South America.[58]

More than a half-million Central Americans live in Los Angeles. Substantial numbers also reside in San Francisco, Houston, Washington, DC, New York, Chicago, New Orleans, and Miami. As the largest Central American group in the United States, Salvadorans usually constitute the majority of Central Americans in most cities, followed by Guatemalans (Table 6). Among Central Americans, Nicaraguans predominate in Miami, however, and Hondurans in New Orleans.

DOMINICAN AMERICANS

Nearly 1 million Dominican immigrants have left their Caribbean homeland for the United States since 1980, in recent years averaging more than 46,000 annually—which makes the Dominican Republic second only to Mexico as a source of Spanish-speaking immigrants to the United States. Of the 1.6 million Dominican Americans, approximately

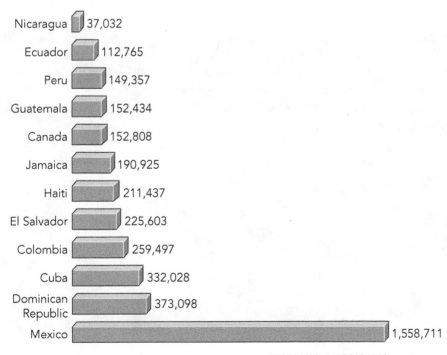

HISPANIC AMERICANS

FIGURE 6 Leading Western Hemisphere Countries for Immigrants, 2003–2012

Source: U.S. Office of Immigration Statistics.

TABLE 6 Number of Central and South Americans
Living in the United States, 2010

Central Americans	3,998,280
Costa Ricans	126,418
Guatemalans	1,044,209
Hondurans	633,401
Nicaraguans	348,202
Panamanians	165,456
Salvadorans	1,648,968
Other Central Americans	31,626
South Americans	2,769,434
Argentineans	224,952
Bolivians	99,210
Chileans	126,810
Colombians	908,734
Ecuadorians	564,631
Paraguayans	20,023
Peruvians	531,358
Uruguayans	56,884
Venezuelans	215,023
Other South Americans	21,809

Source: U.S. Census Bureau, *2011 American Community Survey.*

two of every three live in New York State. Most live in New York City, particularly in Washington Heights in Manhattan and in the Bronx, where Dominicans are a majority in the borough. Other primary areas of residence are New Jersey, Florida, and Massachusetts.

Dominicans more likely are to live and interact within their own ethnic neighborhoods than to integrate into mixed Hispanic neighborhoods. A common pattern is to co-exist alongside Puerto Ricans, each ethnic group keeping mostly to itself. As Puerto

More than one million Dominican Americans live in the greater New York metropolitan region. Especially concentrated in New York City's Washington Heights area in Manhattan and in the Bronx, they comprise approximately one-eighth of the city's population, where the Dominican Independence Day parade along Grand Concourse is one of the city's largest.

HISPANIC AMERICANS

Ricans move out of ethnic neighborhoods into urban or suburban neighborhoods with a significant white or multiethnic presence, Dominicans have replaced them in the older, more segregated neighborhoods.[59]

Most Dominicans are people who have fled the poverty of their land. Because many lack specialized skills, they have a high unemployment rate and often live in poor urban neighborhoods, suffering the deprivation and family disruption so common among people with low levels of education and job skills. More than one in four lives in poverty. Second-generation Dominican Americans, however, tend to be more educated, be employed in skilled or professional occupations, and earn higher incomes. Fifteen percent have college degrees or higher, slightly below Puerto Rican Americans but higher than that for Mexican Americans.[60]

SALVADORAN AMERICANS

Several push factors account for the large-scale Salvadoran emigration to the United States. Agricultural modernization and expansion of property holdings by the landowning oligarchy displaced tens of thousands of rural peasants. Relocating to such urban centers as San Salvador, many of these dispossessed poor could not find work despite the growing industrialization. Conditions deteriorated when the Salvadoran government responded to protests and demonstrations with severe repression. Paramilitary death squads composed of members of the ruling elite, as well as regular security and military forces, targeted peasant leaders, union militants, and political activists. Revolutionary movements arose, and guerrilla offensives in the 1980s prompted escalating violence by the security and military forces and the death squads. Large-scale attacks against civilian populations in rural areas occurred, including massacres of entire villages believed to be sympathetic to the guerrillas. As a result, 20 to 30 percent of the population fled the country.[61]

As a stream of undocumented Salvadorans fled into the United States, immigration agents sought to apprehend and return them, denying them refugee status. The Reagan-era State Department argued that, although El Salvador might be a war-torn country, none of those who left could prove that they specifically had been singled out for persecution and thus did not have the necessary "well-founded fear of persecution" to qualify for political amnesty. Out of this conflict was born the **sanctuary movement** in the United States: Clergy defied the government, hiding Salvadoran refugees in churches and homes. The clergy and members of their congregations provided food, shelter, and clothing and secretly helped the refugees get to safe locations. At first living as a "secret" population, these refugees were among the 143,000 Salvadoran successful applicants for amnesty and permanent residence in the United States.[62]

Although the political situation improved in El Salvador in the 1990s, most Salvadorans in the United States remained, putting down roots and enjoying the support system within their tight-knit ethnic communities. Through chain migration, other relatives and friends join them, continuing a steady migration flow that ranks El Salvador third among Western Hemisphere countries providing immigrants to the United States in recent years. Approximately 2 million Salvadorans live in the United States, with large population clusters in California, Texas, and the New York and Washington, DC, metropolitan areas.[63]

NICARAGUAN AMERICANS

Nicaraguans have entered the United States as immigrants, refugees, asylees, and undocumented aliens. A **refugee** is an alien outside the United States who is unable or unwilling to return to his or her country because of persecution or a well-founded fear of persecution. An **asylee** is similar to a refugee but physically is in the United States or one of its embassies, or at a port of entry when requesting refuge.

HISPANIC AMERICANS

Worldwide, professional soccer is extremely popular, but in the United States it appeals primarily to ethnic Americans, for whom it serves as a rallying point for ethnic identity and pride to cheer for one's homeland. Here, enthusiastic El Salvador fans celebrate their team's victory over Costa Rica in a 2009 Gold Cup game in Los Angeles.

After the Sandinistas came to power in Nicaragua and the Contras undertook a guerrilla war against the new government, more than 46,000 middle-class refugees entered the United States between 1980 and 1990. Simultaneously, another 79,000 Nicaraguans streamed into Texas, filing asylum applications. Most of this latter group, unlike the refugees, consisted of poor, unskilled, and illiterate *campesinos* from the countryside.[64]

Drawn by the Latin American population and the already established Nicaraguan communities in Miami and southern California, most refugees chose one of those two destinations. Miami–Dade County schools, for example, experienced almost a quadrupling of their Nicaraguan student enrollment. With no previous educational experience, most of the 13- to 15-year-olds were illiterate and had to be taught the basics of reading and arithmetic.[65] Sweetwater, a western suburb of Miami, almost completely became Nicaraguan, earning the nickname "Little Managua."

When the Sandinista regime ended in 1990 and the Contra war fizzled out, the 11-year-long exodus of refugees subsided. Some Nicaraguans returned to their homeland, but most chose to stay in the United States.[66] All Nicaraguan refugees and asylees since have received permanent resident status. The immigrant stream in recent years is steady, approximately 3,500 annually, and more than 387,000 now claim Nicaraguan ancestry. About 21 percent hold a bachelor's degree or higher, while 19 percent lived in poverty in 2011.[67] Most live either in Florida or California. Other states with sizable population concentrations include New York, Texas, New Jersey, Maryland, and Virginia.

COLOMBIAN AMERICANS

Among South American countries, Colombia supplies the most immigrants to the United States—more than 280,000 since 2000.[68] Population pressures, the promise of better economic opportunities abroad, and chain-migration networking have increased the annual immigration totals, which now are in the tens of thousands yearly. Of the 995,000 Colombian Americans now residing in the United States, approximately 64 percent are foreign born. Most of the remainder are children born to these first-generation Colombian Americans.[69]

Socioeconomically, Colombians are a mixture of educated professionals and low-skilled peasants seeking a better life (see the Ethnic Experience box). Both their 13 percent poverty rate and 31 percent holding bachelor's degrees or higher are slightly

HISPANIC AMERICANS

the ETHNIC experience

Cultural Traits and Adjustment

"The Colombians here are the poor people. They are the ones who had no chance for an education in Colombia. They are the ones who—because they had no education—their pay was very meager. And so over here, they have a better life than they would in Colombia. So over here, they really—if you can call it the American Dream—has been fulfilled in them."

"Emotionally they're very attached to their country. See, this is the thing that is very hard for people to understand. They want them to become American and to forget everything. You can't! The ties—the blood ties—are too strong! You just can't become—as I said, I cannot even become an American. I can't! Even if I wanted to. You would have to make me all over again. And I love this country and I choose to stay in this country."

"Now with these people—take some of them. They have come because of necessity—sheer necessity. We criticize them because they don't love America, but I don't think that is the fact. Also, if you notice the kind of people that come here. For instance, I had students who were the children of my father's workers on the coffee plantation. Now in my country, they were tilling the soil. You know, the children of the owner go to school. The children of the worker go to till the soil. They had no chance of an education. They had huts up in the mountains where they had no running water, no electricity. Now they come here and they have all the conveniences. If they live poorly, Americans criticize them, but they don't realize where they were living before. If they're not clean and spotless, and they don't keep the shades the right way—but these people have been doing this for a hundred years! The people who just came in never even had a shade to talk about. They never had a venetian blind. They never even had a window to talk about!" [Laughs.]

"I think we have to be careful because we often make the mistake of imposing our way to the people. Now you could say, we're not going to them, they're coming here. But if you accept them in the country, I think you also have to accept a big risk. I think the melting pot idea is not the prevalent idea. It is not a workable idea. Each one has a culture. Each people has a culture and if you want them in America, if you allow them to stay here, you have to work something by which each one is able to live. I don't mean to say that we have independent little countries, but that they are comfortable. Because you cannot remove—those are strong things that you cannot remove from a person."

Source: Colombian immigrant who came to the United States in 1952 at age 16. Taped interview from the collection of Vincent N. Parrillo.

above the national norm.[70] Living mostly in urban neighborhoods near other Hispanics, they form their own social clubs, institutions, and celebrations, attempting—as all first-generation Americans do—to preserve their culture. Colombian Americans mostly are concentrated in New York City (especially in Queens), South Florida, Northern New Jersey, Washington, DC, and California.

A minuscule percentage of Colombians are involved in the cocaine trade and in related drug-war killings. The high profile of this small number of criminals unfortunately smears the rest, just as Italian Americans have suffered from a nationality stereotype because of the Mafia. In reality, nearly all Colombian Americans are decent, law-abiding people who work hard to make a life for themselves in their adopted country. As is the case with many Central and South Americans, the Colombian population can have ancestry that is *mestizo* (mixture of European and indigenous), Spanish, Afro-Colombian, indigenous, and Syrian or Lebanese.

STUDENTS SPEAK "I came to the USA in 2006 when I was 17 years old. Ever since I was five, my grandmother had been telling us we would go to the USA, so this thought was long in my head. I dreamed to be here and I wanted to get out of Peru. Once here, the first problem was assimilating. Everything was new and different: the streets, the housing, the way people drive, the weather, and the radio and TV stations. So, yes, it was definitely very hard to adapt to a new country, but if I'm here, it is for a reason. I have to take advantage of the opportunity life is presenting me."

—Erick Gonzales

HISPANIC AMERICANS

REALITY check

Places and Politics: A Geo-Political Profile

As discussed earlier, Hispanics are settling in all 50 states although three-fourths of them live in only seven states (see Figure 7). However, something else also is occurring. The Hispanic settlement pattern most closely resembles that of the nineteenth-century Germans. In both instances, large numbers settled in cities, creating vibrant neighborhoods with strong ethnolinguistic marks, and in rural areas, bringing a significant ethnic presence to areas long dominated by non-Hispanic whites, and fueling population growth in some of these areas or offsetting population decline in others.

Although mainly living in urban areas, Hispanics now are the fastest-growing group in rural and small-town America. Doubling their numbers in nonmetropolitan areas in the past two decades, most are recent U.S. arrivals, some undocumented, with limited English proficiency and low-education levels. Changing from their traditional pattern of settling in the Southwest, many live elsewhere, such as North Carolina, Georgia, Minnesota, Nevada, and upstate New York. Approximately one in seven works in agriculture; many others are employed in such industries as animal slaughtering and processing, carpet and rug manufacturing, and construction.

Long an influential minority in California and New Mexico, Hispanics continuously have been represented in the U.S. Congress since 1931. Nearly all have been Mexican Americans throughout the years, but Puerto Ricans and Cuban Americans also have served in one or both houses. Hispanics, now 16 percent of the total population, constituted 10 percent of U.S. voters in 2012, and have three U.S. senators and 28 congressional representatives in the 113th Congress, an all-time high in both houses. At the state level, Latinos currently have a combined total of 70 state senators and 206 representatives in 36 state legislatures. Courted by politicians from both political parties, the Latino vote is a greater voice in those seven states where their greatest population concentrations are, but it is only a matter of time before Latino political power is an even more widespread and influential force.

Sources: Adapted from Huffington Post, "Latino Congress Members: 2012 Election Sets a New Record with the Most Latinos Elected to U.S. Senate, House In History." (http://www.huffingtonpost.com); PRNewswire, "Latinos to Serve in State Legislatures of 36 States." (http://www.prnewswire.com); U.S. Census Bureau, The Hispanic Population:2010 (May 2011).

Assimilation

5 Compare and contrast assimilation paths followed by Hispanic Americans.

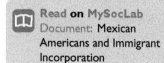

Read on MySocLab
Document: **Mexican Americans and Immigrant Incorporation**

As with all immigrant groups, any discussion of assimilation must take into account the cultural diversity among the groups identified as "Hispanic," as well as other variables such as length of residence, place of residence, social class, family structure, and education of parents (see the Reality Check box and Figure 7). Those differing socioeconomic characteristics among the various Latino groups, as discussed in earlier sections, affect integration into the societal mainstream. Because Hispanics can be of any race, we also must consider that variable in any discussion of assimilation. Consequently, Hispanic Americans can be found at all stages along the pluralism–assimilation continuum. Within the broad range of areas of assimilation, the social institutions of education and family provide valuable insights.

EDUCATION. One means of interpreting rapid assimilation to the United States is educational attainment. Unfortunately, high school age immigrant youths are far more likely than their native-born ethnic peers to drop out of school; some Hispanic groups have above-average levels of school attrition. The most serious problem exists among Mexican teenagers, where nearly half of Mexican-born 15- to 17-year-olds are not in school. Central American youths, especially those from El Salvador and Guatemala, also have

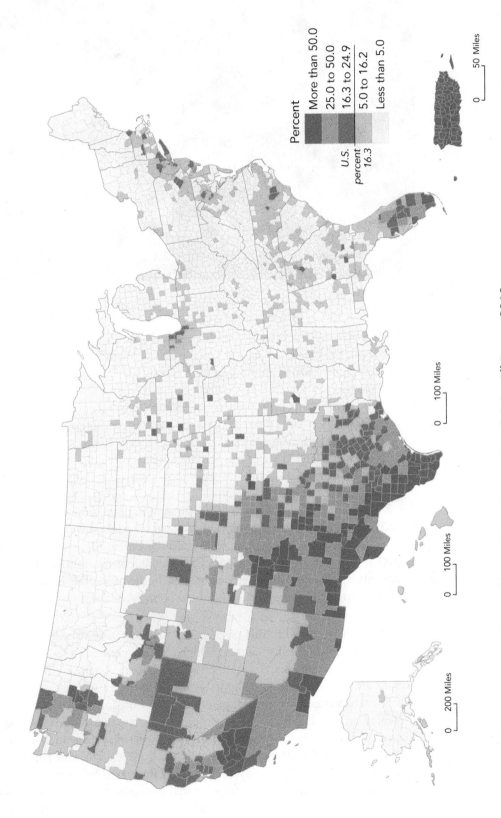

FIGURE 7 Percentage of Population, Hispanic or Latino Origin, All Races, 2010

Source: U.S. Census Bureau.

Percent

More than 50.0
25.0 to 50.0
16.3 to 24.9
5.0 to 16.2
Less than 5.0

U.S.
percent
16.3

50 Miles

100 Miles

100 Miles

200 Miles

In the 2012 presidential election, the growing political power of Latinos was evident, as a record 11.2 million voted, a 15 percent increase over 2008. In battleground states like Colorado, Florida and Nevada, the Latino electorate was particularly decisive, providing the margin of victory in a number of key municipal, state and federal elections.

high dropout rates (less than half are high school graduates). However, if any of these youths immigrate before the start of their schooling, then they are no more likely than native-born Americans to drop out of high school, partly because the younger arrivals become proficient in English more easily.[71] National origin and age of entry therefore are significant variables in the effectiveness of education as an agent of assimilation.[72]

An exception to this pattern occurs among groups concentrated in central cities and attending schools with a demoralized educational climate. In this setting, longer duration of residence in the United States may lead to greater acculturation to U.S. society but not necessarily to better enrollments and the middle-class ideal of high educational aspirations among these groups.

Some analysts argue that the social position of Latino Caribbean populations in the United States today continues relationships rooted in racial hierarchies produced by centuries of European colonialism. Thus, they identify Puerto Ricans as colonial racialized subjects in the Euro-American mindset but Dominicans as transformed into colonial immigrants in the New York metropolitan area. In their view, this legacy of colonialism affects the social acceptance of racially distinct Latino Americans.[73]

FAMILY. As often stated in this chapter, intermarriage patterns are important indicators of assimilation. Recent studies show high rates of intermarriage with non-Hispanics among Cubans, Mexicans, Central Americans, and South Americans. Puerto Ricans and Dominicans have exceptionally high rates of intermarriage with each other, but lower rates of intermarriage with other Hispanics and non-Hispanics.[74] About 15 percent of all Hispanic marriages in recent years have been to non-Hispanics.[75] Third-plus-generation Hispanics especially are increasingly marrying other third-generation co-ethnics and whites.[76] Considerable intermarriage also occurs within the Hispanic population among the different national origin groups, significantly influenced by a pan-ethnic identity of being "Hispanic" that transcends different national origins.[77] Puerto Ricans, though, tend to have greater self-esteem if more attached to their culture and so resist this pan-ethnic identity.[78]

Language acquisition is an obvious factor in the assimilation process. As with past European immigrants, the continual influx of large numbers of new Hispanic immigrants serves to reinvigorate the use of Spanish in everyday life. Its presence has triggered English-only and Official English movements. Nevertheless, even as recently arrived adults have limited English proficiency, Hispanic children—as youngsters always do—learn the new language easily and assimilate more readily than their parents.

Without question, cultural pluralism is an everyday reality among many Latinos and Latinas whose ethnic identity is a vibrant dynamic. A steady influx of newcomers and the presence of many first-generation Hispanic Americans mean continuance of that pattern. However, it would be a mistake either to conclude that the forces of assimilation are not at work, especially among the second generation, or to ignore the assimilation of many Hispanic Americans because of their length of residence and socioeconomic status.

Sociological Analysis

Like other immigrant groups before them, the new arrivals from Latin America are changing the face of the United States, making their distinctive contributions to the neighborhoods in which they live. But with their growing numbers, they also are encountering the hostility historically accorded to almost all newly arriving ethnic groups. Applying sociological perspectives can place their current experiences in a comparative context.

6 Discuss insights gained through sociological analysis.

THE FUNCTIONALIST VIEW

Rapid population growth has been a mixed blessing for these newcomers. They have been able to develop supportive ethnic subcommunities, providing social institutions and an interactive network that ease adjustment to a new country. Cuban settlement in deteriorated urban neighborhoods revitalized those areas and inevitably brought interethnic assistance to other Hispanic groups. Currently, Hispanics are increasingly moving to rural areas, attracted by the low cost of living outside metropolitan areas, and so are helping offset population losses in those communities and transforming the social and economic fabric of many small towns.[79] Because approximately four-fifths of all Hispanics live in nine states (California, Arizona, Colorado, New Mexico, Texas, Illinois, New York, New Jersey, and Florida), they quickly are realizing their potential political power, enabling them to improve their life situation. Concern exists that their numbers and common language may be dysfunctional, delaying assimilation and creating an "Hispanic Quebec" within the United States.

Immigrants with lower levels of educational attainment often fill the needs of industries on the periphery, such as garment factories, restaurants, and hotels, which depend on low-skilled workers, even undocumented aliens and minors. This segment of the labor market prefers to hire immigrants with less than a high school education, as evidenced by the fact that immigrants with less than a high school diploma (except Dominicans, Puerto Ricans, and Russians) have higher rates of labor-force participation than U.S.-born people in the same category and slightly higher earnings. These advantages decrease with increased education, suggesting that, in the less competitive, lower-status jobs, Latin American immigrants have become the highest earners as they fill manual labor jobs needed by labor-intensive industries.[80]

Rapid social change is the key to functional analysis of existing problems. The rapid influx of large numbers of immigrants and the changing occupational structure of U.S. society have prevented the social system from absorbing so many low-skilled workers right away. How can we ease Hispanic newcomers into the societal mainstream? We can either take a *laissez-faire* attitude, allowing the passage of time to produce acculturation and economic improvement, or we can seek an interventionist means of resolving the problems. Advocates of the latter approach argue that, through bilingual and other educational programs, job-training programs, and business investment incentives for more job opportunities, we can improve the system to help newcomers realize the American Dream that brought them here.

THE CONFLICT VIEW

Although Robert Blauner first applied the concept of internal colonialism to the black ghetto, Chicano activists found the idea appealing because it coincided with the legacy of Anglo takeover and domination of the Southwest in 1848 and continued Anglo control of the barrios in the cities of the region since that date. They readily embraced the concept of the barrio as an internal colony, dependent on Anglo investment and subservient to Anglo domination of municipal government and commerce. They criticized the concentration of the Mexican American working class in poor urban barrios and the exodus of the Anglo and Latino middle class to the suburban fringe. In these economically weakened barrios, Mexican Americans struggled against larger economic and political trends.

Analysts of internal colonialism maintain that the continued residential segregation of Hispanic Americans in ghetto areas of many U.S. cities is unlike the pattern experienced by European immigrants to the United States. In the case of Europeans, the level of segregation declined with length of residence in the United States. However, with the newer immigrants, instead of seeing a gradual acculturation or structural assimilation process, these analysts see the persistence of subordination, with Latinos confined to certain areas of rental properties controlled by absentee landlords and restricted to low-paying job opportunities, inferior schools, and many other forms of discrimination.

Economic exploitation is another dimension of conflict analysis. Mexicans, Central Americans, and other Latinos work as migrant farm laborers in many places under abysmal conditions for meager pay despite repeated exposés. City sweatshops employing thousands of undocumented aliens, refugees, and low-skilled legal immigrants operate in clandestine settings, prospering from the toil of low-wage employees. The rise of an ethnic bourgeoisie—the *padrino* in urban or farm settings, the token elite among the Chicano population, or the small middle class with other Hispanic groups—only helps control the rest and does not signal an economic upgrading and assimilation of the remaining group members.

Resolving the problem of this low social status of millions of Hispanic Americans, according to this view, will occur only through protest movements, organized resistance to exploitation, and the flexing of ever-strengthening political muscle. New citizens need to realize more fully their commonalities, taking a lesson from the Irish and using their ballot power to create the necessary changes to benefit themselves. If they effectively wield their political clout, as demonstrated in the 2012 presidential election, they can overcome the power differential that exists in the social and economic spheres as well.

THE INTERACTIONIST VIEW

Anglo–Hispanic relations often are strained by inaccurate perceptions. Members of the dominant group tend to think that there is but one Spanish-speaking public, when actually a variety exists, each preferring different foods, music, and recreation and having different cultural attributes. Too many Anglos view Hispanic ethnic subcommunities, parallel social institutions, and limited command of English as detrimental to the cohesiveness of U.S. society, failing to realize that more than one-third of Hispanics are first-generation Americans repeating a resettlement pattern of earlier European immigrants. Extensive poverty among many Hispanics often invites outsiders to blame the victim or to engage in culture-of-poverty thinking. Instead of confronting the problems of poor education and lack of job skills and job opportunities, some find fault with the group itself, reacting with avoidance, indifference, or paternalistic behavior.

In our earlier discussion about eye contact, physical proximity, the notion of hurrying, and the relevance of time, we identified a few areas of potential cultural misunderstanding. Add to this Anglo impatience with language problems, African American concerns about economic competition, taxpayer resistance to welfare costs, labor union fears that wages will be undermined by cheap labor, and nativist alarm at the failure of the melting pot to "melt" the Hispanics, and you have further reasons for non-Hispanics to stereotype Latinos as an increasing social problem. Because perceptions influence interaction patterns and social policy, the potential for tensions and conflict is strong.

Witnessing extensive Spanish-language usage no doubt is the main "hot button" that triggers nativists' ire more than any other ethnic manifestation by Hispanics. Similar reactions once occurred when German and Italian newcomers concentrated in large clusters and their languages were everyday commonalities. Language and culture share an interdependent relationship; each fosters the other, with both usually ebbing through the assimilation process throughout the generations.

For Hispanics, clinging to the old country's culture and ethnic identity is a matter of pride and personal commitment to a rich heritage. Some find it their only solace against discrimination, and even those who achieve economic mobility retain a strong ethnic identification. Washed afresh with new waves of Hispanic immigrants, the ethnic communities retain their vitality, prompting even successful Hispanics to hold onto their ethnic traditions. Interactionists thus point to the resilience of an ethnic self-definition, which is somewhat at odds with assimilationist views.

Retrospect

In many ways, recent Hispanic immigrants repeat the patterns of earlier racial and ethnic groups. Coming in large numbers from impoverished lands, many enter the lowest strata of society, cluster together in substandard housing units, and face the problems of adjustment, deprivation, frustration, and pathology (sickness and crime). Marked as strangers by their language, customs, and physical appearance, they face difficulty in gaining acceptance and achieving economic security. The Hispanic poor face the same problems and criticisms as earlier groups. They also are criticized for failing to overcome these problems immediately, even though other groups often took three generations to do so. The dominant–minority response patterns in this case thus are quite similar to those of earlier immigrant peoples.

Particularly significant for the Hispanic immigrants, in comparison to other groups, are the changed structural conditions. The restrictive immigration laws of the 1920s drastically curtailed the great influx of southern, eastern, and central Europeans. Consequently, the immigrants already here did not receive continuous cultural reinforcement from new arrivals. But among Hispanics, there is a sizable flow of new arrivals, and rapid and inexpensive communications and transportation encourage return trips to the not-so-far-away homeland. In addition, earlier European immigrants sometimes encountered heavy-handed attempts at Americanization, whereas today's immigrants live in a time when pluralism and ethnic resurgence are common among members of the dominant group.

Other crucial changes in structural conditions are in technology and the job market. When the European poor came to the United States, they could find many unskilled and semiskilled jobs. Despite many evils and abuses in industry, an immigrant could secure a little piece of the American Dream through hard physical labor. The immigrant today enters a labor market where technology has eliminated many of those types of low-skill jobs, but others remain or have taken their place: construction, installation, home maintenance, and service industries. Through hard work, they follow a path that many other immigrants pursued to gain economic security.

During the mass European migration, the fledgling labor unions successfully struggled to improve the economic condition of the immigrant workers. Nowadays, unions have limited means to help newcomers, and the federal government is less inclined to offer welfare aid than in the 1960s, when the government encouraged individuals to apply for welfare by liberalizing eligibility requirements. With structural unemployment leaving no alternative, the system maneuvers many Hispanic newcomers into a marginal existence.

Highly visible because of their numbers, language, culture, and poverty, many Latinos find themselves the objects of resentment, hostility, and overt discrimination from the dominant society. The familiar pattern of blaming the victim results in negative stereotyping, social segregation, and all shades of prejudice and discrimination against the Hispanic and Caribbean poor.

Not all are poor, of course. For those who are not, attaining economic security means a very different life experience. Other positive factors offer some promise of easing the transition to life in the United States: bilingual education, increased public awareness, a greater tolerance for cultural pluralism, and civic and government programs. Serious problems remain for a disproportionate number of Hispanic Americans, however, and it is too soon to tell whether new legislation designed to control the influx of undocumented aliens will have any positive impact on the Hispanic poor.

On MySocLab

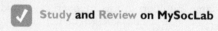 Study **and** Review **on MySocLab**

KEY TERMS

Asylee	*Marianismo*	Refugee
Dignidad	Marielitos	Sanctuary movement
Emigration	Miscegenation	Shuttle migration
Machismo	Pentecostalism	Undocumented alien

DISCUSSION QUESTIONS

1. The beginning of the chapter offers a sociohistorical perspective as well as information on racial attitudes and cultural differentiation. What was one striking or surprising piece of information you picked up here?

2. In this chapter we offer various social indicators by which we measure the degree of mainstreaming that has occurred for any minority group (in this case, Hispanic Americans). What conclusions can you draw from these data? Have we made progress in recent decades? Where do the main problems still remain? What would you expect future data to show? Why?

3. Various Hispanic ethnic groups are discussed in the remainder of the chapter. From reading about them, what observations can you make?

4. A common criticism of Hispanic Americans centers on their not assimilating. Based on the material under the heading "Assimilation" earlier in the chapter, what comments can you make?

5. The end of the chapter offers three theoretical analyses. How did one of these theories become more meaningful or relevant to you in its application to the Hispanic experience?

HISPANIC AMERICANS

INTERNET ACTIVITIES

1. Want to see the Census Bureau's latest report on U.S. Hispanics? Click on "Hispanic Population in the United States" at http://www.census.gov/prod/cen2010/briefs/c2010br-04.pdf, and you will have access to the latest information on their demographic and socioeconomic characteristics.

2. Explore the Internet a little and see what's out there offering information, support, and assistance to the Hispanic American community. For example, click on "Latino/Hispanic Resources" at http://www-bcf.usc.edu/~cmmr/Latino.html, and then check out some of the links. What are you finding? Do you see some common themes or patterns? What groups are better represented than others? What are the primary resources offered?

NOTES

1. William D. Carrigan and Clive Webb, "The Lynching of Persons of Mexican Origin or Descent in the United States, 1848 to 1928," *Journal of Social History*, 37 (2003): 411–38; and Wayne Moquin, *Documentary History of the Mexican Americans* (New York: Bantam Books, 2000).

2. Population Reference Bureau, *2012 World Population Data Sheet*. Retrieved November 12, 2012 (http://www.prb.org).

3. U.S. Office of Immigration Statistics, *2011 Yearbook of Immigration Statistics* (Washington, DC: U.S. Government Printing Office, 2009), Table 34, pp. 92–93.

4. José Vasconceles, *The Cosmic Race* (Baltimore: Johns Hopkins University Press, 1998).

5. See Julia Preston and Fernanda Santos, "A Record Latino Turnout, Solidly Backing Obama," *New York Times* (November 8, 2012), p. P13.

6. See Matthew C. Gutmann, *The Meanings of Macho: Being a Man in Mexico City*, 10th anniv. ed. (Berkeley: University of California Press, 2006); Rafael L. Ramirez, Rosa E. Casper, and Peter J. Guarnaccia, *What It Means to Be a Man: Reflections of Puerto Rican Masculinity* (New Brunswick, NJ: Rutgers University Press, 2000).

7. U.S. Census Bureau, *2011 American Community Surveys*, Table S0201.

8. See Ismael Garcia, *Dignidad: Ethics through Hispanic Eyes* (Nashville, TN: Abingdon Press, 1998).

9. See, for example, Mark Q. Sawyer and Tianna S. Paschel, "'We Didn't Cross the Color Line, the Color Line Crossed US': Blackness and Immigration in the Dominican Republic, Puerto Rico, and the United States," *Du Bois Review: Social Science Research on Race*, 4 (2007): 303–15.

10. See Lee M. Penyak and Walter J. Petry (eds.), *Religion in Latin America: A Documentary History* (Maryknoll, NY: Orbis Books, 2007).

11. Pew Hispanic Center, "Changing Faiths: Latinos and the Transformation of American Religion." Retrieved November 13, 2012 (http://www.pewhispanic.org/2007/04/25/iv-the-renewalist-movement-and-hispanic-christianity); Pedrito U. Maynard-Reid, *Diverse Worship: African-American, Caribbean, & Hispanic Perspectives* (Downers Grove, IL: Intervarsity Press, 2000), pp. 171–82.

12. See H. B. Cavalcanti and Debra Schleef, "The Case for Secular Assimilation: The Latino Experience in Richmond, Virginia," *Journal for the Scientific Study of Religion*, 44 (2005): 473–83.

13. For some excellent cross-cultural analyses of attitudes regarding distance between people, see Edward T. Hall, *The Hidden Dimension*, reprint ed. (Mangolia, MA: Smith Publishing, 1992); and *The Silent Language*, reprint ed. (Westport, CN: Greenwood Press, 1980).

14. U.S. Census Bureau, *2011 American Community Survey*, Table S0201.

15. U.S. Census Bureau, *The Hispanic Population: 2010*, Census Briefs, Table 5, May 2011.

16. See Alejandro Portes and Rubén G. Rumbaut, *Immigrant America: A Portrait*, 3rd ed. (Berkeley: University of California Press, 2007).

17. U.S. Census Bureau, *2011 American Community Survey*, Table S0201.

18. Ibid.

19. Pew Hispanic Center, "Educational Attainment: Better Than Meets the Eye, but Large Challenges Remain." Retrieved November 12, 2012 (http://pewhispanic.org/files/factsheets/3.pdf).

20. U.S. Census Bureau, *The Hispanic Population: 2010*, Table 4.

21. See Roberto M. De Anda, *Chicanas and Chicanos in Contemporary Society*, 2nd ed. (Lanham, MD: Rowan & Littlefield, 2005), Chapters 5 and 7.

22. See Francisco E. Balderrama and Raymond Rodríguez, *Decade of Betrayal: Mexican Repatriation in the 1930s*, revised ed. (Albuquerque: University of New Mexico Press, 2006).

23. See Avi Astor, "Unauthorized Immigration, Securitization, and the Making of Operation Wetback," *Latino Studies*, 7 (2009): 5–29.

24. Carey McWilliams with an update by Matt S. Meier (ed.), *North from Mexico* (New York: Praeger, 1990), pp. 223–25.

25. See, for example, Jack Schneider, "Escape from Los Angeles," *Journal of Urban History*, 6 (2008): 995–1012.

26. U.S. Census Bureau, *2011 American Community Survey*, Table S0201.

27. Zulema Valdez, "Segmented Assimilation among Mexicans in the Southwest," *The Sociological Quarterly*, 47 (2006): 397–424; and Elaine M. Allensworth, "Earnings Mobility of First and '1.5' Generation Mexican-Origin Women and Men: A Comparison with U.S.-born Mexican Americans and Non-Hispanic Whites," *International Migration Review*, 31 (1997): 386–410.

28. See MALDEF (http://www.maldef.org) and National Council of La Raza (http://www.nclr.org); also Peter Skerry, "Racial Politics in the Administrative State," *Society*, 42 (2005): 36–45.

29. See Robert Bauman, "The Black Power and Chicano Movements in the Poverty Wars in Los Angeles," *Journal*

of *Urban History*, 33 (2007): 277–95; Joseph A. Rodriguez, "Ethnicity and the Horizontal City: Mexican Americans and the Chicano Movement in San Jose," *Journal of Urban History*, 21 (1995), 597–621.

30. National Association of Latino Elected and Appointed Officials, *National Roster of Hispanic Officials*. Retrieved November 12, 2012 (http://www.naleo.org/ataglance.html).

31. U.S. Census Bureau, "Illinois," *2011 American Community Survey*.

32. U.S. Census Bureau, *Current Population Survey, 2011*, Annual Social and Economic Supplement, released November 2012.

33. See, for example, Robert K. Ream and Russell W. Rumberger, "Student Engagement, Peer Social Capital, and School Dropout among Mexican American and Non-Latino White Students," *Sociology of Education*, 81 (2008): 109–39; Mira Mayer, "The Dropout Rates of Mexican American Students in Two California Cities," *Research for Educational Reform*, 9 (2004): 14–24.

34. See Jossianna Arroyo, "'Roots' or the Virtualities of Racial Imaginaries in Puerto Rico and the Diaspora," *Latino Studies*, 8 (2010): 195–219.

35. Mireya Navarro, "For Many Latinos, Racial Identity Is More Culture than Color," *New York Times* (January 13, 2012), p. A11.

36. Joseph P. Fitzpatrick, *Puerto Rican Americans*, 2nd ed. (Englewood Cliffs, NJ: Prentice Hall, 1987), pp. 106–7.

37. U.S. Bureau of Labor Statistics, *Economy at a Glance: Puerto Rico*. Retrieved November 12, 2012 (http://stats.bls.gov/eag/eag.pr.htm).

38. U.S. Census Bureau, *2011 American Community Survey*, Table S0201.

39. See Elizabeth M. Aranda, "Class Backgrounds, Modes of Incorporation, and Puerto Ricans' Pathways into the Transnational Professional Workforce," *American Behavioral Scientist*, 52 (2008): 426–56.

40. Gina M. Prez, *The Near Northwest Side Story: Migration, Displacement, and Puerto Rican Families* (Berkeley: University of California Press, 2004).

41. See Oscar Handlin, *The Uprooted*, 2nd ed. (Philadelphia: University of Pennsylvania Press, 2002), pp. 105–28.

42. Nathan Glazer and Daniel P. Moynihan, *Beyond the Melting Pot*, 2nd ed. (Cambridge, MA: MIT, 1970), pp. 103–4.

43. See Edna Acosta-Belen and Carlos E. Santiago, *Puerto Ricans in the United States: A Contemporary Portrait* (Boulder, CO: Lynne Rienner Publishing, 2006).

44. U.S. Census Bureau, *The Hispanic Population: 2010*, Census Briefs (May 2011), Table 4.

45. See Arlene Dávila, *Barrio Dreams: Puerto Ricans, Latinos, and the Neoliberal City* (Berkeley: University of California Press, 2005).

46. U.S. Census Bureau, *2011 American Community Survey*, Table S0201.

47. Ibid.

48. Ibid.

49. U.S. Census Bureau, *Statistical Abstract: 2012*, Table 37, p. 42.

50. See Cecilia Rodríguez Milanés, *Marielitos, Balseros, and Other Exiles* (Brooklyn, NJ: Ig Publishing, 2009).

51. Robert M. Levine, *Cuban Miami* (New Brunswick, NJ: Rutgers University Press, 2001).

52. See Juan Gonzalez, *Harvest of Empire: A History of Latinos in America*, rev. ed. (New York: Penguin, 2011), Chapter 6; Alejandro Portés and Alex Stepick, *City on the Edge: The*

Transformation of Miami (Berkeley: University of California Press, 1994).

53. Marta Diaz Fernandez, "Intergenerational Dynamics in the Cuban Community in Southern Florida: Identity and Politics in the Second Generation," *Cuban Studies*, 31 (2001): 76–101.

54. See C. Alison Newby and Julie A. Dowling, "Black And Hispanic: The Racial Identification of Afro-Cuban Immigrants in the Southwest," *Sociological Perspectives*, 50 (2007): 343–66.

55. U.S. Census Bureau, *2011 American Community Survey*, Table S0201.

56. Ibid.

57. See Louis A. Pérez, Jr. *On Becoming Cuban: Identity, Nationality, and Culture* (Chapel Hill: University of North Carolina Press, 2008); and Alejandro Brice, *An Introduction to Cuban Culture for Rehabilitation Service Providers* (Buffalo, NY: Center for International Rehabilitation Research Information & Exchange, 2002), pp. 8–10.

58. U.S. Office of Immigration Statistics, *20011 Yearbook of Immigration Statistics*, Table 2.

59. Arun P. Lobo, Ronald J. O. Flores, and Joseph J. Salvo, "The Impact of Hispanic Growth on the Racial/Ethnic Composition of New York City Neighborhoods," *Urban Affairs Review*, 37 (2002): 703–27.

60. U.S. Census Bureau, *2011 American Community Survey*, Table S0201.

61. See Carlos B. Cordova, *The Salvadoran Americans* (Westport, CT: Greenwood Press, 2005).

62. See Susan Bibler Coutin, "Falling Outside: Excavating the History of Central American Asylum Seekers," *Law & Social Inquiry*, 36 (2011): 569–96; Cecilia Mejivar, "Family Reorganization in a Context of Legal Uncertainty: Guatemalan and Salvadoran Immigrants in the United States," *International Journal of Sociology of the Family*, 32 (2006): 223–45.

63. See Claudia Dorrington, "Salvadoran Immigrants and Refugees: Demographic and Socioeconomic Profiles," pp. 393–424, in *Asian and Latino Immigrants in a Restructuring Economy* (Stanford, CA: Stanford University Press, 2001); U.S. Census Bureau, *2011 American Community Survey*, Table S0201.

64. See Jennifer H. Lundquist and Douglas S. Massey, "Politics or Economics? International Migration during the Nicaraguan Contra War," *Journal of Latin American Studies*, 37 (2005): 29–53.

65. See Dorothy Norris-Tirrell, "Immigrant Needs and Local Government Services: Implications for Policymakers," *Policy Studies Journal*, 30 (2002): 58–69.

66. Mireya Navarro, "After Year in Exile in South Florida, Nicaraguans Feel the Tug of 2 Homes," *New York Times* (March 21, 1995).

67. U.S. Census Bureau, *2011 American Community Survey*, Table S0201; U.S. Office of Immigration Statistics, *2011 Yearbook of Immigration Statistics*, Table 2.

68. U.S. Office of Immigration Statistics, loc. cit.

69. U.S. Census Bureau, loc. cit.

70. Ibid.

71. Ibid.; Dylan Conger, "Testing, Time Limits, and English Learners: Does Age of School Entry Affect How Quickly Students Can Learn English?" *Social Science Research*, 38 (2009): 383–96.

72. Charles Hirschman, "The Educational Enrollment of Immigrant Youth: A Test of the Segmented-Assimilation Hypothesis," *Demography*, 38 (August 2001): 317–36.

73. Ramon Grosfoguel and Chloe S. Ramon, "'Coloniality of Power' and Racial Dynamics: Notes toward a Reinterpretation of Latino Caribbeans in New York City," *Identities,* 7 (March 2000): 85–125.

74. See Hyoung-jin Shin, "Intermarriage Patterns among the Children of Hispanic Immigrants," *Journal of Ethnic & Migration Studies,* 37 (2011): 1385–1402.

75. Sharon M. Lee and Barry Edmonston, "Hispanic Intermarriage, Identification, and U.S. Latino Population Change," *Social Science Quarterly,* 87 (2006):1263–79.

76. Daniel T. Lichter, Julie H. Carmalt, and Zhenchao Qian, "Immigration and Intermarriage among Hispanics: Crossing Racial and Generational Boundaries," *Sociological Forum,* 26 (2011): 241–64.

77. Michael J. Rosenfeld, "The Salience of Pan-National Hispanic and Asian Identities in U.S. Marriage Markets," *Demography,* 38 (May 2001): 161–75.

78. Irene Lopez, "'But You Don't Look Puerto Rican': The Moderating Effect of Ethnic Identity on the Relation between Skin Color and Self-Esteem among Puerto Rican Women," *Cultural Diversity & Ethnic Minority Psychology,* 14 (2008): 102–8.

79. See William Kandel, Jamila Henderson, Heather Koball, and Randy Capps, "Moving Up in Rural America: Economic Attainment of Nonmetro Latino Immigrants," *Rural Sociology,* 76 (2011): 101–28.

80. U.S. Census Bureau, *American Factfinder.* Retrieved January 12, 2013 (http://factfinder2.census.gov).

GLOSSARY

Asylee An alien found in a country or port of entry who is unable or unwilling to return to his or her country of origin, or to seek the protection of that country, because of persecution or a well-founded fear of persecution.

Dignidad Hispanic cultural value that the dignity of all humans entitles them to a measure of respect.

Machismo Value orientation defining masculinity in varying terms of virility, honor, and providing for one's family.

Marianismo Value orientation defining feminine virtue as accepting male dominance and emphasizing family responsibilities.

Pentecostal faith A form of evangelical Christianity that inspires a sense of belonging through worship participation.

Refugee Any person outside his or her country of origin who is unable or unwilling to return because of persecution or a well-founded fear of persecution.

Sanctuary movement A 1980s religious and political movement of hundreds of Protestant and Catholic congregations that sheltered Central American refugees from immigration authorities.

Shuttle migration Large-scale movement back and forth between two countries.

PHOTO CREDITS

Credits are listed in order of appearance.

Michael McCann Photography/Getty Images;
New York City/Alamy;
Barry Austin Photography/Riser/Getty Images;
Paul Conklin/PhotoEdit;
Joe Sohm/The Image Works;
AP Photo/Arizona Daily Star/Chris Richards;
Mario Algaze/The Image Works;
Mariela Lombard/ZUMAPRESS/Newscom;
Mark Ralston/AFP/Getty Images;
AP Photo

TEXT CREDITS

Credits are listed in order of appearance.

University of New Mexico Press (Rights);
McWilliams, Carey; Praeger Publishers;
Parrillo Vincent;
MIT Press.

The 1970s and 1980s: Redefining the 1960s

The timeline calls to mind the impact that the 1960s, the Vietnam War, the youth rebellion, and the Civil Rights movement had on the decade of the seventies. The school walkouts of 1968 politicized thousands of Chicana/o students throughout the country, which led to their involvement in issues such as the Vietnam War and Civil Rights movement in the 1960s. Because of the sacrifices of the Chicana/o and the preceding generations, more Chicanos and Chicanas entered college after this point than at any time in history. The expectations of the community increased as more people started thinking in terms of constitutional rights and control over their own lives. However, the timeline also resembles the decades of the 1920s and the 1950s, which followed the two major wars and were marked by a growing Euro-American xenophobia and a renewal of big businesses' war on the working class.

The intense demands for human and constitutional rights caused a backlash among President Richard Nixon's supporters. The white establishment resisted reform, resulting in friction with Chicanos and other minorities. As the community's awareness expanded, race, gender, and economic issues competed with the Vietnam War for attention. Chicanos became more cognizant of their dependency and their exploitation by the U.S. economy. Finally, many Latinos also shared the dream of the martyred Che Guevara of a united Latin America.[1] They were outraged by world events in general and the complicity of the Central Intelligence Agency in the 1973 overthrow of Chilean President Salvador Allende in particular.[2]

1968	1969	1970	1972	1973	1974	1975	1976	1977	1978	1979

From Chapter 14 of *Occupied America: A History of Chicanos*, Eighth Edition. Rodolfo F. Acuña. Copyright © 2015 by Pearson Education, Inc. All rights reserved.

The 1970s and 1980s: Redefining the 1960s

Scores of Chicanos continued to organize along national lines, believing that change was possible through unity among Chicanas/os and through the identity politics of the 1960s. *La Raza Unida* Party (LRUP), founded in 1970, was an expression of this nationalism. It was a political party formed to end the marginalization of the Chicana/o community perpetuated by the two major parties; the two parties elected white candidates and kept Chicanas/os powerless. Some Chicanas/os sought to build revolutionary cells, while others preferred working within established organizations. Large numbers of Mexican immigrants continued to enter the country; they benefited from the entitlements brought about by the struggles of earlier Mexican American and Chicana/o generations, often without understanding their legacy. Meanwhile, the entry of larger numbers of Chicanas and Chicanos into college, and their graduation, brought about a slight widening of the Chicana/o middle class. The end of the 1970s saw the election of more Chicanos to political office. However, the agenda of the movement was also changing.

The 1965 amendments to the Immigration Act dramatically changed the mix of immigrants. In the 1950s, 53 percent of immigrants were from Europe, 25 percent from Latin America, and 6 percent from Asia. By the 1980s, only 11 percent of immigrants came from Europe, whereas 42 percent came from Latin America and 42 percent from Asia.[3] This was a result of changing U.S. admission policy from national origins to family preferences. The bulk of the Latin American immigration was from Mexico—a result of Mexico's high birth rate, modernization of agriculture, and a decline of ruralism. Even more Mexicans would have migrated to the United States had it not been for Mexico's economic growth of the late 1970s based on the "Oil Boom." The presence of more foreign-born people meant an increase in U.S. nativism, as politicos and journalists without substantiation criminalized Mexican immigrants. This racist nativism pressured the Immigration and Naturalization Service (INS) to become more aggressive. Thus, by necessity, immigration took its place along with farmworker issues as a priority among Chicanos.

The redefining of the Chicano identity began even before 1970. Government and the media moved to homogenize all Spanish speakers under the classification of Hispanic, and then Latino. Another attempt at redefinition came from within the Chicano community itself. Large waves of immigrants during the 1970s and 1980s rejected the term *Chicano*, which had been viewed as pejorative among first-generation immigrants since it was first proposed in 1969. In the first part of the 1970s, massive social unrest and ethnic pride increased unity within the movement itself, boosting acceptance for the term Chicano. This unifying moment came in the aftermath of the demonstration of August 29, 1970. However, it was doused by the police and the media that manipulated the facts of what happened on August 29. The assassination of journalist Rubén Salazar intimidated some, but more tragic was that the media's suppression of the facts repressed the memory of progressives and thus helped institutionalize racism.[4]

Instead of addressing the grievances of youth, the media portrayed young Chicanos as malcontents who wanted to destroy society. This historical distortion allowed for the redefinition of the 1960s; the death of Rubén Salazar thus became merely an unfortunate accident and racism became an aberration rather than a systemic problem. The lack of a coherent memory of the gains of the 1960s led to a fractionalization of the Chicana/o community. The quickness of this reversal caught most Chicanos unprepared and by July 25, 1983, a *Los Angeles Times* poll showed that 25 percent of Chicanos preferred the designation "Mexican"; 23 percent, "Mexican American"; 18 percent, "Latino"; and 14 percent, "Hispanic." The reversal followed a decade of persistent propaganda blurring the definition of the term *Chicano*, or even *Mexican*.[5]

This was not the first time in history that conservatives derailed the nation's commitment to values such as equality and social justice. After World War II, capitalists exaggerated the Communist threat and labeled New and Fair Deal programs as socialistic and a threat to American democracy. Soon after the 1960s, a similar phenomenon was observed: the right wing moved to weaken the Great Society's civil rights legislation and the decade's commitment to equality and justice for all. In order to change the common perception among the Euro-American public, words such as *racism* and *victim* were redefined. For example, during the 1960s many Americans challenged beliefs such as "every American is equal" and claims that "if the poor are poor, it is because the poor do not want to work." Liberals countered that this point of view blamed the victim; they claimed that programs such as affirmative action brought minorities into the mainstream.

Meanwhile, white homeowners and big business led an assault to shift the burden of funding social programs from themselves to the middle class, thus eliminating many social and educational programs. The recessions of the 1970s spawned the so-called taxpayer revolts. California's Proposition 13 in 1978 limited taxation to 1 percent of the full value of the property at the 1975 assessment, or the assessment after a later ownership change or construction, giving tax advantages to property owners who had purchased before the initiative was passed. Proposition 13 represented windfall profits to commercial, industrial, and landlord interests; it cut services to the majority and shifted the property tax burden to renters and those buying homes after 1978. Consequently Proposition 13 ravaged the public school systems where Latino students were in the majority.[6]

The *Bakke v. University of California* case (1978) was a victory for big business. It was part of a well-funded campaign waged by conservatives to manipulate public opinion. They saturated the air ways with the message that the poor were poor because they wanted to be poor, adding a new twist: it was an insult to call anyone a victim because this implied that the poor were passive. With this logic the conservatives concluded that racism was no longer a problem; the problem was programs designed to end racism: these programs ended up discriminating against white males and promoting mediocrity. The result was clichés such as "reverse racism."

Redefining Racism

During the 1960s, *racism* was a dirty six-letter word; to be called a racist was offensive. In the 1970s, popular culture played a role in this watering down of the term *racism*. Symbolic of this change is the television character Archie Bunker in *All in the Family*, which debuted in January 1971.[7] Norman Lear, a man of impeccable liberal credentials and intentions, produced the series, which premiered during the twilight of the Vietnam War protest movement. Archie Bunker, a lower-middle-class hard hat, hated African Americans, Latinos, and Jews, and had a strong antipathy toward social and political reform. Lear intended Archie's son-in-law, Michael, and daughter, Gloria, to ridicule Archie's outlandish prejudices and make the audience laugh at Archie's racism. In retrospect, just the opposite happened as Archie gave bigotry respectability. The fact is that Archie became so popular that there were a few spin-offs and copycats—*Maude, The Jeffersons, Sanford and Son*—all except *Maude* featured African American bigots.[8]

At the same time, Mexican Americans went against the tide, became more sensitive to racial stereotypes, and protested against them. They demanded more Mexican Americans and Latinos in the media.[9] However, they were not as successful as African Americans because they lacked the moral authority that the Civil Rights movement gave blacks. There were other factors too. For example, Mexican Americans were still a regional minority. In 1970, the African American population numbered 22.6 million, about 11 percent of the total U.S. population. That year, the Mexican origin population numbered just under 4.5 million, a fifth of the black population, and thus did not have the national clout to make politicos do the right thing.[10]

Government Legitimizes Racism

In the summer of 1969, presidential advisor Arthur Burns defined *poverty* as an "intellectual concept"; Nixon later appointed Burns to head the Federal Reserve and manage the nation's economy. The Supreme Court also altered its approach, with the Warren Burger Court being less interested than that headed by William Douglas in improving access for minorities. During the 1970s, the courts actively took the teeth out of the *Brown v. Board of Education* case (1954) decision and moved to criminalize the undocumented worker. Both the courts and Congress criminalized unauthorized immigrants. Initially, at least in the field of voting rights and bilingual education, Mexicans and other Latinos fared well in the courts, but by the 1990s these laws and safeguards were neutralized.[11]

Chicanas/os continued to struggle to end discrimination through the courts. However, the nation based its laws on an either-or standard—one was either black or white. At first, Mexican Americans had followed the strategy that they were white and thus entitled to the protections of the constitution. However, the public did not consider them white and the courts accepted subterfuges that Mexicans were separate because of language deficiency. After World War II, Mexican American organizations adopted the "other white" strategy, and in the 1950s it was accepted that Mexican Americans were "a class apart"; consequently, succeeding cases did not include Mexican Americans under the dicta of *Brown v. Board of Education* (1954), and the school districts distorted the status of Mexican children.

In 1968 José Cisneros and other Chicano parents filed suit against the Corpus Christi Independent School District. Attorney James de Anda abandoned the "other white" strategy and argued that Mexican Americans were an identifiable minority group and that the Corpus Christi Schools segregated Mexicans, denying them equal protection under the 14th Amendment of the U.S. Constitution. The court found for the plaintiffs: Mexican Americans were an identifiable minority group based on physical, cultural, religious, and linguistic distinctions, with a history of discrimination against them. *Cisneros v. Corpus Christi Independent School District* was the first case to entitle Mexican Americans under the *Brown* decision. It replaced the "other white" findings of *Hernández v. State of Texas*.[12]

The Politics of Cynicism: Nixon's Hispanic Strategy

In 1968, presidential candidate Hubert Humphrey received 90 percent of the Mexican vote. Analysts concluded that if Nixon had received 5 percent more of the Chicano votes in Texas, he would have carried the Lone Star State. Taking a cue from the 1968 experience, Nixon developed a "Hispanic" strategy: the plan was to court brown Middle America by giving high-level appointments and more government jobs to Mexican Americans.[13]

The next year, President Nixon replaced the Inter-Agency Committee on Mexican American Affairs with the Cabinet Committee on Opportunities for the Spanish-speaking People, broadening the target group from Chicanos to Hispanics. Nixon appointed Martín Castillo the head of the Cabinet Committee. In 1970, Nixon helped form the National Economic Development Association (NEDA), a national organization funded by state and federal agencies to promote private development in low-income areas. Some Mexican American Democrats affectionately called it NADA (nothing). By 1972, Nixon had appointed 50 Chicanos to high federal posts. The president recruited Romana Bañuelos, a Los Angeles food manufacturer, to serve as treasurer of the United States (1971–1974).[14]

The "brown mafia," a network of community leaders tapped by the Nixon administration to capture the Latino vote, played a key role in the Committee to Re-Elect the President (CREEP). Alex Armendaris of South Bend, Indiana, led the brown mafia, which undoubtedly expected to get at least 20 percent of the Latino vote. The Republicans made it clear to the brown mafia that if they did not reach this goal, the administration would cut federal appointments and stop federal funding to Latinos. Nixon received 31 percent of the Mexican vote nationally. Yet, instead of rewarding Latinos, after the election the president dismantled the War on Poverty program (see discussion below). This was a logical political step, since the poorer Chicanos and other so-called Hispanics did not vote for him.[15]

In 1973, Nixon cynically appointed Ann Armstrong, a white woman, to the post of White House Aide on domestic Latino affairs. According to Nixon, Armstrong was qualified because her husband owned a large ranch that employed Mexicans. Nevertheless, because patronage was funneled through Latino Republicans, after this point the Chicanas/os and, especially, Cuban American Republicans gained more influence as power brokers. From 1972 to 1980, the Republican National Hispanic Assembly raised $400,000 to register Republican voters. Nixon promoted programs benefiting the managerial, professional, and business sectors of this community. After reelection in 1972, Nixon launched his New Federalism with renewed vigor. (New Federalism simply meant decentralizing social programs, returning tax moneys to the municipalities and the states, and relying on the city bosses' good faith to care for the poor.)[16]

Dismantling the War on Poverty

Nixon dismantled the War on Poverty and substituted it with block grants to municipalities to spend as they wished. In 1973, Congress passed the Comprehensive Employment and Training Act (CETA), which changed job-training policy. Previous programs had targeted low-skilled, unemployed, nonwhite workers; CETA included other beneficiaries—mostly better-off, white males. The effect of CETA and other government programs was to reduce services to the disadvantaged, giving more control to local politicians and to the private sector. This policy shift was devastating to Chicanas/os as a whole; poverty, inflation, and a sharp rise in the cost of living worsened their plight, and the number of poor and unemployed kept increasing throughout the 1970s and into the 1980s.[17]

Chicano Power

Nationalists of the 1960s felt that they could transform society by organizing around what many called *Chicanismo*. This faction believed that Chicanas/os should continue to organize around Chicano issues and interests and focus on equality for the group. Much like the early utopian societies, they believed that through example, Chicanos would change society. Many supporters of this movement believed unity would come about through embracing a common identity.

A second movement believed that a new understanding of Chicanos' status in the United States had to be placed into the context of historical and materialist explanations. This faction advocated socialist principles, identifying themselves as working-class people, and entered into coalitions with other progressive groups. Equality would come about by totally transforming society—politically, socially, and economically. A third current was perfectly satisfied with society as it was; they believed that with time, Chicanos would be assimilated into the mainstream as racism diminished and more Chicanos became middle class. At the same time, within each of these groups, women were calling for changes in the culture of Chicanos to bring about gender equality.

Nationalists argued that Marxism itself failed to resolve the identity questions—in fact, Marxists undermined the question of identity. Chicanos had to unite around their culture and change society by working to resolve Chicano-specific problems. The counterargument of leftists was that a revolutionary transformation could not be brought about by organizing solely around a Chicano, Chicana, African American, feminist, lesbian, or gay ideology without giving these particular identities an economic definition. The capitalist system must be replaced before equality could be achieved. The assimilation group—or better still, the mainstream group—believed that through individual achievement the group would be lifted; as more educated Chicanos took positions of power, they would resolve many of the ills of society.[18] Chicanas calling themselves feminists were impatient with the persistence of sexism, and the control of the dialogue by males, and they became more vocal—some broke off from these three waves to form a fourth. It is important to note that within each current there was constant agitation and changes that occurred as a result of activism and interaction—not necessarily through theory.

La Raza Unida Party

Early efforts to form LRUP came from Chicanos in Colorado and Texas. On March 30, 1970, activist Corky Gonzales, who had launched the Crusade for Justice organization, announced the formation of the Colorado RUP.[19] At the 1970 Second Annual Youth Liberation Conference in Denver, the 2,500 activists attending endorsed the notion of a Chicano party. The Crusade for Justice Leadership wanted to form the *Congreso de Aztlán*, which would build a Chicano nation. In May, LRUP held a state convention in Pueblo, at which they endorsed candidates for statewide office. Although police authorities continuously harassed this slate, the party was able to run candidates, albeit without success, at all levels of government. LRUP's purpose was not so much to win as to raise the political consciousness of the Mexican-origin community. By 1971, the stress of police interference took its toll; only 500 attended the Third Annual Chicano Liberation Conference.[20]

Texas was a special case. José Angel Gutiérrez raised the notion of LRUP to the Mexican American Youth Organization (MAYO) in 1968; the executive board rejected it. Meanwhile, MAYO's implementation of the Winter Garden Project, the plan to take over south Texas, which was 80 percent Mexican American, led to Chicano electoral victories in Crystal City, Cotula, and Carrizo Springs. Buoyed by success, Tejanos moved to form a third party. The linchpin to the Chicano revolt was the takeover of the Crystal City School Board. In December 1969, at the first and only national MAYO meeting, Chicano activists endorsed the formation of a third party. In 1971, LRUP went statewide as 300 activists gathered in San Antonio on October 31 and formally launched the party.

The Gutiérrezes, José Angel and Luz, had argued that a strong community power base had to be developed before the party went statewide. However, Mario Compeán, a founder of MAYO who was supported by University of Texas professor Armando Gutiérrez, pushed for an immediate statewide party. The Texas LRUP tasted some initial success as it registered 22,388 voters in 1972.[21]

Tejanas were more visible in LRUP than were Chicanas elsewhere, forming *Las Mujeres por la Raza Unida* (Women for the Raza Unida Party), which supported the Equal Rights Amendment. They were led by Marta Cotera, Alma Canales, Rosie Castro, Evey Chapa, and Virginia Múzquiz. The LRUP platform advocated community control of schools, bilingual education, and women's and workers' rights. In 1972, Alma Canales unsuccessfully ran as RUP candidate for lieutenant governor; Cotera unsuccessfully ran for the Texas State Board of Education; and Viviana Santiago successfully ran for the Crystal City Independent School District Board of Trustees. Statewide, attorney Ramsey Muñiz, 29, a former Baylor University football star, ran for governor on the LRUP ticket, accumulating 214,118 votes (6.28 percent). Republicans won the governorship by 100,000 votes.[22]

The California RUP was divided into northern and southern California. Although LRUP registered almost 23,000 voters and ran candidates statewide, the party never really took root in California. Many Chicanos grew disillusioned with LRUP's attempt at electoral politics and gravitated to other groups such as the Labor Committee of LRUP, which became the core of the August 29th Movement (ATM), a Marxist cell. The ATM later merged into the League of Revolutionary Struggle (LRS), which was active almost into the 1990s. Others joined the *Centro de Acción Social Autónoma* (CASA; Autonomous Center for Social Action), which, like the LRS, became an important trainer of union organizers and future politicos in California.

LRUP ran a candidate for the 48th Assembly District on its ticket; the candidate polled 7.93 percent (2,778) of the votes, playing the role of the spoiler and denying Democratic Party candidate Richard Alatorre the victory. The Republican margin of victory was 46.71 percent (16,346 votes) to 42.17 percent (14,759 votes). Alatorre easily won the next election, in which LRUP did not field a candidate. This campaign was controversial because many wanted LRUP to be known more for its principles than as a vehicle for defeating Democrats. They also deplored the lack of consultation with the local LRUP central committee.[23]

Failure to Build a National Third Party

In September 1972, LRUP held its national convention in El Paso. Tragedy marked the event when a white bigot shot and killed Richard Falcón at Orogrande, New Mexico, as he was en route to the convention. Every Chicano leader except César Chávez participated at the convention. (Predictably, Chávez, whose union was part of the AFL-CIO, endorsed George McGovern rather than Richard Nixon.) There was immediate controversy: many delegates wanted to field an RUP presidential candidate, but the majority preferred to stay out of national politics. Another split occurred at the convention when José Angel Gutiérrez defeated Corky Gonzales for the national chair. Although a symbolic show of unity followed, the formation of two camps was irreversible; within two years, the Colorado RUP bolted from the national organization.[24]

Inevitably, factions developed in the Texas RUP. Many within the party looked to Muñiz, a relative newcomer, as leader, while others looked to Mario Compeán, who as a founder of MAYO had a strong following in San Antonio, which had the largest number of Tejanos and voting potential. After Muñiz's unsuccessful run, tension developed between the Compeán and Muñiz camps. Documents obtained by Gutiérrez under the Freedom of Information Act show considerable Central Intelligence Agency (CIA) surveillance of LRUP, suggesting that the CIA considered LRUP an international threat. Moreover, local police provocateurs and an active campaign by the Democratic Party to destroy LRUP accelerated its demise. LRUP was caught in a dilemma: its radical image turned off many U.S. Mexican voters, while efforts to broaden the party's appeal alienated the party's core constituency. LRUP found success in small towns where they had forged a community base for the party, proving that Gutiérrez's original rural strategy was correct. Even in Cristal (Crystal City, Texas), the stress caused by internal divisions was obvious by the mid-1970s. Many Mexican Americans there wanted to be part of the new prosperity—an impossible goal, given the limited resources of the area.

Texas had a larger percentage of second-generation Chicanos than did other states. Outside Texas, LRUP lacked the base and credibility to launch successful candidacies. In New Mexico, progressive Democrats such as Tiny Martínez in Las Vegas, New Mexico, made the launching of a third party impossible. California had capable leaders such as political scientist Armando Navarro and Genaro Ayala, but there was neither the money nor the time to build a base. In California, there were also divisions around the gender question. In the Lone Star State, space was given to women there, and women became candidates. LRUP's legacy cannot be overestimated.[25]

The Last Days of La Raza Unida

Meanwhile, in 1974 the City Terrace chapter unsuccessfully led a drive to incorporate East Los Angeles into a city. Unincorporated East Los Angeles included a population of 105,033 residents, more than 90 percent of whom were Mexican. The initiative lost—3,262 votes to 2,369 votes. There had been other unsuccessful efforts to create a "Chicano city."

As mentioned earlier, Chicanos controlled Democratic Party machines in New Mexico. These state officials branded LRUP members un-American, radicals, and outsiders; in May 1976, Rio Arriba deputies shot two LRUP activists. Since many New Mexicans were already part of the political system, they did not think they needed an alternative party like La Raza Unida to empower them politically.

However, LRUP still exists today. Its national chair is Genaro Ayala, a retired teacher at San Fernando High School, who has served as national chair since 1980. Ayala partly attributes LRUP's failure to "the lack of clarity of ideology."[26]

By 1974, LRUP began to implode, except in limited south Texas enclaves. Ironically, RUP's success led to disunity in Crystal City, Texas, and the party lost its control there in 1977. The emergence of the Southwest Voter Registration and Education Project (founded by Willie Velásquez, a former MAYO activist) led to the defection of some members to the Mexican American Democrats. Meanwhile, the arrest of Ramsey Muñiz on drug charges resulted in a loss of credibility. Nevertheless, a larger core of RUP activists remained in the political arena in Texas than elsewhere. The role played by the Gutiérrezes—both José Angel and Luz—was immeasurable.[27]

Inequality from Within

As in the case of other movements, the question of gender inequality fractionalized the Chicano movement. Some resisted the call for equality of sexes. The reactions differed: Some, like Martha Cotera, criticized LRUP but chose to work within the structure. Others, like Magdalena Mora, a committed student activist and union organizer who died of cancer in 1981 at age 29, chose to work within CASA and write for its newspaper, *Sin Fronteras*, and later for *El Foro de Pueblo*, speaking out against sexism while campaigning for workers' rights. Still others stressed the importance of developing autonomous feminist organizations. Positions often changed, and even when they did not, there were the inevitable personality clashes and egos, which were difficult to untangle. In general, the more to the left the organization, the more inclusive it became of women's issues. To its credit, *The Militant*, published by the Socialist Workers Party, was at the cutting edge of the question of feminism and sexual preferences.[28] By contrast, most leftist groups, while generally progressive in offering lip service to feminist issues, were in the Stone Age when it came to sexual preferences; homophobia was rampant during the 1970s. Nevertheless, the leftist organizations were training grounds for Chicana labor organizers and evolved to extend human rights to all.[29]

Chicana Voices

An important Chicana and Chicano voice was *El Grito del Norte*, a newspaper for which personages such as Enriqueta Longeaux y Vásquez and Elizabeth "Betita" Martínez wrote. In her featured column, Vásquez asked the U.S. Mexican people to "'stand up' and rethink the given social order," including U.S. militarism, interventions in Vietnam and Latin America, the Catholic Church, gringo society, and sexism—forcing many readers to rethink their positions on these issues. Vásquez's work appears as one of the early feminist voices representing the "loyalist" position and supporting nationalism. However, the designation of Vásquez as a loyalist is a distortion. Vásquez, like others, was attempting to reconcile her own evolving political positions with the reality and the political vocabulary of the community of that time, much the same as what Marxists were doing at that time. The question for Vásquez was how to obtain women's liberation, thus transforming the entire nuclear family. Since her involvement lay within Chicano organizations, her focus was on how to change those organizations and the people in them.

Like Marxism and nationalism, feminism had numerous variants. Critics dwell on the fact that Vásquez declared she was a "*Chicana primero,*" claiming that race should take precedence over gender in analyzing oppression. However, within the heat of the debate, myths often crop up. Take, for example, an event at the First National Chicano Youth Conference in Denver, Colorado, in May 1969. When the time came to report on the resolutions formulated at the workshop on the Chicana, Enriqueta Vásquez was shocked at the wording—that the Chicana woman did not want to be liberated. Yet she understood the tremendous pressure from the men in the hall—although she did not agree with the statement. Perhaps the Chicanas present meant that they did not want to be liberated by white women. That this statement was the consensus of the women at the workshop does not hold up.[30]

Inevitable Factions

Every social movement has factions, and the Chicana/o movement is no exception. A series of conferences on the Chicana Question took place in the early 1970s. One of the first activities of Chicanas was the formation of a women's caucus within the Mexican American Political Association (MAPA); women found it necessary to form a pressure group to change MAPA from within. In 1970, the Mexican American National Issues Conference in Sacramento sponsored a workshop on women. Out of this conference formed *La Comisión Femenil Mexicana* (The Mexican Feminist Commission), a group that was important in generating Chicana community programs through government grants; Francisca Flores and Grace Montañez Davis were among the leaders.[31] Meanwhile, Flores edited *Regeneración*, a magazine that published many articles on *la mujer*. That year, local Chicana forums became more popular—for instance, at California State University at Los Angeles, a Chicana forum honored María Cristina de Penichet, Mexico's first woman brain surgeon, and Celia Luna Rodríguez, leader of the Barrio Defense Committee and before that of the Mexican Civil Rights Congress.

In May 1971, over 600 Chicanas from 23 states attended *La Conferencia de Mujeres por La Raza* (the Women's Conference for the Latino People), sponsored by the YWCA in Houston. Some 40 percent of the attendees (300 women)—mostly Tejanas—walked out of the conference and held their own conference in a park. The dissenters charged that the Houston Mexican community had been engaged in a struggle with the YWCA and that, given a lack of Chicanos/as on staff, the YWCA was racist and its staff was elitist and bureaucratic. Those who remained inside claimed that the dissenters were antifeminist, loyalists, and cultural nationalists. Ironically, most agreed on fundamental issues such as abortion but disagreed on tactics and the role of the YWCA.[32]

Chicana groups focused on the special problems of Mexican women. Most topics revolved around male chauvinism, abortion, childcare, and sexism within the Chicano and the white women's movement. The struggle was very intense both within MEChA (*Movimiento Estudiantil Chicano/a de Aztlán*) and within the community. At the universities, because of the establishment of Chicano Studies programs, there was a ready network for the production and consumption of ideas regarding social change. In 1973, Chicanas spearheaded the opposition to the Talmadge Amendment to the Social Security Act, which required mothers on public assistance with children over six years of age to register with the state employment office and to report every two weeks until they obtained work.

As early as 1971, Dorinda Moreno published a journal, *Las Cucarachas* (The Cockroaches). In 1973, she published an anthology, *La Mujer—En Pie de Lucha* (The Woman in Struggle). Moreno also published the newspaper *La Razón Mestiza* (Mestizo Reason) in the San Francisco area in 1974. A recurrent theme in all her works was the unequal status of women.[33] By the late 1970s there was a broader participation of middle-class Chicanas in the women's movement, with Chicana professionals and activists attending the International Women's Year Conference in Mexico City in 1975 and the National Women's Conference in Houston two years later. There was also more popular coverage of the movement in the mainstream press.

Through their actions, women defined a political culture. For example, María Antonietta Berriozábal and Rosa Salazar Rosales set different paradigms for women's role in society. Berriozábal in 1972 founded Mexican American Business and Professional Women, searching for a strategy to empower Chicanas in the business world. Through her involvement with this issue, she developed a support network of women who ultimately got her elected to the San Antonio City Council in the 1980s, where she evolved into one of the most progressive elected officials of her time. (Berriozábal lost her bid for mayor in 1991.)

Rosa Salazar Rosales took another route. Denied entrance to college after high school despite being a brilliant student, she returned to school after becoming a mother and graduated from the University of Michigan. She returned to San Antonio in the late 1970s and became a union organizer; there the work further radicalized her. Both the women had formed strong networks of women and pushed feminist issues within both the Chicana community and the population at large.[34]

Missing in the early Chicana literature were feminist writings in leftist newspapers and journals. The attitude of some Chicanos was that these women gave up their Chicana cultural citizenship when they joined Marxist organizations. However, groups such as the Socialist Workers Party, through their newspaper the *Militant*, published excellent articles on gender and on homophobia, which influenced Chicanas/os during the 1970s and 1980s. The *Militant* was among the first to tackle the abortion issue head on. CASA published *Sin Fronteras*, and the League of Revolutionary Struggle (LRS) published *Unity*. A host of other newspapers were also published; the leftist newspapers far outnumbered the circulation of nationalist newspapers. Although there was tension among many of the groups due to party building, they had a positive impact on the Chicana/o community. The groups' cadres attended conferences and other meetings, pointing out the imbalances of government programs for women's issues. They were very critical of efforts to undo affirmative action programs, as was evident in their campaign against the *Bakke* decision. This body of thought was energized by Rosaura Sánchez and Rosa Martínez Cruz's anthology *Essays on La Mujer*, published by the Chicano Studies Research Center at UCLA in 1977, which gave a materialist interpretation of feminism.[35]

The Birth of Chicano Studies

Chicana/o Studies are one of the few academic programs that were not born within academe. They came together in 1968 as Chicano school walkouts hit California and Texas, and spread throughout the Southwest, Midwest, and Pacific Northwest—receiving much of their initial energy from the farmworker movement and the actions of the Black Student Union that shut down San Fernando Valley State College and San Francisco State College in November 1968 and spread to other colleges.[36] The eye of the storm was in California. In Texas, the MAYO focused on off-campus strategies toward achieving Brown Power and successfully took over local governments and school boards. At the California State Colleges, where most of the Chicano Studies Departments first took root, there were less than 1,000 Chicana/o students enrolled in the spring of 1969 systemwide. The majority of these students had matriculated there in the fall of 1968, as part of the first Educational Opportunity Programs that brought this handful of students to the CSC.[37] The winds that brought Chicano Studies picked up speed after the East Los Angeles school walkouts, and on the campuses Chicano students caught the tailwinds of the black student movement, the farmworker struggle, and the Vietnam War. By the spring of 1969 the small cores of Chicano students were integrated into the National Chicano Student Movement, which, after the Denver Chicano Youth Conference, met at Santa Barbara, California, and formulated the Plan of Santa Barbara that contextualized the disparate efforts of California campuses. For example, California State Colleges at Los Angeles, San Fernando, Long Beach, San Diego, and Fresno had already formulated programs, as had the Universities of California and many junior colleges, where professors such as Gracia Molina de Pick of San Diego Mesa College were pioneers.[38] In general, research institutions formed research centers and state colleges departments. The Plan of Santa Barbara capsulized these movements that spread throughout the Southwest, Pacific Northwest, and Midwest with varying degrees of success.

Centers were more common in Texas, Arizona, and New Mexico. In time, a center was established at the University of Texas, Austin, and at the University of Arizona, while Chicanos elsewhere lobbied for Mexican American programs. Anywhere a handful of Mexicans matriculated, there was the demand for Chicano studies, with varying degrees of success; the most notable efforts were the community colleges. An exception to the general trend of forming Mexican American Research Centers in the Lone Star State was the University of Texas El Paso where a militant but unsuccessful drive for a Chicano Studies department had emerged out of Segundo Barrio after the burning deaths of the three children of Miguel Rosales on January 4, 1967.[39]

What made the formation of Chicano Studies truly extraordinary was that initially it involved so few students. Unlike the Black Studies and Women's Studies programs, Chicanos did not have a large core of middle-class students in college. As mentioned, an overwhelming number of Chicana/o students were first-generation college students, who were children of immigrants. In every southwestern state, with the exception of New Mexico, they comprised less than 5 percent of the students in the state; in the Pacific Northwest and Midwest they formed less than 1 percent of the student community.[40] In 1969, there were an estimated one hundred Mexican Americans with PhDs nationwide. Again unlike the case of Black Studies and Women's Studies, these programs did not have long-standing contacts with the Ford philanthropic foundations, and they received little outside help.

On campus they became foci of Chicano activism and were a training ground for Chicano leaders and cultural workers within the community. Indeed, in the 1980s and 1990s most elected officials and labor and community organizers came out of the Chicano student movement, as did most artists and musicians. The campuses also became laboratories where Chicano and Chicana ideas evolved from a largely nationalist perspective to a more universal school of thought. It was there that sexist and homophobic notions were challenged and in some cases changed. Chicano Studies continuously advocated for the admission of more students of Latino origin, more Chicano Studies programs, appointment of more Chicana/o professors, and financial aid, as well as progressive social causes.

Sterilization: Saving Taxpayers' Money

During the 1970s, the issue of sterilization was a cause of concern. Sterilization has its roots in the social Darwinism eugenics movement of the early twentieth century whereby American eugenicists believed that people could be categorized according to intelligence and that the United States could genetically engineer its racial composition—the extreme position called for sterilization—a notion that was popular through the 1960s. There is evidence that even the members of President John F. Kennedy's Peace Corps, established in 1961, sponsored sterilization programs. Such programs were common in Puerto Rico, and were used as a policy to reduce overpopulation.[41] From 1973 to 1976, medical authorities sterilized one-third of the women of childbearing age in Puerto Rico and more than 3,000 Native Americans.

At the USC/Los Angeles County Hospital (a.k.a. General Hospital), serving the largest Mexican population in the United States, doctors routinely performed involuntary sterilizations during the early 1970s. According to Dr. Bernard Rosenfeld—who strongly objected to the practice as reminiscent of Nazi experimentation with Jews, gypsies, and the mentally retarded—doctors developed the attitude that by sterilizing the breeders the hospital saved the taxpayers millions of dollars in welfare payments.

Los Angeles General Hospital was in the business of training doctors. To gain practice, physicians often persuaded teenagers to authorize tubal ligations and hysterectomies and even rationalized their malpractice: "I want to ask every one of these girls if they want their tubes tied. I don't care how old they are. … Remember, every one you get to her tubes tied now means less work for some son of a bitch next time."[42] Some doctors bragged that they waited to seek permission to perform the operations until the anesthesia wore off. Often, the doctors gave English-language forms to patients who spoke only Spanish. Sterilization of poor minority women became a national issue when two black girls, ages 12 and 14, were sterilized in Montgomery, Alabama. Chicanas who spearheaded a suit against the General Hospital vehemently opposed this practice.

The issue of abortion continued to split the community. Many Mexican Americans were Catholic, and they followed the Church teachings that abortion was a sin. Feminists and many activists considered abortion to be a personal matter in which women should have full control of their bodies. Many Chicanas supported *Roe v. Wade* (1973), the U.S. Supreme Court decision legalizing abortion; however, on the matter of sterilization, activists point out that poor women who did not have a personal physician and did not speak English had less choice.

The Road to Delano

The drama of the 1960s, the antiwar movement, the Chicano student movement, the Raza Unida, and the farmworkers eclipsed the rich history of the Chicanas/os in the U.S. labor movement. After an initial resistance, gradually industrial unions such as the autoworkers, steelworkers, electrical workers, and miners had started admitting Chicanos. Mexican-origin workers played a huge role in building these unions, although union leadership often resisted their inclusion. By the 1970s, their numbers were too large to ignore, as were their demands. With the growth of Chicano membership within these unions, the United Farm Workers (UFW) union found ready allies. An example is the United Auto Workers, one of the UFW's staunchest supporters, as leaders such as Pete Beltrán of Local 645/GM Van Nuys championed the farmworker cause.

This alliance helped the UFW withstand the awesome economic and political power of agribusiness. Because of this cooperation and the moral authority garnered by Chávez, the growers were unsuccessful in 1972 in their push for Proposition 22, an initiative to outlaw boycotting and limit secret ballot elections to full-time nonseasonal farmworkers. Meanwhile, the Schenley Corporation refused to renegotiate with the UFW on these issues, sparking a strike in which police arrested 269 strikers. The Nixon administration nudged the Teamsters and the growers to cooperate. In the spring of 1973, the Teamsters' Agricultural Workers Organizing Committee declared war on the UFW in the Imperial Valley. The Seafarers Union offered to help Chávez get rid of the thugs, but Chávez, committed to nonviolence, refused. Teamster terrorists then brutally attacked farmworkers.

Governor Edmund G. Brown, Jr., helped form the Agricultural Labor Relations Board (ALRB) in 1975 to supervise elections and resolve appeals. The board allowed secondary boycotts only if employers refused to negotiate. After Brown left office, however, the Republican-controlled legislature constantly harassed the UFW, intervening on the side of the growers.

In Ohio, the Farm Labor Organizing Committee (FLOC) not only organized Mexicans in the fields of Ohio and Indiana but also sensitized Midwesterners regarding INS abuses. FLOC, with the Ohio Council of Churches, sponsored a conference on immigration in 1977. The Catholic bishops supported FLOC, which called a nationwide boycott of Campbell's Soup products. Also strengthening FLOC was its affiliation with the UFW in the 1980s. This boycott lasted until the spring of 1986, when FLOC signed a contract with Campbell's.

The UFW was unsuccessful at unionizing Texas farmworkers in the 1960s. Although Chávez wanted to expand operations there, difficulties in securing his California base kept his focus elsewhere. For a time, the UFW left Antonio Orendian in Texas to organize farmworkers. A split developed and Orendian left the UFW to organize a new Texas union: Texas Farm Workers (TFW). However, as times worsened and continual recessions swelled the ranks of labor, the TFW became less effective.[43]

The Farah Strike: The Breaking of Labor

Willie Farah had textile plants in both Texas and New Mexico. At his largest facility and headquarters in El Paso, Farah employed some 9,500 workers—85 percent were female, mostly Chicanas. The Amalgamated Clothing Workers Union of America (ACWUA) began organizing workers in Farah's San Antonio plant in the late 1960s. In October 1970, in an NLRB-supervised election, the cutting department voted to affiliate with the union. Willie Farah refused to bargain in good faith and immediately resorted to reprisals such as firing union loyalists or making them sweep floors. Willie erected barbed-wire fences around his five facilities.

By 1972, 4,000 Farah employees in El Paso, San Antonio, Victoria, and Las Cruces, New Mexico, were striking Farah. In July the union called its nationwide boycott of Farah, which lasted for two years and took a tremendous personal toll on the strikers and their families. The backbone of the strike was the women, who created their own group called *Unidad Para Siempre* (Unity Forever). In 1974, Farah signed a contract with the union but continued to harass union activists. By 1976, he closed his San Antonio factory and began to move his operations across the border. Slowly the workers' support of the union eroded. Part of the problem was that the union failed to develop its leadership or to continue the political education of the workers. The International (the national office of the ACWUA) had never fully appreciated or encouraged local Chicana workers. Another problem was the continued negative portrayal of Mexican American women by the media.[44]

Sin Fronteras

The Border Industrialization Program (BIP) reduced Mexico to a sweatshop equivalent of an underdeveloped nation. Since the *maquiladoras* (assembly factories) imported 98 percent of their raw materials from the United States and Japan, they did little to stimulate other domestic industries. By the end of the decade, Mexico would gain the reputation of paying even lower wages and having lower energy costs than the Far East, attracting more multinational factories.

In 1974, 476 *maquiladoras* operated in Mexico. During the recession of 1973–1975, the number of *maquiladoras* dramatically declined. As worker militancy grew, transnational managers, through the American Chamber of Commerce in Mexico, warned Mexican President Luis Echeverría to intervene on the side of capital investors or lose the *maquiladoras*. Mexico was almost bankrupt. The International Monetary Fund (IMF) and the World Bank refinanced Mexico's loans, forcing the country to agree to an austerity plan that provided for reducing the number of public jobs, producing more oil, and devaluing the peso. Devaluation cut wages in half and revived the *maquiladoras* by doubling their profits.

There was an increase in the migration of Mexicans from the interior to the border areas; however, only a few of them could find employment there, and the rest were forced to cross the border to seek employment. The migration furnished electrical and garment factories in the United States with a surplus of cheap labor. Simultaneously, factories in closed-shop (union) states moved to right-to-work states, which weakened the political and economic power of Chicano-dominated locals.[45]

Nativism Is Racism

The recession of 1973–1974 revived the capitalist "Greek chorus," and nativist politicians blamed their favorite scapegoat for the failures of the marketplace. By the mid-1970s, an anti-immigrant hysteria was in full swing. The country had come full circle since the nineteenth century, when Euro-Americans stereotyped the Mexican as a bandit to justify keeping open military forts so that merchants could make a profit from government contracts. In the 1970s, Mexicans again became bandits, blamed for stealing jobs. The purpose of the criminalization was multiple: For one, it justified paying undocumented immigrants less than other workers. Next, treating them like outlaws justified the increasing budget allocation for the INS. Finally, it provided copy for the media, which sensationalized the threat, playing on the Americans' fear of the "other." Even many poor and middle-class Chicanos "believed" that the undocumented immigrants, like aliens from another planet, had invaded their land and taken their jobs. In the face of this hysteria, Chicano leaders experienced their finest hour.

Centro de Acción Social Autónoma–Hermandad General de Trabajadores

Bert Corona, founder of the *Centro de Acción Social Autónoma–Hermandad General de Trabajadores* (CASA-HGT), led the movement to protect the foreign born, first in California and then nationally. Corona, born in El Paso in 1918, had been active in trade unions and civic and political groups since the 1930s. By the late 1960s, Corona had built a mass-based organization to defend the rights of undocumented workers.

CASA grew, establishing chapters in San Diego, San José, San Antonio, Colorado, and Chicago, and claimed a membership of 2,000 undocumented workers. Along with the charismatic Soledad "Chole" Alatorre, Corona developed an understanding of the undocumented immigrant's plight. Indeed, undocumented immigrants were merely scapegoats for failures in the country's unregulated economic structure.

In 1973, under the leadership of barrio lawyer Antonio Rodríguez, who led *Casa Carnalismo*, the Committee to Free *Los Tres* (a national committee formed after the arrest of three *Casa Carnalismo* members for allegedly killing an undercover agent whom they suspected of selling drugs), joined by *Comité Estudiantil del Pueblo* (CEP) became part of CASA. By the mid-1970s, the young cadre took over the organization, and transformed CASA from a mass-based organization to a vanguard Marxist group. At this point, Corona and Alatorre left CASA, and merged their supporters into *La Hermandad Mexicana Nacional* (Mexican National Brotherhood) that had been formed in the San Diego area in 1951 to protect the rights of the foreign born.

With the change in leadership, CASA members devoted less energy to organizing workers and more to movement-building operations in Chicano communities, forming alliances with North American and Mexican radicals. More time was spent on Marxist study and publishing of the newspaper *Sin Fronteras*, whose editorial staff included Isabel Rodríguez Chávez (who became a civil rights attorney) and Chicana activist Magdalena Mora. CASA trained leaders, some Marxists and some not, and gave Chicanos a global view of society. CASA's legacy is that it politicized a cadre of Chicano and Chicana activists who went on to become labor organizers and politicos in California.[46]

Get the Mexican Bandits: Criminalization of Mexicans

The passage of laws criminalizing the undocumented worker became common. In 1971, California passed the Dixon–Arnett Act, fining employers who hired undocumented workers. (The State Supreme Court declared the act unconstitutional because it infringed on federal powers.) The next year, U.S. Representative Peter Rodino (D–New Jersey) proposed a bill that made it a felony to knowingly employ undocumented workers and specified penalties that ranged from warnings for first-time offenders to fines and jail terms for repeat offenders. Senator Edward Kennedy introduced a similar bill that additionally granted amnesty to all aliens who lived in the country for at least three years. Chicanos opposed the Rodino and Kennedy bills. Senator James O. Eastland (D-Mississippi), chair of the Senate Judiciary Committee and a large grower, killed the Rodino bill in committee.

By 1976, Representative Joshua Eilberg (D-Pennsylvania) successfully sponsored a bill lowering the annual number of immigrants entering from any one country from 40,000 to 20,000. Eilberg's bill was a slap in the face to Mexico because at that time, it was the only Latin American country sending more than 40,000 immigrants. The law further granted preferences to professionals and scientists, encouraging a brain drain from Latin America. Lastly, the law made the parents of U.S.-born children ineligible for immigration. Children had the option of being deported and returning when they reached legal age, or becoming wards of the court.

INS commissioner Leonard Chapman, Jr., manufactured statistics to support his myth of a Mexican invasion and to hide the improprieties uncovered during "Operation Clean Sweep." The INS apprehended 348,178 undocumented workers in 1971, 430,213 in 1972, and 609,573 in 1973. News reporters and scholars attribute this stepped-up activity, in part, to the bureau's effort to divert attention from internal problems, including rapes, prostitution, bribery, and the running of concentration camp–like detention camps. At the same time, there were scholars on the payrolls of nativist research foundations: even respected public foundations like the National Endowment for the Humanities funded anti-immigrant research. The federal government gave Mexican specialist Arthur Corwin grant money to conduct a definitive border study, even though Corwin had little to qualify him as a border expert.

Behind the facade of pure research, Corwin launched an attack on Chicano scholars for questioning the role of the INS. On July 16, 1975, he sent Henry Kissinger a letter demanding action and control of migration from Latin America. According to Corwin, the United States was becoming a "welfare reservation," and if the trend were to continue, the Southwest would become a Mexican "Quebec." Corwin recommended that the president mobilize the Army and that Congress appropriate $1 billion to the INS, so that the agency could hire 50,000 additional border officers. Corwin also advocated the construction of an electrified fence. Fortunately, the Corwin letter fell into the hands of the Mexican press, who discredited him.

Scholars F. Ray Marshall, an economics professor at the University of Texas and secretary of labor under Jimmy Carter, and Vernon M. Briggs, Jr., favored restricting undocumented workers. Expressing concern that undocumented workers took jobs from Chicanos, Marshall and Briggs called for fining employers to discourage migration. Like most advocates of employer sanctions, Marshall and Briggs had not adequately studied the role of U.S. capitalism in creating the phenomenon.[47]

The Media Perpetuates Racist Nativism

The media molded this anti-immigrant ideology, legitimizing the myth of the "Mexican invasion" by uncritically reporting INS propaganda and nativist scholarship. The press and television promoted the idea that undocumented workers caused poverty, were criminals, and took jobs away from North Americans. On May 2, 1977, *Time* magazine ran two articles: "Getting Their Share of Paradise" and "On the Track of the Invader." The press uncritically quoted INS sources, reporting that the "invaders came by land, sea, and air," and that U.S. taxpayers spent $13 billion annually on social services for aliens, who sent another $13 billion out of the country annually. As absurd as the INS propaganda was, North Americans believed it. Thus, employers who could buy their labor power at ever-lower rates could deny these stateless workers, who were isolated from the rest of society, their human rights.[48]

Getting Away with Terrorism

While scholars manipulated statistics, the INS committed flagrant abuses of human rights: in October 1972, border patrol officer Kenneth Cook raped Martha López, 26, and threatened to harm her two children. In the summer of 1976, George Hanigan, a Douglas, Arizona, rancher and Dairy Queen owner, and his two sons, Patrick, 22, and Thomas, 17, kidnapped three undocumented workers looking for work. They "stripped, stabbed, burned [them] with hot pokers and dragged [them] across the desert." The Hanigans held a mock hanging for one of the Mexicans and shot another with buckshot. Judge Anthony Deddens, a friend of the Hanigans, refused to issue arrest warrants. Later, an all-white jury acquitted the Hanigans. Activists on both sides of the border protested the verdict and pressured U.S. Attorney General Griffin Bell to indict them. The Hanigan case went to a federal grand jury, which in 1979 indicted the Hanigans for violating the Hobbs Act, involving interference in interstate commerce (obviously the civil rights of the undocumented workers were not at issue). Another all-white jury was deadlocked in a first trial. At the second trial in 1981, the jury found the Hanigan brothers guilty (the father was dead by that time).[49]

In Defense of the Foreign Born

Meanwhile, the INS harassed groups and individuals who were attempting to protect the rights of the undocumented worker. In the spring of 1976, INS authorities broke into the Tucson office of *Concilio Manzo*, an organization that offered free counseling and legal services to undocumented workers. The INS confiscated files and arrested Marge Cowan, Sister Gabriel Marcaisq, Margarita Ramírez, and Cathy Montano. INS authorities accused the *Manzo* workers of not reporting "aliens" to the INS. The court, after an extended period and the expenditure of funds and time, dismissed the case.

Throughout the 1970s, Chicano organizations mobilized their constituencies in defense of undocumented workers. Support came from every sector of the Chicano community, crossing party and class lines. In October 1977, José Angel Gutiérrez and LRUP held a conference in San Antonio attended by 2,600 Chicano activists from all over the country. The conference was held in response to Jimmy Carter's immigration reform legislation. Even organizations such as the League of United Latin American Citizens (LULAC) and the G.I. Forum criticized anti-immigrant legislation.

In San Diego, more than a thousand activists, led by Herman Baca, Rodolfo "Corky" Gonzales, and Bert Corona, marched against the Ku Klux Klan, which had threatened the safety of the undocumented workers. In December 1977, Armando Navarro of the San Bernardino–Riverside area assembled 1,200 community folk for a conference on immigration. Such unanimity on the issue of immigration came not without a price. CASA and the National Coalition for Fair Immigration Laws had become increasingly critical of Chávez because he wanted to stem the flow of undocumented workers to the fields. By the mid-1970s, a rift had developed with Chávez, as the Republican administration attempted to use him to push anti-immigrant legislation. Denouncing the pending anti-immigrant legislation, the coalition—made up of the G.I. Forum, LULAC, and the *Comisión Femenil*—pressured Chávez for a statement. Chávez went on record that UFW was supportive of progressive legislation protecting the rights of undocumented workers—adding, however, that if there were no undocumented workers, "we could win those strikes overnight."[50]

The Growth of the Chicano Middle Class

The growth of the Chicano middle class was neither all good nor all bad. Indeed, this growth was a natural by-product of urbanization, modernization, and the success of pressuring colleges to open their doors to Latino students. The good part was that it gave Chicanos more of a voice in government and society. The bad part was that middle-class Chicanos often developed social and economic interests differing from those of the working class, and they were coopted by the mainstream, making them agents of social control, intermediary gatekeepers, power brokers, or influence peddlers between the Chicano community and the ruling class.

Chicanas/os as Commodities

For some, the growth of the Mexican American population and the widening of the middle class was a market bonanza. Beer companies distributed calendars with photos of "Hispanics," celebrating them as role models for the community. The term *Hispanic* appealed to many of the marketers; it packaged the Mexican American, the Puerto Rican, the Cuban, and other Latin Americans in one innocuous wrapper. Most of the new heroes and heroines were not activists but business executives, politicians, and political appointees—both Democrat and Republican. Newly formed Chicano and Chicana groups followed this pattern of celebrating the success of those selected by the system. The term *Hispanic* also appealed to this new wave of middle-class Mexican Americans, and this identity was much more in line with their class biases and aspirations.

This change in identity laid the foundation for the Colorado-based Coors Brewing Company deal of October 1984, when the so-called Hispanic organizations called off a boycott initiated by the Chicano community in 1968. Over the years, both the American G.I. Forum and LULAC had negotiated with the beer company, trying to end the boycott. In 1975, the Forum reached an agreement with Coors, but Forum members later rejected it because of a recently called AFL–CIO strike against Coors.

In October 1984, the G.I. Forum, the Cuban National Planning Committee, the National Council of La Raza, the National Puerto Rican Coalition, and the U.S. Hispanic Chamber of Commerce signed a contract with Coors, ending the boycott. The agreement supposedly made Coors a "good corporate citizen." The pact pledged that Coors, from 1985 to 1990, would return $350 million to the community in the form of advertisements in Hispanic media, investments in Hispanic businesses, grants to selected community organizations, and some scholarships. Coors tied how much it would give to the organizations on how much beer the "Hispanic" community would drink.

In this cynical agreement, since they were the largest sector of the pseudo-Hispanic community, Chicanos would, of course, be expected to drink the maximum quantity of beer. LULAC's leadership at first refused to ratify the agreement because the contract linked how much money they received to beer consumption. Coors, according to LULAC, did not insist on the beer-drinking clause when it funded other, non-Latino organizations—such as its grant to the Heritage Foundation, an arch-reactionary think tank. Meanwhile, activists and trade union organizations such as the UFW continued with the Coors boycott. Unfortunately, after the election of new officers, LULAC ratified the pact.[51]

Redefinition of the Political Middle

The formation of LRUP had a positive impact on Chicano politics in Texas. But the formation of a leftist party had its downside. LRUP and much of the Chicano left abandoned traditional Chicano organizations to the far right, which resulted in a redefinition of the political middle ground. Without the left, the former right-of-center became the left-of-center, and the far right became the right-of-center. Without a leftist critique, conservatives increasingly controlled many established organizations such as LULAC and the American G.I. Forum, and Republicans gained new respectability. During the presidency of Lyndon Johnson, these organizations had become dependent on patronage; that dependency continued in the 1970s under Nixon and then Gerald Ford. The only thing that changed was the brokers between the organizations and the party in power.

For instance, LULAC and the G.I. Forum had received heavy government funding since the 1960s, and they were wedded to the Democratic Party. In 1964, LULAC and the Forum began administering the Service, Employment, and Redevelopment (SER) agency. By the end of the 1970s, SER supervised 184 projects in 104 cities with an annual budget of $50 million. LULAC and the Forum obtained these grants because of their Washington connections. With Republicans controlling the Executive Branch for most of the 1970s and all of the 1980s, Latino Republicans took over from the Democrats their positions as government liaisons. These factors made easier the Republican penetration of groups like the Forum and LULAC, and Latino Republicans used War on Poverty programs for offering patronage. This dependency on government funding shaped the organizations' agendas. However, a number of Republicans were offended by what they perceived as the racist policies of their party. Concerned about the growing influence of Republicans, LULAC President Rubén Bonilla broke with the Brown Republicans and criticized U.S. immigration policy and Washington's intervention in Central America. According to Bonilla, many LULAC leaders were unwilling to lose friends in the White House and Austin. By the mid-1970s, the media and the public- and private-sector bureaucracies looked almost exclusively to middle-class Hispanics to represent the community's interests.[52]

Political Gains

By the grace of the Voting Rights Act, the Chicano movement, and the population boom, changes eventually took place, in spite of the dismal record of Chicano elected officials in the early 1970s. In Los Angeles, Chicanos remained unrepresented on the City Council and Board of Supervisors. The situation was similar throughout the Southwest. Just getting people elected was not enough, however. In 1974, both Eligio (Kika) de la Garza and Henry B. González voted against extending the benefits of the Voting Rights Act to Chicanos. Arizona Governor Raúl Castro, who was elected in 1974, spent most of his time supporting the state's right-to-work law and placating Arizona's conservatives. In 1977, Castro resigned under a cloud of suspicion involving mismanagement and became U.S. ambassador to Argentina.

To stimulate broader political gains, several Chicano/Latino lobbying groups formed in the 1970s. In the mid-1970s, *El Congreso* (the Congress) functioned as a Latino clearinghouse for President-elect Jimmy Carter, but it faded away owing to lack of funds. In 1975, Representative Edward R. Roybal formed the National Association of Latino Elected Officials (NALEO).[53] Its goals were to lobby, coordinate voter registration, and get out the vote. By 1980, NALEO had 2,500 members, with a potential of 5,000. In addition, in the mid-1970s, the four Latino members of Congress formed the so-called Hispanic Caucus;

by 1984, the caucus had eleven members. The Hispanic Caucus, however, had neither the muscle nor the ideological clarity of the Black Caucus because the ultra-conservative Cuban American cabal held it captive.[54]

In 1976, Carter received 81 percent of the Latino vote. Chicanos gave him a 205,800-vote plurality in Texas. Consequently, the Carter White House appointed more Latinos than did previous administrations. Although the Latino population's growing size was an influencing factor in these appointments, the appointees themselves were accountable only to those who signed their paychecks. Their positions gave neither the community nor the appointees any real say; thus, the poor had no more access to power than in the past. Some officers under Carter, such as the Special Assistant for Hispanic Affairs, a post held first by José Aragón and then by Esteban Torres (both from Los Angeles), had some power—they could control which lobbyists had access to the president.

The most symbolic appointment during the waning days of the Carter administration was that of Julian Nava (a Mexican American) as ambassador to Mexico. Unfortunately, Nava's successor was John Gavin, an actor whose credentials included the fact that his mother was allegedly Mexican. By contrast to Nava, who built bridges with the Mexicans, Gavin played the role of the Reagan administration's hatchetman. Evidently, according to most Mexican pundits, the fact that Gavin spoke Spanish and was presumably half Mexican was intended to soften the blow.[55]

Education: The Stairway to the American Dream

In 1968, Congress passed the Bilingual Education Act. Title VII set the framework for bilingual instruction. In *Lau v. Nichols* (1974), involving the San Francisco Chinese community, the U.S. Supreme Court unanimously ruled that the school district had the duty to meet the linguistic needs of children who had a limited grasp of English. If the district did not, it deprived the children of equal protection under the Civil Rights Act of 1964.

Lau v. Nichols drove the expansion of bilingual classrooms. By the mid-1970s, Mexican Americans believed that bilingual education was the law of the land. Bilingual education, however, was viewed by many nativist teachers and other North Americans as a threat that challenged U.S. institutions. They believed in the supremacy of the English language and culture; but even more important, they were concerned that they would become obsolete. Their basic argument was simple: Spanish-speaking students lived in the United States, and they held the burden of learning English; teachers had no such duty to learn Spanish.

Education failed many Mexican American students. Some 50 percent dropped out of school, and more than three-quarters of twelfth graders fell into the bottom quartile of reading level. Traditional education had indeed failed. In fact, less than 3 percent of Mexican students in the Southwest had access to the new bilingual education, and programs in English as a second language reached less than 5.5 percent. Many conservative critics tried to make bilingual education itself the scapegoat for this failure, rather than the meager implementation of these programs.

The U.S. Civil Rights Commission found that in the early 1970s some school districts still enforced the no-Spanish rule. In California, 13.5 percent of elementary schools discouraged the use of any Spanish; in Texas, the figure was 66.4 percent. The commission report found that 40 percent of the Chicano students in classes for the developmentally disabled spoke no English. The school districts often mislabeled Spanish-speaking children and put them in classes for the developmentally disabled.

Resistance to bilingual education increased during the Ronald Reagan years. At the beginning of the 1980s, federal appropriations had reached $171 million. However, the Reagan Administration appointed strong opponents to the National Advisory and Coordinating Council on Bilingual Education, consequently the Bilingual Education Act of 1984 lowered its appropriation to $139 million. In marked contrast, community support remained solid. In San Antonio, 65 percent of the Mexican population surveyed believed that the federal government and local schools spent too little on bilingual education; only 6 percent believed that the schools overspent on bilingual education. In East Los Angeles, 55 percent said the schools spent too little, and only 9 percent disagreed. A U.S. Commission on Civil Rights survey showed that 89 percent of Chicano leaders favored spending more money, while 2 percent did not. The report continues that in San Antonio, 93 percent of Mexicans favored bilingual education; in East Los Angeles, 87 percent; and for Chicano leaders overall, 96 percent.[56]

Educational Equity

From 1968 to 1974, U.S. Mexicans made gains in education; after this point, they slipped backward. The dropout rate again began to climb. In 1974–1975, the percentage of Chicanos who had dropped out of high school was 38.7 for 20- and 21-year-olds; the number rose to 44.1 percent in 1977–1978. In Texas the state tied funding to teacher and professional salaries. Consequently, Mexican schools received about three-fifths the appropriations of white schools.

In *Serrano v. Priest,* John Serrano, Jr., in 1968 sued the California Department of Education, claiming that his son had received an inferior education in East Los Angeles because local property taxes financed the schools. Serrano alleged that poor districts received less funding than did the wealthier ones, and consequently, the children received unequal treatment. In 1971, the California Supreme Court held that financing primarily through local property taxes failed to provide equal protection under the law. In short, a district's wealth determined the quality of its schools. Therefore, if equal educational opportunity was a right, the rich and the poor had to be funded equally. The U.S. Supreme Court (1976) upheld the California Supreme Court's ruling in *Serrano*, but it limited its decision to California, holding that the financing system violated the state constitution's equal protection clause by denying equal access to education.[57]

In *San Antonio School District v. Rodríguez*, filed in 1968, the Supreme Court had found that the U.S. Constitution did not include equal education as a fundamental right. San Antonio had multiple school districts, segregated along race and class lines. The poorest, Edgewood, was Chicano; the richest, Alamo Heights, was mostly white. Edgewood parents sued under the equal protection clause of the Fourteenth Amendment. During the 1970–1971 school year, the state allocated Alamo Heights $492 per child and Edgewood, $356. In Texas in 1971, the 162 poorest districts paid higher taxes than did the 203 richest districts. For example, the poor spent $130 a year in property taxes for education on a $20,000 home, while the rich paid $46 a year on the same type of home. In 1973, the Warren Burger Court overturned a court of appeals judgment that found in favor of the Edgewood parents. The Burger Court ruled that the Texas method of funding was imperfect but rational. It refused to consider the question of race discrimination. Thus, the Edgewood school district continued to have fewer counselors, fewer library books, and fewer course offerings—all because of unequal funding.[58]

In 1970–1971, Latinos made up slightly more than 20 percent of the student population of the Los Angeles Unified Schools; by the end of the decade, they approached a majority. *Serrano* had brought few changes, because the wealthier districts still had better facilities as well as more experienced and better-educated teachers. Latino and black schools continued to be overcrowded, and year-round schools in the 1980s were almost exclusively in Latino areas. (Year-round schools often split families who had children on different tracks.) The Chicano school buildings were older; they accommodated more students per square foot and offered smaller recreational areas. Thirty years after the *Brown* case (1954), schools remained separate and unequal.[59]

The Continuing Importance of the EOPs

Again, higher education was one of the avenues to upward mobility. As imperfect as they were, the Educational Opportunity Programs (EOPs) recruited and retained more Mexican American students in the universities and colleges than there were at any time before in U.S. history. More important, their presence created the attitude among Chicano students that it was their right to attend college and to be part of academe. This belief engendered an early idealism that opened the door of opportunity for many who had once felt excluded from the realm of higher education. Between 1973 and 1977, more Chicanos entered graduate and professional schools than ever before. However, after this point, the number of

Chicano and Latino graduate and professional students dramatically declined in inverse proportion to an increase in undergraduate enrollment. An explanation for the increase in Chicano student enrollment at the undergraduate level is the dramatic increase in the number of Mexican and Latin American students in the public schools.

The EOP propped up minority enrollment in the late 1970s. The downside was that financial aid decreased and tuition costs zoomed as significant numbers of minorities arrived on campus. Meanwhile, politicos such as Jimmy Carter, to appease middle-class white Americans, cut into the loans and other aid available to the needy. At a time when Chicano student undergraduate enrollment was growing, government policy was spreading financial aid thinner, making, for example, Vietnam refugees eligible for these funds. The allocations remained relatively the same, and the EOP had to serve more students—with the same budget. The increased costs provoked student militancy because they had to work longer hours to pay tuition and survive.

Along with EOPs, Chicano Studies programs (departments, centers, and institutes) were important during the early years, because they offered students a platform to formulate their academic demands—for Chicano professors and courses that not only focused on Chicano identity but also served the needs of the community. These programs politicized Chicanos and served as a reminder of why and how Chicano students got to the universities. Between 1968 and 1973, institutions of higher learning in California established more than 50 programs. However, by 1973, acceptance of Chicano Studies by universities and colleges had declined: a financial squeeze forced cutbacks, and Chicano Studies programs were the first to be cut.[60]

Competing Ideologies

The experiences of Chicano students on the different campuses varied. Academe provided a climate for experimenting with ideas and exposure to various world visions. Some colleges exposed students to political ideas outside the Euro-American paradigm. These ideologies ranged from highly nationalistic to revolutionary models. Within this discourse, Chicano nationalism underwent changes as competing models influenced it. The Marxist critique of capitalism was popular among a small core of students, and Marxist groups competed for the hearts and minds of Chicano students. These groups were in no way homogeneous; in fact, they competed among themselves. The Sino–Soviet split of the 1960s had led to the formation of many Marxist organizations, but these groups often clashed among themselves and with the nationalists. Of course, not everyone took part in this discourse; in fact, most Chicano students were not involved.

During the 1970s and 1980s, white leftist parties often posed a problem for some Chicanos: their party-building (recruiting) activities interfered with the normal flow of business. Nevertheless, they played an important role in forming the discourse and raising the consciousness of students. Early on, there was rivalry between the Socialist Workers Party (SWP) and CASA, and then between CASA and the August 29 Movement (ATM, which later became the LRS), though the differences were minute in the larger context. The SWP followed the writings of Leon Trotsky; CASA members had ties with the Mexican Communist party; and ATM was Maoist. These organizations vied with other Marxist parties and an array of nationalist groups. The salvation of these leftist parties was that they were key to enhancing the political consciousness of Chicano students.

Many of these progressives warned students about being mainstreamed into the university structure. The leftists perpetuated their ideas through their own newspapers and literature, which reported on labor and other community struggles and instilled a sense of idealism in students. These leftist parties wrote about the working class to which most Chicano students belonged. Their arguments, often heated and polemical, inclined the discourse of students to the left. The polemics developed a framework for understanding questions of racism and gender in relation to class oppression. However, except for the SWP, most of the leftist organizations failed to discuss the pervasive fear of homosexuals within the movement. The contribution of the Marxist organizations was that they forced nationalists to cognize the meaning of liberation. Moreover, although exasperating at times, these leftist organizations played a vital role in defining the Chicano issues and agenda of the 1970s.[61]

The "Pochoization" of the Political Vocabulary

The development of students' political ideology can be compared to the improvement of one's vocabulary. The Spanish vocabulary of many Chicanos, for example, remains at a third-grade level owing to the lack of use of Spanish and the lack of reading in the language. In the same way student activists often fail to enrich their political vocabulary because they do not continue their involvement. Their political vocabulary stagnates once they leave the campus. On the other hand, new students who are not involved neither possess nor acquire the basic vocabulary to understand history or societal inequality. They neither know nor learn about the sacrifices of earlier generations of Chicanos and Mexican Americans made to win them their access to opportunities. Most take college admission for granted. Thus, increasingly, students go to college for material gains rather than to benefit society.

Meanwhile, many Chicano professors over time became more involved with their professional lives, and they had less and less contact with student activists. Although some Chicano and Chicana professors continued to be active and worked along with students, others were consumed by profession-related pressures such as publishing and meeting the criteria set by the universities for promotion and tenure. Many new professors never participated in the Chicano movement and consequently did not identify with student concerns and had a difficult time relating to students. Involvement helps develop one's consciousness, or simplistically, one's political vocabulary. Activism determines how one is professionalized or socialized. Often new professors found student demands and methods of communication difficult to handle. A small percentage believed that their research would stimulate the Chicano movement and influence government policy; therefore, they felt that time spent with students detracted from work that was more valuable in the long run. Some let their egos run wild, rationalizing their own interests, or were divisive and attempted to destroy student organizations such as MEChA by forming counter groups.

The Myth of a Color-Blind Society

The *Bakke v. University of California* case (1976) popularized the absurd notion of "reverse racism" and the assumption that affirmative action discriminated against whites. During 1973–1974, Alan Bakke, a 34-year-old engineer, applied to 13 medical schools, all of which rejected him because of his age. A white administrator at the University of California at Davis encouraged Bakke to sue, since allegedly "less-qualified minorities" had been admitted. Bakke challenged the Davis special admission program, initiated in 1970, which set aside 16 out of 100 slots for disadvantaged students. Before this plan began, only three minority students had ever been admitted to Davis's medical school. A lower court found for Bakke, as did the California Supreme Court, which flatly stated that race could not be used as a criterion for admission.

On June 28, 1978, the U.S. Supreme Court, in a 5–4 decision, upheld *Bakke*. It based its decision on the 1964 Civil Rights Act, holding that using race as the sole criterion for admission was unconstitutional. Justice Thurgood Marshall dissented, stating that the Court had come "full circle," returning to the post–Civil War era when the courts stopped congressional initiatives to give former slaves full citizenship. Justice Marshall's dissent was prophetic. The *Bakke* decision gave racist faculties and administrators an excuse for excluding minorities. *Bakke* became the law of the land, and it signaled an assault on affirmative action that continued into the late 1990s. *Bakke* was part of a "culture war" funded by right-wing extremists opposed to the idea of equity in education.

The need for minority doctors and other professionals speaks for itself. In California in 1975, one Euro-American lawyer practiced for every 530 Euro-Americans; for Asians, the ratio was 1:1,750; for African Americans, 1:3,441; for Latinos, 1:9,842; and for Native Americans, 1:50,000. In primary-care medicine, one white doctor practiced for every 990 whites; the ratio for blacks was 1:4,028; for Native Americans, 1:7,539; and for Latinos, 1:21,245. *Bakke* supporters argued that overall there was an oversupply of professionals and that services did not depend on the professional's ethnic or racial background. Admittedly, little research has gone into this latter area. However, Dr. Stephen Keith of the Charles Drew Post Graduate School in Los Angeles had conducted a study, the findings of which suggest that the probability that African American and Latino professionals would work with the poor and minority clients was much higher than that for their white counterparts.[62]

Legacy Admits

The debate over preferential treatment of minorities continues even today. For many, the use of race as a criterion is a bogus argument, so the controversy will remain. On the other hand, Chicanos point out that other groups, such as veterans, the children of alumni, the children of donors to the university, or those over 65 years of age, receive preferential treatment. Today society has ramps for the handicapped, which some people would call preferential treatment. According to Alex Liebman, for Princeton's class of 2001 the overall acceptance rate was 13 percent; the statistic for "legacy admits" (children of alumni) was 41 percent; and that for minorities (which includes Asians) was 26 percent. The assumption was that Latinos and African Americans were not qualified and that the legacy admits were qualified, which was not always the case. At Harvard University during the 1990s, the children of alumni were almost four times more likely to be accepted than other prospective students. Harvard University admitted about 40 percent of its entering class using the criterion that the student was the son or daughter of an alumnus or donor. In the same period, 66 percent of children-of-alumni applicants were accepted by the University of Pennsylvania whereas the overall acceptance percentage was 11. Admissions officers saved 25 percent of Notre Dame's first-year class openings for the children of alumni.[63] The preferential treatment given to legacy admits highlights the hypocrisy and racial bias of those who challenge affirmative action.

Why Progressive Organizations Fail

Documents obtained under the Freedom of Information Act suggest the extent of federal monitoring of progressive political organizations. José Angel Gutiérrez and Ernesto Vigil are among the few Chicano scholars doing research in the field. However, almost no evidence is available on local police spying. An exception was a suit filed by the American Civil Liberties Union (ACLU) in 1978: *CAPA* (Committee Against Police Abuse) *v. Los Angeles Police Department*. Some 141 plaintiffs, individuals and groups, went to court in an attempt to restrain police infiltration of political organizations.

Suing the police is an almost impossible task because of the deep pockets of big cities. For example, *CAPA v. LAPD* almost bankrupted the ACLU, which paid out nearly $1 million in legal costs before the LAPD settled. The plaintiffs argued that responsibility for spying went all the way to Chief Daryl Gates, and that further discovery would yield even more evidence of police spying. The plaintiffs voted to settle because they did not have the money to go on. The negotiated settlement, however, included extensive guidelines calling for outside monitoring of the LAPD. Further, the court set up an independent committee to conduct the audit of the agency, and for the first time, the court ordered the police department not to investigate private individuals or groups "without reasonable and articulated suspicion."[64]

Violence as an Instrument of Control

In 1978 in Duarte, California, a gang member shot at postal officer Jesse Ortiz and his two stepbrothers, killing Ortiz. That same night, Los Angeles sheriffs' deputies raided a party, arresting Gordon Castillo Hall, 16, and dragging him outside to a makeshift lineup with squad car lights shining in his face. The Laras, Ortiz's half brothers, contradicted an earlier description of the murderer and identified Castillo Hall, who was much smaller than the suspect.

The trial proved to be a farce. The Pasadena attorney defending Castillo Hall did not conduct a proper pretrial investigation, nor did he call witnesses to prove that Hall had not been at the scene of the crime. The judge allowed expert testimony documenting the so-called violent nature of Mexican gang members toward white and black gang members. The prosecution underscored that Castillo Hall, a Mexican, belonged to a gang.

Bertha Castillo Hall, Gordon's mother, sold her home to pay for the trial attorney. Convinced of her son's innocence, she approached Chicano attorney Ricardo Cruz, who agreed to take the appeal; but she had no money for expenses. A committee was formed to help her—The Committee to Free Gordon Castillo Hall—which raised more than $60,000.

With proper representation, stories changed. The Laras told authorities that they had made a mistake in identifying Castillo Hall. The investigating deputies urged that the case be reopened. However, the trial judge and District Attorney John Van DeKamp, at that time running for state attorney general, refused. Cruz filed a motion of habeas corpus. After several years, the State Supreme Court appointed a referee to investigate the case. The referee recommended reopening of the case; he cited an overzealous district attorney, trial errors, and an incompetent defense. Finally, Castillo Hall was released: in 1981, the State Supreme Court overturned Hall's conviction and freed him. Castillo Hall simply said, "They took my youth." Hall sued the Sheriff's Department, which avoided payment through legal maneuvering.[65]

Another example of police brutality involved journalist and long-time Chicano activist Roberto Rodríguez. On March 23, 1979, members of the Selective Enforcement Bureau of the Los Angeles Sheriff's Department severely beat up Rodríguez, who had been photographing the deputies beating innocent people. Rodríguez had to be hospitalized, and police also charged him with assault with a deadly weapon. He sued the sheriffs and, after a seven-year ordeal, eventually won the case.[66]

Conclusion: The Final Year of the Decade

The decade had begun full of hope with Chicanas/os assembling the largest march in Los Angeles history to protest the war. However, as the Vietnam War ended, the fervor seemed to dissipate as class and other differences divided the community into special interest groups and organizations. As in other groups, youth represented different interests, and as their numbers grew in the universities and in the professions, separate islands formed in academe and the community. This was further complicated with the arrival of a million immigrants from Mexico who had not been part of the struggles of the 1960s, and who often did not understand the legacy of the Chicana/o generation.

The final year of the 1970s was an eventful one. By that time, the proportion of Mexican Americans living in metropolitan areas (80 percent) relative to their total numbers exceeded the corresponding proportion for the general population. Because of poverty and ghettoization of Chicanos there was a higher incidence of crime and violence among them. In Los Angeles, Mexican Americans and Latinos were 2.3 times more likely than Euro-Americans to become homicide victims. The largest increase in crime statistics—over 166.7 percent—occurred among Chicanos and Latinos; murders went from 11.1 per 100,000 in 1970 to 29.6 per 100,000 in 1979.[67] On July 17, Nicaraguan President General Anastasio Somoza fled to Miami and the Sandinistas formed a new government. Somoza was one among a string of dictators supported by the United States in Latin America.[68] In the years to come, this event would have far-reaching implications for the Mexican-origin population. During the 1970s, the growing foreign-born population was already changing the Chicano community. The decade closed with the Iran hostage crisis, as 3,000 Iranian students invaded the U.S. Embassy in Tehran and took 90 hostages, 63 of whom were American. This crisis was one of several factors that brought to power a succession of ultra-conservative administrations during the 1980s, which would also affect people of Latin American origin in the United States.[69]

Notes

1. Che Guevara Internet Archive, http://www.marxists.org/archive/guevara/index.htm.
2. Classified U.S. State Department Documents on the Overthrow of Chilean President Salvador Allende, 1973, Peter Kornbluh, Chile and the United States: Declassified Documents Relating to the Military Coup, National Security Archive, New Declassified Details on Repression and U.S. Support for Military Dictatorship, http://www.gwu.edu/~nsarchiv/NSAEBB/NSAEBB185/index.htm. "New Kissinger, 'Telcons' Reveal Chile Plotting at Highest Levels of U.S. Government," National Security Archive Electronic Briefing Book No. 255, http://www.gwu.edu/~nsarchiv/NSAEBB/NSAEBB255/index.htm.
3. David Reimers, "An Unintended Reform: The 1965 Immigration Act and Third World Immigration to the United States," Journal of American Ethnic History 3, no. 1 (1983): 9–28.
4. Marjorie Heins, Strictly Ghetto Property: The Story of Los Siete de La Raza (Berkeley, CA: Ramparts Press, 1972), 11–12, 49–51, 203–6. In 1969, Central American youth from the Mission District of San Francisco were approached by two plainclothes policemen while moving furniture. An altercation resulted and an officer died from a gunshot wound.

Swarms of officers hit the building and fired automatic rifles and flooded the building with tear gas. Seven youths were arrested in Santa Cruz for murder and attempted murder in the case. Gary Lescallett, Daniel Melendez, Jose Rios, Rudolpho Martinez, Jose Martinez, and Danillo Melendez were acquitted; they included four Salvadorans, one Nicaraguan, and one Honduran. The seventh defendant, George López, was never apprehended. They had been involved in a youth group, the Mission Rebels. The Mission District was a mixed Latino *barrio* held together by La Raza. At trial the stories conflicted and the defendants insisted that the police had drawn their guns. They were in plain clothes. The trial lasted a year and a half, and the seven were acquitted. "Los Siete" Defense Committee helped raise the consciousness of youth.

5. "The Word Chicana/o," Chicana Chicano Public Scholar, http://forchicanachicanostudies.wikispaces.com/Chicana+Chicano+Public+Scholar.

6. Isaac William Martin, "Proposition 13 Fever: How California's Tax Limitation Spread," *California Journal of Politics and Policy*, 1, no. 1 (2009), Art. 17, 1–17. California Chief Justice Rose Bird Loses Election, http://www.youtube.com/watch?v=Kd162US36to.

7. Richard Adler, ed., *All in the Family: A Critical Appraisal* (New York: Praeger, 1979).

8. You can view episodes of these sitcoms. See All in the Family—Archie Bunker Meets Sammy Davis, http://www.youtube.com/watch?v=O_UBgkFHm8o.

9. Culture Clash Show—Lalo Sings No Chicanos on TV, http://www.youtube.com/watch?v=JZt6lZ6RDAU.

10. Rocio Rivadeneyra, "The Influence of Television on Stereotype Threat among Adolescents of Mexican Descent" (Ann Arbor: PhD dissertation, University of Michigan, 2001). Frito Bandito 1, http://www.youtube.com/watch?v=fOUilxJWm24.

11. Michael Harrington, *The Other America: Poverty in the United States* (Baltimore, MD: Penguin Books, 1963), x. George Mowry and Blaine A. Brownell, *The Urban Nation 1920–1980*, rev. ed. (New York: Hill and Wang, 1981), 311. All in the Family—Archie's Civil Rights 3-3, http://www.youtube.com/watch?v=ZDuZQabywjw.

12. *Jose Cisneros et al., Plaintiffs-Appellees, v. Corpus Christi Independent School District et al., Defendants-Appellants,* United States Court of Appeals for the Fifth Circuit August 2, 1972, 467 F.2d 142, http://law.justia.com/cases/federal/appellate-courts/F2/467/142/154342/. Neil Foley, "Straddling the Color Line," in Nancy Foner and George M. Fredrickson, eds., *Not Just Black and White: Historical and Contemporary Perspectives on Immigration, Race, and Ethnicity in the United States* (New York: Russell Sage Foundation, 2004), 351–54.

13. Joan Hoff, *Nixon Reconsidered* (New York: Basic Books, 1995), 97–98. Peter Leyden and Simon Rosenberg, "The 50-Year Strategy," *Mother Jones* (November–December 2007), http://www.motherjones.com/politics/2007/10/50-year-strategy-new-progressive-era-no-really. Deirdre Martínez, *Who Speaks for Hispanics? Hispanic Interest Groups in Washington* (Albany: State University of New York Press, 2009), 32–33.

14. Tony Castro, *Chicano Power: The Emergence of Mexican Americans* (New York: Saturday Review Press, 1974), 103, 199–201; Richard A. Santillán, *La Raza Unida* (Los Angeles, CA: Tlaquila, 1973), 80–81.

15. Frank Del Olmo, "Watergate Panel Calls 4 Mexican Americans," *Los Angeles Times* (June 5, 1974). Report of the Senate Select Committee on Presidential Activities, *The Senate Watergate Reports*, Vol. 1 (New York: Dell, 1974), 345–72. Castro, *Chicano Power*, 7–8, 202–3, 210. See also "La Raza Platform Prohibits Support of Non-Chicanos," *Los Angeles Times* (July 4, 1972). Cindy Parmenter, "La Raza Unida Plans Outlined," *Denver Post* (June 20, 1974). Jim Wood, "La Raza Sought Nixon Cash," *San Antonio Express* (November 18, 1973).

16. "Top Woman Aide Gets U.S. Latin Position," *Los Angeles Times* (March 8, 1977). "Spanish-Speaking Aide Hits Cutbacks," *Santa Fe New Mexican* (March 26, 1973). Julia Moran, "The GOP Wants Us," *Nuestro* (August 1980): 26. Joe Holley, "Leading Texas Republican Anne Armstrong," *Washington Post* (July 31, 2008), http://www.washingtonpost.com/wp-dyn/content/article/2008/07/30/AR2008073002605.html. David Binder, "Charles (Bebe) Rebozo, 85; Longtime Nixon Confidant," *New York Times* (May 9, 1998).

17. Moran, "The GOP Wants Us," 26. Grace A. Franklin and Randall B. Ripley, *C.E.T.A.: Politics and Policy, 1973-1982* (Knoxville: University of Tennessee Press, 1984), 12, 67, 120.

18. Carole A. Stabile, "Postmodernism, Feminism, and Marx: Notes from the Abyss," *Monthly Review* 47, no. 3 (July 1995): 89ff. Ignacio M. García, *Chicanismo: The Forging of a Militant Ethos Among Mexican Americans* (Tucson: University of Arizona Press, 1997), 133–45. Antonia I. Castañeda, "Women of Color and the Rewriting of Western History: The Discourse, Politics, and Decolonization of History," *Pacific Historical Review* 61, no. 4 (November 1992): 501–33. Alma M. García, ed., *Chicana Feminist Thought: The Basic Historical Writings* (New York: Routledge, 1997), 3.

19. Christine Marín, *A Spokesman of the Mexican American Movement: Rodolfo "Corky" Gonzales and the Fight for Chicano Liberation, 1966-1972* (San Francisco, CA: R&E Research Associates, 1977), 17.

20. Armando Navarro, *La Raza Unida Party: A Chicano Challenge to the U.S. Two-Party Dictatorship* (Philadelphia, PA: Temple University Press, 2000), 95.

21. Ibid., 41–48, 153–56.

22. Ibid., 70. Naomi Helena Quiñonez, "Hijas De La Malinche (Malinche's Daughters): The Development of Social Agency Among Mexican American Women and the Emergence of First Wave Chicana Cultural Production" (PhD dissertation, Calremont Graduate School, 1997), 175. Armando Navarro, *Mexican American Youth Organization: Avant-Garde of the Chicano Movement in Texas* (Austin: University of Texas Press, 1995), 75–83. Ignacio M. García, *United We Win: The Rise and Fall of La Raza Unida Party* (Tucson: Mexican American Studies & Research Center, University of Arizona, 1989). Evey Chapa, "Mujeres Por La Raza Unida," in A. García, ed., *Chicana Feminist Thought*, 178–79.

23. Castro, *Chicano Power*, 202. Ernesto Chávez, "Creating Aztlán: The Chicano Movement in Los Angeles, 1966–1978" (PhD dissertation, University of California, Los Angeles, 1994), 152–53, 170–71. Mario T. García, *Memories of Chicano History: The Life and Narrative of Bert Corona* (Berkeley: University of California Press, 1994), 266–69; for Corona's story of what happened, see 308–15. Santillán, *La Raza Unida*, 84–86. Navarro, *La Raza Unida Party*, 46–49, 141–44.

24. Navarro, *La Raza Unida Party*, 236–37.

25. Ibid., 41, 46–48. Oral History Interview of Richard A. Santillán, 1989, by Carlos Vásquez, UCLA Special Collections. Chávez, in "Creating Aztlán," says that Santillán concluded that the Republicans funded the RUP 48th Assembly District race. This charge was denied by the candidate. Good coverage in the *Arizona Republic* in 1972.

26. Navarro, *La Raza Unida Party*, 139, 154, 167–73. Jorge García, "Incorporation of East Los Angeles 1974, Part One," *La Raza Magazine* (Summer 1977): 29–33. Frank Del Olmo, "Early Returns Show East L.A. Incorporation Measure Failing," *Los Angeles Times* (November 6, 1974). Frank Del Olmo, "Defeat of East L.A. Plan Laid to Fear of High Property Tax," *Los Angeles Times* (November 7, 1974).

27. William C. Velásquez: 1944–1988, Willie Velásquez Institute, http://www.wcvi.org/wcvbio.htm. Juan A. Sepúlveda, *Life and Times of Willie Velásquez: Su Voto Es Su Voz* (Houston, TX: Arte Público Press, 2005). Navarro, *La Raza Unida Party*, 70–71, 79.

28. The [Puerto Rican] Young Lords Party, Position Paper on Women (May 1971), *Palante*, 11–14, http://younglords.info/resources/position_paper_on_women.pdf. Young Lords Party, Position on Women's Liberation, *Palante* (May 1971), 16–17, http://younglords.info/resources/position_on_womens_liberation_may1971.pdf.

29. Marta (Martha) Cotera, http://www.umich.edu/~ac213/student_projects05/cf/interview.html. Martha P. Cotera, *Diosa y Hembra: The History and Heritage of Chicanas in the U.S.* (Austin, TX: Information Systems Development, 1976). "Remembering a Revolutionary Mujer: Compañera Magdalena Mora," *¡La Verdad!*, http://uniondelbarrio.org/lvp/newspapers/97/janmay97/pg01.html. Rosaura Sánchez and Rosa Martínez, eds., *Essays on La Mujer* (Los Angeles: University of California Los Angeles Chicano Studies Research Center, 1977) and Adelaida R. Del Castillo and Rosa M. Martinez, ed., *Mexican Women in the United States: Struggles Past and Present* (Los Angeles: University of California Los Angeles Chicano Studies Research Center, 1980) were among the first academic contributions on Chicana feminism.

30. Enriqueta Vásquez, *Enriqueta Vásquez and the Chicano Movement: Writings from El Grito del Norte* (Houston, TX: Arte Público, 2006). Alma M. García, "The Development of Chicana Feminist Discourse, 1970–1980," *Gender & Society* 3, no. 2 (June 1989): 174, 218, 224, 232. Dionne Elaine Espinosa, "Pedagogies of Nationalism and Gender: Cultural Resistance in Selected Representational Practices of Chicana/o Movement Activists, 1967–1972" (PhD dissertation, Cornell University, 1996), 149, 150, 152, 155. Enriqueta Vásquez,

"The Woman of La Raza," *El Grito del Norte* (July 6, 1969). F. Arturo Rosales, *Chicano! The History of the Mexican American Civil Rights Movement* (Houston, TX: Arte Público Press, 1996), 183.

31. Maylei Blackwell, "Contested Histories: Las Hijas de Cuauhtémoc, Chicana Feminisms, and Print Culture in the Chicano Movement, 1968–1973," in Gabriela F. Arredondo, Aida Hurtado, Norma Klahn, Olga Nájera-Ramírez, and Patricia Zavella, eds., *Chicana Feminisms: A Critical Reader* (Duke University Press, 2003), 77–78.

32. Lucy R. Moreno Collection, 1971–1997, University of Texas Austin, http://www.lib.utexas.edu/taro/utlac/00103/lac-00103.html. Vicki L. Ruiz, *From Out of the Shadows: Mexican Women in Twentieth-Century America* (New York: Oxford University Press, 1999), 108–9. Marta Cotera, "La Conferencia De Mujeres Por La Raza, Houston, Texas, 1971," in A. Garcia, ed., *Chicana Feminist Thought*, 155–57.

33. *Dictionary of Literary Biography* on Dorinda Moreno, *Book Rags*, http://www.bookrags.com/biography/dorinda-moreno-dlb/. Flor Y Canto, University of Southern California 1973, http://readraza.com/florycanto/index.htm.

34. Rosa Rosales, Interview by José Angel Gutiérrez, University of Texas Arlington, Tejano Voices, http://library.uta.edu/tejanovoices/xml/CMAS_045.xml. Key profiles, Bios & Links Blog, http://key-profiles.blogspot.com/2006/10/profile-rosa-rosales-lulac-national.html. President of LULAC on Homies Nation TV, http://www.youtube.com/watch?v=2JB63EseIJ4.

35. A. García, ed., *Chicana Feminist Thought*, 8. Marta Cortera, "Chicana Identity (platica de Marta Cortera)," *Caracoal* (February 1976), 14–15, 17, 108–09. Quiñonez, "Hijas De La Malinche," 182. Espinosa, "Pedagogies," 176–81. Benita Roth, "On Their Own and for Their Own: African-American, Chicana, and White Feminist Movements in the 1960s and 1970s" (PhD dissertation, University of California, Los Angeles, 1998), 180. Jim Wood, "Report on Bias Against Latinos in Welfare," *San Francisco Chronicle* (July 2, 1972). Rodolfo Rosales, *Illusion of Inclusion* (Austin: University of Texas Press, 2000), 159–77. Beverly Padilla, "Chicanas and Abortion," *The Militant* (February 18, 1972) quoted in A. García, ed., *Chicana Feminist Thought*, 121. Statement by Elma Barrera, First National Chicana Conference-Workshop Resolutions, in Mirta Vidal, *Chicanas Speak Out! Women: New Voice of La Raza* (New York: Pathfinder Press, 1971).

36. Fabio Rojas, *From Black Power to Black Studies: How a Radical Social Movement Became an Academic Discipline* (Baltimore, MD: Johns Hopkins University Press, 2007), 79. SF State Third World Student Strike, http://www.youtube.com/watch?v=7ar2i-G5O-0&feature=related.

37. CSUN student political activism 1960s/70s "The Storm at Valley State" http://www.youtube.com/watch?v=NB3s_3RDEIc. On the Formation of Chicano Studies at Northridge see Miguel Durán, Unrest Documentary: Full Movie, http://www.youtube.com/watch?v=erf3j3UOmWE. Rodolfo F. Acuña, *The Making of Chicana/o Studies: In the Trenches of Academe* (New Brunswick: Rutgers University Press, 2011).

38. Javier Rangel, "The Educational Legacy of El Plan de Santa Barbara: An Interview with Reynaldo Macías," *Journal of Latinos and Education*, 6, no. 2 (2007): 192. Ruben Salazar, "Chicanos Set Their Goals in Education," *Los Angeles Times* (May 4, 1969), G8. *El Plan De Santa Bárbara: A Chicano Plan for Higher Education*, Analyses and Positions by the Chicano Coordinating Council on Higher Education (Oakland, CA: La Causa Publications, October 1969).

39. Acuña, *The Making of Chicana/o Studies*.

40. Adapted Urban Education Inc., Office for Civil Rights Data, pg. 130, Office of Civil Rights, Racial and Ethnic Enrollment Data from Institutions of Higher Education, Fall 1972, OCR-74-12 (U.S. Department of Heath, Education, and Welfare, 1974), 79–80, in Ronald W. López, Arturo Madrid-Barela, and Reynaldo Flores Macias, *Chicanos in Higher Education: Status and Issues*. The National Commission on Higher Education, Monograph No. 7 (Los Angeles: Chicano Studies Center Publications, University of California, Los Angeles, 1976), 63–64, 67–68.

41. "Cabinet Meeting Decisions" (Puerto Rico). October 6, 1960. Women in World History, http://chnm.gmu.edu/wwh/modules/lesson16/lesson16.php?menu=1&s=12. Harriet B. Presser, "Puerto Rico: The Role of Sterilization in Controlling Fertility," *Studies in Family Planning*, 1, no. 45 (September 1969): 8.

42. Norma Solis, "Do Doctors Abuse Low-Income Women?" *Chicano Times* (April 15–29, 1977). "Doctor Raps Sterilization of Indian Women," *Los Angeles Times* (May 22, 1977). "Puerto Rican Doctor Denounces Sterilization," *Sin Fronteras* (May 1976). Dr. Helen Rodrigues, head of pediatrics at Lincoln Hospital in San Francisco, said that by 1968, 35 percent of the women in Puerto Rico had been sterilized. See also Bernard Rosenfeld, Sidney M. Wolfe, and Robert E. McGarrah, Jr., *A Health Research Group Study on Surgical Sterilization: Present Abuses and Proposed Regulation* (Washington, DC: Public Citizens, 1973), 1, 7. Robert Kistler, "Women 'Pushed' into Sterilization, Doctor Charges," *Los Angeles Times* (December 2, 1974). See also Robert Kistler, "Many U.S. Rules on Sterilization Abuses Ignored Here," *Los Angeles Times* (December 3, 1974). Georgina Torres Rizk, "Sterilization Abuses Against Chicanos in Los Angeles" (Los Angeles Center for Law and Justice, December 2, 1976). Richard Siggins, "Coerced Sterilization: A National Civil Conspiracy to Commit Genocide upon the Poor?" (Chicago, IL: Loyola University School of Law, January 15, 1977), 12. Forced Sterilizations of American Indian Women, http://www.youtube.com/watch?v=WadjMamG4eQ. Reproductive Justice for Latinas: Coerced, Forced, and Involuntary Sterilization, http://www.youtube.com/watch?v=tShnkBmoe3Y.

43. Ronald B. Taylor, *Chávez and the Farm Workers* (Boston: Beacon Press, 1975), 278, 289. "A Boost for Chavez," *Newsweek* (May 26, 1975). "California Compromise," *Time* (May 19, 1975). "Chavez vs. the Teamsters: Farm Workers' Historic Vote," *U.S. News & World Report* (September 22, 1975): 82–83. American Friends Service Committee, *A Report of Research on the Wages of Migrant Farm Workers in Northwest Ohio* (July, August 1976), 1–9. Baldemar Velásquez, interview

by Rodolfo Acuña, Toledo, Ohio, August 8, 1977. "Statement of Problem," *Farm Labor Organizing Committee Newsletter* (January 1977). "FLOC: Both a Union and a Movement," *Worker's Power* (May 9, 1977). Thomas Ruge, "Indiana Farm Workers, Legislative Coalition Fights H.B. 1306," *OLA* (April 1977). Jim Wasserman, "FLOC Goal Is Power Base for Migrants," *Fort Wayne Journal-Gazette* (September 14, 1976). Fran Leeper Buss, ed., *Forged Under the Sun/Forjada bajo el sol: The Life of Maria Elena Lucas* (Ann Arbor: University of Michigan Press, 1993). Anon., *The Struggle of the Texas Farm Workers' Union* (Chicago, IL: Vanguard Press, 1977), 4, 14–15. Ignacio M. García, "The Many Battles of Antonio Orendian," *Nuestro* (November 1979), 25–29.

44. Irene Ledesma, "Texas Newspapers and Chicana Worker's Activism, 1919–1974," *Western Historical Quarterly* 26, no. 3 (Fall 1995): 327 Laurie Coyle, Gail Hershatter, and Emily Honig, *Women at Farah: An Unfinished Story* (El Paso, TX: Reforma, 1979). Bill Finger, "Victoria Sobre Farah," *Southern Exposure* 4, nos. 1–2 (1976): 5, 46, 47–49. Numerous articles ran in *San Antonio Express* and *El Paso Times* during 1972 and 1973 on the Farah strike, the boycott, and the closing of the plant. "Fury Stands Pat on Farah," *San Antonio Express* (December 14, 1973), is a solid article that lays out reasons for the bishops' support of the boycott. Laura E. Arroyo, "Industrial and Occupational Distribution of Chicana Workers," *Aztlán* 4, no. 2 (1973): 358–59. Philip Shabecoff, "Farah Strike Has Become War of Attrition; The Worst Part," *New York Times* (June 16, 1973).

45. Peter Wiley and Robert Gottlieb, *Empires in the Sun* (Tucson: University of Arizona Press, 1982), 257, 265. Gay Young, "Gender Identification and Working-Class Solidarity Among Maquila Workers," in *Ciudad Juarez: Stereotypes and Realities*, in Vicki L. Ruiz and Susan Tiano, eds., *Women on the U.S.–Mexico Border: Responses to Change* (Boston: Allen & Unwin, 1987), 105–28. Devon Peña, "Tortuosidad: Shop Floor Struggles of Female Maquiladoras Workers," in Ruiz and Tiano, *Responses to Change*, 129–54.

46. Chávez, "Creating Aztlán," 179–86, 199, 200–01. David G. Gutiérrez, *Walls and Mirrors: Mexican Americans, Mexican Immigrants, and the Politics of Ethnicity* (Berkeley: University of California Press, 1995), 191. David G. Gutiérrez, "Sin Fronteras? Chicanos, Mexican Americans, and the Emergence of the Contemporary Mexican Immigration Debate, 1968–1978," in David G. Gutiérrez, ed., *Between Two Worlds: Mexican Immigrants in the United States* (Wilmington, DE: Scholarly Resources, 1996), 175–209. M. García, *Bert Corona*, 290–95. Carlos Muñoz, Jr., *Youth, Identity, Power: The Vhicano Movement* (London: Verso, 2007), 92–94. See Juan Gómez-Quiñones, *Chicano Politics: Reality and Promise 1940–1990* (Albuquerque: University of New Mexico Press, 1990). Gómez-Quiñones, *Mexican Students For La Raza: The Chicano Student Movement in Southern California 1967–1977* (Santa Barbara, CA: Editorial La Causa, 1978).

47. Rodolfo F. Acuña, *Occupied America: A History of Chicanos*, 2d ed. (New York: Harper & Row, 1981), 168–71. Vernon M. Briggs, "Labor Market Aspects of Mexican Migration to the

United States," in Stanley R. Ross, ed., *Views Across the Border* (Albuquerque: University of New Mexico Press, 1979), 21, 211, 221. Ronald Bonaparte, "The Rodino Bill: An Example of Prejudice Toward Mexican Immigration to the United States," *Chicano Law Review* 2 (Summer 1975): 40–50. Frank Del Olmo, "Softer Penalties in Alien Cases Urged," *Los Angeles Times* (April 20, 1977). Arthur F. Corwin, *Letter to Henry Kissinger* (July 16, 1975), 2–3, 20, 21, 39; photocopy in possession of Professor Jorge Bustamante, University of Nortre Dame, Indiana.

48. David S. North and Marion Houston, "Illegal Aliens: Their Characteristics and Role in the U.S. Labor Market," study conducted for the U.S. Department of Labor by Linton and Co. (November 17, 1975). Vic Villalpando, "Abstract: A Study of the Impact of Illegal Aliens in the County of San Diego on Specific Socioeconomic Areas," in Antonio José Ríos-Bustamante, ed., *Immigration and Public Policy: Human Rights for Undocumented Workers and Their Families,* Chicano Studies Center Document no. 5 (Los Angeles: Chicano Studies Center Publications, University of California Los Angeles, 1977), 223–31. Jorge Bustamante, "The Impact of the Undocumented Immigration from Mexico on the U.S.–Mexican Economics: Preliminary Findings and Suggestions for Bilateral Cooperation," Forty-sixth Annual Meeting of the Southern Economic Association, Atlanta, Georgia, November 1976.

49. Bill Curry, "Alien-Torture Case Ends in Mistrial for 2 Ranchers," *Los Angeles Times* (July 30, 1980). "The Nation; Judge Sets 3rd Trial in Alien Torture Case," *Los Angeles Times* (September 3, 1980). Tom Miller, *On the Border* (New York: Ace Books, 1981), 158–79. *Arizona Republic,* "Third Trial to Begin in Beating of Aliens: Two Arizona Ranchers Have Been Acquitted Once and a 2d Jury Could Not Reach a Verdict," *New York Times* (January 20, 1981). "Rancher in Plea to High Court in Case of Tortured Mexicans," *New York Times* (December 5, 1982). *United States of America, Plaintiff-Appellee, v. Patrick W. Hanigan, Defendant-Appellant,* No. 81-1262. 681 F2d 1127 (1982), http://openjurist.org/681/f2d/1127/united-states-v-w-hanigan.

50. See Ron Dusek, "Aliens Given Deportation Reprieve by Chicago Judge," *El Paso Times* (March 25, 1977). James Sterba, "Alien Ruling Snarls Migrant Job Inquiry," *New York Times* (August 14, 1977). Robert Kistler, "No Effort to Block KKK 'Patrol' of Border Planned," *Los Angeles Times* (October 10, 1977). *CCR Newsletter* (San Diego, October 29, 1977).

51. Gutiérrez, *Walls and Mirrors,* 199. David Reyes, "In Pursuit of the Latino American Dream," *Los Angeles Times* (July 24, 1983), Orange County section. Armando Navarro, *Mexicano Political Experience in Occupied Aztlán: Struggles and Change* (Lanham, MD: Altamira Press, 2005), 519.

52. Juan Gómez Quiñones, *Chicano Politics: Reality & Promise 1940-1990* (Albuquerque: University of New Mexico Press, 1990), 166. Moises Sándoval, "The Struggle Within LULAC," *Nuestro* (September 1979): 30. Navarro, *Mexicano Political Experience,* 519–22. Craig A. Kaplowitz, *Lulac, Mexican Americans, and National Policy* (College Station: Texas A&M University Press, 2005), 153, 194.

53. NALEO Education Fund, http://www.naleo.org/.

54. Congressional Hispanic Caucus Institute, http://www.chci.org/.

55. Ron Ozio, "The Hell with Being Quiet and Dignified, Says Rubén Bonilla," *Nuestro* (September 1979): 31–32. "3 Million Chicanos Voiceless in California," *Forumeer* (October 1971). In California in 1971, out of 15,650 elected and appointed officials, 310—or 1.98 percent—were Chicanos. None of the 46 state officials and none of the advisors to the governor were Mexican. Castro, *Chicano Power,* 106. Andrew Hernández, *The Latin Vote in the 1976 Presidential Election* (San Antonio, TX: Southwest Voter Registration Education Project, 1977), i, 1–2, 9. Choco González Meza, *The Latin Vote in the 1980 Presidential Election: Political Research Report* (San Antonio, TX: Southwest Voter Registration Education Project, January 1, 1981), 13. Julian Nava Collection, Urban Archives, California State University Northridge, http://digital-library.csun.edu/LatArch/.

56. Keith J. Henderson, "Bilingual Education Programs Spawning Flood of Questions," *Albuquerque Journal* (June 11, 1978). Meyer Weinberg, *Minority Students: A Research Appraisal* (Washington, DC: U.S. Department of Health, Education and Welfare, 1977), 287. U.S. Commission on Civil Rights, *The Excluded Student: Educational Practices Affecting Mexican Americans in the Southwest,* Mexican American Education Study, Report iii (Washington, DC: Government Printing Office, 1972); bilingual education reached only 2.7 percent of the entire Chicano population.

57. *Serrano v. Priest,* 5 Cal. 3d 584; 96 Cal. Rptr. 601; 487 P.2d 1241 (1971). David C. Long, "Litigation Concerning Educational Finance," in Clifford P. Hooker, ed., *The Courts and Education* (Chicago, IL: University of Chicago, 1978), 221–29.

58. *San Antonio Independent School District v. Rodriguez,* 411 U.S. 1 (1973), Appeal from the United States District Court for the Western District of Texas, No. 71-1332 Argued: October 12, 1972—Decided: March 21, 1973. *Rodríguez v. San Antonio ISD.* Handbook of Texas Online, http://www.tshaonline.org/handbook/online/articles/RR/jrrht.html.

59. Alexander W. Astin, *Minorities in American Higher Education* (San Francisco, CA: Jossey-Bass, 1982), 29. Meyer Weinberg, *A Chance to Learn: A History of Race and Education in the United States* (Cambridge, UK: Cambridge University Press, 1977), 164, 340–45. Thomas Carter and Roberto D. Segura, *Mexican Americans in School* (New York: College Examination Board, 1979), 233–35.

60. See Astin, *Minorities.* Donald J. Bogue, *Population of the United States* (Glencoe, IL: Free Press, 1959), 570 gives an excellent synthesis of historical trends up to 1980. Alexander W. Astin, *Assessment For Excellence: The Philosophy and Practice of Assessment and Evaluation in Higher Education* (Westport, CT: Oryx Press, 1993), 196, 199.

61. Peter Camejo, (September 14, 2009), http://asitoughttobe.wordpress.com/2009/09/14/peter-camejo/.

62. Rodolfo F. Acuña, *Sometimes There Is No Other Side: Chicanos and the Myth of Equality* (Notre Dame, IN: University of Notre Dame Press, 1998), 21–32. Minority Admissions Summer

Project, sponsored by the National Lawyers Guild and the National Congress of Black Lawyers, *Affirmative Action in Crisis: A Handbook for Activists* (Detroit, 1977); hereafter referred to as *Minority Admissions*. Celeste Durant, "California Bar Exam—Pain and Trauma Twice a Year," *Los Angeles Times* (August 27, 1978). Robert Montoya, "Minority Health Professional Development: An Issue of Freedom of Choice for Young Anglo Health Professionals" (paper presented at the Annual Convention of the American Medical Student Association, Atlanta, Georgia, March 4, 1978). *Regents of the University of California v. Bakke*, 438 U.S. 265 (1978); No. 76–811.

63. Stephen N. Keith, R. M. Bell, A. G. Swanson, and A. Williams, "Effects of Affirmative Action in Medical Schools: A Study of the Class of 1975," *New England Journal of Medicine* 313 (1985): 1519–25. Rodolfo F. Acuña, *US Latinos Issues* (Westport, CT: Greenwood Press, 2004), Chapter 5 on affirmative action. Alex Liebman, "How'd That Guy Get In, Anyway?" *Argos* 1, no. 2 (Summer 1998); hyperlink no longer available.

64. The Federal Bureau of Investigation (FBI), http://www.zoklet.net/totse/en/politics/federal_bureau_of_investigation/index.html. Ernesto B. Vigil, *The Crusade for Justice: Chicano Militancy and the Government's War on Dissent* (Madison: University of Wisconsin Press, 1999). José Angel Gutiérrez, *The Making of a Chicano Militant: Lessons from Cristal* (Madison: University of Wisconsin Press, 1999).

65. The author was part of the Committee to Free Gordon Castillo Hall. Frank del Olmo, "The System Can Be Murder," *Los Angeles Times* (July 16, 1981). Henry Mendoza, "For Gordon Castillo Hall, First Steps Taken in Freedom Are Frightening," *Los Angeles Times* (July 15, 1981). George Ramos, "Justice Takes a Tortuous Route for Latino Man," *Los Angeles Times* (August 9, 1993).

66. Roberto Rodriguez, *Justice: A Question of Race* (Tempe, AZ: Bilingual Review Press, 1997).

67. Homicide-Los Angeles, 1970–1979, *Morbidity and Mortality Weekly Report* 35, no. 5 (February 7, 1986), 61–65, http://www.cdc.gov/mmwr/preview/mmwrhtml/00000841.htm.

68. S. O. B., http://www.youtube.com/watch?v=odRqoMZRm_Y. Anthony Lake, *Somoza Falling* (Boston: Houghton Mifflin, 1989), 94, 186, 260, 273. Anastasio Somoza Debayle, http://www.youtube.com/watch?v=TDRWSFroSbk&feature=related.

69. People and Events: The Iranian Hostage Crisis, November 1979–January 1981, http://www.pbs.org/wgbh/amex/carter/peopleevents/e_hostage.html. U.S. Interventions: 1945–2000, http://www.metacafe.com/watch/1181268/u_s_interventions_1945_2000/.

Becoming a National Minority: 1980–2001

From Chapter 15 of *Occupied America: A History of Chicanos*, Eighth Edition. Rodolfo F. Acuña. Copyright © 2015 by Pearson Education, Inc. All rights reserved.

Becoming a National Minority: 1980–2001

LEARNING OBJECTIVES

- Compare the causes and effects of the massive U.S. immigration from Mexico and Central America.

- Discuss the reasons for deindustrialization and globalization, and the impact on Mexican Americans.

- Tell how immigration became the overwhelming issue in the Mexican American community.

- Explain how immigrants had a positive impact on the American economy.

- Discuss the impact of population growth on the Mexican American community.

- Recognize Propositions 187, 209, and 227 and tell their importance.

- List the most important issues of the period 1980–2001 in a timeline.

The timeline covers two decades—two very hectic periods. For Mexican Americans, population growth contributed to a transformation that saw the community take center stage nationally. In 1980 fewer than 9 million Mexican Americans were counted; they grew to 12.6 million by 1989; and to 20.6 million by 2000. The Latino population as a whole increased from 22.4 million in 1990 to 35.3 million in 2000.[1] The reason for combining decades has to do with history—the events of these two periods are fairly recent, and it takes a bit of distancing for the historian to view the events unfolding decade after decade. Too often historians find themselves so close to the events that the picture blurs.

The population growth put emphasis on the adage *Gobernar es poblar* (to govern is to populate), which in reference to Latinos meant increased involvement in the political process.[2] Increased immigration came from Mexico due to the collapse of the Mexican economy in the 1980s; the civil wars in

1979	1980	1981	1982	1983	1984	1985	1986	1987	1988	1989

1990	1991	1992	1993	1994	1995	1996	1997	1998	1999	2000

Central America uprooted millions of people that joined the polyglot of Spanish-surname people living in the United States. Almost immediately they became the targets of well-funded xenophobic organizations and a rabid press. Most of the media since the 1970s were shallow and pandered to racist nativists. They stereotyped Mexican and Central American immigrants as criminals. Television, radio, and the print media were the important forms of mass communication in the 1980s and 1990s, and viewers, listeners, and readers all depended on them for news.

In 1971 Lewis Powell's political manifesto was a call to action. Over the next years Corporate America created the Heritage Foundation (1973), the Manhattan Institute (1978), the Cato Institute (founded as the Charles Koch Foundation in 1974), Citizens for a Sound Economy (1984), Accuracy in Academe, and other powerful organizations. Massive corporations moved to control communication and war with the reformers. By the 1980s, many of these foundations played on the fears of an aging white population and made war on trade unions and immigrants. To the credit of Latinos as a community, they did not abandon the foreign born.[3]

A study of the files of the *Los Angeles Times* index shows that it first used the term *illegal alien* to refer to immigrants on September 25, 1901. The first reference to Mexicans as illegal aliens was in January 26, 1930; it was only the fourth time it used the term. By 1970, the *Los Angeles Times* had used the phrase 100 times. But from 1970 to mid-1985 it used it more than 6,200 times and by 2006, in an estimated 20,000 documents. By contrast, the *New York Times*, which began publishing in 1851, did not use the term until 1926, when it reported that a man on a bicycle made an unauthorized entry on the Canadian border. By 1970, the *New York Times* had used the term 74 times. From 1970 to 2003, it used the phrase 4,382 times, far less often than the *Los Angeles Times*.[4]

The Decade of the Hispanic

At the beginning of the decade, a prominent Mexican American national leader called the 1980s the "Decade of the Hispanic," suggesting that Mexican Americans would reap the fruits of their struggle for equality. Not quite! Congressional Representative Edward R. Roybal[5] responded at the G.I. Forum Convention in 1980:

> We have been told over and over that the 1980s will be the Decade of the Hispanics. But, we all remember we were told the same thing at the start of the 1970s. The real answer, my friends, is that we have no clout.

The theme of the conference was "Merchandising the Mexican American Market in the United States."[6] In California, despite the hype, Mexicans still had only one congressman, and in Los Angeles, with millions of Mexican Americans, the community did not have representation at the city or county levels.

Later in the 1980s, this disparity was somewhat narrowed thanks to the Voting Rights Act of 1965 and lawsuits brought by the Mexican American Legal Defense and Education Fund [MALDEF].[7] However, many Latino leaders and business persons were oblivious to the inequality and became cheerleaders, hyping the 1980s as the Decade of the Hispanic as if the community were a commodity. *Latino* organizations multiplied, and many Mexican American organizations broadened their trajectory to include new immigrants in order to create a national market. The numbers, rather than a sense of civil rights history or struggle, were the standard for representation. Consequently, Latinos failed to educate the new immigrants about the fact that their entitlements came not from the numbers alone but the struggles of the Mexican American, Chicano, and Puerto Rican movements. The entitlements did not come through the covers of fashion magazines.

The election of Ronald Reagan in 1980 ushered in an era of political and economic privatization and conservatism; like the 1920s and the McCarthy era in the aftermath of World War II, it was a war on the poor, immigrants, and unions. The deindustrialization of the economy, that is, the downsizing of heavy manufacturing, was a blow to the working class, increasingly composed of minorities.[8] Some of the impact on Latinos and minorities was absorbed by the increased numbers in higher education, brought about by affirmative action. Reagan's policies of privatization and deregulation would in the next 20 years dismantle this access. Big Business would refuse to pay for the social costs of production, and transfer the support of public higher education to the middle class and poor in the form of increased tuition fees.

The expansion of farm employment and the growth of light industries during the 1980s attracted immigrants. These sectors paid minimum wages, and most often they did not provide health benefits. What was disturbing to many Euro-Americans was the color of the skin of many of the new immigrants. The Immigration Act of 1965 had opened the door for nonwhite groups. The act also allowed more political refugees to enter the country. As a result, the foreign-born population increased from 9.6 million in 1970 to 22.8 million in 1994—a jump of 137 percent. In 1988, 43 percent of authorized immigrants came from Latin America, 41 percent from Asia, and only 10 percent from Europe; the preferred destinations of 70 percent of these immigrants were in just six states. Increased numbers of darker-skinned people triggered rabid racist nativism, a xenophobia agitated by right-wing think tanks and foundations, as well as by fanatics and conservative extremists. They built their organizations on fear and made a lot of money in the process.[9]

Immigration in the 1980s

The Central American Wave

It is important to reiterate that the reason large waves of immigrants from Central America arrived in the 1980s was not the Immigration Act of 1965, but the civil wars in their countries, principally funded by the United States. Moreover, prior to the civil wars, there was a population explosion in Central America. From 1950 to 1990 the population of the region swelled from just over 9 million to almost 29 million. El Salvador and Guatemala went from 4.1 million and 6 million, respectively, in 1975 to 5.3 million and 9.1 million in 1990. The population explosion led to a flight to the cities, as farming was nearly impossible owing to the monopolization of land by elite families and foreign coffee and banana conglomerates. U.S. corporations owned 400,000 acres in Honduras alone—land obtained free of cost through arrangements with friendly dictators at the beginning of the twentieth century. Owing to the lack of a manufacturing infrastructure, the cities could not absorb displaced Salvadoran and Guatemalan rural workers. These conditions produced unrest, and civil wars followed. In Salvador an estimated 5–20 percent of the total population fled to the United States.[10]

U.S. intervention in Central America was a major cause of the diaspora. The fall of U.S.-anointed Nicaraguan dictator Anastasio Somoza in 1979 intensified civil wars in Central America—especially in El Salvador, Guatemala, and Nicaragua. Central American immigrants differed from the Mexican immigrants in that most Central Americans were political refugees. The overthrow of Somoza weakened North American hegemony in the region, and a domino effect followed as other Central Americans began demanding sovereignty and democracy.

El Salvador had been in a state of flux since the 1920s; peasants wanted land and were tired of exploitation by the *latifundista* (large plantation owners). Farabundo Martí, aided by the Communist Party, led a revolt, which the Salvadoran military sadistically suppressed in 1932. More than 12,000 peasants (mostly Indians) died; Martí was murdered. During the 1960s, influenced by Liberation Theology, Catholic clergy and lay persons formed base communities where the question of inequality was discussed and many peasants were politicized. This led to a reaction by elite groups, and in the early 1970s, the ruling elite subverted elections and sponsored the rise of Roberto D'Aubuisson, a neo-Nazi, who headed death squads that conducted a campaign of terror.[11] In 1977, D'Aubuisson's White Warriors machine-gunned Jesuit Father Rutilio Grande and ordered all Jesuits out of the country. Archbishop Oscar Romero began to speak out against injustice, and in 1980, assassins murdered Romero as he celebrated mass. That year, the Salvadoran National Guard tortured, raped, and killed four North American churchwomen.[12]

In 1980, a coalition of Christian Democrats, Social Democrats, minor parties, trade unions, students, and others formed the *Frente Democrático Revolucionario* (FDR), which joined hands with the *Farabundo Martí Liberación Nacional* (FMLN), the military wing heading the armed struggle. At the same time, to give the government an air of legitimacy, a centrist party took the national presidency. Meanwhile, the right controlled the legislature. The United States financed military operations against the FMLN. Some 50,000 Salvadorans—most of whom were civilians—died during this civil war. Still, unable to find peace at home, hundreds of thousands of Salvadorans fled north.

The U.S. government sent the Salvadoran military $4.2 billion to conduct the war and, consequently, destroy any semblance of a free market. The military, through its surrogate Arena Party, controlled a large bloc of votes during the 1991 elections—which it subverted, committing gross fraud. Nevertheless, the warring factions signed peace accords that year.[13]

Meanwhile, in Nicaragua, the rebels under the leadership of the Sandinista National Liberation Front (*Frente Sandinista de Liberación Nacional*, or FSLN) successfully set up a revolutionary government.[14] The United States, fearing that a Marxist or left-of-center government would threaten its economic and political interests, backed counterrevolutionaries with the purpose of overthrowing the FSLN. (Nicaragua numbered 2.4 million people. The United States had a population of 226.6 million in 1980.) The United States intensified the war in Nicaragua, under the pretext that Nicaragua was a threat to the security of the United States and it was supplying arms to El Salvador's insurgents. Ronald Reagan's 1980 election escalated the war against the Sandinistas. Reagan stationed 2,000 troops in Honduras, where the CIA—with the Contras (the ultraright opposition)—led military operations against the Nicaraguan government. Thus, the CIA openly violated the Boland Amendment, which prohibited the use of U.S. funds to overthrow a foreign government.[15]

Reagan insisted that Soviet and Cuban influence in Nicaragua threatened U.S. security. But just as it did in 1954 in Guatemala, the Dominican Republic in 1963–1965, and Chile on 9/11/1973, the U.S. moved to overthrow the Nicaraguan government. Reagan dubbed the Sandinistas undemocratic. In 1984, the Sandinistas held elections. While Western European and Latin American nations praised the elections for being open, Reagan labeled them a sham. Reagan and then George H. W. Bush isolated Nicaragua, and in 1990, the Nicaraguan people, weary of war, voted for the United Nicaraguan Opposition. The Sandinistas peacefully relinquished power. This ended the dirty little war, which led to an indictment of Ronald Reagan's former Defense Secretary Caspar W. Weinberger on charges that he lied to Congress about his knowledge of arms sales to Iran and efforts by other countries to help underwrite the Nicaraguan war. It was also charged that the CIA allowed illegal drugs to be imported into the United States by the Contras, which were sold and the proceeds used by Contra leaders to buy arms. President George H. W. Bush pardoned Weinberger and five others, thus preventing an airing of evidence that Bush, while he was Reagan's vice president, was involved in the conspiracy. The media called this unconstitutional operation *Iran Contra*.[16]

During 1966–1968, President Lyndon Johnson sent Green Berets to Guatemala, to train government forces against insurgents. U.S.-supported government troops crushed a revolution, which resurged again in the 1980s. Knowing that the rebels had peasant support, the military embarked on a strategy of burning indigenous villages, corralling the natives into key cities. A secret army unit, financed and trained by the United States, operated in the country in the early 1980s, kidnapping, torturing, and executing Guatemalans in a violent campaign against leftists suspected of subversion. This was the longest and bloodiest butchery in Central America, killing more than 200,000 people. Well over 50,000 disappeared in a nation of 11 million. The war displaced about a million and a half Guatemalan peasants as the army pursued a strategy of "permanent counterinsurgency" against the nation's 5 million Maya.[17]

The Mexican Wave

Mexican immigration accelerated in the 1980s. The underlying causes were population growth and a movement of large number of Mexicans to the cities due to the continued commercialization of agriculture. An international crisis devastated Mexico's economy in 1982 and accelerated the push. Outgoing President José López Portillo dramatically devalued the peso, which in the next three years fell from 12.5 pesos to the dollar to more than 700 pesos to the dollar. The reason for the devaluation was to supposedly stop the flight of dollars from Mexico. The country's external debt, both private and public, climbed to $85 billion. Mexico needed the dollars to pay its debt, which by 1986 was approaching $100 billion.

The minimum wage in Ciudad Juárez in 1978 was 125 pesos ($5.30) a day. Three years later 600 *maquiladoras* (assembly plants) operated south of the border, 90 percent of them along the border. They employed 130,000 workers, 75–90 percent of them women, 70 percent of whom were single. The system supported 80,000 workers in Juárez alone and another 5,000 white-collar jobs in El Paso. Mexican *maquila* wages averaged $2 an hour in 1982 before the devaluation; in 1987, they averaged $0.67 an hour, which was lower than Asian wages. By 1986, Ciudad Juárez became a *maquiladora* boomtown. Corporations such as General Motors, which assembled wire harnesses there, maintained large operations all along the border.

By 1986, Mexico defaulted on the loans or declared a repayment moratorium. Mexico's domestic situation worsened—it could no longer comply with the International Monetary Fund (IMF) demands without facing severe internal consequences. The situation was rendered almost impossible by the nearly 50 percent plunge in the price of oil, which furnished 70 percent of Mexico's export exchange and 50 percent of government revenues. Hence, the rich got richer, and by the end of the millennium, there were 13 Mexican billionaires, the highest by far in Latin America (France was 16).[18]

Reaction to the Little Brown Brothers and Sisters

Since the Alien and Sedition Acts of 1798, there has been a pattern of irrational Euro-American angst fed by the notion that someone was taking America away from them. The panic was worse during periods of uncertainty; generally the fear was fanned by the media. As in the case of a horror movie like *Friday the 13th*, the audience's fear reaches its height over anticipated situations. In the case of white suburban women, the fear was that the inner city would catch up to them and dark men would stalk them. The argument that unauthorized immigrants took jobs away from "Americans," and in some way were stealing their "American Dream," was disproven. Americans refused to listen to the evidence and there was a disconnect between reality and myth. For example, California benefited from immigration. In 1984, the Urban Institute of Washington reported that 645,000 jobs had been created in Los Angeles County since 1970; immigrants took about one-third of the jobs. Without immigrants, the factories hiring them would have left the area, resulting in the loss of higher-paying jobs.[19]

Although the availability of an immigrant labor force spurred economic activity for the nation as a whole, nativism became more strident in 1986, as Californians passed the "English Is the Official Language" Proposition 63, which voters approved by a 3 to 1 margin. The campaign was a look into the future; it was based almost entirely on half truths and hate. Within a year, seven other states passed similar measures, and 31 more were considering English Only measures. Yeshiva University Psychology Professor Joshua Fishman questioned the good faith behind the sudden concern for the "functional protection of English." He asked how English was endangered in a country where 97 percent of the population spoke the language. Fishman raised the probability of a "hidden agenda."[20]

About the same time, Congress responded to nation's jingoism by passing the Immigration Reform and Control Act (IRCA), which was a compromise that included employer sanctions as well as amnesty for unauthorized immigrants who had been residents since January 1, 1981, or could prove they had done farmwork for 90 days, from May 1, 1985, to May 1, 1986. By January 1989, some 2.96 million applied for amnesty (about 70 percent of them were Mexican). IRCA allocated $1 billion a year for four years to fund English, U.S. history, and government classes to be administered by the State Legislation Impact Assistance Grant. The classes were mandatory for all amnesty applicants, and organizations such as *Hermandad Mexicana Nacional* and One-Stop Immigration hoped to use the funds to teach the new immigrants English and to assimilate them into the social and political life of Chicanos. The antiamnesty forces were spearheaded by groups such as the American Immigration Control Foundation (AICF) and the Federation for American Immigration Reform (FAIR) whose opposition was ideological rather than based on reason. The Center for New Community reported:

> *Much of the AICF leadership crosses the thin ideological line separating xenophobic nativism and outright white nationalism. Former AICF board chair Sam Francis (1992–1995 . . .), for example, is well-known for his racist and biological determinist positions. Longtime AICF board member Brent Nelson is on the Editorial Advisory Board of the Citizens Informer, the flagship*

publication of the white nationalist Council of Conservative Citizens (C of CC) and often
pens articles for this publication, as does AICF President and Immigration Watch editor John
Vinson. Moreover AICF has received strong financial support from the Pioneer Fund, a
foundation which has been linked to eugenics and other "racial" research.[21]

Equally to blame for spreading panic were elected officials who had nothing to lose, and a lot to gain, by taking cheap shots at immigrants. For instance, Dallas Mayor Pro Tem Jim Hart exploited the fears of the voters and warned that aliens had "no moral values," and that they were destroying Dallas neighborhoods and threatening the security of the city. California Congressman Elton Gallegly (R–Simi Valley) proposed a constitutional amendment to deny citizenship to U.S.-born children of undocumented immigrants. Even California Representative Anthony Bielenson (D–San Fernando Valley), considered a progressive Democrat, raised the bogus prospect of a Mexican invasion.[22] This tension emboldened far-right racists, who began to abuse the initiative and referendum process with impunity. An example was the campaign to dump California Supreme Court Justice Rose Bird and Associate Justices Joseph Grodin and Cruz Reynoso, a highly respected Chicano jurist who had a long history of involvement in public interest law. Nativists lied and exaggerated the votes of these justices against the death penalty to whip up public angst and hatred of the "other." *Los Angeles Times* columnist Frank de Olmo put the campaign to remove Reynoso in the context of Proposition 63.

> *The campaign against Reynoso and his colleagues, including Chief Justice Rose Elizabeth Bird,*
> *is being pushed by law-and-order advocates who claim that the "liberal" justices are lenient on*
> *crime. It has been waged for several years and has been analyzed more than any other issue on*
> *the state ballot—except for a troubling undercurrent that Californians have become too polite*
> *to discuss openly: racism.*
>
> > *I don't mean the ugly racism that motivates some people to burn crosses. The campaign*
> *against Reynoso is more subtle. It indirectly suggests that because Reynoso came from a large*
> *family of farm workers he is not quite as capable as judges with a different (that is, "better") so-*
> *cial background. And it slyly hints that a Mexican-American judge can't analyze cases affecting*
> *poor people dispassionately.[23]*

The Militarization of the Border

Shortly after the Berlin Wall, separating East and West Germany, came down in 1989, the United States built its own wall separating it from the Third World. Border Patrol abuse increased, as did the military swagger of the agency. The official line—that the Border Patrol was fighting a war on drugs—gave the agency tremendous latitude in violating human rights. In 1990, one year after the Berlin Wall came tumbling down, the Defense Department built an 11-mile fence in the San Diego area as part of its war on drugs. Two years later, the Army Corps of Engineers announced plans to place scores of floodlights along a 13-mile strip of border near San Diego to "deter drug smugglers and illegal aliens." A 1992 *Atlantic* piece posited, "It would not require much killing: the Soviets sealed their borders for decades without an excessive expenditure of ammunition," adding that a systematic policy of shooting illegal immigrants would deter most Mexicans, but "adopting such a policy is not a choice most Americans would make. Of course, there would be no question of free trade."[24]

President Bill Clinton, mindful that he had been defeated in his reelection for Arkansas governor because he allegedly did not act quickly enough to put down a riot of Cuban inmates at Fort Chaffee, Arkansas, played Mr. Tough Guy and followed the policies of Reagan and George H. W. Bush. He manufactured a war against undocumented immigrants, ordering Attorney General Janet Reno to begin blockades and roundups in the El Paso and San Diego areas. By the end of the Clinton administration, San Diego became ground zero in the anti-immigrant war. The Clinton administration called it "Operation Gatekeeper": sealing the border in western San Diego County and forcing undocumented immigrants to cross the deadly terrain to the east. The government increasingly commingled crackdowns on immigrants and the war against drugs—falsely equating immigration and drug smuggling and, thus, further criminalizing the immigrant. However, as described later in this chapter, immigration hysteria lessened considerably by 1998—partially because of improved economic conditions, but in good part because of the backlash within the Mexican American and other Latino communities.[25]

Mexican American Labor

Never before in the history of Chicanos were labor unions needed more than in the 1980s and 1990s. The poverty rate went on climbing throughout the late 1970s and 1980s to reach a 27-year high in 1991, with 35.7 million people living below the poverty line—the highest poverty rate since 1964. Frequent economic recessions during the 1980s and early 1990s especially hurt women, most of whom possessed few job skills. From 1973 to 1990, the median salary of female heads-of-households under the age of 30 fell 32 percent in real dollars—more than 50 percent of the Mexicanas in the workforce earned less than $10,000. Close to 50 percent (47.7 percent) of the Mexican households with an absent father lived in poverty; and close to 40 percent (37.3 percent) of Mexican-origin workers who did not have a high school education lived in poverty, versus 16.7 percent in the non-Latino community.

While the white population increased its college enrollment from 31.8 to 39.4 percent during the 1980s, and African American enrollment went from 27.6 to 33 percent, the Latino enrollment fell from 29.8 to 29 percent. And, unlike black school segregation, which had fluctuated within a narrow range over the previous 25 years, Latino segregation kept increasing. In 1970, the typical black student attended a school where enrollment was 32 percent white; by 1994, it was 33.9 percent. On the other hand, for schools attended by Latino students, white enrollment went down—from 43.8 to 30.6 percent. The harshness of the new economy and the growing gap between the rich and poor did not escape Archbishop Roger Mahoney, who in 1985 said, "we cannot evaluate our economy primarily by the extraordinary opportunities it offers a few."[26]

It is not that history repeats itself, it is that we forget its lessons. During the 1950s Republicans sought to dismantle the protections of the New Deal, though the memory of the Great Depression was still fresh. By the 1980s, those memories either faded or were repressed. This historical amnesia gave Reagan the opportunity that reactionaries had waited for 40 years—to dismantle the safety nets for the average American and make the country business friendly. Reagan declared in 1982, as he signed the Garn–St. Germain Depository Institutions Act, lessening regulations on savings and loans and banks, "This bill is the most important legislation for financial institutions in the last 50 years. It provides a long-term solution for troubled thrift institutions.... All in all, I think we hit the jackpot."[27] Reaganomics made all but certain the financial disaster of 2008.

Capitalists hit the jackpot with Reagan's labor policies when in 1981 Reagan declared war on organized labor by firing 11,400 air traffic controllers, decertifying the Professional Air Traffic Controllers Organization (PATCO), and replacing its members with scabs—labor was paralyzed. As a result, during 1980–1987, strike activities fell some 50 percent in selected unions, and the number of strikers that were replaced jumped 300 percent. Union membership declined nationally, with overall union participation in the private sector falling below 15 percent. In the face of this repression, the trade union movement became more submissive, reluctant to strike or fight back.[28]

Much of the credit for organizing during these lean years has to go to immigrant workers. The historical attitude of labor since the nineteenth century has been anti-immigrant. Even progressive unions such as the Western Federation of Miners in the early twentieth century sought to limit immigration and exclude Mexican laborers as retarded and not having a working-class consciousness. As late as the 1980s, labor federations such as the Los Angeles County Federation of Labor lobbied to crack down on undocumented labor. However, amnesty and the waves of immigrants changed this.

Beside the militancy of the immigrant workers, there emerged a new class of organizers, many of whom had been involved in student and popular activism of the 1960s. Some were white and African American, but a large core was comprised of the Chicano student movement leadership of the 1960s and 1970s. For example, the hotel and restaurant labor had a core of Chicano activists: For María Elena Durazo, whose parents were immigrants, her interest in the protection of the foreign born began when she was a student at St. Mary's College and member of CASA (Center for Autonomous Social Action). Durazo worked alongside Magdalena Mora, a dedicated UC Berkeley student from Mexico who died very young of cancer. After working for the International Ladies Garment Workers Union (ILGWU), Durazo was hired in 1983 by Local 11, the Hotel Employees and Restaurant Employees Union (HERE), as a worker representative. Four years later Durazo won the presidency of the local; however, the international put the local into receivership. In 1989, Durazo was reelected as president. Under her leadership, HERE took on business giants such as the Hyatt Hotel chain. The union returned to the basics of militant unionism, picketing and courting arrest to call attention to the plight of the workers. Local 11 played hardball, relentlessly pressuring politicos to support the union. As of 2013, Local 11 is still in the trenches, fighting for immigrant workers. Meanwhile, Durazo was elected Executive Secretary of the Los Angeles Federation of Labor, one of the most powerful positions in California Labor.[29]

Immigrant workers in the cleaning service sector, although one of the most vulnerable workforces, organized across the country. Like the hotel and restaurant workers, they fought not only for decent wages but medical coverage. Membership in Los Angeles Local 399, Justice for Janitors, plunged 77 percent in the 1980s, and by 1987, only 1,500 janitors remained under contract. With the assistance of white and Mexican college graduates, the workers began to organize. The movement also produced rank-and-file organizers such as Salvadoran Ana Navarette and Chicana Patricia Recino. Navarette was active in the Salvadoran liberation struggle; Recino, a product of the Chicano student movement, had been active in various social justice organizations since her teens.

Fearing permanent replacement of its desperately poor members, Local 399 formulated the strategy of going directly to the streets—making it financially dangerous for the subcontractors to get in the union's way. Among the targets were Century City and the International Service System, Inc. (ISS), the world's largest commercial cleaning contractor. On May 15, 1990, 150 armed LAPD officers attacked janitors and their supporters. The officers gave the order to picketers to disperse in English only. A police riot ensued, which resulted in 40 arrests and 16 injuries, with two women having miscarriages after being beaten. The Century City massacre was more vicious but less publicized than the Rodney King beating a year later. The janitors sued the LAPD, and in September 1993 they settled for $2.35 million.[30]

Confrontational tactics helped union organizers in recruiting low-paid minority workers and renewing the cycle of activism. The percentage of union janitors working in major Los Angeles commercial buildings rose from 10 percent in 1987, when Local 399 launched its campaign, to about 90 percent in the mid-1990s. However, tensions between the members and the union leadership began to surface. In June, a 21-member dissident slate called "Multiracial Alliance" won control of the union's executive board. Once in power, the dissident slate "cleaned the house." Regretfully, it fired many leaders who contributed to the success of the union. The new Latino officers (Salvadoran, Guatemalan, and Mexican) accused the former leadership of being paternalistic and racist. Charges and countercharges followed.

When the international headquarters of the janitors' union responded by placing the local union in receivership and naming Mike García of San Jose as the interim head, most of the so-called dissidents left the union, bitter because they won a fair election and were then dismissed. The old guard, in turn, rationalized that nationalism had produced the rupture. In reality, the labor movement was largely to blame for this and other ruptures, for its failure to employ adequate resources where the labor movement was expanding most—among immigrants and Latinos.[31]

In the 1970s, Los Angeles, once known as the Detroit of the West, employed 15,000 autoworkers producing a half million cars annually. Automakers then began to dismantle their California operations; the Ford Pinto factory in Pico Rivera geared down, as did the General Motors plant in South Gate. By 1982, Van Nuys workers saw the handwriting on the wall. They knew it was only a matter of time before GM would shut down that plant.

Led by the United Auto Local 645 president, Pete Beltrán, the workers and the community built a coalition that threatened a boycott if the GM plant was closed. Although the labor/community strategy bore fruit, the UAW international capitulated and sold workers on the notion that if they cooperated the plant would remain open. In the summer of 1991, General Motors announced the shutdown of the Van Nuys plant. Some GM workers, forced to sell their houses, moved to other states where GM employed them;

others collected severance pay for a year while the community inherited a worsening economic situation as more businesses closed down.

Despite the closing, the "Keep G.M. Van Nuys" campaign begot the Labor/Community Strategy Center, under the leadership of Eric Mann, who had spearheaded the campaign to keep the plant open.[32] The center has done outstanding environmental work. In 1992, the Strategy Center initiated a transportation policy group. Two years later, the group began organizing bus riders in the "Billions for Buses" campaign to confront the racism reflected in the policies of the Metropolitan Transportation Authority of Los Angeles (MTA). Membership in the Bus Riders Union has since grown to more than 3,000 dues-paying members and 50,000 self-identified members on the buses. Most of the riders are Latinos and women.[33]

In eastern Arizona, the cradle of the Chicana/o labor movement, in July 1983, 13 unions, led by the steelworkers' Local 616 at Clifton-Morenci, Arizona, struck the workers' old nemesis Phelps–Dodge.[34] Trouble broke out when Phelps–Dodge imported scabs to break the strike. The National Labor Relations Board (NLRB), under the Reagan administration, sided with management, and it conducted a poll in which it allowed only the scabs to vote; they voted to decertify the union. The mineworkers attempted to gain support from outside the area. A ladies' auxiliary led by activists such as Jessie Téllez toured the Southwest, talking to Chicano and labor groups. Despite insurmountable odds, the miners continued to strike, facing eviction and harassment. However, by 1987—still led by the union's president, Angel Rodríguez—the Morenci strike was all but dead. Only the diehards remained, learning from their mistakes and rebuilding their union. Barbara Kingsolver, in her book *Holding the Line: Women in the Great Arizona Mine Strike of 1983*, captures the feelings of women both inside and outside the mine who struggled for their space in the movement.[35]

In San Antonio, Texas, Levi Strauss, the world's largest apparel manufacturer, closed its plant in 1990, resulting in 1,100 layoffs. The plant, acquired in 1981, was the main domestic production facility for the Dockers line of casual pants, which required twice the labor as was needed for jeans. The company produced $70 million worth of Dockers and Officers Corp jeans. The San Antonio plant made record profits in 1989, and it was Levi's largest operation in Texas. To cut costs, Levi transferred the work previously done in San Antonio to independent contractors in the Caribbean and Costa Rica, where wages ranged from 30 cents to $1 an hour, compared with $6–$7 per hour in the United States. The company notified workers 90 days before closing the plant, 30 days more than is required by law. Levi laid off 10,400 workers between 1981 and 1990, and it shut down 26 plants nationwide from 1985 to 1993. The city of San Antonio lost 10,000 jobs in 1990 alone.

Virginia Castillo, a sewing machine operator at Levi Strauss, was still bitter four years after the San Antonio plant closed. The shutdown abruptly ended Castillo's employment of 16 years and began the unraveling of her life as a factory worker, wife, mother, and grandmother. Castillo, 52, was left unemployed. She had limited job and language skills. Her health deteriorated owing to nerve damage to her back and wrists caused by factory work. Her marriage failed. Yet her experiences made Castillo a labor activist. Like many others, she moved to San Francisco to take on Levi Strauss and to tell the world that, despite its socially conscious image and record of philanthropy, the company continues to exploit workers in the United States and abroad.

Castillo belonged to a movement called *Fuerza Unida* (United Strength), a 480-member group of former San Antonio Levi Strauss workers. *Hispanic* magazine voted Levi Strauss one of the hundred best companies in the United States for Hispanic workers, and *Vista* magazine placed it among the top 50 companies for Latina women. The fact remained, however, that Levi Strauss did not act in a socially responsible way toward the San Antonio workers. Most of the women lacked education. Paid on a piece rate, they worked extremely fast and hard. The shutdown caused vast unemployment. The women, hard hit, lost their homes and cars.[36]

Fuerza Unida said that Levi Strauss cheated the former employees of some severance pay, profit sharing, and other pay from pensions, vacation time, holiday overtime, and $500 Christmas bonus promised to each employee the December before the layoffs. In total, the company owed the workers about $4 million. Levi Strauss responded that it had properly compensated its former employees, and a federal lawsuit by Fuerza Unida was dismissed in 1993. Levi Strauss continued its restructuring throughout the decade. In November 1997, it shut down 11 plants in the United States, laying off another 6,395 workers—one-third of its U.S. manufacturing force. The bottom line, according to former Levi workers in San Antonio, was that the 1997 shutdowns alone saved Levi Strauss $200 million. Even before the 1997 shutdowns, Levi made profits, for example, of $357 million on nearly $5 billion in sales in 1991. Closing their plant was not an economic necessity, the former workers say, but a tactic to earn more profits. Meanwhile, under the leadership of Chicanas, *Fuerza Unida* continued its fight-back campaign.[37]

Although César Chávez symbolized the struggle of the Mexican American people for justice, many Americans by the mid-1980s wanted to forget about the sacrifice of farmworkers, and Chávez's personal contributions were eclipsed by those of Julio César Chávez, a boxing champion. It was symptomatic of the times. The two men symbolized different values and different legacies.[38]

A 1985 poll revealed that 53 percent of the general public still favored Chávez, and only 21 percent opposed him. Chávez's organizational problems, related to the length and intensity of the struggle, led to personality clashes and dissatisfaction with the United Farm Workers' (UFW) direction among a minority of the organizers. Compounding the UFW's woes, California Governor George Deukmejian, heavily indebted to agricultural capitalists, torpedoed the Agricultural Labor Relations Board (ALRB) by appointing David Stirling, a grower hatchetman, as general counsel to the board. Under Stirling only 10 percent of the cases reached the ALRB, compared with 35 percent under the appointees of Governor Edmund G. Brown, Jr. Deukmejian cut the ALRB's budget by one-third; by 1986 the board became inoperative when, because of the governor's appointees, it was totally under the growers' control. Government continued to conspire against the UFW.

Simultaneously, President Reagan appointed John R. Norton—head of J. R. Norton Company, one of the largest lettuce producers of the world—as the U.S. deputy secretary of agriculture. This template of Republican–grower complicity continued at the state and national levels through the administrations of California Governor Pete Wilson and President George H. W. Bush.

In 1985, 4,000 farmworkers walked out of the fields in the Imperial Valley. The growers hired armed guards and attack dogs that injured many strikers. A grower's car struck Isauro López and permanently crippled him. Thugs hired by growers shot Rufino Contreras through the head and killed him. Judge William Lehnhardt refused to disqualify himself from the case, even though his wife had worked as a strikebreaker. Lehnhardt ruled that the union was responsible for the violence and crop loss and did not prosecute growers' agents for murder. The union, on the other hand, raised $3.3 million to appeal this perversion of justice and wait for years to get its day in court. The UFW continued to struggle against all odds to organize workers.[39]

The Movement for Inclusion: The Politicos

An essential part of any struggle is political representation—it is a measure of not only the unity within a group but also the group's acceptance by others. Numbers usually determine the success of the out-groups; however, they do not tell the entire story. The majority culture makes the rules, and therefore the dice are loaded in their favor. In the case of Mexican Americans, gerrymandering and other political gimmickry diluted their voting strength. But there were also other factors such as immigrants not being eligible to vote and the relatively lower median age of Mexican Americans. Moreover, white people would not vote for Mexicans. So the Mexican American community took a long arduous path through the courts to get new rules.

One of the few areas where the Reagan administration helped Mexican Americans was in the enforcement of the 1965 Voting Rights Act. Reagan signed the 1982 amendment to the Voting Rights Act into law, and his justice department vigorously enforced the law. This was not an altruistic gesture though. While redistricting, Republicans often sided with Latinos in disputes between them and Democratic incumbents. Mexican Americans took full advantage of these tensions between Republicans and Democrats by using the 1965 Voting Rights Act, and its subsequent amendments by Republicans, as the basis of the Mexican American electoral revolution of the 1990s. Again, as in the case of labor leadership, throughout the country the Latino candidates for office emerged out of the activist core of the 1960s and 1970s.

The Southwest Voter Registration and Education Project (SVREP) and the MALDEF were major players in the movement. The former registered Chicanos to vote, and the latter used court challenges to give them a fighting chance. For example, MALDEF sued the city of Los Angeles for violations of the Voting Rights Acts in its redistricting plans; the result was the formation of two Latino-friendly council districts. SVREP increased Chicano registration from 488,000 in 1976 to over 1 million by 1985. The project published reports and analyses of Chicano voting potential and trends. Along with MALDEF and sympathetic lawyers, the SVREP challenged reapportionment and at-large voting practices that diluted electoral strength of Latinos. Meanwhile, amendments to the Voting Rights Act in 1975 and 1982 made it easier for the SVREP and MALDEF to persuade local municipalities to restructure their electoral units, *por las buenas o las malas* (literally, "the easy way or the hard way").[40]

In 1981, 19 Chicano candidates were elected to local offices in Salinas and the San Joaquín Valley. Latino population increased in 16 districts. The following year, Mario Obledo, former California secretary of health and welfare and cofounder of MALDEF, who had considerable credibility within the mainstream Mexican American community, decided to enter the Democratic Party primary for governor. Liberals criticized Obledo for running against Los Angeles Mayor Tom Bradley. The unsuccessful campaign, however, mobilized Mexican American activists throughout the state, stimulating aspirations about offices statewide. Unfortunately, the new awareness and the relative success of redistricting also started political infighting in East Los Angeles, as elected officials attempted to forge a political machine. An early defector was Gloria Molina, who ran successfully for the State Assembly in 1982.[41]

Assemblyman Art Torres caused some raised eyebrows by successfully challenging State Senator Alex García for his seat. Although criticized at the time, Assemblyman Richard Alatorre, as chair of the Assembly Elections and Reapportionment Committee, managed to add a new congressional seat. Another congressional seat was vacant as an incumbent had retired. Former White House aides Esteban Torres and Matthew Marty Martínez ran successfully for the open congressional seats in 1982.[42]

The prize that everyone wanted was the Los Angeles City Council seat held by Art Snyder for a decade and a half. His political base scared off most Latino challengers. However, in 1983 a relatively unknown urban planner, Steve Rodríguez, challenged Snyder and almost beat him. (The Los Angeles political establishment did not support Rodríguez because he had once been a member of *La Raza Unida* Party [RUP].) This close race raised expectations—especially as Larry González, 27, beat ultraconservative Richard Ferraro for an LA Unified Board seat. Consequently, in 1986, Richard Alatorre was elected to the Council, replacing Snyder, making him potentially the most powerful Chicano politico in California.[43]

Chicanos pressured the Justice Department to file a suit against the City of Los Angeles—*U.S. v. City of Los Angeles* (1985)—alleging that the city violated civil and voting rights guarantees of Latinos under the Fourteenth and Fifteenth Constitutional Amendments and the Voting Rights Acts of 1965, 1975, and 1982. The suit forced the Los Angeles City Council to submit a new plan to the court in 1986. A compromise was reached, and an additional Chicano district was formed, which opened the possibility of another future seat in the San Fernando Valley. Redistricting made it possible for Gloria Molina to be elected to the Council—a second Latino-held seat. Statewide, other patterns were emerging: The Latino population of the San Gabriel Valley, east of East Los Angeles, and of small cities along the San Bernardino Freeway, grew by almost 50 percent. This area was more middle class than the Los Angeles Eastside and was a base of funding support for Chicano politicos.[44]

In 1986, Texas led the nation in the number of Latino elected officials: 1,466, compared with 588 in New Mexico and 450 in California. Tejanos in the Lone Star State made up one-fifth of the voting-age population that year. Tejanos comprised 12.9 percent of the electorate in November 1988, but only 5.6 percent of the Texas city council members were Chicanos. In 1986, 50 percent of Texas first graders were Tejanos, but again only 6.6 percent of Texas school board members were of Mexican origin.

Henry Cisneros was the best known Chicana/o politico in the country in terms of offices held and his national visibility.[45] He rose to become a member of President Bill Clinton's cabinet, as Secretary of Housing and Urban Development. Mexican-dominated San Antonio elected Cisneros to the San Antonio City Council in 1975. He was a crossover candidate favored by the Euro-American elite and their Good Government League (GGL). That year, Mexicans comprised 51.8 percent of the city but only 37 percent of the registered voters; whites made up 39 percent of the population and almost 56 percent of the registered voters. The Cisneros victory inspired more Tejano political participation, and two years later Chicanas/os and African Americans took over the San Antonio City Council.

Mexicans received a big boost from the Justice Department in 1976 when the department halted San Antonio annexations of surrounding areas. Whites used annexation as a device to dilute the voting power of minorities. In Texas, municipalities annexed surrounding neighborhoods to include more whites, invariably absorbing white areas to neutralize the Mexican and black population increases. The rise of the Communities Organized for Public Service (COPS) also played a determining role in politicizing and registering Mexican voters.

In 1981, Henry Cisneros became the first Mexican American mayor of San Antonio since the 1840s. Born in San Antonio, Cisneros attended Central Catholic High and then graduated from Texas A&M. An urban planner, Cisneros received his doctorate from George Washington University and then returned in 1974 to San Antonio, where he solicited GGL sponsorship. Cisneros's father, a retired Army Reserve colonel, worked at Fort Sam Houston; his mother, Elvira Mungía Cisneros, came from an elite family who fled Mexico during the revolution. Cisneros's maternal grandfather, Henry Romulo Mungía, ran a print shop and had close ties with other exiled families, which included a surprising number of the present generation of San Antonio's Chicano leaders. Cisneros was ideologically more Republican than Democrat. He was one of the few politicos who did not have roots in the 1960s era. Cisneros emphasized economic growth, participation in the technological revolution, and the necessity of attracting high-tech business to San Antonio. Cisneros appealed to educated middle-class Mexican Americans, who were becoming a larger proportion of the community.

By the mid-1980s, Texas had 3 Tejanos who were members of Congress, 4 state senators, and 21 state representatives. In 1986, Texas also led in the number of Chicanas elected to public office. As for electoral politics, Texas had a higher percentage of native-born Mexican Americans than any state outside of New Mexico. In 1980, 83 percent of the Latino population of San Antonio was born in the United States, in contrast to 43 percent of the Latino population in Los Angeles. One hundred and fifty years of housing segregation resulted in residential bonding.[46]

The electoral strength of Tejanos stemmed from the activities and the leadership development of the Mexican American Youth Organization and the political successes of *La Raza Unida* Party that pressured the Democratic Party to open its doors wider. In addition, Texas developed a healthy organizational network; the League of United Latin American Citizens (LULAC), the American G.I. Forum, RUP, SVREP, MALDEF, and followers of Saul Alinsky—who founded the Industrial Areas Foundation (IAF) in Chicago and trained community organizers for organizations such as COPS—all originated in Texas. COPS is part of a network of IAF organizations, which have units throughout the Southwest. In the Latino community, the IAF organizations were heavily involved in Catholic Church networks. Ernesto Cortez, head of the IAF, was a major power, negotiating with state politicos to end the "legacy of neglect." Cortez organized in the barrios of the Rio Grande Valley, Houston, San Antonio, and El Paso.[47]

By the 1980s Chicago ranked second in the United States in terms of a Mexican-origin population. It had a unique history, and Chicago Chicanos functioned within a well-defined "patronage system." Its wards clearly defined the boundaries of the city's ethnic neighborhoods. By 1986, Chicago's Latino population was close to 540,000—19 percent of the city's total population; residents of Mexican origin comprised about 60 percent of the Latino group as a whole. In 1983, Harold Washington, an African American, was elected the mayor of Chicago, supported by Mexicans as well as Puerto Ricans, African Americans, and progressive whites. The Pilsen district remained the principal port of entry for Latinos, and housed the greatest concentration of Mexicans. The South Side barrios of Pilsen, Little Village, and South Chicago numbered more Mexicans than other Latinos. A Mexican minority also lived in the North Side, where they shared space with Puerto Ricans and other Latino groups. Although a large percentage of the Mexican population was foreign born, in the mid-1980s the Latino Institute found that 83 percent of the Latino youth were born in the United States.

In 1981, not a single Latino served on the Chicago City Council; that year, council members blatantly gerrymandered the districts, making the future election of a Latino almost impossible. The following year, MALDEF sued the Chicago City Council under the 1965 Voters Rights Act as amended in 1982. The remapping of the district, according to MALDEF, diluted Latino voting strength. Four years later, the court issued a judicial order that created four Latino wards—the 22nd, 25th, 26th, and 31st; the 22nd and 25th were predominantly Chicana/o. A special election took place in March, in which Jesús García and Juan Solíz were elected from the 22nd and 25th Wards, respectively. The creation of the Latino wards was crucial to the growing power of Chicanos and Latinos in Chicago.[48]

In 1982, Mexican Americans and organized labor turned out heavily to elect Toney Anaya governor of New Mexico. Anaya, the former state attorney general, received 85 percent of the manito vote. Anaya was an energetic governor who took strong and controversial stands opposing the death penalty. He declared New Mexico a sanctuary for Central American political refugees, and was pro–foreign born, condemning racist nativism. He was highly criticized for focusing on Latino issues. A bold step in his career was that he appointed manitos to key posts to protect their interests. For instance, Anaya appointed John Páez to the University of New Mexico's Board of Regents in 1983, giving Latinos a majority for the first time. The next year he appointed Jerry Apodaca and Robert Sánchez to the board of regents.

New Mexico was also the home to newcomer Representative Bill Richardson, who was elected to Congress two years after he arrived in 1980. He made friends with the New Mexican power brokers, who supported his rise. Richardson, under Clinton, was named U.S. ambassador to the United Nations and Energy Secretary in 1998. Richardson, a Democrat, was elected to the House of Representatives from New Mexico in 1982 and reelected seven times. Richardson's mother was Mexican, and his Euro-American father was born in Nicaragua, grew up in Boston, and worked for Citibank as an executive in Mexico. Richardson was raised in Mexico City, but moved to Massachusetts at age 13 to attend a Boston-area high school.

Latinos in New Mexico rivaled Mississippi for the highest percentage of children who lived below the poverty line. San Miguel County rivaled the Rio Grande Valley in claiming the worst poverty. How could this be? Nativists could not blame it on the immigrant, as they did in California. The tragedy was that the old *patrón* politics of the nineteenth century still victimized New Mexican politics. People there largely voted according to personal and family loyalties rather than for issues. Sadly, by the 1980s, outsiders—primarily elderly Euro-Americans—were migrating into the state, and the ability to make substantive changes was slipping away.[49]

Not as nationalistic as Texas, Colorado was divided into north and south, with the latter being more like New Mexico than were Denver and the north. Federico Peña, Denver's first Mexican American mayor, was an exile. Born in Laredo in 1947 and raised in Brownsville, Texas, Peña attended St. Joseph's Academy and received his law degree from the University of Texas in 1971. After law school, he moved to Denver, where he was first elected as state representative in 1978 and then as mayor in 1982—79,200 votes to 74,700. At this time, Mexicans made up only 18 percent of the city's population and 12 percent of its voters.

Peña was a young, upwardly mobile urban Latino who migrated to Denver from Texas and built a rapport with the young building developers, who supported economic development. No doubt Peña, a world apart from the Crusade for Justice Chicanos of the 1960s, was a welcome relief to the white establishment. Peña also enjoyed the support of unions and construction companies because he promoted the expansion of Denver's infrastructure, which to them meant contracts and jobs. Although Peña benefited from being Mexican American, attracting national press, locally he played down his ethnicity. Peña did not promote a Mexican agenda, stating, "I am not an Hispanic candidate. I just happen to be Hispanic." Still, Peña's success encouraged other Latinos nationwide. Peña went on to become secretary of transportation in the Clinton administration.[50]

The 1990s was a decade in which Mexican American and Latino candidates made significant electoral gains. The exuberance was expressed by Xavier Hermosillo, a Mexican American Republican from California who said, "We're taking it back, house by house, block by block. . . . We have a little saying here: 'If you're in California, speak Spanish.' . . . People ought to wake up and smell the refried beans: Not only are we the majority of the population, but we're not going anywhere."[51] Because of the growth in population of Mexican-origin people and the enlargement of the Central American population, there was a dramatic increase in the voting power of Latinos. And numbers count in politics. For instance, a presidential candidate needs 270 electoral votes to win an election. Eighty-three percent of Latinos were concentrated in eight states that alone accounted for 187 electoral votes: Arizona held 8 electoral votes; California, 54; Colorado, 8; Florida, 25; Illinois, 22; New Mexico, 5; New York, 33; and Texas, 32. Of these eight states, Latino population was the highest in three—California, Illinois, and Texas.

The growth in Latino population did not immediately translate into elected officials at the national level. There were no Latinos in the 100-member U.S. Senate in 1999, and only 18 Latinos of 435 voting members in the House of Representatives. Eleven of them were from Texas and California. African Americans, on the other hand, that was slightly larger in numbers had 39 seats. Nevertheless, Latino visibility was increasing. As already mentioned, in 1993, Transportation Secretary (later Energy Secretary) Federico Peña and Housing and Urban Development Secretary Henry Cisneros served on the Clinton cabinet. Clinton later appointed UN Ambassador Bill Richardson as Energy Secretary.[52]

The Glass Ceiling

Some scholars characterized Latinas as invisible in politics, which was often true—and often not—before the 1980s. For example, Olga Peña, wife of Bexar County Supervisor Albert Peña, Jr., in Texas, is generally credited with putting together her husband's political machine and getting him elected. By the 1980s large numbers of Mexican American women were attending universities or working outside the household. Their voices grew louder and more persistent in pursuing their interests. Chicanas were developing a profile quite distinct from that of their male counterparts: in Texas and California, for instance, Mexican American women were less likely than Mexican American men to identify with the Republican Party, a trend that was to continue through the end of the century. Studies in the 1990s showed that there was an 18-percentage-point gender gap in party identification among Latino voters: 69 percent of Latinas claimed Democratic Party affiliation compared with 51 percent of Latino men. In 1986, the number of Latino elected officials grew to 3,314, and the number of Latino women in office jumped to 592—a 20 percent increase in one year. Women accounted for 18 percent of all elected Latino officials.[53]

By 1980, 51 percent of Latinas were either unemployed or underemployed; Latinas earned 49¢ to every dollar made by white males, versus 58¢ for white women and 54¢ for black women. Half completed less than 8.8 years of education. Some 67 percent of households were headed by women with children under 18 and they lived below the poverty line. This statistical profile did not change much throughout the next two decades.

Just over 18 percent of Latinas, and 16 percent of Mexican-origin females, were professionals. More than 50 percent were white-collar workers. Between 1980 and 1990, the percentage of Latinas with BA degrees increased from 7.7 to 10. However, not all the statistics were rosy; only a fraction of 1 percent of all PhDs at the University of California were awarded to Latinas in the late 1970s, and universities nationwide awarded Latinas barely 0.4 percent of the doctorates. The achievements were small, but they represented an important avenue for the change of traditional female roles. The growth of this sector produced a market, and by the mid-1980s, even Chicana Republicans claimed space in the "Hispanic women's movement."[54]

Conscious of the disparities, Chicanas challenged inequalities. In 1982, Gloria Molina ran successfully against Richard Polanco in the Democratic primary race for the California Assembly. Chicano politicos tried to dissuade her from contesting, warning that a woman could not win in East Los Angeles, that she was not tough enough to negotiate with the heavyweights, and that she could not raise sufficient funds without their support. Molina was a field representative to Assemblyman Art Torres and had participated in the founding of the national *Comisión Femenil* (Feminist Commission).

The issue that catapulted Molina into local prominence was her opposition to building a prison in downtown Los Angeles. This issue pitted Molina against recently elected Assemblyman Richard Polanco, who had promised that he would vote against the prison but changed his vote. Molina's leadership in the struggle against the prison attracted a constituency of grass-roots activists. Among them were the Mothers of East Los Angeles, a lay Catholic group from Resurrection Parish headed by Father John Moretta, and St. Isabel Parish, whose women members were led by Juana Gutiérrez. During the summers of 1986 and 1987, these groups attracted 1,500–3,000 protesters at their weekly marches.[55]

The coalition fought Governor George Deukmejian for six years, enlisting the support of Archbishop Roger Mahoney for the "Stop the Prison in East Los Angeles" effort. The prison issue provided a springboard for Molina, who in the fall of 1986 announced her candidacy for the newly created First Council District. Molina registered a landslide victory in the contested race in February 1987. In February 1991, Molina was elected to the Los Angeles County Board of Supervisors. At 48, Molina represented 1.9 million people and became one of the five people overseeing a $13 billion budget. Molina developed her own network, surrounding herself with women such as Antonia Hernández, the chief council of MALDEF; Mónica Lozano, publisher of *La Opinión*, perhaps the largest Spanish-language newspaper in the country; and Vilma Martínez, a prominent attorney and former chief counsel of MALDEF.

Texas differed from California and other states. For example, as mentioned, the RUP had a much greater impact on Chicanos in Texas than in California, and Tejanas were more quickly integrated into mainstream politics. The 1970s saw the rise of grass-roots political activists such as San Antonian Rosie

Castro, who in 1971 was one of the first candidates for city council when she ran on a slate with Gloria Cabrerra and two Tejano males. Castro was very active in demanding equality and forging political space for Chicanas in the process. Another activist was María Antonietta Berriozábal, who successfully ran for the San Antonio City Council in 1981—supported by a network of grass-roots Chicanas. This victory led to the election of Yolanda Vera to the council in 1985. Berriozábal's procommunity stances put her at odds with the rest of the council, which tended to favor business interests. In 1991, Berriozábal ran for mayor and came close to becoming the first Chicana mayor of a major city.[56]

In San Antonio Chicanas enjoyed a measure of success in politics; but even there, the success was limited. Outside San Antonio, the problem of exclusion was even more marked. For example, in Texas the most powerful elected position within local government is the county judge. In 1998, Texas had 254 county judges, of whom 23 were white women and 7 were Chicano. Only one, Norma Villarreal of Zapata County, was a Tejana. An obvious impediment was that the election for county judge ran countywide, not only making the race expensive but also diluting the Mexican American voting numbers.

In 1986 in Crystal City, Texas, Severita Lara ran against an incumbent for county judge. On the first count, she won by one vote. On a recount, she lost by two votes. Although there was foul play, Lara did not have the funds to challenge the verdict of the electoral panel, which the incumbent heavily influenced. Lara ended up $7,000 in debt, an amount she had to pay from her pocket. Unlike Molina, she did not have access to funding from feminist groups. Lara was later elected to Crystal City Council and then served as mayor.[57]

Alicia Chacón from El Paso and Enriqueta Díaz from Eagle Pass won races for county judge in the early 1990s; however, both were defeated in reelection. One impediment was that they never became part of the old-boys' network and did not conduct politics in the usual way, which was to go down to the local bar for informal sessions. Chacón was later elected to the City Council.[58]

Norma Villarreal Ramírez made a successful bid for county judge of Zapata County in 1994. Armed with a $20,000 loan from her father, she challenged the county's count in an election, which she lost by 40 votes. The courts found fraud and ordered a recount, which Villarreal won by several hundred votes. However, once she took office, few people came forward to help Villarreal. "The collegial arrangements between male members from the same political affiliation and/or ethnic group do not extend to women either. The men simply do not want the women in charge."[59]

By the 1980s there was a critical mass of Chicanas in politics. Fewer belonged to the generation that was active in *La Raza Unida* or the 1960s and more to the generation that benefited from those earlier struggles. They cut their teeth in more traditional political routes working in campaigns of others before running themselves. Many, such as Elvira Reyna, learned their politics under the tutelage of white politicos. (Reyna later became a state representative.) What they shared with the previous generation was life experiences which in Texas were formed more by the Confederate culture of the state. The socialization of this generation was different: racism was different—you could choose where you would live and what you would join. Elvira was raised in Dallas, picked cotton, but became a Republican. She was married with two kids before she went to college. She began working part time for law-and-order State Representative Bill Blackwood and became a Republican. Elvira first ran for office in 1993. This experience was much different from that of a Rosie Castro or Severita Lara, who formed their worldviews through activism.[60]

Immigrant Women Workers

Due to a lack of education and the absence of skill development programs for immigrant women, the odds of their achieving success were low. Clearly, deindustrialization affected Latinas, as did their defined class roles. Female immigrants provided a large, motivated, inexpensive, and specialized workforce for service and manufacturing sectors, which supported the expanding export-oriented economy of places like Los Angeles, San Antonio, and Chicago. In 1980, only 8 percent of recently arrived European females worked in blue-collar occupations, compared with 62 percent of Mexican female immigrants. Seventy-five percent of the Mexican female immigrants worked in part-time occupations that paid extremely poor wages. They had little education and a limited ability to speak English, and their situation did not improve over time.[61]

Chicanas and Mexican immigrant women had different characteristics. For instance, in 1980 the mean years of schooling among Chicanas was 11.3, compared with 8.3 years among established immigrant women and 6.8 for recently arrived immigrants. Some 36.3 percent of Chicanas did not have a high school diploma, compared with 64.5 percent of established immigrants and 83.8 percent of recently arrived Mexican female immigrants. Of the Chicanas, 4.8 percent held college degrees, compared with 2 percent of the established immigrant women and 1.7 percent of the recently arrived. The only advantage of age was that the older female workers were more likely to organize. Younger workers were generally more passive and naïve, probably not yet realizing they would be subject to the glass ceiling.

Not all immigrant Latina workers were Mexican. In the 1980s, an estimated 500,000 men and women migrated from El Salvador alone. In 1985, 32.4 percent of the Salvadoran population in the United States was under 10 years of age and 57.3 percent was under the age of 20. More than 89 percent of Salvadoran refugees and 95 percent of the immigrants (those arriving before 1980) lived in family-based households. Labor force participation among Salvadoran males was 74 percent for refugees in 1988. For Salvadoran females, it was 66.7 percent, which was higher than the 52 percent for other Latinas. Salvadoran female refugees had the highest unemployment at 16.7 percent. Median age was 27.7 for females and 25.6 for males. In addition to economic deprivation, these refugees suffered from the experiences of civil war, oppression, and trauma.

Latinas of all nationalities engaged in self-help. Libertad Rivera, 28, from Tepic, Nayarit, in Mexico, worked for the Coalition for Humane Immigration Rights of Los Angeles (CHIRLA), educating and uniting domestic servants. Women also worked in AIDS programs. In the United States, 18 percent of all teenagers infected with HIV are Latinos. In Los Angeles, 38 percent of the babies and children infected with AIDS are Latino—more than double the Latino share of adult AIDS cases. At least 40 percent of Latinas with AIDS contracted it through their husbands or boyfriends. Fear of deportation kept many undocumented Latinas away from healthcare systems and other support services.[62]

¿Gobernar Es Poblar?

The 1990 Census showed that 25 percent of California's 29,760,021 inhabitants (an undercount) were Latinos, an increase from 4,544,331 (19.1 percent) in 1980 to 7,687,938 (25.8 percent) 10 years later. This population was heavily concentrated in 10 assembly districts, yet Latinos represented only four of the districts. (The California Assembly had 80 seats.) At stake in any redistricting were seats in both houses of the state legislature and in Congress. The basic problem was that Chicana/os and Latinos did not always vote, for various reasons: many were not citizens, a substantial number were under 18, and 18- to 35-year-olds, which made up a large proportion of the Latino population, overall had lower registration and turnout rates. In 1990, only 844,000 Latinos voted out of a population of 4,739,000 Latinos who were 18 or older. Some 2,301,000 adults were citizens, 1,218,000 of whom were registered to vote. Another problem was incumbency: white politicos stayed in office for years, and it took substantial efforts to win their seats. As always, Democrats in the California legislature protected their own. Meanwhile, Governor Pete Wilson vetoed three proposed redistricting bills, giving the excuse that the Democratic majority was seeking an "unfair partisan advantage."

Because the legislature and the governor could not agree on a plan, the chief justice of the California Supreme Court appointed a panel of three jurists. They remapped districts for the state legislature and Congress. The maps devised by the court made it possible for Latinos to increase their representation by 40 percent in the state legislature. The 1992 elections made room for gains in the Assembly, where seven Latinos won election. Latinos did not do as well in Congress and gained only one additional seat. The Chicano community believed that with proper redistricting it could have gained another congressional seat. Even so, the first Chicana elected to Congress was Lucille Roybal-Allard, the daughter of retiring Congressman Edward R. Roybal. Nationwide, the 1992 election marked the entry of 17 Latinos to Congress. An estimated 1 million Latinos voted in California alone. And, in the spring of 1993, Latinos won some 60 city council elections in Los Angeles County alone.[63]

Up to this point, population growth and the Voting Rights Act of 1965 and its amendments drove Chicano political victories. In Texas, population clusters made it almost impossible to prevent Mexican

Americans getting elected. However, California in 1990 was a closed shop with incumbents monopolizing the election process. In 1990, by a margin of 52 percent to 48 percent, California voters passed Proposition 140, which put term limits on most state offices. Pushed by Republicans in the days when the Democrats held sway over the California legislature, the proposition reflected the mood of Californians, who trusted neither themselves nor politicos to govern. In their usual self-righteous way, California voters thought that by passing an initiative they would empower themselves merely by forcing incumbents out of office.

Term limits opened the door for more Latinos to become involved in politics. The proposition resulted in the election of Cruz Bustamante as the first Chicano speaker of the California Assembly, and term limits forced him to seek higher office. He was elected California Lieutenant Governor in 1998—a first in the twentieth century. His successor as speaker was Antonio Villaraigosa, and the so-called Latino Caucus, for the first time in history, was a "power broker" in the true sense of the word.[64]

During the 1990s, the population of Texas grew by 23 percent, while that of the nation grew by 13 percent. The number of Latinos increased from 4.3 million in 1990 to almost 6.7 million in 2000, a 53 percent rise—one of every three Texans identified as a Latino/a. The white population grew by only 6 percent. Latinos became the largest ethnic group in Houston, Dallas, San Antonio, and El Paso. Seven Tejanos sat in the state legislature in 1960, 6 in 1965, 15 in 1974, 19 in 1983, and 25 in 1992. Elected women officials among Mexican Americans ran ahead of women officials from other groups. The first Chicana elected to the Texas state legislature was Irma Rangel from Kingsville in 1976, and the first elected to the state senate was Judith Zaffirini from Laredo in 1984. Other changes took place, such as most *La Raza Unida* activists joining Mexican American Democrats (MAD). "[By] 1990 more than 1,000 Mexican Americans (not all MAD members) attended the state convention."[65]

The number of Tejano elected officials increased to 2,030 in 1993, more than in any other state. It is estimated that Texas had 40 percent of all Latino elected officials in the country. Latinos, mostly Mexican Americans, made up a quarter of the state's 17 million residents. Some 2,684,000 Latinos were eligible to vote in Texas; 40 percent (1,073,600) were registered. In 1994 the Texas congressional delegation included five Mexican Americans, all members of the House. However, the question remained: Did numbers automatically translate into political power?

Most pundits assume that Mexican American support for the Democratic Party was a matter of fact. However, as José Angel Gutiérrez pointed out during the 1994 national congressional elections, Latino support for the Democratic Party dropped from 72 percent in 1992 to 61 percent in 1994. There was a spillover to state legislative races; of 140 Latino incumbents in nine states, four lost their seats. Nevertheless, as a group, they were effective and brought about reforms. For example, during George W. Bush's terms as governor, the legislative Latino caucus successfully lobbied him for increased funding for education and bilingual programs.[66]

Outside California and Texas, it was more difficult to get Latinos elected to office. For instance, in Iowa the population of Latinos grew 153 percent during the 1990s. They aspired to be represented in the famed Iowa Caucus, since that would have been an indicator of the power of the Latino vote. The numbers were not large enough, however, for representation. Latinos—especially Mexican Americans—were young, with almost 40 percent of the nation's Latinos not yet voting age. Another factor was that many Latinos were not yet citizens.

How important are numbers then? University of Maryland political science professor James G. Gimpel has shown that as of 2004, 70.2 percent of U.S. House campaign contributions came from outside the candidates' districts. So it is no wonder that as much as 90 percent of campaign contributions in Los Angeles City Council is estimated to come from outside the councilmatic districts.[67]

The North American Free Trade Agreement

The North American Free Trade Agreement (NAFTA) was proposed formally in 1991. The Bush administration pressured Congress to put the negotiations for free trade with Mexico on the "fast track"—implying that congressional debate and criticism of the treaty would be minimal. Mexican President Carlos Salinas de Gortari hailed the treaty as the key to Mexico's future. Advocates for NAFTA dismissed questions about its effects on the environment, human rights, political reform,

Mexican workers, and the indigenous populations. The most controversial provision was a change in Article 27 of the Mexican Constitution, the basis for the nation's *ejidos* (communal lands): NAFTA made it possible for *ejido* members to sell or mortgage their land—thus burying the outcome of the Mexican Revolution. As one Mexican scholar put it, "the death of the Mexican Revolution at least deserved a formal farewell."

The debate over NAFTA split the Latino community into ideological camps. Union activists, environmentalists, and human rights groups campaigned against NAFTA. They argued that NAFTA would take U.S. jobs away, threaten environmental laws, and hurt Mexican farmers and workers by privatizing the Mexican economy. Their campaigns, for the most part, were ineffective and often bordered on racism. U.S. labor in general was mainly concerned about job loss and depressed wages. Meanwhile, Bill Clinton became president and brought the hedging Latino organizations into line through aggressive use of patronage. On November 18, 1993, the U.S. House passed NAFTA by 234–200 votes, 16 more than the needed 218; 102 Democrats voted for and 156 voted against it.[68] As expected, the Senate voted for the accord. The Latino vote in the House of Representatives (which was essentially Chicano) included two Chicanos against it— Henry B. González and Marty Martínez.

On January 1, 1994, the day the NAFTA went into effect, the *Ejercito Zapatista de Liberación Nacional* (EZLN; Zapatista National Liberation Army) rebelled in the southern Mexican state of Chiapas, citing the passage of NAFTA and the changes in Article 27 of the Constitution. Their rebellion was logical since NAFTA would encourage the influx of cheap corn into Mexico, underselling the small farmer. The indigenous peoples argued that the privatization of land would lead to the death of their culture.[69]

The Zapatistas raised the "Land and Liberty" banner of Emiliano Zapata. The impact of liberation theology is suggested by the support of Monsignor Samuel Ruiz García.[70] In 1974, Ruiz convened an Indigenous Congress in an attempt to improve conditions for Mexico's indigenous population. The catechisms raised the consciousness of the indigenous communities and encouraged them to organize and to fight for their rights. In 1989, Ruiz García founded the Fray Bartolomé Human Rights Center, which investigates human rights cases and conflicts over land and religion. He saw the NAFTA agreement as the final straw in the systematic destruction of indigenous communities. For his work, Ruiz was labeled a subversive. He became the target of assassination attempts, and his sister also was attacked and wounded.

December 22, 1997, witnessed an event that horrified the world—the Acteal massacre—enacted with the concurrence of government officials. Masked gunmen from a paramilitary group murdered 45 unarmed Tzotzil Indians seeking refuge in a camp on the road to the village of Acteal, some 20 miles north of San Cristobal. Children, women, and old people were massacred while praying and fasting for peace in the chapel of Acteal. The Mexican government charged that the murdered villagers belonged to the Abejas, many of whom were sympathetic to the Zapatistas.

The Zapatista identity was based on the preservation of their communal culture. Being an agrarian, grass-roots peasant movement, they believed that the neo-liberal policies of the Mexican government would destroy their way of life. Hence, they engaged in "low-intensity warfare" to preserve it. They pursued, as much as possible, a nonviolent struggle. They took inspiration as well as their name from Emiliano Zapata, who said, "It is better to die on your feet than to live on your knees!" The Mexican government was duplicitous in its negotiations with the Zapatistas. A stalemate resulted, which still continues, but the Mexican government so far has not mobilized the army to totally crush the movement for fear of worldwide rebuke.

Meanwhile, a demoralization and skepticism spread among Mexicans. They realized that contemporary Mexico was in the hands of extremely wealthy narco-traffickers, or drug lords. Social scientist James Cockcroft likened "the 'narcotics rush' of the late twentieth century . . . [to the] gold rush of the sixteenth century in Mexico." Shortly before President Carlos Salinas de Gortari left office, drug scandals broke out involving his family and his brother Raul was implicated. It was uncovered that Raul Salinas had placed more than $120 million in foreign banks.[71] However, just as NAFTA is in the hands of Euro-American capitalists, which most people in Mexico are aware of, so is control of the drug trade, which depends on a U.S. market and U.S. bankers to launder the money.

"Don't Mourn, Organize!"

In 1993, César Chávez died in his sleep while on union business in Arizona. More than 40,000 mourners attended Chávez's funeral in Delano, California. Chávez followed a Franciscan regimen: he exercised regularly; he ate healthy, vegetarian, pesticide-free food; and he often fasted. However, he died of exhaustion, having pushed his body to its limits. César told his son-in-law the night before his death, "I'm tired . . . I'm really very tired."[72] Chávez's son-in-law, Arturo Rodríguez, assumed the UFW presidency. The union immediately stepped up activity in the fields, launching a major campaign to organize farmworkers in California; the struggle was often bitter. The UFW still relied heavily on its vast network of boycott volunteers. The workers, most of them poor Latinos, earned an average of only $8,500 a season for up to 12-hour days with no overtime or benefits. Growers continually sprayed fields with a cancer-causing pesticide. The first target was California's strawberry industry, producing 80 percent of all berries eaten in the United States and grossing more than $550 million. More than 10,000 workers were concentrated in the Watsonville–Salinas area alone.[73]

The Political Refugees from Central America

The Salvadoran and Guatemalan communities in the United States formed political refugee organizations and integrated themselves into the Protestant and Catholic refugee relief network. North American groups such as the Committee in Solidarity with the People of El Salvador (CISPES) worked full time to counter Reagan's propaganda. Angela Sanbrano, a Chicano originally from the El Paso area, worked as the national director of CISPES. Another Chicano who worked with refugees was Father Luis Olivares, originally from San Antonio, Texas. An adamant critic of U.S. involvement in El Salvador, in 1985 Olivares declared his Placita church in Los Angeles (Our Lady Queen of the Angels) a sanctuary to Central American refugees. Father Olivares died in March 1994 of AIDS. He contracted the disease when he was injected with an unsterilized needle on a visit to Central American refugee camps.[74]

Meanwhile, successive presidential administrations and Congress gave ultraright refugees preferential treatment in immigrating to the United States. Congress passed the 1997 Nicaraguan Adjustment and Central American Relief Act (NACARA) to protect Nicaraguans and Cubans from deportation if they could prove they had fled communism. By contrast, U.S. government policy excluded thousands of Salvadorans and Guatemalans entering the United States without documents. These refugees routinely applied for political asylum and were just as routinely denied. Eventually, Salvadorans and Guatemalans, through Temporary Protected Status (TPS), won the right to go before an immigration judge to prove, on a case-by-case basis, that returning to their countries would cause them to suffer "extreme hardship." Under new rules, the U.S. government presumed that returning refugees to their countries of origin would in itself pose an extreme hardship for them. An Immigration and Naturalization Service (INS) official would hear the cases rather than a judge.

Forging Communities

Central Americans founded organizations such as the Central American Resource Center (CARECEN), *El Rescate* (the Rescue), the Oscar Romero Health Clinic, and the Coalition for Humane Immigrant Rights of Los Angeles (CHIRLA), among others. Many Central Americans were involved in street vending, day labor, and domestic work, and were prime candidates for exploitation by some employers. CHIRLA instructed the workers about the laws that govern all employers, including individual homeowners who routinely hired them for odd jobs.

Apart from a cluster in Los Angeles, Central Americans were spread out in the United States. The Salvadorans were among the most organized groups, and in the early 1980s the FMLN sent organizers without documents to Washington, D.C., to lobby Congress and organize information centers. After the end of hostilities in 1991, most of them stayed and lobbied for domestic programs. In that year, riots broke out in the Mt. Pleasant neighborhood of Washington, D.C., a *barrio* made up mostly of Salvadorans and

Dominicans. A confrontation between residents and the police ensued when police shot a migrant in a *barrio* street. Several days of rebellion followed, which led to confrontations between Latinos and African Americans. (This happened a year before the South Central Los Angeles Uprisings.) Meanwhile, Central American women played a key role. In the Langley Park area of Washington, D.C., Salvadoran women pushed grocery carts loaded with home cooking, selling to immigrant laborers who live in the area. Langley Park's "pupusa ladies" fed their tired, hungry neighbors for a dollar a dish. Most of the women were unwilling to put a sign on their chest begging for work. Many of them came to the United States during and after the war, leaving children behind with grandparents and other relatives, and were sending money back to give them a better life. Guilt about being separated from their children and fear that they might never see them again consumed many mothers.[75]

Believers: Chicana/o Studies

By 1990, the Mexican American student population on university and college campuses had grown dramatically. This was a new generation that did not come of age in the 1960s and did not necessarily call themselves Chicanas/os. They were children of immigrants entering the country during and after the 1960s, who did not know about the sacrifices it took to get them on campus. Others did, but escalating costs of education forced them to drop out of political activities. Along with the Mexican-origin core, there were growing numbers of Central Americans who might call themselves Hispanic in public but sought their own national identification. The generational change and the other factors mentioned above brought about a reduction in the number of activists on campus, and MEChA as an organization shrank as more Latinos joined sororities and fraternities—some in established organizations and others in Latina/o-specific Greek organizations.

Those calling themselves Chicanas or Chicanos were passionate about seeking an identity and getting more Latina/o faculty hired. On many campuses student groups such as CAUSA (Central American United Student Association) were formed, and a few campuses such as California State University Northridge began to call for a Central American Studies Department.[76] Among Mexican American students, a core sought to expand their programs and recapture the mission of Chicana/o Studies, which was to serve the community.[77]

Within this activity a perfect storm was occurring that would affect the history of Latinas/os. The number of students brought here by their undocumented parents had grown dramatically since 1970. Until the 1990s, California colleges and universities allowed undocumented immigrant students to attend as if they were citizens if they could show residence for a year and a day when they applied and declare that they intended to make California their residence. This resulted from a successful 1985 lawsuit known as *Leticia A. v. Board of Regents* brought against the University of California and the California State University Systems for the right of undocumented students to attend as residents.

The backlash began almost immediately; a UCLA employee named David Paul Bradford sued the University of California, alleging that he was coerced to quit because he would not implement the *Leticia A.* ruling. By 1991 the courts found in favor of Bradford; many *Leticia A.* supporters justifiably claimed that the UC system folded under this intense right-wing pressure. The University of California said that after June of 1991 it would classify undocumented students as nonresidents. In 1992, the California Student Aid Commission followed Bradford and stopped awarding Cal Grants to undocumented students. Then the California Community Colleges (CCCs) adopted the UC policy although they were not mentioned in the Bradford ruling. The CSU appealed the decision but lost and in 1995 began implementing it. Many *Leticia A.* supporters believed that all was lost with the passage of California Proposition 187 in 1994. However, a nucleus was growing daily that did not give up hope or abandon their dreams.[78]

Meanwhile, one of the most dramatic events in Chicana/o Studies history was the UCLA Hunger Strike of 1993, which led to the foundation of the Chicana/o Studies Department (the César Chávez Center) at the University of California Los Angeles (UCLA). The hunger strike in May 1993 was led by Marcos Aguilar and Minnie Fergusson who worked about four years to get a Chicano Studies Department. It was an impossible journey in which they braved opposition to the department by Chancellor Charles Young, associate vice-chancellor Raymundo Paredes, and the institution itself. With the exception of Juan

Gómez-Quiñonez and later Leo Estrada, most of the Chicano faculty was divided and did not support the push for a department. In the years preceding the hunger strike, Minnie and Marcos gathered community support, studied curriculum, and held conferences on campus—helping to organize the United Community and Labor Alliance, which was also involved in the campaign to preserve Olvera Street as Mexican cultural space.[79] Marcos was so adamant about a department that after four years he was expelled from MEChA; its members were increasingly concerned that the issue was polarizing faculty members and students, and consequently reducing its membership and influence.

After three years of controversy, Chancellor Young announced on April 28, 1993, that *Chicano* studies "will not be elevated to an independent department at the Westwood campus."[80] For Marcos and Minnie it became a now-or-never moment. Young announced his decision on the eve of the funeral of César Chávez—a slap in the face of the Chicano community.

Without internal support, Marcos and Minnie went on the offensive and formed Conscious Students of Color, a multiracial group of students, most of whom had never been active in campus politics. A rally began at noon on May 11, which attracted about 200 participants. According to the *Los Angeles Times*, "When they were denied entrance to the faculty center, some of the demonstrators broke windows with hammers, chairs and backpacks and about 80 began a sit-in inside." UC campus police, assisted by 200 LAPD officers, arrested 89 students on felony charges. On the second day a rally drew a crowd of 1,000 people to the front of Royce Hall, and, seeing their friends arrested, some Mechistas returned to the fold. Because the quarter end was fast approaching, most observers speculated that the drive to get a department was kaput and that Marcos and Minnie would be scapegoated.[81]

Pushed to the edge by an intransigent administration, on May 25, Marcos, Minnie, sisters Cindy and Norma Montañez, Balvina Collazo, and María Lara—along with Jorge Mancillas, an assistant professor of medical biology, and two other students—started a hunger strike that lasted 14 days.[82] The strike attracted the citywide support of hundreds of thousands of Chicano and Latino students in surrounding high schools and universities, who sporadically walked out of school. Tensions mounted as a 20-mile march from Olvera Street to UCLA in support of the hunger strikers began on the 12th day to pressure UCLA administration to meet with the hunger strikers. The march stimulated community support, and a thousand supporters marched into UCLA. The strike was settled two days later, and UCLA got the César Chávez Center for Interdisciplinary Instruction in Chicano/Chicana Studies. It functioned as a department but was not given full departmental status—Chancellor Young and Paredes were vengeful to the last. When their journey toward a Chicano Studies Department began four years earlier, someone told Marcos and Minnie that it was doable, but that it would take at least five years. They did it before that deadline.[83]

The success of the UCLA strike motivated student hunger strikes at the University of California at Santa Barbara, Columbia, and Princeton, the Claremont Colleges, the University of Texas at Austin, the University of California at Berkeley, and other schools. However, much of the momentum generated by the UCLA Hunger Strike was diverted by the crises in the Chicano community as community activists, labor leaders, politicos, and students turned their attention to combating the siege on the foreign born. The question of immigration eclipsed all other issues.[84] There was the emergence of racists such as California Governor Pete Wilson and media features such as Glenn Spencer's *American Patrol* website, CNN's *Lou Dobbs*, and Fox's *O'Reilly Factor,* which took every opportunity to label MEChA a terrorist organization. By the turn of the century, this rabid right-wing reaction rivaled the McCarthy witch hunts of the 1950s. These hate groups' anti-immigrant, anti–affirmative action, and pro-racist policies took their toll on Chicano student activists, and their numbers temporarily receded.

The Renaissance in Chicana/Chicano Thought and Arts

The impact of Chicana/o Studies goes beyond the formation or lack of formation of Chicana/o Studies programs or even their influence on the campuses. A large number of the murals, paintings, literature, and music in the communities owe their geneses to Chicana/o Studies. For example, El Centro De La Raza in Seattle, the murals on the walls of Chicano park in San Diego, the National Mexican Art Museum in Chicago's Pilsen District, mariachi and Mexican Folk dance groups throughout the country, and many theatre groups have been nourished by Chicana/o Studies. It is the largest market for Chicana/o literature of all forms. Indeed, the main mission of the disparate study programs has been to organize and produce a Mexican American corpus of knowledge. Moreover, these programs have been a source of support for progressive causes such as the Zapatistas. Chicana/o Studies went beyond the walls of academe.[85]

The content of Chicana/o Studies has changed over the years. In the late 1960s and 1970s, the symbol of the farmworker's eagle and the face of César were ubiquitous. Although initially it was an almost all-male club, since the 1990s the main scholarly current has been that of Chicanas. In 1991, a cursory survey of Proquest's 72 dissertations and a smattering of theses in Chicana/o Studies shows that 49 were written by women. In 2008, out of 94 dissertations/MA theses, 70 were written by women; they are also an indicator as to who will be teaching in those programs. Dissertations are important in synthesizing the existing fund of knowledge. Besides the implications of the hegemony of Chicanas in the area of Chicana/o Studies, much of the ideological energy came from Chicanas who raised questions and pushed the parameters.

Historian Emma Pérez, who authored *The Decolonial Imaginary: Writing Chicanas into History*, intertwines modernist and postmodernist theory. Perez analyzes the self-colonization and institutionalization which Chicanas internalize (something that also applies to males). A Chicana lesbian, Pérez writes in a restless style that is reminiscent of African American writers such as Langston Hughes.[86] Noteworthy are the essays, poetry, and playwriting of Cherríe Moraga. She teaches Creative Writing, Chicano/Latino literature, Xicana-Indigenous Performance, Indigenous Identity in Diaspora in the Arts, and Playwriting at Stanford and other universities. She was a founding member of La Red Xicana Indígena, "a network of Xicanas organizing in the area of social change through international exchange, indigenous political education, spiritual practice, and grass roots organizing." Moraga's use of symbols enriches her writing with brilliant colors not frequently found in Euro-American society.[87] It would be easy to draw a shopping list of cutting-edge Chicana scholars, among them Yolanda Broyles-González of the University of Arizona and historian Antonia Castañeda. But this would only take time away from the Great Gloria Anzaldúa.[88]

Gloria Anzaldúa (1942–2004) was a product of the border; she blended this reality with history. A postmodernist, a feminist, and a lesbian, she enjoyed more influence on these fields than any other Chicana/o writer of her time. She was a major force in Chicana cultural theory and queer theory. Anzaldúa was part of those communities, collaborating with writers such as Moraga. Her *New Mestiza* calls for an awareness of conflicting and meshing identities; her point of conflict is the border. Many feminists have interpreted her "new mestiza" as a way of understanding postcolonial feminism. Anzaldúa talked about consciousness and boldly trespasses into space thought to be reserved for indigenists. Anzaldúa was spiritual in a field that was once dominated by materialists, thus resolving the past with the present. She is one of the few Chicana/o scholars to have universal appeal. In a sense she is one of the few Chicanas/os with appeal outside the Latino sphere. Chicano artist Harry Gamboa has said that some artists are weak painters with great messages, and some are great painters with weak messages; Anzaldúa practiced great artistry that expressed great messages.[89]

Hate Is Tax Deductible

Racist nativist anti-immigration groups have spent millions of dollars in framing the immigrant debate—talking incessantly and irresponsibly about the "illegal alien" threat. These organizations received unlimited funds through conservative think tanks that in turn were financed by reactionaries such as Richard Mellon Scaife, Cordelia Scaife May, Charles and David Koch, and Joseph Coors among other billionaires.[90] In a manner, taxpayers pay for the hate campaigns, since the donations to the think tanks are tax deductible. They financed the English Only political campaigns; Scaife May donated $650,000 to U.S. English. She used the severe recession of the early 1990s to fan an anti-immigrant hysteria—encouraging opportunistic politicos and racist nativists to play on the fears of "Americans." As mentioned, supporters contributed hundreds of millions of dollars to these hate groups, which subsidized the research of right-wing scholars. For example, the Heritage Foundation helped fund *The Bell Curve: Intelligence and Class Structure in American Life* (1994) by Richard Hernstein and Charles Murray, a book that argues that inherited intelligence is a prime determinant of success or failure in society. The authors tied the question of intelligence to race and concluded that African Americans were unsuccessful not because society did not invest in them, but because they lacked intelligence.[91]

These and other foundations actively poisoned public opinion toward affirmative action, immigration, and bilingual education by funding vicious campaigns. The Hoover Institution at Stanford sponsored the work of John Bunzell, one of the intellectual godfathers of the anti-affirmative action movement. The Hoover Institution held ties with the National Association of Scholars (NAS), a right-wing professional organization founded with a gift of $100,000 from the Smith Richardson Foundation. The Center for Individual Rights, founded in 1989, also held close ties with the NAS; it led the fight in *Hopwood v. Texas* (1996), a case filed against the University of Texas Law School in 1992, which resulted in a decision that severely limited affirmative action programs nationally. The U.S. Court of Appeals for the Fifth Circuit found that the University of Texas School of Law violated the equal protection clause of the Fourteenth Amendment by denying admission to Cheryl Hopwood, a white woman, and three white men while admitting African American and Mexican American students with lower grade-point averages and test scores. The court held that race could not be used as a "factor in deciding which applicants to admit."[92]

In police code the number 187 means "Murder," referring to the California Penal Code section for *Murder* or *Homicide.* It became an insider joke among the supporters of Proposition 187. The Proposition 63 campaign laid the groundwork for Proposition 187; more than $1 million was spent on the 63 campaign—$500,000 of it from U.S. English, the largest English-first organization in the country. From this point on, the anti-immigrant movement started to pick up speed with angst dollars pouring in from small contributors. The FAIR and extremist groups such as Voices of Citizens Together (VCT) spun statistics manufactured by the INS and the think tanks. Internet fund-raising was also a bonanza for many immigrant hate groups that collected tax-deductible donations.

The draconian SOS (Save Our State) Initiative, Proposition 187, appeared on the November 1994 California ballot. It proposed denying health and educational services to undocumented immigrants. Governor Pete Wilson immediately supported the proposition. Supporters of the breakup of the Los Angeles Unified School District, the voucher campaign, and the "3 strikes and you're out" proposition joined him. Even Democratic candidates opposed to 187 took potshots: in July, U.S. Senate candidate Diane Feinstein ran an ad claiming that 3,000 "illegals" crossed the border each night. "I'm Diane Feinstein and I've just begun to fight for California."

Chicano organizations and individuals in Los Angeles, led by activists from the 1960s, responded to the anti-immigrant hate crimes by going to the streets. In February 1994, a pro-immigrant march in Los Angeles drew 6,000. On May 28, another march attracted about 18,000 people who trekked up Broadway to City Hall. On October 16, more than 150,000 protesters marched down Avenida César Chávez to City Hall. Some Latino leaders feared that the large number of Mexican flags seen on the march would turn off white voters.

On the eve of the election, spontaneous massive walkouts of high school students who opposed 187 caught most people by surprise. Some Latino politicos, worried that the walkouts would turn off white voters, opposed the demonstrations. Walkouts took place at Huntington Park, Bell, South Gate, Los Angeles, Marshall, and Fremont High Schools, and throughout the San Fernando Valley. Police were called out in Van Nuys as students took to the main street; 200 officers were on tactical alert. News sources estimated that 10,000 (on the low side) students walked out of 39 schools.

A September 1994 *Los Angeles Times* poll showed that 52 percent of Latinos supported Proposition 187. However, Latinos were increasingly alarmed by the racist tone of the anti-immigrant rhetoric, and a field poll about a month before the election showed Latinos in California sharply divided over Proposition 187: Latinos opposed the measure by a slight margin of 48 to 44 percent, and white voters favored it by 60 to 17 percent. White support for 187 remained constant, and another *Los Angeles Times* poll showed that Californian whites favored 187 by 65 to 35 percent, and Latinos by 52 to 48 percent. As expected, on November 8 California overwhelmingly passed 187. Only the San Francisco Bay Area voted against—by 70 percent. Los Angeles voted for 187 by a 12-point margin. Exit polls showed Latinos opposing the proposition 77 percent to 23 percent statewide.

Before the election, Cardinal Mahoney said that the measure would undermine "clear moral principles"—stopping just shy of calling it a mortal sin. The victory of 187 was a blow to the moral authority of the Catholic Church. White Catholics voted 58 to 42 percent for 187. To those supporting racism, Catholic bishops did not deny the sacraments, as they did in the case of the abortion issue. Most Protestant churches remained silent on the issue.[93]

On November 5, 1996, California voters passed Proposition 209. The California Association of Scholars, funded by ultraconservative foundations, placed Proposition 209 on the ballot. It said that "preferential treatment" because of race, sex, ethnicity, or national origin was forbidden. In effect, Proposition 209 made anti-discrimination laws moot. Institutions were not required to recruit or enroll minorities; consequently, there were no damages if they discriminated. Proponents of 209 argued that affirmative action went too far and now was resulting in discrimination against whites who were better qualified. The United States was supposedly a color-blind society.

African Americans voted against Proposition 209 by 73 percent and Latinos by 70 percent. Asian Americans also voted against it, although only by 56 percent. Whites made up three-fourths of the voters; white males voted for 209 by a 66 percent margin and white females by 58 percent. The death of an idea such as social justice does not happen by accident. Indeed, it is very difficult to reverse public policy and change basic commitments to ideals such as civil rights.

Proposition 209 was driven by mean-spirited and extremist organizations and people. They ranged from opportunists such as the VCT, led by Glenn Spencer, who ranted and raved about the Mexican invasion of the United States, and the California Association of Scholars, an affiliate of the NAS, which led a well-funded, well-thought-out campaign designed to change the definition of fairness. The message was, "We live in a classless society; there is equal opportunity for all; work hard enough and you'll make it to the middle-class heaven."

Unfortunately, the Latino community did not organize marches of any size against Proposition 209 in California. Latinos, however, held a march in Washington, D.C., in October 1996. More than 50,000 people marched through the capital in support of Latino and immigrant rights. Although it was successful, the march in Washington was criticized. Many activists felt that a march in Los Angeles to protest Proposition 209 would embarrass President Clinton. It was not until the end of the presidential campaign in California, when Clinton was certain to win by a landslide, that the Democratic Party took a more visible stance.[94]

In June 1998, Californians overwhelmingly approved Proposition 227, insidiously called the "English for the Children" initiative. Californians based their vote not so much on the merits of bilingual education, but on numerous untested assumptions that bilingual education was a failure.

Ron Unz, the man behind Proposition 227 and a Silicon Valley millionaire with dreams of running for governor, had opposed 187. He knew that the core constituency of anti-immigrant, anti-minority voters in California was still very much alive, and he did nothing to mute it. Unz was also a contributor to the Heritage Foundation Policy Review. (Ironically, the Heritage Foundation, while against most progressive agendas, favored the family reunification immigration policy.)

Proposition 227 did not enjoy the near-unanimous Republican support that existed for 187 and 209. First, nativism subsided because of the improving economy and the defections among Republicans running for statewide offices or districts with a sizable Latino constituency. Republican candidates were becoming aware of the backlash in the Chicano/Latino community in the aftermath of Propositions 187 and 209. Their nativism was tempered by the realization that they were losing Latino voters, who once marginally supported them.

Exit polls of Proposition 227 showed that the Latinos opposed 227—in fact, some 63 percent of the Latino electorate voted against Proposition 227. Because of the perception that the proposition was racist, some Republican candidates began to distance themselves from the anti-immigrant, anti–affirmative action, and anti–bilingual education sentiments of their party. Attorney General Dan Lungren, aware of the growing antipathy of Chicanos and Latinos toward Republicans, came out against Proposition 227 to try to stem the loss of their support.

Spanish-language media were crucial in informing the public about 187 and 227. Spanish-language reporters identified with the issue. In the Greater Los Angeles area, 9.74 million radio listeners divided their attention among 81 stations, 12 of which broadcast in Spanish. Two of the 10 TV broadcast channels were Spanish in a "designated market area" that encompassed Los Angeles County; all of Orange, San Bernardino, and Ventura Counties; and parts of Kern, Riverside, and San Diego Counties. Los Angeles–based Univision KMEX Channel boasted higher ratings for its 6 p.m. and 11 p.m. newscasts than those for its English-language competitors.[95]

The National Scene: Census 2000

The 2000 U.S. Census counted 35,305,818 U.S. Latinos; Mexicans comprised 20,640,711 or 58.5 percent; the next largest group was "All other Hispanic or Latino," 6,211,800 or 17.6 percent—meaning that the Mexican-origin population was probably larger. While the Puerto Ricans continued to have a presence, for large numbers of peoples other than Mexican and Puerto Rican, the question of identity was much more complex. Taken as a whole, the U.S. Latino population in 2000 was approaching that of Spain, 39.9 million, and would surpass it by 2008. The Mexican American population alone qualified as one of the largest in the United States. This was a far cry from 1970 Census.[96]

According to the 2000 Census, about three out of four U.S. Latinos lived in California, Texas, New York, Florida, Illinois, Arizona, or New Jersey. Half of the nation's Latinos lived in California or Texas, whose populations were heavily Mexican in origin. Although the largest Mexican populations lived in Los Angeles, Chicago, Houston, San Antonio, and Phoenix, countless Mexicans and Latinos were living in small hamlets throughout the Southwest, Midwest, and Northwest. Latinos' voting strength was growing, although at a snail's pace compared to their dramatic jump in numbers. Youth and citizenship remained obstacles, though the Latino population grew everywhere from Oregon to the rural South, which by 2000 was 12 percent Mexican. Nationally, the U.S. Mexican population grew by 53 percent, with registered Latino voters increasing from 5.5 million in 1994 to 8 million in 2000. Hence, the potential for an increased influence of Latino voters became stronger, since the three largest Latino-population states—California, Texas, and Illinois—have nearly half (108) of the 270 electoral votes needed to elect the president.[97]

Latinos cast 1.61 million votes in the 2000 election, representing 15.2 percent of the total votes cast in California and turning out at a rate of 70.4 percent—far higher than the national average of 51 percent. According to the Willie C. Velásquez Institute, "We estimate California Latino registration at 2.3 million as of October 10, 2000. We estimate that U.S. Latino registration is between 7.2 million and 7.7 million." In 2000, the city of Los Angeles was 46 percent Latino, 30 percent Anglo, 11 percent African American, and 10 percent Asian. California had a total population of 33,871,648 residents, of which 10,966,556 were Latino, including 8,455,926 of Mexican origin. There were a significant number of Central Americans: 576,330. Statewide, white non-Latinos comprised only 47 percent of the population; however, they made up 71 percent of the people who voted in the 2000 presidential election. And, with 54 electoral votes, California wields enormous power.

California, Texas, and New York were considered "out of play" in the race of the presidential election of 2000. Al Gore did little campaigning in California, where support for the Democratic Party was thought to be a given, and Texas, where the opposite was true, and committed few resources to the Latino voter, who was largely ignored. Democrats conceded Texas to George W. Bush. This neglect resulted in the building of some support for Bush among all voters. It demonstrates the opportunistic side of politics and a tendency in the Democratic Party since the time of Franklin D. Roosevelt to ignore or take for granted the Mexican American/Latino vote. It takes money and time to maintain an ethnic voting bloc, something that the machine politicians of old understood. The trend has been for Latinos to vote for Spanish surnames, with a lessening of party loyalty. Incredibly, in places like California, Latino politicos who back white candidates over Latino candidates—for personal reasons or because they want support from the white politico—are diluting this unity. A lot more water or "grease" (in dollars) has to be put on the beans before Latinos can fry them.[98]

Latino voting increased nearly 40 percent from 1990 to 1996. New citizens became a factor as more than 250,000 Latinos became citizens in 1996. That year saw four new Latinos elected to the legislature, including the first Latino Republican. There were now 13 Latinos in the California Assembly. The elections elevated Chicanos to significant leadership positions, such as committee chairs. That same year, a Chicano became Speaker of the Assembly, and another, Senate majority floor leader. State Senator Richard Polanco played a key role in molding the Latino Caucus into an influential power bloc.

In Orange County, Loretta Sánchez (D–Garden Grove) defeated right-wing Republican icon Representative Bob Dornan by 984 votes. Sánchez won reelection handily two years later. In 1999 there were 20 Democrats in the two houses, nine of them Latinas. Two years later, there were 15 Latinos in the

Assembly—four of them were women and four others were Republicans. In the State Senate, there were five Latinos, three of whom were women. GOP strategist Tony Quinn acknowledged, "Republicans simply cannot win in California without one-third of the Latino vote."[99]

In 2000, there were 6,669,666 Latinos in Texas: 32 percent of the state population. Victor Morales was a candidate for the U.S. Senate; although Morales lost, he received more than 80 percent of the Latino vote. Despite the bloc voting, Tejanos were still suckers for the old Texas proverb that went "never trust a Mexican smoking a cigar, or a gringo speaking Spanish." Republican Texas Governor George W. Bush pinned his hopes of winning the White House on wooing the Mexican vote. Bush won reelection to the governorship by more than a 2-to-1 margin; he took half the Latino vote and more than a quarter of the black vote, both of which were normally Democratic. (Although the figure is open to scrutiny, Southwest voters' exit polls placed the Latino support at 39 percent.)

By November 2000 the effect of the growth in Mexican population was evident. Mexican American representatives from Texas to the U.S. Congress numbered six (five Democrats and one Republican). In the Texas Senate there were seven Tejanos and in the House, 28. Meanwhile, the campaign for redistricting heated up in Texas. The G.I. Forum and the MALDEF submitted plans that would boost Latino representation in Congress. Crucial was the pairing of candidates with a sufficient percentage of Latinos in a district to ensure the candidate a winning chance. Many districts had a majority Latino population, but because a large number of the residents were under 18 or were not citizens, only 40 percent of the registered voters would have Spanish surnames. Both parties were aware of the dramatic growth in the Latino population, forcing Republicans to look for Mexican American candidates. The stakes were higher than those after the 1980 and 1990 redistricting when Republicans sided with Latinos to ensure Latino districts at the expense of white Democratic incumbents—in 2000 that was not enough. There were now enough Latinos in Republican districts to turn an election, and Mexican American votes were vital statewide: numbers were redefining Tejano politics.[100]

The year 2001 saw the election of a brown diaper baby—Julian Castro—to the San Antonio City Council; in 2002, his twin brother Joaquin was elected to the Texas House of Representatives. Twenty-six years old in 2001, they graduated from Harvard and Stanford Law Schools. Their mother Rosie Castro, a Raza Unida activist who had run for the city council in 1971, inspired the Castro brothers.[101]

The 2000 Census recorded that, of the 35 million Latinos, 4.7 million resided in the Midwest. Since 1990 the Latino population increased by 107 percent in Wisconsin, 166 percent in Minnesota, and 153 percent in Iowa. Organizations such as the National Council of La Raza continued a strong presence in the Midwest and advocated for education, civil rights, the census, welfare reform, economic and community development, health issues, migrant labor, and youth leadership.

Illinois was the state with the third highest Mexican-origin population after California and Texas. By 2000, 63 percent of its counties possessed a Latino population of 5 percent or more. Chicago remained the capital for the Mexican-origin population in the Midwest. According to the *New York Times,*

> *The biggest change in Chicago's population mosaic is the increase in Hispanics, up more than 200,000 from 1990. While partly the result of better counting efforts, demographers say there has been a rapid stream of Mexicans coming from Mexico and from other American cities, and a growing influx of immigrants from El Salvador, Guatemala, Colombia and other countries.[102]*

The first Latino elected to the Chicago City Council—in 1915—was William Emilio Rodríguez, son of a Mexican immigrant father and a German mother. In Chicago in the 1990s, a gauge of power was the vote you brought in—the living and the dead (an allusion to the Daly political machines voting the living and the dead). In the late 1990s, Representative Luis V. Gutiérrez (D–IL), a Puerto Rican, personified coalition politics. Gutiérrez took strong stands for undocumented immigrants. Latino voter turnout had been terrible; but during the 1990s, it began to improve, and Latinos began to make gains. Seventy-eight percent of the white community was of voting age, versus 68 percent of the African American community, and barely 60 percent of the Latino community. This fact and the fact that a high percentage of the voting-age population is recent immigrants and/or undocumented keep the voting strength of Mexicans and other Latinos just a potential rather than a reality.

By 2000, the Latino population began to move to the suburbs, a change that caused another set of problems. During the 1990s, 32 Illinois towns saw their minority populations grow by nearly 45 percent. Although these areas included more than 30 percent Latinos in 2000, only one Latino was elected to office, a trend that would continue into the 2000s. In 2000, seven aldermen on the 50-member Chicago City Council were Latinos—four were U.S. Mexican and three were Puerto Rican. According to the 2000 Census, almost two-thirds of Chicago Latinos were of Mexican origin; 15 percent were Puerto Rican; just fewer than 8 percent were Cuban; 10 percent were of Central and South American heritage.

The political situation of the Chicago area resembled that of most of the United States. Redistricting was on the minds of the Latino political players, who thought that their growth would offset the decline in African American and white populations. Chicago numbered 175,793 Latino registered voters by the year 2000. However, as in Los Angeles, even when they comprised a majority of a ward, they would be outvoted by a minority of white, and sometimes black, voters: a large proportion of the community was too young to vote or undocumented. And the chances of Latinos winning in wards where they were a minority were still remote. In Chicago, there were five wards that had a majority of Latino voters; MALDEF wanted another such ward, and it sued the city.

The court dealt Latinos a setback in 1998, when the U.S. Court of Appeals for the Seventh Circuit ruled that only residents of voting age who are citizens should be counted for remapping purposes. This criterion was of concern, since 60 percent of the Latinos would not be counted, thus drastically reducing their political clout. Taken as a whole, Latinos comprised more than one in five Chicagoans (in a city of 2,896,016 residents), with some 530,462 of the Mexican born making up 75 percent of the Latino population. Of concern to non-Latinos was that any growth in Latino representation would come at the expense of African Americans and whites. Increased gentrification also threatened Latino political power.[103]

The Northwest, once largely a Texas affair, with most migrants coming from the Lone Star State, included more of a mix of Texans and immigrants by 2000. By the 1980 Census the Latino population in Washington had grown to 3 percent of the state's total population—approximately 123,000; by the end of the decade it nearly doubled. The 2000 Census showed it had increased to 441,509. Similarly, neighboring Oregon by 2012 grew to 450,062, which was 11.7 percent of the total population, up from 8 percent in 2000.[104] It is a community in transition, with the Latino population doubling every decade. Although Mexican-origin people make up approximately 80 percent of the Latino population, other Latinos are growing in numbers. The changes taking place are interesting. For example, the number of Mexican *tortillerías* that have sprung up in places like the Yakima Valley of Washington amazes the outsider. Indeed, Latino-owned companies in Washington grew 64 percent between 1992 and 1997, employing 18,830 persons by 1997. The number of Latino farmers there also grew from 378 in 1992 to 625 four years later. Two-thirds of the farmers owned and operated their own farms, 120 were part-time owners, and only 79 were tenants. No longer is the region a stopping-off place for migrants; established communities were formed.

Looking at the Mexican-origin population in the Pacific Northwest, from the vantage point of numbers, they are growing dramatically—this is made more significant by the fact that the percentage of the white population is declining. In 1990 just over 380,000 Latinos, of whom over 80 percent were of Mexican origin, lived in Washington, Oregon, and Idaho (they were 4.4 percent of the total population). Ten years later the Mexican portion had grown to 623,000. Unlike in many other regions of the country, the growth is in agricultural communities where the Latino population is still growing.

In 1980, whites were 90.2 percent of Washington's population. Just two decades later it would dip to 76.2. It was not so much that the white population was falling but that the Latino population, which remained overwhelmingly of Mexican origin, was skyrocketing. Asian and Latino immigration played a huge role, too. In 1980, 5.8 percent of Washingtonians were foreign born; it would double in the next two decades. By 2000, 67.2 percent of Washington's Asian population and 45.6 percent of Latinos were foreign born. However, the 2000 Census indicated 88.64 percent were classified as white.

The Yakima Valley continued to be a major entry port for Mexican migrants. For instance, the town Wapato, according to the 2000 Census, numbered 4,572, of which 76 percent were Latino—and this is not counting undocumented residents.[105] Whites call it "Mexican Town." Mexican residency goes back to World War II when undocumented workers, *braceros*, and Tejanos and Mexican sugar beet workers came to pick crops. In the 1970s cold-storage facilities in Wapato and Union Gap opened new opportunities and made possible year-round employment. In the 1980s Mexican immigrants displaced Chicano migrants as the primary farm workforce. The landscape took on more diversity as local restaurants and tortilla plants run by Mexican immigrants and the cantinas run by Chicanos multiplied. Some Mexicans own farms, but agriculture is still dominated by Euro-Americans.[106]

The largest state in the Northwest is Washington. In 2000, its total population was 5,894,121—of which 441,509 (or 7.5 percent) were Latinos. Mexicans made up 329,934 or just fewer than 75 percent of the Latino population. Puerto Ricans were the next largest group (16,140), followed by Central Americans (12,126). As with other states, the Latino population of Washington doubled during the 1990s. Some 40 percent were under 18, making it the youngest ethnic group. Adams and Franklin Counties in eastern Washington were 50 percent Latino, and Yakima County was 35 percent Latino. Central Americans became more numerous as Guatemalans moved into Shelton and Salvadorans into Aberdeen.

Besides this resident population, 100,000 migrants arrived in Washington annually. Another trend was the in-migration of indigenous Mexicans who knew little Spanish or English. The Spanish-speaking were bound together by a chain of Spanish-language radio stations playing Spanish music. Despite some economic progress achieved, the low educational attainment, with corresponding low income, has contributed to low rates of home ownership in comparison with other groups. The big banana in Washington is Seattle, home of Microsoft. It is a white city, ranking last in terms of percentage of minorities among the 25 most populous cities. "The Times [Seattle] analysis also shows Seattle has earned a distinction as a city short on children. Only about one in six Seattlites is under age 18." Sixty-eight percent of Seattle's population is white. It ranked second in the Pacific Northwest behind Portland, Oregon.

In 2000, Latinos made up at least 20 percent of the school enrollment in 26 Oregon towns—and 65 percent in Woodburn, Oregon. The Latino population of Oregon was expected to grow to 500,000 by 2025. Nevertheless, Latinos lacked political representation.[107]

The town of Salem, Oregon, has experienced dramatic growth in the Mexican-origin population since the 1970s. As in other places in the Pacific Northwest, the roots of the Mexican population extend back into the nineteenth century—but up until recently they have not been strong in terms of numbers. World War II was a turning point, with significant numbers of migrants and *braceros* finding their way into Oregon. By the 1970s, immigrants arrived from Michoacán and Oaxaca to work in tree farms and canneries. A similar growth occurred in surrounding areas, and, by the beginning of the twentieth century, 55,000 Latinos lived in Marion and Polk Counties and over 100,000 lived in Clackamas, Multnomah, and Washington Counties alone.[108] By the beginning of the twenty-first century, the proportion of whites in the population was declining and the growth in the Latino population was taking up the slack. As in the Southwest and Midwest, the Mexican and Latino communities were increasingly divided into those with green cards and those without. On the one hand, more Mexican American students attended universities; on the other hand, like California, Oregon attracted thousands of Mixtec and other Mexican migrants coming to work in the fields. They differentiate themselves from other Latinos, and many do not speak Spanish or English and are the victims of exploitation, living in fear.[109]

As with Oregon and Washington, Mexicans migrated to Idaho for agricultural work.[110] The sugar beet companies recruited Mexicans around World War I as Central European labor was restricted. Mexicans also worked on the railroads. During World War II *braceros* entered the state, as did the Mexican American migrants. The Mexican population changed in the 1960s, 1970s, and 1980s, with the existing Mexican American population settling in and the state's economy diversifying. Mexican American and Latino businesses became more common, and distinct communities formed. These communities grew more conscious of their rights. Migrant workers continued to work in Idaho, where as many as 100,000 arrived in the summer months. The Tejanos continued to be a significant part of the workforce. By 1991, the Idaho Migrant Council estimated that the Mexican-origin population reached more than 58,000 in the southern Snake River Valley.[111]

Political Roundup: 2000

In 2000, Antonio Villaraigosa lost the election for mayor of Los Angeles partially because the then Assemblyman Tony Cárdenas, Los Angeles City Councilman Alex Padilla, and Congressman Xavier Becerra supported Jim Hahn. The rift was personal. Villaraigosa supported a white liberal to replace him as Speaker of the Assembly. This schism gave many white liberals and African Americans an excuse to support Hahn, who ran racist ads associating Villaraigosa with gang members and drug dealers.

California Latinos as a whole were entering a new era, one where money beyond the means of an ordinary politician carried the day. To run successfully for city council or mayor required more money than the Mexican/Latino community could raise independently. To attract such huge amounts of funds, compromises were made with the business community, whose interests did not always coincide with those of Mexican Americans and other Latinos. Term limits, personal ambitions, and the need to raise campaign funds were changing the direction of Chicano politics.

In the years past, nationalism disciplined politicians such as Richard Alatorre. However, times had changed, and by 2000 Mexican Americans and Latinos wanted to believe that they were players. While the redistricting processes in 1980 and 1990 were contentious, this time around the Mexican American community assumed that it was part of the establishment, given its power in Sacramento. Latinos were now incumbents, and incumbents in both parties worked out a bipartisan redistricting plan that protected incumbents. It kept intact 13 seats (7 state senators; 6 members of Congress) currently held by Latinos. The legislature would also create a new Chicano congressional district in Los Angeles County. MALDEF disputed the plan. Considering the growth and size of the Latino population, it was entitled to more.

According to Chicano elected officials, the benefits of multiracial coalitions were huge. They said that in 2002 there were 26 Latino legislators, proof of the effectiveness of coalition politics. Evidently, many elected officials forgot that Chicanos leveled the political field in the courts. In fact, it cost the community a lot of political capital to get them elected.

In June 2002, the Ninth Circuit Court found that the redistricting plan—a blatant deal—was not unreasonable. In effect it held that rules protecting minorities were no longer necessary because of the dramatic political progress Latinos had made in California in recent years—such as winning dozens of seats in Congress and the California legislature and nearly electing a Latino mayor in Los Angeles. This decision was significant since it came from the court's most liberal judges. In the space of just under three decades, society returned to the era of legal gerrymandering.[112]

The success of George W. Bush in cultivating Latino voters formed his base in Texas. Whereas Latinos were not a factor in California, where Gore was the overwhelming favorite, they were much more of a factor in Texas and New York. Nationally, the U.S. Latino community took a huge leap during the 1990s, growing by 58 percent to 35.3 million people; they were 12.5 percent of the population while constituting 7 percent of all voters. However, in some cases increased numbers did not result in Latino representation: despite a 2000 Census count of 30 percent Latino citizens in Fort Worth, Texas, there were no Latinos on the City Council. They did better on the Fort Worth school board where they held three of the nine seats. It was estimated that Latinos needed at least a 60 percent majority to elect a candidate.[113] This was a pattern for Latino politics throughout the country.

Some Things Never Change: Police Brutality

Twenty-five years after the assassination of Rubén Salazar, the justice system was still not protecting the rights of Mexican Americans. In 1995 in Sun Valley, California (a suburb of Los Angeles), William Masters II, 35, killed an 18-year-old tagger named César Rene Arce and wounded his friend, David Hillo, 20. Both taggers were unarmed. Many Euro-Americans applauded Masters, while the Chicano community remained largely indifferent. In the end, the district attorney did not indict Masters for the murder; still the community remained silent.

In 1999, the Los Angeles Police Department's (LAPD) Rampart scandal began when Officer Rafael Pérez, who served as a Rampart Community Resources Against Street Hoodlums (CRASH) antigang officer, copped a plea bargain for having stolen drugs from LAPD evidence lockers—in return for evidence of widespread corruption and brutality in the Rampart CRASH unit. Dozens of police were implicated in numerous crimes and acts of brutality committed while waging a systematic war and shooting down youth in the Pico-Union neighborhood. Only a few Chicanos and Central Americans protested this gross violation of human rights; many Latino elected officials sided with the police.

In Bellevue, a suburb of Seattle, Washington, police killed Nelson Martínez Méndez, 24, an unarmed Guatemalan accused of domestic violence against a cousin. *El Centro de la Raza* of Seattle, led by Roberto Maestas, organized protests against the injustice. In January 2002, an inquest jury ruled it justifiable homicide, and the district attorney refused to prosecute the officer.

In 2005, an LAPD SWAT team killed 19-month-old Susie Lopez Peña in an exchange of gunfire with her father, who was holding her. Police fired over 60 shots at the father, with numerous bullets hitting and killing Susie. Not one politico challenged Police Chief William J. Bratton, who defended his officers.[114]

Race continued to be a factor in society. At the trial of Jessy San Miguel, the prosecutor made a point of emphasizing the so-called Mexican Macho culture. The prosecutor made a reference to "those that cross the border and commit crimes." San Miguel, 28, died from lethal injection, after George Bush refused a stay of execution.[115]

Conclusion: The Problem of Becoming the Nation's Largest Minority

As mentioned at the beginning of the chapter, the timeline encompasses two decades—two very hectic decades. Not only had the population grown dramatically, but no longer could it be assumed that Latinos were a homogeneous population—there were Mexicans, there were Puerto Ricans, and, to a lesser extent, there were Cuban Americans. Neither did these peoples live in exclusive pockets—all Mexicans did not live in the Southwest; Puerto Ricans, in New York; or Cubans, in Florida. By 2000, most Latino groups were scattered throughout the country, with the most dramatic shift taking place in the South. A report of the Pew Hispanic Center wrote:

> The Hispanic population is growing faster in much of the South than anywhere else in the United States. Across a broad swath of the region stretching westward from North Carolina on the Atlantic seaboard to Arkansas across the Mississippi River and south to Alabama on the Gulf of Mexico, sizeable Hispanic populations have emerged suddenly in communities where Latinos were a sparse presence just a decade or two ago.[116]

These new settlement areas differed from California, Texas, and New York, where migrants joined well-established Latino communities with networks of organizations. They posed new challenges to national Latino organizations, a majority of which were still Mexican American. There would also be the challenge of how the member communities of this amorphous group called "Latinos" would relate to each other and how they could find unity and the consensus to develop a common agenda.

Notes

1. Betsy Guzmán, The Hispanic Population: Census 2000 Brief May 2001, http://www.census.gov/prod/2001pubs/c2kbr01-3.pdf.
2. Ibid. Rafael Valdivieso, "Demographic Trends of the Mexican-American Population: Implications for Schools. ERIC Digest," ERIC Clearinghouse on Rural Education and Small Schools, Charleston WV. ED321961 (September 1990), http://www.ericdigests.org/pre-9217/trends.htm.
3. The Powell Memo (also known as the Powell Manifesto). The Powell Memo was first published August 23, 1971. Confidential Memorandum: Attack of American Free Enterprise System, August 23, 1971, TO: Mr. Eugene B. Sydnor, Jr., Chairman, Education Committee, U.S. Chamber of Commerce. FROM: Lewis F. Powell, Jr., In Reclaim Democracy, http://reclaimdemocracy.org/powell_memo_lewis/. Lewis was later appointed to the Supreme Court. Jean Stefanic and Richard

Delgado, *No Mercy: How Conservative Think Tanks and Foundations Changed America's Social Agenda* (Philadelphia, PA: Temple University Press, 1996).

4. Amy Goodman, "The Criminalization of Immigration," *Democracy Now* (September 11, 1997), http://www.democracynow.org/1997/9/11/the_criminalization_of_immigration.

5. Edward R. Roybal, "Hispanic Americans in Congress, 1822–1995," http://www.loc.gov/rr/hispanic/congress/roybal.html.

6. David Reyes, "GI Forum Address," *Los Angeles Times* (August 7, 1980).

7. MALDEF, Mexican American Legal Defense and Education Fund, http://www.maldef.org/.

8. Deindustrialization is the reduction of heavy industry and manufacturing within the country's borders and sending the production abroad. Paul L. Street, *Racial Oppression in the Global Metropolis: A Living Black Chicago History* (Lanham, MD: Rowman & Littlefield Publishers, Inc., 2007), 132. Joan Moore, "Latina/o Studies: The Continuing Need for New Paradigms," Occasional Paper No. 29, Julian Samora Research Institute, December 1997, http://www.jsri.msu.edu/pdfs/ops/oc29.pdf.

9. Jorge Chapa, "The Burden of Interdependence: Demographic, Economic, and Social Propects for Latinos in the Reconfigured U.S. Economy," in Frank Bonilla, Edwin Meléndez, Rebecca Morales, and María de los Angeles Torres, eds., *Borderless Borders: U.S. Latinos, Latin Americans and the Paradox of Interdependence* (Philadelphia, PA: Temple University Press, 1998), 71–82. Stefanic and Delgado, *No Mercy*.

10. Robert W. Fox, "Neighbors' Problems, Our Problems: Population Growth in Central America," Negative Population Growth (NPG) Forum Series, http://www.npg.org/forum_series/BalancingHumansInTheBiosphere.pdf. Thomas F. O'Brien, *The Revolutionary Mission: American Enterprise in Latin America, 1900-1945* (Cambridge, UK: Cambridge University Press, 1999), 51–53. Charles D. Brockett, *Land, Power and Poverty: Agrarian Transformation and Political Conflict in Central America* (Boulder, CO: Westview Press, 1990), 70–76.

11. El Salvador in the 1980s, http://www.youtube.com/watch?v=1bEpEK7uKzE&feature=related. David Kirsch, "Death Squads in El Salvador: A Pattern of U.S. Complicity," *Covert Action Quarterly*, Summer 1990, http://www.thirdworldtraveler.com/US_ThirdWorld/deathsquads_ElSal.html. El Salvador: Civil War, PBS, http://www.pbs.org/itvs/enemiesofwar/el-salvador2.html. Ron Rhodes, "Christian Revolution in Latin America: The Changing Face of Liberation Theology," Part One in a Three-Part Series on Liberation Theology, Reasoning from the Scriptures Ministries, http://home.earthlink.net/~ronrhodes/Liberation.html. Roberto D'Abussion [sic] interview (1984), http://www.youtube.com/watch?v=0e-jnwAwIKE&feature=related.

12. Massacre in El Salvador During Oscar Romero's Funeral, http://www.youtube.com/watch?v=EN6LWdqcyuc&feature=related.

13. I was in El Salvador in the spring of 1991 before the peace accords. Rodolfo F. Acuña, "Column Left; Latin Generals Count on the Wages of War," *Los Angeles Times* (April 1,

1991). Tom Gibb, "US Role in Salvador's Brutal War," *BBC News/America* (March 24, 2002), http://news.bbc.co.uk/2/hi/americas/1891145.stm.

14. Nicaraguan Sandinistas, Latin American Studies, http://www.latinamericanstudies.org/sandinistas.htm.

15. Boland Amendment—Definition and Overview, WorldIQ.com, http://www.wordiq.com/definition/Boland_Amendment. Secrets of The CIA—Nicaragua, http://www.youtube.com/watch?v=zKXZfwG43pU.

16. Lawrence E. Walsh, Independent Counsel, "Final Report of the Independent Counsel for Iran/Contra Matters," in *Volume I: Investigations and Prosecutions,* August 4, 1993 (Washington, DC, United States Court of Appeals for the District of Columbia Circuit Division for the Purpose of Appointing Independent Counsel, Division No. 86-6), http://www.fas.org/irp/offdocs/walsh/. Iran Contra Coverup: Part 1 (All eight can be found on YouTube), http://www.youtube.com/watch?v=35KcYgMPiIM. CIA, Guns, Drugs, Fraud, Iran Contra, http://www.youtube.com/watch?v=bbt9PsaSUiI.

17. Ginger Thompson and Mireya Navarro, "Rights Groups Say Logbook Lists Executions by Guatemalan Army," *New York Times* (May 20, 1999). Rachel Cobb, "Guatemala's New Evangelists," *Natural History* 107, no. 4 (May 1998): 32ff. "Guatemala Civil War 1960–1996," GlobalSecurity.org, http://www.globalsecurity.org/military/world/war/guatemala.htm.

18. "Maquiladoras," *Handbook of Texas Online,* http://www.tshaonline.org/handbook/online/articles/MM/dzm2.html. María Patricia Fernández-Kelly, *For We Are Sold. I and My People: Women and Industry in Mexico's Frontier* (Albany: State University of New York Press, 1983), 45–84. Devon G. Peña, *The Terror of the Machine: Technology, Work, Gender, & Ecology on the U.S.-Mexico Border* (Austin: CMAS Book, University of Texas Press, 1997). James M. Cypher, "Mexico: Financial Fragility or Structural Crisis?" *Journal of Economic Issues* 30, no. 2 (June 1996): 454–55.

19. Thomas Muller, *California's Newest Immigrants: A Summary* (Washington, DC: Urban Institute Press, 1984), ix–x, 7, 13, 28.

20. James Crawford, "California Vote Gives Boost to 'English-Only' Movement," *Education Weekly* (April 1, 1987), http://www.edweek.org/ew/articles/1987/04/01/27useng.h06.html.

21. Leo R. Chávez, "The Power of the Imagined Community: The Settlement of Undocumented Mexicans and Central Americans in the United States," *American Anthropologist* 96, no. 1 (1994): 52–73. Margo De Ley, "Taking from Latinos to Assist Soviet Immigrants—an Affront to Fairness," *Los Angeles Times* (March 19, 1989). A Look at the Forces Behind the Anti-Immigrant Movement, Democracy Now! May 2, 2007, http://www.democracynow.org/2007/5/2/a_look_at_the_forces_behind.

22. Terry Maxon, "Hart Angers Hispanics with Letter on Aliens," *Dallas Morning News* (February 5, 1985). Stephen Moore, "A Pro-Family, Pro-growth Legal Immigration Policy for America," Backgrounder no. 735, The Heritage Foundation (November 6, 1989): 1–7. Elton Gallegly, "Just How Many Aliens Are Here Illegally?" *Los Angeles Times* (March 13, 1994).

23. California Chief Justice Rose Bird Loses Election, http://www.youtube.com/watch?v=Kd162US36to. Cruz Reynoso Honored for Civil Rights Commitments, http://www.youtube.com/watch?v=wViKbfS_Gds&feature=related. Frank del Olmo, "Ugly or Polite, It's Racism," *Los Angeles Times* (October 30, 1986).

24. William Langwiesche, "The Border," *Atlantic Monthly* (May 1992), 69. Sebastian Rotella, "Border Abuses Continue 2 Years, Study Says," *Los Angeles Times* (February 26, 1992). Sebastian Rotella, "INS Agents Abuse Immigrants, Study Says," *Los Angeles Times* (May 31, 1992).

25. Stuart Silverstein, "Years Later, Many Scoff at Immigration Act," *Los Angeles Times* (August 29, 1993). Dan Freedman, "U.S. to Boost Border Patrols," *Los Angeles Daily News* (February 3, 1994). "Southern Exposure—Perspective," *California Journal* (May 1, 1998). "U.S. Border Patrol in S. California Developing Deadly But Ineffective Operation Gatekeeper," *In Motion Magazine*, http://www.inmotionmagazine.com/rm99.html.

26. Robert R. Brischetto and Paul A. Leonard, "Falling Through the Safety Net: Latinos and the Declining Effectiveness of Anti-Poverty Programs in the 1980s," *Public Policy Report 1*, Southwest Voter Research Institute, 1988. Rebecca Morales and Frank Bonilla, "Restructuring and the New Inequality," in Rebecca Morales and Frank Bonilla, eds., *Latinos in a Changing U.S. Economy. Comparative Perspectives on Growing Inequality* (Newbury Park, CA: Sage Publications, 1993), 11–12. Roger M. Mahoney, "Democracy's Obligated to the Poor," *Los Angeles Times* (October 23, 1985). Jason DeParle, "Poverty Rate Rose Sharply Last Year as Incomes Slipped," *Los Angeles Times* (September 27, 1991). James Risen, "History May Judge Reaganomics Very Harshly," *Los Angeles Times* (November 8, 1992). Harry Bernstein, "Closing the Wage Gap: Job Equality," *Los Angeles Times* (April 8, 1993).

27. Paul Krugman, "Reagan Did It," *New York Times* (June 1, 2009).

28. Harry Bernstein, "Put Teeth Back in Worker's Right to Strike," *Los Angeles Times* (July 5, 1993). "Patco: Ex-Controllers Regret Striking in 1981," *Los Angeles Times* (July 17, 1991). Bob Baker, "Workers Fear Losing Jobs to Replacement in Strikes," *Los Angeles Times* (June 7, 1990). Jane Slaughter, "What Went Wrong at Caterpillar?" *Labor Notes* (May 1991). Bob Baker, "Union Buster Turns to 'A Labor of Love,'" *Los Angeles Times* (September 5, 1993).

29. Marita Hernandez, "Latina Leads Takeover of Union from Anglo Male," *Los Angeles Times* (May 6, 1989). "*Raiz Fuerte que no se arranca,*" pamphlet paying homage to Magdalena Mora (Los Angeles, CA: Editorial Prensa Sembradora, 1981). Steve Proffitt, "María Elena Durazo," *Los Angeles Times* (September 27, 1992). Bob Baker, "Union, Hyatt Hotels Still at Odds," *Los Angeles Times* (July 23, 1991). See Rodolfo F. Acuña, *Anything but Mexican: Chicanos in Contemporary Los Angeles* (London: Verso, 1996). Patrick J. McDonnell, "Hotel Boycott Is a High-Stakes Battle for Union. . . ," *Los Angeles Times* (February 3, 1996).

30. Justice for Janitors actions (1990 through 2006), http://www.youtube.com/watch?v=WKfQgUn7UNg. Stronger Colorado/Justice for Janitors Denver Rally, http://www.youtube.com/watch?v=WV_1vb0JDHg. NOW "Janitor Justice?"; PBS,

(October 26, 2007), http://www.youtube.com/watch?v=kdK7Chg7Dm4&feature=related.

31. Sonia Nazario, "Janitors Settle Suit, Involving Clash in 1990," *Los Angeles Times* (September 4, 1990). Rodolfo F. Acuña, "America Retreats on Labor Laws," *Los Angeles Times* (July 16, 1990). Bob Baker, "Tentative Accord Ok'd to End Janitor's Strike," *Los Angeles Times* (June 26, 1990). Sonia Nazario, "For Militant Union, It's a War," Los Angeles Times (August 19, 1993). Harry Bernstein, "It's a Fine Line Between Profit and Greed," *Los Angeles Times* (January 2, 1994).

32. Labor Community Strategy Center, http://www.thestrategy-center.org/project/bus-riders-union.

33. Bob Baker, "L.A.'s Booming Auto Industry Now a Memory," *Los Angeles Times* (July 20, 1991). Henry Weinstein, "Boycott by UAW of GM Threatened," *Los Angeles Times* (May 15, 1983). Eric Mann, *Taking on General Motors: A Case Study of the UAW Campaign to Keep GM Van Nuys Open* (Los Angeles: Center for Labor Research and Education, Institute of Industrial Relations, University of California Los Angeles, 1987), 7–9, 219–50. James F. Peltz, "General Motors Plant in Van Nuys to Close," *Los Angeles Times* (July 2, 1991).

34. Rodolfo F. Acuña, *Corridors of Migration: The Odyssey of Mexican Laborers, 1600–1933* (Tucson: University of Arizona Press, 2007).

35. Robert B. Reich, "Business Dynamism Gone Overboard," *Los Angeles Times* (November 17, 1985). Barbara Kingsolver, *Holding the Line: Women in the Great Arizona Mine Strike of 1983* (Ithaca, NY: ILR Press, Cornell University, 1996). Jonathan D. Rosenblum, *Copper Crucible: How the Arizona Miners Strike of 1983 Recast Labor-Management Relations in America* (Ithaca, NY: ILR Press, Cornell University, 1995) 4, no. 2 (Summer 1988): 251–68.

36. The Women of "Fuerza Unida," http://www.youtube.com/watch?v=TlIODcghnHk.

37. "Texas Plant Closure Still Haunting Levi's" (November 1, 1992). Reese Erlich, "Former Levi Strauss Workers Protest Texas Plant Closing," *Christian Science Monitor* (November 9, 1992). Alexander Cockburn, "Merciless Cruelties of Bottom Line," *Arizona Republic* (Phoenix, May 23, 1993). Suzanne Espinosa Solis, "Rare Shadow on Company's Image: Ex-Workers Take on Levi Strauss," *San Francisco Chronicle* (July 18, 1994). Fuerza Unida, http://fuerzaunida.freeservers.com/.

38. Cesar Chavez Trilogy Cut Version, http://www.youtube.com/watch?v=jZt7g1t1iAo.

39. Harry Bernstein, "Farm Workers Still Mired in Poverty," *Los Angeles Times* (July 25, 1985). Harry Bernstein, "The Boycott: Chávez Gets a Slow Start," *Los Angeles Times* (July 25, 1985). Harry Bernstein, "Growers Still Addicted to Foreign Workers," *Los Angeles Times* (October 2, 1985). Harry Bernstein, "Ruling May Devastate Chávez's Union," *Los Angeles Times* (February 25, 1987).

40. Rochell L. Stanfield, "Reagan Courting Women, Minorities, But It May Be Too Late to Win Them," *National Journal* 15, no. 22 (May 28, 1983): 1118ff. *Dallas Morning News* (October 19, 1984). Juan Vásquez, "Watch out for Willie Velásquez," *Nuestro* (March 1979), 20.

41. Robert Gnaizda, "Mario Obledo, Latino Vote: The 'Sleeping Giant' Stirs," *Los Angeles Times* (November 13, 1983). Gloria Molina interviewed by Carlos Vásquez (1944), Courtesy of the Department of Special Collections/UCLA Library, Calisphere (1990), http://content.cdlib.org/xtf/view?docId=hb8b69p65d&chunk.id=div00011&brand=calisphere&doc.view=entire_text.

42. Chip Jacobs, "Return of the Native," *Los Angeles City Beat* (April 7, 2005), http://chipjacobs.com/articles/profiles/return-of-the-native/. John P. Schmal, "Chicano Representation: Coming into their own (1975–1984)," HispanicVista.com, http://www.hispanicvista.com/HVC/Columnist/jschmal/071805jpschmal1.htm. Acuña, *Anything but Mexican*, 56, 74, 98.

43. Frank del Olmo, "Snyder's Narrow Victory Gives Latino Political Activists a Rude Awakening," *Los Angeles Times* (April 28, 1983). Janet Clayton, "Snyder's Decision Throws Eastside Seat Up for Grabs," *Los Angeles Times* (January 3, 1985). Frank del Olmo, "Alatorre Vs. Snyder . . ." *Los Angeles Times* (January 31, 1985).

44. Douglas Johnson, "Latinos and Redistricting: 'Californios for Fair Representation' and California Redistricting in the 1980s," The Rose Institute of State and Local Government, Claremont McKenna College, July 1991.

45. Douglas Johnson, "Latinos and Redistricting: 'Californios for Fair Representation' and California Redistricting in the 1980s," The Rose Institute of State and Local Government Claremont McKenna College, July 1991. Henry Cisneros Interview: Charlie Rose: July 26, 1996, no longer available on internet.

46. Kemper Diehl and Jan Jarboe, *Henry Cisneros: Portrait of a New American* (San Antonio, TX: Corona Publishing, 1985). Rodolfo F. Acuña, *Occupied America: A History of Chicanos*, 3d ed. (New York: Harper & Row, 1988), 430–37. Marshall Ingersol, "San Antonio's Mayor Is Simply 'Henry' to Everyone," *Christian Science Monitor* (March 24, 1984). James García, "Cisneros Fall Wasn't a Tragedy," *Dallas Morning News* (January 4, 1998).

47. "Where Minority Mayors Ride High," *U.S. News & World Report* (April 22, 1985), 12. Peter Skerry, "Neighborhood COPS; The Resurrection of Saul Alinsky," *New Republic* (February 6, 1984), 27. Peter Skerry, *Mexican Americans: The Ambivalent Minority* (New York: Free Press, 1993), 66. Robert Reinhold, "Mexican-Americans in Texas Move into Political Mainstream," *New York Times* (September 15, 1985).

48. Rita Arias Jirasek and Carlos Tortolero, *Mexican Chicago* (Chicago, IL: Arcadia Publishing, 2001), 135–45. Ray Hutchison, "Historiography of Chicago's Mexican Community," Urban and Regional Studies University of Wisconsin-Green Bay, April 1999, http://tigger.uic.edu/~marczim/mlac/papers/hutchison.htm. Chicago Activist Voices Opinion on Immigration, Online News Hour, PBS, http://www.pbs.org/newshour/bb/social_issues/july-dec06/immigration_08-18.html. Karen Mary Davalos, "Ethnic Identity Among Mexican and Mexican American Women in Chicago, 1920-1991" (PhD dissertation, Yale University, 1993). Latino Institute, *Al Filo/At the Cutting Edge: The Empowerment of Chicago's Latino Electorate* (Chicago, IL: Latino Institute, 1986), 1–6, 11, 14–15, 18–19, 24–26.

49. "New Mexico Offers a Preview of Mobilization," *New York Times* (September 1, 1983); interview with nine academicians within the state. Ted Robbins, "1980 Race Set Tone for Richardson's Political Future," NPR, September 13, 2007, http://www.npr.org/templates/story/story.php?storyId=14361319.

50. Chip Martínez, "Federico Peña: Denver's First Hispanic Mayor," *Nuestro* (August 1983), 14–17. Steve Padilla, "In Search of Hispanic Voters," *Nuestro* (August 1983), 20. "A Mile High: Denver Buys Peña's Dream," *Time* (July 4, 1983), 22. Kenneth T. Walsh, "Minority Mayors on Fast Track," *U.S. News & World Report* (April 7, 1986), 31–32.

51. Bill Boyarsky, "Battle Over Hermosillo: It's Just the Start," *Los Angeles Times*, August 25, 1993.

52. Acuña, *Anything but Mexican,* 152–53. Mark Z. Barabak, "Latinos Struggle for Role in National Leadership, Politics . . ." *Los Angeles Times* (July 7, 1998).

53. Rodolfo F. Acuña, *Sometimes There Is No Other Side: Chicanos and the Myth of Equality* (Notre Dame, IN: University of Notre Dame Press, 1998), 66. Lisa J. Montoya, Carol Hardy-Fanta, and Sonia Garcia, "Latina Politics: Gender, Participation, and Leadership," *PS: Political Science & Politics* 33, no. 3 (September 2000): 555–61. Mary Benanti, "Hispanic Officeholders 'Barometer' of Progress," *USA Today* (September 18, 1987).

54. Sarah Deutsch, "Gender, Labor History, and Chicano/a Ethnic Identity," *Frontiers* 14, no. 2 (1994): 1–9. Virginia Escalante, Nancy Rivera, and Victor Valle, "Inside the World of Latinas," *Los Angeles Times* (August 7, 1983). "For Business: Making Full Use of the Nation's Human Capital. Fact-Finding Report of the Federal Glass Ceiling Commission Release by the Department of Labor," March 1995, Washington, DC, http://digitalcommons.ilr.cornell.edu/cgi/viewcontent.cgi?article=1118&context=key_workplace.

55. Mary Pardo, *Mexican American Women Activists: Identity and Resistance in Two Los Angeles Communities* (Philadelphia, PA: Temple University Press, 1998). Rodolfo F. Acuña's Herald-Examiner articles on the Mothers of East Los Angeles are in his collection at the California State Northridge Library.

56. José Angel Gutiérrez, Michelle Meléndez, and Sonia Adriana Noyola, *Chicanas in Charge: Texas Women in the Public Arena* (Lanham, MD: Rowman & Littlefield, 2007), 106–12. María Antonietta Berriozabal, Tejano Voices, http://library.uta.edu/tejanovoices/interview.php?cmasno=033.

57. Severita Lara, Tejano Voices, UT Arlington, http://library.uta.edu/tejanovoices/interview.php?cmasno=013. Gutiérrez et al., *Chicanas in Charge*, 113, 121.

58. Alicia Chacón, Tejano Voices, UT Arlington, http://library.uta.edu/tejanovoices/interview.php?cmasno=002. Gutiérrez et al., *Chicanas in Charge*, 47–55.

59. Norma Villarreal Ramírez, Tejano Voices, http://library.uta.edu/tejanovoices/interview.php?cmasno=007. José Angel Gutiérrez, "Experiences of Chicana County Judges in Texas Politics: In Their Own Words," *Frontiers* 20, no. IL

(July–August 1999): 181ff. See Tejano Voices, http://library.uta.edu/tejanovoices/gallery.php.

60. Gutiérrez et al., *Chicanas in Charge*, 131–35, 144.

61. Rebecca Morales and Paul Ong, "Immigrant Women in Los Angeles," *Economic and Industrial Democracy* 12, no. 1 (February 1991): 65–81. Benjamin Mark Cole, "Do Immigrants Underpin L.A. Business World?" *Los Angeles Business Journal* (May 27, 1991). Elaine M. Allensworth, "Earnings Mobility of First and '1.5' Generation Mexican-Origin Women and Men: A Comparison with U.S.–Born Mexican Americans and Non-Hispanic Whites," *Internal Migration Review* 31, no. 2 (Summer 1997): 386–410. Elizabeth Martínez and Ed McCaughan, "Chicanas and Mexicanas within a Transnational Working Class," in Adelaida R. Del Castillo, ed., *Between Borders: Essays on Mexicana/Chicana History* (Los Angeles, CA: Floricanto Press, 1990), 31–52. Pierrette Hondagneu-Sotelo, *Gendered Transition: Mexican Experiences of Immigration* (Berkeley: University of California Press, 1994). Rebecca Morales and Paul M. Ong, "The Illusion of Progress," in Morales and Bonilla, eds., *Latinos*, 69–70.

62. Morales and Ong, "The Illusion of Progress," 64–77. Claudia Dorrington, "Central American Refugees in Los Angeles: Adjustment of Children and Families," in Ruth E. Zambrana, ed., *Understanding Latino Families: Scholarship, Policy, and Practice* (Thousand Oaks, CA: Sage, 1995), 111. Claire Spiegel, "Prenatal Care in L.A. Worsening, Report Concludes," *Los Angeles Times* (July 12, 1988). Jill L. Sherer. "Neighbor to Neighbor: Community Health Workers Educate Their Own," *Hospitals & Health Networks* 68, no. 20 (October 20, 1994): 52. Leo R. Chaves, Estebán T. Flores, and Márta López-Garza, "Undocumented Latin American Immigrants and U.S. Health Services: An Approach to a Political Economy of Utilization," *Medical Anthropology Quarterly* 6, no. 1 (March 1, 1992): 6–26. David James Rose, "Coming Out, Standing Out: Hispanic American Gays and Lesbians," *Hispanic* (June 1994): 44ff.

63. Marita Hernandez, "Gloria Molina," *Los Angeles Times* (February 13, 1989). Virginia Escalante, Nancy Rivera, and Victor Valle, "Inside the World of Latinas," in *Southern California's Latino Community. A Series of Articles Reprinted from the Los Angeles Times* (Los Angeles, CA: Los Angeles Times, 1983), 82–91. Daniel M. Weintraub, "Remap Bills Are Vetoed by Wilson," *Los Angeles Times* (September 24, 1991). "Proposed Redistricting in Los Angeles County," *Los Angeles Times* (January 3, 1992). Frederick Muir, "Reapportionment Shuffles the Political Deck," *Los Angeles Times* (January 3, 1992). "Latino Voters in California," *Nuestro Tiempo* (April 30, 1992).

64. "World Politics and Current Affairs," *The Economist* (September 29, 1990). Madeleine May Kunin, "Give Everyone a Turn at the Game; Term Limits . . . " *Los Angeles Times* (September 13, 1991).

65. Britney Jeffrey, "Rangel, Irma Lerma," *Handbook of Texas Online* (http://www.tshaonline.org/handbook/online/articles/fra85), accessed December 5, 2013, Cynthia Orozco, "Mexican American Democrats," *Handbook of Texas Online*, http://www.tshaonline.org/handbook/online/articles/wmm02.

66. José Angel Gutiérrez and Rebecca E. Deen, "Chicanas in Texas Politics" (Occasional Paper No. 66, Julian Samora Research Institute, October 2000). Roberto R. Calderón, "Tejano Politics," *Handbook of Texas Online*, http://www.tshaonline.org/handbook/online/articles/TT/wmtkn.html. Guillermo X. García, "Texas Surpasses N.Y. as Second Most Populous State," *USA Today* (March 13, 2001).

67. Lee Drutman, "The Rise of the Political Donor Class," *Miller-McCune* (August 28, 2008), http://www.psmag.com/politics/the-rise-of-the-political-donor-class-4305 http://www.miller-mccune.com/politics/the-rise-of-the-political-donor-class-562.

68. Marie Claire Acosta, "The Democratization Process in Mexico: A Human Rights Issue," *Resist* (January 1991), 3–6. Bob Howard, "U.S. Latinos Speak up on Free Trade Accord," *Nuestro Tiempo* (November 7, 1991). "The U.S. and Mexico: A Close Look at Costs of Free Trade," *Business Week* (May 4, 1992), 22. Joel D. Nicholson, John Lust, Aljeandro Ardila Manzanera, and Javier Arroyo Rico, "Mexican-U.S. Attitudes Toward the NAFTA," *International Trade Journal* 8, no. 1 (1994): 93–115. Acuña, *Anything but Mexican*, 231–49.

69. North American Free Trade Agreement (NAFTA), Public Citizen, http://www.citizen.org/trade/nafta/. "1994—60 Minutes—Subcomandante Marcos," part#1 of 2, http://www.youtube.com/watch?v=AIi_88YoUFk. Denise Bedell, "Revisiting Nafta." *Global Finance*, 23, no. 3 (2009): 22–24. Garrett Zehr, "On NAFTA." *This*, 42, no. 2 (2008): 20–21.

70. David Agren, "Bishop Samuel Ruiz Garcia, 86, champion of indigenous, dies in Mexico," Catholic News Service, http://www.catholicnews.com/data/stories/cns/1100290.htm.

71. Denise Dresser, "A Painful Jolt for the Body Politics," *Los Angeles Times* (January 12, 1994). Juanita Darling, "With Chiapas Cease Fire, Political Fallout Begins," *Los Angeles Times* (January 14, 1994). Michael Lowy, "Sources and Resources of Zapatism," *Monthly Review* 49, no. 10 (March 1998): 1ff. Catherine Capellaro, "My Visit with the Bishop of Chiapas; Bishop Samuel Ruíz García; Interview," *Progressive* (November 1998), 26ff. J. C. Seymour, "Two-Hearted in Chiapas: After the Massacre; Relations between Indians of Chiapas, Mexico, and the Mexican Government," *Christian Century* (April 1, 1998), 333ff. James D. Cockcroft, *Mexico's Hope: An Encounter with Politics and History* (New York: Monthly Review Press, 1998), 221–22, 336. Andy Gutierrez, "Codifying the Past, Erasing the Future: NAFTA and the Zapatista Uprising of 1994," *West-Northwest Journal of Environmental Law & Policy* 14 (2008): 883–1703.

72. A History of Hispanic Achievement in America—Cesar Chavez, Cesar Chavez Foundation, http://www.chavezfoundation.org/_cms.php?mode=view&b_code=001013000000000&b_no=472&page=4&field=&key=&n=11.

73. Miriam J. Wells, *Strawberry Fields: Politics, Class, and Work in California Agriculture* (Ithaca, NY: Cornell University Press, 1996). David Bacon, "Fruits of Their Labor: In Steinbeck Country, the United Farm Workers Are Battling the Strawberry Growers in the Fields and in the Suites," *LA Weekly* (August 8, 1997).

74. Charles Nicodemus, "FBI Agents Get Training About Rights; Decree Ends 'Spying' Case Here," *Chicago Sun-Times* (December 15, 1997). The FBI admitted misconduct during its probe of CISPES, which sued the FBI in 1988. In March 1983, the FBI accepted unsubstantiated—later discredited—charges by an undercover informant who insisted that CISPES was providing financial support to Salvadoran terrorists. Court documents showed that the local FBI probe targeted dozens of Chicagoans through infiltration; analysis of phone, utility, and banking records; and other covert activities. "Olivares' Legacy," *Los Angeles Times* (March 1, 1994).

75. Little Central America LA—Pico Union/Salvadoran Culture, http://www.youtube.com/watch?v=ylAxy8xYXa0. Salvadoran Riots 1991 Mount Pleason [*sic*] Washington, D.C. Riots, http://www.youtube.com/watch?v=-gpjiUSRA38. José Cardenas, "State Official Tells Day Laborers How Laws Can Work for Them; Jobs: Exploitation All Too Common, Labor Commissioner José Millan Says in Outreach Program Held to Educate Workers," *Los Angeles Times* (June 30, 1998). Pamela Constable, "Central Americans Protest Uncertain Future Under Refugee Amnesty Program," *Washington Post* (October 23, 1994). Philip Pan, "Honorable Work or Illegal Activity? In Langley Park, It's 'Pupusa Ladies' vs. County Agencies, with Latino Officers Caught in Middle," *Washington Post* (August 24, 1997). Lisa Leff, "Sacrifice Through Separation; Salvadoran Women Grieve for Children They Left Behind," *Washington Post* (March 31, 1994). Making pupusas at Chicago's Pupuseria Las Delicias, http://www.youtube.com/watch?v=qe96acRppe0&feature=related. Ana Patricia Rodríguez, *Dividing the Isthmus: Central American Transnational Histories, Literatures, and Cultures* (Austin: University of Texas Press, 2009), 184–85.

76. CAUSA, http://www.csun.edu/cas/causa.html. CSUN Central American Studies, http://www.csun.edu/catalog/centralamericanstudies.html.

77. National Association for Chicana/o Studies, History of NACCS, http://www.naccs.org/naccs/History.asp. Gary M. Stern, "TRENDS: Minority Students Outnumber Whites," *Hispanic Outlook in Higher Education* 6, no. 8 (1995): 6.

78. Dennis López, "Chicano/Latino Coalition for Educational Equity & English Learners of the Inland Empire Practical Issues in Serving Undocumented Immigrant Students," Latino Educational Advocacy Day @ CSU San Bernardino, March 29, 2010. "Undocumented Immigrant Students: A Very Brief Overview of Access to Higher Education in California," http://tcla.gseis.ucla.edu/reportcard/features/5-6/ab540/pdf/UndocImmigStud.pdf.

79. George Ramos, "UCLA Cuts in *Chicano Studies* Hit Education: Protests Have Spread off Campus to Involve Latino Leaders . . . " *Los Angeles Times* (January 9, 1991), 1. Chancellor Young told LA Times editor Frank del Olmo that there would never be a department as long as he was chancellor.

80. Larry Gordon, "*UCLA* Resists Forming *Chicano* Studies Department," *Los Angeles Times* (April 29, 1993), B1.

81. Larry Gordon and Marina Dundjerski, "Protesters Attack UCLA Faculty Center Education: Up to $50,000 in Vandalism Follows the University's Refusal to Elevate *Chicano studies* Program to Departmental Status. Police Arrest 90," *Los Angeles Times* (May 12, 1993), 1. Larry Gordon and Marina Dundjerski, "UCLA Has 2nd Day of Protest over Program," *Los Angeles Times* (May 13, 1993), B1. "UCLA Students Demand Chicano Studies Department," *San Francisco Chronicle* (May 13, 1993), A7. "Reassessment, Please, in UCLA Controversy: Rethinking *Chicano studies* Issue in Wake of Protest," *Los Angeles Times* (May 13, 1993), 6. Rodolfo F. Acuña, *The Making of Chicana/o Studies: In the Trenches of Academe* (New Brunswick: Rutgers University Press, 2011), 179–187.

82. "Chicano Studies Activists Begin Hunger Strike at UCLA," *Los Angeles Times* (May 26, 1993), 4. Mary Anne Perez, "A Hunger for Change Protest: Students from the Central City Join the Fight for Chicano Studies Department . . . " *Los Angeles Times* (June 6, 1993). Raymundo Paredes, "Chicano Studies at UCLA: A Controversy with National Implications," *Hispanic Outlook in Higher Education* 2, no. 3 (November 30, 1991): 10.

83. "A hunger strike ends, a center is born," UCLA History Project, June 7, 1993, http://www.uclahistoryproject.ucla.edu/Fun/ThisMonth_JunTent.asp. Semillas Community Schools, Winter 2008, http://www.dignidad.org/index.php?option=com_content&view=article&id=81&Itemid=55. Acuña, *Anything but Mexican*, chap. 12. Robert A. Rhoads, "'Immigrants in Our Own Land': The Chicano Studies Movement at UCLA," in *Freedom's Web: Student Activism in an Age of Cultural Diversity* (Baltimore, MD: Johns Hopkins Press, 1998), 61–94, http://orion.neiu.edu/~tbarnett/102/race.htm. Marcos Aguilar and Minnie Fergusson interviewed by Rodolfo F. Acuña (August 12, 2009) in El Sereno, California. The César Chávez Center has since achieved full department status. Marcos and Minnie continue to work in the community. They are the founders and directors of the Semilla Charter School, which teaches indigenous cultures along with Spanish, Nahuatl, and Mandarin. Routinely they are libeled by KABC Radio and other right-wing forces.

84. Rodolfo F. Acuña, "Forty Years of Chicana/o Studies: When the Myth Becomes a Legend," http://forchicanachicanostudies.wikispaces.com/Chicana+Chicano+Studies.

85. El Centro de La Raza, Transcript: El Centro de la Raza, NOW, PBS, http://www.pbs.org/now/transcript/transcript_laraza.html. The History of Chicano Park, San Diego, California, http://www.chicanoparksandiego.com/. Mexican Art in the Pilsen District of Chicago, http://artpilsen.blogspot.com/. Harry Gamboa, Chicano Art, http://www.harrygamboajr.com/.

86. Emma Pérez, *The Decolonial Imaginary: Writing Chicanas into History* (Bloomington: Indiana University Press, July 1, 1999), 20. Emma Pérez, "Queering the Borderlands: The Challenges of Excavating the Invisible and Unheard," *Frontiers: A Journal of Women Studies* 24, nos. 2 & 3 (2003): 122–31.

87. About Cherríe Moraga, http://www.cherriemoraga.com/index.php?option=com_content&view=section&layout=blog&id=5&Itemid=53.

88. The title "the Great" is used sparingly, as in the case of La Gran Lola Beltrán.

89. Borderlands/LaFrontera, http://www.youtube.com/watch?v=c2jvSN_-JS4. Gloria Anzaldúa, *Borderlands/La Frontera, The New Mestiza*, 3d ed. (San Francisco, CA: Aunt Lute Books, 2007). Gloria Anzaldua, http://almalopez.com/projects/ChicanasLatinas/anzalduagloria5.html.

90. Who is Richard Mellon Scaife? http://www.youtube.com/watch?v=km_yDCfDNn0. Behind The Veil: America's Anti-Immigration Network, http://www.youtube.com/watch?v=qpiq1nAK4a0. Make Coors pay for funding racism! Defend Affirmative Action Defend the Victory in *Grutter v. Bollinger!* http://www.bamn.com/boycott-coors/. Codewords of Hate, http://www.youtube.com/watch?v=5kCpoXbCpqQ&feature=related. Stefancic and Delgado, *No Mercy*, name most of the early benefactors.

91. "A Look at the Forces Behind the Anti-Immigrant Movement," Democracy Now, http://www.democracynow.org/2007/5/2/a_look_at_the_forces_behind. Excerpt James Crawford, "Hispanophobia," Chapter 6, in *Hold Your Tongue: Bilingualism and the Politics of "English Only"* (Reading, MA: Addison Wesley, 1993), http://www.languagepolicy.net/archives/HYTCH6.htm. An important work in understanding the extent of the new-rights' financing of the "culture war" is Stefanic and Delgado's *No Mercy*. Alexander Cockburn, "In Honor of Charlatans and Racist," *Los Angeles Times* (November 3, 1994). Nina J. Easton, "Linking Low IQ to Race, Poverty Sparks Debate," *Los Angeles Times* (October 30, 1994). Richard Hernstein and Charles Murray, *The Bell Curve: Intelligence and Class Structure in American Life* (New York: Free Press, 1994).

92. Laura C. Scanlan, "Hopwood v. Texas: A Backward Look at Affirmative Action in Education," *New York University Law Review*, 71, no. 6 (1996): 1580–1633. Lawrence S. Wrightsman, *Judicial Decision Making: Is Psychology Relevant?* (Springer 1999), 29–30.

93. Wilson's Re-Election Ads on Illegal Immigration, http://www.youtube.com/watch?v=o0f1PE8Kzng&feature=related. Barbara Sellgren, "California's Proposition 187: A Painful History Repeats Itself," *U.C. Davis Journal of International Law & Policy*, 1 (1995): 153–331. Richard D. Lamm and Robert Hardway, "Pro 187 Opposition Has Origins in Racism," *Daily News* (November 22, 1994). Patrick J. McDonnell, "March Just 1st Step, Latino Leaders Vow," *Los Angeles Times* (June 4, 1994). Ed Mendel, "Voters Still Favor Pro 187 but Field Poll Finds Latinos Split on Issue," *San Diego Union-Tribune* (September 27, 1994). Paul Feldman, "Times Poll: Pro 187 Is Still Favored Almost 2 to 1," *Los Angeles Times* (October 15, 1994). Howard Breuer, "Voters Approve Pro 187, Lawsuits to Follow," *Los Angeles Daily News* (November 9, 1994). John Dart, "187 Shows Clergy's Weak Influence on Electorate," *Los Angeles Times* (November 19, 1994).

94. Acuña, *Sometimes There Is No Other Side,* chap. 1. Juan González, "In Washington, Latino Chorus Lifts Its Voice," *New York Daily News* (October 15, 1996). Amy Pyle, Patrick J. McDonnell, and Hector Tobar, "Latino Voter Participation Doubled Since '94 Primary," *Los Angeles Times* (June 4, 1998). Patrick J. McDonnell and George Ramos, "Latino Voters Had Key Role in Some States . . . ." *Dallas Morning News* (November 10, 1996). Linda O. Valenty and

Ronald D. Sylvia, "Thresholds for Tolerance: The Impact of Racial and Ethnic Population Composition on the Vote for California Propositions 187 and 209," *Social Science Journal* 41, no. 3 (2004): 433–46.

95. Pyle et al., "Latino Voter Participation." McDonnell and Ramos, "Latino Voters." Dave Lesher and Mark Z. Barabak, "Gubernatorial Hopefuls Hold Landmark Forum . . . ," *Los Angeles Times* (May 24, 1998). Jeffrey L. Rabin, "Elusive Univision Chairman Spreads Wealth Around in Gubernatorial Race," *Los Angeles Times* (March 2, 2001); the chair of Univision was A. Jerrold Perenchio, an Italian American. He donated $1.5 million to defeat 227. However, he also donated $1,040,000 in support of vouchers for private schools, and $425,000 to support school board members for the L.A. school districts who were on a slate supported by L.A.'s former Republican mayor, Richard Riordan. A Proposition 227 Story, http://www.youtube.com/watch?v=TQwKrz_6dRY.

96. Center for Latin American, Caribbean, and Latino Studies: Latino Population of the U.S. Data Bases, Census 2000, http://web.gc.cuny.edu/lastudies/census2000data/Latinodatabases.htm.

97. The Hispanic Population: Census 2000 Brief (May 2001), http://www.census.gov/prod/2001pubs/c2kbr01-3.pdf. "Latino-Origin Populations Revisited: Estimating the Latino-Origin Group Populations at the National Level and for Selected States, Counties, Cities, and Metro Chicago," Research Reports, Vol 2005.1, Inter-University Program for Latino Research, see http://latinostudies.nd.edu/publications/.

98. Diane G. Thomas, "Hispanic Voter Project at Johns Hopkins University," http://learningtogive.org/papers/paper242.html. Antonio Gonzalez, The Rise of the California Latino Vote, Willie Velasquez Institute, www.wcvi.org/data/election/PR_021108_CALatinoVote.doc.

99. Jodi Wilgoren, "California and the West; Sanchez Elated as Probe Is Dropped . . . ," *Los Angeles Times* (February 5, 1998). Roxanne Roberts, "House Mates Loretta and Linda Sanchez Are Congress's First Sister Act . . . ," *Washington Post* (December 11, 2002). Phil García, "Latino Voters Showing Strength," *Sacramento Bee* (November 14, 1996). Anthony York, "Latino Politics," *California Journal* (April 1, 1999). Hugo Martin, "Power of Polanco Evident in Alarcón's Victory . . . ," *Los Angeles Times* (June 22, 1998).

100. John P. Schmal, "The Tejano Struggle For Representation," Hispanics in Government, Houston Institute for Culture, http://www.houstonculture.org/hispanic/tejano4.html. R. G. Ratcliffe, "Congressional Fate in Hands of Court/Democratic Judge Has Until Oct. 1 to Rule on State Redistricting Plans," *Houston Chronicle* (September 23, 2001). Eduardo Porter, "Hispanics Seek Increased Representation, and Republicans are Very Eager to Help," *Wall Street Journal* (April 2, 2001).

101. Dane Schiller, "Castro Upholds Family's Involvement Tradition," *San Antonio Express-News* (May 6, 2001).

102. Illinois Hispanic Population as a Percentage of Total Population (2012), Illinois Hispanic Population as a Percentage of Total Population (2000). Pam Belluck, "Chicago Reverses 50 Years of Declining Population," *New York Times* (March 15, 2001).

103. Georgia Pabst, "La Raza Meeting to Draw 12,000," *Milwaukee Journal Sentinel* (July 8, 2001), 1B. Danielle Gordon and Natalie Pardo, "Hate Crimes Strike Changing Suburbs," *Chicago Reporter* (September 1997). Manuel Galvan, "Hispanics in Chicago from Central America Take First Steps to Political Empowerment," http://www.lib.niu.edu/1993/ii931134.html. Juan Andrade, "Latinos Must Beware of Redistricting," *Chicago Sun-Times* (January 4, 2002). Rick Pearson, "Latinos Seek More Power in Remap," *Chicago Tribune* (Internet Edition, July 25, 2001). "State Profile—Illinois" http://www.cnn.com/ALLPOLITICS/1996/states/IL/IL00.shtml. The Chicago Reporter, 2001 Back Issues, http://www.chicagoreporter.com/issue/index.php?y=2001. Nacho González, "Latino Politics in Chicago," *CENTRO: Journal of the Center for Puerto Rican Studies* 2, no. 5 (1990): 47–57. "Gentrification in West Town: Contested Ground," University of Illinois at Chicago, Nathalie Voorhees Center of Neighborhood and Community Improvement (September 2001), http://www.uic.edu/cuppa/voorheesctr/Publications/Gentrification%20in%20West%20Town%202001.pdf.

104. Jerry Garcia, "History of Latinos in the Northwest," https://www.k12.wa.us/CISL/pubdocs/HistoryLatinoPacificNorthwest.pdf. Nikole Hannah-Jones, "Oregon's 2010 Census Shows Striking Latino and Asian Gains," *The Oregonian* (February 23, 2011), http://www.oregonlive.com/pacific-northwest-news/index.ssf/2011/02/2010_census.html.

105. Washington County Selection Map, U.S. Census Bureau, http://quickfacts.census.gov/qfd/maps/washington_map.html.

106. Carlos Arnaldo Schwantes, *The Pacific Northwest: An Interpretive History*, Revised and Enlarged ed., (Lincoln: University of Nebraska Press, 1996), 6, 450. Gonzalo Guzmán, Wapato—Its History and Hispanic Heritage, HistoryLink.org 7937, September 16, 2006, http://www.historylink.org/index.cfm?DisplayPage=output.cfm&file_id=7937. Mexican Americans in the Columbia Basin, Washington State University, http://www.vancouver.wsu.edu/crbeha/ma/ma.htm. Chicano/Latino Archive, Evergreen State College Library, http://chicanolatino.evergreen.edu/introduction_en.php.

107. Florangela Davila, "Spanish Definitely Spoken Here: State's Hispanics Gain Numbers, Clout," *Seattle Times* (Online, March 26, 2001). U.S. Census Bureau, Grant County, Census 2000 PHC-T-10, Hispanic or Latino Origin for the United States, Regions, Divisions, States, and for Puerto Rico: 2000. Florangela Davila and Susan Gilmore, "Big Racial Gap Remains in State Homeownership," *Seattle Times* (Online, July 16, 2001). Stuart Eskenazi, Justin Mayo, and Tom Boyer, "Seattle Behind Other Cities When It Comes to Diversity," *Seattle Times* (Online, March 31, 2001). Steve Suo, "Oregon Surge Has Mexican Roots," *Oregonian* (Portland, May 10, 2001).

108. Oregon County Selection Map, http://quickfacts.census.gov/qfd/maps/oregon_map.html.

109. Latinos in Salem, http://www.salemhistory.net/people/latinos.htm. Modern Society in the Pacific Northwest: The Second World War as Turning Point, http://www.washington.edu/uwired/outreach/cspn/Website/Classroom%20Materials/Pacific%20Northwest%20History/Lessons/Lesson%2020/20.html. Oregon State University, Bracero Collection, http://library.state.or.us/repository/2008/200805231544055. Gosia Wozniacka, "Hispanic Surge Is Reshaping Oregon," *Oregonian* (May 13, 2009), OregonLive.com, http://www.oregonlive.com/washingtoncounty/index.ssf/2009/05/2008_census_estimates_hispanic.html. Robert Bussel, ed., *Understanding the Immigrant Experience in Oregon: Research, Analysis, and Recommendations from University of Oregon Scholars* (Eugene: University of Oregon, [No Year]), http://library.state.or.us/repository/2008/200805231544055/index.pdf. Lynn Stephen, "Globalization, the State, and the Creation of Flexible Indigenous Workers: Mixtec Farmworkers in Oregon," The Center for Comparative Immigration Studies, University of California, San Diego, Working Paper 36, April 2001, http://escholarship.org/uc/item/4wd691zw.

110. Idaho County Selection Map, http://quickfacts.census.gov/qfd/maps/idaho_map.html.

111. Errol D. Jones, Invisible People: Mexicans in Idaho history, http://web1.boisestate.edu/research/history/issuesonline/fall2005_issues/1f_mexicans.html. Mexicans figured in Idaho events of Frontier Days, Idaho Digital Resources, http://idahodocs.cdmhost.com/cdm/singleitem/collection/p4012coll2/id/103. Amando Alvarez, The Mexican Experience in Idaho, http://www.angelfire.com/journal2/luz/cuentos04.htm. Idaho History, Raices, http://raices2.obiki.org/approach/cluster_sites/idaho.html.

112. David Rosenzweig, "Judges Asked to Postpone Voting in 4 House Districts . . . ," *Los Angeles Times* (November 1, 2001). Thomas B. Edsall, "A Political Fight to Define the Future; Latinos at Odds over California's Two New Democratic Congressional Districts," *Washington Post* (October 31, 2001). Carl Ingram, "Davis OKs Redistricting That Keeps Status Quo . . . ," *Los Angeles Times* (September 28, 2001). Frank del Olmo, "Getting away with a Blatant Gerrymander for the Record," *Los Angeles Times* (June 16, 2002).

113. Ambika Kapur, "Encouraging the Latino Vote," *Carnegie Reporter* 1, no. 3 (Fall 2001): http://carnegie.org/publications/carnegie-reporter/single/view/article/item/38/. Richard Gonzales, "Where Are the Latino Office Holders?" *Fort Worth Star-Telegram* (December 9, 2001).

114. Stuart Eskenazi, "150 Years of Seattle History: Familiar Landscape Lured Scandinavians," *Seattle Times* (Online, November 4, 2001). Robin Fields and Ray Herndon, "Segregation of a New Sort Takes Shape; Census: In a Majority of Cities, Asians and Latinos Have Become More Isolated from Other Racial Groups," *Los Angeles Times* (July 5, 2001). Gordy Holt, "Hetle Again Spurns Shooting Review; But Bellevue Officer Meets Arbitrator on Another Matter," *Seattle Post-Intelligencer* (January 11, 2002).

115. T. Christian Miller, "Race Issues Raised in Latest Texas Death Penalty Appeal," *Los Angeles Times* (June 29, 2000).

116. Rakesh Kochhar, Roberto Suro, and Sonya Tafoya, "The New Latino South: The Context and Consequences of Rapid Population Growth," Pew Hispanic Center (July 26, 2005), http://pewhispanic.org/reports/report.php?ReportID=50. "U.S.-Born Hispanics Increasingly Drive Population Developments," Pew Hispanic Center, http://pewhispanic.org/files/factsheets/2.pdf.

Diversity in America - Third Edition

1

Perception and Reality

"Café Wall Illusion," a well-known visual illusion, depicts the difference between perception and reality. Things are not always as they appear to be. In this case, the horizontal lines are parallel to one another, even though they seem not to be, even after you know they are.

1

Emblazoned in virtually every individual's mind is the knowledge that the United States is a nation of immigrants. That realization—taught in our schools and reinforced in political speeches, particularly on the Fourth of July—serves as a source of nationalistic pride for all Americans, even those who trace their ancestry back to 17th-century colonists. The American Dream—that promise of freedom of choice, education, economic opportunity, upward mobility, and a better quality of life—inspires many to come here. It also serves as the underpinning for basic value orientations that are the foundation of American beliefs, behaviors, definitions of social goals, and life expectations.

Today, immigrants continue to arrive in pursuit of that dream, just as others have done for more than 200 years. Yet these newcomers frequently generate negative reactions among native-born Americans despite their common pride in belonging to a nation of immigrants. In all parts of the United States, we often find frequent expressions of fear, suspicion, anxiety, resentment, hostility, and even violence in response to the immigrant presence. Immigrants are not the only group triggering a backlash, however. African American and Native American assertiveness often provokes resistance. Challenges to the status quo by feminists and gay rights activists also regularly induce adverse responses.

Why this contradiction? If Americans value their nation's immigrant heritage and ideals of equality and opportunity, why do they begrudge those traveling the same path to the same destination? Answers come readily from the critics. It is different now. When earlier immigrants came, they learned the language, worked hard, and became Americanized. We are getting too many immigrants now. They take away jobs from Americans. They drain our tax dollars through health and welfare benefits and schooling for their children. They do not want to assimilate or even learn English, and therefore they present a threat of unraveling the fabric of our society. Too many people today are just lazy and want a handout. Too many want undeserved privileges at the expense of everyone else. They want the rewards without earning them.

At least partially fueling these everyday conversational complaints by the citizenry are provocative stories in the media or public pronouncements from reactionaries and immigrant-bashers. Sometimes, however, even respected scholars are in the forefront. Noted historian Arthur M. Schlesinger, Jr., for example, denounced "the cult of ethnicity" (an insistence on maintaining vibrant ethnic subcultures) as a forerunner to the imminent "balkanization" of U.S. society.[1] His reference to the hostility that led to intense violence among Bosnians, Croats, and Serbs in the Balkan Peninsula is a scary one. No one wants U.S. society disintegrating into a collectivity of groups hostile to one another. Nor do they want the "snuffing out" or "shipwreck" of the

American republic by new immigrants that Peter Brimelow, ironically himself an immigrant (from England), warned us about with apocalyptic rhetoric in *Alien Nation*.[2]

Minority actions also reinforce nativist perceptions. The rhetoric of leaders from the National Council of *La Raza* and from the League of United Latin American Citizens (LULAC) for the maintenance of Spanish language and culture at public expense, in both the schools and the workplace, demonstrates to native-born Americans an unwillingness to assimilate.[3] The insistence of some African American leaders for slavery reparation payments to all Blacks enrages many Whites as an unreasonable demand. The "clannish" retail shopping patterns of Asian Americans and their noninvolvement in community activities annoy many local residents and merchants. News reports about militant actions, public mayhem, street crimes, and mob violence all trigger other negative reactions against minorities.

Once we talked about the United States as a melting pot. Now there is something called multiculturalism, which Schlesinger and others fear is undermining the cohesiveness of U.S. society.

What is happening? Are such instances illustrations of a different pattern emerging than in previous generations? Are we witnesses to a new social phenomenon? Is a flood of immigrants who do not wish to integrate overwhelming us? Are they and the people of color born in the United States pursuing separatist paths that will lead to the disuniting of our society? Is the land of *e pluribus unum* ("from the many, one") therefore disintegrating into *e pluribus plures* ("from the many, many") right before our very eyes, as Diane Ravitch warned?[4]

What This Book Is All About

These questions and issues reflect real concerns. They require responses that are more than subjective impressions of the current scene, for what people may think is happening is not necessarily what is actually occurring. This book is an attempt to provide those responses.

The famed Roman orator Cicero once remarked, "Not to know what happened before we were born is to remain perpetually a child." Just as children gaze with wonderment on new sights, so too can adults react to social phenomena as new and different unless they recognize these phenomena as variations of past patterns. It is my contention that the perception of many Americans is tainted because (a) they lack an accurate understanding of past U.S. diversity, and (b) they fail to view contemporary events in a larger context.

As mentioned in the Preface, this book is about race and ethnicity in the United States and the interaction of gender relations within that context. As such, it does not include other aspects of diversity (aged, disabled, and gays) found in other books on the subject. The book's origins trace back to my replies to the many concerned (and similar) questions asked of me during a U.S. State Department–sponsored lecture tour in 1993 throughout Canada and Western Europe. Just as Alexis de Tocqueville attempted to explain our form of government in *Democracy in America* in the 1830s, I have sought to explain our diversity—past, present, and future—in this book, deliberately titled *Diversity in America,* in homage to Tocqueville, although some may criticize my use of *America* because there are other Americas in the Western Hemisphere.

A central thesis of this book is that multiculturalism has always been part of the U.S. scene and is no more a threat to the cohesiveness of society today than at any time in the past. Rejecting claims that modern circumstances create a different situation than in the past, this book shows parallels, similarities, and continuities. It also shows instances when U.S. society was actually more multicultural than today.

Another central tenet of the book is that assimilation and pluralism are not mutually exclusive entities, nor are they necessarily enemies of one another. They have always existed simultaneously among different groups at different levels. Whether they are persistent or multigenerational convergent subcultures, culturally distinct groups have always existed. Even when their numbers have been great, they never threatened the core culture. Assimilation remains a powerful force affecting most ethnic groups, although it has been less effective in enabling racial minorities to achieve full integration. Proponents of one position may decry the other, but both pluralism and assimilation have always been dual realities within U.S. society.

The idea behind this book, then, is to place the current debate on immigration and multiculturalism in a proper sociohistorical perspective. Within a sociological context of social patterns and social change, the historical record of past and present cultural diversity in the United States is presented. Included are factors such as economic conditions, elitism, nativism, racism, social class biases, and the struggle for power that mitigate against harmonious intergroup relations.

The first half of this book contains a brief portrait of U.S. diversity through five eras: Colonial, Early National, Growth and Change, Industrial, and Information Ages. These chapters outline how cultural diversity has always been characteristic of U.S. society. They also show the continuity of various social patterns from one era to the next, down to the present.

Women, of course, have constantly been an integral part of the U.S. experience, although their efforts often received little public attention until recent decades. Partly to compensate for that neglect, the period portraits in the following chapters include information about women during these times. My intent is to emphasize more fully their gender experiences of status, power, and influence within a sociohistorical framework as a prelude to understanding today's feminism.

In these discussions of women, you will learn how women's experiences varied greatly depending on their locale, social class, and length of residency in the United States. Indicators of how they fared compared to men delineate gender diversity in terms of rights and power. Explanations about women's social activism also show a parallel to the militancy of other minority groups seeking equal treatment.

Seeing Is Believing, but Is It Knowing?

Some people believe what they see, but appearances can be deceptive, as are optical illusions or mirages. Magicians are human illusionists, and the good ones can stupefy us with their artful tricks on a grand scale. We know they tricked us, but we don't know how.

In everyday life, we think we know what we see, but here, too, we may be deceived. As Peter Berger once observed, "The first wisdom of sociology is this—things are not what they seem."[5] He was suggesting that social reality has many layers of meaning, and as you discover one layer, your perspective of the whole changes. So, perceptions about diversity or anything else change with increased knowledge. Seeing is not enough. You need to know what it is that you are seeing.

To understand how people could mistakenly accept a reality as natural or obvious requires an understanding of *social constructionism*. The major focus of this perspective is that an individual's views form through social interaction, interpersonal communication, and cultural influences. What emerges is a perceived reality, one that societal members have created and institutionalized into a shared tradition and understanding. Like the perceived reality presented to us by the illusionist, another social reality of the past or present may possibly exist "out there" independent of the cultural view that dominates people's interpretation and acceptance. However, the only reality that matters to societal members is the one on which they agree. This social construction of reality thus serves as the basis for their approval or criticism, acceptance or rejection of events and/or groups that complement or run counter to the "facts" as they see them.

Another dimension exists that may affect whether what we believe from what we see is actually what we truly understand. Complementary to Berger's statement is the aphorism, "You can't see the forest for the trees." Its message is clear. When you are too close to the situation, you can't see the entire picture. You can't get a sense of the whole because you are caught up in the small details. It is necessary to find a detached viewpoint if you are to comprehend what you see. (Later in this chapter, we discuss the reverse problem of perception and reality, that believing is seeing.)

That detached viewpoint can be found in the sociological perspective, which provides, says Berger, "a special form of consciousness" (p. 23). It enables us to focus objectively on aspects of our social environment that may have previously escaped our notice, allowing us to interpret them in a different, meaningful way. If we add a historical frame of reference along with a sociological analysis to our study of diversity, we gain a valuable dimension to observe what continuities and changes are occurring.

The Cultural Homogeneity Myth

Diversity has been an ongoing social reality in the United States, not just since its inception as a nation, but even in its primeval colonial cradle. This viewpoint is not the prevalent one. The prevailing belief that this nation was essentially a culturally homogeneous launching pad for the new nation is steeped in the historic myth that the 13 colonies were almost entirely populated by English immigrants and their descendants. Such was not quite the case. As we see shortly, this "historic reality"—this fallacy of cultural homogeneity—changes under careful sociohistorical analysis.

That we are a nation of immigrants is an undeniable fact, but often not connected to the current multicultural picture. Contemporary public views on multiculturalism often assume erroneously that what occurred in the past were fleeting moments of heterogeneity that yielded to fairly rapid assimilation. Today's cultural diversity is misperceived as different, more widespread, and resistant to assimilation—something to be celebrated, respected, and maintained, say its proponents—thus making it, in the eyes of alarmed others, not only a new construction, but somehow also a threat to the cohesiveness of society.

Only an objective analysis that peels away layers of myths, assumptions, presumptions, and misconceptions can provide an accurate assessment. To do so, we must take a sociohistorical perspective, moving beyond only present-day realities and noting instead long-term patterns throughout the nation's history. In this way, we can put the current scene in a wider context and determine more precisely how unique our situation is.

Before we can embark on this examination of our past and present, however, we must first address three areas that affect judgments about diversity in the United States. The first of these is the changing views about minority adaptation to U.S. society. The second is the melting pot concept and its limitations of application. The last, but an extremely important area, is the Dillingham Flaw, in which perceptions about immigrants can be misdirected through faulty comparisons.

The Rise, Fall, and Rise of Pluralism

Because the term is of recent vintage, many incorrectly conclude that *multiculturalism* is therefore a fairly new social phenomenon, the product of a changing world and of changing government policies. But as Nathan Glazer (1993) and Peter Rose (1993) correctly assert, *multiculturalism* is actually a refashioning of an older concept of cultural pluralism.[6]

Early Advocates

In the early 20th century, educator John Dewey and social worker Jane Addams both spoke out against assimilation destroying the cultural values of immigrants. In 1915, Horace Kallen, an immigrant from Eastern Europe, advocated this ideology in an essay in *Nation;* by citing the persistence of cultural identity among the Irish in Massachusetts, Norwegians in Minnesota, and Germans in Wisconsin, he promoted a multicultural society, a confederation of national cultures.[7] As Peter Rose puts it:

> To Kallen . . . the United States was not a fondue of amalgamation but a symphony of accommodation. Pushing his own metaphor, Kallen saw the orchestra—that is, the Society—as consisting of groups of instruments—nationalities—playing their separate parts while together making beautiful music resonant with harmony and good feeling.[8]

Kallen's ideas, expanded in his seminal work on cultural pluralism, *Culture and Democracy in the United States* (1924), contained only incidental references to racial groups.[9] Foreshadowing today's opponents to multiculturalism, part of Kallen's focus was on public concern that the recent arrivals of his time might not integrate fully into society.

Assimilationists Prevail

Despite the pluralist advocates, a chain of events encouraged assimilation over ethnic persistence. Patriotic hysteria following U.S. entrance into World War I effectively ended the German subculture. Restrictive immigration laws in the 1920s, a world depression in the 1930s, and World War II in the 1940s dramatically reduced immigration. With little new blood to keep everyday ethnicity viable, with the second generation growing up as Americans, and with the housing and education entitlements offered to GIs, White ethnics by mid-century had moved closer to the center, loosening their ethnic ties as they did.

As the old idea of America as a melting pot seemed to reaffirm itself, major books by sociologists Robert E. Park[10] and Milton M. Gordon[11] influenced social scientists to think more about assimilation than pluralism.

In *Race and Culture* (1950), Park offered a universal cycle theory suggesting that all groups go through a progressive, irreversible process of contact, competition, accommodation, and eventual assimilation. Park acknowledged that the process might take centuries, possibly even including a semipermanent racial caste system, but ultimately even racially subordinate groups would assimilate.

Gordon delineated, in *Assimilation in American Life* (1964), seven processes of group adaptation to the host society. Most important was his distinction between cultural and structural assimilation, showing how a group can change its cultural patterns but not yet mainstream into primary relationships in the cliques and associations of the society.

The Reassertion of Pluralism

Just as a series of social changes enabled assimilationists to prevail over the pluralists, a new set of circumstances reversed the situation. The civil rights movement of the 1960s and the White ethnic revival of the 1970s were precipitating factors. However, a major element was the third wave of immigration that began after the 1965 immigration law removed national quota restrictions, opening the door to millions of developing world immigrants.

Pluralism flourished at a time of peak immigration to the United States and ebbed when immigration declined. With a new influx of culturally distinct immigrants, it flowered again. Renamed multiculturalism, its advocacy of the preservation and appreciation of ethnic cultures and identities, as well as peaceful coexistence among groups, echoed the sentiments of Kallen, Addams, Dewey, and other cultural pluralists.

This time, however, the movement included people of color, not just White ethnics. Some arrived with a strong background that empowered them economically, allowing them to organize more effectively and assert themselves more so than past immigrants. Their ranks included educated, articulate spokespersons who used TV and computerized direct mailings to reach millions of potential members whom their predecessors could not.

Yet even as pluralism gained new advocates, another influential socio-logical voice reaffirmed assimilationist patterns. In *The Ethnic Myth* (1981), Stephen Steinberg argued that pluralism only appeals to groups that benefit from maintaining ethnic boundaries.[12] Disadvantaged groups, he main-tained, willingly compromise their ethnicity to gain economic security and social acceptance. Moreover, he claimed, the United States was closer than ever before to welding a national identity out of its mélange of ethnic groups.

The Multiculturalist Challenge

Nevertheless, with minority group assertiveness, massive immigration, and bilingual/pluralist government policies, the change in popular usage from *cultural pluralism* to *multiculturalism* helped suggest to some that a new era for social consciousness of diversity had arrived. To others, it signaled that the disuniting of America through "ethnic tribalism" was upon us. The bat-tle was joined and still continues.

Multiculturalism is especially strong on college campuses, where the ranks of multiculturalists include many college professors whose advocacy in their teaching and publications has spread the doctrine far and wide to millions of others. They have challenged the once-prevailing idea of the United States as a melting pot, a concept many social scientists now regard as an idealized myth.

The Melting Pot

In an often-quoted passage in *Letters from an American Farmer* (1782), Michel Guillaume Jean de Crèvecoeur, an immigrant to the United States from France, defined an American and popularized the concept of America as a melting pot:

> What is an American? He is either a European, or the descendant of a European; hence that strange mixture of blood which you will find in no other country. I could point out to you a man whose grandfather was an English-man, whose wife was Dutch, whose son married a French woman, and whose present four sons have now four wives of different nations. . . . Here individu-als of all nations are melted into a new race of men, whose labors and poster-ity will one day cause great changes in the world.[13]

Overstating Ethnic Intermarriages

Even if Crèvecoeur actually knew of such an exogamous family and did not invent it to illustrate his idealized concept of a melting pot, he was not accurately portraying the reality of his times. His would have been an atypical family in the late 18th century because most White ethnics then did not intermarry. In-group solidarity—based on nationality, clustering, geographic separatism, and most especially religion—mitigated against personal social interaction among the distinct groups, let alone intermarriage.

When Crèvecoeur spoke of those English, Dutch, and French intermarriages, he was covering a considerable span of the 18th century and most likely including several religious faiths in a time when religious ecumenicism was unknown. Religious tolerance may have slowly evolved out of a period of bigotry, close-mindedness, and intolerance just a few generations before, but that hardly meant that the ethnocentric barriers had vanished and amalgamation was flourishing.

No Racial Minorities

The greatest problem with Crèvecoeur's melting pot model is his omission of African and Native Americans.[14] Was this omission a reflection of his ethnocentrism or a deliberate choice to augment his concept? Surely he was aware of their presence in significant numbers throughout the colonies. Perhaps he thought they were not relevant to the destiny of a nation struggling to be born.

Many shared this attitude. The framers of the Constitution, in Article I, Section 2, excluded "Indians" and counted each slave as three fifths of a person to determine a state's representatives. In 1790, the First Congress passed the Naturalization Law, which limited citizenship only to free White aliens. Until passage of the Fourteenth Amendment in 1868, people of color born in the United States were not citizens.

Crèvecoeur's melting pot model was not accurate for several reasons. By restricting its application only to those with political power (Whites), it excluded a sizable segment of the population (people of color). Thus, it did not describe a society that had "melted." Moreover, even in its narrow focus on Whites, the model ignored the existing cultural diversity and social distance existing among the diverse White groups.

Emerson's Vision

Crèvecoeur influenced others who helped popularize the image of the United States as a melting pot. Ralph Waldo Emerson, for example, struck a similar theme in 1845:

> Well, as in the old burning of the Temple at Corinth, by the melting and intermixture of silver and gold and other metals, a new compound more precious

than any, called Corinthian brass, was formed; so in this continent—asylum of all nations—the energy of Irish, Swedes, Poles, and Cossacks, and all the European tribes—of the Africans, and of the Polynesians, will construct a new race, a new religion, a new state, a new literature, which will be as vigorous as the new Europe which came out of the smelting-pot of the Dark Ages, or that which earlier emerged from Pelasgic and Etruscan barbarism.[15]

Emerson's private journal entry is interesting for several reasons. He "hated" the "narrowness" of nativist reactions against immigrants as "precisely the opposite of true wisdom." Significantly, he included people of color (but not Native Americans) in his vision of an amalgamated society, and it was a vision of the future, not a pretense about his times or of Crèvecoeur's time 63 years earlier. For Emerson, America as a melting or smelting pot was a tomorrow to come, not a reality that was.

Turner's Frontier

In contrast, Frederick Jackson Turner saw the American frontier as the catalyst that had already fused the immigrants into a composite new national stock. His frontier thesis of 1893 followed the 1890 declaration of the Census Bureau that the "unsettled area has been so broken into . . . that there can hardly be said to be a frontier line."[16] Unlike Emerson's private musings known only to a few, Turner's update of Crèvecoeur's melting pot greatly influenced historical scholarship for more than 40 years.

Thus, the Middle West was teaching the lesson of national cross-fertilization instead of national enmities, the possibility of a newer and richer civilization, not by preserving unmodified or isolating the old component elements, but by breaking down the line fences, by merging the individual life in the common product—a new product that held the promise of world brotherhood.[17]

The previous quotation is taken from Turner's 1920 book, *The Frontier in American History,* where he expanded on his 1893 essay. He argued that, because pioneers confronted many problems and harsh conditions, their adaptation necessitated innovative solutions that they shared with others. Out of this mutual assistance evolved a new and distinct culture, a blend of shared cultural contributions, but noticeably different from any of their source cultures.

Turner's argument popularized further the romanticized notion of a melting pot, but it also did not accurately reflect frontier reality any more than Crèvecoeur had depicted his times. The pioneers did adapt to their new environment, but the culture remained Anglo-American in form and content.

Furthermore, in many areas of the Middle West that Turner speaks about, culturally homogeneous settlements of Germans or Scandinavians, for example, often maintained distinct ethnic subcultures for generations.

Zangwill's White Fusion

Another voice raised in support of the melting pot was Israel Zangwill in a 1908 play appropriately called *The Melting Pot.* Some of its oft-quoted lines are these:

> Ah, what a stirring and a seething—Celt and Latin, Slav and Teuton, Greek and Syrian. America is God's Crucible, the Great Melting Pot where all the races of Europe are melting and reforming!

> ... Germans and Frenchmen, Irishmen and English, Jews and Russians, into the Crucible with you all! God is making the American!

> ... the Real American has not yet arrived. . . . He will be the fusion of all races, perhaps the coming superman.[18]

The term *race* once referred more loosely to either racial or ethnic groups. So, Zangwill appears to mean only White ethnic groups in the melting or fusion of all races when he speaks of the "races of Europe" and excludes any specific example of people of color. Although he curiously includes Syrians as Europeans, Zangwill's words nonetheless echo those of Crèvecoeur in describing the melting pot as a White ethnic phenomenon, thereby implying that an American is a White person.

In this book, we use the contemporary applications of race and ethnicity. A *racial group,* therefore, is one in which its members share visible biological characteristics and regard themselves or are regarded by others as a single group on that basis. An *ethnic group* is one in which its members share a common culture, language, nationality, and/or religion. Of course, members of a racial group are also members of an ethnic group, and vice versa. What clouds this distinction, however, is that members of the same racial group can be members of different ethnic groups (e.g., Black Americans, Haitians, Jamaicans, and Nigerians), and members of one ethnic group can be members of different racial groups (i.e., Hispanic Blacks, Whites, and mulattos).

Recent Studies on Intermarriage

The White ethnic intermarriage that Crèvecoeur prematurely asserted as evidence of his melting pot is now a reality. Alba (1991) reported that only half as many third-generation Italians of unmixed ancestry born after 1949 had spouses of unmixed Italian ancestry, compared with third-generation Italian males born before 1920.[19] Lieberson and Waters (1988) found significant declines in endogamous marriages among virtually all White groups.[20] In Census 2000, 58 percent of the U.S. population identified only one ancestry.

Although such intermarriage patterns provide support for melting pot proponents, they do not necessarily indicate assimilation. As Lisa Neidert and Reynolds Farley (1985) reported, third-generation members of second-wave ethnic groups were not indistinguishable from the core English group, although they had been successful in their occupational achievements.[21] That is, they remained distinct, and a considerable social distance existed between them and mainstream society. Furthermore, within-group marriages are still fairly common among people of unmixed ethnic ancestry.

When race and culture are similar, marital assimilation is more likely. If the past patterns of 19th- and 20th-century White Americans are an indicator, however, this process may require three or more generations to blend together the post-1965 ethnic groups.

The Dillingham Flaw

The continuing debate between assimilationists and pluralists revolves around the issue of cultural homogeneity. Part of those polemics often contain what I identify as the *Dillingham Flaw,* an erroneous way of comparing people from one time period with people living in the present. As a consequence, one group usually suffers in the comparison and is judged negatively.

The Dillingham Commission

Senator William P. Dillingham of Vermont chaired the House–Senate Commission on Immigration (1907–1911), which listened to the testimony of civic leaders, educators, social scientists, and social workers. It even made on-site visits to Ellis Island and New York's Lower East Side, where hundreds of thousands of impoverished immigrants lived. When its investigation was completed, the Commission issued a 41-volume report, part of which was based on social science research and statistics.

Unfortunately, the report was flawed in its application and interpretation of the data. It was more than the fact that the Commission members, however well intentioned they may have been, reflected the perceptions and biases of their times. The Dillingham Commission committed several errors of judgment that led them to conclude that the immigration from southern, central, and eastern Europe was detrimental to U.S. society. Their conclusion led them to recommend the enactment of immigration restrictions.

The Commission erred in its use of simplistic categories and unfair comparisons of the "old" and "new" immigrants, thus ignoring differences of technological evolution in their countries of origin. It also erred in overlooking the longer time interval that immigrants from northern and western Europe had to adjust, as well as the changed structural conditions wrought by industrialization and urbanization.

No doubt influencing the Commission members were the highly reported intelligence test findings. By 1908, Alfred Binet and Thomas Simon had developed the intelligence quotient (IQ) measurement scale. Using an alpha test (for those literate in English) and a beta test (for those illiterate or non-English-speaking), the low scores of newly arriving southern, central, and eastern Europeans, in contrast to higher scores by native-born Black and White Americans, seemingly gave "scientific evidence" that mentally deficient ethnic groups were entering the United States.

Although many social scientists today recognize that cultural biases affected those outcomes, controversy continues about whether intelligence measures reveal genetic or environmental differences. This "nature versus nurture" issue boiled over in the 1960s with the writings of Arthur Jensen and William Shockley, and again in 1994 with the publication of *The Bell Curve* by Richard Herrnstein and Charles Murray. Each of these writers argued that genetic differences existed between Black and White Americans, a point fiercely contested by many others.

Back in 1911, however, these test results were unquestioned and were just one more aspect to convince Commission members about the rightness of their views. The social conditions in 1911 help explain how such flawed conclusions were accepted so easily. President Theodore Roosevelt had called for the Commission to address the "immigrant problem," thereby creating a mind-set about the situation in the first place. Both he and the Commission reflected the biases and perceptions of most native-born Americans witnessing the unprecedented mass influx of immigrants who were culturally, and often physically, different. The Commission's findings reinforced public opinion and were therefore readily accepted.

The Concept of the Dillingham Flaw

In our society, similar errors of thinking also influence people's perceptions of outgroup members. An *outgroup* is any group with which an individual does not identify or belong. In our discussion, we are referring to the foreign born as the outgroup to native-born Americans of different backgrounds.

Because some of today's negative judgments flow from the same faulty logic as that of the Dillingham Commission, I call this weakness the *Dillingham Flaw*. Quite simply, this term refers to inaccurate comparisons based on simplistic categorizations and anachronistic observations. We make these comparisons when we apply modern classifications or sensibilities to a time when they did not exist, or, if they did, they had a different form or meaning. To avoid the Dillingham Flaw, we must avoid the use of modern perceptions to explain a past that its contemporaries viewed quite differently.

One example of an inappropriate modern classification would be the term *British* to describe colonial Americans from the British Isles. Today, this word refers collectively to the people of Great Britain (the English, Welsh, Scots, and Scots-Irish). However, in the 18th century, *British* had the much narrower meaning of only the English and for good reason. The English, Scots, and Scots-Irish may have been English-speaking, but significant cultural and religious differences existed among them. Moreover, the geographic segregation, social distance, and even hostility that existed between English Anglicans and Scots-Irish Presbyterians created a wide cultural gulf between them. They did not view each other as similar. Among the English, divergent religious beliefs created various subcultures whose shared sense of identity, social insulation, and endogamy resulted in limited social interaction. *Ecumenicism,* the tendency toward greater Christian unity that is occurring in our times, is a far cry from the antipathy among the Protestant sects of colonial America.

Religion, a meaningful component of everyday life in the 18th century, was cause for outgroup prejudice and avoidance, and we must not overlook its significant impact on intergroup relations. It would be a mistake to presume that the English were a single, cohesive entity.

It also is misleading to speak broadly of either African slaves or Native Americans as single entities. In a period of White dominance and racial exploitation, ethnocentric generalizations such as these failed to pay heed to the fact that these groups consisted of diverse peoples with distinctive cultures. Similarly, European immigrants were not alike despite their collective grouping by mainstream society. Instead, all of these groups—African American, Native American, and immigrant—were diverse peoples with linguistic and cultural distinctions that set them apart from one another.

The Dillingham Flaw Chain Reaction

Once someone falls victim to the Dillingham Flaw, other misconceptions usually follow about one's own time. This phenomenon is to be expected.

Such victims falsely believe that they understand their nation's past and so confidently assess their own world in what they presume is a wider context. Certain that they have a knowledgeable, objective frame of reference, they tend to be highly critical of the present scene because they perceive it as different from the past.

However, because their observations and reactions are predicated on a reference point rendered inaccurate by the Dillingham Flaw, they are more likely to reach incorrect conclusions. Like that old congressional commission, they are susceptible to mistaken impressions about a threat posed by recent immigrants whose presence and behavior they view as different from past immigrants.

For instance, some people suggest that today's steadily increasing ranks of Asians, Hispanics, and Muslims present an unprecedented challenge to an integrative society. The undercurrent of this thinking includes the continuing large numbers of new arrivals, their racial group membership and/or non-Judeo-Christian background, and their alleged nonassimilationist patterns.

Such concerns and fears are echoes of those raised about earlier groups, such as the racist responses to the physical appearance of southern Europeans or the anti-Semitic reactions to eastern European Jews. Or, consider the petition to Congress by 19th-century Germans in the Northwest Territory to create a German state with German as the official language; it easily matches the fear of some nativists that Florida may become "America's Quebec."

Believing Is Seeing

In writing about the improper use of biology as ideology to justify the naturalness of gendered behavior and social statuses, Judith Lorber (1993) informed us that the way we think about a particular social phenomenon affects what we actually see or at least what we think we see.[22] The actions of the Dillingham Commission and the politics of those times are another illustration of this concept. When we feel most threatened by outsiders who are different because of their religion, skin color, or social class, we may see different things in the current immigration (they are a threat because there are too many of them and/or they "fail" to assimilate) rather than see other things (ourselves, our ancestors, past generations of immigrants, new workers, new consumers, new taxpayers, human capital to fuel our economic growth).

In other words, the two major themes of this book are interconnected. The political controversies swirling around the assimilation/pluralism debates affect how people think about and react to diversity in society at any given time. Thus, the influence of beliefs on perceptions and reactions is an important element in understanding why some groups or issues become problematic and others do not.

The Boundary Flaw

With the oldest democratic constitution among all nations and its centuries-old experience of accepting tens of millions of immigrants from all parts of this planet, the United States certainly offers a rich reservoir of history, social change, and patterns of intergroup relations. Furthermore, it was the first to offer the promise of freedom and opportunity to one and all while showing the rest of the world its willingness to accept and include foreigners within its societal mainstream. Yet, however special many of these elements may have been, they did not occur in a global vacuum. A second flaw we must thus avoid is the *boundary flaw,* the assumption that we can explain everything solely in the context of internal social dynamics unique to U.S. culture.[23]

Virtually nothing has ever occurred in the United States that was self-contained or universal within its borders. In the early stages of its sociocultural evolution, when it was a minor player on the world stage and there was no such entity yet as a global community, regional—even local—cultural differences abounded. In the sociocultural epochs described in the next six chapters, the United States went through changing positions in the world order even as it was buffeted by external social forces that affected its citizens' sense of self and perceptions of demographic and technological changes.

This interplay of regional, national, and global forces often generated tensions as sociocultural changes occurred and new migration patterns emerged. Part of the explanation for the dualities of, and conflicts between, assimilation and pluralism trends lies in recognizing this process.

In each of the following chapters, then, we attempt to identify the place of the United States in the world system as a key referent to understanding more fully the developing themes of this book.

Understanding Today by Knowing About Yesterday

Understanding the past sociohistorical reality of U.S. diversity allows for a more accurate comparison with today's multicultural society without falling victim to either the Dillingham Flaw or the Boundary Flaw.

In this way, we can avoid those flaws and debunk the cultural homogeneity myth. It is essential to know truly what we were if we are to comprehend what we are now and what we are becoming.

Telecommunications today enable each of us to bear witness to many aspects of our multicultural society, but our knowledge about our nation's past comes to us chiefly through the words of others whose ethnocentric perceptions often hid from us what truly was that reality. Although rarely presented in the comprehensive form found in this book, enough data exist to peel away the layers of nationalist myth-building to get at the sociocultural actualities about our multicultural past.

What follows is not an exercise in revisionist thought, but a sociohistorical analysis of the past and present. Hopefully, this book provides the perspective that diversity is the nation's strength, not its weakness.

Notes

1. Arthur M. Schlesinger, Jr., *The Disuniting of America: Reflections on a Multicultural Society* (Knoxville, TN: Whittle Communications, 1991).

2. Peter Brimelow, *Alien Nation: Common Sense About America's Immigration Disaster* (New York: Random House, 1995).

3. Hispanic leaders' views on language maintenance appear in Linda Chavez, "Hispanics vs. Their Leaders," *Commentary* (October 1991): 47–9.

4. Diane Ravitch's much-discussed views appeared in her article "Multiculturalism: E Pluribus Plures," *American Scholar*, 59 (1990): 337–54.

5. Peter Berger's thoughts are expressed in his wonderful sociological primer, *Invitation to Sociology* (Garden City, NY: Doubleday, 1963), 23. Another classic on perception and reality is Peter L. Berger and Thomas Luckmann, *The Social Construction of Reality* (New York: Doubleday, 1966).

6. The comparison of multiculturalism and cultural pluralism by Nathan Glazer and Peter Rose appeared in the special issue edited by Peter I. Rose, "Interminority Affairs in the U.S.: Pluralism at the Crossroads," *The Annals of the American Academy of Political and Social Science, 530* (1993). The two articles are Nathan Glazer, "Is Assimilation Dead?" 122–36; Peter I. Rose, "Of Every Hue and Caste," 187–202.

7. Horace Kallen, "Democracy versus the Melting Pot," *Nation*, February 18, 1915, pp. 190–4, and February 25, 1915, pp. 217–20.

8. Peter Rose, "Of Every Hue and Caste," *The Annals of the American Academy of Political and Social Science, 530* (1993): 193.

9. Horace Kallen, *Culture and Democracy in the United States* (New York: Boni & Liveright, 1924).

10. The posthumous publication of Robert E. Park's writings is *Race and Culture: Essays in the Sociology of Contemporary Man* (New York: The Free Press, 1950).

11. Milton Gordon's seminal work on assimilation is *Assimilation in American Life* (New York: Oxford University Press, 1964).

12. Stephen Steinberg, *The Ethnic Myth* (New York: Atheneum, 1981).

13. Crèvecoeur's famous statement appears in *Letters from an American Farmer* (1782; reprint, New York: Alert and Charles Boni, 1925), 54–5.

14. Observations about Crèvecoeur's omission of racial minorities first appeared in Vincent N. Parrillo, *Strangers to These Shores* (Boston: Houghton Mifflin, 1980), 98, and then in all subsequent editions; Nathan Glazer's "Is Assimilation Dead?" *The Annals of the American Academy of Political and Social Science, 530* (1993): 124.

15. Emerson's recorded thoughts appear in *The Journals and Miscellaneous Notebooks of Ralph Waldo Emerson*, eds. Ralph H. Orth and Alfred K. Ferguson (Cambridge, MA: Belknap, 1971), 9:299–300.

16. James A. Henretta et al., *America's History Since 1865* (Homewood, IL: Dorsey Press, 1987), 588.

17. Frederick Jackson Turner, *The Frontier in American History* (New York: Henry Holt, 1920), chap. xiii.

18. Israel Zangwill, *The Melting Pot: Drama in Four Acts* (New York: Macmillan, 1921), 33.

19. The intermarriage findings of Richard D. Alba are reported in "The Twilight of Ethnicity Among Americans of European Ancestry: The Case of the Italians," *Rethinking Today's Minorities*, ed. Vincent N. Parrillo (Westport, CT: Greenwood Press, 1991), 29–62.

20. The study by Stanley Lieberson and Mary C. Waters is *From Many Strands* (New York: Russell Sage Foundation, 1988).

21. Lisa Neidert and Reynolds Farley, "Assimilation in the United States: An Analysis of Ethnic and Generation Differences in Status and Achievement," *American Sociological Review, 50* (1985): 840–50.

22. Judith Lorber, "Believing Is Seeing: Biology as Ideology," *Gender & Society*, 7 (1993): 568–81.

23. I am indebted to Gonzalo Santos for suggesting this concept.

7

Diversity in the Information Age

This earth satellite station in Andover, Maine, began a new era in telecommunications when in 1962 it successfully beamed a television picture of an American flag to an orbiting Telstar satellite, which relayed it to a similar facility in Pleumeur-Bodou, France.

117

As early as 1948, the invention of the transistor signaled the dawn of an electronic revolution. In the 1950s, numerous advances—the discovery of the structure of the genetic material DNA, the first successful transplant of an organ (the kidney), the development of an effective polio vaccine and an oral contraceptive, the building of atomic energy plants, and the successful orbiting of *Sputnik,* the first artificial earth satellite—all expanded the horizons for human achievement.

The 1960s, an incredible decade of turbulence and reform, also heralded new accomplishments once the sole province of science fiction. We developed the laser beam, transplanted hearts, and launched communication satellites instantly linking the world with images and sound from anywhere. Sending men in space and landing on the moon fired our imaginations even more. In the 1970s came microprocessors, test tube babies, space shuttles, and the eradication of smallpox. On the heels of those advances arrived VCRs, CDs, and personal computers in the home and workplace, utilizing the Internet and the information highway.

The Larger Context

In this era, the United States became a global, hegemonic power, particularly after the collapse of the Soviet Union. Changes in immigration laws, declining birth rates in Europe, and numerous push factors in the developing world—high birth rates, weak economies, and political unrest, to name a few—resulted in a new migration flow to the United States. Asia and Latin America surpassed Europe as the primary sending areas of new immigrants, a process intensified by the chain migration pattern of family members reuniting with those who arrived before them. Living conditions in Mexico prompted an unauthorized migration flow northward across a convenient, porous border. The violence of wars in Vietnam, Bosnia, and Kosovo (or civil wars in Angola, El Salvador, Peru, and Sierra Leone) forced refugees to flee and played an additional role in further changing the population composition of the United States.

Technological advances led to the evolution of a global economy, enabling companies to market their goods and services throughout the world. Newly industrialized countries (NICs)—notably Brazil, China, India, Malaysia, Mexico, the Philippines, South Africa, Thailand, and Turkey—have lower labor costs, thereby giving them a comparative advantage over more developed countries (MDCs) in exporting their products, thereby stimulating their rapid economic growth. As a postindustrial society, the United States has a declining manufacturing sector. Once dominant in global exports, the United States fell to third place in 2006, behind the European Union and China. Japan, Canada, Korea, and Hong Kong complete the list of the top seven countries.[1] This development has an impact on such countries and their populations.

Globalization—whether through economic changes, rapid air travel, instant telecommunications, or borderless Internet activity—has shrunk the world irrevocably. Practically everyone everywhere is now aware of the diversity of people and cultures elsewhere. Foreign lands no longer seem to be so remote, prompting in many the desire to travel or migrate. Multinational companies are the norm, as are transnational families maintaining strong links to their homeland as well as building new lives in their adopted country. Despite their inevitable adapting to their new culture, recent immigrants find through technology the means to retain their own multicultural reality through a psychological nearness to others they left behind, as well as in the reinforced ethnic vitality they experience among compatriots who have made the same migrating journey.

The Human Element

This exciting world of scientific advancement is, of course, only one part of the human dimension, and in many ways, other aspects of life are unchanged from past generations. People in the world still suffer from hunger, deprivation, persecution, and repression. They still dream of a better life for themselves and their children. For many, that dream has a name: America.

In July 1963, when President John F. Kennedy urged an end to national quota restrictions in a special message to Congress, he initiated a change in our immigration policy that culminated with President Lyndon B. Johnson symbolically signing the new bill in 1965 on Liberty Island at the base of the Statue of Liberty. With his signature, he ended a discriminatory immigration policy that emphasized place of birth and not individual worth or family reunification.

Unexpected Consequences

Most government officials expected the new legislation to open the doors to increased European migration. After all, there was an extensive waiting list for visas in many European countries severely restricted under the old quota system. Yet in a typical year, the British Isles, for example, was sending less than 40 percent of its allotted quota.

Immigrants from some countries—namely, Greece, Italy, Poland, Portugal, Spain, the Soviet Union, and Yugoslavia—did increase notably.

However, the "push" factors to leave were now greater in other parts of the world, and soon European migration was quickly eclipsed. By the 1980s, European immigration represented only 10 percent of the total, with countries such as Greece, Italy, and Yugoslavia declining significantly in the number of emigrants leaving for the United States.

In the 1960s, emigrants from the Caribbean and Latin America outnumbered Europe for the first time and have done so in increasing proportion ever since. European immigration was more than two and a half times Asian immigration in the 1960s, but only slightly more than half the Asian total in the 1970s. In 2006, Europe accounted for 13 percent of all legal immigration, Asia for 33 percent, and the Caribbean and Latin America for 41 percent. Canada, Africa, and Oceania accounted for the remaining 13 percent.

A Different America

The high-tech age dramatically altered U.S. society just as the industrial age had. Previous emigrants from agrarian Europe had to make a triple adjustment to a new culture, an urban environment, and an industrialized society. Many of today's emigrants also make a triple adjustment, but for some the third part is often a bigger leap, from a preindustrial background into a postindustrial society.

Gone are many unskilled and semiskilled jobs enabling the newcomers to gain even a toehold in their new society. Many factory and mill jobs, once plentiful in the cities a short distance from where immigrants clustered in ethnic urban neighborhoods, are now often in industrial parks away from where many of today's immigrants can afford to live. New types of jobs now exist in the building improvement, landscaping, and food service sectors, but many are low-paying, dead-end jobs.

Some immigrants, however, arrive possessing entrepreneurial skills or the education and training needed for higher status, higher paying positions. Their income enables them to settle in residential areas unaccustomed to the presence of first-generation Americans, particularly racially and culturally distinct Asians. Many rural and suburban areas now have a racial and cultural diversity once mostly confined to our cities.

Today's diversity is visible everywhere, not just in a few geographic locales. Some states receive more immigrants than others, and some have greater numbers of one or more groups than others, but no state is immune to the influx of developing world immigrants. Each of the 50 states now contains an unprecedented mixture of racial and ethnic groups that reflects current immigration patterns.

For Americans lulled by previous decades of lower immigration totals and new arrivals primarily from the traditional sending countries of Europe, the presence of so many different groups and languages is strange, but it is *déjà vu* for this nation. Some of the groups may be new to the U.S. scene, but the patterns of acculturation and ethnogenesis among them and of negative dominant responses are replays of yesteryear.

However, this latest manifestation of pluralism also comes with some new ingredients. Government policy now supports pluralism instead of forced assimilation. Bilingualism in ballots, driver education manuals, education, and other public aspects are controversial realities. Social legislation from the 1960s ensures minority rights and opportunities as never before. Because diversity is more visible and protected than ever, some Americans fear the loss of an integrative, assimilationist force in the land.

Institutionalizing Minority Rights

Significant legislation passed in the 1960s brought American ideals about equality closer to reality for minorities long denied their rights. The Civil Rights Act of 1964 was the most far-reaching law against racial discrimination ever passed. It dealt with voting rights, employment practices, and any place of public accommodation, whether eating, lodging, entertainment, recreation, or service. It gave broad powers to the U.S. Attorney General to intervene in private suits regarding violation of civil rights and it directed federal agencies to monitor state and local recipients of federal funds and withhold monies wherever noncompliance was found.

In 1965, Congress simplified judicial enforcement of the voting laws and extended them to state and local elections. In 1968, new legislation barred discrimination in housing and gave Native Americans greater rights in their dealings with courts and government agencies. Affirmative action, initiated by an executive order in 1963 by President Kennedy, became a powerful tool toward reducing institutional discrimination in hiring, promotion, and educational opportunities for minority group members or women.

In the decades since, important gains have been made, some of which are delineated in the following sections on specific groups. For women, whether of the majority or minority groups, we note some progress now.

Females have achieved near parity with the males of their race in the level of educational attainment. A greater proportion than ever before are in the labor force, with growing numbers of women entering male-dominated occupations, including such advanced degree professions as medicine, dentistry, law, and engineering. Whereas only 9 percent of bachelor's degrees in business and management were awarded to women in 1971, about half now are. Even in the male domains of mathematics and the physical sciences, where women earned 13 percent of the degrees in 1971, they now earn more than 42 percent and are steadily increasing in numbers.[2] The 110th Congress (2007–2009) has the most female senators (16) and representatives (74) in its history, and the number of women serving in state legislatures is four times greater than the number 20 years ago. However, only one woman now serves on the U.S. Supreme Court, but thousands of others hold judgeships at the federal, state, county, and local levels.[3]

All of these gains and many others too numerous to mention are encouraging, yet many disquieting signs exist as well. Workplace gender bias contributes to the continuing wage gap. For example, in June 2007, women earned 81 cents for every dollar a man earned.[4] Many occupational fields remain mostly sex-segregated, usually with lower pay levels than comparable male sex-segregated fields. Women face a "glass ceiling" in upward mobility, as illustrated by the highly publicized class action in 2007 on behalf of 1.5 million women against Walmart for sex discrimination.[5]

Women of racial minority groups face the double problem of racism and sexism. As in generations past, women from affluent, mainstream groups enjoy greater advantages and are often social activists in quest of gender equality. Many women have not yet reached that destination, but their journey is nearer its destination than ever before.

The Europeans

Although Europe is no longer the principal sending region for immigrants to the United States, it still continues to send a sizable number. Between 1997 and 2006, almost 1.4 million European immigrants arrived. Included were approximately 161,000 Russians, 157,000 Ukrainians, 137,000 British, 121,000 Poles, 111,000 Bosnia-Herzegovinians, 72,000 Germans, 57,000 Romanians, and 42,000 Bulgarians.[6]

California, Texas, and New York, in that order, are typically the primary places of intended residence for Germans. For the Irish, it is New York, Massachusetts, and California. Polish immigrants prefer Illinois, New York, and New Jersey, whereas former Soviet Union immigrants like better the states of California, New York, and Illinois. British immigrants mostly choose California, New York, and Florida.

According to the 2000 census, the states with the highest density of people with English ancestry were Utah (30 percent), Maine (25 percent), and

Idaho (22 percent). Highest German densities were North and South Dakota (46 percent each), Wisconsin (43 percent), and Minnesota (38 percent). Highest Irish densities were Massachusetts (23 percent), New Hampshire (21 percent), and Rhode Island (20 percent).

Other significant ancestry densities were the Italian in Rhode Island and Connecticut (20 percent), New Jersey (18 percent), and New York (15 percent); the French in Vermont and New Hampshire (27 percent), Maine (25 percent), and Rhode Island (20 percent); and the Polish in Wisconsin and Michigan (9 percent), Connecticut (8 percent), and Illinois and New Jersey (7 percent).

Asians and Pacific Islanders

The Information Age has witnessed Asia surpassing Europe as a sending area of immigrants to the United States. In the 1960s, about 1 in 10 immigrants came from Asia. In the 1970s, however, Asians became one in every three immigrants, a ratio generally unchanged since then. As they naively once did with the Native Americans and the southern, central, and eastern European immigrants, today many Americans view Asian Americans as a single cultural entity because they are of the same race. In fact, they are quite different from each other in their histories, languages, religious beliefs, and cultural attributes.

The earliest of the Asian immigrant groups to put down roots in the United States, the Chinese have become a strong presence, numbering now more than 3.3 million. Although Chinese Americans live in all 50 states, their greatest concentrations are in California and New York, with high aggregates also found in Massachusetts, Illinois, New Jersey, and Texas. A bipolar occupational distribution exists for Chinese Americans. Their ratio in the management and professional occupations is higher than that of the non-Hispanic White labor force (52 to 38 percent), but they also have more living in poverty (13 to 9 percent), among the highest for Asian Americans.[7]

Other than Mexican Americans, no other foreign-born group is as heavily concentrated in one state as are the roughly 1 million Filipinos in California. Other states where the remainders of the 2.2 million total live are Hawaii, New York, Illinois, New Jersey, Washington, Texas, and Virginia. Mostly Roman Catholics, American-born Filipinos tend to have less education and fewer occupational skills than do newcomers from the Philippines, and so many work in low-paying, private-sector jobs. Some of the new arrivals find work in professional and technical fields, especially in health care. Because of licensing and hiring problems, many are underemployed and unable to secure jobs comparable to their education, skills, and experience. Filipino Americans are fragmented linguistically, politically, and socially. Although they have strong loyalty to their family and the church, they generally avoid group separatism or an ethnic advocacy group. Although fraternal and social organizations do offer ethnic interaction opportunities, most Filipinos seem more desirous of broader participation in nonethnic associations.

Asian Indians are another sizable presence, now numbering about 2.3 million. California is home to the largest cluster of Asian Indians, with other high population totals found in New York, New Jersey, Illinois, and Texas. Most Asian Indian immigrants are Hindi-speaking, but many others arrive who speak Gujarati, Punjabi, or Bengali. More than 60 percent of all working Asian Indians are in managerial or professional occupations, greater than any other group in the United States, including Whites. They also are the most highly educated of all U.S. groups; about 68 percent of all adults over age 25 are college graduates, compared to 30 percent of non-Hispanic Whites.[8] About 20 percent of the nation's convenience stores, gas stations, or family-managed hotels and motels are operated by Asian Indians, giving them a family-labor economic niche. This ethnic group has the smallest proportion of its members in low-paying, low-status jobs.

In 1970, Japanese Americans constituted the largest Asian American group, totaling 591,000. However, with negative population growth in Japan, its emigrants to the U.S. are presently about 9,000 annually, which is far below other Asian-sending nations. Now numbering over 832,000, Japanese Americans rank sixth, behind the Chinese, Asian Indians, Filipinos, Vietnamese, and Korean Americans. As with other Asian groups, the largest concentration of Japanese Americans resides in California. Other high-population areas are New York, Hawaii, Texas, and Washington. Although a significant presence in some states, Japanese Americans are the most widely dispersed of all Asian groups throughout the 50 states. Younger Japanese Americans seem more interested in their structural assimilation, as indicated by their high rates of outgroup dating and marriage.

Korean Americans are the fifth largest Asian American group, with their immigration presently exceeding 20,000 annually. Among first- and second-generation Korean Americans, 33 percent live in California, 11 percent live in New York, and about 4 percent live in each of the following states: New Jersey, Texas, Virginia, Washington, and Maryland. About 70 percent of the 1.2 million Korean Americans are Christians, mostly Methodist and Presbyterian. Church affiliation is about four times greater than in Korea because the church also serves as a communal bond for ethnic identity and culture.[9] Koreans can be found in a variety of occupations, but one striking aspect is their self-employment rate of about 12 percent, far greater than any other group. One out of eight Korean Americans is a business owner. These family-owned businesses are found in both cities and suburbs, more likely serving other minority customers or mainstream Americans than fellow Koreans.

Vietnamese Americans, now exceeding 1.2 million, live in all 50 states. Half of them live in California, with 10 percent in Texas and other sizable numbers in Virginia, Washington, New York, and Pennsylvania. Their acculturation is similar to other Asian groups. The older adults—particularly the women, who are less likely to be in work situations interacting with out-group members—display little grasp of English or American ways, but the children and younger adults, more exposed to American life, learn quickly. Scholastic achievement by Vietnamese youth is strong, well above the national average.[10]

More than 226,000 Laotians, 195,000 Cambodians, and 130,000 Thai also call the United States home. Many of the first wave were refugees, but more recent arrivals are either part of the U.S. family reunification program or else immigrants motivated by the same forces that attract others. Also comprising part of the cultural diversity of Asian Americans are more than 20,000 Afghanis, 17,000 Burmese, 52,000 Indonesians, 11,000 Malaysians, and 209,000 Pakistanis, about half of whom live in California.

Black Americans

Use of the term *African American* is somewhat problematic because we must distinguish among those who are American-born of long-ago African ancestry, those who are recent African immigrants, and those who are from an Afro-Caribbean background. Even within these three main groupings, enormous diversity exists in the lives of the different social classes of American-born Blacks and in the languages, cultures, and adjustment patterns of Black immigrants from the different countries. Moreover, as with other racial groups, social stratification creates separate worlds for the American-born, and ingroup loyalty and social isolation among many first-generation Americans often keeps them apart from others.

U.S. society is far from eliminating racism as a serious social problem, and Black Americans still remain disproportionately represented among the nation's poor, with all the attendant problems of that sad reality. Despite the spending of billions of dollars on social welfare programs and economic incentives, one fourth of Black Americans remain mired in poverty. Yet this is not the complete picture. Black America is really two societies: one poor and the other nonpoor. Thanks to civil rights legislation and other social reforms, remarkable gains have been made, especially in education and occupational representation. Nevertheless, a disturbing gap remains between Black Americans and White Americans.

One of the more encouraging social indicators for Black Americans is educational attainment, but even here the message is mixed. From a 1980 high school dropout rate of 16 percent, compared with 11.3 percent for Whites, both are now closer—9.2 percent for Blacks and 7.9 percent for Whites in 2005.[11] In 1970, 4 percent of Blacks and 11 percent of Whites completed college; by 2006, this level was achieved by 18.5 percent of Blacks and 28.4 percent of Whites, or a quadrupling of the Black rate to a doubling of the White rate.[12] Black enrollment in college among recent high school graduates increased from 43 percent in 1980 to 56 percent in 2005. However, this increase has not kept pace with that of White students, whose college enrollment grew from 50 percent to 73 percent in the same period.[13]

Black representation in managerial and professional specialties is steadily growing, now at about 22 percent for males and 31 percent for females. About 18 percent of the males and 32 percent of the females are in technical, sales, or administrative support positions. For Black females, this is a dramatic change in occupation patterning from just a little more than one generation ago, when two in five worked in domestic service. As of now, Black and White females are less different from one another than are the males. About two out of five Black males work in service or blue-collar jobs, compared with two out of three White males working in white-collar jobs.[14]

The continued increase in the number of Black elected officials is another positive indicator. With 40 of 435 representatives in the 110th Congress, Blacks are nearing a total proportionate to their population ratio, although only one presently serves in the U.S. Senate. More than 9,000 elected Black officials now serve in the U.S. or state legislatures, in city or county offices, and in law enforcement or education. This number has grown consistently for more than three decades.

On the negative side are the data for Blacks living in the central cities: higher rates of poverty, unemployment, infant mortality, miscarriages, and mortality than Whites. Of particular concern is the high proportion of female-headed families. Of the 8.9 million Black families in 2004, women headed 45 percent of them, compared with a total of 13 percent female-headed White families. Adding strength to some Black American families, however, is the extended family household. About 12 percent of children with only the mother present live in a household with at least one grandparent present as well.[15]

Many Black immigrants add to the diversity found among the U.S. Black population. About 91 percent of the more than 550,000 Haitian Americans now in the United States are Roman Catholics and are concentrated in just four states: New York, Florida, Massachusetts, and New Jersey. Most live in tightly clustered neighborhoods. Speaking Haitian Creole, most newcomers have a limited command of English and usually work in low-paying jobs in service industries or as farm laborers.

Jamaican Americans are the largest non-Hispanic group from the Caribbean now living in the United States. Of the approximately 737,000 here, about 80 percent are foreign-born. Jamaicans continue to grow as a sizable minority group; for instance, nearly 25,000 arrived in 2006. About 40 percent of all Jamaican Americans live in New York. Florida is home to another 26 percent, with other large Jamaican populations found in New Jersey, Connecticut, California, Maryland, Massachusetts, and Pennsylvania.

Immigration from Africa remained low until the 1980s, but since 1980, about 1 million immigrants have arrived. Nigerians constitute the largest group, with about 165,000 claiming Nigerian ancestry in the 2000 census, compared with 78,000 Ethiopians and 42,000 Ghanaians. African immigrants face two handicaps in culturally adjusting to life in the United States. In their homelands they were a racial majority, but here they are not. In various social and work settings, many encounter racism for the first time. Second, because of their cultural distinctions, many Africans do not identify with either American Blacks or Afro-Caribbeans. Successful native-born Blacks interested in helping the less fortunate of their race usually concentrate on the American-born poor, not on newcomers from Africa. As a matter of preference and necessity, the African immigrants seek out one another for mutual support and refuge.

An important lesson emerges from the last point. Culture is *the* important determinant in how groups relate to one another. *Black* may be a convenient racial category, but it is a simplistic generalization that ignores cultural differences. Blacks born in Ethiopia, Ghana, Haiti, Jamaica, Nigeria, the United States, or any other country belong to distinctive groups whose cultural differences make them unlike one another and, to some extent, more likely to have social distance barriers between them. Multiculturalism thus takes many forms, both between and within all races.

Hispanic Americans

Hispanic is a broad term that encompasses the *Hispanos* of the Southwest whose family roots predate the nation's expanding borders, U.S. nationals such as the Puerto Ricans, Spaniards from Europe, Latino immigrants and refugees, and their descendants. This generic term suggests a common

Spanish language and cultural influence, but it is deceptive because it ignores the Portuguese Brazilians and the many cultural and class distinctions among the various Spanish-speaking nationalities.

Although some non-Hispanic Americans view the Hispanic American population as a collectivity of similar groups, their differences are consequential enough to prevent the evolution at this time of a cohesive entity. Cultural orientations, social class divisions, and first-generation American ingroup loyalties create considerable diversity within this rapidly growing ethnic group, presently comprising about one tenth of the total U.S. population.

Excluding the Mexican Americans, more than 6 million people are foreign-born or native-born Americans from Central or South America.[16] Salvadorans are the largest group, with about 803,000, followed by Colombians with about 584,000, and Guatemalans with about 464,000. Other larger groups include those from Ecuador (323,000), Peru (293,000), Honduras (267,000), and Nicaragua (230,000). Central and South Americans are diverse and defy generalization, except to say that they tend to be better educated and less susceptible to poverty than all other Latinos except Cubans, and they also fall behind Anglos in both categories. Otherwise differences in the economic development in their homelands, rural or urban backgrounds, social class, or racial composition make for numerous dissimilarities.

Since 1980, more than 452,000 Cubans have come to the United States, and those of Cuban ancestry now exceed 1.1 million. Two out of every three Cuban Americans live in Florida, with other large concentrations in New Jersey, New York, and California. In Miami, the Cubans have stamped a positive imprint. Its "Little Havana" section is now a 600-block area, and more than 25,000 Cuban-owned businesses operate in the Miami metropolitan area. The Cuban influence has transformed Miami from a winter resort town to a year-round commercial center with linkages throughout Latin America and has made it into a leading bilingual cultural center. Cubans have a lower fertility rate and a much higher proportion of people 65 years old and older than other Hispanic groups. They also have a lower unemployment rate, higher median family income, and greater middle-class composition.

A major sending country of recent immigrants is the Dominican Republic, which has sent more than 764,000 immigrants since 1980. Two out of every three live in New York. Their large numbers (nearly 1 million now) and settlement patterns have enabled the Dominicans to establish viable ethnic neighborhoods, often adjacent to Puerto Rican ones. Although the two groups coexist and essentially keep to themselves, intergroup marriages and consensual unions are becoming common. Low educational attainment and limited job skills result in high unemployment rates and poverty-level living standards among many Dominicans.

Most of the 30 million Mexican Americans are concentrated in the southwestern states, with the largest concentrations in California, Texas, and Arizona. All 50 states contain appreciable numbers of Mexican Americans, with the largest concentration living outside the Southwest in Illinois (about 1.5 million). Nine out of 10 reside in metropolitan areas, and some of them are realizing the American Dream in rising educational levels, occupational opportunities, and incomes. However, Mexican American gains as a group have not kept pace with Anglo gains because of the large influx of unskilled, poorly educated newcomers. Almost half of urban Mexican Americans live in central cities where, for many, life in the barrio is one of substandard housing, high unemployment rates, poverty, school dropouts, crime, and gang violence. One source of strength, however, is the family. Mexican Americans' divorce rate is well below the national level, and the percentage of their family units headed by both a husband and a wife is comparable to the national average.

Of the 3.7 million Puerto Ricans living on the mainland, one third of them live in New York. Other states with large concentrations are Florida, New Jersey, and Pennsylvania. In comparison to other Hispanic groups, Puerto Ricans have the lowest median family income, the highest poverty rate, and the highest proportion of female-headed families. Puerto Ricans have a higher educational attainment level on average than Mexicans, but lag far behind non-Hispanic Americans. As with the Mexican American urban poor, the Puerto Rican urban poor live in areas of limited job opportunities, making them more vulnerable to welfare dependency. Some segments of the Puerto Rican community are doing well. Almost 40 percent of all Puerto Rican families earn as much or more than the national median family income level, and about 10 percent have incomes that classify them as affluent.

The rapid increase in the Hispanic population (a 58 percent increase from 22.4 million in 1990 to 35.3 million in 2000, and another 18 percent to 43.2 million in 2006) makes them the largest minority group in the United States. Because of a higher birth rate than African Americans, a high immigration rate, and a low average age of these immigrants (nearly 40 percent are under age 21), the Hispanic American population will continue to grow significantly in the foreseeable future.[17] Their growing numbers have enabled them to gain political power in many cities and have increased their labor market competition. Both of these developments have occasionally generated some tensions with the African American community, and it remains to be seen whether such problems are fleeting adjustment issues or a portent of greater problems to come in minority relations between African Americans and Hispanic Americans.

Perhaps the analogy of the *nopales* is apt here.[18] Nopales are cactus with a rather prickly exterior, but they also are edible treats if one proceeds with patience, caution, and determination. In previous eras, a new group's arrival often created tensions with an older minority group, particularly in economic competition, but in time the situation improved as both groups moved past the sharply contested points and "digested" their share of the American Dream. That was not always simply accomplished, but neither was it usually a prolonged encounter. Hopefully, African and Hispanic Americans will similarly move past the prickly experience in short fashion and into that place where both can enjoy the fruits of their labors.

North Africans and Middle Easterners

Immigration from Islamic countries of North Africa and the Middle East has been of such sustained strength that these ethnic groups have become a visible presence in many states. More than 182,000 immigrants arrived in the 1970s, followed by the next wave in the 1980s that increased to almost 343,000, with a slightly higher number coming in the 1990s, and that trend continuing in recent years. Not all are Muslims, particularly the many Christians from Lebanon and Coptic Christians from Egypt.

Although the single largest concentration of Arab Americans is the more than 250,000 living in southern Michigan, the largest proportion of the approximately 1.2 million Americans claiming Arabic ancestry in the 2000 census are the 27 percent living in the Northeast. About 24 percent live in the Midwest, 26 percent in the South, and 22 percent in the West. More than one third of all Arab Americans, about 440,000, are of Lebanese descent. Syrians are the next largest group, approximately 143,000. Other sizable groups are Egyptians, Palestinians, Jordanians, Moroccans, and Iraqis.

Largest of all groups, but neither Arab nor Arabic-speaking, are the Iranians. With their distinct culture and Farsi language, about 60 percent of the more than 338,000 Iranian Americans live in California. Other large enclaves are in the New York and Washington, DC, metropolitan areas. Many are middle-class professionals, and their children are becoming extensively Americanized despite their parents' efforts to preserve their culture.

Turks also are neither Arabs nor Arabic-speaking, but tend to settle near other Arabic and Islamic immigrants in working-class urban neighborhoods. Along with their Arabic neighbors, they often work in the mercantile and building trades.

Over 1,200 mosques now dot the U.S. landscape, two thirds of them built since 1981. Muslims are but one of many conservative groups in the United States, but in attempting to retain their values and practices, their visibility—particularly since 9/11—often elicits suspicion and hostility, a subject we examine more closely in chapter 10.

Native Americans

In 2000, the Native American population increased 19 percent, rising from 2.1 million in 1990 to 2.5 million, thanks to a birth rate higher than the national average. Their quality of life varies from tribe to tribe. Some reap large profits from gambling casinos, whereas others languish in poverty. Nationwide, the Native American poverty rate hovers at nearly three times the national average. Equally depressing are statistics showing Native American life expectancy about 2.4 years less than the national average, and their infants die at a rate of nearly 10 per every 1,000 live births, compared with 7 per 1,000 for the U.S. total population. Moreover, their death rates are higher than other Americans for tuberculosis (500 percent), alcoholism (550 percent), diabetes (200 percent), unintentional injuries (150 percent), homicide (100 percent), and suicide (60 percent).[19]

Twenty percent of Native Americans are ages 10 to 19, compared with 14 percent of other U.S. racial/ethnic groups. Yet compared with those same minority groups, fewer Native American teens will graduate from high school (72 percent vs. 84 percent), and fewer still will complete college (12 percent vs. 27 percent) given current patterns.[20]

Disputes about water rights, fishing rights, natural resources, landfills, and upwind or upstream pollution of tribal lands continue in many states. However, legal efforts to honor treaty rights have been more numerous and successful in recent years.[21] Those successes have led state officials to respect the growing power of Native Americans and to negotiate directly with tribes in their borders to avoid costly and possible court defeats on environmental issues, health policy, child welfare agreements, and water rights.

Religious Diversity

The United States is now probably the most religiously diverse country in the world, with more than 1,500 religious groups. About 200 of these are conventional Christian and Jewish denominations, with 26 of them having memberships exceeding 1 million.[22] Although the country remains mostly Christian

(83 percent claim this faith), the forces of immigration, intermarriage, and disenchantment with some of the oldest religious institutions are redefining the country's religious composition. For example, the United States now contains 7 times more Muslim Americans (6 million), 10 times more Buddhists (2 million), 9 times more Hindus (1 million), and 220 times more Sikhs (220,000) than it did in 1970. Religions once on the periphery of mainstream Christianity are growing vigorously: Mormons by 90 percent, Jehovah's Witnesses by 162 percent, and the Pentecostal Assemblies of God by 267 percent. In contrast, the once dominant Episcopal, Presbyterian, and Congregational churches have declined in membership by 20 percent to 40 percent.[23]

A curious paradox now exists. Perhaps the fastest growing group of all are those opting not to belong to any church, these "unaffiliated" now totaling 49 million Americans, including 17 percent of all Christians.[24] Nevertheless, religion remains an important aspect of U.S. culture. In a 2007 Gallup poll, 86 percent said they believe in God, and 59 percent said that religion is "very important" in their lives, a fairly consistent proportion for decades and two to three times higher than in other Western nations.[25] Although the proportion of Americans attending a weekly worship service may appear low at 42 percent, it is by far the highest of all developed countries; for example, only 20 percent of Canadians and 8 percent of the British go to church weekly.[26]

The growing diversity in religion and its increased importance for many often have a pronounced effect on numerous societal issues and on race and ethnicity. Such "hot-button" topics as abortion, gay marriage, Nativity displays on public property, and school prayer, for instance, fuel intense and bitter debate, political pandering, and extensive lobbying. Erection of non-Western houses of worship in mostly Christian suburban communities can trigger a backlash of resentment and hostility. Seemingly minor issues, such as Sikh males insisting on maintaining their religious beliefs in wearing a turban and having the right to be, say, a police officer, can spark controversy and criticism.

In many ways, U.S. society is more religiously tolerant than in past centuries. However, the efforts of some religious groups to impose their values on the rest of society create both division and conflict. A multicultural society continually faces the moral challenge of encouraging norms and laws for the common good while respecting the different religious values of others.

The Next Horizon

A new wave of immigrants arrives on U.S. shores in pursuit of the same dreams of a better life that motivated millions of other immigrants before them. A new generation of native-born Americans, the descendants of those older immigrants, observes the present immigration with apprehension, concerned and alarmed about what they fear is an undermining of the American culture and character. That also was the past nativist reaction to previous immigrations.

Some demographers, historians, and politicians point with alarm to tomorrow's reality given today's trends. Misgivings about the multiple losses of White numerical superiority, preeminence of Western culture and the Judeo-Christian heritage, and preservation of the existing social order are heard from many sections of the country. There is distress about group separatism and use of languages other than English. On another front, feminist advocacy also draws negative responses in some quarters.

Some of the resistance is from well-intentioned individuals who view the changes as altering the nation's identity too dramatically. Some of that concern is rooted in racial fears, as the White majority sees its numerical superiority and its economic and political dominance threatened by the continued arrival of so many non-White immigrants.

At the heart of most of these feminist, ethnic, and racial issues is the struggle for power. Challenges to the status quo—as vocal and visible minority groups seek economic, political, and social power—prompt resistance by those unwilling to yield their advantages. Their real fears of loss of hegemony are masked in dire predictions about loss of societal cohesion.

Multiculturalism is evident in the land once again, and we can find many examples of both accommodation and conflict. Which trend will prevail? Will our future be one of greater discord or greater unity? What does lie beyond the next horizon? Fortunately, we have some clues from our past and present that may offer us a glimpse of that future. In the remaining chapters, we seek that understanding.

Notes

1. Finfacts, "China Overtakes US in Global Export Rankings in 2006." Accessed at http://www.finfacts.com/irelandbusinessnews/publish/article_10009747 .shtml [October 20, 2007].

2. National Center for Education Statistics, *Digest of Education Statistics, 2006* (Washington, DC: U.S. Government Printing Office, 2007).

3. Center for the American Woman and Politics, Eagleton Institute of Politics. Accessed at http://www.cawp.rutgers.edu/ [October 20, 2007].

4. U.S. Department of Labor, Employment & Earnings, June 2007, Table 39.

5. See, for example, Mark Trumbull, "For Women, Glass Ceiling Still an Issue," *Christian Science Monitor* (February 8, 2007): 1, 11.

6. U.S. Department of Homeland Security, *Yearbook of Immigration Statistics: 2006* (Washington, DC: U.S. Government Printing Office, 2007), Table 3.

7. U.S. Bureau of the Census, *The American Community—Asians: 2004* (Washington, DC: U.S. Government Printing Office, 2007), 16.

8. *Ibid.*, 15.

9. See, for example, Okyun Kwon, "The Role of Religious Congregations in Formation of the Korean American Community of the Washington, DC Area," in *Korean-Americans: Past, Present, and Future*, ed. Ilpyong J. Kim (Elizabeth, NJ: Hollym International Corporation, 2004), 239–70.

10. Min Zhou and Carl L. Bankston, *Growing Up American* (New York: Russell Sage Foundation, 1999).

11. U.S. Census Bureau, *Statistical Abstract of the United States: 2008* (Washington, DC: U.S. Government Printing Office, 2008), Table 265.

12. U.S. Census Bureau, *Educational Attainment in the United States: 2006* (Washington, DC: U.S. Government Printing Office, 2007), Table 1a.

13. National Center for Education Statistics, *Digest of Education Statistics* (Washington, DC: U.S. Government Printing Office, 2007), Table 187.

14. U.S. Census Bureau, *The Black Population in the United States: March 2004* (Washington, DC: U.S. Government Printing Office, 2005), Table 11.

15. U.S. Census Bureau, *America's Families and Living Arrangements: 2006* (Washington, DC: U.S. Government Printing Office, 2007), Table C3.

16. U.S. Census Bureau, *The Hispanic Population of the United States: 2006* (Washington, DC: U.S. Government Printing Office, 2007), Table 8.1.

17. *Ibid.*, Table 1.1.

18. My thanks to Gonzalos Santos at California State University, Bakersfield for suggesting this concept.

19. Indian Health Service, "Facts on Indian Health Disparities." Available at http://info.ihs.gov/Files/DisparitiesFacts-Jan2007.doc [accessed October 24, 2007].

20. U.S. Census Bureau, "The American Community—American Indians and Alaska Natives: 2004," *American Commmunity Survey Reports* (May 2007): 13.

21. See "Dances with Lawyers," *The Economist* (August 10, 1991): A18.

22. Eileen W. Lindner, ed., *Yearbook of American and Canadian Churches, 2004* (Nashville, TN: Abingdon Press, 2004).

23. Mary Rourke, "Redefining Religion in America," *Los Angeles Times* (June 21, 1998): 1.

24. *Ibid.*

25. The Gallup Organization, Religion. Accessed at www.pollingreport.com/religion.htm [October 24, 2007]; CBS News Poll, "For Almost All Americans, There Is God." Available at www.cbsnews.com/stories/2006/04/13/opinion/polls/main1498219.shtml [accessed October 24, 2007].

26. Charles Moore, "Is Christianity 'Almost Vanquished'?" *Western Catholic Reporter* (October 15, 2001): 1.

8

Intergenerational Comparisons

"Generations" by noted photographer Gordon Parks (1942) depicts Mrs. Ella Watson of Washington, D.C., with three grandchildren and her adopted daughter, together with a photograph of either her parents or herself and her husband.

135

Each generation of Americans experiences anew the influx of immigrants arriving in pursuit of the American Dream. Each new generation also contains native-born Americans who have not only been denied fulfillment of that dream, but also witnessed newcomers who succeed where they do not. This has been the case since colonial beginnings and appears likely to continue far into the future. It is an old story and yet incredibly fresh each time to those who live or observe it.

When we examine what has prompted people, past and present, to forsake their homelands and begin new lives elsewhere, we find a remarkable consistency in their motives.[1] Many people entered on their own initiative, lured by the promise of a better life. Others were recruited by labor agents, enticed by the media, or encouraged to leave by their own governments that were seeking a lessening of social unrest or economic distress. Still others, forced to flee their native lands as refugees, had little choice.

Whatever the reason and whenever the time, the United States has always served as a destination for these adventurous, desperate, or determined people. Yet despite the immigrant ancestry of most Americans, many times in the past and present they have wanted to pull in the welcome mat for new immigrants.

Why Are Voices Raised Against Immigration?

Too often the native-born react with fear and anxiety, perceiving some groups as "unassimilable" and their presence in large numbers as a threat to societal cohesion.[2] Other Americans are apprehensive about these groups' possible integration, believing that such an eventuality would somehow destroy or undermine the "purity" of the American character. So it was with American ambassador to England Rufus King, who wrote in 1797 to Secretary of State Timothy Pickering that the Irish immigrants would "disfigure our true national character."[3] Ever since, others have expressed concerns about this or that group of immigrants as wrong for the nation's well-being.

Religious, Racial, and Cultural Biases

Sometimes these reactions reveal a religious bias: against Quakers, Shakers, or Catholics in the 18th century; against Catholics, Jews, or Mormons in the 19th century; or against Catholics, Jews, or Sikhs in the early 20th century. Other negative responses reflect a racial bias: against African and Native Americans throughout the nation's history, and against Asians and dark-complexioned southern Europeans in the late 19th and early 20th centuries. There have been other varieties of bias: religion and race (Rastafarian) and culture and religion (Irish and Italian). Today, other nativist voices express the old fears about other religiously, racially, or culturally different newcomers: Muslims, Asians, or Latinos.

Economic Competition

Past or present targets also have induced alarm because others see them as a danger to their own livelihood. This perceived economic threat may result from the scarcity of jobs, affirmative action hiring or promotion policies, or the recruitment of cheaper labor or strike breakers. Since the mid-19th century, employers have often used newly arrived groups, including migrating Black Americans, to keep wages low or to break a strike.

The resulting ethnic antagonism can be of three types. Native-born Americans may resent the immigrant influx, as when West Coast labor unions in the late 19th and early 20th centuries fought against Asian workers. An interethnic rivalry may develop, such as the importation of Syrian-Lebanese immigrants in an effort to break the 300-mill shutdown in the Paterson, New Jersey, region in 1913, caused by striking European immigrant textile workers. Same-group members can pose a third variation of an immigrant economic threat. Economist Vernon Briggs, for example, has shown the negative influence on employment conditions for legal Mexican Americans by undocumented Mexicans working in the food and fiber industry.

The "Tipping Point"

Sometimes biases are so deeply ingrained that people will respond negatively to the presence of even one member of a despised outgroup. More often, however, if the number of outgroup members is few, people tend to be more receptive to less-alike strangers or at least indifferent or begrudgingly tolerant. When the numerical increase reaches the tipping point, hostile responses become more likely. As Luigi Laurenti's classic study on property values and race revealed, that tipping point has no exact number; it is a perceptual stage when the ingroup believes "too many" of "those people" are in its midst and "something needs to be done."[4]

Today Isn't Yesterday, or Is It?

If 10 generations of Americans have followed similar patterns of response to immigrants who have subsequently blended into the mainstream, why can't we recognize that fact and be less fearful about today's newcomers?

Today's nativists dismiss any effort to compare past immigrant concerns with their own. Past objectors, they argue, were narrow-minded bigots opposed to people who have since proven their ability to assimilate. They contend that today we are "inundated" with racially different Asians who lack a Judeo-Christian heritage and whose culture is radically different from ours.

Hispanics, they add, are holding on to their language and customs, thereby presenting a real threat to the cohesiveness of U.S. society.

With the 1990s now the decade of the greatest number of immigrants ever to arrive (9.1 million), and with about four in five from developing world countries, nativists consider current immigration as a serious threat to the population composition of U.S. society as we have long known it. Furthermore, with a lower national birth rate among the native-born, the higher birth rate among the foreign-born enables them to have a stronger impact on natural population growth. Moreover, the nation has not satisfactorily dealt with the unemployment and poverty of its native-born Americans, they contend, to continue to admit large numbers of immigrants to intensify further an already difficult problem.

Questions about America's racial mix, natural population increase, unemployment, and poverty do offer some new wrinkles to old arguments and need to be addressed. However, despite nativist disclaimers of new and different elements, these arguments share many commonalities with those of similar-minded alarmists of previous generations. All have seen newcomers as a threat to the "purity" of the American character and to the stability and economic welfare of the society. All have seen the newcomers as inferior additions and complained about their retention of language and customs. All have assumed acculturation and assimilation would not occur. As Rita J. Simon states,

> These have been the arguments used against all of the "current cohorts" from the time the new immigrants began arriving, first from Ireland, then a decade or two later from Southern and Eastern Europe. . . . Contemporary immigrants are no less popular than the immigrants who began coming to this country after the Civil War and for all the years in between. The only popular or valued immigrants are those who came long ago, whenever "long ago" happened to be.[5]

I would suggest that, when nativists argue that today's situation is far different from past years, their perception reflects the Dillingham Flaw. They tend to view past fears as ignorant or irrational nativism against White ethnics who actually shared far more similarities with their hosts than any differences. However, what we perceive today as their mutual similarities were not viewed as such in those times. It is past perception—not present-day perception—that matters when examining past behaviors.

So are things different today or not? We need some comparative data to determine where the truth lies. To relate the present with the past, I focus on several aspects of nativist fears: the significance of immigration totals, the foreign-born presence, racial population changes, and assimilation.

Immigration Rate

As specified by the Immigration Act of 1990, an annual limit of 675,000 immigrants currently exists. Because immediate family members are not included in these caps, yearly totals have actually been higher, as they were in 2006, when 1.27 million legal permanent residents entered the United States. In 2005, that number was 1.12 million, higher than the 958,000 who entered in 2004. Such numbers provoke that nativist alarm, but these are misleading statistics by themselves. Much more informative about the impact of immigrants on society is the immigration rate. This measurement tool allows for comparisons of different eras while enabling us to specifically address vague nativist fears that the United States is being overwhelmed by a large influx of foreigners. It thus serves as a concrete aide in objectively describing a reality that may or may not differ from perceptions.

The immigration rate per 1,000 persons in the general population is computed by dividing the sum of the annual immigration totals by the sum of annual U.S. population totals for the same number of years. Collection of such data began in 1820, when new regulations required shipmasters to submit passenger lists to customs officials. What is particularly useful about this measurement tool is that it allows us to relate immigration totals to population totals and to do so in a way that provides a comparative means for analysis. Immigrant totals for any particular year or decade become more relevant if we know the size of the population the newcomers are joining. To be more specific, if 1 million people enter a society that totals 50 million people, the immigrants' presence will be more keenly felt than if 1 million people enter a society that has a population of 250 million.

As seen in Fig. 8.1, the 1990s were the decade with the highest total number of immigrants arriving. However, in terms of its immigration rate of 3.4, the 1990s actually tie for ninth out of the 17 decades. Immigrants in the 1990s were less than one third the proportion found in 1901–1910, and so the influx of 8.8 million immigrants in that decade resulted in an immigration rate of 8.795. In comparison, the immigration rate for 2001 to 2005 was 3.4.[6]

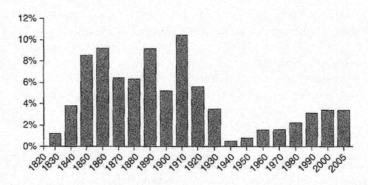

Figure 8.1   Immigration Rate, 1820–2005

SOURCE: U.S. Census Bureau, *Statistical Abstract of the United States: 2007* (Washington, DC: Government Printing Office, 2007), Table 5, p. 8.

What are we saying? First, the earlier waves of immigrants in each of the decades between 1841 and 1920 had a more immediate effect on the nation's population composition. That is, the ratio of immigrants to the population receiving them was greater in the past. Such a higher ratio means that those immigrants from 1840 to 1920 proportionately and visibly changed America's population mix to a greater degree than the recent immigrants have.

Second, a major factor in examining the immigration rate is immigration law. With the current ceiling of 675,000 immigrants annually, the general population will experience natural increases annually while the immigration cap remains constant. The result therefore must be a decline of the immigration rate in the years to come, as the population (denominator) increases while the number of immigrants (numerator) remains fairly constant. (In 2003, for example, the immigration rate dropped to 2.4 after a 3.7 rate for the previous 2 years.) Until new legislation raises that immigration cap, we can expect a steady reduction in the immigration rate, one measurement of alien impact on the host society.

Immigration Rate Caveats

Although the legal immigration rate is a helpful comparative measurement, it cannot stand alone. Too many other factors need to be considered as well. Perhaps most important is how much immigration contributes to population growth in an era of declining birth rates. Because immigrants have a higher birth rate than the native-born, their group numbers will grow at a faster rate. Using a formula of births plus immigration minus deaths and emigration, the Population Reference Bureau reports that immigrants currently account for about one third of U.S. population growth.[7] Demographer Leon F. Bouvier says immigration will thus affect the nation's future ethnic population mix, a topic addressed in the last chapter.

We also must consider illegal immigration in any discussion of the presence in the United States of the foreign-born. Although undocumented immigrants have always been a presence since the first immigration laws, their numbers—now estimated in excess of 11 million—have never been so high. If immigration remains at present levels, the projection for the percentage of first-generation Americans (the foreign-born) in 2025 is about 15 percent, which is up from the current 12 percent.[8]

Another consideration is that the United States is now a postindustrial society. Many manufacturing jobs no longer exist that immigrants with few skills and limited command of English could once attain. The ability of a nation to absorb its newcomers is thus dependent on how well they can find their niche in the workplace, as well as on the proportion of immigrants to the total population. Legal and illegal immigration added as much as $10 billion to the Gross Domestic Product (GDP)—the value of goods and services produced in the United States—in the mid-1990s in an $8 trillion U.S. economy. Both legal and illegal immigrants are responsible for paying taxes, including sales and income taxes, but they are not eligible for some tax-supported services, which further increases their positive fiscal effects.[9]

Foreign-Born Population

A companion set of data to immigration rates is the foreign-born population in various time periods because they represent the cumulative totals of immigrants residing in the United States. Therefore, by determining what percentage of the general population is foreign-born at any given time, we can discern the extent of their presence as a basis for comparing the past with the present.

Data on the foreign-born were not gathered until the 1850 census. This year marked the close of the first decade with more than 1 million immigrants—1.7 million to be exact. (In the 1830s there were about 600,000, and in the 1820s there were about 143,000.) Hence, 1850 serves as a good starting point for examining times of higher immigration.

Because immigration rates were higher in the past than in the present, as we have just seen, it is therefore not surprising to see in Fig. 8.2 that the foreign-born segment of the population has been higher in 10 of the past 15 decennial censuses, consecutively from 1850 to 1940.

Figure 8.2 shows that the percentage of foreign-born living in the United States between 1860 and 1930 was greater than in 2000. In the 1890 and 1910 censuses, one in seven was foreign-born; in 1860, 1870, 1880, 1900, and 1920, it was one in eight. The Pew Hispanic Center, a respected non-partisan research organization, reported that the foreign-born population in 2005 totaled 35.8 million, or 12.4 percent of the population, a lower percentage than existed between 1860 and 1920.

At the beginning of the 20th century, most cities in the Northeast contained a foreign-born population that comprised two thirds to three fourths of the cities' total populations. In contrast, the cities in 2000 with the most foreign-born populations were Miami (60 percent), Los Angeles (41 percent), San Francisco (37 percent), and New York (36 percent).[10] Although these are significant proportions, they pale alongside the data of 100 years ago.

From another viewpoint, the aforementioned 35.8 million foreign-born are the largest numerical total ever, but in proportion to the entire population, that figure ranks seventh among the 16 decades for which this information is available.

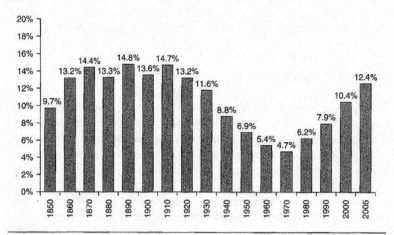

Figure 8.2   U.S. Foreign-Born Population as a Percentage of the Total Population, 1850–2005

SOURCES: "The Foreign-Born Population in the United States: 2003," August 2004. U.S. Census, Series P20–551; Pew Hispanic Center, A Statistical Portrait of the Foreign-Born Population at Mid-Decade (2006): Table 1, accessed online at www.pewhispanic.org on October 27, 2007.

Because these statistics do not include U.S.-born children raised in immigrant family households, the proportion of those living in various ethnic subcultures has been greater, especially among past generations, when family size was typically larger than today. Regardless of acculturation patterns, different languages, customs, and traditions from the old country have always prevailed to some extent among a sizable part of U.S. society, more so in the past than the present.

At its lowest point in 1960, the foreign-born component has since been moving upward again, reflecting the recent increases in the immigration rate. Similarly, the foreign-born percentages will continue to rise for a while, but will eventually level off and decline for the same reasons enumerated for the immigration rate.

Race in America

U.S. race relations have a violent, exploitative past and an often-troubled present. Racism finds many forms of expression ranging from verbal putdowns to killing, producing disturbing consequences not only for its victims, but also for the society itself in economic, health, and social welfare costs.

At first, only Whites among the native-born enjoyed the privileges of citizenship and voting rights, and only White aliens could become naturalized citizens. In time, following the pain of the Civil War, the 14th Amendment (1868) granted citizenship to anyone born or naturalized in the United States, and the 15th Amendment (1870) extended voting rights to every male regardless of race or color. After an arduous struggle, non-White exclusion yielded under force of law to inclusion.

Advances against other areas of exclusion—notably in education, employment, housing, and public accommodation—occurred only a generation ago, growing out of the civil rights movement of the 1960s. Gaining legal rights and political participation did not necessarily mean social acceptance, however. Just as Crèvecoeur overlooked the disenfranchised racial U.S. minorities of his time, so too have many White Americans avoided any inclusion of non-Whites in their daily lives. Lack of interaction helps perpetuate stereotypes and allows racial prejudice and discrimination to thrive.

Although succeeding generations of America's people of color have made significant gains in education, employment, income, and political participation, problems remain. Many forms of institutionalized racism have been eliminated, but structural discrimination—the differential treatment of racial groups that is entrenched in our social institutions—remains. About one in four African Americans and one in five Hispanic Americans still lives in poverty, more than twice that of Whites.

Racism manifests itself in negative reactions to the number of immigrants in general who are non-White, or of one race such as Asians, or of one group such as Haitians. It finds expression also in fears that the racial mixture of U.S. society is changing too dramatically.

If we look at some of the data about past and present racial groups in the United States, we can dispel some of the generalizations and unfair comparisons (the Dillingham Flaw) that engender some of the unfavorable responses to the presence of people of color. Our focus once again will be on proportional representation within the total population through the years. Is the non-White to White ratio greater than ever? Exactly how is our society changing in its racial mixture?

After increasing proportionately since 1790 and peaking in 1940 at 89.8 percent, the nation's White population has since been decreasing steadily, as Fig. 8.3 reveals. In 2004, the total White population (including Hispanic Whites) was 80.4 percent, a slightly higher portion of the total population than the 79.3 percent of Whites living in the United States in 1790. [11]

The reason there was a smaller percentage of Whites in 1790 is that there was a greater percentage of Blacks. Then African Americans constituted almost one in five residents, at 18.9 percent. That was the peak year for African Americans. Thereafter, elimination of the slave trade in 1808 and mostly White immigration slowly but steadily reduced African American apportionment within the society.

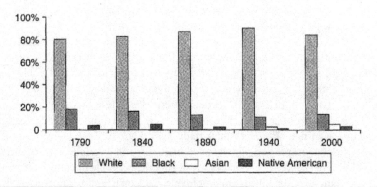

Figure 8.3   U.S. Population by Race as a Percentage of the Total Population

SOURCES: U.S. Bureau of the Census, *Historical Statistics of the United States, Part I*, Series A91–104 (Washington, DC: Government Printing Office, 1976); *Statistical Abstract of the United States: 2007* (Washington, DC: Government Printing Office, 2007), Table 13.

Although the percentage of African Americans continually declined until reaching its lowest point in 1940 at 9.8 percent, their percentages did not drop below current figures until 1890. Before then African Americans comprised a greater share of the total population.

Since 1950, their ratio has been slowly climbing from 9.9 percent to 12.8 percent in 2004, with the Census Bureau projecting an increase to 15 percent by 2050. Part of that increase is due to the presence of more than 1.3 million residents of West Indian ancestry and more than 1 million immigrants from Africa.

Virtually nonexistent in the United States in 1790, Asians have been steadily increasing in numbers and proportion since their first tallies in the 1860 census. Since the liberalization of immigration regulations in 1965, their growth has been dramatic, and their visible concentration in certain regions of the country—particularly on the east and west coasts and in the Chicago metropolitan region—makes their 4 percent of the total population seem much greater to residents of those areas.

After experiencing a calamitous decline in population from first contact with Europeans until the 20th century, Native Americans have a high birth rate and are now steadily increasing their numbers. Their recent population growth has stabilized their proportional place in U.S. society at 1 percent.

What can we conclude from this information? Perhaps one surprise is that the United States is less Black today than it was from 1790 to 1890. However, it is also true that the White population percentage of the total is shrinking and the Black population percentage is increasing. Also, the increase in Asians, Hispanics (who can be of any race), and Native Americans—when combined with the increase in African Americans—means that the United States today is more of a multiracial society than ever before. What will the changing racial composition mean for the future of race relations? As the ratio of Whites declines, Whites will no doubt become more aware of their race instead of just paying attention to the visibility of other racial groups. Will this lead to greater understanding or to a racial backlash? This is part of the challenge before us.

In the last chapter, we explore more fully the implications of current birth and migration rates on the future of U.S. society, including racial composition.

Mainstream Americans

Rarely are cultures or societies static entities. In the United States, the continual influx of immigrants has helped shape its metamorphosis. Part of this tempering has been the evolving definition of the mainstream ingroup or identifying who was "really an American."[12]

In the initial conception of mainstream Americans, the English comprised virtually all of this ingroup. Gradually, this ingroup expanded from English American exclusivity to British American or White Anglo-Saxon Protestant, thus including the Scots-Irish and Welsh previously excluded. This reconceptualization was triggered by the rapid Americanization of these groups after the Revolutionary War and by nativist reaction to the first large-scale wave of immigrants whose culture, religion, and, in the case of the Irish, peasant class set them apart from the mainstream.

By 1890, the "mainstream American" ingroup did not yet include many northwest European Americans. Although some multigenerational Americans of other than British ancestry had blended into the mainstream, millions had not. These Americans remained culturally pluralistic, their separateness resulting from race, religion, or geographic isolation. In addition, more than 9 million foreign-born—one in seven, perhaps one in five if we include their children—also lived outside this mainstream society then.

In 1890, the "melting pot" had not yet absorbed the 80,000 Dutch, 200,000 Swiss, or 1.2 million Scandinavians in the Midwest, most of whom had arrived after 1870. Likewise, the 150,000 French immigrants, 200,000 Cajuns in Louisiana, and 500,000 French Canadians in New England and the Great Plains remained culturally, linguistically, and religiously separated from the larger society. So, too, did many of the 8 million Germans in the rural Midwest or who were concentrated in many large cities. Their poverty and Catholic faith kept 6 million Irish in the Northeast and 300,000 Mexican Americans in the Southwest in social isolation. About 7.5 million African Americans, 248,000 Native Americans, and 110,000 Asians also lived as mostly impoverished racial minorities separate from the mainstream.[13]

Race, culture, and/or social class origins shaped group relations in the United States in 1890, keeping the nation a patchwork quilt of cultural diversity. All three variables influenced perceptions, receptivity, and interaction patterns.

In the 1890s, the tide of immigration began to change. The turning point came in 1896, when immigrants from the rest of Europe surpassed those from northern and western Europe. These "new" immigrants soon caused a redefinition of a mainstream American, bringing those of north and west European origins (including Australian and Canadian) into this classification in contrast to the newer, "less desirable" newcomers. Because this redefinition did not necessarily reflect cultural or structural assimilation in 1890, however, Fig. 8.4 suggests the perceptual reality of that time.

By 1970, a new turning point in immigration had been reached, with developing world immigrants outnumbering European immigrants. Once again, partly through a reaction to this change and partly due to acculturation, education, and upward mobility, the concept of *mainstream American* expanded. This time it included anyone of European origin, thus setting them apart from the people of color now arriving in great numbers, as well as the still nonintegrated African Americans and Native Americans.

Mainstream American Caveats

Figure 8.4 illustrates these mainstream American and outgroup classifications. Admittedly, these groupings are somewhat arbitrary. For example, some non-English were clearly mainstream Americans in 1790, such as Welsh Americans William Floyd, Button Gwinnett, Thomas Jefferson, Francis Lewis, and Lewis Morris—all signers of the Declaration of Independence. However, there still were many 18th- and 19th-century segregated Welsh settlements of Quakers, Baptists, or Congregationalists scattered in numerous regions where Welsh-language newspapers, even books, helped maintain a distinct ethnic minority group. Similarly, 19th-century German industrialists such as H. J. Heinz, Frederick Weyerhauser, John J. Bausch, and Henry Lomb typify non-British individuals who wielded considerable power and influence; yet most Germans remained socially isolated in rural or urban subcommunities.

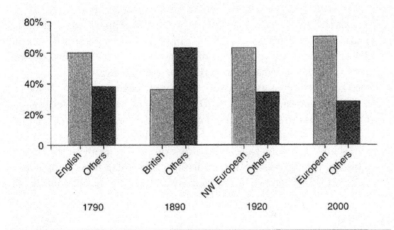

Figure 8.4   Mainstream Americans, by Ancestry Group

SOURCES: Based on data from U.S. Census Bureau, *Historical Statistics of the United States, Part I*, Series A91–104 (Washington, DC: U.S. Government Printing Office, 1976); *Statistical Abstract of the United States: 2007* (Washington, DC: U.S. Government Printing Office, 2007).

The 2000 mainstream category also is an arbitrary oversimplification because it overlooks the religious and cultural differences among White ethnics that set them apart from fully assimilated European Americans. For example, mainstream Americans view the Amish, Mennonites, and Hasidic Jews as culturally distinct groups living within their own subcultures outside the mainstream. Therefore, the categories cannot be taken literally.

Even so, these categories still serve a useful purpose. They address the perception, acceptance, social distance, and therefore the basis on which people react positively or negatively to physically or culturally distinct others. Some people here included in the mainstream group may not actually be a part of it and vice versa, yet these groupings offer an approximation of who are seen as "Americans" and who still remain as outsiders. The social distance scores reported by Emory Bogardus and other researchers since 1926 are a helpful indicator of these groupings.[14] Comparatively, the studies reveal a lessening of social distance among all groups through the decades, but nevertheless a consistent clustering of non-White groups farther away in social acceptance than White ethnic groups.

Of course, one can create other configurations and numbers. For example, one could introduce social stratification as a variable and make an effective argument for social class designation affecting mainstream acceptance and thereby altering the ingroup–outgroup memberships. Such a position has some merit, although it opens the door for counterarguments involving racism and structural assimilation, which would affect acceptance regardless of social class. Even so, with a smaller proportion of people living in poverty today than in 1890, and less in 1890 than in 1790, the pattern shown in Fig. 8.4 of an increased proportion of mainstream Americans through the centuries would likely remain and perhaps be even greater.

These statistics serve as a guide to our understanding and not as an absolute identification. Avoiding the Dillingham Flaw and identifying mainstream Americans through the eyes of each period's contemporaries, we find that the expanding American identity has resulted in a greater ingroup totality today than ever before. Despite recently expressed fears about the United States becoming a polyglot society of dissimilar people (a historically recurring anxiety), the nation's mainstream group has expanded, not contracted.

The "Wall"

What do we learn from this focus on mainstream Americans? As the nation's population mix has changed through the generations, so, too, has its definition of national cultural identity. Groups once excluded, once considered unassimilable, and even sometimes reviled, became included. In time, this socially constructed new reality seemed natural, especially with the appearance of a new group perceived as "different" and/or as economic competitors. A long, sometimes conflict-ridden process unfolded. Eventually, the newer group also became part of the ingroup and was replaced by another outgroup.

The concept of an expanding mainstream American identity is similar to the history of the walled medieval cities. Only so many inhabitants could fit within the protective wall that surrounded the city. The lack of available space forced newcomers to settle outside in *fauborgs* (the first suburbs), where they could participate in the city's daily activities, although they were not really a part of the city.

Hawking their wares as merchants inside the city's gates, they no doubt were resented by some as economic competitors. When trouble came in the form of marauders, all united in a common cause, but the newcomers were more likely to suffer the most in loss and destruction of their property outside the walls. In time, as the outsiders became a more integral part of the city, a new encircling wall was built farther out as the old wall was torn down. With the previously excluded inhabitants now safely ensconced within the city's new walled perimeter, others would soon settle outside and begin the process anew.

The wall is an apt metaphor. In intergroup or gender relations, too often we still build protective walls of isolation, avoidance, or exclusion. Whether physical or social, walls do more than separate people: They limit one's field of vision, restrict movement, create a "they" and "we" mentality, and inspire conflict. Walls of prejudice keep people apart from one another, making those on one side more susceptible to victimization, as those *fauborg* dwellers once were. Just as economic growth brought the medieval walls down, so, too, does it help bring down our walls of prejudice. Conversely, economic decline helps erect walls between groups as people compete for jobs.

The social barriers we erect can sometimes be just as insurmountable and long lasting as many of those medieval walls still standing these many centuries later. Sometimes, however, those walls can be scaled, their gates opened, and the ramparts destroyed. It is a paradoxical tribute to the dynamics of U.S. society that its cultural identity walls of exclusivity have been weak enough to overcome several times, thereby producing a stronger nation and a more vibrant American character than could have existed without such expansiveness.

Perception and Reality

Americans' perception of the foreign-born population is affected by how they become aware of that diversity within the United States. The growing presence of first-generation Americans in previously homogeneous small town and suburban locales brings a changed reality into the residents' taken-for-granted world. How that translates into interaction patterns helps determine whether the interactions are positive or negative. However, news about "illegal aliens" almost always triggers a negative response because Americans typically resent people violating their laws who also cost them money as well.

Concern about unauthorized immigrants is nothing new. After passage of the Chinese Exclusion Act in 1882, Americans reacted strongly against the problem of Chinese illegally entering the United States through British Columbia. Today, with a porous border with Mexico, unauthorized crossings are constant. Federal agents now apprehend around 1.2 million aliens each year, but an estimated 200,000 successfully elude detection.[15]

Controversy about these unauthorized immigrants—particularly with the education, health, and social welfare costs they create—distorts the public image of authorized immigrants, resulting in mixed public opinions on the issue of immigration. For example, in a 2007 CBS News/*New York Times* national poll, 57 percent of respondents said they felt that recent immigrants contribute to the country while 28 percent thought they caused problems. When specifically asked how serious a problem they thought illegal immigration was, 61 percent viewed it as "very serious," and another 30 percent said it was "somewhat serious."[16] Yet in a June 2007 NBC News/*Wall Street Journal* national poll, a more even split occurred, with 46 percent saying immigration helps more than it hurts the United States, whereas 44 percent thought the opposite.[17]

Those expressing negative views frequently cite reasons such as immigrants lacking job skills and using too many tax-supported services, factors that are more likely to be associated with unauthorized immigrants than the immigrants whose skills or family sponsorship clears them for admission legally. Unfortunately, many Americans do not make a distinction between these two different groups of newcomers.

The Larger Context

The United States is certainly not the only country undergoing a significant foreign-born influx that prompts native-born citizens to compare their present-day scene with their nation's past. For example, many Western European countries, mostly homogeneous in the past, now find themselves confronting the large-scale presence of racially and culturally distinct others. This situation has necessitated changes in government policies to maintain societal cohesion in the face of such unprecedented diversity.

Following World War II, England experienced a major change in the size of its non-White population. Numbering in the low thousands in 1945, by 1970, they numbered about 1.4 million, one third of them actually born in the United Kingdom.[18] Enacting strict controls on immigration in the 1970s and race riots in the early 1980s, the British government sought to improve the situation. Because many Britons viewed the new minorities as not belonging, although growing numbers of the second- and third-generation minority citizens had only lived in the United Kingdom, the government acted to change this mind-set. With passage in 1976 of the Race Relations Act, all official reports thereafter use the term *ethnic minority* instead of *immigrant* and expanded the concept of discrimination to include indirect discrimination (those seemingly neutral rules that have an indefensibly discriminatory effect). Although problems remain, race relations have improved and non-White citizens now serve in the British Parliament.

Industrialization in early 20th-century France attracted millions of Italian, Polish, and Spanish immigrants to work in the factories. Yet despite their common Catholic faith and shared continental heritage, they were not easily able to join the French mainstream. In a country that for many years enforced a language policy even against regional dialects, foreigners discovered that Franco-conformity (assimilation) was the only allowable choice, not pluralism. Today, about 5 million immigrants (8 percent of the population) live in France, most of them from Muslim North Africa. With so many foreigners in their midst who differ in appearance, language, religion, and values, many French worry that their nation is losing its cultural identity. Three weeks of rioting in 2005 by alienated Muslim youth were a clear signal that the fabric of French society was, at the least, badly frayed. A hopeful note, however, was the beginning of a new chapter in French history with the 2007 election of Nicholas Sarkozy as president, a man who is the son of Hungarian immigrants.

In Germany, an acute labor shortage after World War II prompted the government to invite foreign guest workers from several countries to help rebuild the country. Most notably, beginning in 1961, it officially invited Turkish workers to replace East Germans no longer able to work in the factories after the communists built the Berlin Wall. These "temporary immigrants" elected to stay and soon sent for their families. Under previous German law, children born to foreigners in Germany were still not citizens, so over time even the third generation born there remained outsiders, typically living in ethnic enclaves and socially segregated from the mainstream. Although many in the second and third generations only know Turkey secondhand, they have not felt fully accepted by German society and so have strongly identified with their Turkish roots and culture. Now numbering over

2 million, they constitute more than one fourth of all foreigners in Germany. To address the societal schism, in 2000, the government conferred German citizenship on children of all foreigners born in Germany, thereby helping more and more to think of themselves as Turkish Germans, not Turks.

Today's Patterns in Perspective

Many Americans believe we are living in the midst of the greatest immigration ever. In actual numbers, that appears to be true, but in relation to the total population, the current immigration rate is lower than that of an 80-year period stretching from 1840 to 1920. Those higher rates meant a much greater ratio of immigrants to the population than at present.

Similarly, today's foreign-born population, so easily visible, is, in fact, less in relation to the native-born population than in 8 of the last 16 censuses. Put plainly, we have a lower foreign-born ratio today than we have had throughout most of the past 150 years.

We are indeed becoming a more multiracial society, and we have more Africans, Asians, and Hispanics than ever before. The trend toward more people of color will continue. As Whites decline as a percentage of the total, they may feel threatened economically and politically and could act to reverse or slow down this demographic change. Perhaps California, where Whites first became a minority, will become the bellwether state for a national response. Florida and Texas are other states to watch for nativist reactions.

Acculturation and assimilation have resulted in a greater inclusiveness of previously excluded groups into the mainstream American category. Up until now, however, that process has not included people of color. If the process is to continue, a sea change in racial attitudes will be required to allow today's outgroup members to become part of the American mainstream.

Our discussions about the statistics relating to immigration, foreign-born census counts, and racial proportions all addressed aspects of the pluralism that has been, and continues to be, the reality of the United States. Commentary on the expanding definition of mainstream Americans points to the ongoing assimilation process that continues through the generations. So, while dispelling some of the myths that immigration will get out of hand or that the proportion of foreign-born is higher than ever, the data also offer quantitative insights for avoiding the Dillingham Flaw. Peter Berger was right. Things are not necessarily as they seem. The pluralism of today in many ways does not surpass that in our nation's past, and assimilation is not endangered by numbers because it has successfully continued as a dynamic force under more overwhelming proportionate numbers of years ago.

Left unsaid in this discussion is whether the agendas of separatist multi-culturalists create a real danger to societal cohesiveness regardless of comparative statistics. We turn next to that topic.

Notes

1. See Vincent N. Parrillo, *Strangers to These Shores*, 9th ed. (Boston: Allyn & Bacon, 2009), 167–8, 304, 402–3.

2. See John Higham, *Strangers in the Land: Patterns of Nativism, 1860–1925* (New York: Atheneum, 1971).

3. James M. Smith, *Freedom's Fetters* (Ithaca, NY: Cornell University Press, 1956), 25.

4. Luigi Laurenti, *Property Values and Race: Studies in Cities* (Berkeley: University of California Press, 1960).

5. Rita J. Simon, "Old Minorities, New Immigrants: Aspirations, Hopes, and Fears," *The Annals of the American Academy of Political and Social Science*, 530 (1993), 65, 73.

6. U.S. Census Bureau, *Statistical Abstract of the United States: 2007* (Washington, DC: U.S. Government Printing Office, 2007), Table 5, p. 8.

7. Philip Martin and Elizabeth Midgley, "Immigration: Shaping and Reshaping America," 2nd ed., *Population Bulletin*, 61 (December 2006), 16.

8. *Ibid.*, 17.

9. *Ibid.*, 17, 22.

10. U.S. Census Bureau, "The Foreign-Born Population in the United States: 2003," *Current Population Reports*, Series P20–551, August 2004.

11. U.S. Census Bureau, "Race and Hispanic Origin in 2005," *Population Profile of the United States; Dynamic Version*, Table 1.

12. Martin E. Spencer, "Multiculturalism, 'Political Correctness,' and the Politics of Identity," in Vincent N. Parrillo (ed.), "Multiculturalism and Diversity," *Sociological Forum*, 9 (1994): 547–67.

13. James S. Olson, *The Ethnic Dimension in American Society*, 2nd ed. (New York: St. Martin's Press, 1994), 102–4.

14. Emory Bogardus, "Comparing Racial Distance in Ethiopia, South Africa, and the United States," *Sociology and Social Research*, 52 (1968): 149–56; Carolyn A. Owen, Howard C. Eisner, and Thomas R. McFaul, "A Half-Century of Social Distance Research: National Replication of the Bogardus Studies," *Sociology and Social Research*, 66 (1981): 80–97; Vincent N. Parrillo and Christopher Donoghue, "Updating the Bogardus Social Distance Studies: A New National Survey," *Social Science Journal* 42:2 (2005): 257–71.

15. U.S. Department of Homeland Security, *Yearbook of Immigration Statistics: 2006* (Washington, DC: U.S. Government Printing Office, 2007), Table 35.

16. "Immigration." Available at www.pollingreport.com/immigration.htm [accessed December 28, 2007].

17. "Immigration: Overview." Available at www.publicagenda.com/issues [accessed December 28, 2007].

18. British Broadcasting Company, *Short History of Immigration*. Available at news.bbc.co.uk [accessed November 2, 2007].

9

Is Multiculturalism a Threat?

"Double Lightning in Glyfada-Athens" by Niko Silver (2006) illustrates the theme of this chapter: determining whether or not what appears on the horizon should be a matter of concern or enjoyed for what and how it presents itself to the beholder.

155

Multiculturalism is taught in academia, debated in government, promoted by ethnic leaders, reported by the media, and discussed among the citizenry. Few are indifferent to a subject with so many proponents and opponents. Some see multiculturalism as the bedrock on which to build a society of true equality, whereas others see multiculturalism as a sinkhole that will swallow up the foundation of U.S. society.

At its core, the multiculturalism debate is a polarization of the centuries-old dual American realities of pluralism and assimilation into competing forces for dominance. As this book has shown, pluralism has been a constant reality in the United States since colonial times, and assimilation has been a steady, powerful force as well. There have always been both assimilationist and pluralist advocates, as well as both nativist alarmists and minority separatists.

Resentment and hostility about multiculturalism result from several factors. Rapid communication and televised images have heightened public consciousness of the diversity within U.S. society, but without placing it in the continuity of the larger historical context. Government policies and programs, particularly those dealing with bilingualism, become controversial when viewed as more than transitional aids by both pluralists and assimilationists. Vocal advocates for each position arouse strong feelings in their listeners in suggesting an either-or stance of supposedly diametrically opposing forces.

Raising reactions toward multiculturalism to a firestorm level are still other factors. First are the radical positions either anti-immigrant or racist or else anti–White male or nonintegrationist.[1] Another is revisionist history or literary anthologies that downplay dead White males (DWMs) or else Western civilization and heavily emphasize women, people of color, and non-Western civilization. Add furor about political correctness, whether in the guise of speech or behavior codes, curricula offerings, or selective emphases. The result is controversy of a (dare I say it?) white-heat intensity.

Multiculturalism is a stance taken by pluralists. Does that mean it imperils the process of assimilation? Basically, the answer is no, but the explanation is a complicated one. Multiculturalism, as mentioned in the first chapter, is a newer term for cultural pluralism, not a new phenomenon. Large foreign-speaking communities, foreign-language schools, organizations, houses of worship, and even pluralist extremists are not new to U.S. society. Is, then, the new version not to be feared any more than its precursor or is this more than a "new suit"? Is this thing we call *multiculturalism* a clear and present danger? Before we can address this concern, we need to understand exactly what multiculturalism is.

The Umbrellas of Multiculturalism

Multiculturalism does not mean the same thing to everyone. Even the multiculturalists do not agree with one another as to what they are advocating. Before we can address the advantages or disadvantages of a multicultural society, therefore, we need to understand these differing viewpoints.[2]

The Inclusionists

During the 1970s, multiculturalism meant the inclusion of material in the school curriculum that related the contributions of non-European peoples to the nation's history. In the next phase, multiculturalists aimed to change all areas of the curriculum in schools and colleges to reflect the diversity of U.S. society and to develop in individuals an awareness and appreciation for the impact of non-European civilizations on American culture.[3]

Inclusionists would appear to be assimilationists, but they are more than this. Assimilationists seek the elimination of cultural differences through the loss of one's distinctive traits that are replaced by the language, values, and other attributes of mainstream Americans. Although inclusionists share assimilationists' desire for national unity through a common identity, they also promote a pluralist or multiculturalist perspective. This notion finds expression by recognition of diversity throughout U.S. history and of minority contributions to American art, literature, music, cuisine, scientific achievements, sports, and holiday celebrations.

In the 1990s, this viewpoint perhaps found its most eloquent voice in Diane Ravitch.[4] She also emphasized a common culture, but one that incorporated the contributions of all racial and ethnic groups so that they can believe in their full membership in America's past, present, and future. She envisioned the elimination of allegiance to any specific racial and/or ethnic group, with emphasis instead on our common humanity, our shared national identity, and our individual accomplishments.

Inclusionist multiculturalists thus approach pluralism not with groups each standing under their own different-colored umbrellas, but of all sharing one multicolored umbrella whose strength and character reflect the diverse backgrounds but singular cause of those standing under it together.

The Separatists

The group of multiculturalists that generates the most controversy is people who advocate "minority nationalism" and "separate pluralism."

They reject an integrative approach and the notion of forming a common bond of identity among both the distinct minority groups and mainstream Americans. Instead of a collective American national identity, they seek specific, separate group identities that will withstand the assimilation process. This form of multiculturalism is the most extreme version of pluralism.

To achieve their objective and create a positive group identity, these multiculturalists seek to teach and maintain their own cultural customs, history, values, and festivals while refusing to acknowledge those of the dominant culture. For example, some Native Americans raise strong objections to Columbus Day parades, while Afrocentrists downgrade Western civilization by arguing that it is merely a derivative of Afro-Egyptian culture—a claim, by the way, that is not historically accurate.[5]

Separatist multiculturalists do not want to stand with others under one multicolored umbrella. Not only do they wish to be under their own special umbrella, but they also want to share it only with their own kind and let them know why it is such a special umbrella. One may walk the same ground in the same storm, but shelter is to be found under a group's personal umbrella.

What particularly infuriates the assimilationists about the separatists' position is their concern that such emphasis on group identity promotes what Arthur Schlesinger called "the cult of ethnicity." In *The Disuniting of America* (1991), a book widely discussed in both Europe and North America, Schlesinger warned that the Balkan chaos at that time could be America's prologue.[6]

It is precisely that devastating warfare in the Balkans among Bosnians, Croatians, and Serbs in the former Yugoslavia that prompted so many voices in Canada, Europe, and the United States against multiculturalists who espouse separate pluralism. The "balkanization of society" is the most common expression that critics of multiculturalism use to suggest the threat to the social fabric supplied by a divisive policy promoting group identity over individual or societal welfare.

When Hispanic leaders from groups such as LULAC insist on "language rights"—the maintenance of the Spanish language and Latino culture at public expense—the assimilationists warn of an emerging "Tower of Babel" society.[7] When Afrocentrists such as Molefi Asante and Leon Jeffries emphasize the customs of African cultures over those of the dominant culture, their stress on African ethnicity provokes disapproval from critics such as Schlesinger, who complain that they drive "even deeper the awful wedges between races" by exaggerating ethnic differences.

The Integrative Pluralists

In 1915, Horace Kallen used the metaphor of a symphony orchestra to portray the strength through diversity of U.S. society.[8] Just as different groups of instruments each play their separate parts of the musical score, but together produce beautiful music of blends and contrasts, so, too, he said, do the various populations within pluralist America. Kallen's idea of effective functional integration but limited cultural integration, however, was essentially a Eurocentric vision and reality. People of color were mentioned only incidentally and were typically not allowed to sit with, let alone join, the orchestra.

Harry Triandis not only added an interracial component to this view of integrative pluralism in 1976, but he also suggested that the majority culture is enriched by "additive multiculturalism."[9] By this comment he meant that one can get more out of life by understanding other languages, cultural values, and social settings. He hoped for society becoming more cohesive by finding common superordinate goals without insisting on a loss of Black identity, Native American identity, Asian identity, or Hispanic identity. Arguing that mainstream Americans, secure in their identity, need to develop new interpersonal skills, Triandis maintained that the essence of pluralism is the development of appreciation, interdependence, and skills to interact intimately with persons from other cultures. He added,

> The majority culture can be enriched by considering the viewpoints of the several minority cultures that exist in America rather than trying to force these minorities to adopt a monocultural, impoverished, provincial viewpoint which may in the long run reduce creativity and the chances of effective adjustment in a fast-changing world. (p. 181)

This argument of cultural enrichment from diverse subcultures found another form of expression in *Beyond the Culture Wars* (1992) by Gerald Graff.[10] He suggested that exposure to differing cultural views will revitalize education by creating the dynamics of dialogue and debate. As Socrates once encouraged his students to search for truth through intellectual clashes, so, too, Graff maintained, can multicultural education help students overcome relativism so they can become informed about different positions.

Ronald Takaki echoed Graff's idea by recommending that the university become the meeting ground for different viewpoints.[11] He believes that American minds need to be opened to greater cultural diversity. U.S. history, like the country, does not belong to one group, says Takaki, and so a change in the status quo is needed. Instead of a hierarchy of power headed by a privileged group, greater cross-cultural understanding and interconnected viewpoints are necessary.

Integrative pluralists envision a multitude of distinctive umbrellas each containing a different group, but with the umbrellas' edges attached to each other, so that, collectively, they embrace everyone. Guided equally by the many handles of the interconnected umbrellas, one can look around to see where another group is coming from within the framework of the whole.

The Larger Context

Although the United States has always been a nation of immigrants and a land of diversity, some of its citizens nevertheless have continually spoken and acted against what they perceived as threats from multiculturalism. Similarly, in the other traditional immigrant-receiving nations—Australia, Canada, and England—outcries against multiculturalism have occurred in the past several decades.

In Australia, historian Geoffrey Blainey's book, *All for Australia* (1984), severely criticized that country's immigration and multiculturalist policies, paving the way for the formation in 1997 of the One Nation Party, which stressed national unity over multiculturalism. Although that political party no longer exists, the federal government enacted many of its policies. In England, rising tensions led to a riot in 2001 in the working-class city of Bradford, involving about 1,000 South Asian youth and about £27 million in damages. In recent years, British politicians have debated whether their current policy of cultural diversification requires change to increase societal cohesion. Canadian multiculturalism, cited by many admirers as the world's best model of pluralism, nonetheless has its critics who believe it promotes divisiveness. They contend that such policies and practices force individuals to be ethnics forever even if they want to assimilate.[12]

In Europe, multiculturalism is a different concept compared with the United States. The U.S. concept of citizenship is that anyone from anywhere can become naturalized, but the European conception, for the most part, rests on ethnic heritage, language, and culture. I have seen this firsthand through interactions with politicians and nonpoliticians alike in numerous European countries. One can be a third-generation Turk in Germany or Hungarian in Romania, for example, and still not be considered a German or Romanian, respectively, by others or even by oneself. Generally, multiculturalism in Europe means psychological isolation and social distance between groups, rather than any growing cohesiveness.

Currently, low birth rates have resulted in the reality that not a single European country has people having enough children to replace themselves when they die.[13] Beginning in the 1990s, the resultant influx of foreigners to meet labor demands intensified this us-and-them mentality, generating in the 1990s and afterward xenophobic reactions, ethnoviolence, the rise of right-wing reactionary political parties, and efforts at new restrictive immigration laws. For example, in Germany during a wave of violence in 1992–1993, more than 1,800 attacks on foreigners and 17 deaths occurred. In France, the far-right Nationalist Front political party finished second in the 2002 election with 18 percent of the vote. Similar parties—the Free Party in Austria, the Flemish block in Belgium, and MSI in Italy—have all received increasing support in recent years.

Europeans use the term *racism* more generally to refer to negative attitudes or actions toward any ethnic group, whereas Americans tend to use its narrower connotation to refer only to physically distinct groups. Yet racism by its American definition also is a factor in European xenophobia. In Italy, for example, many of its non-White citizens complain of treatment as inferiors or as children without respect shown to them. As Italy struggles to absorb its recent influx of developing-world migrants, many Italians avoid interactions with them and little mixing occurs other than through mercantile encounters.[14]

Roses and Thorns

Cultivated for almost 5,000 years, roses were known to the ancient Persians, Greeks, and Romans. One of our most popular flowers, the rose now comes in more than 8,000 varieties. Yet as beautiful and romantic as most people find roses to be, their thorns can hurt.

Roses seem a particularly apt analogy in any discussion about multiculturalism. Both require warmth and nurturing to bloom fully. The stronger their roots, the more they thrive. A variety of species is common to both, yet universal treatment gives vibrancy to all. Both also contain beauty and danger. Focusing only on the rose when reaching for it often brings flesh into painful contact with a thorn; focusing narrowly on racial or cultural differences often causes the pain of isolation or conflict.

Some proponents of multiculturalism (the separatists) want to focus on only one variety of "rose" among many, whereas other advocates (the inclusionists) stress the commonality in origin that so many kinds of "roses" share. The third group of multiculturalists (the integrative pluralists) emphasizes the overall beauty of "roses" of different colors and varieties sharing the same "garden." The critics of multiculturalism, however, seem only to see its "thorns."

Completely ignoring the thorns needlessly places one at risk. If we look only at the thorns, we miss the beauty of the rose. If we pay heed to the thorns or remove them, as florists so thoughtfully do for their customers, they cannot hurt us, and our appreciation for the rose remains unspoiled. We now look first at the thorns, the negative side of multiculturalism, and then at the roses, the positive side.

The "Thorns" of Multiculturalism

The "thorns" of multiculturalism are primarily those of immigration, language, culture, and race. Other thorns could undoubtedly be named, but these are the most important because it is primarily in them that some Americans find the threat to U.S. society.

The "Immigrant Thorns"

Make no mistake about it. Continuing high immigration fuels the debate about multiculturalism because this subject is about much more than simply preserving one's heritage. It is about power struggles among groups. It is about economics, jobs, social welfare, and tax dollars.

Concern about large numbers of immigrants arriving each year is likely to instill antipathy in many native-born White and Black Americans toward any manifestation of foreign origins through multicultural policies or programs. With more than 23 million immigrants arriving since 1980, a sizable proportion of the U.S. public thinks there are too many immigrants in the country. Such anti-immigration sentiments have sounded in the land almost continually since large numbers of Irish Catholics began entering the United States in the early 19th century.[15]

Public opinion polls conducted by the Roper Center in 1981 and 1982 found that two thirds of all Americans favored a decrease in immigration. That heavy anti-immigration response should be understood in the context of the 1980–1982 recession and the influx of more than 200,000 Vietnamese "boat people" and 125,000 Cuban "Marielitos" within this 2-year period.

Today, Americans have mixed opinions about immigration. A May 2007 CBS News/*New York Times* national poll, for example, found that 57 percent of respondents said they felt that the most recent immigrants contribute to the country, whereas 28 percent thought they caused problems. Yet in a June 2007 NBC/*Wall Street Journal* national poll, a more even split occurred, with 46 percent saying immigration helps more than it hurts the United States, whereas 44 percent thought the opposite. On the subject of unauthorized immigration, 61 percent viewed it as "very serious," and another 30 percent said it was "somewhat serious."[16]

One multigenerational pattern about the public response to immigration needs mentioning. Contemporary immigrants of any time period have almost always received negative evaluations by most native-born Americans, many descendants of earlier immigrants once castigated by other native-born Americans. With the passage of time, people view these now "old" immigrant groups as making positive contributions to the cultural and socioeconomic well-being of society as they transfer their negative perceptions to new immigrant groups. Numerous anti-immigration organizations have emerged to lobby for restrictive laws to curtail immigration. The largest of these are the American Immigration Control Foundation (AICF), the Foundation for American Immigration Reform (FAIR), and the Center for Immigration Studies (CIS).

Although these and other anti-immigrant groups vary in the intensity of their views, they all see the present immigration as a threat to the United States. Their opposition rests on their belief that immigrants either take jobs away from Americans, often from poor people who are forced onto welfare, or else go on welfare. Either way, these groups insist, the immigrants drive up social welfare costs. Other arguments include the assertion that immigrants strain law enforcement resources, contribute to an overpopulation problem through their higher birth rates, and deplete our natural resources.

Some states—such as California, Florida, Illinois, New Jersey, New York, and Texas, which are the destinations of about 80 percent of all immigrants—clearly feel the impact of immigration more than other states. In 2004, FAIR estimated that—in just the areas of education, emergency room medical services, and incarceration—illegal immigration costs taxpayers about $36 billion annually.[17] Such reports and claims of high costs for the taxpayer provide ready ammunition for immigration critics.

If multiculturalism means favoring an immigration that places a financial hardship on the American worker and taxpayer, then many Americans oppose multiculturalism.

The "Language Thorns"

Foreigners speaking a language other than English have been a thorn in the side of many Americans for more than 200 years. In 1750, Benjamin Franklin expressed concern about the prevalence of the German language in Pennsylvania, and George Washington wrote to John Adams in 1798 against encouraging immigration because, among other things, the new arrivals "retain the language . . . which they bring with them."[18] No doubt these men spoke not only for themselves, but also for a great many of their contemporaries as well.

Such complaints have reverberated down through the generations to the present day. They are now also louder and more numerous given current migration trends. Two out of every three immigrants speak Spanish, and, as a result, more than 28 million Americans 5 years and older speak Spanish. Another 7 million speak an Asian or Pacific Island language. Education officials expect more than 5 million children speaking more than 150 languages to enter the nation's public schools in this decade.

With the prevalence of so many non-English-speaking youngsters and adults, Americans have done more than complain. For example, Japanese American S. I. Hayakawa, a former U.S. Senator from California and former president of San Francisco State University, founded U.S. English, an organization dedicated to making English the nation's official language; eliminating or reducing bilingual education programs; and abolishing bilingual ballots, government documents, and road signs. By late 2007, it claimed 1.8 million members. English-only laws have been introduced in dozens of state legislatures since the late 1980s. Although 13 states rejected English-only legislative proposals, by 2007, 30 states had English as their official language.

Many Americans are impatient with those who are unable to speak English. Their contention is that anyone living in this country should speak its language. Believing that our schools provide the "heat" for the melting pot, they are particularly irked about bilingual education programs. Critics see bilingual programs as counterproductive because they reduce assimilation and cohesiveness in U.S. society while isolating ethnic groups from one another. It is here that opponents use the terms *ethnic tribalism* and *classrooms of Babel* to argue that bilingual education fosters separation instead of cultural unity.[19] When LULAC leaders and others call for language and cultural maintenance programs at public expense, the monolingual adherents see red.

If multiculturalism means that English proficiency is not a priority, then many Americans oppose multiculturalism.

The "Cultural Thorns"

A monthly average of 105,000 new immigrants—about 75 percent of them Asian or Hispanic—now arrive in the United States. Ethnic resiliency in language, ingroup solidarity, and subcultural patterns is both sustained and enhanced by the steadily increasing size of each new immigrant group.

Without this constant infusion of newcomers, acculturation would inexorably lessen each group's cultural isolation. Group members would gradually learn to speak English and function more fully within the larger society. Even if such factors as limited education, poor job skills, and discrimination were present to prevent economic mainstreaming, greater cultural fusion would most likely occur over time.

Instead, we have large-scale immigration from Asian and Latin American countries revitalizing ethnic subcommunities with their language usage and cultural patterns. Differences in physical appearance, non-Western traditions, and religious faiths—together with the prevalence of languages other than English, especially Spanish—suggest to some Americans that, unless immigration is significantly curtailed, American culture and society are in danger of fragmenting.

What makes the cultural thorns even sharper is the new ethnic presence in our small towns and suburbs. Once the almost exclusive sanctuary of homogenized Americans, many of these communities are now the residential areas of choice for tens of thousands of first-generation Americans of non-European, mostly Asian, origin. Educated business and professional persons, seeking out desirable communities with excellent school systems, have brought racial and ethnic diversity to towns unaccustomed to such a multiethnic mix, sometimes erecting a mosque or Sikh temple, with its unique architecture, in contrast to other structures in the community.

It is not simply the presence of visibly distinct newcomers that creates tensions. These first-generation Americans live in the community, but they are not of it, because they seldom interact with neighbors. Instead, they maintain an interactional network within their own group scattered throughout the area. This informal social patterning is reminiscent of other immigrants who have lived in recognized territorial subcommunities. However, because these middle-class suburban ethnics live among homogenized Americans, their lack of involvement in community life encourages social distance and grates on others' sensibilities.

Besides a normal first-generation immigrant preference to associate with one's own people, some pragmatic elements deter suburban ethnic social interactions. Often the wife, filling the traditional gender role as the nurturer, has limited command of English and feels insecure about conversing with neighbors. The husband is usually at work for long hours and has little free time except to spend with the family.

Joining social organizations is a strong American orientation, as noted by Tocqueville and many others. Possessing neither time nor yet fully acculturated, few Asian Americans get involved in such typical suburban activities as parent-teacher organizations, team sports coaching, or scouting leadership.

In time, this situation will probably change, but the present noninvolvement maintains Asian social distance from other Americans in their local communities. In response, suburbanites often view the Asians as not giving to, but only taking from, the community. This reaction is especially acute when Asian American children, reflecting the high motivation and goal achievement instilled in them by their parents, appear overrepresented in garnering awards and recognition in scholarships and music.

If multiculturalism means maintenance of an alien culture and lessening community cohesiveness, then most Americans oppose multiculturalism.

The "Racial Thorns"

Except for extremist groups like the Ku Klux Klan, the National Association for the Advancement of White People, and neo-Nazis, few talk openly of race in their opposition to multiculturalism. Nevertheless, race is an important component of the multiculturalism debate.

The United States may be a less racist country than in earlier years if civil rights legislation, public opinion polls, and the social indicators of education, occupation, income, and elected officials serve as a barometer. Yet racism still exists, perhaps less intensely in some areas than others, but it remains nonetheless, and flares up occasionally as in the 2007 case of the Jena 6. It also can be found in numerous conversations, avoidance responses, subtle acts of discrimination, and myriad interaction patterns.

Institutional racism—the established laws, customs, and practices that systematically reflect and produce racial inequities in society—is a more significant factor than individuals committing overt racist actions, however. Biases remain built into the social structure, causing many individuals unknowingly to act without deliberate intent to hinder the advancement of non-Whites.

Although the Commission on Civil Rights (1981) identified areas where affirmative action could take aim at institutional racism (job seniority rules, nepotism-based recruitment or union membership, bank credit practices, culturally biased job performance tests), more than a quarter century later, some of these remain problem areas. De facto housing segregation and disparities in school funding for urban and suburban schools are other examples of the multigenerational continuation of a subtle, structural racist practice. The pervasiveness of institutional racism remains both an obstacle in the path of upward mobility to many racial minority group members and a basic impediment to better interracial relations.

As successful as the United States has been in assimilating national minorities, it has been far less successful in assimilating racial minorities.

African and Native Americans are still not fully integrated as mainstream Americans. Because we have never fully resolved our centuries-old twin problems of race relations and racial integration, the growing presence of people of color from developing world countries exacerbates the matter.

Racial tensions have heightened in some areas because of the influx of racially distinct, "clannish" strangers into neighborhoods unaccustomed to their presence. When this influx has occurred in previously homogeneous middle-class suburbs, the reactions may be more subtle, but the resentment is real and finds expression in avoidance responses, zoning regulations, and verbal complaints within one's circle of family, friends, and neighbors.

If multiculturalism means an increased racial presence and/or increased racial power that puts their own racial group to any disadvantage, then most Americans oppose multiculturalism.

The "Roses" of Multiculturalism

Roses bud, bloom, and fade away. Rosebuds give us the promise of new beauty about to arrive, and when the flowers are in full bloom, their contribution of beauty to our lives has to be experienced to be fully appreciated. Gradually, however, the roses fade and their petals gracefully fall to the ground, covering the dark earth with their pastel colors. With modest pruning, the gardener can coax other roses to appear and repeat the process again and again.

Multiculturalism, however, is not a rose that will fade away in the United States, which has always been a land of diversity and destination for millions of immigrants. However, some "blooms" of ethnicity do fade away as, for example, we presently witness what Richard Alba calls "the twilight of ethnicity" among European Americans.[20] Moreover, what appear to some people as thorns may actually be roses instead. Let us extend our metaphor of roses onto the four types of thorns just discussed.

The "Immigrant Roses"

If a nation's strength lies in its people, then the strength of the United States clearly lies in the diversity of its people. Immigrants from all over the world have come here, and in one way or another, each group has played some role in the nation's evolution into its present superpower status.

Past immigrants built our cities, transportation systems, and labor unions and enabled us to come of age both agriculturally and industrially. Many of today's immigrants have revitalized our cities; helped our high-tech industries remain competitive; and pumped billions of dollars annually into the national economy through their businesses, occupations, and consumerism. Combating negative stereotyping, societal ostracism, and fear about their growing size, each immigrant group then and now has worked hard to survive and put down roots. Viewed as a threat, each has proved to be an asset.

Although the immigrant roses bloom, others do not often appreciate their beauty. It is the exceptional individual who admires immigrants when they are immigrants. Only after the immigrant rose fades and its falling petals mingle with the soil that contains all our roots do we look back and cherish the bloom that is part of our heritage.

The "Language Roses"

Unlike the people of most nations who are at least bilingual, most Americans are monolingual. This limitation encourages ethnocentrism and provincialism and places the business community at a disadvantage in the global marketplace. Mastery of a second language enhances one's mental mobility while enriching cultural insights and perspectives.

If Americans were to become proficient in a second language, encouraged to do so by the Asian and Latino population cohorts now living here, the result could easily be a society reaching greater maturity and tolerance in its intergroup relations. Most Europeans have long been at least bilingual, and their cultures and societal cohesion have not suffered. Bilingual advocates argue that bilingualism would not undermine U.S. culture either, only enrich it.

For those who do not buy into bilingualism for all citizens, the consistent findings of public opinion polls and scientific studies about English language acquisition offer comforting news. A 2003 Public Agenda study funded by the Carnegie Foundation revealed that 87 percent of immigrants polled said it was extremely important for immigrants to be able to speak and understand English.[21]

Today, first- and second-generation Americans become fluent in English at a faster pace than did past immigrants. In one of the largest-ever longitudinal studies of second-generation Americans (5,200 immigrant children in Miami and San Diego), Rubén Rumbaut and Alejandro Portés found that 99 percent spoke fluent English and less than one third maintained fluency in their parents' tongues by age 17.[22] In a different study, Rumbaut determined that 73 percent of second-generation immigrants in Southern California with two foreign-born parents preferred to speak English at home instead of their native tongue. By the third generation, more than 97 percent of these immigrants—Chinese, Filipino, Guatemalan, Korean, Mexican, Salvadoran, and Vietnamese—preferred to speak only English at home.[23]

Despite all fears of Asian and Hispanic immigrants posing a threat to the English language, assimilation is still, as Nathan Glazer (1993) asserted, "the most powerful force affecting the ethnic and racial elements of the United States."[24] As the American Jewish Committee stated, "The use of additional languages to meet the needs of language minorities does not pose a threat to America's true common heritage and common bond—the quest for freedom and opportunity."[25]

To allay further the anxieties of those who fear that the large Hispanic American presence is an unprecedented threat simply because of its size, we have a comparable example in our past, with the almost 4.9 million Germans who entered the United States between 1841 and 1900. Keep in mind that the U.S. population was much smaller then (23.1 million in 1850 and 62.9 million in 1890, compared with 203.3 million in 1970 and 303.2 million at the beginning of 2008). Also, today's films, TV, music, and Internet are ever-present English-learning aids that were unknown at the time of this large German presence.

In the mid- to late 19th century, so many hundreds of thousands of Germans lived in the area lying among Cincinnati, Milwaukee, and St. Louis that it became known as the "great German triangle."[26] Because so many German children attended public schools in the German triangle, the states passed laws permitting all academic subjects to be taught in German whenever the demand was sufficient to warrant it. Ohio passed its statute in 1837, and the others followed in the 1840s.

Consider the enormity of this action. In major cities, as well as in rural regions, the states of Ohio, Missouri, and Wisconsin (other states, too) authorized German as an official language for all classroom instruction. Cultural diversity, including that of language, was not only tolerated, but also encouraged.

The use of German in the public schools served a purpose other than academic instruction. It was intended to preserve the whole range of German culture even more so after the unification of Germany in the 1870s. With an increased pride in their origins, German immigrants and their children developed a greater sense of their ethnicity than they possessed before their emigration. Because language enhanced their sense of being German, the German Americans continued to speak their language in their schools, homes, churches, and everyday business transactions.

As extensive German immigrant settlement in the region continued decade after decade, German-language instruction in all subjects continued in the public schools. Such was the case in the private schools as well. By 1910, more than 95 percent of German Catholic parishes had parochial schools taught in German, and more than 2,000 parishes conducted

German-language services, much to the consternation of the Irish American church hierarchy. During World War I, however, patriotic hysteria to drive the "Hun" language out of the schools prompted states such as Ohio and Nebraska to pass laws prohibiting instruction in German in all schools, public and private. A legal challenge to this action reached the U.S. Supreme Court in *Robert Meyer v. Nebraska* (1923).

Although the Court upheld the states' right to determine public school instruction in English only, its ruling on private and parochial schools was an important one with regard to language rights. Ruling that all state laws prohibiting the teaching and use of German in private or parochial schools were in violation of the 14th Amendment and therefore unconstitutional, the Court declared that the rights of both parents and private/parochial schools to teach their children in a language other than English was within the liberty guaranteed by that amendment.

Despite (a) the institutionalization of academic instruction in German, (b) the steady influx of large numbers of German immigrants, and (c) more than 60 years of German language maintenance, German language usage declined. That process had already begun by 1885, as indicated by the complaints then of German American leaders that the younger generation was losing the German tongue and that parents no longer insisted on their children studying German in the schools.

As with other ethnic groups, English gradually replaced the homeland language, even among the millions of Germans so heavily concentrated in regions such as the German triangle. The German language rose once bloomed mightily in the United States, but it has faded, its petals drifting downward and blending with others that fell earlier. Perhaps the Spanish language is another such rose.

The "Cultural Roses"

The United States contains many persistent subcultures, people who steadfastly adhere to their own way of life as much as possible, resisting absorption into the dominant culture. These are usually religious groups—such as the Amish, Hutterites, Mennonites, and Hasidim—or groups whose ancestors predate the United States, such as the Native Americans and Spanish Americans in the Southwest. One also could argue that a persistent subculture exists among one fourth of the Black Americans mired in poverty for multiple generations. Until society finds an effective means to end their deprivation, these hard-core Black poor will continue to subsist within a subculture necessary for their survival.

Most racial and ethnic groups, however, are part of a convergent subculture gradually disappearing as its members become integrated into the dominant culture. For some their "cultural roses" bloom longer than others, but at some point the roses do fade. Besides the Germans just discussed, we have dozens of other examples of once-vibrant ethnic subcultures, ones that contemporary native-born Americans considered both persistent and a threat to the dominant culture, but that eventually converged into the mainstream.

Ethnic subcultures do not undermine the dominant culture. The United States has always had them, and at the time of their growing strength and vitality, they often contained separatist advocates. It is not uncommon for outsiders to become anxious about subgroup loyalties posing a danger to the larger society. Theodore Roosevelt's famous remark that "there is no room in this country for hyphenated Americanism" spoke to the same fears of subversion of American culture that Schlesinger addressed as the "disuniting of America."[27]

When immigrants come to the United States, they come to join us. In forsaking their ancestral lands, they pay us the highest compliment: They want to spend the rest of their lives with us in a country where they hope to realize their dreams of a better life. They come to be a part of us, an "us" they have imagined after exposure to thousands of pictures, films, TV shows, stories, letters, and rumors. They come to join us, not to keep separate from us. It may take some time, longer than some Americans' patience, but for most that integration into the dominant culture occurs.

The falling petals of fading cultural roses also mingle with the soil containing all our roots. U.S. society, reflecting its multicultural past and present, continually becomes even more enriched with architecture, art, creative works, cuisine, music, and other cultural contributions from the diversity of its people.

The "Racial Roses"

Here we have a rare species of rose because its bloom in a multiracial setting in the United States is difficult to produce. Filling too much of our past and present has been racial animosity, exploitation, and violence. As I said earlier, we have never fully resolved the twin problems of race relations and racial integration in our society.

Part of our problem has been our cultural mind-set. With a simplistic White and non-White racial classification system, we have insidiously enmeshed race within our social structure. We have created and consistently reinforced the us-and-them mentality that manifests itself in social distance, differential treatment, deprivation, and suffering. Furthermore, our monora-cial categories ignore the multiracial backgrounds of millions of African Americans, Filipinos, Latinos, Native Americans, and Whites. We have taken a step forward in the deconstruction of race with the multiple racial census choices and in the growing recognition of the millions of biracial Americans.

As changing demographics make an increased multiracial society more evident to Americans, perhaps we shall see the removal of the weeds of racism (particularly the rooting out of institutional discrimination) and the blooming of the racial roses. Such a change will not be easy. But as the non-White segment of the U.S. population increases, so may the multiracial com-ponent of the American identity. If no longer relegated to the periphery, racial groups will be more at the center, and at the center one finds both power and integration.

Increased racial tensions remain a distinct possibility, however, and we certainly find examples of that today. However, with the greater sharing of power that must come, that very same sharing of power could also cause greater racial acceptance.

At the risk of being accused of wearing rose-colored glasses in depicting the racial roses, I would suggest that if we can get the racial roses to bloom in this land—get to that point where each of the races displays its full beauty—then we can look past that point to the next horizon. When the racial rose petals fall and mingle with the soil common to us all, we will have moved past race as a divisive aspect of our society. This was Martin Luther King's dream, that one day his children would be judged by the content of their character instead of the color of their skin.[28]

Is Multiculturalism the Enemy?

On the battlefield of multiculturalism, pluralists and assimilationists wage war, but neither side will vanquish the other. As always, both forces will remain an integral part of U.S. society. The United States will remain a bea-con of hope to immigrants everywhere, keeping the rich tradition of plural-ism alive and well. Assimilationist forces, as consistently demonstrated for centuries, will remain strong, particularly on immigrant children and their descendants. Multiculturalism will no more weaken that process any more than the many past manifestations of ethnic ingroup solidarity have.

Social observers of different eras—Alexis de Tocqueville, Gunnar Myrdal, and Andrew Hacker, among others—have commented on the separate racial worlds within the United States. These separate worlds are not the result of multiculturalist teachings. Only when we break down the remaining racial barriers, eliminate institutional discrimination, and open up paths free of obstacles to a good education and job opportunities for everyone will racial integration improve. Afrocentrist schools do not undermine a cohesive society any more than Catholic schools, yeshivas, or other religious schools do. Multiculturalism is not the enemy; systemic racism is.

Notes

1. John Leo, "The Hijacking of American History," *U.S. News & World Report* (November 14, 1994): 36.

2. Ronald Takaki, ed., *From Different Shores: Perspectives on Race and Ethnicity in America*, 2nd ed. (New York: Oxford University Press, 1994), 283–95.

3. Martin E. Spencer, "Multiculturalism, 'Political Correctness,' and the Politics of Identity," ed. Vincent N. Parrillo, "Multiculturalism and Diversity," *Sociological Forum, 9* (December 1994): 547–67.

4. Diane Ravitch, "Multiculturalism: E Pluribus Plures," *American Scholar, 59* (1990): 337–54.

5. Molefi K. Asante, *The Afrocentric Idea* (Philadelphia: Temple University Press, 1987).

6. Arthur M. Schlesinger, Jr., *The Disuniting of America: Reflections on a Multicultural Society* (Knoxville, TN: Whittle Communications, 1991).

7. See Linda Chavez, "Hispanics vs. Their Leaders," *Commentary* (October 1991): 47–9.

8. Horace Kallen, "Democracy versus the Melting Pot," *Nation* (February 18, 1915): 220.

9. Harry C. Triandis, "The Future of Pluralism," *Journal of Social Issues, 32* (1976): 179–208.

10. Gerald Graft, *Beyond the Culture Wars: How Teaching the Conflicts Can Revitalize American Education* (New York: Norton, 1992).

11. Ronald Takaki, "Multiculturalism: Battleground or Meeting Ground?" *The Annals of the American Academy of Political and Social Science, 530* (1993): 109–21.

12. Irene Bloemraad, *Becoming a Citizen* (Berkeley: University of California Press, 2006), 235–6.

13. Michael Specter, "Population Implosion Worries a Graying Europe," *New York Times* (July 10, 1998): A1.

14. Sophie Arie, "Italy Takes Heat as Racist Voices Rise," *The Christian Science Monitor* (August 9, 2004): 6.

15. See Rita J. Simon, "Old Minorities, New Immigrants: Aspirations, Hopes, and Fears," *The Annals of the American Academy of Political and Social Science, 530* (1993): 62–3.

16. "Immigration." Available at www.pollingreport.com/immigration.htm [accessed January 2, 2008].

17. Federation for American Immigration Reform, "The Cost to Local Taxpayers for Illegal or 'Guest' Workers." Available at http://www.fairus.org/site/PageServer?pagename=research_localcosts [accessed January 2, 2008].

18. Vincent N. Parrillo, *Strangers to These Shores*, 9th ed. (Boston: Allyn & Bacon, 2008), 131, 146.

19. Connie Leslie, "Classrooms of Babel," *Newsweek* (February 11, 1991): 56–57.

20. Richard D. Alba, *Italian Americans: Into the Twilight of Ethnicity* (Englewood Cliffs, NJ: Prentice Hall, 1985).

21. Public Agenda, "Immigrants Dispel Negative Stereotypes." Available at www.publicagenda.com/press/press_release [accessed December 27, 2004].

22. Rubén G. Rumbaut and Alejandro Portés, *Ethnicities: Children of Immigrants in America* (Berkeley: University of California Press, 2001).

23. Rubén G. Rumbaut, "A Language Graveyard? Immigration, Generation, and Linguistic Acculturation in the United States," paper presented to the International Conference on The Integration of Immigrants: Language and Educational Achievement," Social Science Research Center, Berlin, June 30–July 1, 2005.

24. Nathan Glazer, "Is Assimilation Dead?" *The Annals of the American Academy of Political and Social Science, 530* (1993): 123.

25. "English as the Official Language" (New York: American Jewish Committee, 1987).

26. Carl Wittke, *We Who Built America*, rev. ed. (Cleveland, OH: Case Western Reserve University Press, 1967), 196–9.

27. Roosevelt's remarks come from a speech he gave in 1917 and preserved in Ralph Stout, ed., *Roosevelt in the Kansas City Star* (Boston: Houghton Mifflin, 1921), 137.

28. King's famous "I Have a Dream" speech was delivered on August 28, 1963, during the March on Washington for Jobs and Freedom. His actual words were, "I have a dream that my four little children will one day live in a nation where they will not be judged by the color of their skin but by the content of their character."

The Chicago Manual of Style

Chicago Manual (CM) Style

In disciplines such as history and other humanities, the preferred style is that of *The Chicago Manual of Style* (16th ed., 2010). This style is also explained in the *Student's Guide to Writing College Papers* (4th ed., 2010) by Kate L. Turabian et al. You can find news and updates for the *Chicago Manual of Style* on its Web site (http://www.chicagomanualofstyle.org) as well as on its Twitter page (twitter.com/ChicagoManual) and Facebook page.

When you use CM style, you may use notes or endnotes to acknowledge sources in the text (see a), or you may use in-text citations that refer the reader to a bibliography at the end of the paper (see b).

a NUMBERED NOTES

- *Numbering in the text.* Numbered notes are used to indicate publication information. They also add explanations and other material that would otherwise interrupt the main text. Citations should be numbered consecutively with superscript numbers ([1]). Put the note number at the end of the sentence or end of a clause immediately following the punctuation mark. Don't insert a space between the punctuation mark and the superscript number.

  > Appropriate government regulation may be the key to turning resource-rich countries into successful, profitable economies for its citizens.[6] Peter Maass has noted that "countries dependent on resource exports . . . are susceptible to lower growth, higher corruption, less freedom, and more warfare."[7]

- *Placing notes.* Notes appear at the bottom of the page as footnotes or at the end of the essay as endnotes.

- *Spacing notes.* Single-space within each note, and insert one blank line between each note. Indent the first line of each note the same number of spaces that you indent paragraphs.

- *Ordering the parts of notes.* Begin with the author's first and last names, add the title, and then include the publishing information and page numbers.

- *Punctuating, capitalizing, and abbreviating.* Use commas between elements, and put publishing information within parentheses. Include the page number, but omit the abbreviation *p.* or *pp.* Italicize titles of books and periodicals. Capitalize titles of articles, books, and journals. Use quotation marks around titles of periodical articles and sections of books. And end with a period.

From Chapter 72 of *Prentice Hall Reference Guide*, Eighth Edition. Muriel Harris, Jennifer L. Kunka. Copyright © 2011 by Pearson Education, Inc. Published by Pearson Prentice Hall. All rights reserved.

APA, CM, and CSE Documentation

- *Using a bibliography page.* A bibliography page is usually added to a paper containing notes (for a title, see the next page).

- *Adapting the style to the source material. Chicago Manual* style allows for some flexibility in creating bibliography entries, particularly for works accessed online. In bibliography and notes entries, include all relevant material needed to retrieve the source.

Ordering Notes in a Paper

The first time you cite a source, include the authors' full names, followed by a comma; the full title, followed by a comma; publication information, enclosed in parentheses; and the page or pages being cited, omitting *p.* or *pp.* Later citations include authors' last names, a shortened version of the title, and page numbers.

Use *Ibid.* to refer to the work in the directly preceding note or, if the page is different, use *Ibid.* followed by a comma and the page number.

6. Paul Collier, *The Plundered Planet: Why We Must—and How We Can—Manage Nature for Global Prosperity* (New York: Oxford University Press, 2010), 5.

7. Peter Maass, *Crude World: The Violent Twilight of Oil* (New York: Knopf, 2009), 6.

8. Collier, *Plundered Planet,* 132-33.

9. Ibid., 122.

10. Maass, *Crude World,* 7.

b AUTHOR-DATE CITATION FORMAT

The author-date citation format requires both in-text citations and a bibliography page. In-text citations in *Chicago Manual* style are similar, but not identical, to those in APA style.

- Up to three authors are cited by last name. If there are four or more authors, list only the first author's last name followed by *et al.*

- The date of publication is given next, with no intervening punctuation.

- If a page number is required, it is given following a comma.

Here are some typical author-date citations in CM style:

(Patel 2010, 18)

(Newhouse and Zuzu 1889)

(Baez et al. 2009, 244)

As explained by Patel (2010, 18), . . .

For online or electronic works without page numbers, indicate the section title (if available) under which the specific reference can be located:

> (Quinn 2010, under "Espionage")

If you are not using numbered notes, every work cited in the body of your paper must have an entry in the Bibliography at the end of the paper, and every work appearing in the Bibliography must be cited at least once in the body of the paper.

Note that the *Chicago Manual* also permits bibliography entries to follow the order and capitalization scheme of APA style, with one major difference: the date is *not* enclosed in parentheses.

C   BIBLIOGRAPHY ENTRIES

There are some stylistic differences between footnotes or endnotes and Bibliography entries. Whereas the names in notes appear in natural order (first name, then last name), the bibliography inverts the first author's name, with last name first. Elements in the bibliography are separated by periods, not commas and parentheses.

> Gladwell, Malcolm. *Outliers: The Story of Success.* New York: Little, Brown, 2008.

Title your list "Bibliography," "Works Cited," or "References."

Start the first line of each entry at the left margin, and indent all other lines in the entry. Double-space all bibliography entries in academic papers. Indent each line after the first with the same spacing used in indenting paragraphs. Include all of the same elements as in a note for that source, but do not put parentheses around the publishing information.

Italicize titles of books and periodicals. Use quotation marks around titles of periodicals and sections of books.

Parts of the Bibliography Entry for a Book

Information appears in the order given here.

| Author. | Give the full names of all authors (or editors or translators).

| *Title: Subtitle.* | Give the full title, including subtitle, in italics. If adding an editor, end with a comma instead of a period.

| Editor, compiler, or translator. | List these, if any, if in addition to the author.

| Volume number. | For a multivolume work, give the total number of volumes if the work is being referred to as a whole. If a single volume is being cited, identify only that one by number.

| Title of individual volume. | List the volume title, if applicable. If adding page numbers for a specific work, end with a comma instead of a period.

City: Publisher, Year. Include the city, the publisher's name (not abbreviated), and the date of publication. For an online book, add the electronic address, and place the access date in parentheses.

Page numbers. Give page numbers when a chapter or other section of a book is being cited. Use an inclusive number format (write 211–40, not 211–240).

DOI or URL. For works accessed online, add the Digital Object Identifier (DOI) number (doi:10.xxxx.xxxxx). If no DOI is available, give the full online address (URL) instead (http://xxxxxx.xxx/xxxx).

Notes and Bibliography Examples

In the examples, *N* stands for note format and *B* stands for bibliography format. See the note in b for information on parenthetical citations. Notes and bibliography entries may be either single-spaced or double-spaced in manuscripts, but *The Student's Guide to Writing College Papers*, 4th ed., by Turabian et al., indicates notes should be single-spaced and bibliography entries should be double-spaced in student papers, as shown below.

Books

1. One Author

N: 1. Evan Thomas, *The War Lovers: Roosevelt, Lodge, Hearst, and the Rush to Empire, 1898* (New York: Little, Brown, 2010), 20.

B: Thomas, Evan. *The War Lovers: Roosevelt, Lodge, Hearst, and the Rush to Empire, 1898*. New York: Little, Brown, 2010.

2. Two Authors

N: 2. Torben Iversen and Frances Rosenbluth, *Women, Work, and Politics: The Political Economy of Gender Inequality* (New Haven: Yale University Press, 2010), 50.

B: Iversen, Torben, and Frances Rosenbluth. *Women, Work, and Politics: The Political Economy of Gender Inequality*. New Haven: Yale University Press, 2010.

3. Three Authors

N: 3. Douglass C. North, John Joseph Wallis, and Barry R. Weingast, *Violence and Social Orders: A Conceptual Framework for Interpreting Recorded Human History* (New York: Cambridge University Press, 2009), 174-76.

B: North, Douglass C., John Joseph Wallis, and Barry R. Weingast. *Violence and Social Orders: A Conceptual Framework for Interpreting Recorded Human History*. New York: Cambridge University Press, 2009.

CM: Citing a Book

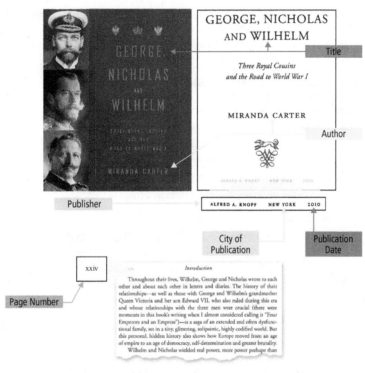

CM Notes Format:

1. Miranda Carter, *George, Nicholas, and Wilhelm: Three Royal Cousins and the Road to World War I* (New York: Knopf, 2010), xxiv.

CM Bibliography Format:

Carter, Miranda. *George, Nicholas, and Wilhelm: Three Royal Cousins and the Road to World War I.* New York: Knopf, 2010.

In-Text Example:

Miranda Carter writes that the story of King George V, Tsar Nicholas II, and Kaiser Wilhelm II "is a saga of an extended and often dysfunctional family, set in a tiny, glittering, solipsistic, highly codified world."[1]

APA, CM, and CSE Documentation

4. Four or More Authors In the notes format, list the first author and add *et al.* with no intervening punctuation.

N: 4. James A. Baker III et al., *The Iraq Study Group Report: The Way Forward—a New Approach* (New York: Vintage, 2006), 27.

In the bibliography format, list all authors for a work with between four and ten authors. If the work has eleven or more authors, list the first seven authors and add *et al.* with no intervening punctuation.

B: Baker, James A., III, Lee H. Hamilton, Lawrence S. Eagleburger, Vernon E. Jordan Jr., Edwin Meese III, Sandra Day O'Connor, Leon E. Panetta, William J. Perry, Charles S. Robb, and Alan K. Simpson. *The Iraq Study Group Report: The Way Forward—a New Approach.* New York: Vintage, 2006.

5. Book with an Editor

N: 5. George Ritzer and Zeynep Atalay, eds., *Readings in Globalization: Key Concepts and Major Debates* (Malden, MA: Wiley/Blackwell, 2010), 1.

B: Ritzer, George, and Zeynep Atalay, eds. *Readings in Globalization: Key Concepts and Major Debates.* Malden, MA: Wiley/Blackwell, 2010.

6. Second or Later Edition

N: 6. Mark T. Gilderhus, *History and Historians: A Historiographical Introduction,* 7th ed. (Upper Saddle River, NJ: Prentice Hall, 2010), 139-41.

B: Gilderhus, Mark T. *History and Historians: A Historiographical Introduction.* 7th ed. Upper Saddle River, NJ: Prentice Hall, 2010.

7. Reprinted Book

N: 7. F. Scott Fitzgerald, *This Side of Paradise* (1920; repr., New York: Penguin, 2009), 64-65.

B: Fitzgerald, F. Scott. *This Side of Paradise.* 1920. Reprint, New York: Penguin, 2009.

8. Selection or Book Chapter in an Anthology/Scholarly Collection

N: 8. Holly Brewer, "Apprenticeship Policy in Virginia: From Patriarchal to Republican Policies of Social Welfare," in *Children Bound to Labor: The Pauper Apprentice System in Early America,* ed. Ruth Wallis Herndon and John E. Murray (Ithaca, NY: Cornell University Press, 2009), 184.

APA, CM, and CSE Documentation

B: Brewer, Holly. "Apprenticeship Policy in Virgina: From Patriarchal
            to Republican Policies of Social Welfare." In *Children Bound
            to Labor: The Pauper Apprentice System in Early America*,
            edited by Ruth Wallis Herndon and John E. Murray, 183–197.
            Ithaca, NY: Cornell University Press, 2009.

9. Multivolume Book If the individual volume has a title different than the whole collection, list the individual volume title before the collection title. However, when citing a book without an individual volume title, omit the volume number after the book title. Instead, after the facts of publication, insert the volume number, followed by a colon, and the page numbers (i.e., 2:45–96).

N: 9. Howard Spodek, *Since 1300*, vol. 2 of *The World's
            History*, 4th ed. (New York: Pearson, 2010), 850-51.

B: Spodek, Howard. *Since 1300*. Vol. 2 of *The World's History*.
            4th ed. New York: Pearson, 2010.

10. Government Publication

N: 10. Office of Management and Budget, *A New Era of
            Responsibility: Renewing America's Promise* (Washington, DC:
            Government Printing Office, 2009), 11.

B: Office of Management and Budget. *A New Era of Responsibility:
            Renewing America's Promise*. Washington, DC: Government
            Printing Office, 2009.

11. Article in a Reference Book Don't include the volume or page number. In the notes, cite the term in the reference book under which the information is contained. Use the abbreviation *s.v.* for *sub verbo*, meaning "under the word," and place the term in quotation marks. List the whole text in the bibliography. Popularly used reference books are usually cited just in the notes rather than in the bibliography.

N: 11. *Encyclopaedia Britannica*, 15th ed., s.v. "Parks, Rosa."

12. Biblical or Other Sacred Work Include the book (abbreviated with no underlining or italics), chapter, and verse, but no page number. References to sacred works are usually cited only in a note or a parenthetical citation.

N: 12. Gen. 21:14–18.

Periodicals

13. Article in a Journal If no issue number is available, the year of publication follows the volume number.

N: 13. Dennis F. Thompson, "Constitutional Character: Virtues
            and Vices in Presidential Leadership," *Presidential Studies
            Quarterly* 40, no. 1 (2010): 24.

B: Thompson, Dennis F. "Constitutional Character: Virtues and
        Vices in Presidential Leadership." *Presidential Studies
        Quarterly* 40, no. 1 (2010): 23-37.

14. Article in a Magazine Referenced page numbers should be included
in the notes entry. Omit page numbers for the bibliographic entry.

N: 14. Connie Bruck, "The Influencer," *New Yorker,* May 10,
        2010, 66.

B: Bruck, Connie. "The Influencer." *New Yorker,* May 10, 2010.

15. Article in a Newspaper No page numbers are listed. If you are
citing a specific edition of the paper, you may add a comma after the
year and list the edition (e.g., late edition, Southeast edition), followed
by a period.

N: 15. Julie Creswell, "The Trades of a Lifetime in 20 Minutes."
        New York Times, May 8, 2010, national edition.

B: Creswell, Julie. "The Trades of a Lifetime in 20 Minutes."
        New York Times, May 8, 2010, national edition.

16. Book Review

N: 16. Evan Rhodes, review of *Fight Pictures: A History of
        Boxing and Early Cinema,* by Dan Streible, *Modernism/
        Modernity* 17, no. 1 (2010): 264-66.

B: Rhodes, Evan. Review of *Fight Pictures: A History of Boxing and
        Early Cinema,* by Dan Streible. *Modernism/Modernity* 17,
        no. 1 (2010): 264-66.

Online and Electronic Sources

Try This

**TO CITE ARTICLES LOCATED IN A LIBRARY DATABASE
OR SUBSCRIPTION SERVICE**

Start your notes or bibliography entry by following the citation format for
the print version of the text. Include an access date only if a publication
date is not available. For sources available only by subscription or for
material that does not contain a stable URL or DOI, name the database
at the end of the entry, followed by a period. If the source contains a stable
URL or a digital object identifier (DOI) number, list it instead of the one that
appears in your Internet browser.

17. Journal Article Located in a Library Database or Subscription Service If the article has pages that are numbered (including those you can see in a PDF file), include them after the year of publication. Name the article's Digital Object Identifier (DOI) number at the end of the entry. If no DOI is available, name the database in which you located the article.

N: 17. David Lewis, "High Times on the Silk Road: The Central Asian Paradox," *World Policy Journal* 27, no. 1 (2010), 39-49, Project Muse.

N: 18. Marc F. Plattner, "Populism, Pluralism, and Liberal Democracy," *Journal of Democracy* 21, no. 1 (2010), 81-92, doi:10.1353/jod.0.0154.

B: Lewis, David. "High Times on the Silk Road: The Central Asian Paradox." *World Policy Journal* 27, no. 1 (2010): 39-49. Project Muse.

B: Plattner, Marc F. "Populism, Pluralism, and Liberal Democracy." *Journal of Democracy* 21, no. 1 (2010): 81-92. doi:10.1353/jod.0.0154.

18. Magazine Article Located in a Library Database or Subscription Service If the magazine has numbered pages, provide a page reference in the notes. Otherwise, provide a reference to headings or numbered paragraphs, if available, in the notes. Name the article's Digital Object Identifier (DOI) number at the end of the entry. If no DOI is available, name the database in which you located the article.

N: 19. Sean McLachlan, "Roman History: Hiking across History on the Hadrian's Wall Path," *British Heritage,* May 2010, 38, 27, Academic OneFile.

B: McLachlan, Sean. "Roman History: Hiking across History on the Hadrian's Wall Path." *British Heritage,* May 2010. Academic OneFile.

19. Newspaper Article Located in a Library Database or Subscription Service

N: 20. Susan Saulny, "Tough Look Inward on Oil Rig Blast," *New York Times,* May 12, 2010, LexisNexis Academic.

B: Saulny, Susan. "Tough Look Inward on Oil Rig Blast." *New York Times,* May 12, 2010. LexisNexis Academic.

APA, CM, and CSE Documentation

Hint

CITING MATERIALS ACCESSED ONLINE

When citing sources that you accessed online, additional information may be needed in your notes and bibliography entries.

Digital Object Identifier (DOI) Number—A DOI number is a unique code a publisher assigns to a book, journal article, or other source. If a DOI number is available for your source, list it at the end of your entry. (See entries 20 and 23.)

URL—If no DOI is available for your online source, include the full URL (or online address) at the end of your entry. (See entries 20 and 23.)

Date of Access—If your online source does not contain a date of publication or update, or if your instructor requests it, include the date you accessed your source. In notes entries, after the source title, include *accessed* and the date, followed by a comma. In bibliography entries, after the source title, include *Accessed* and the date, followed by a period.

20. Article from an Online Journal with a DOI or URL If the article has pages that are numbered (including those you can see in a PDF file), include them after the year of publication. Name the article's Digital Object Identifier (DOI) number at the end of the entry. If no DOI is available, provide the full URL for the article.

N: 21. Robert M. Haberle and Melinda A. Kahre, "Detecting Secular Climate Change on Mars," *MARS: The International Journal of Mars Science and Exploration* 5 (August 2010): 69, doi:10.1555/mars.2010.0003.

N: 22. Irene Watson, "Aboriginality and the Violence of Colonialism," *Borderlands* 8, no. 1 (May 2009): 6, http://www.borderlandsejournal.adelaide.edu.au /vol8no1_2009/iwatson_aboriginality.pdf.

B: Haberle, Robert M., and Melinda A. Kahre. "Detecting Secular Climate Change on Mars." *MARS: The International Journal of Mars Science and Exploration* 5 (August 2010): 68-75. doi:10.1555/mars.2010.0003.

B: Watson, Irene. "Aboriginality and the Violence of Colonialism." *Borderlands* 8, no. 1 (May 2009): 1-8. http:// www.borderlandsejournal.adelaide.edu.au /vol8no1_2009/iwatson_aboriginality.pdf.

21. Article from an Online Magazine If the magazine has numbered pages, provide a page reference in the notes. Otherwise, provide a reference to headings or numbered paragraphs, if available, in the notes. Name the article's Digital Object Identifier (DOI) number at the end of the entry. If no DOI is available, provide the full URL for the article.

N: 23. Andrew Blum, "Cold Comforts: Antarctic Research Bases Are Seriously Self-Sustaining," *Wired,* April 19, 2010, http://www.wired.com/magazine/2010/04/ff_antarctica/.

B: Blum, Andrew. "Cold Comforts: Antarctic Research Bases Are Seriously Self-Sustaining." *Wired,* April 19, 2010. http://www.wired.com/magazine/2010/04/ff_antarctica/.

22. Article from an Online Newspaper

N: 24. Corey Williams, "Daunting Task Ahead to Secure Detroit's Future," *Washington Post,* May 3, 2010, http://www.washingtonpost.com/wp-dyn/content/article/2010/05/02/AR2010050201833.html.

B: Williams, Corey. "Daunting Task Ahead to Secure Detroit's Future." *Washington Post,* May 3, 2010. http://www.washingtonpost.com/wp-dyn/content/article/2010/05/02/AR2010050201833.html.

23. Online Book with a DOI or URL When accessing a book online, include the book's Digital Object Identifier (DOI) number at the end of the citation. If the book has no DOI number, include the book's URL at the end of the citation.

N: 25. William Caferro, *Contesting the Renaissance* (Malden, MA: Wiley/Blackwell, 2011), 62, doi:10.1002/9781444324501.

N: 26. Edith Wharton, *The Age of Innocence* (New York: Appleton, 1920), 64, http://www.bartleby.com/1005/.

B: Caferro, William. *Contesting the Renaissance.* Malden, MA: Wiley/Blackwell, 2011. doi:10.1002/9781444324501.

B: Wharton, Edith. *The Age of Innocence.* New York: Appleton, 1920. http://www.bartleby.com/1005/.

24. Book for an Electronic Reader Name the edition type at the end of the citation.

N: 27. Michael Lewis, *The Big Short: Inside the Doomsday Machine* (New York: Norton, 2010), Kindle edition.

B: Lewis, Michael. *The Big Short: Inside the Doomsday Machine.* New York: Norton, 2010. Kindle edition.

25. Online Government Document

N: 28. National Commission on Children and Disasters, *Interim Report* (Washington, DC: National Commission on Children and Disasters, October 14, 2009), 3, http://www.childrenanddisasters .acf.hhs.gov/20091014_508IR_partII.pdf.

B: National Commission on Children and Disasters. *Interim Report*. Washington, DC: National Commission on Children and Disasters, October 14, 2009. http://www.childrenanddisasters .acf.hhs.gov/20091014_508IR_partII.pdf.

26. Page on a Web Site Give information for the specific page you used in the notes, and provide the name of the site provider or publisher (if available). List the date of publication or last revision in the notes. If neither is available, list the date you accessed the site. Include the citation for the full Web site in the bibliography.

N: 29. "Banking on the Seed Bank Project," *San Diego Zoo*, Zoological Society of San Diego, accessed May 12, 2010, http://www.sandiegozoo.org/conservation/plants/seedbank _project/banking_on_the_seed_bank_project/.

N: 30. Andrew Hollinger, "United States Holocaust Museum Decries Eviction of Aid Agencies in Darfur and Southern Sudan," *United States Holocaust Memorial Museum*, March 5, 2009, http://www.ushmm.org/museum/press/archives/detail.php ?category=03-coc&content=2009-03-05.

B: *San Diego Zoo*. Zoological Society of San Diego. Accessed May 12, 2010. http://www.sandiegozoo.org/.

B: *United States Holocaust Memorial Museum*. Accessed May 1, 2010. http://www.ushmm.org/.

27. Blog Entry Start the entry with the name or pseudonym of the writer. Add the word *blog* in parentheses after the title of the blog. Provide specific citation information for the notes, but give information only about the blog's home page in the bibliography.

N: 31. The Little Professor, "Authorial Intent," *The Little Professor* (blog), April 23, 2010, http://littleprofessor.typepad .com/the_little_professor/2010/04/authorial-intent.html.

N: 32. McBride, Bill, "Unemployment: Geographic Mismatch," *Calculated Risk* (blog), May 13, 2010, http://www .calculatedriskblog.com/2010/05/unemployment -geographic-mismatch.html.

CM: Citing a Page on a Web Site

CM Notes Format:

> 2. Karla Murthy, "Bridging the Gender Wage Gap," *Need to Know,* PBS, May 20, 2010, http://www.pbs.org/wnet/need-to-know/economy /bridging-the-gender-wage-gap/835/.

CM Bibliography Format:

Need to Know. PBS. Accessed June 1, 2010. http://www.pbs.org/.

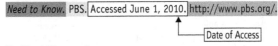

In-Text Example:

For each dollar earned in the workforce by an American man, an American woman receives only 77 cents on average for performing the same work, resulting in a more than $400,000 income disparity over a 40-year span.[2]

Courtesy WNET.org (http://www.pbs.org/wnet/need-to-know/economy/bridging-the-gender-wage-gap/835/)

CM: Citing a Page on a Website: Courtesy WNET.org. (http://www .pbs.org/wnet/need-to-know/economy/bridging-the-gender-wage-gap/835/)

APA, CM, and CSE Documentation

B: The Little Professor. *The Little Professor* (blog). Accessed
   May 2, 2010. http://littleprofessor.typepad.com.
B: McBride, Bill. *Calculated Risk* (blog). Accessed May 14, 2010.
   http://www.calculatedriskblog.com.

28. Comment on a Blog Start the notes entry with the name or pseudonym of the commenter. Add the word *blog* in parentheses after the site title. Provide specific citation information for the notes, but give information only about the blog's home page in the bibliography.

N: 33. Zhiv, April 27, 2010 (7:08 p.m.), comment on Little
    Professor, "Authorial Intent," *The Little Professor* (blog), April 23,
    2010, http://littleprofessor.typepad.com/the_little_professor
    /2010/04/authorial-intent.html#comments.
N: 34. Wisdom Seeker, May 13, 2010 (9:59 p.m.), comment
    on Bill McBride, "Unemployment: Geographic Mismatch,"
    Calculated Risk (blog), May 13, 2010, http://www.hoocoodanode.org
    /node/9746.

B: The Little Professor. *The Little Professor* (blog). Accessed May 2,
   2010. http://littleprofessor.typepad.com.
B: McBride, Bill. *Calculated Risk* (blog). Accessed May 14, 2010.
   http://www.calculatedriskblog.com.

29. E-Mail Message or Posting to a Mailing List E-mail messages and postings to mailing lists usually appear only in the notes or parenthetical citations, not in the bibliography. Add an electronic address and access date at the end of the entry if the posting is archived on a Web site.

N: 35. Dora Dodger-Gilbert, e-mail message to Veterinary
    Questions and Viewpoints mailing list, January 3, 2010.
N: 36. Daniel Kaplan, e-mail message to the author,
    September 23, 2009.

30. Podcast, MP3, or Other Downloaded Material Add the provider and file format at the end of the entry.

N: 37. Melvyn Bragg, Carolin Crawford, Paul Murdin, and
    Michael Rowan-Robinson, "The Cool Universe," *BBC Radio 4:
    In Our Time* (May 6, 2010), iTunes MP3.
N: 38. Kanye West, *808s and Heartbreak* (New York:
    Roc-a-Fella Records, 2008), iTunes MP3.

B: Bragg, Melvyn, Carolin Crawford, Paul Murdin, and Michael Rowan-Robinson. "The Cool Universe." *BBC Radio 4: In Our Time.* May 6, 2010. iTunes MP3.

B: West, Kanye. *808s and Heartbreak.* New York: Roc-a-Fella Records, 2008. iTunes MP3.

Other Sources

31. Television Interview

N: 39. Joe Biden, interview by David Gregory, *Meet the Press,* NBC, February 14, 2010.

B: Biden, Joe. Interview by David Gregory. *Meet the Press.* NBC. February 14, 2010.

32. Personal or Telephone Interview In the author-date format, personal communications are acknowledged in the text and notes but usually not in the bibliography.

N: 40. Kenneth Autrey, interview by the author, May 2, 2010, Florence, South Carolina.

N: 41. John Sutton, telephone interview by the author, April 29, 2010.

33. Film on Videotape or DVD

N: 42. *The Young Victoria,* directed by Jean-Marc Vallée (2009; Culver City, CA: Sony Pictures, 2010), DVD.

B: *The Young Victoria.* Directed by Jean-Marc Vallée. 2009. Culver City, CA: Sony Pictures, 2010. DVD.

34. Sound Recording Include the product number (often located on the spine of a CD) after the publisher's name. Add the medium of publication at the end of the entry.

N: 43. Wolfgang Amadeus Mozart, *Clarinet Concerto in A; Violin Concerto No. 3,* Royal Philharmonic Orchestra, dir. Thomas Beecham, Discover Classical B003UYV188, 2010, compact disc.

B: Mozart, Wolfgang Amadeus. *Clarinet Concerto in A; Violin Concerto No. 3.* Royal Philharmonic Orchestra, dir. Thomas Beecham. Discover Classical B003UYV188, 2010, compact disc.

APA, CM, and CSE Documentation

35. Source Quoted from Another Source Quotations from secondary sources should ordinarily be avoided. If, however, the original source is unavailable, list both sources in the entry.

N: 44. H. H. Dubs, "An Ancient Chinese Mystery Cult," *Harvard Theological Review* 35 (1942): 223, quoted in Susan Naquin, *Millenarian Rebellion in China: The Eight Trigrams Uprising of 1813* (New Haven, CT: Yale University Press, 1976), 288.

B: Dubs, H. H. "An Ancient Chinese Mystery Cult." *Harvard Theological Review* 35 (1942): 223. Quoted in Susan Naquin, *Millenarian Rebellion in China: The Eight Trigrams Uprising of 1813*. New Haven, CT: Yale University Press, 1976, 288.

36. Television Episode Begin the entry with the name of the writer. End the entry with the network and original air date.

N: 45. Matthew Weiner, "Public Relations," *Mad Men,* season 4 episode 1, directed by Phil Abraham, AMC, aired July 25, 2010.

B: Weiner, Matthew. "Public Relations." *Mad Men,* season 4, episode 1. Directed by Phil Abraham. AMC, July 25, 2010.

37. Advertisement List advertisements in the bibliography only if they are retrievable.

N: 46. Sony Bravia, "Play-Doh," television advertisement, Fallon London, directed by Juan Cabral, 2008.

B: Sony Bravia. "Play-Doh." Television advertisement. Fallon London, directed by Juan Cabral, 2008.

Index